An Introduction to Social Anthropology

Sharing our Worlds

Second edition

Also by Joy Hendry

Marriage in Changing Japan: Community and Society (1981)

Becoming Japanese (1986)

Interpreting Japanese Society: Anthropological Approaches, *edited with Jonathan Webber* (1986)

Understanding Japanese Society (1987)

Wrapping Culture: Politeness, Presentation and Power in Japan and other Societies (1993)

An Anthropologist in Japan (1999)

The Orient Strikes Back: A Global View of Cultural Display (2000)

An Anthropology of Indirect Communication, *edited with C. W. Watson* (2001)

Japan at Play, *edited with Massimo Raveri* (2002)

Dismantling the East–West Dichotomy, *edited with Heung Wah Wong* (2005)

Reclaiming Culture: Indigenous People and Self-Representation (2005)

An Introduction to Social Anthropology

Sharing our Worlds

Second Edition

Joy Hendry

First edition 1999
This second edition published 2008 by
PALGRAVE MACMILLAN
Houndmills, Basingstoke, Hampshire RG21 6XS and
published in the USA in 2008 by New York University Press under the title *Sharing Our Worlds: An Introduction to Cultural and Social Anthropology*.

PALGRAVE MACMILLAN is the global academic imprint of the Palgrave Macmillan division of St. Martin's Press, LLC and of Palgrave Publishers Ltd. Macmillan® is a registered trademark in the United States, United Kingdom and other countries. Palgrave is a registered trademark in the European Union and other countries.

ISBN-13: 978–0–230–00526–6 (hardback)
ISBN-10: 0–230–00526–8 (hardback)
ISBN-13: 978–0–230–00527–3 (paperback)
ISBN-10: 0–230–00527–6 (paperback)

The book is printed on paper suitable for recycling and made from fully managed and sustained forest sources. Logging, pulping and manufacturing processes are expected to conform to the environmental regulations of the country of origin.

A catalogue record for this book is available from the British Library.

A catalog record for this book is available from the Library of Congress.

10   9   8   7   6   5   4   3   2
17   16   15   14   13   12   11   10   09
Printed and bound in China

In memory of Dennis,
who shared several worlds,
past and present

I thoroughly commend this revised and expanded edition of Joy Hendry's acclaimed book. It is without doubt one of the best introductory texts to social and cultural anthropology that exists. Written in lucid, jargon-free prose and in a style that is both personal and engaging, Hendry once again demonstrates her extraordinary gift for explaining and rendering accessible even the most complex ideas and arguments. This book goes a long way towards bridging the gap between the general public and academic anthropology. It is essential reading for any newcomer to the subject.

Professor Cris Shore, University of Auckland

This is an indispensable text. Hendry conveys key principles in an accessible way without ever losing sight of what it is that makes anthropology such a dynamic and exciting field.

Dr Cathrine Degnen, University of Newcastle

From my own experience I know this book works well with students – and indeed with anyone who is curious about what anthropology is. Hendry deals with a broad range of topics – from what it means to do fieldwork to the classical contributions that have shaped anthropological discourse; from individual symbols to larger constellations of cultural and social organization. The further research sections at the end of each chapter add to the value of the book and the two new chapters, on tourism and on globalization, draw us further into how anthropologists seek to understand contemporary realities. The enlarged new edition of this useful and informative book is easy to recommend.

Professor Leif Manger, University of Bergen

It is very nice to see that my words have been reproduced without editing, without changes, and without interpretation. These are words direct from someone to whom people rarely listen and I appreciate the opportunity to offer something other than romantic nonsense about Travellers' ways.

**Mick Ganly, English Traveller, author of one of the
first-hand accounts featured in the book**

A lively and accessible introduction to the discipline. Hendry's revised text combines overview and explanation, looking back to anthropology's achievements and forward to the ways in which anthropologists today, and tomorrow, might engage a mobile, connected and globalized world. A very welcome second edition.

Dr Tom Hall, University of Cardiff

A lovely, accessible and engaging introductory book. Hendry's friendly style, together with the clear on-page glossary, personal accounts and useful collections of additional resources, including films and novels, make this an excellent gateway to the world of anthropology.

Gemma Jones, Royal Anthropological Institute

Contents

List of Figures and Maps   xi

List of Photographs   xii

List of First-hand Accounts   xiv

Acknowledgements   xv

Preface   xviii

Introduction   1

What Anthropologists Do   1

A Brief History of Social (and Cultural) Anthropology   8

The Content of this Book   13

1   Seeing the World   17

Souvenirs and Handkerchiefs   17

Learning to Classify   20

Life, Death and Burial Alive   21

Cultural Relativism and the Anthropologists' Bias   23

Changes in Systems of Classification: The Issue of
    Gender   30

2 Disgusting, Forbidden and Unthinkable 36

Challenging Some Ingrained Ideas 36

Taboo 38

Pollution 41

Purity and Classification 42

Animal Categories and Verbal Abuse 45

3 Gifts, Exchange and Reciprocity 51

The Anthropologist's Arrival 51

Gifts 52

The Indian Gift 58

Exchange 62

Reciprocity 64

Objects Inalienable, Entangled and Wrapped 67

4 The Ritual Round 73

Shoes and the Empty Ritual 73

Definitions of Ritual 75

Rites of Passage 77

5 Society: A Set of Symbols 93

What is a Symbol? 93

Bodily Symbols 95

Symbolising Relationships 102

Group Symbols and Their Interpretation 104

Anthropological Interpretation of Symbolism 105

6 Beauty and Bounty: Treasure and Trophies 110

Seeing and Value 110

Living Art 112

Art for Gaining Access to 'Seeing the World' 115

Art and Status: The Status of Art 117

Art and Meaning 122

Aesthetics 123

Definitions of Art 125

7 Cosmology I: Religion, Magic and Mythology   129

Religion, Science and Cosmology   129
Definitions and Distinctions   130
Origins of Religion   133
Explanations of Religious Phenomena   136
Cults: The Persistence of Religious Movements   142

8 Cosmology II: Witchcraft, Shamanism and Syncretism   150

Indigenous Categories of Cosmology   150
Terminology   151
Roles of Witchcraft and Sorcery Beliefs   153
Reactions and other Theories of Witchcraft   155
Possession and Shamanism   158
Syncretism   160

9 Law, Order and Social Control   170

Rules and Norms   170
Sanctions   173
Order and Dispute   178
Contested Norms and Social Control in a Context   181

10 The Art of Politics   187

Political Possibilities   187
Types of Political System   189
Acquiring and Achieving Political Power and Status   201

11 Family, Kinship and Marriage   207

Varieties of Kinship   207
Classifying Kin Relations   213
Unilineal Descent Groups   216
Kinship in a Multicultural Context: A Case Study   219
Marriage   224
Endogamy, Exogamy and Incest   226
Marriage as Exchange – Dowry and Bridewealth   227
Locality of Marriage Residence   231
Monogamy and Polygamy   232

12   Economics and the Environment   236

Introduction   236
Subsistence and Survival   237
Property and Tenure   241
Market Economics   244
Social Views of the Environment   247
Environmental Influence in Social Life   251

13   Tourism and the Intercultural Encounter   256

Cultural Difference for Recreation   256
The Study of Travel and Tourism   258
Play and Rites of Passage   263
Ecotourism and Sacred Places   265
Performance, Identity and Authenticity   271
Theme Parks, Museums and Material Culture   273

14   Transnationalism, Globalisation and Beyond   280

Anthropology for the Future   280
People on the Move and Transnational Connections   281
Globalisation of Business, Objects and Ideas   283
New Themes and Methods for Anthropology   289
The Value of Anthropology in our Future World   294

Map of Peoples and Places Mentioned in this Book   302

Glossary   304

Index   310

Index of Authors and Film Makers   310
Index of Peoples and Places   314
General Index   318

List of Figures and Maps

Figures

1.1   English and Welsh colour classifications   27

3.1   Reciprocity and kinship residential sectors   66

10.1 A representation of the social and political organisation of the Nuer   198

10.2 The segmentary system   198

11.1 A standard English family   214

11.2 Patrilineal and matrilineal descent   215

11.3 A unilineal descent group   216

11.4 Cross-cousins and parallel-cousins   218

11.5 Direct (sister) exchange   229

11.6 Matrilateral cross-cousin marriage   230

Maps

12.1 A view of the world from the Southern hemisphere   252

World Map   Peoples and places mentioned in this book   302

List of Photographs

1.1   A Japanese souvenir handkerchief   18

1.2   A bereaved woman's long-term commitment in Greece   32

2.1   A pig sacrifice in East Nepal   39

2.2   How to classify a dog   45

3.1   Selling pots in the market in Texcoco   63

3.2   Wrapping for a Japanese gift   68

4.1   Shoes in the entrance to a Japanese home   74

4.2   A Church of England wedding   76

4.3   Piercing as a rite of passage?   85

5.1   A Wahgi man from the Highlands of New Guinea   97

5.2   Symbolism of the tattoo   98

6.1   An example of Dinka cattle   113

6.2   Details of a Kwoma ceremonial men's house, Sepik region, New Guinea   116

6.3   A totem pole on display in the Pitt Rivers Museum, Oxford   121

8.1   An offering made on the Day of the Dead in Mexico   161

8.2   An example of syncretism in the Kathmandu Valley   162

9.1   The ruined house at Hampton Gay, Oxfordshire   175

9.2   Nunavut Legislative Assembly symbolism   179

10.1   Slash-and-burn cultivation in Surinam   193

11.1   A mosque in Oxford, England   219

11.2   A Jain wedding, in northern India   227

12.1   Dividing up a whale in Indonesia   251

13.1   The Ponte della Paglia in Venice, bulging with tourists   259

13.2   Māori greeting at the Māori Arts and Crafts Institute in Thermal Valley, Rotorua, New Zealand   270

13.3   A reproduction of the home of William Shakespeare in Maruyama, Japan   275

14.1   Mobile phone restrictions in Japan   285

14.2   A lacquerware chest transformed from Japan to Europe   290

List of First-hand Accounts

1 Wong Si Lam on *Feng Shui* 28

2 Mick Ganly on Cleanliness among Travellers 46

3.1 Manuka Henare on *Hau*: The Ethic of Generosity and Spirituality of Māori Gift Exchange 56

3.2 Maria Guadalupe Hernandez White on Mexican Gifts that need no Return 60

4 Hiroko Ford on Rituals Associated with Pregnancy in Japan 82

5 Lesikar Ole Ngila on Maasai Initiation 100

6 Raymattja Marika on Art through Indigenous Science 124

7 Timothy Jenkins on Anglicanism and Anthropology 138

8 Bhawana Tuladhar-Douglas on Syncretism in Nepal 163

10 Merinto Taje Tarëno, on Slash-and-Burn Cultivation in Surinam 194

11.1 Mary Martha Beaton on Same-Sex Parentage 210

11.2 Ashini Kothari on Jain marriage 224

12 Laara Fitznor on Space–Place–Location and Sacredness 242

13.1 Ashraf Tageldeen on Tourism and the Case of Cultural Encounter in Egypt 260

13.2 Chellie Spiller on Sustainable Māori Cultural Tourism 268

14.1 Wong Si Lam on Transnational Identity 287

14.2 Harvey Whitehouse on the Future 292

Acknowledgements

I must again acknowledge my enormous debt to the people whose worlds I have been privileged to share. These include some who barely receive a mention in the text, for I did not eventually pursue further the study of their worlds, but they undoubtedly influenced my initial discovery of the subject. First, the various people of Morocco amongst whom I lived and travelled in 1966–7, and the French family to whom I became attached on that occasion and who have made me welcome ever since in Paris and les Alpes Maritimes; secondly, the again various people I encountered while living in French Canada in 1967–8, including a Canadian godfather who happened to visit my father, his wartime friend, at the time I was born, and the staff and pupils of Beth Jacob School in Outrement, where I taught for the second two-thirds of an academic year which included the Six Days War in Israel, who introduced me to the (female) world of a highly protected orthodox Jewish community. In Mexico, where I lived and worked from 1968 to 1970 and again in 1972, I discovered the subject of anthropology, which I pursued formally with a period of fieldwork in Texcoco and the formerly Nahuatl community of San Nicolas Tlaminca. Finally, I have shared in many worlds in Japan over the years, but of these I have published: a farming community in Yame, Kyushu, a seaside community in Tateyama, Chiba, and many friends and colleagues in Tokyo and other university cities. To all these and many more casual acquaintances, I record a deep gratitude to them for allowing me to share their lives.

Since the first edition of this book was published I have built up another series of debts to the many Indigenous people with whom I have been working, and who have undoubtedly influenced my thinking about anthropology as well as about their situation. I have tried to name as many as possible of them in my book *Reclaiming Culture*, and as the acknowledgements there are of record length I probably should not repeat the exercise, though my gratitude is none the weaker, and I thank them all again.

The decision to include in this edition first–person accounts of various important issues is also related to my more recent research, and I would like to express a real heartfelt thanks to those people who agreed to write these texts. There was little in it for them – I promised them a copy of the book, that is all – so I thank them warmly for their contributions, which certainly enliven and add authority to the whole book. For help with finding and encouraging some of these people, and proposing others who didn't in the end make it, I would like to thank Gemma Burford, Elizabeth Cory-Pearce, Philippa Deveson, Helen Ganly, David Gellner, Katie Hayne, Gwyneira Isaac, Douglas Johnson, Cees Koelewijn, Howard Morphy, Josephine Reynell, Peter Rivière, John Ryle and Andre Singer.

More people than I can possibly list have influenced my understanding of the social anthropology I present here, and some may anyway feel that I have oversimplified it in an attempt to make the subject accessible to anyone who feels inclined to pick up the book. However, I must at the very least mention my own first supervisor, Peter Rivière, whose words have undoubtedly appeared inadvertently in these pages, so firmly ingrained were some of them in the recesses of my mind, and Rodney Needham, whose work on symbolic classification clearly inspired the whole basis of the original lecture course and therefore the approach of the book. The influence of cultural anthropology came after I published the first edition of this book, when I attended an enlightening course offered by Laura Peers at the Pitt Rivers Museum and, at her introduction, spent a couple of semesters visiting McMaster University in Canada.

For practical help with reading, suggestions and comments on various stages of the whole process, I am indebted to Ross Bowden, Jeremy MacClancy, Howard Morphy and Mike O'Hanlon for help with Chapter 6, Nazia Tenvir and Haroon Sarwar with Chapter 11, and, more generally, to Renate Barber, Genevieve Bicknell, Annabel Black, Paul Collinson, Martin Flatman, Ian Fowler, David Gellner, Clare Hall, Renee Hirschon, William Kay, Tammy Kohn, Chris McDonaugh, Andrew McMullen, Diana Martin, Lola Martinez, Peter Parkes, Bob Parkin, Sue Pennington, Josephine Reynell, Peter Rivière, Alison Shaw, Cris Shore and Felicity Wood. For comments and suggestions on various aspects of the second edition, I would like add Jan Harwell, Garry Marvin and Jacqueline Waldren for Chapter 13, Mitch Sedgwick for Chapter 14, and more generally, Mary Martha Beaton, Mary Louise Bracho, Udi Butler, Hilary Callan, Ericka Chemko, Audrey Colson, Michael Herzfeld, Roger Just, Emiko Ohnuki-Tierney, Laura Rival and Phil Sawkins. Students over the years have also added helpful comments and Peter Momtchiloff at Oxford University Press kindly read and discussed a draft of the first edition when he took on the anthropology list. I must also acknowledge the detailed, helpful and incisive comments and suggestions of the several anonymous readers of the draft of this edition, and thank them for some of the examples I have incorporated into the final text.

Thanks, too, to various friends and colleagues for the generous loan of their photographs, which are credited individually, but especially to the Pitt Rivers Museum for allowing me to publish my snapshot of the totem pole, and also to Michael O'Hanlon, the director, and Jeremy Coote, curator, who have allowed me to use formerly published photographs. For technical support, I would like to thank Bob Pomfret and Lisa Hill for help with the photographs, Gerry Black, who made the original figures and world maps, and Bev Massingham, Kirsten Brown, Maggie Kleszczewska and other Social Sciences staff for general secretarial support.

Specific help with the final stages of the second edition, sometimes quite late in the day, came from Chantal Butchinsky, who responded with amazing calm and speed to requests for help with updating reading lists, films and, particularly, finding websites; Susanne Hammacher, for RAI film lists in the midst of preparing for the annual RAI film festival; Gemma Jones for more helpful websites and a fund of other interesting ideas; and Catherine Travers at Palgrave Macmillan, who offered the most wonderfully cool and organised author support as well as long lists of helpful comments and suggestions on the draft text. To all these, I am especially grateful.

Finally, I would like again to thank my father and mother, whose pleasant but unashamedly chauvinistic bickering about their respective origins in Scotland and Yorkshire made me aware of cultural boundary marking before I had any idea what it was, and helped me to keep at bay the tendency to exoticise anthropology long before it became politically important to do so. Dennis, my husband, and his family made me aware of a special cultural quality that is shared in Liverpool, and James and William, our sons, ensure that I don't forget about it now that he is no longer with us.

Preface

Anthropology is one of those fields that many people have vaguely heard of, but few know how to define. Even students of the subject dread that inevitable party-stopping question: 'Just what is it that you are studying?' and several rather pat answers have been invented to snuff out the interest. Once started on an explanation, however, an enthusiastic student may be hard to stop and, for many, anthropology comes to change their lives in a profound and irreversible way. It may still be difficult to say quite why, but they will share an understanding of life with others who have ventured into the same pastures, an understanding which will also stand them in good stead in all kinds of future endeavours, including when they enter the workplace.

Social and cultural anthropology – the focus of this particular volume – is not an esoteric, difficult subject, however. Quite the contrary, it is concerned with the most mundane aspects of everyday life and it should, up to a fairly advanced point, be relatively easy to understand and absorb. Those who have been brought up bilingual, or in a multicultural school aware of its advantages, or in a society different from that of their parents may have an initial advantage in this respect, for they will have begun to appreciate some of the implications of cultural diversity. Indeed, social anthropology may help them to find a niche of their own in the world. Those who have pondered intriguing differences they encounter during travels abroad may also find they have taken the first steps into the field. For others, novels may have opened the gates.

This book is written to create order out of these initial experiences. It does not aim to be comprehensive, or even to give a broad summary of the basic works in the field. References to the anthropology discussed are provided at the end of each chapter, along with some ideas for further reading, and together these should offer a sound introduction to anyone embarking on the study of the subject. The later chapters also cover several of the traditional sections into which the field is divided. The main aim, however, is to help the initiate over some of the first hurdles they are likely to encounter. My own first professor warned me to expect to be confused for the best part of a year, and some difficulty may be inevitable because of the very nature of the subject, but this book aims to smooth the way.

initiate – a person joining a new stage of life, typically learning in order to be an effective member, sometimes through certain trials and ordeals.

The text is written primarily for students taking up the study of social and/or cultural anthropology, or thinking about taking it up, but it is also written for their mothers, brothers and friends, and for their potential future employers to see how broadly beneficial such a background may be. It is written (I hope) in a style open to any to follow, making no assumptions about prior knowledge or background, and it is written in such a way that one can use it to refer back to the parts one feels unsure about later. Most of all, however, it is written in an effort to make the whole venture enjoyable. It is a subject I discovered almost by chance when, during my youth, I was setting out to enjoy myself. Imagine my delight when I found I could spend the rest of my life doing just that for a career!

This book was inspired by a series of lectures presented annually to first-year students at Oxford Brookes University, lectures that are only part of their learning experience. The students also play games, watch films, read other books and articles, answer short computer-aided tests, and write essays about what they are learning. During the later part of their university career some of the same students go out into the city or further afield to carry out their own investigations, and over the years these have included studies of greyhound racing, public houses, churches, witches' covens and college dinners. In contemporary global society, there are plenty of different 'worlds' to share and to learn about and I am sure that each of you readers will find some interest of your own to follow up, whether it be in your family, among your friends, or in some new world you will discover. I hope that this book will help you to do that in a respectful and egalitarian way.

Preface to the Second Edition

Planning and writing the second edition of this book has been a great opportunity to bring into the text some up-to-date research, some new attitudes to anthropology, and some now quite well-established changes in the approach of potential students. All three of these innovations reflect a rapidly growing awareness around the world of the diversity of people who share it with us, whoever we are, and the book seeks to foster a greater knowledge about our common humanity as well as our continuing cultural differences.

Much anthropological research has moved into a mode which could be described as global, just as there is a wider awareness of its value, and students now often come to the classroom with experience of travel, relocation of their families, and first-hand encounters with worlds that differ from their own. This offers a wealth of experience to bring to discussions, and I have added some end-of-chapter questions to encourage readers to consider how the issues raised may manifest themselves in their own lives. The approach still aims to be directly accessible to those with no prior knowledge, gradually introducing more complex issues once the basic building blocks have been laid, but the questions also encourage a deeper consideration of the issues raised. Another innovation for the new edition is the glossary at the end of the book, which defines terms used in the text. These terms appear in bold type at first mention, with an immediate definition to hand in the margin.

A prime aim of the social and cultural anthropology I present here is that we learn to respect and value all peoples equally, an aim that is vitally important in the transnational, global world in which most of us now live and work. A new feature of this second edition about which I am particularly pleased is to be found in the first-hand accounts that have been presented within most of the chapters. These were planned to recognise the essential contributions made by those whose lives anthropologists have described in developing the subject, and to give a few of them a chance to speak directly to the reader without the intervention of the anthropologist along the way. I tried where possible to invite members of groups discussed in the text, and this is particularly valuable when the anthropology is classic, and therefore rather dated, for it allows the reader to get a feel for what has happened to the people since the initial studies were made.

We have also introduced references to new books, articles and films and, of course, generally updated the text to reflect changes in the field. However, we have not interfered with the overall structure of the book, which was and still is designed to form a coherent whole with logical links between chapters building towards an ever-greater understanding of the subject.

Two completely new chapters have been added at the end. Both reflect the place of anthropology in an increasingly globalised world, but they approach it from contrasting angles.

The first of these chapters, 'Tourism and the Intercultural Encounter' (Chapter 13), addresses directly the way in which peoples of different backgrounds are in general much more likely than they were in the past to encounter cultural variety in their worlds. Of course, there have been multicultural regions since time immemorial, and there have for long been those who catered to travellers of one sort or another, but the movement that has become known as tourism has really only burgeoned in the last few decades. This is largely because of technology that has enabled cheap and fast movement around the globe, but the interest in cultural variety is also found at home, as we shall see. This chapter will offer many insights, then, but its base in the new field of Tourism and Anthropology should be of particular interest to those who include a gap year of travel in their lives.

The second new chapter, 'Transnationalism, Globalisation and Beyond' (Chapter 14), examines ways in which social life has been altered since rapidly changing technologies have enabled people in different parts of the world instantly to be in touch on a regular basis. It discusses the consequences, positive and negative, of how people have reorganised or rearranged their lives, and looks at some of the new and often quite interesting situations that have arisen. It also examines how the work of anthropologists has adapted to these new arrangements, and how new roles have emerged for us to play. The playing of some of them is still at an early stage, however, and at the end of this new edition, I merely throw out a few ideas about how a neophyte anthropologist, perhaps like yourself, may take forward the knowledge you will acquire as you tread this path. Undoubtedly, you will think of many others!

Introduction

What Anthropologists Do

Anthropology comes in a variety of different forms, and the Greek basis of the term, which simply means the study of human beings, doesn't really help to narrow things down much, especially when we find that some anthropologists work with monkeys and other non-human primates more than they work with people! The term is used in different ways in different countries, and there are even subtle differences within the same country. You will probably be happy to hear, then, that there is also a broad understanding among anthropologists about how to proceed, and in this opening section, we will focus on the kinds of things that anthropologists do in order to earn that title.

In this book, our prime focus is actually on social and cultural anthropology, and we will therefore not be discussing archaeology, which is a closely related subject that is sometimes included under the term anthropology, but which has its own experts and methods. Nor will we much discuss biological anthropology, which is again quite closely related, but which is concerned with human anatomy and physiology, and, like archaeology, with examining ancient remains and artefacts in order to draw up theories about human evolution. In the United States, linguistics is also regarded as a separate branch of anthropology, and we will touch on this field, but only where it helps us to understand the social and cultural aspects of human life that form *our* main focus.

What social and cultural anthropologists generally share, then, is an interest in different ways people have of looking at the world they live in. These different ways are not individual idiosyncrasies, but different views of the world learned as people grow up in different societies, or within one of the different groups that make up one larger society. It may be the differences between people who live in Birmingham and Brighton, or between those in Bermuda and Bangkok, or even the variety of views across a number of diverse groups within one of those places. There is an almost unlimited variety of world views for us to look at, and each anthropologist tends to specialise, at least for a time, in looking at one of them.

Most social anthropologists gain their specialist knowledge by going to live in a society they have negotiated to work in. They don't just go there for a week or two with an interpreter and a set of questionnaires. They go for a year or more, seek to set up home with the people they are interested in, and try to live as far as possible as those people do – in every respect. The idea is to find out exactly what it is like to be a member of the society in question, and anthropologists operate on the assumption that the best way to do this is to live with those people and seek to share their lives. This form of investigation is called participant observation, because the observer finds out what he or she wants to know by participating in the lives of the people under study.

participant observation – a method used by anthropologists to learn about a people and their activities by observing at the same time as participating in their lives.

Anthropologists participate in the regular routines of everyday life, perhaps trying out the activities of a number of different members of the society, as well as asking permission to take part in their rites, and observe as far as possible their most intimate ceremonies. If the people they are concerned with get up early, they get up early; if they stay up all night, the anthropologist should do the same. If some of the people take hallucinogenic drugs, the anthropologist might legitimately argue that they should do the same, for the activities that are banned in one country may be accepted in another, although a newcomer should always be careful. If the people they choose to work with stand for long periods of the night in a freezing stream, so should the observer (this example may sound far-fetched, but it was part of a study carried out in the Andes on which a book called *The Coming of the Sun* is based [Tayler 1997]). The idea is to experience what it is like to be a member of the world under study, for otherwise one could not begin to understand how it looks and feels.

An important part of this exercise, more technically though rather quaintly known as fieldwork, is to learn the language of the people concerned. This was absolutely vital in the early studies of peoples with whom the outside

fieldwork – carrying out practical investigations necessary to a particular study chosen by an anthropologist.

world had previously had little contact, but it is essential anywhere to gain an understanding of the way the world is seen and described. Anthropologists have found that working with interpreters gives a wholly inadequate view, for first-hand knowledge of a language is the only way to become fully aware of the meanings and implications of the words used, and these might be very different from the straight translations presented in a dictionary.

This concern with language is important even for anthropologists who choose to work in a society where their own idiom is the native tongue, for there are many versions of any particular language. Teenagers who claim that their parents do not understand them, for example, are not merely being adolescent and rebellious. They are also usually quite accurately referring to differences in language (and values) which develop between generations. Within the English language there are also clear regional differences, and differences based on other allegiances such as ethnic origins, class and occupation. An anthropologist working in his or her own mother tongue must be especially careful to look out for these sometimes rather fine distinctions. Consider the difference between American, British and Australian humour, for example.

Anthropologists may experience other difficulties in finding ways to fit into a society of their choice. People may (quite rightly) be very suspicious of a stranger whose main aim in life seems to be to poke their nose into the affairs of those around them, and they are entitled to feel resentful of such interference into their lives. It is important, then, for an anthropologist to consider these feelings, to take care to explain their intentions, and to respect requests from the people they work with not to publish and broadcast all that they learn. It is not only polite, but also ethically essential to discuss with people how the knowledge they share might subsequently be used, and in recent years people generally check back what they write with those who helped them with the work (see Cooper 2007 on this subject, however).

In remote areas, before travellers and television crews became commonplace almost anywhere, a stranger who appeared out of the blue was usually treated to food and accommodation by local people. Anthropologists benefited from this human hospitality, and they learned to carry gifts or medicines to offer thanks, and to make an initial bid for acceptance. In some cases, local people would adopt an anthropologist as a fictitious relative so that others would know how to relate to them, and this helped with their own local learning. Others failed to achieve this kind of trust, and some were even killed. One I know, who went to work in the South American rain forest, claimed he had spent several weeks living off food thrown out for dogs until the local people accepted that he shared human qualities.

Nowadays, it is rare to find a place where people are unaware of the wider world. Communication technologies have penetrated even the most isolated of areas, and outsiders are unfortunately often associated with unwelcome intrusions, such as industrial construction and environmental destruction, into the lives of local people. It is unsurprising then if the old hospitality to strangers has become rare. Anthropologists also work in cities and other places where their business may be confused with that of less welcome visitors, such as tax inspectors, evangelists or political activists. It is important then to devise strategies to gain the trust and confidence of the people with whom they hope to work.

Many anthropologists have found it useful to arrive with their family. This seems less threatening, and helps to overcome problems of crossing local barriers of age and gender. In some parts of the world, men and women lead very separate lives, and a man may find it virtually impossible to investigate the lives of women, and vice-versa. A female anthropologist who worked in Mexico reported that she found it essential to adopt an 'anomalous sexless' role so that women would not be jealous of her talking to men, and men would not misinterpret her intentions. In rural Japan, at gatherings where men and women sat separately, but in age order, I used to be seated between the youngest man and the oldest woman, so my role must have been ambiguous in this respect too. Later, working with my children in Japan opened doors to subjects I had never even anticipated (see Hendry 1999 for examples).

My own experiences were at first relatively easy: in Mexico, where anthropologists are thick on the ground even if the local interpretation of the word (*antropologia*) is closer to archaeology, and then in Japan, where the pursuit of academic inquiry of any kind seems to be regarded with great respect. In both cases, I received much cooperation from the start, but each had its own problems too. In Mexico, people would sometimes express their suspicion of outsiders asking questions by telling quite blatant lies, even in matters as basic as the number of their children. In Japan, people were more likely to tell me things they thought I'd like to hear – a more subtle form of deception. More recently, I have been working with Indigenous people who have sometimes built up a negative view of anthropologists, largely based on their association with the activities of colonial powers.

Indigenous People – a term adopted collectively by those, also called **Aboriginal** or **First Nations**, whose territories have become subsumed into nations built around them, and who are seeking various 'rights' through international bodies like the United Nations.

All of these problems, and indeed many others encountered by anthropologists, are solved at least to some extent by the fact that their initial study at least is carried out over a longish period of time. A year is regarded as a bare minimum in order to see the complete cycle of annual events, seasons and so forth, but many spend much longer, especially if they are starting from scratch with a new language. Thus the initial reservations of the informants (a word that has long been used for members of the society under study) are usually dispelled, and their views become more transparent as they relax and operate in normal everyday life. In recent years, in response to some who complain that their ancestors shared too much of their lives with outsiders,

informants – the word used for members of the society under study by anthropologists.

who then disappeared to publish their knowledge, the word collaborators has been used for those with whom we work, and increased possibilities for return visits and long-distance communication make the practice more collaborative too.

collaborators – a term used recently in anthropology to describe those with whom we work, who collaborate in our research, to replace the less equal-sounding term **informant**.

Other aspects of the method of investigation help to smooth relations as well, for it has been common to choose a relatively small group of people to work with so that the anthropologist can get to know everyone well. This allows relationships to be observed first hand, as well as to be described, and differing views may be compared. The group could be a village, a school, perhaps an occupational unit such as a factory, bank or advertising agency, or a large extended family. One of my acquaintances took up the study of a group of criminals, whom he used at first to meet largely in pubs, although later he had to spend a lot of his time in prisons. Another decided to observe an enclosed order of nuns. The authors of two PhD theses I have examined on Japan worked in a bridal parlour (see Goldstein-Gidoni in Chapter 12) and a regional museum.

In all such cases, the anthropologist is observing people in what we call 'face-to-face' relations (though recent technology, and websites like *facebook*, have introduced a new meaning to that phrase, which we discuss in Chapter 14). This is a great advantage, not least because people will talk about each other as well as about themselves, which gives the anthropologist more in-depth, interlocking and complex information than can be gleaned from a few one-to-one interviews. More importantly still, however, members of such groups are likely to share a system of values, and although they might disagree with one another on specific issues, they will draw upon a set of underlying assumptions in their communication with each other. It is this set of shared assumptions which defines in broad terms the language they use and the way they see the world through that language.

The anthropologist learns that language, and the world view it portrays, by living amongst the people. They may start out by asking questions – indeed most do, for there are a lot of practical details to amass. Later, however, they may find they learn more by sitting quietly and listening, by joining in with the work of the day, or even by simply observing the activities of others. In Japan, as elsewhere, much is communicated at a non-verbal level, perhaps in silence, in slight movements of the body, or by exchanging gifts or other material goods such as plates of food. Too much verbosity could blind the investigator to this level of interaction.

Listening also allows one a chance to check the validity of statements made in answer to questions. In Japan, for example, there is something of a controversy about whether love marriages are better than those arranged by elders. One old man told me how much he approved of love marriages, winking and confiding that his own had been such. Later I learned that he had refused to consent when his own daughter wanted to have such a marriage, and, even later, I heard him telling one of his friends how dangerous he thought it was for young people to initiate their own relationships. This man was often sought as a go-between, as it turned out, undoubtedly because of his charm and diplomacy – the same qualities which probably lay behind his initial reaction to my investigations, since he knew love marriages were the norm where I came from.

It is this kind of information which adds an extra dimension to the findings of anthropologists who carry out long-term participant observation, and it goes beyond the more limited fieldwork or statistical surveys of the sociologist or economist. There are of course drawbacks, because much depends on the character and interests of the investigators, and their own cultural background. The depth of understanding anthropologists are able to gain, which enables them to see beyond the cool front of a diplomat, has a value that should not be underestimated, however – especially in the global, multicultural world in which most of us now live. To respond to criticisms about the personal bias involved, anthropologists now usually provide information about their own background and experience when they write up their work. This subject is discussed again in Chapter 1.

Translation is the anthropologists' next task. After learning how to live with the people under study, they must return to their own societies and explain what they have found in their own languages. They must discover ways to analyse and make sense of their findings that are comprehensible to their colleagues and compatriots, which is not as easy as it may sound. Other anthropologists who have parallel experiences provide models in their own work for the subsequent reports from the returned fieldworker. These basic accounts are called ethnography, literally writings about a particular 'ethnic' group of people, though ethnicity has been defined in different ways (see Banks 1996). Groups may also be characterised in other ways, as we saw for the criminals and nuns mentioned above (and see MacClancy 1996, in relation to sport).

translation – for anthropologists, this practice involves much more than finding an equivalent word in a different language; gaining an understanding behind the meaning of words and phrases, is an important part of anthropological work.

ethnography – literally, writings about a particular 'ethnic' group of people, the descriptive part of what anthropologists provide in their reports of fieldwork. The term is also used in other disciplines to describe research methods that resemble those of anthropologists.

Comparisons are usually made with previous work, and much time may be spent trying to assess the extent to which areas of apparent similarity are comparable with phenomena observed elsewhere. Findings that seem to be peculiar to a particular group may be especially interesting, but they may also dissolve into general features of society which are manifested under a different guise in other places. It is beneficial to both sides if anthropologists return to the place of their research after some years have elapsed. On the one hand, the people can see at first hand what they helped to achieve in terms of books, films, articles and so forth, and, on the other, they can comment on its accuracy and help to place the initial findings in a long-term context.

The more accomplished scholars use their material to contribute to or to formulate general theories about social life and human behaviour, and this venture has been one of the most important aims of social and cultural anthropology. We are all interested in difference and diversity in the people with whom we carry out our work, but ultimately we are also keen to identify underlying principles in the way that human beings put together and enact their social, political and ritual life. We may be fascinated by the variety and ingenuity we discover – and this is one of the aspects of the subject that can be shared beyond the field – but to make general theory about the human condition is a bigger aim that is not always so easy to transmit.

It is this part of our work that may irk our informants, or 'collaborators', because the published material will carry 'their' knowledge that they have 'shared' with us into a more esoteric form of analysis that may seem to leave them in an inferior position. (This feeling of inferiority on the part of the collaborators stems from the fact that they may feel excluded by the language of academic anthropology – but in reality, all spheres, academic or otherwise, have their own specialist language and terminology: just as anthropologists may use terms with which their collaborators are not familiar, so archaeologists or biologists may understand different, specialist language which is unfamiliar to the anthropologist.) We will return to this issue several times, for there are also historical reasons for this perception of a power differential. In the meantime, for you, the reader, an important aim of the present book is to introduce some of the specialist language anthropologists share, and some of the theoretical advances that they have made.

It should be emphasised straight away, however, that anthropological theories do not always build upon one another. Indeed, many set out to contradict those of previous scholars; this critical approach is part of an anthropologist's training and we will begin to introduce it here (see Sykes 2005, for another example). There are some classic works, which are accepted by most people in the field, and these will be discussed quite early on in this book. There are also several areas where different interpretations exist side by side, and there is no consensus about which is better. Some of these will be mentioned too. This book is inevitably informed by the British anthropological traditions which exist in Oxford, where I was trained, but it is intended as an introduction to the subject that is accessible and engaging no matter what the reader's background. An important thing to remember, however, is that the study of society is not simply the learning of a body of facts. The study of ourselves and our social worlds is an area of much interpretation and many differing views.

Writing for the general public, on the one hand, or working with them, on the other, is less often the aim of anthropologists, at least at first: rather, they tend to write for and work with colleagues who share much of the same background and have parallel experiences on which to draw. This book is an attempt to bridge the first of those gaps, however. A growing number of anthropologists afterwards bridge the second by putting their new understanding into practical applications in the wider world, an area known as applied anthropology, which we will consider in the last section of Chapter 14 of this book. Some also make, or advise on, television documentaries about the area where they worked, and there is now a superb worldwide collection of visual ethnography (see Banks 2001; Pink 2001). Reference to a selection of films, some of them now classic, is made at the end of each chapter of this book, and some general distributors and anthropological film festivals are listed at the end of this chapter.

> **applied anthropology** – using knowledge gained through the academic study of anthropology out in the public arena, usually to the benefit of people there.

Many students of anthropology go out into the world to do quite unrelated tasks, but always informed by the knowledge that *their* world, *their* way of thinking, is only one of many. They are equipped with the skill to see the other's point of view, whether the other be Chinese, Czech or from Church Hanborough, and it is this skill which can be acquired through the study of social and cultural anthropology. Even without becoming a professional anthropologist, a student of the subject can gain a great deal from at least a smattering of practical experience, carrying out a project in a 'world' different from their own. This book offers only the first key to the first door to this experience, but it is a door that many people fail ever to open.

A Brief History of Social (and Cultural) Anthropology

We have so far made no distinction between the terms 'social' and 'cultural' in qualifying the subject of anthropology, and indeed, there is not a great deal to distinguish the two approaches to the field in the way it is practised today. In this section we will see that they have had rather different histories, reflecting in some ways the locations where they were developed, and in others, the theoretical interests of those who built them up. *Social anthropology* is a more accurate name for the practice I have described so far, as *cultural anthropology* has a greater concern with collecting material objects, and did not always involve such long periods of fieldwork. In practice, the terms 'society' and 'culture' have been much discussed in ways that need not concern us at this stage. Taking a look at the history of the field will give us a basis for a later understanding, however.

The subject as practised today actually developed only within the last hundred-odd years, and some of the stages in its development will be illustrated in the chapters that follow. However, its intellectual foundations go back a little further and it has recently been subjected to considerable critical self-scrutiny, so it is useful before embarking on these chapters to lay out some of this general background. A thorough history of anthropology would form the subject matter of a book in its own right, and indeed, several have been written (an accessible one is *A History of Anthropology* by Eriksen and Nielson, published in 2001). This section seeks only to summarise some of the issues that have been addressed, and to place them in the context of changes that have affected and improved our work.

People have undoubtedly speculated about neighbours they considered strange since time immemorial, and travellers' tales have always been popular, but the European interest in social life became more focused when the tales of explorers and adventurers began to show striking similarities between societies found in different parts of the world. Many such societies fell prey to the destructive European battles for colonisation, largely because their technological resources were inadequate to resist the Europeans who arrived on their shores. The more sympathetic invaders consoled themselves with the thought that they were bringing 'civilisation' to those whose lands they were claiming, and they collected information about the people they met as they realised that their worlds were being irrevocably changed. Theories were also developed about how studies of these so-called 'primitive' people could shed light on the prehistorical past of the investigators' own worlds.

These theories built on the establishment in the eighteenth century of the 'rational' way of thinking of the natural sciences (the period in which this approach developed is described as 'Enlightenment', so important was the understanding scholars felt they were gaining of the world around them). Laws were proposed and tested to explain the physical, chemical and biological worlds, and it came to be thought that society could be regarded as a natural system too. In France, for example, Montesquieu set out to discover the laws of social life by analysing and comparing various types of political institutions, and examining religious beliefs as social phenomena, which he argued were usually suited to the society in which they were found and therefore difficult to transport.

In Scotland, during the same period, David Hume was investigating the origins of religion in human nature, and he posited a development from polytheism through monotheism to the inevitable decline of religion. He was part of the school of Moral Philosophers, which also included Adam Smith, who founded the discipline of economics, and Adam Ferguson, one of the early thinkers to argue that contemporary 'primitive' society could throw light on the past history of 'higher' societies. It was in France, though, that a science of society was seriously proposed. First, Saint-Simon built on an assertion made by Condorcet that social phenomena were just as natural as those of organic and inorganic sciences were, and he suggested therefore that they should be studied by the same methods. The subject was named *sociology* by Comte, who drew up a ranking of sciences ranging from mathematics and astronomy as the most general, through to psychology and sociology at the extreme of greatest complexity. His laws of social life were based on the assumption that all societies evolved through the same stages, and that the human species has a fundamental tendency to ameliorate itself.

polytheism – a belief system that holds that there are multiple gods.

monotheism – a belief system that holds that there is only one God.

This evolutionary approach characterised the wider thinking of the nineteenth century, when several systematic attempts were made to trace the development of social institutions through different stages. J. F. McLennan made a study of marriage, for example, and Henry Maine made one of law. In Britain the most influential theoretical writer of the time was probably Herbert Spencer, whose ideas about the 'survival of the fittest' were later attributed to that other great evolutionist of the nineteenth century, Charles Darwin. Spencer made many biological analogies in his consideration of society as 'superorganic', and he also advocated looking at how the parts of a society related to one another rather than taking them out of context as others were wont to do.

This was later to be the cornerstone of two schools of anthropology known as functionalism and structural functionalism, led by twenti-eth-century scholars Bronislaw Malinowski and A. R. Radcliffe-Brown, respectively. These approaches, each seeking an explanation of social behaviour within a particular society at a particular time, were something of a reaction to the previous evolutionary method, although they were later criticised for neglecting history. They entailed spending a long time with a particular people and really learning their language in all its complexity, and this came to distinguish *social anthropology* from *sociology*.

Malinowski, a Polish-born anthropologist, was the first major proponent of the value of this long-term study in Britain. He had been interned in Australia at the start of the First World War, and spent several years in the Trobriand Islands, where he discovered the great advantages of a long stay for properly understanding the ways of thinking of another people. The functionalist approach he advocated was grounded in the idea that all social and cultural behaviour could be explained as responding to human needs. He taught social anthropology at the London School of Economics (LSE) on his return to Europe, and inspired a whole cohort of anthropological fieldworkers who produced a body of detailed ethnography. Some of Malinowski's work is discussed in Chapters 3 and 7, and that of other members of the continuing LSE department throughout the book.

Radcliffe-Brown's long-term fieldwork was carried out in the Andaman Islands (Bay of Bengal) from 1906 to 1908, although it was less intensive than that of Malinowski. His interests were in the value of social behaviour for the maintenance and well-being of a network of social relations he called the social structure – hence the phrase structural functionalism. He taught in Sydney, Capetown and Chicago, so his work was very influential around the world. It has remained known as British social anthropology, though it is less often referred to in Britain now than elsewhere, and in the United States, at least, a reaction to the closed nature of his analysis still continues.

functionalism – a word used to describe theories that explain social behaviour in terms of the way it appears to respond to the needs of members of that society, as advocated by Bronislaw Malinowski and his followers.

structural functionalism – a theory of explanation of social behaviour which examines the way that components of a particular society functioned to maintain the **social structure**. It was developed by Radcliffe-Brown and applied for a while by his followers.

Social structure – a way of describing the make-up of the features of a society in order to devise general theories that could be applied to specific cases, but also allow cross-cultural comparison.

We will look at an example of Radcliffe-Brown's work in Chapter 9, and illustrate its inapplicability to the contemporary world in Chapter 14.

In the United States, the emphasis on intensive fieldwork dates back to the earlier work of Franz Boas, a German immigrant of Jewish origin, who argued in 1896 that all cultures were equal but different, and a great deal of work needed to be applied to each one. He spent long periods of time studying with groups of Native Americans, and trained his followers to collect detailed empirical data about their material culture, as well as language and social behaviour. His work became known as *cultural anthropology*, and he introduced the idea of cultural relativism, which argues that because cultures are based on different ideas about the world, they can only be properly understood in terms of their own standards and values, although this does not mean that outsiders cannot learn to decipher those meanings.

cultural relativism – a term devised by Franz Boas to explain that as cultures are based on different ideas about the world, they can only be properly understood in terms of their own standards and values. The phrase has been misunderstood to deny human universals, and to suggest that cultures cannot change.

Ruth Benedict, a student of Boas, continued his efforts to demonstrate the basic equality of different cultural forms, and avidly to collect materials about peoples who were coming under the threat of contradictory assimilation policies that still operated on the assumption of an evolutionary superiority. Like most anthropologists, she opposed war as an expression of this kind of posture, an important stance in the build-up to race-based fascism in Europe. Although she was employed by the United States War Office to study the enemy Japanese during the Second World War, her book (1954[1946]) makes a plea for 'a world made safe for cultural difference'. It was also later described by a Japanese anthropologist as a 'consistently balanced contrast between America and Japan' (Aoki 1994: 5). Almost contemporary with Benedict was the anthropologist Margaret Mead, who brought her writings about Pacific peoples in Samoa and Papua New Guinea so much into the American public domain that she remains famous to this day.

In Europe, a French sociologist who had a profound influence on the evolving subject of social anthropology in the early part of the twentieth century was Emile Durkheim. His concerns were still evolutionary, but he insisted that society must be looked at as more than the sum of individuals who make it up. He advocated the identification of social facts, which exist outside the individual and exercise constraint 'like moulds in which our actions are inevitably shaped'. Examples are legal and moral regulations, religious faiths, financial systems, and taste in art, all of which form part of our socialisation and education in a particular society. He led a group of scholars who were, sadly, largely wiped out in the First World War. Some of the work he wrote with another member, Marcel Mauss, will be discussed in Chapter 1, and Mauss will reappear in Chapter 3.

social facts – the proper materials, which 'exist outside the individual and exercise constraint', to be collected by sociologists and anthropologists, as advocated by Emile Durkheim.

The first chair in anthropology was created in Oxford at the turn of the twentieth century, and it was held by Edward Tylor, who also reacted negatively to the idea that 'savages' were somehow different from 'civilised' people. He had travelled in Mexico as a young man and he continually argued that 'human nature is everywhere similar'. He encouraged the comparison of 'primitive' and 'civilised' practices, but he was still an evolutionist. Another school of thought – the Diffusionists – argued for a cradle of civilisation from which practices had spread or *diffused* around the world, as people influenced and copied one another. Eventually, another influential Oxford professor of anthropology, Edward Evans-Pritchard, pointed to a futility in the speculation about how societies had developed, or evolved, and even rejected the idea of social laws.

He argued that societies are systems only because human beings need to order the world rationally, and anthropologists should study this structural order, and seek *meaning* (rather than *function*) for the elements that make up that order in the context of a particular society. He advocated representing a particular society by establishing sets of related abstractions, which could then be compared with those of other societies. These structures could undergo transformations, which would represent change, an advance on the earlier structural functional explanations, which seemed to ignore history. Some examples of his work are discussed further in Chapter 7 and Chapter 10 of this book.

One of the most influential anthropologists to date has been another Frenchman, Claude Lévi-Strauss, whose name will pop up in several chapters. Among other things, he marvelled at the human capacity to devise, tell and pass on stories, the structure of which he analysed in fine detail. His brand of structuralism was different again from that of Evans-Pritchard and Radcliffe-Brown, however, as he was seeking to explain human behaviour through universal qualities of the human mind. Professors of social anthropology who built on the work of Lévi-Strauss include Mary Douglas in London, Rodney Needham in Oxford, and Edmund Leach in Cambridge, although all three moved on in their own distinctive ways, and we will also see the influence of their thinking in several chapters.

structuralism – a method, originally developed in linguistics, of analysing elements of social phenomena for their meaning in displaying the framework of society as a set of structural relations which express a universal human capacity to classify and construct such systems of thought.

It is hard to know where to draw to a halt in laying out the history of an ongoing field, and much more could have been covered in this brief introduction, but I think that enough background has been presented to give an idea of where social and cultural anthropology has come from. In the academic year that this book goes to press, Mary Douglas and Rodney Needham have passed away, and with them goes a period that will never be repeated. Throughout the subsequent pages of this book the work of many living anthropologists will be discussed, alongside other influential characters from the history of the subject, and towards the end we will look towards the period when these will all become part of history – but for the time being let us examine how the book will be laid out.

The Content of this Book

Because anthropology can be quite complex, and therefore possibly daunting, I have organised the presentation of chapters in a way that will, I hope, start with things that all readers can find familiar and relatively easy to understand. The discussion questions at the end of each chapter are designed to encourage individual readers to consider how the general issues raised apply in your own lives, and these will also offer opportunities for comparison in class, and among friends and fellow students. More complex issues are introduced gradually, once the basic building blocks have been laid, and the material is presented in such a way that theoretical influences we touched upon in the history section should become clearer in the context of specific cases.

The order of the chapters is not entirely chronological, but the material has also been arranged to offer a sense of the way the subject has developed, bringing some of the classic contributions in at the start, and ending with the consequences of recent technological change. It also moves from a consideration of how anthropologists go about their work, to a discussion of various important themes and issues that concern them, and ends with the two new chapters that bring the second edition up to date with various changes in the field. Some of the issues raised are covered only superficially here, partly for lack of space, but also because the aim of the text is to give an overall introduction, and those who wish to can pursue their studies elsewhere. The questions and readings at the end of the chapters are designed to help also with this.

In fact there is much material presented at the end of the chapters, and readers need to take care to evaluate the types of knowledge they will acquire in following up the suggestions. The first section, headed 'References and Further Reading', offers directly the sources of the anthropology discussed in the body of the chapter, as well as other anthropology that pursues the same themes. It is divided into books that present thorough coverage of the various issues, and articles that will give a briefer, though not necessarily easier take on the themes. There then follows a list of novels, which usually do offer easier reading, and which may give a great insight into the aspects of life in question, but which are not anthropology, as such.

The films provide a mixture of the above, but in a different medium. Thus, there are feature films, which offer a level of knowledge that may be compared with the novels, and these can usually be hired in video stores, or downloaded from the internet. Then, there are documentary films, made by professional film-makers, often for release on television, but also sometimes easily available, and these may be quite controversial from an anthropological point of view and, in some cases, we have offered articles discussing such films. There are a few films made by people about themselves (see *Redskins, Tricksters and Puppy Stew*, below, for example), sometimes together with an anthropologist, and then there are films made by anthropologists as part of the work they do. This last is material, like the books and articles listed, that illustrates the work that anthropologists do, in this case known as visual anthropology.

Finally, there are some limited listings of internet sites, and again these are quite varied in quality and content. Some are illustrative of points being made in the text, some go further into the issues, but less authoritatively than the published books, and others provide reading lists and other useful information. These lists of internet sites are only really indicative of the kinds of things that can be found in cyberspace, which actually come and go, and so may not be available for long, but it will be easy enough to find others for yourselves as you go along. Try to ascertain the nature and source of the site before you take the content too seriously. Some are excellent resources, others are less valuable, but there is plenty to choose from out there.

Throughout the body of the text, 'personal accounts' bring first-hand illustrations or modifications of the ideas being presented, mostly from the point of view of people whose forebears have been studied and described by anthropologists, although one or two take a different approach. These are there for three main reasons. First, they make it possible in several cases to see that the people on whose lives anthropologists built their theories, sometimes quite long ago, still exist and still share an identity, though their lives may have changed. Secondly, they add examples of the raw material that anthropologists work with, the real people on whose cooperation we depend. Lastly, and in a way most importantly, they add an authority that no amount of second-hand recounting can do, and I hope that their contributions will help to bring the text alive as you venture into this new field.

References and Further Research

Books

Banks, Marcus (ed.) (1996) *Ethnicity: Anthropological Constructions* (London: Routledge).

Banks, Marcus (2001) *Visual Methods in Social Research* (London: Sage).

Baumann, Gerd (1996) *Contesting Culture: Discourses of Identity in Multi-ethnic London* (Cambridge: Cambridge University Press).

Benedict, Ruth (1954) *The Chrysanthemum and the Sword* (Tokyo: Tuttle).

Davies, Charlotte (1999) *Reflexive Ethnography* (London: Routledge 1999).

Eriksen, Thomas Hylland, with Finn Sivert Nielson (2001) *A History of Anthropology* (London: Pluto Press).

Hendry, Joy (1999) An Anthropologist in Japan (London: Routledge).

MacClancy, Jeremy (ed.) (1996) *Sport, Identity and Ethnicity* (Oxford: Berg).

Pink, Sarah (2001) *Doing Visual Ethnography: Images, Media and Representation in Research* (London: Sage).

Sykes, Karen (2005) *Arguing with Anthropology: An Introduction to Critical Theories of the Gift* (London: Routledge).

Tayler, Donald (1997) *The Coming of the Sun: A Prologue to Ika Sacred Narrative* (Oxford: Pitt Rivers Museum Monograph Series, no.7).

Tuhiwai-Smith, Linda (1999) *Decolonizing Methodologies: Research and Indigenous Peoples* (New York: Zed Books).

Articles

Aoki Tamotsu (1994) 'Anthropology and Japan: Attempts at Writing Culture' *Japan Foundation Newsletter* **XXII** (3): 1–6.

Bourdieu, P. (2003) 'Participant Objectivation', *Journal of the Royal Anthropological Institute* (n.s.) 9: 281–94.

Cooper, M. (2007) 'Sharing Data and Results in Ethnographic Research: Why this Should Not be an Ethical Imperative'. *Journal of Empirical Research on Human Research Ethics*, 2(1): 3–19.

Eriksen, Thomas Hyland (2005) 'Nothing to Lose But our Aitches', *Anthropology Today*. 21(2): 1–2.

Hart, Keith (2004) 'What Anthropologists Really Do', *Anthropology Today*. 20(1): 3–5.

Hendry, Joy 1996 'The Chrysanthemum Continues to Flower: Ruth Benedict and Some Perils of Popular Anthropology', in Jeremy MacClancy and Chris McDonaugh (eds), *Popularising Anthropology* (London: Routledge), pp. 106–21.

Mills, David (2006) 'Trust Me, I'm an Anthropologist', *Anthropology Today*, 22(2): 1–2.

Whisson, Michael G (1986) 'Why Study Anthropology?', *Anthropology Today*, 2(1) 23–4.

Novels

Forster, E. M. (1998 [1924]) *A Passage to India* (London: Penguin,) provides insight into the encounter between Western, colonial values, and Indian society pre-Independence.

Lewycka, Marina (2006) *A Short History of Tractors in Ukrainian* (Harmondsworth: Penguin,) gradually reveals the story of a Ukrainian family and its adjustments to life in Britain.

Lodge, David (1989) *Nice Work* (Harmondsworth: Penguin) is an amusing fictional account of an anthropologist and a businessman who trail each other at work.

Tan, Amy (1994) *The Joy Luck Club* (London: Minerva) is a novel touching on problems of cultural identity in the relationship between Chinese women and their Chinese–American daughters.

Films

The 'Strangers Abroad' series (André Singer, 1985) introduces five of the early anthropologists and their influence on the subject. *Off the Verandah*, about Bronislaw Malinowski, demonstrates the value for British colonists of getting down off their verandahs and living with the people they were describing. *Fieldwork*, about Sir Walter Baldwin Spencer, pursues the theme by illustrating his work with the Arunta and other Australian Aboriginal peoples. There are also films about W. H. R. Rivers (see Chapter 11), Margaret Mead, and Edward Evans-Pritchard. The work of Rivers is introduced in Chapter 1.

Firth on Firth (Rolf Husmann, Peter Loizos, Werner Sperschneider, 1993) a film in which Sir Raymond Firth (see Chapter 5) talks about his life, social anthropology under Malinowski at the London School of Economics, and his fieldwork.

Redskins, Tricksters and Puppy Stew (directed by Drew Hayden Taylor for the National Film Board of Canada, 2000), in which the Ojibwe director presents a humourous account of life in Native Canada.

Good sources of anthropological/ethnographic films include:
Asian Educational Media Services (AMES) www. Ames.uiuc.edu

Documentary Educational Resources (DER) http://www.der.org/
Royal Anthropological Institute (RAI) http://www.therai.org.uk/film/film.html
The National Library of Australia http://www.nla.gov.au/film/
Granada Centre granada.centre@manchester.ac.uk
Life on Lens http://www.lifeonlens.org/ (though not specifically anthropological, this
    charity is dedicated to documenting humanitarian achievements on film and contains
    interesting material.

There are also a number of international ethnographic film festivals:
AA (Screenings of the Visual Anthropology Association at the American Anthropological
    Association congresses, annual) http://www.societyforvisualanthropology.org
Astra Film Festival (Northwest Romania, annual) http://www.astrafilm.ro
Beeld voor Beeld (Amsterdam, annual) http://www.beeldvoorbeeld.nl
Göttingen International Film Festival (Germany, biennial) http://www.iwf.de/giff/
Margaret Mead Film & Video Festival (New York, annual) http://www.amnh.org
Mostra Internacional do Filme Etnográfico (Rio de Janeiro, biennial) http://www.
    mostraetnografica.com.br/
Nordic Anthropological Film Association festival (peripatetic, biennial) www.nafa.uib.no/
International Festival of Ethnographic Film, Royal Anthropological Festival (peripatetic,
    biennial) www.raifilmfest.org.uk
Taiwan International Ethnographic Film Festival (Taipei, biennial) http://www.tieff.sinica.edu.
    tw/

Websites

http://www.anthrobase.com/Browse/Thm/index.html – a limited index of references to
    anthropological works in a variety of European languages.
http://www.as.ua.edu/ant/Faculty/murphy/436/anthros.htm – a site prepared by students for
    students about anthropological theories.
http://www.sas.upenn.edu/~nsalazar/anthropology.html – a site with lots of links useful for
    students of anthropology.

Seeing the World

Souvenirs and Handkerchiefs

Visitors to foreign countries very often return with a selection of objects collectively known as souvenirs. These are items acquired on the journey. They may be received as gifts, purchased in a tourist shop, or even just picked up on the beach. Their economic value is not necessarily important, for these objects are not usually for resale. Instead, they are essentially material reminders of the experience of the traveller. The objects may also be chosen for a variety of other reasons – for some perceived intrinsic beauty, to show off to friends, to give as a gift, or just to stand on the windowsill and bring out one of the colours in the curtains. However, all will be chosen because they are in some way remarkable, and because they stand for the place in which they were acquired.

The same objects, taken individually, will have different meanings to the people for whom they are a part of everyday life. In tourist resorts, local business people become astute at anticipating the interests of visitors, and many secure their living by making available a range of local goods, as we will discuss again in Chapter 13. Some goods may be designed for the purpose, but the best bargains – or business prospects, depending on who notices first – are those goods which are mundane locally, but unusual and appealing to outsiders. Objects that are taken for granted and perhaps readily produced in one place may be rare and charming in another. They may also have quite different uses.

To take a simple example, there are in Japan some light and relatively cheap souvenirs known as *hankachi*. These are neatly finished squares of soft cloth, often individually packed in cellophane, and characteristically printed with a Japanese motif such as an *ukiyoe* print (see Photograph 1.1) or a local view. These *hankachi* are actually named after 'handkerchiefs', but they are often so exquisitely soft and beautiful that it would seem a positive injustice to apply them to a runny nose. Indeed, they may well be inadequate for the task, for in Japan 'handkerchiefs' are for delicately dabbing at a sweaty brow on a hot summer's day. In Japan, the

Photograph 1.1

This Japanese handkerchief makes a good gift or souvenir, but it would hardly serve for blowing the nose (photograph: Lisa Hill)

whole idea of blowing one's nose into a piece of cloth, and storing the subsequent contents in a pocket, is seen as quite disgusting.

This single example illustrates a basic principle underlying the whole subject of anthropology, namely that different people *see* things – or, in anthropological terms, classify things – in different ways. For a foreign visitor to Japan, the *hankachi* is, at least at first, a member of the class of objects known as souvenirs. It may also belong to a *class* known as gifts, which could be shared at least superficially by both Japanese donor and foreign recipient. Once received, however, the same object may be further *classified* together with other similar objects in several different categories, depending on local ideas about usage. Moreover, a possibility amongst one particular people – that of containing nasal mucus and storing it in a pocket – invokes extremely negative reactions in another people.

The handkerchief continues to be a good illustration of principles underlying this subject even within one country, for different segments of the population may well have different ideas about handkerchiefs. A generation ago in Britain, for example, people were brought up to regard 'a clean hankie' as a vital part of their daily dress. Indeed, our mothers (or teachers) would chastise us if we were found to be without one. Thus some older members of the community continue to carry handkerchiefs, as they were trained, while younger people rarely use more than the paper tissue which has come to be a more convenient, if less environmentally friendly, substitute.

These paper tissues – at least the ones known by the brand name Kleenex – were originally designed in America in 1924 for women to use to remove face cream. In the 1930s, when people began also to use them as handkerchiefs, the American company Kimberly-Clark seized upon the idea and created the advertising slogan 'the handkerchiefs you can throw away.' According to an American friend/informant, the replacement of handkerchiefs with paper tissues was fostered by an increasing sensitivity in America to infection. Another tells me they are mostly used by 'older aunts and grandmothers', but an exception is the male gay community, who have a colour-coded use of handkerchiefs 'to indicate their availability and preferences'.

During the heyday of handkerchiefs, there was great variety in the quality, and people would judge one another's taste and affluence according to the type they carried. Perhaps associated with this idea, it used to be part of smart dress among some groups of men to wear a handkerchief peeking out of their top pocket. Others would avoid the custom, seeing it as ostentatious or crude. Some people would carry handkerchiefs made of silk, others would have them embossed with their initial, and some would tie knots in the corners of them and wear them on the beach to keep off the sun. People who thought of themselves as 'ladies' would display the delicate lace edging of their handkerchiefs by wearing them in the front of their low-cut dresses, or by dropping them at strategic moments for passing men to pick up.

Different ideas about these small squares of cloth indicated information about the social allegiances of their owners, and thus provided ways of *classifying* other people according to their upbringing, generation and status. The use of handkerchiefs was thus rather appropriately associated with the *class* system in Britain, and parallel distinctions elsewhere. Nowadays, they are much less used, but beautiful lace hankies are still a popular gift from Venice or Brussels and, in the airport in Beijing, they come in a range of qualities so that they can be given as change in a country which forbids the export of much of its currency. In a 'progressive' kindergarten in Japan, which has done away with the use of uniforms for its charges, the children who go there must nevertheless wear a hankie pinned to their clothes to indicate their membership of a particular *class*.

Learning to Classify

We have see, then, that classification in an anthropological sense is concerned with the way different people *see* the world. This is because people divide up the world into categories of objects and categories of living beings in ways that differ from the ways other people do it. Time and place are classified in a variety of ways, as we shall shortly illustrate in more detail. A system of classification is something that is shared by members of a particular society. It is among the most fundamental characteristics of that society, and it is acquired by children growing up to be members of that society. It is, indeed, the basis of the socialisation of a child, the conversion of a biological being into a social one, who shares a system of communication with those who surround it.

classification – a system of organisation of people, places and things shared by all human beings, but in ways that differ in different societies, which therefore forms a subject of interest to anthropologists.

socialisation – the inculcation into a child of a society's systems of classification and ways of behaving so that it is converted from a biological being into a social one. The term may also be used for adults acquiring a new set of social rules and mores.

As babies learn their first words, they learn simultaneously a range of meaning for the sounds they enunciate. They learn to use the 'label' of each word for a particular 'category' of meaning. Anyone who has spent time with babies will know that this category and its meaning may for some time be rather different from that of the adults around, and parents are usually required to 'translate' the baby's utterances. A classic and potentially embarrassing example is the way some babies learn the word 'Daddy' and then apply it indiscriminately to sundry other men they meet. The baby has learned the label 'Daddy', which applies to a particular man they probably know rather well, but they are not yet aware of any of the further detail about the meaning of the word. They may have in mind a category closer to 'man', or perhaps 'young man with blond or black hair', nothing which they could possibly explain, but some part of the world which they link with that label. Later, they will come to associate much more meaning to the label, and realise to whom it makes an appropriate address. But all this takes time.

In some languages, the label which corresponds to 'Daddy' actually applies to a range of people, as we will discuss in more detail later on, and the baby in that society will eventually learn who those people are and how they are to be distinguished from other people. In both cases, the babies are learning to classify people. They will also learn any number of other terms, together with the characteristics that define them. Just as they learn language, then, they are learning a system of classification shared by other people who use that language. In complex, multicultural societies, like many of those where English is spoken, there will be variations in both the language and the system of classification, and these may be related, rather appropriately again, to class distinctions.

Our first system of classification is usually learnt so early that it becomes deeply ingrained. Until we think about it, it seems as natural as eating and sleeping. We have notions of people, classified as relatives, friends or strangers, with further subdivisions depending on various other characteristics, and we have ideas about the expectations of those categories; we also classify places, again with expectations about them – for example, we may learn to drop our voices or remove shoes when we enter a place of worship, call out a greeting as we enter a house, and perhaps to salivate for popcorn when we enter a cinema. Things of one sort or another are classified as nice or nasty, clean or dirty, safe or dangerous.

Until we travel outside our own society we tend to take for granted that our system of classification is universal. Even then, we may learn differences only rather reluctantly, and some notions are very hard to shift. We may find countries foreign to us, or even just foreign neighbours, 'smelly', 'dirty', or simply 'strange'. For anthropologists to learn the system of classification of another people, they must first learn to stand outside their own system and to reject notions of revulsion or disapproval based on their early upbringing. As a baby learns to classify in its own society, the anthropologist must learn all over again the new system of classification of the people under study.

In the introduction to his translation of a book on the subject of classification, Rodney Needham compares the anthropologist, setting out to study a strange people, with a person blind from birth who is suddenly given sight. In the latter case, the first impression is apparently of a

> painful chaos of forms and colours, a gaudy confusion of visual impressions none of which seem to bear any comprehensible relationship to the others. (Needham in Durkheim and Mauss 1963: vii)

Just as the previously blind person needs to learn to distinguish and classify objects, the 'culturally blind' anthropologist needs to learn to make sense of 'a confusion of foreign impressions, none of which can safely be assumed to be what they appear' (ibid.).

Life, Death and Burial Alive

The task of understanding fully the categories of another society is a very difficult one. Indeed, the whole enterprise is relatively recent, and tended for some time to concentrate on so-called 'primitive' people. In the early twentieth century the French philosopher Lucien Lévy-Bruhl (1910) wrote a book about what he called the mentality of primitive people, which he described as 'pre-logical'. At that time descriptions of people in remote parts of the world were based on limited observation, often without the benefit of language, and their practices sometimes seemed to defy the cherished systems of logic that were held to underpin all 'civilised' thought. As explained in the Introduction, Europeans of the time saw themselves at the pinnacle of development, and they saw people who were technologically less advanced as radically different.

In fact, this 'civilised thought' was actually the thought of Western Europeans. W. H. R. Rivers questioned the idea that there was a fundamental difference between the logic of primitive people and that of their observers. In an essay entitled 'The Primitive Conception of Death' (1926), he suggested that deeper investigation would reveal logic quite recognisable to the Western mind if due consideration was given to the fact that things might be *classified* differently. Drawing on his own experience among Melanesian people in the Solomon Islands, he addressed some apparent contradictions in the use of a local word, *mate*, used to translate 'dead', but also applied to people who by his standards were patently still living.

It might be thought at first sight that the distinction between life and death is rather clear. A person is either alive, or they are dead. Their heart is beating or it is not. This is simply one way in which to classify death as a state, however, and even this has been brought into question since the introduction of life-support machines. A state of 'brain death' might now justify the stopping of a heartbeat sustained by such a machine, and this possibility has brought to the surface a general degree of woolliness in the definition of death. Amongst the Melanesians, Rivers suggested that the category *mate* also included the idea of 'very ill' and 'very old', so that the dividing line between that and the opposite *toa* (*alive*) is drawn in a different way to the distinction between life and death in Europe at the time.

His own distinction was a biological one, based on certain observations of the body perceived through a fairly sophisticated understanding of its component parts. It also involved, more subtly, notions set in a historical and philosophical context about the heart and the soul. Elsewhere, the distinction may be concerned with socioeconomic value, and a scarcity of resources. Japanese folk tales recount a custom of leaving old people up on a mountain once they had reached a certain stage of frailty and inability to contribute to the needs of family life. In Melanesia some people were being buried alive, by a European system of classification, as they were reported to have been in parts of Africa.

Notions of life and death are related to notions of the afterlife, and what becomes of people after they 'die'. Europeans were profoundly shocked in the sixteenth century when they discovered human sacrifice practised among the Aztecs, and they tried immediately to put a stop to it. The Aztec people saw human sacrifice as an essential part of the appeasement of their gods, however, and it was thought to be a noble way to die, which would give one a special, honoured position in the next life. They understood that if they failed to 'feed' their gods in this way, the world would come to an end. As it happened, they were proved right in a way. The Spaniards put a stop to the practice and that particular Aztec world was indeed destroyed. There are people today attempting to recreate Aztec dancing and other practices, but the old Aztec 'civilisation' was indeed destroyed by the arrival of the Europeans.

Prior to the colonisation of the Sudan, when the practice was also prohibited, the Dinka people are said to have preferred to bury members of their priestly class while they were still alive. Godfrey Lienhardt, who did not witness the custom, but analysed it in his immensely readable book *Divinity and Experience*, quotes one of his informants as follows:

> When a master of the fishing-spear has fallen sick and is becoming weak, he will call all his people and tell them to bring his whole camp (tribe or subtribe) to his home to bury him whilst he lives. His people will obey him and quickly come, for if they delay and the master . . . dies before they reach him, they will be most miserable . . .
> And he will not be afraid of death; he will be put in the earth while singing his songs. Nobody among his people will wail or cry because their man has died. They will be joyful because their master . . . will give them life so that they shall live untroubled by any evil.   (Lienhardt 1961: 300)

Lienhardt's book contains much information about these masters, and their role in performing myth and ritual, when they are seen to embody the traditions of the Dinka people. He is thus able to interpret this practice as a representation to the Dinka people of a renewal of their own collective life (ibid. 301).

In the case of the Melanesians, Rivers puts the distinction between *mate* and *toa* in the context of different ideas about stages of life, and, again, about what happens to human beings after death. He also suggests that a clearer understanding of a different system of classification in this respect could perhaps explain events which had horrified European travellers and missionaries when they had observed the funerals and burials of people who, for them, were still alive.

He also points out, incidentally, that Melanesians use different systems from Europeans to classify their relatives, applying the term 'father' to the brothers of their fathers, by his reckoning, and also to the husbands of their mother's sisters (systems we will discuss further in Chapter 11). This is related to a wider system, which makes clear distinctions between generations, and between relatives on the mother's and father's side of the family. Rivers makes some amusing speculations about what Melanesians might make of the local system of classifying relatives were they to come and study English people, who, for them, apply words (like cousin, uncle and aunt) indiscriminately across these boundaries. He suggests, not altogether frivolously, a possible native view that 'the hyperdevelopment of material culture has led to an atrophy of the thought processes' – perhaps a 'post-logical mentality' (1926: 45).

Cultural Relativism and the Anthropologists' Bias

Rivers himself betrays a system of classification common amongst writers of the time by describing peoples as 'primitive' or 'savage', as if this in itself allows a degree of generalisation. Although he is arguing against Lévy-Bruhl's ideas of 'pre-logical mentality', he still tends to assume that the Melanesians he describes will share certain forms of classification with other people of 'lower orders'. This broad classification of peoples is related to technological achievements, but it also illustrates the idea of the time that an understanding of earlier stages of development of more 'advanced' peoples could be sought in the practices of the more 'primitive'.

The best-known book which addresses directly the subject of classification, written in French at the turn of the twentieth century, reflects this notion that peoples could be fitted onto a scale of civilisation, with the European scholarly elite (particularly the French) at one end, and the so-called 'primitive' people at the other. Durkheim and Mauss (1963), in their book entitled *Primitive Classification*, turn to 'primitive' society in an attempt to demonstrate their idea that the origins of mental categories are to be found in society. Nowadays social anthropologists are less concerned with origins than they used to be, but they are of necessity concerned with modes of classification, and the book also gives some very good examples of how various these may be.

The first two chapters are concerned in particular with the *classification of other human beings*. They discuss various systems reported from Australian Aboriginal groups, which divide themselves into marriage classes and clans associated with animals. The whole society may also be divided into two major classes described by the observers as *moieties*. The consequences of such a system for the people concerned are multiple, but major ones include a division of all other human beings into those one may and those one may not marry. Some people also have groups into which marriage is preferred. This will have further ramifications as the system operates to produce relatives of one sort or another, and these will fall into indigenous categories quite impossible to translate accurately into the usual English system of names for relatives (see Chapter 6, p. 124, for a first-hand account of Yolngu moieties).

Anyone can approach an understanding of such a system when thinking of which members of their own families would be prohibited to them for marriage, and a reader's own native tongue may more explicitly classify relatives in a parallel way. Regular English terms for relations make few distinctions according to the marriage links involved, however, and these would probably not affect further decisions about marriage with people to whom one can trace no genealogical link, except perhaps for categories such as 'blood brothers'. The Australian groups described, on the other hand, classified everybody within the group as part of the overall marriage system, and all had to fit into the scheme.

Everyone also belonged to one or other of the animal clans, and both of these allegiances may indicate further rules about what in the environment people may or may not eat. A member of the snake clan may be prohibited from eating snake, or they may be the only people allowed to; either way, they are seen as having a special relationship with the snake, just as members of the opossum clan are expected to have a special relationship with opossum. Creatures in the environment may well also be allocated membership of the moieties, as may meteorological phenomena such as wind and rain, and distant objects such as the sun and stars.

The authors then turn to discuss a system they describe as more complex, which also brings into the arrangement the *classification of space*. This is the system observed among the Zuni, a group of Pueblo Indians of North America, whom they describe, with quotations from Cushing, the original ethnographer, as follows:

> ... what we find among the Zuñi [sic] is a veritable arrangement of the universe. All beings and facts in nature, 'the sun, moon, and stars, the sky, earth and sea, in all their phenomena and elements; and all inanimate objects, as well as plants, animals, and men', are classed, labelled, and assigned to fixed places in a unique and integrated 'system' in which all the parts are co-ordinated and subordinated to one to another by 'degrees of resemblance'.
>
> In the form in which we now find it, the principle of this system is a division of space into seven regions: north, south, west, east, zenith, nadir and the centre. Everything in the universe is assigned to one or other of these seven regions. To mention only the seasons and the elements, the wind, breeze or air, and the winter season are attributed to the north; water, the spring and its damp breezes, to the west; fire and the summer, to the south; the earth, seeds, the frosts which bring the seeds to maturity and end the year, to the east. The pelican, crane, grouse, sagecock, the evergreen oak, etc. are things of the north; the bear, coyote, and spring grass are things of the west. With the east are classed the deer, antelope, turkey, etc. Not only things, but social functions are also distributed in this way. The north is the region of force and destruction; war and destruction belong to it; to the west peace ..., and hunting; to the south, the region of heat, agriculture and medicine; to the east, the region of the sun, magic and religion; to the upper world and the lower world are assigned diverse combinations of these functions.   (Durkheim and Mauss 1963: 43–4)

This division of the universe into seven classes is also associated with colours, so that, for example, south is red, the region of summer and fire, the north is yellow, and the east is white. A comprehensive system of classification such as this is again learned very early, and an investigator could not expect members of the society necessarily to be able to explain it in an analytical form. It would nevertheless underlie a lot of communication within that society, and until the ethnographer pieced it together, much communication could be lost. The use of the word 'yellow' could, for example, have connotations based on other associations with north, so that a person described as 'yellow' could be fierce and destructive, rather than cowardly, as is the case in the English language, though again native speakers may not know why.

In fact, colours themselves are classified differently in different societies, and even by different groups within the same society. Newton's classification of bands of the spectrum into the seven 'colours of the rainbow', identified by scientific measurements, is widely accepted now, but there are different indigenous systems still in existence at a colloquial level. For example, the Japanese word *aoi* may be applied to something described in English as 'blue' (a rather light blue), as 'green', (the colour of pine trees, a 'go' traffic light, or a person feeling sick), or as 'pale' (the same person, slightly less sick). The colour blue, even in English, has a huge number of subdivisions, especially for professional artists or designers.

According to a study by Edwin Ardener (1971), the Welsh language used to have only two words for the colours described in English as grey, brown and black, with *du* for a colour covering part of the range described in English as black and part of 'brown', and *llwyd* covering another aspect of 'brown', and part of grey, which also shaded off into *glas*, a colour including hues described as blue and even green in English. Gradually the Welsh have come to adopt the English word 'brown' into their own language, and the shades covered by the modern colloquial Welsh words are much closer to their nearest English equivalents, probably to avoid confusion since Welsh speakers are almost always bilingual (see Figure 1.1).

Durkheim and Mauss (1963) also bring the *classification of time* into consideration in their description of Chinese ideas collectively known as *taoism*. This is a system of classification independent of social organisation, they explain, but it orders and affects many details of daily life. It also comprises a division of space into four cardinal points, again associated with animals and colours, and a division of objects into associations with five elements, namely earth, water, wood, metal and fire, and a further cycle of twelve signs of the Chinese zodiac. There is also a now widely known huge bipartite division of almost everything into *yin* and *yang*, sometimes also described as female and male, negative and positive, younger and older, or passive and active.

The system is used to classify divisions of years, days and even smaller units of two hours within the day, where each is assigned an animal of the zodiac and an element in its *yin* or *yang* form. Taken together with the classification of space into four cardinal points, an immensely complex system of divination (known as geomancy), developed in ancient China, was consulted in all kinds of endeavour and influenced much behaviour, particularly of a ritual kind. The system affected many parts of the Far East and even in today's technological super-states such as Japan and Hong Kong, activities like choosing sites and times for building, arranging weddings and funerals, and investigating unexpected misfortune, will involve consulting almanacs and experts in this ancient lore for advice (see First-hand Account 1 overleaf)

An example quite recognisable to members of Western societies who consult astrological charts is the way people's characters are supposed to be related to the year and time at which they were born. The animal associated with a particular year is said to have an influence, so that a person born in the year of the ox is said to be very patient and to speak little, and one born in the year of the tiger is sensitive, short-tempered and given to deep thinking. Certain pairs of people are also said to be better suited to marriage than others, and a geomancer may advise a change of name to offset a disadvantage of this sort. A Japanese woman born in the year of the horse, which also falls in the active

ENGLISH	STANDARD WELSH	MODERN COLLOQUIAL WELSH
green	gwyrdd	gwyrdd
blue	glas	glas
grey		llwyd
brown	llwyd	brown
black	du	du

Figure 1.1 English and Welsh colour classifications

Source: Edwin Ardener (ed.), *Social Anthropology and Language* (1971), p. xxi, by permission of Tavistock Publications.

aspect of fire, is still said to be a very bad bet for marriage. A general indication of the seriousness with which these ideas are taken can be found in a sharp drop in the birth rate during those years. On the other hand, this book goes to press in the Chinese year of the 'golden pig', a combination of pig and fire, which is said to be auspicious for babies and therefore a rise in the birth rate is expected.

It is clear, then, that technological advance is not necessarily accompanied by a convergence of ideas about the ordering of space, time and social relations. Some elements of systems of classification may be displaced as societies influence one another, such as the example of the use of 'brown' in Welsh, but others persist, and observers of other societies must try to avoid making assumptions based on their own system of thought. The classic work of Durkheim and Mauss (1963) not only provides us with examples of widely different systems of classification found in societies at that time relatively untouched by outside influence; it also illustrates a system of classification shared by scholars of the period in which it was written.

Anthropologists have recently been much concerned with examining their own preconceptions, and several works published in the last few years illustrate a concern with the way the background, age, gender and theoretical approach of the ethnographer might affect the results of their work. Different ethnographies of the same people were of particular interest, especially where these presented conflicting views, and two studies of the same village in Mexico, by Robert

Like everyone else in Hong Kong and Macau, I have been familiar with the term *Feng Shui* since I was little. Whenever my family moved house, my parents would invite a *Feng Shui* master to come and show us how we should arrange the furniture. When there are big events like weddings and funerals, my family would consult a master to pick an auspicious day and hour. They believe that an auspicious timing for a marriage would make the marriage happy and one for a funeral would make the family happy and prosperous. 2006 was said to be an auspicious year for

First-hand account 1:
Wong Si Lam, Chinese from Macao* – on Feng Shui

marriage so the marriage registry offices in both Hong Kong and Macau were filled with bookings from the beginning of the year! During Chinese New Year, I listen to the radio programmes about the Chinese horoscope in order to find out whether I am having a good or bad year and how I can attract more luck and avoid bad fortune.

Feng Shui, which is literally translated as 'wind' and 'water', is about how the *chi*, or the energy of the life force, flows around us and influences our lives. It is a practice used to make adjustments to improve the naturally occurring *chi* of a place. This practice is estimated to be more than four thousand years old by the Chinese. Basically, it is a Taoist practice of positioning and arrangement of space to achieve comfort, balance and harmony with the environment. *Feng Shui* was a guarded secret in ancient China and was not accessible to the public. The teachings were transmitted orally from a master to a limited number of students, and confidentiality was strictly required. In ancient times, *Feng Shui* masters never took women as their students because Confucianism did not promote the transmission of important and sacred knowledge to females, as it was said: 'teach sons, not daughters'. Today, there are many female *Feng Shui* practitioners and masters around the world.

In Hong Kong, *Feng Shui* is everywhere. For example, there are television programmes about *Feng Shui* everyday in the afternoon, teaching people how they should arrange their home

CHINA

Macao

©MAPS IN MINUTES™ 2008

in order to receive the best *chi* and to avoid 'dirty stuff', meaning bad luck, disease, injuries and spirits. These programmes are even more popular during the Chinese New Year period when the *chi* of the year changes. There are also radio programmes hosted by *Feng Shui* masters, who would answer personal questions such as whether the colour and the licence number of one's car are harmonious with the owner. There are also *Feng Shui* schools and a large range of *Feng Shui* books available in the bookstores. Moreover, many buildings and sites in Hong Kong were built according to *Feng Shui* theories. A recent and famous example is Hong Kong Disneyland.

* See First-hand account 14.1 for a fuller discussion of her national identity.

Redfield and Oscar Lewis, provide a classic example. The first study described a positive, cheerful people, with many mechanisms of cooperation; the second concentrated on negative aspects of the same society, illustrating the poverty of the people and a grasping, competitive character.

Various theories were put forward to explain these divergent results, and one put the difference down to changed demographic and economic conditions. Others saw the discrepancy in the character of the ethnographers. A third explanation might be related to the prior interests of each (Martin 2005 examines the issues). A more general literary examination of the work of anthropologists suggests that those who made most impact in the subject were simply good writers. The social and cultural features of the people they chose to study have therefore taken on a disproportionate value in the subject because of the clear and arresting language in which they were described (see, for example, Clifford and Marcus 1986). This is not necessarily a disadvantage, however, if it helps other people become aware of the relative nature of their own social and cultural assumptions, and therefore to understand the depth of difference which may exist in the views of their neighbours.

In another collection, anthropologists were invited to use autobiography, of themselves and of their informants, as a means to tackle head-on this problem of personal involvement in the research they carry out (Okely and Callaway 1992), and the resulting book has become a valuable aid to field work. Most anthropological studies make serious attempts to counteract the inevitable bias of the human studying humans – a phenomenon not unlike that known in physics as the Heisenberg uncertainty principle, which recognises the need to introduce a change to particles of matter in order to observe them. In a similar way, students of anthropology can learn from and about their own experience in the process of understanding people elsewhere.

Changes in Systems of Classification: The Issue of Gender

It was, in my view, no coincidence that this last collection of papers, about the personal involvement of the ethnographer, was edited by two women, for one of the biases identified in the work of their earlier colleagues was towards allocating much more importance in any society to the activities of men than to those of women. Sometimes the equally important roles of women even passed completely unnoticed. Steps have been taken to rectify this practice in the last few decades – steps that reflect an area of quite noticeable change in the wider systems of gender classification in the so-called 'civilised' societies from which the observers hailed. Indeed, the recognition of gender as a culturally relative notion has added a new dimension to the ideas of 'sex' as a biological feature. Here we can see the role of anthropology as a discipline that has forced its practitioners to challenge and reconsider their own assumptions about everyday life.

gender – a term of classification used to refer to conceptions of male and female, or masculinity and femininity in any society, and 'gender studies' refers to research and teaching that makes this distinction its primary focus.

This example also illustrates the way in which changes can be brought about in systems of classification over time within a particular society, or indeed through the influence of one people on another. One of the major distinctions learned is that between men and women, or, more importantly in this context, between the roles assigned to each of the categories. Within only one or two generations, there have been great changes in these roles in Western societies. Women have secured for themselves a much greater part in public life than their mothers and grandmothers played, and men are now much more likely than their fathers were to be found contributing in a significant way in the home.

This has been no mean feat, since the pioneers of women's 'liberation' found themselves fighting against the constraints of all sorts of 'social facts', in Durkheim's terms: legal and moral regulations, customs, and other collective representations about appropriate attitudes and behaviour. My own maiden aunt lamented the three years she spent waiting to marry and take care of a fiancé (who died while they were saving money) because, as a teacher in Scotland in the 1930s, she would have to give up work on marriage. My mother gave up her job as a nurse to

collective representations – symbols understood and used for communication between members of a particular social group (after Durkheim).

marry, and, throughout her life, saw her role in the 'work' of 'running the home'. The men of their class and generation were expected to provide for the whole family, and for long after women did begin to go out to work, it was still the men who were obliged, by law, to take care of the tax return in the United Kingdom.

In my own generation, expectations changed markedly, and some women experienced disapproval if they did not keep up their economic activities after marriage and even childbirth. We had been trained in the 'female' roles of housework, caring and comfort, but once we won our places in the wider world we were expected to maintain them, as well as attend to our homes and children. Some men were overtly supportive, but many found it difficult to do more than 'help' with the household tasks. Outside, men still tended to see other men as appropriate people to promote. Nowadays, men and women do, at least in some families, play an equal part in the rearing of their offspring, who will be unlikely to carry the same clear ideas in their heads as their grandparents did about 'men's and women's work'.

Anthropologists who noticed the male bias in their colleagues' work, perhaps projecting Western ideas onto the people of their studies, have over the years published a great deal of interesting material about women from different parts of the world, as well as attending to their own roles in society. In the wake of the early feminist works of influential writers such as Simone de Beauvoir, Kate Millet and Germaine Greer, two ground-breaking collections of anthropological articles appeared, first in America in *Women, Culture and Society* (Rosaldo and Lamphere 1974), and then, shortly afterwards, in the UK, in *Perceiving Women* (Ardener 1975). The latter was the first of a series of publications to come from a group of colleagues who eventually founded a Centre for Cross-Cultural Research on Women, later to become The International Gender Studies Centre.

Another of the early ones in this series, *Defining Females: The Nature of Women in Society*, originally published in 1978, examined the way in which even the so-called biological characteristics of women are culturally constructed:

> perceptions of the *nature* of women affect the shape of the *categories* assigned to them, which in turn reflect back upon and reinforce or remould perceptions of the *nature* of women, in a continuing process. (Ardener 1993:1; cf. Caplan 1987)

Hirschon's paper about a Greek community, for example, explains ideas about the appropriate behaviour for women in terms of beliefs about their sexuality. Only women are thought to be able to control their sexual urges, so both men and women should be married at an early age, and respectable women must be kept out of the way of other men, who might lead them into temptation. If a husband strays from the straight and narrow – in other words, from fidelity to his wife – it is the other woman who is blamed. Keeping their houses immaculate, cooking complicated dishes, preserving fruit in sweetmeats and cakes, and sewing and embroidery, are all time-consuming ways of keeping women occupied, and off the street (Hirschon 1993: 51–72; see also Photograph 1.2).

Documenting the roles of women, their variety, and their changes has meant there is now a veritable plethora of books and articles. These publications were for some time distinguished from regular anthropology by being called 'women's studies', but gender now forms just one type of social differentiation, alongside others based on age, generation, kinship, race, ethnicity, religion, region and social class. Women concerned with their own liberation from the constraints of Western society sometimes tended to focus overly on their counterparts in other

Photograph 1.2 Bereaved women in Greece express their loss by wearing black for at least three years as widows, sometimes for the rest of their own lives for other family members (photograph: Karpathos Island, Greece by Renee Hirschon).

societies, ignoring areas shared by men and women. They have also been accused of imposing, as universal, models subordinating women to men, whereas the situation in any one society might be much more subtle, even lacking hierarchical organisation at all.

Gullestad also advocates looking at gender 'in such a way that it is possible to study changes of cultural categories', pointing out that changes sought by women in their roles and definitions of themselves 'will have profound implications for the definitions of masculinity as well' (1993: 129). The Oscar-winning film *The Full Monty*, about a group of redundant steel workers seeking to reinstate their self-respect, is a poignant popular representation of this situation in the English city of Sheffield in the late 1990s. Anthropologists have now turned their attention to the new roles of men, and one interesting book, *Dislocating Masculinity: Comparative Ethnographies* (Cornwall and Lindisfarne 1994), is a re-examination of the notions of masculinity which have been displaced and replaced as women have moved into many of the spheres which were previously closed and almost sacrosanct to men.

Conclusion

In this chapter we have discussed systems of classification which affect and constrain the way in which people 'see' and understand 'the world'. We have considered various examples of difference in modes of classification: of objects, of life and death, of people, of space and time, and we have looked at how these may change. We have identified classificatory constraints (or bias) in the anthropologists as well as in the people they study, and pointed out the inevitability of this when human beings set out to study other human beings. In the next chapter, we begin to look at ways in which systems of classification are expressed, and in this and the following two chapters, the various ways in which anthropologists gather information about them.

 ## Discussion Questions

1   Have you got a souvenir of somewhere you have visited that you feel is particularly representative of that place? Try to write down some of the reasons why you chose that object, and why it is special and different for you.

2   Make a list of words for colours which are also used as descriptions of sentiments, or have other meanings. Can you suggest reasons for the association? Do you know anyone who has different associations? You might want to compare your ideas.

3   Think of ways in which you have felt constrained to behave in a particular way because of your gender, age or religious background. Did the same constraints apply to your parents? Will you (or do you) impose them on your children?

4   In what way does *Feng Shui* offer an illustration of ideas about classification? Take a look at the First-Hand Account 1 on p. 28 for some more information. Can you imagine any instances where *Feng Shui* might influence an anthropologist's investigation? Should they try to avoid this and if so, how? Now look again at your answers to question 3, above, and consider how the constraints you have identified might influence your own thinking about anthropology.

References and Further Research

Books
Ardener, Edwin (ed.) (1971) *Social Anthropology and Language* (London: Tavistock).
Ardener, Shirley (ed.) (1975) *Perceiving Women* (London: Malaby Press).
Ardener, Shirley (ed.) (1993 [1978]) *Defining Females: The Nature of Women in Society* (Oxford: Berg).
Barley, Nigel (1997) *Dancing on the Grave* (London: Abacus).
Caplan, Pat (ed.) (1987) *The Cultural Construction of Sexuality* (London and New York: Tavistock Publications).
Clifford, James and Marcus George. E. (1986) *Writing Culture: The Poetics and Politics of Ethnography* (Berkeley, Los Angeles and London: University of California Press).
Cornwall, Andrea and Lindisfarne, Nancy (1994). *Dislocating Masculinity* (London: Routledge).
Durkheim, Emile and Mauss Marcel (1963) *Primitive Classification*, translated, with an introduction, by Rodney Needham (London: Cohen & West).
Gell, Alfred (1992) *The Anthropology of Time: Cultural Constructions of Temporal Maps and Images* (Oxford: Berg).
Hertz, R. (1960) *Death and the Right Hand*, translated by R. and C. Needham (London: Cohen & West).

Lévy-Bruhl, Lucien (1926 [1910]) *How Natives Think* (New York: A. A. Knopf; original text published in 1910 as *Les fonctions mentales dans les sociétés Inférieures*).

Lienhardt, Godfrey (1961) *Divinity and Experience: The Religion of the Dinka* (Oxford: Clarendon Press).

Martin, JoAnn (2005) *Tepoztlán and the Transformation of the Mexican State: The Politics of Loose Connections* (Tucson: University of Arizona Press).

Moore, Henrietta L. (1988) *Feminism and Anthropology* (Cambridge: Polity Press).

Needham, Rodney (1973) *Right and Left: Essays on Dual Symbolic Classification* (Chicago: Chicago University Press).

Okely, Judith and Callaway, Helen (eds) (1992) *Anthropology and Autobiography* (London: Routledge).

Rosaldo, Michelle Zimbalist and Lamphere, Louise (eds) (1974) *Woman, Culture and Society* (Stanford, Calif.: Stanford University Press).

Articles

Fukuda Kaoru (1997) 'Different Views of Animals and Cruelty to Animals: Cases in Fox-Hunting and Pet-Keeping in Britain' *Anthropology Today*, 13(5): 2–6.

Gullestad, Marianne (1993) 'Home Decoration as Popular Culture. Constructing Homes, Genders and Classes in Norway', in Teresa del Valle (ed.), *Gendered Anthropology* (London: Routledge), pp. 128–61.

Hirschon, Renee (1993) 'Open Body/Closed Space: The Transformation of Female Sexuality' in Shirley Ardener (ed.), *Defining Females: The Nature of Women in Society* (Oxford: Berg), pp. 51–72.

Rivers, W. H. R. (1926) 'The Primitive Conception of Death', in *Psychology and Ethnology* (London and New York: Kegan Paul and Trench Trubner).

Sherif, Bahira (1999) 'Gender Contradictions in Families: Official v. Practical Representations among Upper Middle-Class Muslim Egyptians', *Anthropology Today*, 15(4): 9–13.

Novels

Barker, Pat (1992) *Regeneration* (Harmondsworth: Penguin), is a trilogy of novels about the First World War, which feature W. H. R. Rivers, although not much direct mention is made of his anthropological work until the third book, the *Ghost Road*, where the effects of a British ban on head-hunting in the Solomon Islands are juxtaposed with reports of the atrocities taking place in war-torn Europe.

Bowen, E. Smith (1954) *Return to Laughter* (London: Victor Gollancz) is a fictionalised account of fieldwork amongst the Tiv of Nigeria by Laura Bohannan.

Durrell, Lawrence (1968 [1962]) *The Alexandria Quartet* (London: Faber and Faber) explores the encounter between 'Western' and 'Eastern' outlooks, through portraying events from a variety of different perspectives.

Mahfouz, Naguib (1994) *Palace Walk* (London: Black Swan), the first of the Cairo Trilogy, illustrates particularly well the contrasting life of men and women in a traditional Egyptian Muslim family.

Pamuk, Orhan (2001) *My Name is Red* (London: Powell's), a murder mystery that examines Islamic values in sixteenth-century Turkey as the Ottoman Empire declines.

Films

Doctors of Two Worlds (Natasha Solomons, 55 minutes, 1989) is about an English doctor administering health care in mountain villages of the Bolivian highlands who shares ideas and methods of healing with the local healer (*curandero*).

The BBC TV series *Life on Mars* (2006–7) was a popular series about a detective who was thrown back to the past, to 1973, where 'things were done differently' and many interesting culture clashes ensue.

Websites

http://www.relst.uiuc.edu/durkheim – The Durkheim Pages has extensive bibliographies and access to original texts.

http://durkheim.itgo.com/ – the Durkheim Archive, specifically for undergraduates.

http://www2.pfeiffer.edu/~lridener/DSS/INDEX.HTML – this link is for the Dead Sociologists Index – Durkheim pages written by L. A. Coser.

http://www.hewett.norfolk.sch.uk/curric/soc/durkheim/durk.htm – good introductory pages to Durkheim's ideas.

2

Disgusting, Forbidden and Unthinkable

Challenging Some Ingrained Ideas

One of the ways in which anthropologists find out about a system of classification is by looking at ideas which are strongly held by the people concerned. These are likely to be learnt early in life and are difficult to dislodge even when one becomes aware of the fact that they are culturally relative. They include ideas that would provoke expressions of shock and disgust should they be contravened – ideas which are at the root of prejudice and discrimination – for people who engage in practices contradictory to one's own may well seem barbaric and uncivilised.

In practice, these cherished ideas are usually challenged whenever we travel abroad. A resident of Southern England, for example, may need only to cross the Channel to France to find toilets which seem not only dirty, but constructed in a fashion unpleasant to use, to discover people relishing the consumption of creatures they cringe at the thought of eating, and to encounter customs that appear strange, perhaps even obsessive. They might be surprised, at least at first, to discover that their friends in France find a number of English habits disgusting too. Further afield, in India, for example, some of the activities taken for granted in

Europe are regarded as seriously polluting. A separation of the uses of the right and left hands, for eating and cleaning the body respectively, make passing food with the left hand seem quite disgusting.

Certain practices are also quite simply forbidden in the law and custom of each society. In many countries, it is against the law to appear in public in the nude, and 'streakers', who gain a few seconds of attention by running naked across a cricket pitch or other public place, would be promptly arrested. Those who wear very few clothes are accepted to different degrees in different places, and company on a beach will be much more tolerant than in a kindergarten, for example. Some exclusive clubs and restaurants have rules about dress, where men may be turned away if they have no jacket and tie; in Oxford, undergraduates are refused entry to the examination hall if they are not wearing the appropriate gowns and black and white clothes; and in my own London college in the 1960s, women were forbidden from appearing in jeans, or indeed, any trousers – though I found no serious sanctions came into operation when I decided to put the rule to the test.

Some of these regulations may sound quaint and perhaps old-fashioned to foreign visitors to Britain, even former compatriots whose families settled in Australia or the Americas, but there are conventions of dress everywhere which are difficult for people to break, even if there is no hard and fast rule. It would be 'unthinkable' for a man in most societies to turn up to work in a skirt – even in Scotland, kilts are usually only worn at weddings and other special occasions – and mothers who dress their daughters in dungarees, so as not to distinguish them overly from their brothers, would probably baulk at the idea of dressing their sons in little frocks. In some Islamic communities, women cover themselves from head to foot, a custom causing concern in Europe as this book was being written. In other parts of the world – the rain forest in South America is one example – it is acceptable for them to be quite bare down to the waist (see First-hand Account 10 on p. 194).

Men kissing in public is pretty unusual in Western countries (though this is another area which has been changing, along with new ideas about gender roles), but it is positively expected in greetings in other parts of the world. In much of the Middle East, men are freer about their bodily interaction than they are in northern Europe, but in the Far East kissing was not really a custom at all until recently, although men and women might think nothing of falling asleep on the shoulders of strangers in an underground train. In Japan, men and women used to bathe together in public until they saw how shocked Western visitors were in the nineteenth century. Now they bathe on different sides of a partition, but courting couples feel free to cuddle in public places, which they did not previously do, even until the early 1970s.

It is ideas such as these, which may form the basis of prejudice and suspicion when people from one culture visit, or move to live amongst members of another, that provide good starting places for anthropological investigation. Notions of pollution and taboo, which are essentially institutionalised versions of an antipathy towards 'dirt' and the 'unthinkable', are particularly useful in this respect because not only are they firmly held, they are also greatly concerned with classification. Things which are taboo and things which are regarded as polluted or polluting are very often things which fall between important categories. Thus, by studying the notions a people have about pollution (or dirt), and the things which they regard as taboo (or forbidden), we can learn more about the system of classification of that particular society.

pollution/ purity - a pair of terms used by anthropologists to describe institutionalised ideas about dirt and cleanliness in any particular society, especially where these have connotations with notions of spiritual power.

taboo - something prohibited, usually for reasons associated with a wider system of classification, perhaps related to ideas of pollution, or with notions of the **sacred** in any society.

Taboo

'Taboo' is a word which was brought back by Captain Cook from his voyages in the South Seas. His sailors noticed that in Polynesia the use of this word designated a prohibition and they found it useful themselves when they wanted to keep visitors off the ship, or reserve a particular girl for themselves. It was also a word for which they had an existing category, though they may have found this new word more instantly expressive and appealing than previous ones like 'prohibited' or 'forbidden', just as their countrymen did when they returned to introduce it to the English language. In any society certain things may be regarded as taboo.

In fact there are several possible translations of the word, as was discussed in some detail by Franz Steiner in another classic little book, named simply *Taboo* (1956). Its use in Fiji, for example, had been translated as 'unlawful', 'sacred' and 'superlatively good'; in Malagasy (Madagascar), a closely related word is translated as more like 'profaned' or 'polluted'. In either case, some special category is indicated, though the translations may seem opposed to English speakers. Steiner suggested that the best etymology is one which divides the word into two parts, where *ta* means 'to mark off', and *bu* is simply an emphatic suffix, so that the whole word means 'to mark off thoroughly' or 'to set apart'.

sacred/ profane - this dichotomy is used by anthropologists to describe a variety of distinctions made between things, people and events that are set apart (sacred) from everyday life (profane), though the deeper meanings vary between societies, some of which have no such distinction, and they always require further study.

Steiner went on to show that there was a great range of types of taboo. In Polynesia, for example, a close association with political authority meant that the taboos a person could impose provided a measure of their power (or *mana* – see Shore 1989 and Chapter 3 in this book). To quote:

> The power to restrict was the yardstick by which power was measured; here was the social manifestation of power. Second, the exercise of this veto was in terms of taboo, that is, the actual sphere of any person's office or office's power was delimited by the kinds of taboos he could impose.

Taboo thus provided the means of relating a person to his superiors and inferiors. One can imagine a Chancellor of the Exchequer declaring eight or nine shillings in every twenty taboo as a measure of the power conferred on him. It takes a stretch of the imagination to realize that in the Polynesian system this power could have been conferred on him only by somebody exercising an even more awful taboo, and that the Polynesian chancellor would use the same term for his share in your pound as for the rights of his superiors, because these rights would concern him only as infringements of his own rights, just as taking away eight shillings is a restriction on your use of your twenty shillings. (1956: 39)

For a chief or king, this power could be so great and terrible that anything he touched immediately became polluting and dangerous for ordinary people. This explained why people of extremely high rank – including visiting members of the royal family in former British colonies – had to be carried by slaves. As these were owned by the king, polluting them did not cause too much inconvenience, otherwise the visiting dignitaries would pollute for everyone else the ground on which they had walked. Clearly these taboos are helping to delineate categories of social ranking in that particular society. In today's world, when widely shared ideas such as these can be less well relied upon, persons of high status and power are very often separated from their people by a ring of armed body guards, not only to protect them, but literally to 'set them apart'.

Further powerful examples of distinctions of classification based on taboos of one sort or another are to be found in rules about food. Hindus, for example, are

Photograph 2.1 The Yakha of East Nepal sacrifice pigs as well as other animals such as buffalo for the Hindu festival of Dasain, though the subsequent feast would be taboo to their Hindu neighbours (photograph: Tamara Kohn).

brought up always to use separate pots to cook meat and vegetables, a practice which expresses an idea so strong that many feel they cannot eat at all in non-Hindu restaurants which serve meat in case this rule may have been ignored. Amongst themselves, Hindus have a variety of food taboos, depending on their caste associations, which affect who cooks the food and who may eat with whom, as well as a series of complicated rules about what may or may not be eaten at any one time. The cow is sacred, so beef is taboo, but a dairy product like butter protects food fried in it, which can then be shared across caste lines. Food distinctions therefore express social divisions within Hindu society (see Photograph 2.1).

Muslims, on the other hand, who may live in close proximity to Hindus, have a taboo against eating pork, but this time it is because the pig is regarded as unclean. Although these animals appear to have been forbidden for different reasons from the Hindus' sacred cow, they are both 'set apart' and therefore 'taboo'. In both cases, too, the prohibition makes an important distinction between the categories of people involved. Other peoples have different food taboos. Orthodox Jewish rules prohibit eating meat and dairy products at the same meal, for example, and they also proscribe eating meat which has not been drained of blood, or made kosher. Jeremy MacClancy, in a book entitled *Consuming Culture*, describes these arrangements very colourfully:

> The Jewish dietary laws do not stop at the curly tail-end of a pig. They are made up of a whole set of kosher dos and dont's, of which the ban on pork and the separation of meat and milk are merely the most well known. Though these dietary rules are still central in the lives of many Jews, they were even more important in Jesus's time, when each Jewish sect interpreted God's gastronomic intentions in its own way. What foods you ate and with whom you ate them were a key means of saying what particular group you belonged to. The Essenes would only have a meal among themselves, and neither they nor members of the Pharisees, the Maccabees, the Sadducees, the Hasidim, the Sicraii, the Herodians, the Hellenists, or the Therapeutae, would even think of sitting down at the same table with a gentile. For Jews, their food rules came to stand for the whole of their law, and violating any of them was seen as equivalent to leaving the faith. God had founded his Covenant with His chosen people through the medium of food, and His followers were not going to break this holy agreement by nibbling the wrong edible in the wrong company. When forced to eat swine by the Romans, some chose to die rather than pollute themselves and profane their sacred pact with the Almighty. (1992: 33–4)

In many parts of the world there are taboos associated with the body and bodily functions, typically with pregnancy, childbirth and menstruation for women, and illness and death for anyone, regardless of gender. A study of pregnancy and childbirth amongst the Chinese in Hong Kong, by Diana Martin (1994), describes an abundance of food prohibitions during pregnancy, even amongst the most highly educated women. Martin discovered that her informants were expected to hand over the care of their babies and tiny infants to others almost as soon as they were born, and noted that the food and other taboos were observed openly in public situations. She suggests, therefore, that the prohibitions are an open expression of the fact that a woman is about to become a mother during the only time she has total responsibility for her offspring.

As for menstruation taboos, women in many societies are excluded from certain activities during their monthly periods. They may be required to live in a separate house for the duration, perhaps with other women in the same situation, or they may simply be banned from the fishing boats or not allowed to enter the temple. *The Red Tent*, a novel by Anita Diamant (2001) set in the biblical time of Dinah, sister of Joseph of the coat-of-many-colours fame, is much concerned with the lives of women in such a society, and vividly depicts the periods they spent in the separate quarters described in the title. Here, too, they gave birth, and attended to each other's feminine needs.

In rural Japan, where I did fieldwork in the 1970s, women observed taboos on certain foods, on bathing, and even on watching television for a period of 31–33 days after childbirth. After a death in the family, the bereaved relatives would avoid certain foods for up to 49 days. These customs were explained in terms of the relationship between the soul and the body. The soul of a person who has recently died is said to be prone to stay around the house for a while, and the taboos are concerned with avoiding trouble and seeing that a complete separation occurs. In the case of a baby, the soul is in danger of escaping in the early stages, and the prohibitions are to help avoid this kind of disaster. An examination of these ideas is thus revealing of Japanese notions about the constitution of the person, the relationship of humans with the spiritual world, and, by further examination of the range of people affected by the taboos, of the make-up of the Japanese family.

Pollution

Anthropologists use the word 'pollution' to describe ideas found to be held strongly in various parts of the world about the destruction of a parallel notion of purity. In most cases, purity denotes cleanliness, but in many societies there are religious associations with this concept so that it would perhaps be more accurately translated into English as 'sanctity'. It may be the case that rituals of purification precede any communication with the spiritual or supernatural world, for example, but in some societies there are strongly held views about the avoidance of pollution and polluting behaviour for reasons connected with ideas about social relations. In either case these are inevitably concerned with local systems of classification.

In the Japanese case above, taboos related to birth and death may also be explained in terms of the protection they will provide for others, since those observing the taboos may also be regarded as polluting at these times. Women after childbirth are thus prohibited from preparing food, entering a public bath, or participating in ritual activities, which they may spoil due to their polluted state. Similarly, a girl whose father had recently died had to instruct a group of friends in the plaiting of a straw rope for the shrine festival from a position just over the wall and therefore out of the sacred area that she would defile if she entered. After a death in Japan, a notice is posted on the front door of the house of the deceased to warn visitors of the polluting situation.

In the Indian subcontinent, on the other hand, the food taboos we discussed above express more permanent notions of pollution associated with a caste system which divides all human beings into classes of people conceptually distinguished from one another in such a way that the word 'class' seems inadequate (see Dumont 1980 and Quigley 1993 for two interpretations). The strength of the danger of pollution is evident in the existence of a caste of 'untouchable' people who are employed specifically to protect others (Deliege 1997). They sweep, clear sewage, deal with dead animals, and make leather goods, all tasks which are thought to be polluting for those of other castes. Brahmins, for example, must have nothing to do with excrement, an idea so firmly ingrained that a Brahmin girl working in a nursery in England preferred to alienate all her workmates rather than break the taboo and agree to change the nappies of her charges.

Such ideas of pollution demonstrate very clearly ways in which people divide themselves up, in this case initially into castes, an ancient system understood and observed in its own local context, but in practice in another society creating new reasons for emphasising old divisions. Actually, it is precisely for deeply ingrained ideas such as these that foreigners are regarded with suspicion, and often with distaste, wherever they are found. The system of classification, particularly when it is reinforced with taboos associated with ideas of pollution, is very hard to dislodge. It expresses the way the world is perceived, and changes in it can lead to a good deal of confusion, even to shock – that American phrase, 'culture shock', is no trite description.

The novels of Paul Scott's *Raj Quartet*, which were televised under the title of the first in the series, *The Jewel in the Crown*, opened with a forcible illustration of ideas such as these. Hari Kumar, a British public schoolboy of Indian parents, is returned to his relatives in India when his father dies suddenly, leaving no provision for the rest of his education. He finds himself in a society which includes people brought up like himself, but the colour of his skin excludes him from their company. His kinsfolk find his lifestyle entirely alien and indeed polluting to them, and they force him to drink the urine of the sacred cow, an abhorrence to him, but for them the only way to purge Hari of the pollution he has picked up by living overseas.

Purity and Classification

Various theories have been advanced to explain particular notions of pollution and taboo, but Mary Douglas has pointed out in her book *Purity and Danger*

(1966) that they all form part of a wider system of classification. The taboos, and the ideas about purity and pollution, are thus themselves fertile areas of investigation for anthropologists, who try to set them in the context of other knowledge about the peoples in question, and about the historical influences they have experienced. The analysis of the 'Abominations of Leviticus' in the same book is one of the best-known attempts to interpret an extremely complex and otherwise seemingly random system of rules and restrictions of this sort.

The lists of animals which were prohibited in the biblical book of Leviticus are many and varied, and previous attempts to make sense of them had been rather unsuccessful, according to Douglas. She argues, however, that they must not be considered piecemeal. Within the context of God's order for the world, laid out in the book of Genesis, important distinctions are to be made between the components of the threefold classification of the world into the earth, the waters and the firmament. Living beings which reside in each medium are described according to their type: flesh, fish and fowl, respectively, and each has an appropriate means of locomotion. In the firmament, for example, two-legged fowl fly with wings, in the water scaly fish swim with fins, and on the earth four-legged animals hop, jump or walk.

Those creatures which are forbidden turn out to be anomalous according to this system, Douglas argues. This includes four-footed creatures which fly, and creatures with two hands and two feet who move about on all fours. It particularly forbids creatures which swarm because these are neither fish, flesh nor fowl. They are matter out of place, and therefore forbidden.

> If the proposed interpretation of the forbidden animals is correct, the dietary laws would have been like signs which at every turn inspired meditation on the oneness, purity and completeness of God. By rules of avoidance holiness was given a physical expression in every encounter with the animal kingdom and at every meal. Observance of the dietary rules would thus have been a meaningful part of the great liturgical act of recognition and worship which culminated in the sacrifice in the Temple. (Douglas 1966: 72)

Mary Douglas's book has become a classic, and it was one of the first works to argue that rituals of purity and impurity create unity of experience in any society, not just those formerly regarded as 'primitive'. It brings the ideas discussed in this chapter right into the most domestic sphere, because in it she writes about *dirt* in a European household, or, to be more precise, in *her* type of household, since the ideas may not be shared by Europeans of all classes and ethnic origins; however, this anthropologist provides an excellent example of how the principles learned in exotic places may be most aptly applied in any society, including one's own.

She points out that cleaning is as much concerned with *order* as with hygiene. There is no such thing as absolute dirt, she tells us, 'it exists in the eye of the beholder', and if we abstract pathogenicity and hygiene from our notion of dirt we find it is simply 'matter out of place'. Cleaning expresses our own system of classification, so that an object likely to confuse it is regarded as *polluting*, that is, *dirty*.

> Shoes are not dirty in themselves, but it is dirty to place them on the dining-table; food is not dirty in itself, but it is dirty to leave cooking utensils in the bedroom, or food bespattered on clothing; similarly, bathroom equipment in the drawing room; clothing lying on chairs; outdoor-things in-doors; upstairs things downstairs; under-clothing appearing where over-clothing should be, and so on. In short, our pollution behaviour is the reaction which condemns any object or idea likely to confuse or contradict cherished classifications. (1966: 48)

In Japan, as elsewhere, shoes should not be brought into the house at all, and this is a rule enforced so strictly that even tiny children must obey it as soon as they are able to walk. A foreigner who stepped across a Japanese threshold with shoes on would soon be hustled back out again, for this error would contravene deeply ingrained ideas about dirt and cleanliness which further reflect a pervasive Japanese distinction between *inside* and *outside*. Shoes are to be left in the doorway to the outside world, where they should be donned before stepping out again. Within the house itself, there are further distinctions to be made between areas where slippers may be worn, and the fine floor matting which should only be crossed in stockinged feet.

The force of this distinction was illustrated clearly in the writings of Fukuzawa Yukichi, one of the first Japanese to visit America in the nineteenth century when the country was opened to the outside world after two hundred years of virtual isolation. He was shocked to see people going inside the houses in their shoes, which had come directly in from the outside world, but he was particularly affected to notice them walking on great areas of soft material (i.e. carpets) that looked to him identical to a substance highly valued in Japan for making small purses.

These foreigners seemed dirty to the Japanese just as people in Britain classify 'gypsies' as dirty because they throw rubbish out of their caravan windows and leave it behind when they move on. Judith Okely, who made a study of Traveller Gypsies in Britain in the 1970s, has nevertheless demonstrated forcibly how clean these people are within their own system of classification. Again, they make a clear distinction between the inside and the outside, this time of their caravans. Beyond the window is not their world, but within it they have such strict rules about cleanliness that if a dog were to lick a human plate, the owner would feel obliged to break the whole set.

This is part of a strict code of purity and pollution shared by the Traveller Gypsies, who keep their homes immaculate. They separate bowls for washing clothes (outside) from bowls for washing up pots (which hold food which goes inside), and they separate male and female washing as well. For them, cats are regarded as dirty because they lick their own fur and confound the distinction between inside and outside, whereas other members of the surrounding society admire cats for keeping themselves clean. Dogs are dirty, too, and should live out-side; members of the wider society who allow cats and dogs to live in the house and eat off human plates fill the Travellers with disgust (see First-hand Account 2 on p. 46 and Photograph 2.2).

Photograph **2.2** Dogs are classified in very different ways by different peoples. To some, they are pets, though not always treated in the same way (see Fukuda 1997 in Chapter 1), to many they are work animals, including the hunt scenario pictured above, where they are referred to as hounds, and for others they are simply food (photograph: Robert Davis and Garry Marvin).

Animal Categories and Verbal Abuse

Edmund Leach wrote an interesting article about the role played by tabooed words in language. He was concerned with obscenities – dirty words, blasphemy and words of abuse – words that are unmentionable in some company, and there-fore used to shock or impress in other circumstances. He argued that language in general is like a grid, in which words provide labels for important categories and break up the social and physical environment, which would otherwise be a continuum, into discrete, recognisable things. Words that are regarded as taboo help to reinforce this system and prevent confusion by inhibiting the recognition of the parts of the continuum that separate the things.

His first illustration of the argument concerns the boundary of the human being within its environment, particularly important, again, as a baby is learning

In a world where a cup of tea requires no more than the turn of a tap and the flick of a switch, it is easy for old ways to die, and equally easy to regard as quirky the way of life that went with them. For me, it is unthinkable to eat from a plate or cup or any other utensil that has been touched by a dog or cat; indeed, if I were aware of any such contact, I would break and discard the utensil so defiled. Horses and cattle would not cause such a reaction because they are clean or 'sweet' animals, but cats, dogs, pigs and many other animals are regarded as unclean or 'mockerdy', and by

First-hand account 2:
Mick Ganly, English Traveller – on Cleanliness among Travellers

definition, anything they touch becomes 'mockerdy covel', or a dirty thing. Likewise, when I eat I need to know that my eating utensils have been cleaned or, if you like, purified, in running water. I am aware in my rational mind that my prejudice no longer has a valid foundation in hygiene but something very deep rooted keeps it alive.

Equally difficult to overcome (actually, more so) was the matter of menstruating women, who were not welcome in the wagons when I was a boy, and who could not eat with us until they became 'clean' again, nor, might I add, were they encouraged to buy or handle food. Another section of society, subject to a variety of beliefs, placed somewhere between dogs and menstruating women, were those with mental impairments, i.e. Down's syndrome, madness in its various forms, or the downright simpleton. These were (and are) known as raji, or radgy people, and it would be a grave misfortune to have them handle one's food. The same sort of beliefs, I am told, are common in India, but that may be wholly untrue. In the matter of personal hygiene, things were equally clear cut. One's feet, mouth and private parts were cleaned scrupulously both morning and evening, but it is true to say that other parts of the body were not quite so important. This, I suspect, had as much to do with every drop of water having to be found and carried, and the same for firewood. There were no taboos, as far as I know, with regard to food itself.

England

If it ran, swam, flew or grew, we killed it and ate it – in fact, I still do – but it is interesting that one could and would happily eat a hare or rabbit killed by a dog, or a bird killed by a cat, yet not eat the same hare or rabbit from a plate touched by its executioner.

Photograph taken by Władislaw Szulc

to see and label the surrounding world. Here taboos are clearly associated with what Leach refers to as exudations of the body – 'feces, urine, semen, menstrual blood, hair clippings, nail parings, body dirt, spittle, mother's milk' is Leach's list (1966: 38), although in the case of the baby, vomit and nasal mucus could well be added. In an essay which was initially read to an audience, Leach notes that

> so strong is the resulting taboo that, even as an adult addressing an adult audience, I cannot refer to these substances by the monosyllabic words which I used as a child but must mention them only in Latin.   (Ibid.)

The child is not born with these inhibitions, of course, and it is an important aspect of the training of small children to see that they don't pay inappropriate attention to these same exudations of the body, which are apparently part of them, but which must be carefully separated from them. Failure to learn these practices would be regarded as dirty, although the behaviour regarded as 'clean' and appropriate is of course variable from one society to another. The substances themselves may also be regarded as powerful in some societies, like the cow's urine above, and hair and nail clippings are sometimes the focus of mystical attack. In any case, words for the substances may be used to make a forceful exclamation, and they are also inclined to provoke expressions of disgust.

Leach's second set of tabooed words comprises those which in a religious context would be described as blasphemous. He points out that although life and death are in fact inseparable, religion always tries to separate them, and the gap between this world of 'mortal men' and the next, inhabited by 'immortal nonmen (gods)' is bridged by beings who are ambiguous in terms of such regular systems of classification. Thus we find incarnate deities, virgin mothers and supernatural monsters which may be half-human/half-beast. These ambiguous creatures mediate between the two worlds, but they are also the object of the most intense taboos, and to speak in an inappropriate fashion about them may be regarded as a particularly dangerous endeavour.

The bulk of Leach's essay is about animal categories, and how these relate to categories of human being. Any number of animals are called into play – cow, pig, bitch, cat, rat, filly – but it is worth drawing attention to the fact that all the animal terms which are used to address or describe human beings, either in a derogatory or a familiar fashion, are those for beasts to be found in the households or countryside of Britain. An immediate concern is to distinguish between the human and animal worlds, then, and since it would be impossible to confuse animals from further afield with ourselves, it would therefore be less than forceful, as he points out, to address someone in Britain as a polar bear.

Leach chose to focus on the language of British English to illustrate his argument, but he suggests that similar mechanisms operate everywhere, and provides a further example in a consideration of the Kachin language of the people he worked with in Southern Burma. Leach's argument was later heavily criticised in an article in the anthropological journal *Man* (Halverson 1976), but the ideas do provide a forceful (if inaccurate) linguistic example of the general way in which taboos and ideas of pollution and purity help to delineate systems of classification.

Conclusion

It is clear that a look at ideas of dirt, cleanliness and prohibitions opens up avenues to the understanding of different systems of classification, which can evidently exist side by side, even within the same society. It is also clear how strong and powerful these ideas may be. Within one society, where such notions are shared, rules seem natural and normal. To members of other societies, however, the same rules may well appear unnecessarily strict, burdensome barriers to friendship and integration. In Chapter 4 we will return to these ideas when we look at ritual activities, but in the meantime, we turn to further aspects of social relations, this time expressed through material objects.

Discussion Questions

1   Think of a culturally variable situation you have found repulsive, perhaps in a foreign country. Think about why. Now try and imagine something a person from that country might find repulsive in your lifestyle.

2   Do you alter your greeting behaviour depending on who you are meeting and how well you know them? How would you greet the Queen of England, for example, or the Emperor of Japan? What about your own president or prime minister? Or a friend's spouse? Would you greet a strange child in the same way you would greet the child of a friend? Think about what a greeting can tell us about relationships.

3   Try out Leach's idea by making a list of words you might avoid in front of your mother. Consider when and whether you might use them and what force they might have. Do they illustrate Leach's categories of distinction?

References and Further Research

Books

Deliege, R. (1997) *The World of the 'Untouchables': Paraiyars of Tamil Nadu* (Delhi: Oxford: Oxford University Press).

Douglas, Mary (1966) *Purity and Danger* (Harmondsworth: Penguin).

Dumont, Louis (1980) *Homo Hierarchicus: The Caste System and Its Implications* (Chicago and London: University of Chicago Press).

MacClancy, Jeremy (1992) *Consuming Culture: Why You Eat What You Eat* (New York: Henry Holt & Company).

Martin, Diana (1994) 'Pregnancy and Childbirth among the Chinese of Hong Kong', DPhil thesis, University of Oxford.

Masquelier, Adeline (ed.), (2005) *Dress, Undress, and Difference: Critical Perspectives on the Body's Surface* (Bloomington: Indiana University Press).

Okely, Judith (1983) *The Traveller Gypsies* (Cambridge: Cambridge University Press).

Quigley, Declan (1993) *The Interpretation of Caste* (Oxford: Clarendon Press).

Steiner, Franz (1956) *Taboo* (Harmondsworth: Penguin).

Articles

Fassin, Didier (2001) 'The Biopolitics of Otherness: Undocumented Foreigners and Racial Discrimination in French Public Debate', *Anthropology Today*, 17(1): 3–7.

Gaborieau, Marc (1985) 'From Al-Beruni to Jinnah: Idiom, Ritual and Ideology of the Hindu–Muslim Confrontation in South Asia', *Anthropology Today*, 1(3): 7–14.

Halverson, J. (1976) 'Animal Categories and Terms of Abuse', *Man*, 11: 505–16.

Hendry, Joy (2007 [1984]) 'Shoes, the Early Learning of an Important Distinction in Japanese Society', in G. Daniels (ed.), *Europe Interprets Japan* (Tenterden: Paul Norbury Publications), reprinted in D. P. Martinez (ed.), *Japanese Culture and Society* (London, Routledge, 2007).

Leach, Edmund (1966) 'Animal Categories and Verbal Abuse', in Eric H. Lenneberg (ed.), *New Directions for the Study of Language* (Cambridge, Mass.: MIT Press).

Radcliffe-Brown, A. R. (1952) 'Taboo' chapter in *Structure and Function in Primitive Society* (London: Cohen & West).

Shore, Bradd (1989) '*Mana* and *Tapu*', in Alan Howard and Robert Borofsy (eds), *Developments of Polynesian Ethnology* (Honolulu: University of Hawaii Press).

Novels

Diamant, Anita (2001) *The Red Tent* (Pan). A novel built around the story of Dinah, who makes a brief appearance in the Bible; at the same time a well-researched account of the life of women at the time.

Fatima Altaf, (1993) *The One Who Did Not Ask* (translated from Urdu by Rukhsana Ahmad) (London: Heinemann), tells poignantly of the problems experienced by the daughter of a well-to-do Indian family when she breaks some of the taboos of her high class upbringing.

Hugo, Victor (1831) *The Hunchback of Notre-Dame*, is the story of Quasimodo, a man whose deformity causes others to reject him and to assume he is monstrous.

Scott, Paul (1996) *The Jewel in the Crown* (London: Mandarin) is the first of a series of four novels entitled *The Raj Quartet*, which depict, amongst other things, reactions to the breaking of unwritten taboos in the life of British India.

Films

Caste at Birth (Mira Hamermesh, 1990) explores the complexities of the caste system in the Indian subcontinent. It illustrates in particular taboos surrounding 'untouchables'.

The Lau of Malaita (Leslie Woodhead and Pierre Maranda, 1987), a film in the Granada

'Disappearing World' series, provides information about taboos amongst a group of Solomon Islanders and tells of how their long-standing 'Custom' is being defended (or otherwise) against Christian missionaries in the area.

Some Women of Marrakesh (Melissa Llewelyn-Davies, 1977), another 'Disappearing World' film, penetrates the enclosed world of female society in the male-orientated Muslim state of Morocco.

Websites

www.guardian.co.uk/obituaries/story/0,,2082621,00.html# – obituary for Mary Douglas, *Guardian*, May 2007.

www.samvak.tripod.com/taboo.html – taboos around the world and their history.

www.philosophersnet.com/games/taboo.htm – exercise to get one thinking about taboos.

www.catohoeben.com/lafti_film and www.lifeonlens.org/index.php?option=com_content&task=view&id=35&Itemid=37 – two films about the movement to raise the living standards of 'untouchable' people.

3

Gifts, Exchange and Reciprocity

The Anthropologist's Arrival

With all the complexity of possibility discussed in the last chapter, an anthropologist arriving in a society to make a study might well feel daunted by the task ahead. Where to start? This is a pertinent question and many students worry a great deal about it before they leave for fieldwork. In practice, once they arrive and settle in, there are so many details of daily life to be seen to that the work just seems to take on a pace of its own. In a strange situation, one must first of all learn to cope with very basic needs – eating, of course, but also cooking, bathing, laundry, disposing of refuse – all these things are highly relevant to an ethnographer, as we have seen, and for the participant observer, the work is begun.

While coping with the mundane, the fieldworker is also bound to enter into communication with other members of the society concerned and this forces an immediate consideration of the nature of social relations. My first days of fieldwork in Japan were greatly eased by the good nature and friendship of my next-door neighbour, whom I visited to inquire about refuse collection. To my good fortune, he not only explained carefully about dividing waste into the burnable and the unburnable (which began to indicate information about local systems of classification), but he also instructed me about the more orthodox way of introducing oneself to new neighbours – namely, by calling round with a small gift, such as a towel.

This turned out to be an important custom in a Japanese context, for it allows a relationship to be opened. Some foreigners return from working or studying in Japan complaining sadly that they never made any progress with their neighbours – they had lived there for a year, maybe more, but they had neglected to take that first important step of self-introduction. For an ethnographer, who can only begin to learn properly about the people under study through social interaction with them, the principle of opening relations is a vital one, and if the neighbours are part of the study, as they were in this first fieldwork of mine, it is an advantage to start out in a way that they can comprehend and appreciate.

Social relationships are themselves an important part of the study of social anthropologists, of course, but they are not actually visible without being signified in some way. The presentation of gifts or, indeed, any movement of material objects from one person to another can provide an observer with information which they can record, if only later to analyse and understand. It gives access to a visible medium of communication, and in the early days of study in a community, when only a limited amount of the spoken language may be understood, details about the movement of objects can help an ethnographer to build up a map of social ties between the people who live there.

Gifts

Gifts are also given at rather specific times, and an examination of the occasions involved may also help lead to an understanding of important events and stages in the lives of the people concerned. Gifts to individuals may be marking changes of status; exchanges within wider groups may be celebrating occasions important in their society. In many places, presents are given as one grows up and grows old, year by year; they are given as one attains important goals, like entry to a school or university, or achieving a new position at work; many are given if one decides to move from being single to being married, although rather fewer are given if the marriage breaks down; many are also given to mark a new life, and to mark the end of a life.

Gifts are also presented when one couple, or family, visits another, especially if they are to eat together, or to spend a weekend or holiday in the other's home. House-warming presents are made to families who have recently moved in most English-speaking countries, just as such families are expected to visit their neighbours in Japan. At certain festivals, everywhere, friends and relations express their relationships by making gifts to each other, or to each other's children, and Christmas has become such a global example of this custom that non-Christians may join in simply for the purpose of reinforcing their own social relations.

This has been described by Baumann in his study of Southall, mentioned in the Introduction (see Chapter 4, Baumann in de Coppet 1992).

All this gift exchange must be examined very carefully, however, for things that look familiar may be misleading. In theory, at least in some places, gifts are given voluntarily, but there are always rules and conventions involved. As well as knowing when it is appropriate to give gifts, and to whom, it is important to know how valuable they should be, how they should be received, and how and when they should be repaid. In some societies gifts are ignored by the recipient in front of the donor, in others they must be opened and admired, whether they actually bring pleasure or not. These rules vary from one society to another, and there are also sets of conventions about how the gift should be presented, and what form of words should accompany the presentation.

Another study which has become a classic in the field of social anthropology, and continues to invite comment, addresses precisely this subject. This book, *The Gift*, by Marcel Mauss, was written in 1925, at a time when Europeans still sought to learn about their own past by looking at so-called primitive or 'archaic' people. Mauss was interested in examining 'the realm of contract' and systems of 'economic presentation' by isolating

> one important set of phenomena: namely, prestations which are in theory voluntary, disinterested and spontaneous, but are in fact obligatory and interested. The form usually taken is that of the gift generously offered; but the accompanying behaviour is formal pretence and social deception, while the transaction itself is based on obligation and self-interest. (Mauss 1970: 1)

Through an examination of the practices found in various parts of the world, Mauss suggests that in small-scale 'early' societies, gift exchange is particularly important because it is a total phenomenon which may involve simultaneous expressions of a religious, legal, moral and economic nature. He argues further that exchange may often be between whole groups, through their chiefs, and may involve not only goods, wealth and property, but also courtesies, entertainment, ritual, military assistance, women, children, dances and feasts. These 'total prestations' are again in theory voluntary, but here, more than ever, strictly obligatory, with possible sanctions of private and open warfare.

total phenomenon – a social phenomenon that is found to involve all areas of life in a particular society. The term was chosen by Marcel Mauss in the case of *le don* – translated as gift or 'prestation' – which he saw involving simultaneous expressions of a 'religious, legal, moral and economic' nature.

He proposed that there are three clear obligations involved:

1 the obligation to give
2 the obligation to receive and
3 the obligation to repay

and examples of the mechanisms of gift exchange in several different societies illustrate the significance it may hold in the wider arenas of social life. In all cases, ethnographers have returned again and again to the societies he chose, and knowledge about the people concerned has been greatly deepened, but three examples from Mauss's material lay out an agenda for further discussion. They also illustrate principles which arise in all societies in one way or another – quite an achievement.

The first of these is the case of the *kula*, a system of gift-giving found in the Trobriand Islands and described and analysed in detail by Malinowski (1922), of whom we heard in the Introduction. He entitled his first book *Argonauts of the Western Pacific* after people who build elaborate boats and make long journeys to visit other islands in the area. The ostensible purpose of their voyages is to make gifts, gifts which are passed on to further islanders in time by the recipients, and which continue around in a wide circular progression. The gifts are made of local shells, and in one direction travel necklaces, called *soulava*, and in the other, expressed as a return for the first, according to Malinowski, armbands called *mwali*.

Despite a show of disinterest in the gifts when they arrive, often to be thrown down disdainfully, the *mwali* and *soulava* are greatly prized by the local people. The community as a whole is said to gloat over them while they are in their possession, handing them round with affection, wearing them as adornment, and even placing them over the sick to help them recover. Some of these objects have legends attached to them, and are particularly prized, but it is important not to keep the gifts too long before passing them on. The objects move around a much wider area of the ocean than any of their 'owners', but people gain status by being involved in the *kula*, and they take a lot of trouble to set up the voyages.

In practice, each visit involves considerable preparation, for the elaborate canoes must be built and maintained, and the presentation of gifts is accompanied by the regular exchange and barter of a multitude of other objects, or 'utilities', as Malinowski terms them, which are 'often unprocurable in the district to which they are imported, and indispensable there'.

> The Kula is thus an extremely big and complex institution, both in its
> geographical extent, and in the manifoldness of its component pursuits.
> It welds together a considerable number of tribes, and it embraces
> a vast complex of activities, interconnected, and playing into one
> another... (Malinowski 1922: 83)

Mauss's first example thus demonstrates that this system of ceremonial gift exchange is ensuring *communication* amongst island people who would otherwise be widely separated. The gifts are surely expressing social relationships.

The second example from Mauss proposes to help understand the force of obligation associated with gift-giving, which he finds lacking in Malinowski's account of the *kula*. He turns to Polynesia to consider practices and ideas of the Māori people, and those of Samoa, where spiritual forces are held to attack a person who fails to repay a gift received. Within the local system of thinking a person builds up a kind of honour or prestige, known as *mana*, which is conferred by wealth but lost if suitable gifts are not returned. This is said to be because *mana* includes a magical or spiritual element transmitted through the vehicle of *taonga*, which may be property, labour or merchandise, that has the power to turn and destroy the recipient if appropriate repayment is not made.

A part of the giver is thought to be sent with the gift, which gives him or her a kind of hold over the person who receives it, and also over anyone who may steal it! This view thus represents an explicit expression in spiritual terms of the obligation to repay goods or services received, which Mauss argues exists to some extent everywhere. It also demonstrates very clearly the way those who are unable to repay gifts received, for whatever reason, lose face and prestige within their own society. Indeed, the term *mana*, which is related to ideas of *tabu*, as we discussed in the last chapter, is sometimes translated as 'face' (see First-hand Account 3. 1 overleaf for the interesting 2007 interpretation of a Māori scholar).

This principle is illustrated forcibly in the third example we take from Mauss, namely the case of *potlatch*, which he explains was originally a Chinook word meaning to 'nourish' or 'consume', but that had come to describe competitive feasts held amongst peoples of northwest America like the Tlingit, Haida and Kwakiutl of Alaska and British Columbia. As elsewhere, the political hierarchy was based on wealth, which was said to indicate proof of favour with the spirits, and people would demonstrate their status in this respect by inviting each other to feasts during the cold winter months. Gifts would be handed out, and those who couldn't afford to repay would lose face, and could even be enslaved for debt.

The chiefs of each group invited would sometimes sit in hierarchical order at these gatherings so that everyone could see their ranking, and trade and marriage arrangements would depend upon an internally recognised relative standing of the groups involved. These people collectively became so rich during the late nineteenth and early twentieth centuries due to their skills at trapping animals whose furs were highly prized in the wider world, that their winter celebrations became extremely lavish, and they even began to destroy valuable goods to demonstrate their immense wealth. Beautiful blankets would be burned, and huge copper plates hurled over the cliffs, in their agonised efforts to humiliate one other.

This is evidently an exaggerated case, but the principles are quite recognisable. Where wealth is a mark of status, it is not enough to have the resources; others must be made aware of the fact. The notion of conspicuous consumption was discussed some time ago by Veblen (1899) for Western societies, and the wanton destruction of valuable goods is an extension of spending wildly to impress. In British society, there are subtle ways to gain status through diverting wealth into children's education, club membership, or perhaps land, sometimes even leaving a shortage of ready cash, a state which may be contrasted snobbishly with an excessively obvious display of wealth.

conspicuous consumption – the ostentatious consuming of food, drink or other goods interpreted (initially by Veblen) as a way of demonstrating wealth, or laying claim to a wealthy group or society.

Tikanga hau, the 'spirit of gift exchange' or the ethic of generosity, and its associated values are identified in my current research as a principal motivation of Māori business and cultural leaders. This is evident in economics, and significantly also in the politics of social relations. In anthropology, especially in the work of Marcel Mauss, who was informed on Māori thinking by Tamati Ranapiri of the Ngāti Raukawa tribe, exchange theory and gift exchange are often presented in the form of the following propositions: that exchange is a fundamental social system; that gift exchange is a prior economic system; that a gift economy is animated by the spirit of the gift (*hau*); that the spirit of the gift creates an indissoluble bond between persons engaged in the exchange, and that it was Western societies which were responsible for the separation of persons and things.[1]

First-hand account 3.1:
Manuka Henare, Māori – on *Hau*: The Ethic of Generosity and Spirituality of Gift Exchange

However, a focus solely on material and cognitive anthropology of gift exchange and generosity without recourse to its metaphysics and spirituality, or *wairuatanga*, is not adequate in the mind of Māori of Aotearoa New Zealand. While Mauss has, in my analysis of the Ranapiri letters of 1907, remained close to Ranapiri's metaphysics and indeed was informed by it, other commentators have concentrated on the material and social aspects of gift exchange, disputing a metaphysical explanation at all. Severe critiques were made by Raymond Firth, Claude Lévi-Strauss and Marshall Sahlins on Mauss's hermeneutics and treatment of *hau*, which reflect utilitarian, materialist, secularist, and psychological and Western rationalist critiques of Māori metaphysics as understood by a French scholar. The only ethnographer to have worked from the original Tamati Ranapiri letters was Elsdon Best, as they were in correspondence with each other. As far as I know, none of the commentators read or accessed the original letters in Māori of Tamati Ranapiri. They

Aotearoa
New Zealand

all therefore depended upon the accuracy of Elsdon Best and his transcribing and translating the letters correctly.

I found that Best had, when transcribing the letters and preparing extracts ready for publication in *Māori Forest Lore* (1909), made significant changes to key phrases. The effect of Best's changes turned Ranapiri's hermeneutics about Māori metaphysics into a secular materialist's explanation, thus reflecting Best's views more so than those of Ranapiri. The error was partly corrected by Mauss, albeit somewhat intuitively, but Firth, Lévi-Strauss and Sahlins followed Best's edited translation of the Ranapiri letters and the former's phenomenological approach. Many others have followed suit, including Weiner (1992) and Parry (1986). Following Best, Firth, Lévi-Strauss and Sahlins challenged Mauss's interpretation and his idea of the spirit of the gift itself. According to Firth: 'When Mauss sees in gift exchange an interchange of personalities, a "bond of soul", he is following not a native belief, but his own intellectual interpretation of it' (1972: 418).

Claude Lévi-Strauss wrote:

> Hau is not the ultimate explanation for gift exchange; it is the conscious form whereby men of a given society, in which the problem had particular importance, apprehended an unconscious necessity whose explanation lies elsewhere.   (Cited in Schrift 1997: 55–6)

Finally, Marshall Sahlins presents a rationalist utilitarian criticism:

> Since Mauss ... anthropology has become more consistently rational in its treatment of exchange. Reciprocity is contract pure and mainly secular, sanctioned perhaps by a mixture of considerations of which a carefully calculated self-interest is not the least.   (Cited in Schrift 1997: 93)

Ranapiri wrote of two distinct *hau* associated with a *taonga*, or the gift. The first is the *hau* intrinsic to the *taonga* itself, which is the *hau* infused at the creation of the *taonga*. The second *hau*, advises Ranapiri, is the original donor's *hau* that is associated with his or her possession or ownership of the taonga. Thus in Māori belief exchange and its spiritual–moral bases are therefore a central theme in contemporary social relations and economics. It is a Māori view of the exchange and its moral bases of the human action that matters. *Tikanga hau*, exchange or generosity, spirituality and morality, is part of a matrix of some thirteen associated ethics, which constitutes a moral system, based on a plurality of ethics.

Despite Elsdon Best's mistake in the translation of Ranapiri's explanation of *hau*, Marcel Mauss' intuitive explication of the meaning and significance of *hau* was correct all along and captured the spirit of Ranapiri's 'text capitale.'

Note
1. My thanks to Dr Amiria Salmond, Anthropology Department, Cambridge University, England for discussions on these points in 1999 and in New Zealand in 2000.

Dr Manuka Henare is associate dean of Māori and Pacific Development at the University of Auckland Business School. See the Henare entry under the 'References and Further Research' section at the end of this chapter to read about his research.

In 1928, the practice of potlatch was banned in British Columbia, by a Canadian government taking measures to try and assimilate their Native populations, and responding to complaints from local churchmen about the extreme measures being taken to acquire the necessary goods. The anthropologist Franz Boas wrote in defence of the system as an important part of the socioeconomic organisation of those peoples, but the ban was not lifted until the 1950s and masks confiscated at the time of the ban not returned until later (the film *Box of Treasures*, listed below, is the story told from the perspective of the Kwakwaka'wakw people, described by Mauss as Kwakiutl). The practice was in many cases continued in secret, for potlatch feasts also mark important occasions in people's lives.

Today, the gifts given include modern consumer goods such as coffee pots and tea towels, and the occasions include university and school graduation, marking the agreement of a land claim treaty, and memorials for people who have passed away. Jonaitis (1991) is a good source of information about the continuing feasts and their associated material culture.

The Indian Gift

Since Mauss's time there have been many refinements to the ethnography he used, but his ideas are still discussed, sometimes critically. One important contribution was made by anthropologists who have worked in India, where the obligation to repay gifts received is shown to be not as universal as Mauss seemed to be suggesting. Here a form of gift known as *dân* or *dana*, made to a priest or members of a different caste who can deal with residual pollution, is positively not to be repaid, because it is thought to carry away inauspiciousness and sin, which one would not want back. An interpretation of the Indian situation depends on an understanding of notions of purity and pollution, which are inextricably linked with the caste system, as introduced in the previous chapter.

This subject was the focus of a book called *The Poison in the Gift*, by Gloria Goodwin Raheja, who argued that the close examination of gift-giving in the North Indian village where she worked revealed a new theoretical interpretation of caste, based on the centrality of the landowners called Gujars:

> The structural position of Gujars in the caste configuration of the village and the region is dependent not only on their possession of the land, but also on the pattern of their relationships with the other castes in terms of the giving and receiving of specific named prestations, as the 'protectors' ... of the village.
>
> .... Gujars have a 'right' to give *dân* ... and it is always given in the context of ritual actions that are said to promote the 'well-being [achieved through] gift-giving' (*khairkhairât*) and 'auspiciousness'(*śubh*) of the Gujar donors through the transferral of inauspiciousness (*nâsubh*) to the recipients. (Raheja 1988: 18–20)

Raheja argues that her observations and analysis of the movement of objects, including gifts, reveals a new understanding of the relations between caste groups. She thereby challenges the previous work of both Mauss and Dumont (see Chapter 2), and her work is an excellent example of the value of the analysis of material culture for understanding social relations.

Jonathan Parry (1986) also discusses the *dana* gifts which positively reject a return. He proposes a rereading of Mauss's ideas to remind the reader that the ideological distinction between 'free gift' and 'economic self-interest' was part of Mauss's own society, distinguished from the practices of his ethnographic subjects by his choice of the word *prestation* to describe them. In the case of gifts unreciprocated materially, Parry points out that the act of giving builds up not only auspiciousness or status for the donor, but also allows them to accrue credit in their *karmic* destiny:

> I am suggesting, then, that an elaborated ideology of the 'pure' gift is most likely to develop in state societies with an advanced division of labour and a significant commercial sector. But what is also in my view essential to its articulation is a specific type of belief system, as is suggested by the fact that in all of the major world religions great stress is laid on the merit of gifts and alms, ideally given in secrecy and without expectation of any worldly return. (Parry 1986: 467)

In the world religions mentioned by Parry, teachings suggest that the donors might reasonably expect to build up credit for the afterlife for their generosity, and although the giver may never express things in this way, indeed it may be regarded as counterproductive to do so, the objective possibility of an eventual return of a non-material nature does conserve the principle of reciprocity. First-hand Account 3.2 overleaf provides an excellent Mexican example of the care and attention people may put into giving gifts that have no tangible return in view.

Another example of imbalance of this sort is where a person aspiring to leadership may give gifts in order to build up a following and, in this case, loyalty is the return that is expected. Indeed, in this last case, the return must necessarily

In Mexico, on 12th December we have one of our biggest celebrations: it's the day of our Lady of Guadalupe. We honour her as our mother, in a similar way as mother's day is celebrated basically around the world. People prepare gifts for her months in advance and they can take diverse forms.

Knitted tablecloths (similar to lace made in Bruges-Brussels) are one of the most popular gifts that our Lady of Guadalupe receives. They cover the permanent (or temporary) altar that some families have at their homes, where a picture or statue of the Virgin is placed and surrounded by fresh flowers – roses most of the time – and candles. Depending on the altar's size, women (mainly) start knitting the new gift several weeks or even months in advance, and every year they made a new one. The type of work can vary, but many of the pieces made are delicate, beautiful and perfect, and they should be white, meaning the purity of the Virgin. I had the opportunity to see an example of this work in progress. It was planned to be as grand as 4 × 3 metres approximately, requiring around 2 months of work, and consisted of small squares of 10 × 10 centimetres in a beautiful pattern. I was impressed both by the process and the final work.

First-hand account 3.2:

Maria Guadalupe Hernandez White, Mexican – on Gifts that need no Return

Another special gift for her is live music called a *serenata*. On the first minute of 12th December *mariachis* (a folkloric music band), soap opera stars, musicians, pop singers, composers and members of the general public go to *La Basilica de Guadalupe* (the Church dedicated to the Virgin) to sing *las mañanitas* – the Mexican happy birthday song – to the *Virgen* and thousands of people around the country follow the event by TV broadcast and sing along. Afterwards, a celebration with more songs and dances lasting more than one hour is performed in *La Basilica*.

Serenatas can also be offered to people on special occasions – always in the evening or at midnight. Mothers can receive *serenatas* on mother's day as a gift from their children; a woman (mainly) on her birthday or saint's day, when the first song is always *las mañanitas* followed by other favourite tunes of the one who is receiving the *serenata*. A long time ago someone offered me a *serenata*, and that has been one of the most beautiful gifts that I received in my life: I love music and it was a very nice surprise.

Another reason for offering a *serenata* is when a man is wooing a woman, but contrary to the other events, the first song is not *las mañanitas*; it is different and it used to be one that the woman likes very much.

We also offer gifts on *el Dia de los Muertos* (The Day of the Dead). It is a complex celebration, very deep with meaning, that happens from the evening of 31st October until the evening of 2nd November. People elaborate an *ofrenda* (an offering in the form of an altar) dedicated to relatives and also loved friends who have died. An *ofrenda* consists of cooked food like *mole*, *tequila* and *pulque* (drinks), soft drinks, tea, coffee, *atole* (a corn-based drink), cigarettes, candies, fruits, and special bread baked for the dead. *Ofrendas* are made at home and also placed on graves in the cemeteries (see photograph 8.1 on p. 161).

At home, *ofrendas* are decorated with photographs of the people honoured and, as in graves, with objects they liked and used when they were alive, for instance toys for dead children. Other common gifts are candles, pottery, clothes, punched tissue paper with special designs related to death in a comic way; burning incense and myrrh; special flowers that are used only on this occasion: *cempansuchiles* – very similar to marigolds, skulls made from sugar and from *papier mâché*. Sometimes, both at home and at mausoleums, music bands offer live music also.

be blurred to avoid accusations of corruption, although views on what constitutes bribery are culturally variable, as can often be seen in reports of international politics. We will return to consider the question of power in Chapter 10, but the principles raised here are of course directly relevant, whether it be at an individual level, or in relations between nations. Those who can accumulate a surplus of wealth in any society are in a position to use that wealth to secure power in all kinds of ways, but it is sometimes necessary to be quite careful that the transactions not be too overt. The immense wealth that has been accumulated by the United States makes possible a political edge in all kinds of international negotiations, but, as the second edition of this book goes to press, many of the activities of that nation, under the presidency of George W. Bush, have gone way beyond the bounds of acceptable interaction for many onlookers, inside and out.

Exchange

In a wider interpretation of social life, gifts may be seen to form just one material part of a complex system of exchange, which is found in all societies in one form or another. Whether made in material form or not, exchange is an important means of *communication* which expresses social relationships at various levels. Within Western society, some of the ways in which social relationships are fostered are through dropping in to drink cups of tea or coffee together, inviting people to dinner (and other) parties, writing letters, sending Christmas cards, making telephone calls, buying drinks and doing favours.

In each of these cases, a degree of exchange is usually expected, and people would soon become tired of someone who was only on the receiving side or, indeed, only on the offering side. There are exceptions, but generally for a friendship or other relationship to develop, there needs to be a two-way flow. It need not be identical. One person may be better at writing, another at 'phoning; one may enjoy preparing dinners for their friends, another prefer spending time in the pub; but unless an individual has an extraordinarily magnetic personality, or a very depleted bank account, they would usually expect to engage in some level of give and take.

Even at the level of conversation, a social relationship does not usually thrive on one-way flow, and a person who failed to reply to an opening gambit could well be expressing a rejection of the relationship offered. This is of course always a possibility, and unwelcome overtures from strangers may be snuffed out by silence. Greetings are forms of exchange of a very basic kind, and it is not necessary to know someone well to say hello to them on a corridor. Refusal to reply, on the other hand, can be offensive. To try it out with people you see often is an excellent (if unpleasant) way to test the force of exchange in maintaining relationships!

In Japanese, even the smallest 'favours' are expressed in a giving or receiving verb which qualifies the main action verb and makes clear who is obligated to whom. Thus 'I'll carry your bag for you' is literally 'I'll carry-give your bag'; and 'Will you hold my books' is difficult to write literally because it asks the other person to hold the books but expresses the obligation using a word more akin to 'receive' in expressing the obligation incurred. Of course, it is not necessary to repay exactly every tiny favour in Japan, but the explicit language used is undoubtedly related to the very careful accounting found amongst Japanese people about the exchange of one sort or another in which they are involved.

Such precise accounting may seem more appropriate for economic transactions, but there is an overlap between the social and the economic in more societies than the so-called primitive ones that Mauss identified. In Mexico and Guatemala, for example, an interesting system developed in some regions which ties a number of villages into a single socioeconomic community. This is achieved by the fact that villages specialise in making only one particular product – bread,

Selling pots from the Mexican village of Santa Cruz de Arriba, at the central market in Texcoco (photograph: Joy Hendry).

pots, woollen goods, flowers, even fireworks. In order to provide for the necessities of life, then, the people of these villages must communicate with each other and this usually takes place at markets. Sometimes these circulate, visiting one village after another, nowadays usually arriving at the same place on a particular day of the week, although the system pre-dates the European calendar. In larger centres, a regular market attracts villagers from the whole area (see Photograph 3.1). In pre-Columbian times, the market day was also a day for sports and festivals, adding to its social function.

In areas where such a circulating marketing system operates, people tend to marry within the community so that they can use the skills of their own speciality and pass them on to their children. In other parts of the world, a preference for marriage outside the community may provide the means of communication across a wider area, and here *marriage* is sometimes interpreted as a form of exchange. This is usually described as an exchange of women, perhaps largely because the anthropologists were men and saw the world through the eyes of the men, as we discussed in Chapter I, but it may also be that this is the way the people (men?) themselves described the situation.

The influential French anthropologist Claude Lévi-Strauss identified two main types of exchange of this sort. One he called restricted (or direct) exchange, which may be a straight swap between brothers of their sisters, or anyway between women of one community for those of another. The other he called generalised (or indirect) exchange, where women move in one direction only, but several communities are eventually linked into a circle or more complicated arrangement. These different arrangements will be discussed in more detail in Chapter 11. Once marriages have been set up, further communication is effectively maintained through visiting, exchange of gifts, and probably further marriages in future generations. Again, this is a way in which smaller communities are drawn into larger systems with those around.

exchange, direct/ indirect, restricted/ generalised – words used to describe types of social interaction between individuals or groups, ranging from gift giving to marriage.

Reciprocity

In all the cases of exchange described above, some degree of reciprocity is necessary for the communication to continue in an amicable way, and the ultimate sanction for failing to maintain reciprocity may be, as Mauss predicted, private or open warfare. Warfare is itself a form of exchange, although in this case the reciprocity could be described as negative. Some villages of the Yanomamö Indians (in Brazil and Venezuela) go through cycles where they trade with

reciprocity – a return for something given, often part of a continuing arrangement expressing social relations, and analysed by Marshall Sahlins into three types: generalised, balanced and negative.

one another for a while, even arrange marriages, but then relations break down and they go to war. Eventually they may patch up their quarrels and go through the cycle again, and there is even evidence that villages develop specialities and shortages which they didn't previously have so that they are forced to look for, or manage without, trading partners (Chagnon 1983: 149–50).

Reciprocity may be of various kinds, then, with more or less of a time factor involved and greater or fewer social or moral implications attached. An immediate exchange is less likely to represent a social relationship than a delayed one, since the transaction will be completed on the spot and there is no need for further communication. A small shopkeeper who gives credit is likely to be one with whom customers also have a social relationship of some sort, whereas it is possible to make purchases in a supermarket – an immediately agreed form of reciprocity – without even exchanging greetings with the cashier. Unbalanced reciprocity, on the other hand, is more likely the greater the strength of the relationship.

In another classic piece of work, entitled 'On the Sociology of Primitive Exchange' (1974), Marshall Sahlins drew up a typology of reciprocity, according to the social distance represented. Again, he is talking of so-called 'primitive people', but there are clear parallels with wider situations, and the article raises a number of examples which are quite transferable to any society. He identifies three main types of reciprocity, but he emphasises that these are the extremes and the mid-point of a spectrum of possible types to be encountered in practice.

The first type, which he calls generalised reciprocity, not to be confused with generalised exchange, as discussed above, is that found at the 'solidary extreme', that is amongst those with, or wishing to express, the closest social relations. In this case, there is no return stipulated and no definite obligation; indeed the return may never actually be fulfilled. Sharing of goods within a family is the example Sahlins gives as the extreme, where 'the expectation of a direct material return is unseemly. At best ... implicit' (1974: 147). In practice, the return is related to the circumstances of the recipient rather than to the value of that received, and failure to reciprocate does not necessarily stop the giving.

The mid-point of the continuum Sahlins calls balanced reciprocity and this is where goods of equal worth pass immediately between two parties, with no time lag and no moral implications. Here, we are more in the realm of economic than social transactions 'from our own vantage point', as Sahlins puts it, and while generalised reciprocities are characterised by a material flow sustained by social relations, balanced exchange is where social relations hinge on the material flow. The type of exchange involved will be akin to trade, but may also include peace treaties or alliances, some marital transactions, and compensation payments.

Sahlins's third type, at the 'unsociable extreme' of the spectrum, is negative reciprocity:

> the attempt to get something for nothing with impunity, the several forms of appropriation, transactions opened and conducted toward net utilitarian advantage. Indicative ethnographic terms include 'haggling' or 'barter', 'gambling', 'chicanery', 'theft', and other varieties of seizure. Negative reciprocity is the most impersonal sort of exchange. In guises such as 'barter' it is from our own point of view the 'most economic'. The participants confront each other as opposed interests, each looking to maximise utility at the other's expense. Approaching the transaction with an eye singular to the main chance, the aim of the opening party or of both parties is the unearned increment. . . . negative reciprocity ranges through various degrees of cunning, guile, stealth, and violence to the finesse of a well-conducted horse-raid. . . the flow may be one-way once more, reciprocation contingent upon mustering countervailing pressure or guile. (1974: 148–9)

Sahlins goes on to argue that the spectrum of reciprocity he has outlined may be related to degrees of social distance within any particular social world. In a well-known diagram, which applies to a tribal model of social relations (Figure 3.1), he maps the spectrum of types of reciprocity onto a series of concentric spheres moving out from the home, through to unrelated people from other tribes. Within the home, village, or even lineage, generalised reciprocity is expected, while for the rest if the tribe, a balanced arrangement is sufficient. Outside the tribe, with 'other' tribes or peoples, anything goes, and the moral system is, in effect, suspended. Sahlins's scheme also considers social ranking, relative wealth and the nature of the goods exchanged.

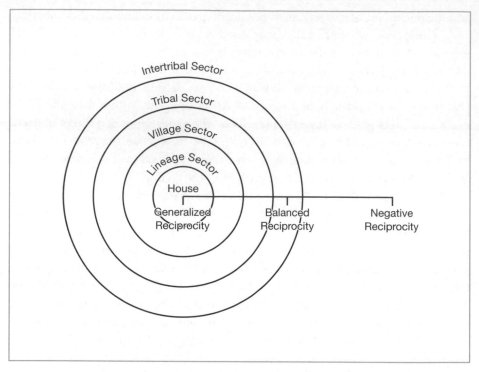

Source: This has been adapted from Marshall Sahlins, 'On the Sociology of Primitive Exchange', in Michael Banton (ed.), *The Relevance of Models in Social Anthropology* (1974), p. 152, by permission of Tavistock Publications.

Figure 3.1 Reciprocity and kinship residential sectors

The basic principles outlined here are rather crude, and in any specific situation the details would need to be modified, but they give a feel for the contribution an anthropological approach can make to areas which have become associated with economists. Sahlins suggests that 'trade' should be classified as balanced exchange, but in an actual trading situation social factors are hard to eliminate, and in the global community, rules will vary depending on the nature of the market concerned. The capitalist world is full of people trying to make something out of other people, and social distance is invariably a factor, which may have little to do with geographical distance. It will also be related to perceived relative wealth and status. Former schoolmates, now trading between London and Auckland, New Zealand, for example, may well be kinder to one another than either will be to their Japanese business partners, but both could probably be persuaded to make concessions to a 'Third World' economy.

Neither should 'barter' always be classified as 'negative reciprocity', just because it does not involve a third medium of exchange, such as money. It may be part of a highly moral system in various parts of the world, including domestic babysitting circles in the English-speaking world, and exchanges of labour in Asia and South America. Furthermore, money may itself be valued in different ways in different parts of the world, and in the same parts of the world in different contexts (see Parry and Bloch 1989). Wrapping a bank note up in a special envelope, or placing a larger sum in a 'trust', may convert it into a gift, for example, and we are back to the various social and moral implications we considered above.

Objects Inalienable, Entangled and Wrapped

It is many years since the classic works referred to here were written, and their messages are clearly powerful, for they have probably inspired more reactions in the work of later scholars than any other related collection of ideas to be found in the subject. Some seek to refine the theoretical ideas put forward; others insist on a more thorough understanding of the ethnography, and, in between all this, the commentators comment on each other's reactions. It is particularly interesting to see whether the original peoples cited are still engaged in the forms of exchange described above, how they have been affected by outside influences, and whether subsequent studies have cast new interpretations on the material they collect.

One interesting study, which challenges the theories of both Mauss and Malinowski, was that carried out by Annette Weiner, who also travelled to the Trobriand Islands for her fieldwork, but who chose to spend more time with women than Malinowski did. She published several books, examining various aspects of the lives of Trobriand women, but most relevant to this discussion is a book entitled *Inalienable Possessions: The Paradox of Keeping-While-Giving* (1992), which puts forward theory based on practices observed throughout Oceania. The Maori and Samoan ideas of *taonga* and *mana*, examined by Mauss, are considerably refined in this book, as are the notions of reciprocity advocated by both writers.

The basic principle she advocates is a distinction between objects which can be given away, or perhaps consumed, and those that remain what she calls 'inalienable', even though they may be passed to another person. In other words, the first person retains ownership of the object, and therefore a kind of domination over the person to whom it is passed. Inalienable objects include mats, cloths and other materials made by women, each of which retains a special quality of its own, and the continued possession while passing around of these goods gives women a powerful political role previously ignored by ethnographers. Thus, not only were women ignored by a male bias in the early work of anthropologists, but, according to Weiner,

> the tenacious anthropological belief in the inherent nature of the norm of reciprocity ... impedes the examination of the particular cultural conditions that empower the owners of inalienable possessions with hegemonic dominance over others. (1992: 149–50)

Another study which attacks the notion of reciprocity is again located in the Pacific, but Nick Thomas (1991) focuses on the different uses Pacific Islanders and Europeans have made of each other's material artefacts. Entitled *Entangled*

Objects: Exchange, Material Culture and Colonialism in the Pacific, this book examines the way material objects are allocated significance in social life, but appropriated in different, but nevertheless entangled ways by the various parties caught up in the colonial endeavour. Thus objects may become something quite else from what they were made to be, depending on the context in which they are found, and they may be interpreted in different ways, depending on political factors inseparable from their acquisition or appropriation.

To make clearer some of the ideas behind both of these studies, consider the hypothetical case of a beautiful cloth, which forms part of a museum collection in a country that had colonised the island where it was made. The object, transformed into a work of art, adds kudos to the museum, and possibly also enhanced the reputation of the traveller who donated it. The traveller may have perceived the acquisition of the cloth as a purchase, or a straight exchange, whilst the producer expected continuing influence with the apparently powerful outsider. In the long run, the producer, or her descendants, may be right, as museums now find themselves negotiating terms with indigenous people seeking to repatriate objects they describe as their stolen heritage.

Situations of intercultural encounter are fertile areas for contemporary anthropologists to examine, and they may provide an interesting zone of contested

Photograph 3.2 A Japanese gift very often transmits more information in the wrapping than in its content. These envelopes simply enclose cash, but their size and shape is formal, probably the outer of three layers, and the decoration – of a turtle and a crane created out of special celebratory cord – symbolise a long and happy life for a couple getting married.

understanding in the global marketplace. In Japan, all sorts of social encounters are marked with gifts, and they are often presented in quite beautiful and elaborate wrapping (see Photograph 3.2). This *wrapping* conveys meaning way beyond the mere role of hiding the object inside, indicating the degree of formality, and whether the occasion is a happy one of celebration, or a sad one of condolence. This attention to presentation in Japan often delights the unsuspecting foreigner, but if they are serious about future relations with their Japanese partners, they should be aware of possible further meaning in the gift.

In Japan, the receipt of a gift is less likely to bring pleasure than a feeling of obligation, and this is the kind of information anthropologists could bring to people engaged in intercultural communication, who would be wise to be aware of such nuances. The Japanese donor is very likely to be aware that a gift will bring pleasure to a Westerner, so it is vital for the recipient to understand the reasons behind the overtures. The value of the gift will indicate the importance of the link, and although the price tag may not be there, the wrapping paper will probably display the name of the store where it was purchased, a clear indication to those who take the trouble to appreciate the significance of gifts.

It is also usual in Japan for the donor to belittle their own gift, as do the Trobriand Islanders, protesting in response to thanks that the object is nothing of value, even though it may actually be quite the opposite. This may be interpreted as another form of wrapping, namely the *social wrapping* of politeness formulae, and I have discussed the importance for anthropologists of looking beyond this social deception in a book entitled *Wrapping Culture: Politeness, Presentation and Power in Japan and Other Societies* (1993). Another example from the Japanese case is when you are invited to a meal, only to be greeted with the apology, 'There is nothing for you', whereas in fact the table is groaning with an abundant feast.

In Mexico, on the other hand, you are invited to make a house you are visiting your own: 'You are in your house', they assure you, although they would almost certainly be alarmed if you began to unpack your bags. 'It is at your service', they reply if you admire something, even a garment, though you would not usually expect to take up the offer. Little conventions like this are only gradually acquired during the course of field research, and investigators may make many social gaffes in the early stages, but they are usually indulged, as outsiders, for at least an initial period. Eventually, the social deceptions may turn out to have rather deep and vital significance, as I discovered to be the case in Japan, where non-verbal communication can be as important, if not more so, than verbal exchanges.

As the world is increasingly open to intercultural encounters of a social, economic and political kind, it provides a tremendous advantage to be aware of differences in the expectations of the people with whom one is dealing. This is a subject to which we will return in more detail in Chapter 14. As an anthropologist who has worked in Japan, my hunch is that many Japanese travelling abroad are more aware of local expectations than foreigners visiting Japan tend to be. This is because they are aware of some of their own idiosyncrasies – indeed they have been accused of being obsessed by their 'uniqueness' – so they take the trouble to find out how things are done elsewhere.

Some of my own compatriots have been known to be less humble. British business people travelling abroad sometimes don't even recognise a need to know much beyond the polite form of greeting in the countries they visit. As for bothering to understand local systems of distribution, or notions of value that might influence their marketing strategies, they are liable to dismiss 'all that' as meaningless cultural relativism. This is an area where anthropological knowledge can have very practical advantages, however, and the HSBC advertising campaign that sets out to demonstrate their care in such matters was actually informed by the advice of one of my students. Those who take the trouble to consult someone with such a speciality in their area of interest would be quite likely to reap benefits.

Conclusion

At the start of this chapter, I mentioned a small gift I was advised to take to my new neighbours in Japan – 'a towel or something'. The gift in this case could be quite small; indeed it *should* be quite small, for a larger one would incur unnecessary and possibly unwanted feelings of obligation, an issue I have discussed further in a whole paper about towels (Hendry 1995). The purpose is to open relations, but to do it too forcibly could be counterproductive, as we have also seen where wealth is used in the exercise of power. Just as presents may have many layers of wrapping, each with a meaning, exchange can be a complicated issue, with much subtle variation. A polite form of greeting may have different manifestations, too, with a multitude of further implications. The next chapter addresses these and many other such issues from the perspective of ritual activity.

Discussion Questions

1   Consider your own gift-giving behaviour. When do you give gifts? To whom? How do you know how much to spend? What do your answers tell you about your own social circle? And how do they fit into Mauss's theories?

2   How about receipt of gifts, or other goods and favours? Are there people to whom you feel no obligation to return? And when would you invite back someone who had you to their home for a meal? How does the gift-giving described in Maria Guadalupe Hernandez White's first-hand account (p. 60) relate to other theories discussed in this chapter, and your own? Try to draw a Sahlins-type map of your own social world in terms of reciprocity and social distance.

3   Now consider the power related to giving. To whom are you in debt? Have you considered the power they have over you? Do you ever give strategically? Why, and with what aims in mind? How do these obligations affect social life?

References and Further Research

Books

Chagnon, Napoleon (1983) *Yanomamö: The Fierce People* (New York: Holt, Rinehart & Winston).

Firth, R. (1972 [1929]) *Economics of the New Zealand Māori,* 2nd edn (Wellington: A. R. Shearer, Government Printer).

Hendry, Joy (1993) *Wrapping Culture: Politeness, Presentation and Power in Japan and Other Societies* (Oxford: Clarendon Press).

Jonaitis, Aldona (1991) *Chiefly Feasts: The Enduring Kwakiutl Potlatch* (Seattle: University of Washington Press).

Lévi-Strauss, Claude (1969) *The Elementary Structures of Kinship* (London: Eyre & Spottiswoode).

Malinowski, Bronislaw (1922) *Argonauts of the Western Pacific* (London: Routledge & Kegan Paul).

Mauss, Marcel (1970) *The Gift*, translated by I. Cunnison (London: Cohen & West).

Parry, J. and Bloch, M. (1989) *Money and the Morality of Exchange* (Cambridge: Cambridge University Press).

Raheja, Gloria G. (1988) *The Poison in the Gift* (Chicago: University of Chicago Press).

Schrift, Alan D. (ed.) (1997) *The Logic of the Gift: Toward an Ethic of Generosity* (New York: Routledge).

Thomas, Nicholas (1991) *Entangled Objects: Exchange, Material Culture, and Colonialism in the Pacific* (Cambridge, Mass.: Harvard University Press).

Veblen, Thorstein (1899) *The Theory of the Leisure Class* (New York: Macmillan).

Weiner, Annette B. (1992) *Inalienable Possessions: The Paradox of Keeping-While-Giving* (Berkeley, Calif.: University of Callifornia Press).

Articles

Benthall, Jonathan (2001) 'Time to Look "The Gift" in the Mouth', *Anthropology Today,* 17(4): 1–2.

Foster, Robert J. (2005) 'Commodity Futures: Labour, Love and Value', *Anthropology Today,* 21(4): 8–12.

Henare, Manuka (2001) '*Tapu, Mana, Mauri, Hau, Wairua*: A Maori Philosophy of Vitalism and Cosmos', in John A. Grimm (ed.), *Indigenous Traditions and Ecology: The Interbeing of Cosmology and Community* (Cambridge, Mass.: Harvard University Press for the Center for the Study of World Religions), pp. 197–221.

Hendry, Joy (1995) 'The Ritual of the Revolving Towel', in Jan van Bremen and D. P. Martinez (eds), *Ceremony and Ritual in Japan* (London: Routledge), pp. 210–26.

Lévi-Strauss, Claude (1997) 'Selections from *Introduction to the Work of Marcel Mauss*', in Alan D. Schrift (ed.), *The Logic of the Gift* (New York: Routledge) pp. 45–69.

Liep, John (2001) 'Airborne Kula: The Appropriation of Birds by Danish Ornithologists', *Anthropology Today,* 17 (5): pp. 10–15.

Parry, Jonathan (1986) 'The Gift, the Indian Gift and "the Indian Gift"', *Man,* 21: 453–73.

Riches, D. (1975) 'Cash, Credit and Gambling in a Modern Eskimo Economy: Speculations on Origins of Spheres of Economic Exchange', *Man,* 10: 21–33.

Sahlins, Marshall (1974) 'On the Sociology of Primitive Exchange', in Michael Banton (ed.), *The Relevance of Models in Social Anthropology* (London: Tavistock).

Schrift, Alan D. (1997) 'Introduction: Why Gift?', in A. D. Schrift (ed.), *The Logic of the Gift* (New York: Routledge).

Novels

McCullers, Carsten (2000 [1940]) *The Heart is a Lonely Hunter* (London: Penguin) is a novel about people giving companionship to one another.

Steinbeck, John (2000 [1945]) *Cannery Row* (London: Penguin Modern Classics) is a story about the attempts of a group of unemployed men to organise a party for their friend, the Doctor.

Wendt, Albert, (1994) *Leaves of the Banyan Tree* (Honolulu: University of Hawaii Press) is a poignant novel about a Samoan family struggling to balance the influence of outside ideas, notably Christianity, and their indigenous values.

Films

Box of Treasures (U'Mista Cultural Centre, Alert Bay, Vancouver Island) is a film about the return of the potlatch masks confiscated when the practice was banned by the Canadian government in 1928, but later returned when a culture centre was built to house them.

The Feast (Timothy Asch and Napoleon Chagnon, 1970) is a classic 28-minute film, a combination of stills with explanation, and moving pictures without, about exchange of goods, feasts and warfare amongst the Yanomamö people of the Venezuelan-Brazilian borderlands.

In Search of the Hamat'sa: A Tale of Headhunting (Aaron Glass, 33 minutes, 2004) traces the history of anthropological depictions of the Hamat'sa (or 'Cannibal Dance') – the most important and highly represented ceremony of the Kwakwaka'wakw (Kwakiutl) people of British Columbia – and how, through the return of archival materials to the community, diverse attitudes towards this history inform current performances.

The Kawelka: Ongka's Big Moka (Charlie Nairn and Andrew Strathern, 1974) is a Granada 'Disappearing World' documentary about assembling pigs and other goods for a feast which forms part of a long-term exchange system amongst the Kawelka of New Guinea.

See *Off the Verandah* (Chapter 1) for more detail about the *kula*.

Trobriand Cricket (Gary Kildea and Jerry Leach, 1975) is an amusing film about the introduction and adaptation of cricket to these same people.

The Trobriand Islanders (David Wasan, 1990), a 'Disappearing World' film, made with the help of anthropologist Annette Weiner, focuses on the female exchanges which complement the more famous *kula* practices.

Websites

http://www.peabody.harvard.edu/potlatch/default.html – gifting and feasting in the Northwest Coast Potlatch.

http://www.altruists.org/ – Altruists' International website!

http://rsnz.natlib.govt.nz/volume/rsnz_41/rsnz_41_00_003410.html – gives access to the article on Māori Forest Lore, by Elsdon Best, referred to in First-hand Account 3.1 on pp. 56–8.

4

The Ritual Round

Shoes and the Empty Ritual

Ritual is sometimes described as 'empty', or meaningless, and there are people who make conscious efforts to pare it away. They may decide to have a simple wedding 'without any fuss', or a small family funeral, with 'no flowers please'. Some Christian churches make a virtue out of simplicity of design, cast away the ecclesiastical robes, and even abandon their notion of an order of service on some especially open occasions. In each case, there is an expression of rejection of the more complicated forms which may be regarded as wasteful of time and resources, or unnecessary adornment of the event. In a way, it's like leaving the wrapping off a gift in the interest of saving trees ... but let us look at ritual a little more closely.

We talked in Chapter 1 about the importance of understanding systems of classification in order to understand the way in which people in different societies divide up the world into categories, and, in Chapter 2, about notions of pollution and taboo which may be associated with the places which fall between those categories. The places and situations which fall between categories, the interstitial places as they may be called, are also often associated with danger in any society, and a common response to this kind of danger is to institute some sort of ritual. By looking at ritual, then, we can again learn a lot about the system of classification held by a particular people.

To illustrate this idea, we can return briefly to the example of Japanese shoes. It is an inviolable custom in Japan to remove your shoes before entering someone's house, as was discussed earlier. The place in which you remove your shoes is usually a porch, which separates the inside of the house from the outside world, and this space may be described as an interstitial place between those two worlds (see Photograph 4.1). The act of removing shoes thus emphasises the importance of the distinction between them, and it is an act so firmly prescribed by society that in the Japanese case it may be regarded as having the force of a ritual act. In fact we find that further rituals very often accompany the removal or donning of shoes in that space.

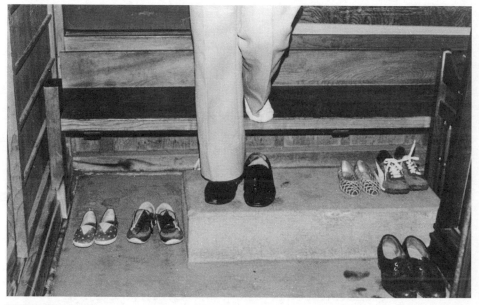

Photograph 4.1 Shoes must be removed before entering a Japanese home so there is always a 'liminal' space between the outside world and the inside of the home where these may be removed and put back on.

These include greetings, with fixed words, depending on whether one is coming in or going out, and there is a response, again fixed, from anyone who is inside the house. The announcement of an arrival literally means 'now', and the response is something like 'welcome'. The call on departure means 'I go and come back'. A visitor to the house calls out 'I make disturbance' as they enter, and 'I make rudeness' as they leave. Mothers with small children will call out these greetings as they go in and come out whether there is anyone inside or not, because the rituals of crossing the threshold of the household are part of the training they feel they need to give to their child.

Further elements may be added to the ritual, such as the changing of clothes on returning home, and many mothers insist that their children also wash their hands and gargle. Husbands returning home from work may well head straight for the bath as a regular feature of their arrival, and some will change from their city suits into Japanese garments. The ritual for greeting guests includes bowing, and in the rural area of Japan where I did my first fieldwork, this was an elaborate performance involving kneeling on the ground and bringing one's head almost into contact with the floor. The guests would return the compliment, so this exchange would take place after the person had climbed up onto the matted floor.

Definitions of Ritual

It may be objected at this point that some form of greeting is carried out anywhere on entering or leaving a house, and people may also adjust their bodily attire. Why then should this be regarded as ritual? Let us turn first, then, to examine what exactly is meant by the term ritual in anthropology. In fact, there are several definitions of 'ritual', some of which restrict its use to describing behaviour of a religious nature (see, for example, Lewis 1980: 6–38 de Coppet 1992) but most anthropologists these days prefer to adopt a broader one which can include secular activities like greetings. For example,

> **ritual** - behaviour prescribed by society in which individuals have little choice about their actions; sometimes having reference to beliefs in mystical beings or powers.

> Ritual is behaviour prescribed by society in which individuals have little choice about their actions.

To test a form of behaviour to see whether it might qualify to be called ritual or not, one could try to change it, or omit it, and see how others would react. As mentioned in the previous chapter, refusing to reply to a greeting could be seen as most offensive. Omitting to greet someone on entering their house would seem churlish at the very least. In Japan, a visitor is expected to utter the appropriate phrases, and a child who failed to wash would soon be hustled into the bathroom, though the husband might get away with the odd lapse so that perhaps his practice would better be termed a routine, or custom, though a wife might read meaning into a lack of greeting anywhere! With this definition, rules about gift exchange can also be included, as can secular special occasions such as birthday parties.

After all, a birthday party, especially for a child, would hardly qualify to be such if it lacked certain elements: balloons, cards, presents, the cake, candles, the singing of a special song, and possibly the playing of games as well. In some areas, there are further expectations, perhaps about the provision of increasingly large gifts to take home, the wrapping up and distribution of pieces of cake, and a ceremony when the birthday presents are opened, one by one, to a series of 'oohs' and 'ahs' from the assembled company. A parent who put on a party without the appropriate paraphernalia would run the severe risk of disapproval on the part of their own offspring, and possibly voluble complaints from the young guests.

A more restricted definition of ritual, which several anthropologists have used and which may therefore be referred to, is:

> prescribed formal behaviour for occasions not given over to technological routine, having reference to beliefs in mystical beings or powers.   (Turner 1967: 19)

Even in the case of religious ritual, the rites themselves must be examined separately from belief that may be associated with them, since people may participate for entirely social reasons. A funeral, for example, is attended by those who were close to, or who wish to express their respect for the deceased. Such participants will mourn, wear black or some other sombre colour and, if appropriate, they will attend a religious service. This says nothing about the individual beliefs of the participants with respect to God or gods and the service they are attending. It may not even say very much about their feelings for the dead. Perhaps they are attending to express sympathy for the bereaved.

Similarly, in the case of a marriage, or a christening, the participants may have very different views amongst themselves about the religious nature of the event. As the social anthropologist Edmund Leach (1969) pointed out, a Church of England wedding tells us nothing of the bride or her beliefs, only about the social relations being established (Photograph 4.2). In other words, we must separate personal beliefs from the social aspects of ritual behaviour. The latter is the domain of interest of the social anthropologist.

Photograph 4.2 According to Edmund Leach, a Church of England wedding tells us nothing of the bride and her beliefs, but only of the social relations being established.

Rites of Passage

Much has been written on the subject of ritual, and there have been many theories about its interpretation, but there is one classic work that has stood the tests both of time and of further research. This is the study by Arnold van Gennep, first published in 1909, in French, and translated into English in a book called *Rites of Passage* (1960). Again, this writer refers to the people under discussion as 'primitive', and he talks mostly of people in small-scale society, but his theories have been shown to have applicability in any society in any part of the world. Van Gennep's notion of ritual is also closer to the second definition about religious behaviour, but it applies to ritual which fits the first in many cases as well.

These rites of passage are those which accompany the movement from what van Gennep describes as 'one cosmic or social world to another'. In the terms we have been using in this book, it involves a move from one social category to another, the passage of a person or persons in a society from one *class* to another. There are four main types of move:

> **rites of passage** – rites that celebrate and protect the move of an individual or a social group from one 'class' or social category to another.

1. The passage of people from one *status* to another (for example, marriage or initiation to a new social or religious group).
2. The passage from one *place* to another (for example, a change of address or territory).
3. The passage from one *situation* to another (for example, taking up a new job or starting at a new school).
4. The passage of *time* (when the whole social group might move from one period to another, for example at New Year, or into the reign of a new king/queen or emperor).

If we think of occasions in our lives, and in those of people around us, when we might engage in some form of ritual, they are very often precisely the sort of passages which fit these descriptions. For example:

- birth, marriage, death
- christening, initiation, bar mitzvah
- changes of school, job or house
- going away, coming back
- birthdays, anniversaries, graduation
- changes of the seasons, New Year.

We ritualise these occasions in various ways, but some elements on which we draw are:

- dressing up
- sending cards
- giving presents
- holding parties

- making and consuming special food
- making resolutions
- ordeals.

By examining reports of rites of passage from various parts of the world, van Gennep noticed that certain characteristic patterns recurred in the order of the ceremonies even from places much too far apart to have influenced one another. First of all, there would be rites of separation from the old class or category, and these, he argued, are very often characterised by a symbolic death. There would also be rites of incorporation into the new class or category, and these would be characterised by a symbolic rebirth. Most striking, however, was the fact that these sets of rites would almost always be separated by a transition period when the participants would belong to neither one nor the other.

These rites he named as follows:

- Rites of Separation *or* Preliminal Rites
- Rites of Transition *or* Liminal Rites
- Rites of Incorporation *or* Postliminal Rites

Not all of these rites would be equally developed in each ceremony, since they would be of differing importance depending on the nature of the ceremony – for example, one might expect funerals to have more developed rites of separation – but van Gennep argued that this general structure is characteristic of rites of passage everywhere. Moreover, if the liminal or transition period is a particularly long one, for example during betrothal or pregnancy, there might be a set of each of the three types of rite at each end of it. He also noted that other kinds of rites – perhaps for fertility at marriage, or protection at birth – may be superimposed on the rites of passage. Let us examine some examples of the types of rite of passage he proposes.

Territorial Rites of Passage

Van Gennep's book is full of examples of rites of passage of different types, but most of these are set in small-scale societies which, he argues, imbue all such movements with ideas of a magico-religious variety. Since his book is still available and in print, let us turn here to examining some examples of secular rites of passage which may be familiar to a wider range of readers. The prototype for rites of passage is, according to van Gennep, a territorial passage from one social space such as a village to another, a passage which he argues often involves passing through a transitional area which belongs to neither side, a kind of no-man's-land in the middle.

Van Gennep discussed passages from one tribal area to another, or between different inhabited regions, but his ideas also work in a consideration of the bureaucratic rituals associated with making a passage from one nation to another. First of all, it is necessary to acquire a passport, sometimes quite a complicated and time-consuming process. In the case of many countries, it is also necessary to acquire a visa for entry. If the journey is to be of a considerable duration, friends and relatives may hold a farewell party and offer gifts and cards of good wishes. The moment of parting, at the airport, dock or station, will be marked with kisses, embraces and/or handshakes, and the passenger will be exhorted to telephone, text or e-mail on arrival.

In an airport, one is then forced to pass through a series of physical barriers involving the showing of passports and visas, the checking of luggage (and the body) through security screens, and, until arrival at the point of destination, one is quite literally in a zone of transition. Airlines use a technical explanation to account for their requests for mobile phones and other electronic equipment to be turned off during a flight, but the fact of doing it adds to the sense of liminality. The rituals of departure are repeated in reverse on arrival, and if friends or relatives are waiting, despite a high probability of fatigue and overindulgence in food and drink, it would be regarded as most unfriendly to refuse the welcoming rituals of hospitality. The phone call of arrival is a reassurance for those left behind that the zone of transition is safely crossed, that the traveller has entered another social world. It may be a world relatively dangerous and unknown, but at least it is a world!

liminality – a term used by anthropologists to describe something separate from, or on the periphery of the wider society; thus used to describe those set apart during the period of transition in a rite of passage, or a people marginalised in a particular social situation.

Van Gennep also discusses rites for crossing thresholds, and the Japanese example given above would fit his theories perfectly. The zone of transition is most clear at the entrance to a Japanese house, and it is often filled with shoes, but there are parallel rites for entering a Jewish house, where the Mezuzah must be touched, and churches, mosques and temples have some form of ritual act as one moves from a profane space to a sacred one. This may involve the removal of pollution, with a touch of holy water; it may involve a bow, a sign of the cross, the removal or donning of shoes or headgear, or simply a lowering of the voice. Again, the crossing of the threshold involves a passage from one cosmic world to another, and visitors might be expected to observe the conventions regardless of their own religious allegiances. In Chapter 13, we will discuss a couple of examples of rites imposed on tourists visiting a specific cultural area that they should respect the rules and customs of that world.

These rites also represent a form of security for the world which is being entered. In the case of countries, the checking of the passport is a way of controlling immigration; in the case of a sacred building, there is an opportunity to remove the pollution of the mundane outside world. In any house or community a stranger may represent a threat, and ritual is a way of neutralising the potential danger. Van Gennep describes society as 'similar to a house divided into rooms and corridors' (1960: 26) and territorial rites of passage associated with entering and moving about in a house may thus be seen as a model in spatial form of the rites which accompany moves from one section of society to another.

Pregnancy and childbirth

The arrival of a completely new member of society is an occasion for ritual observance anywhere, and it also provides a threat to the mother who will give birth. In some societies women are regarded as polluting throughout their pregnancy and they must live in a special hut removed from the public arena. They are thus removed physically from their normal lives to live in a 'liminal' part of their social world. They participate in rites of separation before they go, rites of transition while they are there, and only become incorporated back into society after the baby has been born. The baby, too, must be welcomed into society through rites of separation from the mother and rites of incorporation into the new social world it has joined.

Although there are few formal periods of separation for pregnant mothers in the cosmopolitan world, the English language does still contain the telltale word 'confinement' which refers back to a period when it was considered inappropriate for heavily pregnant women to be out in the world at large. Moreover, pregnant women in almost all societies do observe various restrictions on their usual behaviour, perhaps in variations to their culinary practices, as we saw in Chapter 2, or the avoidance of alcohol and smoking, as well as the careful control of drugs and other remedies. Others who are aware of their condition will carry heavy objects for them, seek out titbits for them to consume, and generally offer special care during this transitory period. Women who suffer high blood pressure and other serious complications may be literally removed from society to hospital for the waiting period.

In Japan, many women bind themselves up in a special corset during pregnancy, and the first donning of this garment may be accompanied by a party which makes official the announcement of the impending arrival. The celebration is held on a day of the dog, according to the Chinese calendar, because dogs are said to give birth relatively easily and it is hoped that this birth will be likewise (see First-hand Account 4 overleaf). Women also often return to the homes of their own parents in order to give birth and they may stay away from their marital home for up to a month afterwards. Their return is celebrated with a visit to the local shrine to present the baby to the local protective deity, and a party will also be held to incorporate mother and child back into the community.

In most societies there is some form of celebration following a birth. Amongst Christians, the christening is a formal naming ceremony in the church as well as a presentation of the child to God, and the Church of England used to have a ceremony for mothers known as 'churching', which incorporated them back into normal life. During the christening service the baby is taken from its mother by the minister, who holds it throughout the most crucial part of the ceremony, and it may be handed to a godparent as well. Elsewhere, there is a rite of separation of the baby from its mother associated with the cutting of the cord, and the cord itself may be buried in a special place with some significance for the future. The

Jewish practice of circumcising a baby boy is also an important early rite of passage.

In some societies in South America, the father of a baby goes through a series of rites parallel to those undergone by the mother, partly as a way of expressing and confirming his paternity. This practice, known as couvade, implies the idea that the father shares substance with the mother and the unborn child, and they restrict their behaviour to avoid ill-nesses, particularly to avoid the child taking on the charac-teristics of animals eaten by humans. Although for very different reasons, this practice could be compared to the way fathers in the UK, USA and elsewhere attend and par-ticipate in antenatal classes with their pregnant partners so that they may assist at the birth of their children. These classes sometimes demand quite serious commitment on the part of the fathers, who must carry out breathing and relaxation exercises along with the mothers.

couvade - a practice in some societies in South America where the father of a baby goes through a series of rites parallel to those undergone by the mother as a way of expressing and confirming his paternity.

A role has been created here which has little to do with the 'safe' delivery of the baby in a purely medical sense. Rather it was created to provide psychological support for the mother in a highly intimate situation, which had become almost entirely impersonal. Before hospitals were deemed the appropriate place for childbirth, other women would usually surround and help a woman giving birth, and although a specialist may have been called in, it was for close kin to provide more familiar backup. The newly created role for the father reflects the increasing importance and isolation of the nuclear family unit, as well as a breakdown in the sexual division of labour which used to separate men from the care of their young in many societies.

Initiation Rites

During childhood, rites are held in different societies to mark various stages of development that are regarded as important. These may include regular events such as birth-days, or accomplishments such as a first outing, first food, first haircut, first teeth (or loss of same), first day at school, and so forth. In some societies physical changes are made, such as circumcision or ear piercing. The periods which are marked reflect the local system of classification of life into stages and some societies are divided into age sets where groups of children born within a particular period move through the stages together. Others move through on an individual basis. In either case, there will be rituals to mark the passages from one stage to another.

age set - a term used to describe a group of people who share a social position that cuts across kin ties. It is based on their birth within a particular period and they are therefore approximately the same age. Members of such a group share certain obligations to one another, and usually pass through age grades together.

Social recognition of the physical changes of puberty provide widespread

In Japan, it is common for an expectant mother to wear an *obi* (sash) or *haraobi* both to protect the baby and keep the mother's tummy warm. The ceremony associated with this is called *obiiwai* and is held on the day of the dog in the fifth month of pregnancy, according to the Shinto religious calendar. It is said that dogs give birth easily and women hope that their experience will be the same.

Obiiwai marks the official announcement of pregnancy in Japan not only to the family and friends, but also to neighbours. In general, women keep it secret until this time, from when a miscarriage is less likely. In some parts of Japan, the expectant mother and the baby's maternal grandmother distribute rice cakes (*mochi*) or red rice (*sekihan*) to neighbours as they announce the pregnancy.

First-hand account 4:

Hiroko Ford, Japanese – on Rituals associated with Pregnancy

Japan

Traditionally, the baby's maternal grandmother presents the *obi*. She and her daughter go to a Shinto temple together to get the obi from the priest and have it blessed, so that it has a sacred quality. Also, they bless pregnancy and pray for a good birth together. In general, it costs 5000 yen (£25) to be blessed. The *obi* is about 2 metres long and often has written on it 安産 'easy birth' or 寿 'celebration'. A formal *obi* consists of three sashes, two in red and white silk and one in white cotton. The imperial family celebrate the *obiiwai* in the ninth month of pregnancy as well, and when Princess Kiko reached that stage, the Emperor and Empress presented her an *obi* that was 4.5 metres long and had one side of white silk and the other red silk.

In modern Japan, more pregnant women wear a so-called pregnancy girdle instead of an *obi*, not only because it is fashionable to do so, but also because it takes less time to put it on. This is a significant factor for the increasing number of pregnant women who continue working during pregnancy. These days, there is a wide range of fashionable girdles in various styles – corset type, colours (pink, yellow, green), materials (cotton, lace, mesh) costing between 4000 yen (£20) and 12,000 yen (£60).

Most of my friends used the girdle type one instead of a traditional *obi* and I myself started to wear a maternity girdle on the day of the dog in my fifth month of pregnancy. My mother bought me three different maternity girdles at a department store where I saw some other pregnant women, accompanied by their mothers (or mothers-in-law), choosing maternity girdles. From my experience, wearing a maternity girdle was very comfortable and I felt very stable especially during later pregnancy when my tummy got bigger.

examples of clearly defined rites of passage which ritually turn children into adults, and these may again involve a substantial period of separation and/ or special treatment. Amongst African tribes such as the Maasai of the Kenya/ Tanzania borders, and the Ndembu of Zambia, for example, young men are turned out to fend for themselves in 'the bush', and they may be regarded as dead for the duration. Special rites precede and follow their absence, and their physical appearance will reflect their stage in the process (see First-hand Account 5, on p. 100). The Maasai allow their hair to grow long and unkempt in the bush, but shave completely on their return, painting their bare heads with shining ochre to mark their rebirth into society. The Ndembu have female puberty rituals which take place when a girl's breasts begin to form. They are confined to the village, but the girl is wrapped up in a blanket and lain under a tree where she must remain motionless for the whole of a very often hot and clammy day while others perform ritual activities around her (see Chapter 5 for further detail).

This kind of ordeal is characteristic of many initiation rituals, which may again involve mutilations of the body of one sort or another. The proximity of these events to the flowering of sexual maturity may focus attention on the genitals in the practice of circumcision again, or even clitoridectomy. This last practice has incurred something of a backlash from women around the world, although there have been fewer protests about the former, male practice. In some societies, incisions in the face will leave permanent scarring, indicating membership of a particular tribe or lineage. Undergoing the ordeal associated with these practices is supposed to demonstrate the readiness of the child for adulthood, and the permanent markings left behind will illustrate their new status once and for all.

Education of some sort is also often involved, and youths may be taken for the first time into the men's hut to be shown ritual objects, or taught tribal lore to be kept secret from the women and children. Likewise, girls may be taught certain esoteric elements of female life. In many societies, these young initiates are regarded as immune to social sanctions for the period of transition, and they may engage in all sorts of outrageous antisocial behaviour. Even if they are not in the bush, they may live for a period in a special house where they can experiment with adult activities and practise various social aberrations while they are in the intermediate stage between two categories.

Something of the same tolerance is accorded to youths for certain periods in many societies. For example, in universities in Britain, Holland and Ireland, an annual institution known as 'rag week' is the occasion for the tolerance of all kinds of scrapes and usually illegal activities in the interest of raising money for charity. For a few years in Britain, there was also an extraordinary amount of tolerance for a practice known as 'joy-riding', during which youths sometimes as young as 12 years of age would steal expensive cars and drive them wildly around the countryside before abandoning them. The vehicle would usually be returned to the owner within a few days, somewhat worse for wear, and even if the culprits were caught they were often let off with little more than a warning. They were too young to charge, and had few resources to pay for the damage they caused, so society seemed for a while to tolerate the practice.

Whether this represented a stage of transition between childhood and adulthood is a matter open to debate, but if the youths were not seen as responsible for their own behaviour, and their parents were not held responsible for them, it seems that they must have fallen between the categories of childhood and adulthood, at least in the legal system. In the more acceptable version of education, these youths may or may not have been doing well, and they may still have been living at home, but they were gaining the skills of theft and manipulation of powerful motor cars at an extremely early age, and they were exposing themselves to the risks and ordeals that other societies institutionalise for their youngsters.

The recent popularity of voluntarily piercing various parts of the body in countries such as North America, Britain and Australia is interesting in that these societies now have few clear ritual occasions to mark the transition from childhood to adulthood. The bar and bat mitzvah celebrations for the Jewish attainment of adulthood is an exception to this general rule, and some Native Americans and First Nations in Canada also practise their own versions of marking the occasion, but a 'Coming of Age' seems to be practised only rather sporadically now. In Britain, at least, it is not clear whether this should be at the eighteenth or the twenty-first birthday, since legal changes have scattered the rights, and neither has clear rules of procedure (and see Photograph 4.3). There is a sense of special occasion, and woe betide a parent who fails to do anything unusual on both occasions, but they are difficult ages at which to please. It may be that the people engaging in 'piercing' or possibly tattooing are actually trying to express independence from the parental fold by inventing an ordeal for themselves. In Chapter 13 we will return to this subject to consider another recently popular form of youthful activity as a rite of initiation into adulthood.

Other forms of initiation to secret societies or esoteric bodies such as priesthood, as well as the enthronement ceremonies for a king or emperor, follow the same principles as initiation to adulthood. There are rites of separation of the principals from their previous lives, periods of transition involving education and

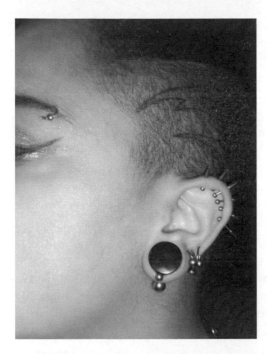

Photograph 4.3

'Piercing has become a prized activity among many young people, possibly as an expression of independence, and solidarity with friends, even a rite of passage (photograph: Tim Bauer, courtesy of Kaley Davis and Tiger Lily, Oxford).

training, and rites of incorporation representing a rebirth into their new roles. In some societies the period of interregnum between one ruler and his successor allows antisocial behaviour for the whole people, and steps are sometimes taken to keep the death of a king secret until the arrangements are in place for a quick succession, in order to cut down on the disorder.

Marriage Rites

Marriage is a most important transition in most societies and it may coincide with the attainment of adulthood so that the rites associated with the wedding come at the end of the period of separation associated with the initiation into adulthood. In other societies there will be a long period of betrothal, which may be regarded as a period of transition with rites at the beginning and end. In any case, this is a passage well marked with rites of separation, transition and incorporation in most societies, although the details may differ.

In Mexico, for example, a party held for girls who have become engaged is called the *despedida de soltera*, or seeing off of the state of being single. Friends of approximately the same age gather to drink and eat together, and they dress up and act out some of the events which will follow for the bride, an occasion usually of considerable laughter and frivolity. The 'shower' for girls in the USA serves a similar role, and in the UK there is a 'hen party'. These rites separate the bride from her previous life in preparation for the new state to come. The version for the bridegroom is also commonly an all-male occasion known as a 'stag party' where serious drinking seems to be the order of the day.

In the country in Japan, where I did my own fieldwork, there were several rites of separation before the bride left her village to marry into a house elsewhere. A party would be held for her age-mates, both boys and girls this time, and there would be a display of the betrothal gifts she had received and the clothes and furniture she would take with her. Friends and neighbours would call round to see them, bringing gifts of money to send her on her way. On the morning of the wedding, there would be a farewell breakfast with the closest relatives, who would then travel together to the ceremony, and the bride would say a formal prayer of departure to the ancestors in the household Buddhist altar. After she had left, her rice bowl would be broken, just as if she had died to the house.

The bride in Japan wears a white garment under her colourful wedding kimono and this is said to represent a clean slate for her new life. In this way she resembles a corpse, as she dies to her old house, and a baby, to be born again into the new one. After the ceremony itself, the bride goes through a series of rites of incorporation into the new house and community, greeting her new ancestors, visiting the new local shrine, and being introduced to the new neighbours. According to Walter Edwards, in a book about modern Japanese weddings, the bride and groom are ritually separated from the rest of the party for the sharing of cups of *sake*, the crux of the marriage itself:

> In ethnographic accounts of pre-war and early post-war home weddings, ... the exchange is described variously as taking place in a separate room; as occurring behind a screen; and as being attended only by the *nakōdo* [go-between] or someone to pour the *sake*. In the contemporary Shinto ceremony the physical isolation is less extreme, but it is there nonetheless. Together with the *nakōdo*, the bride and groom sit in the center of the shrine room, apart from the rest of the group.   (Edwards 1989: 107–8)

In many parts of the world it is customary for the bride and groom to go away for a honeymoon after their wedding and this practice can be seen as a rite of transition for the couple as a new unit. This time they will be formally separated from the crowd of family and friends who have come to wish them well, and various rites may be practised as they leave. Throwing of confetti is one example, tying boots to their car another. Some people go much further, and in Scotland my brother was kidnapped by his old friends, who tied his hands and feet together and hailed a passing van to drive him away around the streets of Glasgow. Again, this is a period of liminality when few rules apply. Later the couple will be regarded as properly married and treated as such. In the meantime, there would seem to be no end of fun to be had.

In recent years, there has been a noticeable breakdown in the institution of marriage in several countries. Many couples live together now without undergoing any formalities at all, and may split up just as easily if things don't work out. Even those who do marry seem to find themselves as likely to be divorced after a few years as to be still married, so the whole exercise seems rather hollow. Marriage is by no means disappearing, however, and people seem still to be happy to spend vast sums of money on their weddings. According to one of my students, a 'hand-binding ceremony' has also recently been instituted for a short-term union, and various rites of divorce are discussed from time to time in the media.

Funerals

Rites of separation are highly developed at a funeral, but there is again a period of transition, both for the deceased on his or her way to the afterlife, and for those who remain behind to come to terms with their loss. At Christian funerals, the custom of throwing a little earth into the grave is a way of saying farewell, as is the practice in Japan of adding a pinch of incense to the burning pile. In Roman Catholic and Afro-Caribbean communities, the custom of holding a wake allows a more elaborate venue for the final farewells, and elsewhere there is open house for the bereaved to receive the condolences of their friends and relatives.

During the period of mourning, people may alter their lifestyles, refraining from celebrations and jollification perhaps, and making regular visits to the grave of the loved one. In Japan, a notice is pasted to the door which not only identifies the house as one in mourning but also makes explicit the idea of pollution associated with the period in question. During this time, no meat is to be eaten, and there is a special diet for the bereaved. Various rites are held to mark stages in the progress of the soul, and these coincide with gatherings to thank those who helped at the funeral, and generally to redefine the social relations of the members of the family left behind. In some countries in southern Europe, a widow continues to wear black for the rest of her life, but in most cases there is a means of incorporating the living back into normal life.

Festivals and the Passage of Time

Finally, most societies have regular rituals to mark the passage of time. These reflect the classification of time in the way that the rituals associated with territorial passage reflect the classification of space into homes, villages, countries and so forth. As with the rites of passage through life, these events regularise in a social form natural cycles, though this time of the earth and moon, rather than the human body. Thus, the year is divided in various ways depending on the local climate, though provision is usually made for a festival to mark the harvest, at least in agricultural communities, and in countries with a severe winter there is usually a rite to herald the arrival of spring.

In the summer, in Europe, the year is clearly broken with holidays, and this ritual break in the normal routines of life is especially marked in countries such as France and Italy where there is a long and serious period of play which is virtually compulsory in its effective interruption of the ordinary. In France, the motorways are cleared of large trucks and roadworks, and it seems as though the entire population heads south to the sea and the sunshine. Certainly it is difficult to get anything done in government buildings, or, indeed, any number of other city offices. In Chapter 13 we consider further the way that tourism may be interpreted as a rite of passage.

The pattern of breaking work with play is of course repeated weekly in many parts of the world, but this is a system of classification originally based on the biblical story of the creation of the world. Elsewhere the breaks will come at different times. The lunar month is a more universal segment, and, especially before the advent of electricity, many people would organise events to coincide with the light of the full moon. Approaching the equator there is little difference in the climate between winter and summer, and seasons and their markings may be organised instead around wet and dry periods, or some other local climatic variable.

In many parts of the world, the year is broken clearly during the season of Christmas and New Year, when schools close and many government activities are suspended for a period of about two weeks, all preceded by preparations which may last for a couple of months. This 'festival' is, strictly speaking, a celebration of the birth of Jesus Christ, but it takes place at a time chosen by early Christians to coincide with winter solstice celebrations in northern Europe, and for many of its participants it is characterised as much by feasting and resting from usual routines as for any religious rites. Moreover, followers of other faiths observe their own rituals, such as the Jewish Hanukah and Hindu Diwali, close to the winter break, and a popular greeting card message, especially in the United States, has become 'Happy Holidays'.

These local differences are not actually as new as they may seem, for the Scots have long distinguished their winter celebrations from those of the English by placing greater emphasis on Hogmanay, celebrated on New Year's Eve, than on Christmas, whether they are Christians or not. Brought up as an ex-pat Scot in England, myself, I was made aware of this distinction from an early age, and our annual Hogmanay party encapsulated very clearly the elements of van Gennep's scheme: the old year seen off with a rendering of 'Auld Lang Syne', a liminal period passed listening to the chiming of Big Ben, and then greetings, accompanied by handshakes, hugs and kisses signalling a communal incorporation into the New Year which had opened.

At our parties, we would follow all this with a wild Eightsome Reel, as fellow Scots kicked their heels in an expression of togetherness as Scots, as well as to their specific friends and relatives. Although some English people I know have chosen to celebrate the New Year in this Scottish celebration, and they dress themselves in kilts and other 'Scottish' garments, they draw the line at a dance so common and apparently unrefined. These groups practise weekly all manner of complicated Scottish dancing, and although they incorporate a rite of 'first-footing' into their Hogmanay celebrations (another Scottish practice which echoes the theories of van Gennep), their togetherness is actually based on excluding dances that any outsider can do, just because they happen to be Scottish.

The element of abandonment which the Eightsome Reel signified for me, growing up, and which is expressed by the only element of Hogmanay that all Scots agree about – namely, that one must get very drunk – is a characteristic of the liminal period of many festivals for the people concerned, as were initiation rites for youths passing into a transition state before becoming adults. This is well illustrated by carnivals such as Mardi Gras, another Christian feast that has taken on wider appeal, but which is actually the beginning the period of fasting called Lent, and another example of a rite of passage marking a longer period of transition, culminating in Easter in the Christian calendar.

Edmund Leach (1961) wrote an interesting little article entitled 'Time and False Noses', where he examines the way people dress up, sometimes smartly and sometimes in quite bizarre ways, during ceremonies and festivals which mark the passage of time. He notes also that people sometimes even perform roles quite the opposite of their usual ones on these occasions – men dressing as women, kings as beggars, and vice versa. His thesis is that where rites of passage are marked by these examples of *formality* and *masquerade*, they form a pair of contrasted opposites to stand at either end of ritualised breaks in the passage of time. *Role reversal*, on the other hand, marks the middle period when normal time has stopped – another example of the period of liminality.

The British custom of performing plays known as pantomimes during the Christmas period is a good illustration of this phenomenon, for there is always a 'Dame', a buxom female role played by a man, and the main male role – who may be a prince in disguise as a pauper, for example – is very often played by a young woman. There is usually a 'princess', or some other female role played by a girl, too, so that the love scenes between her and the lead 'male' may seem physically homosexual, though the symbolism is clearly heterosexual. The general entertainment value of pantomime, carnival, holidays and the original holy days is commented upon in studies made around the world, and ritual, however solemn, usually has its fun side too, as Leach suggests.

Not surprisingly, then, an interest amongst anthropologists in the study of theatre, media and other types of performance is related to ritual (see, for example, Hughes-Freeland 1998). This, too, marks – for the audience, if not for the players – a break from the routines of working life. Like ritual, performances of one sort or another provide a place and period of separation from 'real life', a break in the relentless passage of time. For the players, theatre and media allows a period of (artistic) licence to behave quite outside the regular norms of social life, and in both ritual and theatre, people take on the task of performance of one sort or another.

My own research on theme parks was precisely about places which allow everyone to participate in a world of fantasy whenever they feel inclined – or, at least, when they have the funds available to take a holiday. Here, too, individuals may choose their own breaks in routine, but still with the possibility of reversing usual roles, and removing themselves from the exigencies of 'real life'. Some of the parks in Japan that I studied recreate the experience of visiting a foreign country, inviting their customers to spend a day or more imagining themselves to be in Canada or Spain, Germany or Holland, even dressing up to play the part of a native.

The apparent allure of cultural themes is found in many other countries, local culture being displayed for visitors in Taman Mini Indonesia Indah, just outside Jakarta, and parks in Taiwan, Singapore and China, although Shenzhen has a funfair of global culture in a park called Windows of the World. In Hawaii, there is a popular Polynesian Cultural Centre, and theme parks in other places offer a trip back in history, sometimes preserving buildings in the process. Colonial Williamsburg and Upper Canada Village in North America, Sovereign Hill in Australia, and Skansen in Sweden are all early examples of places which encourage visitors to remove themselves, temporarily, to a former period in time.

Conclusion

Rituals, wherever they are found, mark out the social categories for the people in question. They may be more or less related to the natural cycles of the seasons, the moon and the human body, but they will always order them in a cultural way related to ideas about the social world in which they are found. The range of possibilities offers an element of choice which might seem to contradict our initial definition of ritual, but the appearance of fixed elements of culture in a slippery flexible world may be the attraction to people seeking an identity to espouse – especially if they feel that more traditional rituals have become empty. In Chapter 13, we will look at some of the ways in which tourism has become a ritualised activity associated with the confirmation of identity, but meanwhile, in the next chapter, we look at some of the detail of ritual by turning to the subject of symbolism.

Discussion Questions

1   On what occasions do you dress up and/or cook special kinds of food? Make a list, and consider the extent to which they mark a point in the passage of life, yours or that of someone else. Are there elements of separation? transition? incorporation? See if van Gennep's scheme works in your life!

2   Have you been invited to a wedding or a funeral by friends in another social or religious setting to your own? How did you behave? Consider the constraints you felt, and compare them with an experience within your own family.

3   How is the year marked out where you live? What are the ritual events, and how do they make distinctions between participants? Do you know of any new events? Consider ways in which these reflect changes in the surrounding societies.

References and Further Research

Books

Bloch, Maurice (1989) *Ritual, History and Power* (London: Athlone Press).

Bloch, Maurice (1991) *Prey into Hunter: The Politics of Religious Experience* (Cambridge: Cambridge University Press).

Cannadine, David and Price Simon, (1987) *Rituals of Royalty: Power and Ceremonial in Traditional Societies* (Cambridge: Cambridge University Press).

de Coppet, D. (1992) *Understanding Rituals* (London: Routledge).

Edwards, Walter (1989) *Modern Japan through Its Weddings* (Stanford, Calif: Stanford University Press).

Fienup-Riordan, Ann (1994) *Boundaries and Passages: Rule and Ritual in Yup'ik Eskimo Oral Tradition* (Oklahoma: University of Oklahoma Press).

Van Gennep, Arnold (1960) *Rites of Passage* (London: Routledge & Kegan Paul).

Hendry, Joy (1986) *Marriage in Changing Japan* (Tokyo: Tuttle).

Hughes-Freeland, Felicia (1998) *Ritual, Performance and Media* (London: Routledge).

Huntington, Richard and Metcalf, Peter (1979) *Celebrations of Death* (Cambridge: Cambridge University Press).

La Fontaine, Jean, (1985) *Initiation* (Harmondsworth: Penguin).

Lewis, Gilbert (1980) *Day of Shining Red: An Essay on Understanding Ritual* (Cambridge: Cambridge University Press).

Ortner, Sherry (1977) *Sherpas through Their Rituals* (Cambridge: Cambridge University Press).

Turner, Victor (1969) *The Ritual Process* (London: Routledge & Kegan Paul).

Turner, Victor (1967) *The Forest of Symbols: Aspects of Ndembu Ritual* (Cornell, NY: Cornell University Press).

Articles

D'Alisera, JoAnn (1998) 'Born in the USA: Naming Ceremonies of Infants among Sierra Leoneans Living in the American Capital', *Anthropology Today*, 14 (1): pp.16–18.

La Fontaine, Jean (1986), 'Invisible Custom: Public Lectures as Ceremonials', *Anthropology Today*, 2(5): pp. 3–9.

Leach, E. R. (1961) 'Two Essays Concerning the Symbolic Representation of Time: (ii) Time and False Noses', in *Rethinking Anthropology* (London: Athlone Press).

Leach, Edmund (1969) 'Virgin Birth', in *Genesis as Myth and other Essays* (London: Cape Editions).

Sprenger, Guido (2006) 'Out of the Ashes: Swidden Cultivation in Highland Laos', *Anthropology Today*, 22(4): pp 9–13.

Novels

Tartt, Donna *The Secret History* (London: Penguin, 1992) is a novel about a small group of college students who try to enact a Dionysian ritual, with some disastrous consequences.

Films

Adhiambo – Born in the Evening (Ruth Prince, Wenzel Geissler and Ruth Tuchtenhagen, 66 minutes, 2001) is a personal account of a woman's life, motherhood, children and the maintenance of bodily health in rural western Kenya. Set among the Luo, it follows NyaSeme, a married mother and grandmother in her late thirties, during the last month of her pregnancy and through the first weeks of her newborn daughter's life.

The Day I Will Never Forget (Kim Longinotto; Consultants: Fardhose Ali Mohamed and Eunice Munanie N'Daisi Kwinga, 92 minutes, 2002) is a documentary that explores the local dimensions of the female circumcision debate in Kenyan societies.

Imbalu: Ritual of Manhood of the Gisu of Uganda (Richard Hawkins and Suzette Heald, 69 minutes, 1988) is an insightful documentary about the male circumcision ritual among the Gisu of Uganda. The narrative follows one male participant through the ritual and contrasts his hopes and anxieties on this important day of his life with the expectations of the rest of the village.

Osōshiki ('Funeral, Japanese-style'), a 1987 Itami Juzo feature film, is an irreverent but interesting depiction of events surrounding death in modern Japan.

Masai Manhood (Chris Curling and Melissa Llewelyn-Davies, 1975), another classic 'Disappearing World' – film about initiation amongst these pastoral people of East Africa, also demonstrates cattle values, male–female relations and the power and influence of the elders. There is a companion film called *Masai Women*, made by the same team.

Good-bye Old Man (David MacDougall, 70 minutes, 1977). A last request of a Tiwi man on Melville Island was that a film be made of the *pukumani* (bereavement) ceremony to follow his death. The film follows his family, from the days of preparation to their final leave-taking of the old man.

The House-opening (Judith MacDougall, 45 minutes, 1980). When Geraldine Kawanka's husband died, she and her children left their house at Aurukun on Cape York Peninsula. In earlier times a bark house would have been burnt, but today a 'house-opening' ceremony – creatively mingling Aboriginal, Torres Strait and European elements – has evolved to deal with death in the midst of new living patterns.

Waiting for Harry (Kim McKenzie, and Les Hiatt, 1980, 57 minutes (AIATSIS-RAI). Set in Arnhem Land, east of Maningrida, we witness Frank Gurrnanamana as he prepares the final mortuary ceremonies for his dead brother, assisted by anthropologist Les Hiatt. The coffin is to be a hollow log covered with meticulous paintings. At the climax of the ceremony, all his close kin will be expected to be present, including Harry Daima, nephew of the dead man. As the relatives gather from outlying regions, Harry's unexpected absence provides a test of Frank's organisational ability. This film gives a view of the social context of Arnhem Land art, music, dance and song.

The Wicker Man, a feature film, directed by Robin Hardy (1973), in which an unsuspecting policeman falls prey to a ritual sect on an isolated Scottish island.

Websites:

http://www.msu.edu/~jdowell/miner.html – Horace Miner's brilliant 1956 paper in the *American Anthropologist* entitled 'Body Ritual among the Nacirema' (read the title backwards for a clue to who features here).

http://www.swcp.com/~ldraper/slim/biblios/morris.html – bibliography of social anthropological theories of ritual meaning and function.

5

Society: A Set of Symbols

What is a Symbol?

In the last chapter we talked of examining ritual to help our understanding of systems of classification. We referred to the scheme identified by Arnold van Gennep which seems to recur throughout the world in rites of passage, and we discussed various examples which would appear to illustrate it. This scheme makes sense of a wide variety of behaviour in an overall way, but let us turn now to see how we interpret these rituals in practice. What we can most easily look at when examining ritual behaviour are the material objects involved, the fixed elements of human behaviour, and the way the humans dress themselves. We divide the whole performance into small units – the clothes, the cards, the gifts, the food – all of which may be seen and interpreted as symbols. Symbols may be regarded as the smallest units of ritual and we can learn a lot by examining them in their own right.

symbol – a thing regarded as typifying, representing or recalling something else by possession of analogous qualities or by association in fact or in thought (*Concise Oxford Dictionary*). Symbols are particularly significant in the interpretation of rituals, but also as the visible features of invisible aspects of social organisation.

Symbolism is of course a huge subject which crops up in almost every sphere – in literature, art, religion and psychology, as well as in anthropology. There are certain differences in the way we interpret symbols in these different subjects, and there are various sorts of symbols to be interpreted. For example, there are private symbols which refer to emotional aspects of human behaviour and fall more into the domain of psychology or psychiatry. The symbols which interest social anthropologists are public symbols, shared by members of particular social groups. They express aspects of the ideology of the group, understood and interpreted within a specific social and moral system, and the same symbols may mean something quite different to members of another social group, or even different social groups within a single broad social system, such as a nation.

public symbols – are those shared by members of a particular social group, usually meaningful to all members of that group, though possibly in different ways.

Symbolism pervades human behaviour, at even the most mundane levels, and the ability to use symbols, including speech, is one of the ways in which the behaviour of humans is said to be distinguished from the behaviour of other animals. We have already seen examples of symbolism in the use of greetings and gift exchange, where we noted that social relationships would be invisible without some clearly defined way of expressing them. In anthropology we are particularly concerned with the variety of ways in which symbols may be interpreted in different societies, and between different groups in the same wider society. A large part of our work is to make sense of these units of communication in social life.

The definition of a symbol given in the *Concise Oxford English Dictionary* (1951) is:

> a thing regarded by general consent as naturally typifying or representing or recalling something by possession of analogous qualities or by association in fact or in thought.

These associations are specific to a particular society, though the analogous qualities could be clear to an outsider, and the 'general consent' is of course only general within a particular social or linguistic group. It is interesting that the definition uses the word 'naturally' because it is often the case that people within one society remain blissfully unaware of the relativity of their symbols. A connection which seems natural to one people may be quite contrived to another.

A sign is rather similar to a symbol, but it is a much more straightforward representation of something which is easy to describe in other ways. A symbol, on the other hand, is more open to different interpretations. It generally has more semantic content, more meaning, than a sign. As Jung put it (although he was referring to the analysis of dreams):

> The sign is always less than the concept it represents, while a symbol always stands for something more than its obvious and immediate meaning. (1964: 55)

A traffic light is a sign – red means 'stop', green means 'go' – now quite universally, though it is hardly natural. The wearing of red and green may be open to much more complicated interpretation – it may be nothing more than a fashion statement, or it may be associated with Christmas, or with the colours of a European flag. It could also be criticised, for there is a saying in the English language which goes: 'Red and green should never be seen except on an Irish Queen' – an Irish Queen?

Because public symbols are shared by members of a particular society, it is essential that an anthropologist studying that society learn to use them too. They are the visible features of invisible aspects of social organisation, as was demonstrated in the case of gifts. They provide objects of study, and of discussion, which lead to an understanding of that society. Symbols in any society must be used in a systematic way, or the members would be lost, just as the outsider feels lost on first exposure to the society. Within larger groupings, such as cities, nations, and now even cyberspace and the 'global village', people will also use symbols to express distinctions between differing social units. As in the case of language, an anthropologist must be careful not to make early assumptions about them. Let us examine some examples.

Bodily Symbols

Individuals in Western societies like to think of themselves as unique. They choose clothes and accessories to express their personalities, and they wear their hair in a style which they feel suits them personally. They are expressing themselves through the symbols of the society in which they live, however, and their range of choice for dress and adornment is limited to what is acceptable in that society. Even the most outrageous outfits must cover certain areas of the body, and a person who painted themselves and appeared on the streets with no further apparel would, at least in cities, be arrested unless the painting looked like very convincing clothes. Elsewhere, paint may be the appropriate attire for the most formal occasion.

Bodily attire provides a huge range of possibilities for symbolic communication, some relatively permanent, some entirely temporary, and the messages which are expressed may be interpreted at different levels by different groups of people within the same wider society. In societies less concerned with individualism as an ideology people are happy to dress much as their neighbours do, and they will express allegiances to certain groups in their appearance, or perhaps be more concerned to demonstrate the nature of an occasion in the way they present themselves. They may also indicate their level of status within their own society in the way they appear.

In markets in rural Mexico, for example, groups of Indigenous people may easily be identified because of the clothes they wear. Those groups who still live in relatively isolated communities continue to wear colours and styles that identify their groups rather than their personalities, and they may be picked out easily in a mixed crowd. Mexicans who have become part of the wider community have adopted more universal clothing, which may be judged according to taste and quality, but they would not necessarily be picked out in a cosmopolitan city as Mexicans – unless, of course, they chose to wear the sombrero, which has become a symbol of the Mexican people!

In some cities, people from different religious groups are easily identifiable by the clothes and hairstyles they choose to wear. In Jerusalem, for example, ortho-dox Jews may be picked out by the hats and black garments which symbolise their allegiance to the faith, and priests of the Armenian Church wear tall hats which distinguish them from other Christian groups who reside there. Visitors from religious orders, men and women, may also choose to wear the habits which express their particular allegiance in this holy city. In each case, the individuals express their membership of a religious order over any other allegiance. Here, too, however, the street vendors become adept at assessing the nationality of the tourists from their apparel so that they can guess what language to use in their sales patter.

These distinctions are more subtle, because the individuals concerned prob-ably didn't get up in the morning intending to dress in their national costume. They may be wearing clothes to express their individuality, but their choices will reflect to an outsider something about their social group, national and regional. Many of them will be wearing jeans, a kind of universal unisex garment, it could be thought, but sometimes worn with sandals, sometimes with high-heeled shoes, sometimes with boots, and sometimes with trainers. Some jeans are shrunk, some are purposely faded, some are chosen for their designer label, and some are worn with colourful patches or indecently open holes in them. They may be worn with smart shirts and jewellery, or with a nondescript baggy T-shirt.

Some of these differences indicate information about the wearers which they may not consciously have thought about, although people are usually influenced by the way they think others will perceive them. Another almost universal gar-ment is the two-piece (or three-piece) suit, yet almost no one would be willing to go to work in any garment just because it fell into that category. The tie is a particularly useful piece of apparel to be used symbolically, especially in Britain, where men express their allegiances to clubs, schools and colleges in the more traditional examples of the genre, assess one another's taste and judgement in the more decorative versions, and reject the whole system by leaving them off altogether. On special occasions the long variety is replaced by a bow, of course, and in some parts of North America the usual version is an object which would be used to lace shoes in the British Isles.

Within particular groups, different messages are communicated from those picked up by outsiders. Consider the case of headgear: although both may be Scottish, and sold to tourists for that reason, a deer-stalker – the mark of a coun-try gentleman – tells quite a different story internally to a tartan cap with a peak at the front; in the England of Charles Dickens, a top hat would have conveyed different information from a bowler, though both are now sold as souvenirs in London. A Jewish skull cap will tell a non-Jew only that the wearer is probably Jewish. Within a particular Jewish community, however, these small items, where possible carefully crocheted in the home, allow women great scope to transmit messages, both to their menfolk for whom they make them, and to the wider world about their men's caretakers and loved ones. As a corollary of this, women are also said to be quite prone to judge one another on the basis of the skill they witness in these rather neat exhibitions of their handiwork (Baizerman 1991).

Jewellery and other types of adornment are highly symbolic, too. There is a kind of thick, gold jewellery abundantly available in airport shops which is a clear, international expression of wealth, just as designer scarves and handbags are. Amongst the nomadic Fulani people of West Africa, women wear coins in their hair to express the same meaning, and the Bella, their former slaves, decorate their hair with buttons to follow the style but without the same resources. The Rendille women of Kenya wear arm bands to show that they are married,

Photograph 5.1

A Wahgi man from the Highlands of New Guinea, in full festive adornment (photograph courtesy of Michael O'Hanlon, Pitt Rivers Museum, Oxford)

just as men and women elsewhere wear rings on their fingers, but the Rendille add further bands to demonstrate the stage of life their sons have reached. They also wear their hair in an enormous coxcomb from the birth of their first son.

In the Highlands of New Guinea, amongst the Wahgi people, men wear beautiful headdresses made of the feathers of local birds, and adorn their skin with the shiny fat of the pigs they value so highly. These forms of display (see Photograph 5.1) worn on certain special occasions, symbolise political and military might as well as status in the community. Michael O'Hanlon devotes a whole book, *Reading the Skin: Adornment, Display and Society among the Wahgi*, to the subject, but a few of his words give a feeling for the communicative possibilities:

> in a turbulent social landscape of shifting alliances and insistent rivalries, impressive displays are felt to intimidate rival clans, and to deter enemies from attacking ... the appearance of those displaying is thought of as an external reflection of their inner moral condition ... evaluations of adornment and display emerge as a dynamic idiom in terms of which moral issues are discussed ... in the rivalrous Wahgi social environment, displays are credited with exerting a direct influence over the military policies of spectator clans. (1989: 124–5)

In Polynesia, people tattoo themselves to make a more permanent statement about their role and place in society (see, for example, Gell 1993). In Japan, too, some gangsters wear beautiful tattoos which cover a large part of their bodies and depict scenes from the country's abundant religious and mythological artistic repertoire, but they keep them hidden under their clothes most of the time because the wider society finds them offensive and disgusting. To have one done – a painful process of more than a year – therefore symbolises an irreversible commitment to the life of the underworld, and could be seen as part of a rite of passage of initiation into the group. Even just part of such a tattoo, revealed at a strategic moment, makes a powerful statement about the allegiance, a statement sometimes illustrated in films about the Japanese underworld. In contrast, those with less extensive tattoos in Japan may merely be expressing a liking for a Western fashion, although this has in itself been much influenced by Japan over the years.

Hair on the head is an excellent medium for making symbolic statements of a striking if only semi-permanent nature. Shaving the head is a custom associated with initiation in several parts of the world, for example, as was seen with the Maasai in the last chapter, where leaving the hair to grow in an unruly fashion was also part of the process (see First-hand Account 5 overleaf for more detail about this symbolism). Where there is a prevailing custom about hairstyle, such as the short-back-and-sides arrangement for men, some people can express a rejection of the mainstream by allowing their hair to grow long. When this practice was first coming into its own in Britain, Raymond Firth (1973: 272), who had been working in Tikopia, an island in Polynesia, noticed that there had been a curious reversal of custom between the two places. When he left for fieldwork, men in Britain had worn their hair short, and women very often long, whereas in Tikopia he found this convention reversed. During his stay, the Tikopians began to follow outside influence and cut their hair to coincide with the Western way of doing things. Firth was surprised on his return to Britain to find that the situation seemed to have reversed there, too, at least among some of his students.

Young people in Britain have been through various stages since that time, often choosing a style that contrasts sharply with the previous generation of youth. The long-haired beatniks whom Firth encountered were a complete change from the 'Teddy' boys and girls who preceded them, with their neat quiffs and hair grease. These in their turn were rejected and opposed by the short-haired 'mods' who came afterwards, themselves contrasted with the unkempt 'rockers' of the same generation. Skinheads and 'bovverboys' wear their hair short to look threatening, as do the more lavishly turned-out punks, clearly expressing something animal or 'primitive' in their elaborate coxcombs, rejecting the society of both their parents and other elders. Variants of these differences are found in other Western countries, and young people travelling abroad may well identify potential allies by the way they cut and wear their hair.

This is not always the case, however, and one of my students recounted during a lecture on this very subject how he had chosen a punk hairstyle in order to be 'different' from everyone else. He was disappointed, however, for when visiting a night club he found the whole floor to be seething with variants of himself. As

Photograph 5.2

Tattoos can have various meanings for various people. What do you think this one might mean? (photograph by Tim Bauer, courtesy of Kaley Davis and Tiger Lily, Oxford).

The day after my friends and I were circumcised, other *isipolio* (new initiates) came to fetch us, and showed us how to tie cloths around the wounds. They brought us ostrich feathers to wear in our hair. We also had to put on the *esurutiei* necklace worn by women and the leather belt worn by young girls, and to carry the sticks of adult men. We would keep these things for several months. For the Maasai, the new initiates symbolically bring together all the different sections of society – men and women, young and old, humans and the environment – so that we were dressed as 'four in one'. With the *esurutiei* necklaces, we became bound by the same taboos as women, in that we weren't allowed to see any meat that would be eaten by the fully fledged warriors.

First-hand account 5:
Lesikar Ole Ngila, Maasai – on Initiation

As the new generation of warriors, *isipolio* are the future guards of the community, so during the first few weeks after circumcision we were greatly respected. While dressed in the black clothes of *isipolio* we were free to go wherever we wanted, like tourists, and nobody could harass us. New initiates aren't allowed to go to bed hungry, but nor can they handle blood themselves, so the warriors and elders had to slaughter rams and goats for us. We painted our faces with elaborate patterns in white chalk (*enduroto*) mixed with water, to symbolise the different birds, and greased our bodies with a mixture of sheep fat and charcoal to make them even blacker than usual. On our feet, we wore traditional leather sandals, to remind us of the old days when the Maasai pastoral economy was strong and nobody had rubber-soled shoes.

Tanzania

Four months after my circumcision, I asked my father to shave off my hair. Newly initiated warriors usually let their hair grow for a whole year, so that it becomes matted into something called *almasi*, and they aren't supposed to wash it. He had already bent the rules by allowing me to wash mine, as I was beaten in school for looking dirty. Now I needed to be shaved at home, because the teacher believed that the traditional Maasai education was outdated and should be left behind. 'If you waste your time with those old customs', he was fond of saying, 'you won't be able to focus on your studies'. So he had been going around with his scissors, chopping off the long hair of *isipolio* while they stood in lines, taking away the black jewellery that had been given to them by their elders as a blessing, and throwing all of it down the latrine.

One day a group of our *isipolio* age-mates, who weren't students at the school, had gone there to sing to him, 'Mr George, the curse of the *almasi* of the *isipolio* will follow you for the rest of your life, because of your disrespect! How could you throw our friends' hair into the latrine, instead of putting it in a safe place that is cold like the sacred *oreteti* tree?'

Mr George may have been cursed, but my friends and I believed that it would be a disaster for us too, if we were to fall victim to those scissors instead of following the proper customs. Every time we saw the other students standing in line, we would run away. My father, along with many of the other elders, thoroughly disliked the teacher and didn't want that fate for me, so he agreed to shave me at home even though it wasn't really the right time.

Lesikar Ole Ngila is the Director of Aang Serian, which means House of Peace, an organisation that has set up a school to value indigenous knowledge in Tanzania, among other things. See http://www.aangserian.org.uk/ *for further details.*

he put it, 'it seemed I had joined a convention of parrots'. He then decided to try another tack in his quest for individuality, and attended the same venue wearing a short haircut and a three-piece suit. He certainly looked different then – so different that he was beaten up.

In nineteenth-century Japan, people wore particular hairstyles to show their social status, and children in that world celebrated stages of life by altering their hair, the first haircut being a sort of initiation into childhood. Members of the *samurai* class had a topknot which was not allowed to lesser mortals, and although unmarried women could wear their hair loose, once married they were obliged to keep it in a kind of bun. In the film *Shinjū*, a couple who run away to commit suicide together, because they have developed a socially impossible relationship, let their hair down and cut it off to symbolise their rejection of society before they carry out the desperate act.

This relationship between hair, power and sexuality has been reported widely. For example,

> In pre-Christian Polynesia, the head was *mana* ... The Samoan word for head (*ulu*) can mean 'head' or 'hair'. Not surprisingly, hair was treated as if it too were *mana*. The hair of Samoan chiefs, for example, was cut by special attendants ... *Mana* was associated with the vital energies of the natural world and was synonymous with fecundity ... In pre-contact Samoa, women grew their hair long only during pregnancy ... The implication is that long hair alluded to the pregnant or fecund state. (Mageo 1994: 410)

Several anthropologists have put forward theories about the way hair is used symbolically, some suggesting universal ideas, and Mageo's (1994) article examines these in the light of Samoan material she gathered over a period of eight years' residence there. This is particularly interesting because, like the Tikopian case mentioned above, the way hair is worn in Samoa has changed greatly over the period of colonial influence. Christian morals have come to play an important part, so that the positive role of fecundity has become tarred with a negative attitude towards excessive sexuality. Mageo also addresses the question of overlap between public and private symbols.

Symbolising Relationships

We have pointed out already that relationships are expressed in various symbolic ways, notably in Chapter 3 where we discussed gift exchange. We examined how gifts are given on particular occasions, perhaps wrapped in a locally appropriate fashion, so that the object and its presentation make statements about the relationship between donor and recipient. We discussed the importance of reciprocity in the exchange of gifts, and other modes of communication, if a relationship is to proceed smoothly, and we considered the problems that may arise when people from different cultural backgrounds misinterpret the significance of presents they may receive.

Again, the symbols are part of shared meaning peculiar to a particular society, and it is another role of the anthropologist to examine the local significance of such exchanges. Japanese people are well known for their generous and beautiful gifts to foreigners who have even the most tenuous of social relationships with them, but, as we mentioned, few foreigners are aware of the importance attached to the practice of gift-giving in Japan. Those who simply try to keep up with or outdo the cost of gifts they have received, and neglect factors such as relative status and non-material favours when they make their returns, could find themselves in a rapidly escalating and quite inappropriate contest of affluence.

Relationships may also be modified in a subtle manipulation of the local practice of gift exchange. An unexpected gift could, of course, signal a desire to intensify a relationship, but it could also mark the end of a series of exchanges, or be a way of expressing empathy for a situation difficult to discuss. Gifts of perishable food received may provide a good excuse to express friendship by inviting round a neighbour or colleague on the pretext of avoiding waste, but also purposely to further the acquaintance. A usual gift withheld, or noticeably cheaper than expected, can create distance when a relationship is becoming too close, or symbolise a rejection of an unwanted approach. A gift returned may seem like a clear symbol, but it must be interpreted within the range of possibilities of a particular social system.

Greetings are another important way of expressing relationships, and again these can be manipulated for more subtle communication within a particular society. The handshake has become an international symbol of agreement and accord, so that important treaties may be sealed in such a way, and photographs of handshakes frequently embellish the world press. Within Europe, customs vary, but generally handshakes express goodwill. In some countries they are practised daily within the family, in others they are reserved for first meetings and special occasions such as the conferment of a degree or a prize. People use them to seal a new arrangement, or to express the resumption of good relations after a quarrel.

In some situations a handshake would be too cool a greeting, however, and while hugging seemed to be rather common among the First Nations and others with whom I worked in Canada in 2003, various forms of kisses are practised within the continent of Europe. The lips are usually involved, though they may merely be pursed in the air as cheeks brush gently together, especially when women kiss one another in public. In some social circles, it is imperative to kiss on either cheek, and in Poland, at least according to my Polish niece-in-law, it is usual to kiss three times. This practice varies between different classes within Europe, as well as between regions, and people can express various degrees of intimacy by the kind of kisses – or hugs – they exchange within one group. The significance of a kiss in sexual relationships is also culturally variable, which may come as a surprise to some readers. In pre-modern Japan it was not even thought to be particularly erotic.

Kissing and hugging are rather intimate symbols in Western society, and they still don't seem to be practised as often between men as between women, as was discussed in Chapter 2, but in parts of the Middle East they may be more usual than a handshake, even in public situations. Before the historic meeting in 1993 between the Israeli Prime Minister Yitzhak Rabin and the leader of the Palestinian Liberation Organisation Yasser Arafat, speculation was rife about how their greeting would be expressed. Many hoped for a hug, but this was not forthcoming. Their handshake was celebrated all over the world, but for local people it may have seemed rather cool. The continuing differences between these two peoples reinforce the disappointment … oh, for that hug!

In Japan, the usual form of greeting is a bow, and this has many variations. From a standing position the depth of a bow indicates the degree of deference, and two people bowing to one another will indicate their relative status in the angle of their acknowledgement. It is also expected that the lower-ranking person will allow the superior to rise first, so the situation can become quite comical if both parties are trying to defer to the other. In a *tatami*-matted room, where people habitually sit on the floor, there are various types of formal bows which may be carried out, and these involve bringing the head almost in contact with the floor. It is said that men in *samurai* times were taught to keep their eyes on their greeting partners, however, in case they proved to be enemies who would take advantage of the defenceless position.

Symbols are, of course, also used to express enmity and ferocity, and the *samurai* man would wear a pair of swords to demonstrate his invulnerability in this respect. The sword would also demonstrate his status in society, but in premodern Japan it could be used with impunity to decapitate a disobedient sub-ject. In the United States, it is more acceptable to carry a gun than in some other countries, although the gentlemen's duel at dawn was for long a highly ritualised and therefore symbolic way of resolving a dispute in European countries. Suits of armour, now thankfully usually only on display in museums and castles, are also a repository of symbolic power and helmets or breast pieces very often sport a mark of allegiance as well.

Group Symbols and Their Interpretation

In battles and warfare, symbols such as these abound, representing the whole social group involved. Flags and banners represent a nation, town or the par-ticular people concerned, and the human beings are decked out in clothes which make their adversarial activity their prime purpose. Battledress comes in a vari-ety of forms, and uniform – or, previously, armour – is a powerful symbolic tool in rallying people to a cause. It clearly subordinates the individual to a greater social entity, in which personal qualms must be set aside for the wider common good. In such a guise human beings can carry out acts of terrible violence which would abhor them in normal life and which could well bring about their arrest and imprisonment. Similarly, police in uniform are empowered to pick up people who are disobeying laws agreed within a country, and to lock up people if they think they have committed a crime.

National anthems and marching songs are designed to invoke a pride of par-ticipation in those who listen to them, as are words of rhetoric turned out to whip up enthusiasm for a cause, whether it be bellicose or peaceful. The ban-the-bomb symbol has been one of the best known and most powerful in the last couple of generations, though it has various origins and interpretations in different parts of the world, for those who take the trouble to inquire. Anthropologists analyse the language and paraphernalia of the social groups they study in order to identify symbols that are important to the people concerned. These can in turn lead to an understanding of the ideology or ideologies they live by, and may be related to other aspects of social life.

A useful book, set in Britain and compiled and edited by Anthony Cohen, is entitled *Symbolising Boundaries* (1986). It considers the symbolism used to express and identify differences within communities, between the worlds of men and women in Devon, between households in Yorkshire and Battersea, between neighbouring settlements in Lewis, in the Outer Hebrides, and between Catholics and Protestants in Northern Ireland. The articles examine and illustrate the complexities and ambiguities of these distinctions. The second part of the book moves into the mechanisms used by certain groups to express their distinctions within the wider society, for example by adolescents in an adult world, by suburban occupants of a northern city, and by Glaswegians in reference to the image they portray abroad.

Cohen introduces the interesting idea of the malleability of symbols in a complex community:

> The efficacy of symbols which we recognise here is their capacity to express in ways which allows (sic) their common forms to be retained among the members of a group, and among different groups, whilst not imposing upon these people the yoke of uniform meaning. Symbols, being malleable in this way, can be made to 'fit' circumstances. They thus provide media through which individuals and groups can experience and express their attachment to a society without compromising their individuality. (1986: 9)

Anthropological Interpretation of Symbolism

Much has been written on the subject of symbolism, and there has been some dispute amongst anthropologists about how far an outsider should go in the interpretation of the symbolism of another people. As Cohen puts it:

> The ethnographic difficulty for us, therefore, is that not only is symbolism a matter of interpretation (as it is everywhere); but the interpretation of behaviour as symbolic in character is itself a matter of conjecture and judgement which is only demonstrable through notions of plausibility or of theoretical 'fit' ... The danger is, of course, that rather than using my imagination as an interpretive resource, I risk allowing it to constitute the data themselves ... I have written about the croft, the spree, the burial as symbolically significant... But significant for whom? The people we are supposedly describing. Or ourselves? (Cohen 1986: 7)

Victor Turner is one of the anthropologists who has made a great contribution in this field. In his book *The Forest of Symbols*, he suggested that the structure and properties of ritual symbols could be inferred from three classes of data:

1 external form and observable characteristics;
2 interpretations offered by specialists and by laymen;
3 significant contexts largely worked out by the anthropologist (1967: 20)

It is this last category which is most contentious, because it goes beyond the second, and sometimes even contradicts it. Different anthropologists also disagree at this level, although this is not unusual in this subject, as was pointed out at the beginning of the book. Turner stresses the importance of putting sets of symbols in the total context of the ritual in which they appear, other rituals and their performance, and the wider society of which they form a part, including notions of class, lineage, generations and so forth. This, he argues, is easier for an outsider than for a subjectively involved participant, as the latter regards as axiomatic the ideals, values and norms expressed or symbolised.

Turner gives as an example the case of the Ndembu girls' puberty ritual, which was mentioned in the previous chapter, where a girl lies under a tree for a whole day. The tree, which is called a *mudyi* tree, exudes milky beads when the bark is scratched, and this, for the Ndembu, is its most important 'observable characteristic'. Women explain that this liquid stands for breast milk, and indeed, for the breasts which supply it. They further explain that the tree represents the relationship between mother and child, and the continuing line from woman to woman which stands for the tribe itself, including the men. When observing the ritual, however, Turner noticed that it actually serves to symbolise the separation of mother and daughter as the latter reaches puberty, to separate women from men, and even to separate some groups of women from others.

This was clear to him in the following ways. First, the mother of the initiate is excluded from the group of women who dance around the motionless girl under the tree. She is not allowed to participate in this important part of her daughter's puberty rite. Secondly, men are excluded from the ritual altogether, and the matter is handled entirely by women. Thirdly, when the mother brings out food for the participants, there is a kind of competition to be the first to take some, for that person's origin is said to indicate where the girl will marry. The Ndembu informants were unable to recognise these apparent contradictions, and Turner argues that it is only possible to infer them with a wider knowledge of the society, which is also made as a relatively objective outsider.

In societies which have a large number of Christians, a parallel may be made when anthropologists take a look at Christianity. Edmund Leach (1969) upset a lot of people in England when he discussed Christian practices in anthropological terms, writing essays entitled 'Genesis as Myth' and 'Virgin Birth', which will be considered in Chapter 7 of this book. His intentions were seriously academic ones, but putting Christian rituals in the context of those held in societies regarded as 'pagan' by Christian believers undoubtedly offended against their systems of classification, and struck a chord of taboo. Those people who are committed to one form of religious worship may find it difficult to stand back and view their practices in the context of other forms.

Nor may they necessarily understand all the elements of their activities. As John Beattie pointed out long ago, in an excellent article about ritual, the fact that a Christian communicant may not understand the doctrine and full meaning of the Eucharist (or Holy Communion) doesn't mean that it does not have such a meaning (1966: 67). Even specialists may disagree in explaining ritual events, and the Eucharist is a good example again, for while a Protestant minister will explain that the bread and wine represent (or symbolise) the body and blood of Jesus Christ, a Roman Catholic priest will say that the bread and wine *become* the body and blood of Jesus Christ. There is a fundamental difference of views here, which makes it difficult for believers and participants alike to make an objective analysis.

In Japan a similar problem may be observed. After the Second World War, the indigenous religion, Shinto, was officially denigrated as being associated with the notion of a divine emperor and the whole disastrous war effort. Buddhism, on the other hand, was unaffected in this way, and for many years people would talk only of Buddhism as religion, tending to describe Shinto activities, which did continue, as 'superstition'. It was thus rather easier to investigate Shinto practices than Buddhist ones, for the former had been stripped to some extent of their mystical elements. The mysticism attaches an awe to elements of religious faith which may make it difficult for people to discuss them without offending their own system of classification. They have been affected by the kind of taboos we discussed in Chapter 2.

Not so sacrosanct are secular elements of rituals, and people are usually quite happy to speculate about things such as the cakes and special clothing that mark rites of passage. An anthropological study carried out by Simon Charsley in Glasgow examined the meaning and purpose of the wedding cake in Scottish weddings. In fact, he was disappointed by the lack of ready interpretation of this apparently essential feature of the great day, but some ideas of his own were quite fruitful, if only in a negative way. He was impressed by the idea that the white wedding cake might stand for the white-clad bride, and 'cutting the cake', actually 'plunging the knife' into the centre of the cake, would then clearly represent a breaking of the 'virginal white outer-shell' (1987: 106).

Much of Charsley's article is a discussion about the degree to which an anthropologist is legitimately entitled to interpret beyond the explanations of the participants, just as Turner suggested, and an interesting twist to his investigation occurred when a couple actually came up with this meaning for the cake. They had heard it from someone else, but they were so horrified by the inequality they felt it expressed between bride and groom that they decided to do away with a cake altogether. Charsley then examines the interesting question of whether a rite can only be practised if a possible meaning for its symbolism has not been noticed. He rejects this idea, however, pointing out that it was not the idea of virginity and its loss that upset this particular couple, but the idea of inequality which they themselves felt it represented.

Interestingly, many people are more concerned in the arrangements of their own weddings, and even more so with those of their children, that things should be done 'properly'. They seek the 'right' way to do things, rather than examining the meanings in order to impose their own interpretations. A veritable barrage of wedding magazines stand ready at bookshops and newsagents to provide instant advice, and most people are quite happy to be informed of the appropriate etiquette. Rather than do away with a wedding cake, then, people may use it to express something personal about their relationship, according to Charsley's research, and he reported one couple who chose the icing decoration of a sofa depicting themselves and their children by previous marriages. British friends of mine who had worked in Japan chose to cut their cake with a *samurai* sword.

Conclusion

Ideas for symbolism may be discussed, then, and alternatives considered, but in any society there will be a set of underlying notions which form the basis of these deliberations. It is fine to be outrageous, if that is understood, and some may express messages selectively to a close group of friends or relatives, but it would be pointless in terms of communication to do something so unusual and different that nobody could discern the meaning at all. These basic tools of communication are the **collective representations** we discussed in Chapter 1, following Durkheim's terminology. They include the 'set of symbols' after which we named the chapter, and they form some of the most basic subject matter of social anthropology.

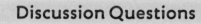

Discussion Questions

1   Can you think of an occasion when you, or someone you know, has described some kind of behaviour as 'natural'? Think again! Is it really universal to human life?

2   Do you think there is a symbolic element to body modifications such as tattoos and piercing? Think about what they might be at (a) an individual level, (b) a group level, or c) a relational level.

3   Do you think it legitimate for an anthropologist to go beyond the explanation of a member of another society in interpreting symbolic behaviour? How far?

References and Further Research

Books
Basso, Keith (1996) *Wisdom sits in Places: Landscape and Language among the Western Apache* (Albuquerque: University of New Mexico Press).
Cohen, Anthony (1986) *Symbolising Boundaries: Identity and Diversity in British Cultures* (Manchester: Manchester University Press).
Douglas, Mary (1975) *Implicit Meanings* (London: Routledge & Kegan Paul).
Eicher, Joanne B. (ed.) (1995) *Dress and Ethnicity* (Oxford: Berg).
Firth, Raymond (1937) *We, the Tikopia* (London: Allen & Unwin).
Firth, Raymond (1973) *Symbols, Public and Private* (London: Allen & Unwin).
Gell, Alfred (1993) *Wrapping in Images* (Oxford: Clarendon Press).
Jung, Carl G. (ed.) (1964) *Man and His Symbols* (London: Aldus Books).
Leach, Edmund (1969) *Genesis as Myth and Other Essays* (London: Cape Editions).

Needham, Rodney ((1979) *Symbolic Classification* (Santa Monica, Calif: Goodyear).

O'Hanlon, Michael (1989) *Reading the Skin: Adornment, Display and Society among the Wahgi* (London: British Museum Publications).

Turner, Victor (1967) *The Forest of Symbols: Aspects of Ndembu Ritual* (Cornell, NY: Cornell University Press).

Articles

Baizerman, Suzanne (1991) 'The *Kippa Sruga* and the Social Construction of Gender', in Ruth Barnes and Joanne B Eicher, *Dress and Gender: Making and Meaning* (Oxford: Berg).

Beattie, John (1966) 'Ritual and Social Change', *Man*, 1:60–74.

Charsley, Simon (1987) 'Interpretation and Custom: the Case of the Wedding Cake', *Man*, 22:93–110.

Edwards, Jeanette and Simpson, Anthony (1998) 'Diana and the Popular Imagination: An ICCCR Workshop' *Anthropology Today*, 14(3): p. 15.

Mageo, Jeanette Marie (1994) 'Hairdos and Don'ts: Hair Symbolism and Sexual History in Samoa', *Man*, 29:407–32.

Moretti, Daniele (2006) 'Osama Bin Laden and the Man-eating Sorcerers: Encountering the "War on Terror" in Papua New Guinea', *Anthropology Today*, 2006, 22(3): 13–17.

Watson, C. W. (1997) '"Born a Lady, Became a Princess, Died a Saint": The Reaction to the Death of Diana, Princess of Wales' *Anthropology Today*, 13(6): 3–7.

Novels

Lethem, Jonathan (2005 [1997]) *As She Climbed Across the Table* (London: Faber & Faber) is a campus novel, which mocks postmodernism through a symbolism of emptiness.

Mann, Thomas (2001 [1912]) *Death in Venice* (London: Vintage) is a novella about beauty and mortality, with multi-layers of symbolism.

Films

Altar of Fire, directed by Robert Gardner (1976), is a film about the performance of a Vedic ritual of sacrifice by Mambudiri Brahmins in Kerala, southwest India, known as the Agnicayana.

A Celebration of Origins: Wai Brama, Flores, Indonesia (E. Douglas Lewis, Patsy Asch and Timothy Asch, 45 minutes) is a record of rituals that also examines ceremonial leadership and the role of evolving religious practice in a changing society.

The Seventh Seal is a 1958 existential film directed by Ingmar Bergman, depicting a medieval knight playing chess with Death.

Shinjū: Ten no Amajima is a 1969 film, directed by Masahiro Shinoda, about the circumstances leading up to a double suicide set in eighteenth century Japan.

Websites

www.aangserian.org.uk/ – the website for Aang Serian (House of Peace), a Tanzanian non-governmental organisation dedicated to 'preserving indigenous traditions and knowledge, developing culturally appropriate programmes of education and training, and promoting inter-cultural dialogue across the world.'

http://hirr.hartsem.edu/ency/geertz.htm – an entry about Clifford Geertz in the *Encyclopaedia of Religion and Society*.

www-personal.si.umich.edu/~rfrost/courses/MatCult/content/Geertz.pdf – a reproduced online version of a famous paper on the symbolism of the Balinese cockfight by the American anthropologist Clifford Geertz.

6

Beauty and Bounty: Treasure and Trophies

Seeing and Value

An interesting aspect of the interpretation of objects and symbols in a particular society is the aesthetic one, and the anthropology of art and aesthetics is a particularly lively branch of the subject. There are various reasons for this, but one of the most important is reflected in the title of this chapter. One person's art is for another a commodity to be exploited, and the world of 'art' has truly become a *global* concern. At the beginning of Chapter 1 we talked of souvenirs and different ways of 'seeing the world', and then we went on to examine various ways of understanding these different worlds. In this chapter we return to 'seeing', but add the subject of value, notably but not exclusively aesthetic value.

In the cosmopolitan world, there are people who make a very tidy living by being acquainted with the value of *objets d'art*, while others feel excluded and possibly diminished by being

commodity – this word is used to describe articles designated an economic value, usually for the purpose of trade, and it may be applied to people and inanimate objects as well, if such an economic value is assigned.

objets d'art – literally, an object with artistic value, but used here in French to suggest the way that people in the world of very expensive art create a language of their own to make decisions about what (and who) may and may not qualify for inclusion.

uninformed on this subject. The value of art objects is, however, entirely relative to the place they are assigned in this exclusive world, and some people are able to take advantage of others in manipulating this system of categorisation which has come into existence. Indigenous (or, earlier, 'primitive') art has been increasingly valued in this cosmopolitan world, but in recent years some Indigenous artists have begun to join the fray, with interesting effects.

The value of objects for gaining access to an understanding of people and their views is still of prime concern, but it is also important to realise that interpretations may be seen in a particular light. Some people may feel aggrieved or misrepresented by the way in which their objects are used, and they may disagree with the interpretations assigned to them, whether by anthropologist or art historian. When people become aware of the value assigned elsewhere to their work, they may be influenced to respond to an apparent need, especially if it is economically or politically beneficial to them to do so. The outsiders, in their turn, may feel aggrieved that the 'pure' art forms of the people concerned have been corrupted. A good example of this phenomenon forms the subject matter of an ethnography of Japanese potters whose work gradually changed when it was chosen as the epitome of Japan's 'folk art' (Moeran 1984).

The relationship between art and the spiritual or transcendental is another source of interest to anthropologists, and this chapter will try to show how difficult it may be to separate works of art from their cosmological context. In practice, some objects have acquired different levels of interpretation in different situations, and the art of the Australian Aboriginal people is a case in point. Spiritual meaning is preserved for the artist and those of his or her own society while explanations provided for the tourist are much more limited, which would seem to be quite appropriate in a society that attaches value to secrecy, as is the case in many Aboriginal communities.

It is possible that there is also a certain attraction for the consumer in knowing that their purchase may carry some esoteric value, and although the layers of meaning may not be appreciated by indigenous artists, it is likely that their advocates are aware that those who wish to acquire it may be seeking more than just an attractive souvenir. Early Western paintings of the native inhabitants of the various idyllic isles discovered by Captain Cook and his sailors depicted people in a situation resembling the Garden of Eden, a fictional paradise quite in keeping with the Rousseauan ideas of the noble savage current at the time. Indigenous art may still carry a tinge of spiritual healing, which appeals to those seeking solace from the fast city life of the high-tech world.

Aboriginal refers to the first status of **Indigenous** peoples around the world, used by explorers and travellers who arrived in their lands. Its negative connotations in the English language made it an unacceptable term in many countries for years, though it was still used in Australia. Now it has become a preferred term again by some of the people themselves (e.g. Aboriginal Peoples Television Network in Canada).

Living Art

The anthropology of art is not confined to the study of marketable objects, however. In many societies people assign aesthetic qualities to the decoration of their own bodies, sometimes spending days in the preparation of a particular display. Some cases of bodily decoration, and its symbolic associations, were raised in the previous chapter, but a particularly striking example of the aesthetic appreciation of bodily decoration is to be found amongst the Nuba people of Southern Sudan. Here, young men and women spend time every day making themselves up and rubbing oil into their whole bodies to make them shine, some of the most attractive designs being found amongst pubescent boys between the ages of about 15 and 20.

According to the anthropologist J. C. Faris (1971), this activity is purely aesthetic, to express the beauty of healthy nubile bodies, which are idealised in this society. The attachment of aesthetic value to an idealised form of the human body is of course found in many societies, possibly universally, and examples probably overlooked by art historians abound in television series such as *Bay Watch* or *Footballers' Wives*, where the story line would seem much less important than the health and youthful vigour of the characters on display. The technical term for displaying and admiring nubile bodies in their physical and sexual prime is ephebism, although how the ideal body is conceptualised will vary from culture to culture.

> **ephebism** – displaying and admiring nubile bodies in their physical and sexual prime, although how the ideal body is conceptualised will vary from culture to culture.

Tattoos are a permanent type of bodily adornment requiring considerable investment of time and resources which may also bestow a long-term political advantage, as we discussed in the previous chapter. In some societies they express a man's place in a hierarchical scheme, in others they are chosen to demonstrate a kind of *macho* ability to endure pain, but people also choose them for their aesthetic appeal. The 'disgusting' Japanese tattoos we mentioned draw on the same fund of mythological inspiration as do woodblock prints, exported as examples of Japanese cultural achievement, and tattoo artists around the world have chosen elements of them to offer their clients, along with a range of examples from other cultural sources.

Aesthetic appreciation can also be expressed towards aspects of everyday life which might, by others, be considered mundane or functional; for example, Jeremy Coote (in Coote and Shelton 1992) shows how Nilotic herding people such as the Nuer and the Dinka demonstrate an artistic focus of attention on colour, shading, shapes and patterns of the cattle which form the basis of their livelihood (see Photograph 6.1). The languages of these people have extensive vocabulary with which to discuss and express the finer variations of the animals' markings, and a conversation about them is said rather to resemble one of antique dealers or wine connoisseurs than what might be expected elsewhere from stockbreeders. In the Nuer and Dinka languages, words which might be translated as 'piebald' and 'guernsey' take on a whole new set of values.

An example of Dinka cattle, whose aesthetic qualities are discussed in this chapter (photograph courtesy of Jeremy Coote)

Another interesting area of living art brings us back to a most conventional form for Europeans, namely the area of gardens and landscape. The story of decorative gardens is a history of cultural influence, appropriation and creativity, and signs of the Far Eastern influence in European countries provide a good example of the process. Indeed, many of the flowers which are highly valued by horticulturalists have their origins in China, as do features of the Japanese garden to which they attribute many favoured varieties of trees and shrubs. Several wealthy families in Europe and elsewhere in the nineteenth century created Japanese gardens, and finding and restoring these has become an aim of the Japanese Garden Society, created in Britain in 1993.

The appeal of these Japanese gardens does not often derive from a wider interest in Japanese culture, but their intrinsic aesthetic qualities seem to offer something intangible to their aficionados, sometimes described as 'haunting' or 'spiritual'. They provide a way of creating a 'scene' or a possibly miniature 'landscape' which has been a European endeavour for centuries. Whether in practice in a tiny space or a country estate, or in two-dimensional form in a painting, creating a landscape has been an important part of the artistic worlds in the East, too, and this has been an area of the deepest cultural reciprocity. It is not necessarily the way in which the world is depicted or perceived in all societies, however.

In several of the major galleries of Australia (and undoubtedly other countries with a similar history) it is possible to observe a selection of depictions of the local landscapes made through the period of colonisation and beyond by artists who variously came from Europe, were born in Australia, and those whose origins are largely Aboriginal. Since many of the galleries also boast a collection of European art, it is quite easy to discern the same periods and styles in the early European paintings of Australia, and distinguish these from the later Australian schools which developed as people born and brought up in the Australian landscape perceived their surroundings in a way less dominated by European traditions.

The stark contrast with Aboriginal depictions of some of the same scenery, which forms much of the subject matter of Howard Morphy's (1991) book *Ancestral Connections*, immediately opens up questions about the systems of classification which underlie the whole endeavour of two-dimensional representation of an environmental landscape (see First-hand Account on p. 124 for an Aboriginal account). Landscape paintings, like maps, illustrate a culturally specific form, dating back to classical antiquity in the West, where it was rediscovered in the Renaissance, but even the idea of a landscape is not as universal as might be imagined. The collection of papers in *The Anthropology of Landscape* (Hirsch and O'Hanlon 1995) provides some excellent examples of alternative ways in which this notion, which the editors see as a relationship between ideas of 'place' and the here-and-now of foreground actuality, and 'space' of background potentiality, may be understood.

> The model of landscape developed ... is one predicated on the idea of landscape as process ... this process is one which relates a 'foreground' everyday social life ('us the way we are') to a 'background' potential social existence ('us the way we might be'). It is a process that attains a form of timelessness and fixity in certain idealized and transcendent situations, such as painted landscape representation, but which can be achieved only momentarily, if ever, in the human world of social relationships. (1995: 2)

One paper, which discusses the Piro people of Amazonian Peru, makes the point that in the rain forest the horizon does not recede away from the point of observation. The vegetation pattern that surrounds villages is 'seen' in terms of kinship and past activities associated with it:

> It is hard to see Amazonia as a landscape ... The land does not recede away from a point of observation to the distant horizon, for everywhere vegetation occludes the view. (Gow 1995: 43)
>
> For the native people of Bajo Urubamba, the local environment is a lived space. It is known by means of movement through it, seeing the traces of other people's movements and agency, and through the narratives of yet other people's agency. (Ibid. 59)

In Australian examples, too, notions of kinship are intimately bound up with ideas of place and space, through the ancestral connections with which they are attributed, and these are also bound up with notions of time and the passage through life and death. In another paper about a people who inhabit dense forest, this time Papua New Guinea, we are told about the importance of sounds to an understanding of the landscape. Here 'hiddenness' is perceived as inaudibility, rather than invisibility, and the landscape is one of 'articulation' (Gell 1995: 238). Clearly, the way that our senses are trained locally to perceive aesthetic value can be quite variable.

Art for Gaining Access to 'Seeing the World'

As an anthropologist embarks upon a study, however, material objects in any society provide a useful focus for attention, a concrete set of phenomena for investigation and discussion with informants, and a fertile source of information about the people who make and use them. Local interpretations and evaluations of objects offer an excellent way to gain access to indigenous systems of classification, which underpin the modes of thought and expression of the people under study. As Coote and Shelton point out in the introduction to their book on the anthropology of art and aesthetics, 'the art of a society can provide a fruitful starting-point for the analyst's explication of its world-view' (1992: 5).

A good explicit example of this is to be found in the paper by Ross Bowden in the same book, on the art and architecture of the Kwoma people of the Sepik River region of Papua New Guinea. Bowden (1983) has also written a fascinating book about the sculpture found amongst these same people. In all cases – art, architecture and sculpture – intricately carved and painted material objects strike the visitor as the epitome of what we have come to call primitive or tribal art, and examples are to be found on display in the most famous museums of the Western world. For the Kwoma themselves, these objects are assigned quite different value – political, spiritual and symbolic – and they thus offer a particularly enlightening window to understanding the way they 'see the world', or their **collective representations**.

Bowden argues, for example, that the lavishly decorated ceremonial houses form visual counterparts for the roles men, in contrast to women, play in the structure of Kwoma social groups. These houses, where male members of a community meet for informal social interaction and to perform ceremonies, are located in the centre of villages, a geographical location which corresponds to the structurally central position men have in clan organisation. Villages are made up of a group of related men, who remain together throughout their lives, and women move in and out of the village on marriage, which, in a society where divorce is common, may be quite a frequent occurrence.

Reflecting this, domestic homes, where individual men live with their wives and children, are scattered adjacent to the forest on the margins of the village. Unlike men, women do not form groups except in relation to those of their husbands, and they are excluded from the ceremonial house. Bowden argues that women's peripheral geographical position within a village expresses their 'peripheral' position structurally: that is the way they, as wives, form the links between groups rather than constituting their residential and social cores. Interestingly, Kwoma women display the art with which they are associated in the form of elaborate decorative scars on their own bodies (Williamson 1979), art works which are of course carried with them when they move.

The construction of the ceremonial house, on the other hand, expresses male attributes sought and admired in Kwoma society. Men aspire to be killers in warfare, and to produce many children and great gardens, and these same qualities of homicidal aggression and human and horticultural fertility are attributed to ceremonial houses as well. This is explicitly expressed in the choice of timbers used to construct the elaborately carved and painted ridge pole and the longitudinal side beams, customarily made from the wood of a tree which in myth is ascribed superabundant masculine sexual potency. In the story this tree stands

Photograph 6.2

Detail of the sculptures and bark paintings that decorate the ceiling of the Kwoma ceremonial men's house named Wayipanalin Bangwiss village, 1973. The sculpture depicts a clan spirit and the paintings are clan totems (photograph courtesy of Ross Bowden).

beside a forest track and whenever a woman, or girl, steps over one of its roots she immediately becomes pregnant, but girls who are not yet sexually mature are condemned to die in childbirth.

The splendid figures found in the carvings on the posts and beams in these buildings (see Photograph 6.2) also depict culture heroes which feature in Kwoma myths about the creation of fundamental features of Kwoma culture, such as the types of plants on which Kwoma rely for food, sago plants, which yield the highest quantities of edible starch, and the central role played by exchange in the structure of Kwoma society. The literally hundreds of bark paintings on the ceilings illustrate the species of plants and animals that belong to the different clans, and Kwoma people say that any knowledgeable person who walks into these buildings can immediately determine the clan composition of the community from the paintings on display.

Art and Status: The Status of Art

An important aspect of the way in which objects may be interpreted in an ethnographic context is to see how they express and relate to systems of hierarchy and power. Amongst the Kwoma, described above, the Yena sculptures represent the spirit world which guarantees the continued fertility of the gardens and people, and underpins their system of morality and law. In the men's house they look down on discussions of social concern, and protect the human protagonists who may not strike one another in the presence of the spirits. They stand for the authority and continuity of the wider community, and the skills men display when carving and painting these objects are thought to come directly from the supernatural world.

Elsewhere, notably in Africa, masks are used to disguise individuals handing down the judgements of the ancestors or spirits, and to separate the authoritative role being played from the person who is called upon to play it. The voice used during judgement will also very often be changed. Some art objects are shown only to people in certain positions in society. In several parts of the world it is an important feature of adult initiation rites to reveal ritual objects, which are often so beautifully carved that they are also easily classified in the West as works of art. Antony Forge wrote of the Abelam people, again in Papua New Guinea, that showing the ritual objects for the first time towards the end of a traumatic initiation procedure heightens their apparent power, as well as increasing the significance of the whole ritual. Knowledge of how to perform such rituals, and even more of the creation of the art objects, demonstrates a special relationship with the supernatural world and a sure way to success in the local system of politics.

We will return in the next section to examine further the meaning of art objects in a particular context, but it is interesting that an association with secular art is also capable of bestowing status. It was mentioned in the introduction that in cosmopolitan societies people accrue considerable status, and potentially wealth, through knowledge of the value and authenticity of *objets d'art*. Furthermore, those in the most powerful positions influence the extent to which a work will be assigned a high value in artistic terms, or even whether it will be classified as art at all. In an exhibition I once saw at the Victoria and Albert Museum in London, one of the most appealing exhibits was an arrangement of garden gloves. For a collection of garden gloves to be deemed a work of art requires not only the declaration of the artist, but the agreement of a number of other agents along the way. In this case, members of the viewing public seemed to acquiesce with the decision, but they are sometimes left bewildered as to why mundane objects are attributed such status.

In practice, it is not even necessary for people to understand why art is assigned a high value in order to acquire status through its ownership or display. Collections of art are commonplace in the homes of the wealthy, and in the public rooms of royal palaces and other aristocratic houses, where they may also express a family heritage, but it has become fashionable for companies to buy and display paintings in their foyers and executive rooms as an expression of sophistication and economic power. The ownership of these paintings says little about the understanding of the company employees of the aesthetics and meaning of the object, rather the aim is to demonstrate corporate access to the elite and expensive world of high art with which it gains kudos by association.

We should perhaps, therefore, not be surprised to discover that some Indigenous people also display apparently meaningful objects largely for the kudos they acquire, rather than for any deep significance they display in the designs. According to Anderson (1989), an example of this is to be found in the elaborate totem poles owned by Northwest American Indian peoples such as the Kwakiutl (now corrected locally as Kwakwaka'wakw), Tlingit and Haida (whom we met in Chapter 3). They depict animals and, possibly, characters from their folk tales (see Photograph 6.3). These features are sometimes quite stylised, and they are open to symbolic interpretation, but their chiefly owners are said to be much more concerned with the status they represent than with any stories they might depict:

> **totem** – thought by some early anthropologists to be a sacred symbol, which represented a specific part of society known as a clan, but eventually discovered to have more complex meanings, which were different in Australia and in North America.

> A piece carries with it a message that bears no palpable resemblance to the image itself: It is a 'status symbol'. The totem poles, houseposts, and most of the masks were signs of the high social standing of their owners. Even if a native viewer did not accurately decipher the iconic message of a given art work, he or she undoubtedly appreciated the social significance of the piece. The quantity and elaborateness of the works of art possessed by a person were public statements of the individual's relative position in the social hierarchy. As we know, members of Northwest Coast

Photograph 6.3

This Haida totem pole, originally from Queen Charlotte Islands, (now Haida Gwaii), British Columbia, was acquired by Edward B. Tylor, and is now on display in the Pitt Rivers Museum, in Oxford (photograph: Joy Hendry, with permission of the Pitt Rivers Museum).

societies were vitally concerned with their relative social standing, so to them the symbolic messages transmitted via their art were far from trivial. (Anderson 1989)

In both cases, corporate art and totem poles, the iconography is supposed to be less significant than the possession of the objects, but another factor has become important since Anderson published his book. Many of the totem poles that once stood proudly on the Northwest Coast are now to be found in museums (as in Photograph 6.3) around the world and, in some cases, members of the groups that once made those poles are seeking to have them returned. A major reason for this is that the displays are of old, sometimes rotting poles, and give the impression (as does Anderson's use of the past tense) that the practice has died out. In fact, in one case in Sweden, a new pole was carved to replace the old one. Poles are carved and raised to this day to mark important occasions, and they can be seen in many locations in Northwest Coast Canada and in Haida Gwaii (formerly the Queen Charlotte Islands).

In an international context, people allocate one another status in a preconceived view of aesthetic value, and evidence of a highly developed aesthetic sense may be cited as an index of civilisation. The reciprocal influences which have run between East and West for millennia are an illustration of this process, and in Europe the value placed on the acquisition of Chinese ceramics and Turkish carpets are just two examples where status has been assigned in one society to an art form developed in another. This is an area open to considerable negotiation, of course, and Japan now sports many art forms originally developed in China as characteristically Japanese.

Indeed, some Japanese writers claim that their country is superior to all others because their artistic accomplishments are developed in such subtle and deceptively simple ways. A single leaf, or a simple twist of paper, may be regarded as aesthetic achievements of the highest quality, and attention accorded to the wrapping and presentation of objects and ideas, as already discussed, is said to be greater than in any other civilisation. Even objects wrapped for the most mundane reasons will receive a meticulous care – demonstrating the same kind of attention to detail which has brought Japan into the forefront of microchip technology – but it is the appreciation of aesthetic qualities which raises the level of civilisation in a Japanese view.

One Japanese author who has written on this subject is Iwao Nukada (1977) who proposes an evolutionary theory that wrapping was first used everywhere for practical reasons: to carry food safely from the fields to the home, to keep the body warm in winter, and to protect from the elements. With the development of spiritual and religious ideas, this material form acquired all kinds of new significance in the realm of the sacred, he argues, and he cites examples from different parts of the world. The third and fourth stages of development, in his view, are those of art and courtesy. The wrapping forms took on an aesthetic quality, and provided a medium for the elaboration of beauty, but they also enabled their creators to communicate deeper expressions of concern and appreciation. They offered a way to communicate the status which an appreciation of beauty implied, both on the part of the donor and in recognition that the efforts would be appreciated by the recipient.

This kind of subtlety of communication is highly regarded in a Japanese view, and it is by no means limited to material culture. The choice of words and language is also tinged with an aesthetic quality, even in everyday discourse, as is the choice of clothes and interior design. These concerns are not, of course, unique to Japan, but the areas of artistic achievement recognisable in a Western context bring Japan into a universe of discourse more readily shared in the cosmopolitan world than are some of those found in societies technologically less developed. The Dinka appreciation of the beauty of their cattle might be one example. This apparent Western understanding of Japan is deceptive, however, because it may well mask some of the deeply ingrained differences, which could thus be overlooked.

Art and Meaning

In Chapter 3 I gave some examples of the kinds of meaning that may be transmitted in the wrapping of a gift, but it is important to remember that the whole notion of gift wrapping may carry different messages in a Japanese view from that expected in many Western countries. In formal presentations, the wrapping may even be more important than the gift inside, and I know several Japanese people who put away the gifts they receive without even opening them, perhaps to use again when they need to make a presentation. The wrapping is not 'mere decoration' to be ripped off and thrown away. It is itself, in all its glory, the medium of the message of the gift.

This quality of what outsiders may see as 'mere decoration' to carry deep and meaningful messages was raised in the last chapter when we considered the work of Michael O'Hanlon (1989) in his book about the Wahgi people of the Highlands of Papua New Guinea. Like Japanese wrapping, the adornment provides the medium which carries the message, the beautiful headdresses exhibiting directly the political clout of their wearers, and the use of the special shining qualities of pig's fat to embellish the skin is a direct demonstration of the health and fertility of the most important medium of wealth and exchange in this society. O'Hanlon elsewhere examines the implications of this lack of exegesis about artistic accomplishments among the peoples of Papua New Guinea (O'Hanlon 1992).

Also talking of Papua New Guinea, other writers have emphasised the competitive element of the ritual bodily attire. Just as gifts from one group to another are lined up in an ostentatious display of wealth, one of the aims of the headdress is to impress and overawe the spectators who attend. The body is decorated to an enhanced, idealised form, which in this case is a general representation of the collective health and prosperity of the wider group. In the Trobriand Islands, it is the canoe boards which play this role:

> The function of the Trobriand canoe-boards is to dazzle their owners' Kula trade partners, making them take leave of their senses and trade more of their valuables than they otherwise would have done. The designs on the canoe-boards identify the boat with the original flying canoe of Trobriand mythology, and symbolise slipperiness, flowing water, and wisdom, all of which help to attract the luxury goods the expedition hopes for. In this example, the form and content of the art work together to produce magical, aesthetic effects. (Coote and Shelton 1992:9)

This is essentially the same competitive element mentioned above in reference to corporate art, and bodily and other art is also found in complex societies as an index or reflection of structural divisions within that society. The hairstyles discussed in the previous chapter provide an excellent example, as do other forms of bodily attire. People in complex societies do not necessarily share taste and the fact that punk bodily art differs from more acceptable tastes expresses their rejection of wider society. Similarly, if one section of society expresses a preference for art forms of a certain kind, another section may well define their own boundaries with that section by belittling it. Popular music is a particularly apt example.

The notion of 'taste' underlies this phenomenon, as social groups express their shared ideas in terms of what they admire and seek to acquire. 'Taste' becomes a way of expressing values which are clearly 'contested' by different social groups, and this notion of contested value is an area of recent interest for anthropologists. The French anthropologist Pierre Bourdieu wrote a classic text entitled *Distinction: A Social Critique of the Judgement of Taste* in which he relates the idea of taste to the way people classify one another in a particular society, and hence to the classes into which society divides, or 'distinguishes' itself.

> Taste classifies, and it classifies the classifier. Social subjects, classified by their classifications, distinguish themselves by the distinctions they make, between the beautiful and the ugly, the distinguished and the vulgar, in which their position in the objective classifications is expressed or betrayed. (Bourdieu 1992 [1984])

Lines along which divisions of opinion occur indicate lines of education and social class. Interestingly, however, artistic taste would seem to be one area where there is little difference based on gender.

Aesthetics

These aspects of the communicative properties of art and decoration are again difficult to describe in detail. Why one object should be regarded as tasteful by one social group and distasteful by another is beyond easy explanation. Indeed, the explanation may be couched in terms of upbringing and education. One learns how to recognise a valuable object by being around objects assigned value in a similar value system. One acquires a gut reaction which will coincide with those whom one respects and admires, or, in the case of punk and other revolutionary art, one specifically sets out to flout those accepted values and produce something that will shock. In all these cases, there is meaning which lies embedded in the art itself, and one area of meaning is concerned with the quality we call aesthetic. This is an area about which anthropologists themselves disagree.

aesthetics – strictly speaking, a branch of philosophy concerned with beauty and the physical ability to recognise it.

On the one hand, there is the view that the whole idea of aesthetics is culture bound, like the notion of taste, so that an aesthetic appreciation is itself a product of a particular society which can only be properly applied within that social context. Those who hold that view see others applying this culture-bound aesthetic sense in other societies, but feel that their judgements are misplaced. They may even feel that the idea of universality of aesthetic sense is a kind of faith, held in the context of art as theology is with religion. Alfred Gell, who expressed this view in his paper in the Coote and Shelton book, goes on to suggest that art has become a sort of religion, whose shrines are theatres, libraries and art galleries, and whose priests and bishops are the painters and poets.

The other view is that there exists a universal aesthetic sense possessed by human beings, whatever their society, although it will of course be interpreted and evaluated in socially appropriate ways. This view argues for a human capacity to appreciate beauty and experience a sensory reaction to the physical qualities of an object, such as form and texture, which will be related to non-material aspects of that object within its cultural system of knowledge. In his introduction to *Anthropology of Art*, Howard Morphy (1994) gives an example of the way a particular aesthetic effect, namely that of shimmering or shining brilliance, may be highly valued, but with different interpretations, in three different societies.

Amongst the people with whom he himself worked, the Yolngu of Northern Australia, the shimmering effect applied to paintings with a cross-hatching technique is interpreted as the power of the ancestral beings shining out of a creation which is anyway seen as a manifestation of their existence. The value of brilliance is reiterated in myth and song in Yolngu social life. The Wahgi, too, value a shining effect, this time created on their bodies, as described above, but here the association is with health and fertility, with the power and strength of the group as a whole. Morphy's third example is of the shining effect of a black mask valued by the Mende people of Sierra Leone, particularly during a ritual dance display as an expression of female health.

In all these cases, shining is itself a quality selected for particular note. Elsewhere, efforts may be made to reduce shine, such as when a woman powders her nose, or a set of photographs is ordered with a matt finish. The value of shine has undergone a major change in Western society, perhaps reflecting an underlying economic and political shift of values. Hard polished wood is still highly prized in antique furniture, but there has been a shift of appreciation towards the originally cheaper pine, which is not only easier to care for, but also more politically correct. In the days of shiny polished hardwood, and bronze and silver ornaments, their ownership and display was a way of demonstrating the economic resources to engage staff to maintain their quality. Interestingly, the lower-quality wood, which has been stripped of its glossy paint, is now quite expensive to acquire!

Definitions of Art

The problem with defining the notion of aesthetics is only part of the wider problem of defining the notion of 'art'. We have been applying both terms throughout this chapter, without pausing to define them, partly because an understanding of some of the issues we have raised is vital to an appreciation of this problem.

In the Yolngu worldview there are two moieties, one is Yirritja and the other is Dhuwa. They are two halves of one whole. Our view of the world is holistic. All knowledge is interconnected. Art is connected to songs and songs are connected to people. People are also connected through song lines and stories. Stories are connected to art and art is connected to country and land through clans and totems. Everything in our world is linked to all these things. Our Yolngu world view consists of all these things.

First-hand account 6:

Raymattja Marika, Yolngu – on Art through Indigenous Science

Everything in the Yolngu world view is made up of two moieties. One is Yirritja and the other one is Dhuwa. Dhuwa and Yirritja make up our worldview. They are two halves of our holistic world view.

Yirritja and Dhuwa are a bit like ying and yang. They fit together perfectly. Everything in Yirritja and Dhuwa is connected. For example, Yirritja and Dhuwa intermarry into each other and vice-versa.

Everything in the land is Yirritja and Dhuwa. *Yothu-yindi* and *mari-gutharra* are the two main relationships for Yirritja and Dhuwa. *Mari* and *gutharra* means grandmother and grandchild relationship. *Yothu* and *yindi* means mother and child relationship.

Everything in our world view is interrelated. For example, Yirritja land and Dhuwa land can come together at a certain point and that land becomes Dhuwa and Yirritja. Also, Yirritja country being looked after by a Yirritja clan, that has a *mari-gutharra* connection (grandmother and grandchild). Yes, Yirritja and Dhuwa have these relationship terms, through *yothu-yindi* and *mari-gutharra*.

This world view is expressed through songs, through stories, through art, through rituals, and through paintings. Paintings consist of maps, abstract maps of the land, trees, the animals, the plants, the rocks and so on. All have meaning, they're either Yirritja or Dhuwa. So everything is integrated – science, language, culture, law, they're all integrated – whereas in the non-Aboriginal world view all these things are taught separately.

Northern Territory

AUSTRALIA

Science is taught differently, language is taught differently, art is too, they are all taught in their own components. For Yolŋu, in the Yolŋu world view everything is interconnected and interrelated in a holistic way.

This piece was videotaped in May 2002 at Yirrkala, Community Education Centre, by Katie Hayne.

Many of the books cited below tackle the issue of definition, and you may pursue the ideas presented for yourself, but in the end the whole endeavour of definition is also so culturally bound that it seemed better not to engage in it at the outset. The next chapter is almost entirely devoted to the problems of defining the term 'religion' which runs into parallel problems, and the reader will probably find that exercise taxing enough.

A few words are in order, however, by way of summary, for the main problem centres around the varying and disputed attitudes to the concept of art in European languages. Morphy (1994) points out that in the nineteenth century a Western definition of art involved such a strong notion of civilisation that the idea of 'primitive art' was almost a contradiction in terms. Even now, the three aspects of a European definition of art that he identifies are very revealing of European ideas: first, the institutional one, whereby objects are deemed art or otherwise depending on whether they are chosen to be displayed in galleries as opposed to museums, and therefore classified as 'fine art' as opposed to 'folk art' or 'craft'; secondly, a definition in terms of attributes makes reference to aesthetics again, but also skills and semantic properties; and finally, Morphy sees the *intent* of the artist as important:

> art objects are ones that are *intended* to be works of art by their makers. With most types of object, intention is subordinate to functional or institutional specification – the intention to make a boat is insufficient if the object is incapable of floating. In the case of art objects the individual has a little more freedom, since the category is always open to persuasion   (1994: 652)

This leads to the extraordinary situation we find in art galleries where almost anything, or indeed, nothing, can be designated as 'art'.

The boundaries that exist between fine arts, crafts and artefacts are now beginning to break down, however, since no clear distinction, anyway often a product of Western hegemony, is made in all social settings. The garden gloves referred to earlier were part of an interesting exhibition of Japanese 'Studio Crafts', which combined a wonderfully irreverent mix of functional artefacts, sometimes called 'traditional', with a dramatic display of abstract 'modern' artistic constructions, one of which, a steep upward slope, is entitled *The M25*, presumably after the usually clogged London ring-road. As mentioned above, Japan is a country where the beauty of an apparent simplicity of form has for long been recognised amongst the most mundane objects, as well as in the creations of the aristocracy, a point illustrated in a book now well known in many countries, entitled *How to Wrap Five Eggs* (Oka 1967).

Intent is therefore also a problem, although this is also cited in Layton's (1991) introduction to the anthropology of art, where he gives a possible definition as concerned with objects made primarily to be aesthetically pleasing rather than for a pragmatic functional purpose. He considers discussions of ancient Greek philosophy about the formal properties of beauty, but also the capacity of art to represent the world around us in a way which enhances our perceptions of it and, indeed, which induces emotional response. Art historians in the Western world look for innovation in artistic accomplishments, and associate these advances with particular periods in the past. Their approach is premised in an idea of the creativity of the artist.

This premise is not necessarily shared by people in other societies whose work has been deemed 'art' by the outside world. In some societies, including those of Australian Aborigines and the Sepik people discussed above, any one of them is thought capable of creating their painting and sculpture. Indeed, the skills are not thought to be talents given only to certain individuals, but to be revelations of the spiritual world through the human beings involved. Neither is there an indigenous concept of originality in art, for since the source of the works is to be found in the spirit world, it is regarded as vital to replicate them to keep them in good order. Thus, the older Kwoma houses are burned down to be rebuilt; and ancient sculptures sold to early travellers, and now maybe carefully guarded in Western museums, are apparently less valuable to the people whose ancestors made them than some purists might think. Indeed, letting them rot away back into the earth that provided the source material might well be thought the most appropriate treatment for them once they have lost their lustre.

Conclusion

In the Western world, replication of a work of art is considered acceptable as part of the learning process, but passing it off as one's own would be a forgery. Of course, in the past, schools of a single artist produced work now attributed only to that one name, and during certain periods art was also much more closely associated with religion than it is now. Some Western people might still argue that they receive their artistic talent from God, but those whose 'art' is a revelation of the spiritual world would possibly not classify their work as art in a Western sense at all! In the next chapter we turn our attention to what it is we mean by the term 'religion'.

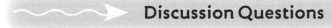

Discussion Questions

1 Consider the meaning of the word 'art' in your social world. Does it apply only to things that are beautiful? Who has authority in that art world and how much status do they have?

2 What is a craft? If a craftsperson is good at their job, would their production need to be beautiful? How beautiful would it need to be before it became classified as 'art'? What are the cultural implications of this classificatory device?

3 Do you agree that aesthetics has a universal value? Is a cow aesthetically pleasing to you? How would you make a judgement about that?

References and Further Research

Books

Anderson, R. L. (1989) *Art in Small-Scale Societies* (Englewood Cliffs, NJ: Prentice Hall).

Banks, Marcus and Morphy, Howard (1997) *Rethinking Visual Anthropology* (New Haven and London: Yale University Press).

Bourdieu, Pierre (1992 [1984]) *Distinction: A Social Critique of the Judgement of Taste* (Cambridge, Mass.: Harvard University Press).

Bowden, Ross (1983) *Yena: Art and Ceremony in a Sepik Society* (Oxford: Pitt Rivers Museum).

Coote, Jeremy and Shelton, Anthony (1992) *Anthropology, Art, and Aesthetics* (Oxford: Clarendon Press).

Faris, J. C. (1971) *Nuba Personal Art* (London: Duckworth).

Hirsch, Eric and O'Hanlon, Michael (1995) *The Anthropology of Landscape: Perspectives in Place and Space* (Oxford: Clarendon Press).

Layton, Robert (1991) *The Anthropology of Art* (Cambridge: Cambridge University Press).

Moeran, Brian (1984) *Lost Innocence* (Berkeley, Los Angeles and London: University of California Press).

Moeran, Brian (1997) *Folk Art Potters of Japan: Beyond an Anthropology of Aesthetics* (Richmond, Va.: Curzon).

Morphy, Howard (1991) *Ancestral Connections: Art and an Aboriginal System of Knowledge* (Chicago and London: University of Chicago Press).

Nukada Iwao (1977) *Tsutsumi* (Wrapping) (Tokyo: Hosei Daigaku Shuppansha) – in Japanese.

Oka, Hideyuki (1967) *How to Wrap Five Eggs: Japanese Design in Traditional Packaging* (New York: Weatherhill; Tokyo: Bijutsu Shuppansha).

Articles

Bowden, Ross (1992) 'Art, Architecture, and Collective Representations in a New Guinea Society', in Jeremy Coote and Anthony Shelton, *Anthropology, Art and Aesthetics* (Oxford: Clarendon Press), pp. 67–93.

Gell, Alfred (1992) 'The Technology of Enchantment and the Enchantment of Technology', in Jeremy Coote and Shelton, Anthony, *Anthropology, Art and Aesthetics* (Oxford: Clarendon Press) pp. 40–63.

Gell, Alfred (1995) 'The Language of the Forest: Landscape and Phonological Iconism in Umeda', in Eric Hirsch and Michael O'Hanlon, *The Anthropology of Landscape* (Oxford: Clarendon Press), pp. 232–52.

Gow, Peter, (1995) 'Land, People and Paper in Western Amazonia', in Eric Hirsch and Michael O'Hanlon, *The Anthropology of Landscape* (Oxford: Clarendon Press), pp. 43–62.

Forge, Anthony (1970) 'Learning to see in New Guinea', in Philip Mayer (ed.), *Socialisation: The Approach from Social Anthropology* (London: Tavistock).

Morphy, Howard (1994) 'The Anthropology of Art', in Tim Ingold (ed.), *Companion Encyclopedia of Anthropology* (London: Routledge).

O'Hanlon, Michael (1992) 'Unstable Images and Second Skins: Artefacts, Exegesis and Assessments in the New Guinea Highlands', *Man* (n.s.), 27: 587–608.

Scheper-Hughes, Nancy (2003) 'Anatomy of a Quilt: Civil Rights, Art and Anthropology', *Anthropology Today*, 19(4): 15–21.

Schneider, Arnd (1993) 'The Art Diviners', *Anthropology Today*, 9(2): pp. 3–9.

Strathern, Marilyn (1979) 'The Self in Self Decoration' *Oceania*, 49: 240–56.

Williamson, Margaret Holmes (1979) 'Cicatrisation of Women among the Kwoma', *Mankind*, 12: 35–41.

Novels

Carey, Peter (2007) *Theft: A Love Story* (Canada: Vintage) is a novel centred around the themes of art and fraud.

Chevalier, Tracy (2006) *Girl with a Pearl Earring* (London: HarperCollins) is a novel that speculates about the relationship of a servant and muse to the artist Vermeer.

Ishiguro, Kazuo (1986) *Artist in a Floating World* (Harlow: Faber) is a novel that illustrates the relationships between Japanese artists in the turbulence of pre-Second World War Japan.

Films

The Wodaabe (Leslie Woodhead and Mette Bovin, 1988), a film in the Granada *'Disappearing World'* series, is about the nomadic lives of a Fulani people of Nigeria who are described as 'obsessed with male beauty'. A part of the film is devoted to the extraordinary facial decorations they apply.

Parts of the *Strangers Abroad* film on Sir Walter Baldwin Spencer (see Chapter 2) is about Australian Aboriginal art and its meaning.

Deep Hearts is a (1981) film directed by Robert Gardner about a male 'beauty contest' among the Bororo Fulani of Niger.

In and out of Africa (Ilisa Barbash and Lucien Taylor, 59 minutes, 1993) – the negotiation of cultural values between European and American collectors and African artists and traders is revealed by following Nigerian Gabai Baare, from the Ivory Coast to Long Island, USA, as he conducts transnational trade of African art.

Singing Pictures – Woman Painters of Naya (Lina Fruzzetti and Ákos Östör, 45 minutes, 2005) illustrates the daily lives of Muslim Patua women from West Bengal, who have formed a scroll painters' cooperative, thus following the generations of the Patua (Chitrakara) communities of painters and singers of stories depicted in scrolls.

Websites

http://www.societyforvisualanthropology.org/ – Society for Visual Anthropology.

http://www.socialsciences.manchester.ac.uk/visualanthropology/ – Visual Anthropology Centre at Manchester (UK) University.

http://nymag.com/arts/art/features/16542/ – Article about the Western art world.

http://www.iep.utm.edu/a/aestheti.htm – history of Western aesthetics.

7

Cosmology I: Religion, Magic and Mythology

Religion, Science and Cosmology

Until the last chapter, we were looking rather broadly at the way in which anthropologists observe and make sense of particular societies, the way they try to understand systems of classification and value, and the social relationships into which they enter. In Chapter 6 we began to look at contested ideas about objects and their meaning. It was mentioned at the outset of this book that another important task for anthropologists is the translation back of their findings into their own language and their own system of categories. This is what makes it possible to compare their findings with those of people working elsewhere, or, at least, to present a description capable of comparison with those produced elsewhere.

Important categories of analysis have therefore been those which represented divisions made in the societies of the academics doing the analysis – religion, politics, economics – and broad headings for the chapters which follow include these very three. However, as we have begun to see, problems arise when anthropologists try to fit the indigenous categories of other parts of the world into their own clearly defined notions, and all kinds of other descriptions are needed to describe local ideas. In the pages that follow we will examine some of these problems as well as some of the descriptions, and we will introduce some analytical notions which have fewer restricting connotations to detract from our understanding of people with very different ideas.

This and the next chapter are concerned with what anthropologists have come to call cosmology, or, in other words, broad ideas and explanations which people have about the world in which they live and their place in that world. These include ideas about the creation of the world, or the arrival of the people in question into that world. They include notions of other worlds, worlds from which they may believe they have come, and to which they go after death in this world, or indeed during transcendental experiences in this world. Until now we have concentrated on social relations between living beings, but in all cultures there are notions about beings beyond that living world, about places and events beyond those of the strictly tangible, and these are usually related to explanations about life itself.

> cosmology – broad ideas and explanations that people have about the world in which they live and their place in that world

We are in the area of *religion*, but, as we shall see, some of the theories and practices found around the world make the drawing up of a valid universal definition a virtually impossible task. In this chapter we will consider some of the problems of definition of the categories used in the European world of the first anthropologists, in the English language in this text, sometimes translated from French, but also undoubtedly influenced by Scandinavian ideas as well as those of Latin and Greek. In the next chapter we will turn to examine examples of non-European indigenous ideas and some actual situations. We are also in the area of *science*, and some readers may feel that this is where we should now turn for answers to all the above questions. A minimal definition of science is 'a body of knowledge', with further qualifications about observation, experiment and induction, but let us examine that concept too.

Definitions and Distinctions

Various attempts have been made to define the word '*religion*'. Edward Burnett Tylor tried to be very broad when he suggested religion be defined as 'the belief in spiritual beings' (1913: 8). A problem arises immediately, however, for there are plenty of people whose devout religious activities involve no spiritual beings. Buddhists, for example, are concerned with achieving a state beyond the spiritual, a state which does not require the intervention of a god or gods. Indeed, a Buddhist specialist working in Sri Lanka enjoys telling people about how two different monks there told him quite clearly that the word usually translated as 'religion' has nothing to do with gods (Gombrich 1971: 46).

This statement may sound crazy to a reader brought up in the Abrahamic religious traditions of Islam, Judaism and Christianity, but it makes perfect sense in the local language of Sinhala where 'religion', as far as Buddhism is concerned, refs to a path leading beyond this world. Other ideas about spirits and gods are part of worldly life and defined quite differently. The names of some of the gods come from Hinduism, but this set of beliefs is not classified as 'religion' as far as local Buddhists are concerned. As discussed in Chapter 5, a parallel situation was found in post-Second World War Japan, where Buddhism is again regarded as 'religion', but indigenous ideas about gods and spirits, which form part of a complex known as Shinto, were described by many as 'superstition'.

Tylor's definition above may also include notions such as *magic* and witchcraft, which many would object fall outside the area of' 'religion' as such, and a category was subsequently developed of *magico-religious beliefs* which was broad enough to include all the above phenomena as well as ideas of pollution and taboo. Perhaps because of their own prejudices, based on deeply felt distinctions, several scholars tried to find ways of distinguishing between magic and religion, however (see Tambiah 1990 for a detailed historical analysis of this propensity from a Sri Lankan anthropologist). Sir James Frazer, whose monumental 12-volume The Golden Bough, addresses just these issues, argued for the following distinction:

> *Magic* assumes that in nature one event follows another necessarily and invariably without the intervention of a spiritual or personal agency. Thus its fundamental conception is identical with that of modern science; underlying the whole system is a faith, implicit but real and firm, in the order and uniformity of nature. (1922: 49)

In contrast,

> *Religion* is a propitiation or conciliation of powers superior to man which are believed to control and direct the course of nature and of human life. Thus defined, religion consists of two basic elements, a theoretical and a practical, namely a belief in powers higher than man and an attempt to propitiate or please them   (ibid. 50)

With an abundance of examples, Frazer demonstrates that there are but two basic principles underlying the practice of magic. The first is that like produces like, so that a magician trying to bring about an effect may imitate the effect he wants to produce, for example by sticking pins into a model of the victim. This is what he calls *homeopathic* or *imitative magic*. The second, *contagious* magic, assumes that 'things which have once been in contact with each other continue to act on each other at a distance'. Thus, acting on something which was once part of a person will still affect that person even when no longer attached to them, leading to spells involving the hair, finger nails and so forth.

Frazer was writing in the evolutionary mode characteristic of his time when he suggested that there had been, everywhere, an Age of Magic, which was followed by an Age of Religion, when at least the more intelligent people realised the falsity of some of these theories and turned instead to superior beings. This move involved an assumption that nature is to some extent elastic or variable and subject to deflection by a mightier power, the opposite of the assumption which underpins both magic and science. Close observation proved this to be untrue, he argues, so thinking people moved into a third Age of Science, which rejects both the previous modes of thought. He then makes a wonderfully futuristic statement:

> Yet the history of thought should warn us against concluding that because scientific theory of the world is the best that has yet been formulated, it is necessarily complete and final. We must remember that ... the generalisations of *science*, or, in common parlance, the laws of nature are merely hypotheses devised to explain that ever-shifting phantasmagoria of thought which we dignify with the high-sounding names of the world and the universe. In the last analysis magic, religion, and science are nothing but theories of thought; and as science has supplanted its predecessors, so it may hereafter be superseded by some more perfect hypothesis ... (Ibid. 712)

In practice, it seems that magic and religion persist, even in a world dominated by scientific thought, and the 'more intelligent', or 'thinking people', as Frazer would have them, are by no means excluded. Malinowski took up this subject, and argued moreover that scientific thought exists everywhere, alongside ideas about magical powers. Based on his own experience with the 'savage' people of the Trobriand Islands, he argued in his essay *Magic, Science and Religion* (1974) that they were aware of and distinguished all three modes of thought, as defined above, demonstrating the existence of 'rational' explanations for technological routines, which form a body of knowledge easily comparable with what we call *science*.

He argued for a clear distinction between these and ideas of *magic* and *religion* to which people turned in times of uncertainty, and explains that Trobriand Islanders fishing in a lagoon, where conditions are known and quite safe, practise no magic, but when they venture out into the ocean, where there may be sudden changes in the weather, they take ritual precautions to seek to avert the possible danger. Furthermore, on the subject of the failure of magic always to succeed, he wrote:

> we should vastly underrate the savage's intelligence, logic and grasp of experience if we assumed that he is not aware of it and that he fails to account for it. (1974: 85)

Malinowski's distinction between magic and religion refines Frazer's on two levels. He proposes:

> *magic* as a practical art consisting of acts which are only means to a definite end expected to follow later on; *religion* as a body of self-contained acts being themselves the fulfilment of their purpose ...
>
> *Magic* ... had to be handed over in direct filiation from generation to generation ... it remains ... in the hands of specialists ... *Religion*, on the other hand, ... is an affair of all, in which everyone takes an active and equivalent part. (Ibid. 88–9)

One of the problems here is that, according to Malinowski's distinction, some of the practical aspects of religious worship in Roman Catholic countries look pretty much like magic: for example the conversion of bread and wine into the body and blood of Jesus Christ is an act with a very specific end, as are rites of exorcism, and so forth, and they are both carried out by priests who have been given much training, in other words experts whose role is hardly 'equal' to that of their parishioners.

Durkheim had proposed a similar distinction to the second half of Malinowski's one, however, when he insisted that religion needs a moral community, whereas in magic, laymen are merely clients. He formulated a definition of *religion* as:

> A unified system of beliefs and practices relative to sacred things, that is to say, things set apart and forbidden – beliefs and practices which unite into one single moral community called a Church, all those who adhere to them. (1915: 47)

This definition, while useful, presupposes the acceptance of a universal division of the universe into the two categories, sacred and profane, as well as a very corporate concept of the community, neither of which always hold up in practice. Indeed, in several societies the sacred, as we might understand the term in English, is found to pervade all spheres of life, and religious practice, where there are ascetics and other individuals who seek personal salvation, may also be found to be a very lonely and isolated pursuit. The case of Buddhism is a very pertinent one again, for the search for *nirvana* is precisely concerned with removing oneself from the social, though those who achieve it may be expected to return to help others along.

It has, over the years, proved very difficult to find an acceptable universal definition of religion, though there are clearly resemblances between the ideas of these different thinkers. Before continuing with the examination of indigenous ideas, let us turn to examine some of the ways in which those who drew up the definitions have investigated ideas about 'religion'.

Origins of Religion

In the nineteenth century people were greatly concerned with the origins of religion and they looked to the so-called primitive societies for ideas about how religion might have developed. This approach reflected contemporary scientific advances which were apparently disproving religious beliefs. By their very nature, these theories were speculative, but some of them had a great impact on the thinking of the time, and a few influenced social anthropology in quite a profound way. The various theories are discussed in a very readable manner in the book by Evans-Pritchard entitled *Theories of Primitive Religion* (1965) where they are divided into the psychological and the sociological.

Notable amongst the psychological were the rather similar, though independently developed theories of Herbert Spencer and Edward Tylor, which argued that notions of the spiritual were derived from the apparent existence of a dual self. There was the self of the waking world and the self of dreams, trances and death, as Spencer imagined the primitive person reasoning. He argued that as dead people could appear in dreams, the earliest idea of the supernatural must be associated with ghosts, so that ancestor worship must have been the first form of religion. It was inevitable, he argued, that ghosts would develop into gods, so that the offerings to the dead to please them would gradually become libations and sacrifices to the gods to propitiate them.

Tylor's theory was also rooted in the idea of a self of dreams, but he focused on the notion of a soul which could act separately from the body. He saw primitive people attributing souls also to animals and even to inanimate objects. These ideas constituted a primitive religion known as animism, according to Tylor, and these souls became the spirits of his minimal definition, which eventually developed into the gods and God of more highly developed religions, in which they took control of the destiny of man. Although anthropologists have come up with detailed descriptions of religions of this sort, which show great differences between them, common parlance still seems to describe animism as a kind of universal earlier form of religion.

animism – the attribution of souls or a spiritual existence to animals, plants and other natural objects, such as mountains and rocks, thought by early anthropologists to be an early stage of religion, a theory now shown to have no supporting evidence.

Evans-Pritchard points out that in both cases the arguments were mere speculation. Each of the writers simply imagines himself in the shoes of some so-called primitive man, but neither has any evidence at all that things did indeed develop in this way. Dreams may have led to speculations about souls and ghosts, but there is no real way of knowing, and there is no particular reason why these should have developed into gods. There were many other attempts to explain religion in this 'psychological' way, but Evans-Pritchard dismisses them all, pointing out that psychological states vary from one individual to another, and in one individual from time to time; therefore these states could not serve to explain social behaviour which exists independently of the psychological states it might or might not induce:

> in an individual's experience the acquisition of rites and beliefs precedes the emotions which are said to accompany them later in adult life. He learns to participate in them before he experiences any emotion at all, so the emotional state, whatever it may be, and if there is one, can hardly be the genesis and explanation of them. A rite is part of the culture the individual is born into, and it imposes itself on him from the outside, like the rest of his culture. It is a creation of society, not of individual reasoning or emotion, though it may satisfy both; and it is for this reason that Durkheim tells us that a psychological interpretation of a social fact is invariably a wrong interpretation. (1965: 6)

Evans-Pritchard goes on to discuss sociological theories, and the most ingenious is that of Durkheim himself explained in his book *Elementary Forms of the Religious Life* (1915), where he also proposed the working definition quoted above. Durkheim was convinced that the simplest form of religion was a system known as a *totemic clan cult*, found amongst Australian Aborigines called the Arunta, and also in North America. This religion brought together the worship of ancestors with the notion of a totem to represent them. The totem was a sacred symbol which stood for the clan that it represented, and rites of worship served to recharge the sense of belonging and solidarity of the clan itself. God, for these people, was simply the clan itself divinised.

Durkheim argued that all the elements of more advanced religions were to be found in this system, which had elsewhere gradually developed over time, so that other religions were simply more complicated versions of the same idea. He marshalled evidence to demonstrate that rites in any religious system served to draw people together and to renew in them a sense of solidarity and communality as they worshipped their gods, which stood for the society, and eventually God, when **polytheism** gave way to **monotheism**. These actions were carried out by individuals, but they existed in collective form which transcended individual participation. The driving force was society itself, also the object of worship, so that God was simply society divinised.

Durkheim argued that in secular times the same function could be performed by patriotism. In the French Revolution a cult had arisen around the notions of the Fatherland, Liberty and Equality, and he hoped that humanitarian values would replace the spiritual ones. Evans-Pritchard admires Durkheim's 'brilliant and imaginative' theory, but he calls it yet another 'just-so story', based on insufficient and atypical ethnographic evidence (1965: 64). He chose totemism to discuss, assuming people with simple technology would have a similar simple religion, but this is only one kind of totemism, and even in other Australian groups it was quite different, nor was it particularly characteristic of all people with simple technology.

totemism – a term used by Émile Durkheim to describe what he thought was the earliest form of religion, which brought together the worship of ancestors with the notion of a **totem** to represent the clan to which they belonged.

Indeed, as we saw in the previous chapter, the 'totem' poles of Northwest America, where the word originated, have no such function. Again, the seeking of origins must be little more than conjecture, Evans-Pritchard argues. The theories may be true, but equally they may be false. As for totemism, the whole subject became something of an anthropological red herring, eventually dispensed very firmly by Lévi-Strauss in the early 1960s, when he applied his (then) new form of **structural analysis** to the subject to argue that theories about it said more about the theorists than the people under consideration, illustrating views prevalent at the time. In Europe, anyway, the word seems less used now than animism, and totem poles are, in popular thought, probably firmly back in place in Canada.

In the period since the first edition of this book was published and the second edition goes to press, there has again been some serious research on the evolution of religion, this time drawing on advances in cognitive science and cultural transmission. It is still an area of much discussion and debate, but one of its chief protagonists, Harvey Whitehouse, has set up two research centres on the subject called the Institute of Cognition and Culture and the Centre for Anthropology and Mind (websites listed below). More recently still, he has set up a new Institute for Cognitive and Evolutionary Anthropology to be headed up by the distinguished evolutionary anthropologist Robin Dunbar. Whitehouse's own theories focus on two divergent 'modes of religiosity', which he calls the imagistic and the doctrinal, around which different kinds of activity cluster depending on how behaviours are remembered. In the first case, highly arousing ritual plays a stronger part, leaving a lasting visual impression on the mind; the second is more concerned with the teaching, learning and interpretation of doctrine and narrative. Both draw on the findings of evolutionary psychology, and, as these theories develop, we may well have a new approach to this theme (see First-hand Account 14.2 on pp. 292–4 for further detail).

Explanations of Religious Phenomena

Eventually, anthropologists turned from trying to establish the origins of religious phenomena to seeking explanations of them within their social context. Durkheim's grand evolutionary religious theory may have foundered, but his insistence on the identification of **social facts** in any study continued to be much more influential. Instead of working out explanations of behaviour by trying to enter the mind of those participating, he urged researchers to seek social constraints which exist outside the individuals. Religious faiths and moral systems provide a rich source of such constraints into which any one individual is gradually socialised, and these also provide the social facts an anthropologist should seek.

The interpretation of these facts within the wider social context falls into various types, two of which have subsequently been described as '**functional**' and '**structural**', though they are not completely separate and the latter has at least two distinct forms. Examples of these will be given below, along with an attempt to explain this classification. We will also examine briefly the association of religious phenomena with moral systems, a subject which will recur in Chapter 9, and we will look at explanations of some new manifestations of religious phenomena which have arisen in times of great social change. Other examples of reactions to social change will emerge in the next chapter.

Functional Explanations

One set of sociological explanations of religion seeks to analyse religious rites for their capacity to promote social cohesion, to encourage a spirit of cooperation, and to support the social structure of a particular society, just as Durkheim proposed. These explanations also sought to relate religious systems to the social and political system in which they were found, and, as detailed ethnography became available, religious behaviour could be analysed as part of the total set of **social facts** to form a coherent system. Radcliffe-Brown's work was of this type, and his analysis of the religious life of the Andaman Islanders was a specific example of his more general theory on the subject, later to be dubbed **structural functionalism**.

Malinowski's approach, on the other hand, related religion, magic and the related subject of mythology to very specific human needs, providing what became known as essentially functional explanations. For example, he explained the magical practices associated with fishing at sea, where sudden storms might bring danger, as efforts to control adverse, unknown factors as opposed to the predictable ones associated with fishing in the safer lagoon. *Mourning rites* he explained as serving to reintegrate the group's shaken solidarity on losing a member, and to re-establish the morale of the community. There were personal benefits in comforting the bereaved, Malinowski argued, but he also saw the anthropologist's job as showing the value of phenomena for social integrity and the continuity of culture.

mythology – a term used by anthropologists to describe the study of myths, bodies of stories held by a people about themselves and their origins, described by Malinowski as a codification of belief, which acted as a charter for ritual, justifying rites, ceremonies and social and moral rules.

Mythology he saw as a 'codification of belief', which acted as a 'charter for ritual', justifying rites, ceremonies and social and moral rules. Thus, for example, myths about the points of origin of local groups he explained as justification for the clan hierarchy, and myths concerned with death as a kind of screen between man and 'the vast emotional void' which would otherwise gape beyond death (1974: 38). It may sound sacrilegious and somewhat trite to say so, but this line of argument brings the great books of world faiths, such as the Bible and the Qur'an, into the category of mythology, because they serve much the same purpose. We need to recognise that the English-language use of the word 'mythology' implies a disbelief which is disrespectful of people who may hold their own myths as truth.

Following the line of argument which sees *science* as another type of faith, we can better understand the conflicts and rows which arose in the nineteenth century when Darwin proposed a theory of evolution which appeared directly to disagree with the explanation of the origins of the human race propounded in Genesis. Those who took both seriously felt they had to decide which one to 'believe', and this period could be seen as a turning point in the dislocation of security. In complex societies, people have come to live with apparently conflicting world views, and their cosmologies may include elements which could also be described as 'scientific', 'religious' and even 'magical'. Indeed, in Japan, a sick person may well consult a diviner as well as a doctor, as we will see in the next chapter, and he or she may also visit a shrine or temple to pray for recovery (Ohnuki-Tierney 1984).

Let me start from the perceived tension between objective analysis, on the one hand, and belief and participation in a religious 'world view', on the other (see p. 137) for this is matter on which I have had to reflect, being both an ordained Anglican priest and a trained academic anthropologist.

It is worth observing that different Churches and Denominations hold different and distinctive attitudes towards the world, towards the society they are part of and the political structures of that society. Different Denominations will find specific social scientific approaches attractive as being compatible with their particular approach; Anglicanism finds its broad world view readily supported and confirmed by the practices and concerns of (British) social anthropology.

(see p. 137)

First-hand account 7:

Timothy Jenkins, English – on Anglicanism and Anthropology

I have found the experience of fieldwork a good preparation for parish ministry, and there is compatibility between the tasks of the priest and those of the anthropologist. For example, the clergy live in their parishes, taking an interest in the well-being of the place and the people it contains over a long period of time, just like anthropologists. But more importantly, there is a congruency in the two disciplines of paying attention to a place and the forms of life that it contains, and to the resources for living well or badly that underwrite these forms. Clearly, the knowledge is not required for the same purposes, but it is the same kind of knowledge.

The task of the priest is to enter into the lives of the people who make up the parish, to understand their concerns, limits and opportunities, and to respond to some of these concerns on the basis of the Christian tradition they represent. For example, the occasional offices concerned with marriages, births and deaths cannot be conducted well without involvement in and knowledge of the lives of those who attend the services. A parish ministry from this perspective might be seen in terms of a double apprenticeship of the meanings both of those lives and of the ceremonies themselves.

England

From an anthropologist's point of view, it is a good thing to have a particular role to fulfil – in my case, that of a priest – which also gives a privileged access to all kinds of institutions, lives and activities. But the priestly task always takes precedence over anthropological interest, both at the time and in any writing up, and this imposes clear restrictions upon what can be said. However, these constraints operate in all kinds of knowledge; all human knowledge is ethical, and everyone has to judge what may be said under the particular circumstances they are in. In this sense, the good informant, the good priest and the good anthropologist are all in the same situation: the information they give will be on the basis of a series of judgements and responsible decisions. Anthropology as a human science is inescapably concerned with moral knowledge.

Doubts as to whether the anthropological conflicts with the priestly task may also be expressed from the Christian side, on the grounds that it is not a priest's task simply to understand, but also to make a difference and to cause an alteration in the circumstances being considered. There is a tension observed between the 'is' of description and the 'ought' contained in a particular Christian world view. This perspective, of course, mirrors the reservations implied in the sociological account; the fear that an objective account will be interfered with by the demands of faith matches the resistance to a properly objective account on the part of believers. And the same sort of answer can be given in either case: knowledge of any kind, including objective knowledge, is constructed through complex, collective moral practices, and sound or reliable knowledge is constructed carefully in each case, while unreliable knowledge is constructed hastily and without due procedure.

So the contrast is less between the motivated nature of faith engagements and the objective nature of sociological ones, than between good judgement and less well-founded judgement in either case. In short, truth – whether religious or sociological – is a difficult business; what matters is the calibre of the persons you deal with rather than their presuppositions about what counts and does not count as knowledge. Participation and belief are, indeed, an integral part of objective knowledge, and not to be contrasted with it.

See the Jenkins entries under the 'References and Further Reading' section at the end of this chapter to find out more about these views.

In some ways, Malinowski went too far in making such a clear distinction between magic, science and religion, because his definitions did not always apply elsewhere, as we noted above. However, it is useful, if sometimes a little alarming, to consider that even experimentally based 'science' is part of a wider cosmology, in the same way as magic and religion. They all aim to provide theories about the world, as Frazer suggested, and they all also offer practical, functional ways of dealing with problems. After all, for many readers, 'science' may also be rather mystical, even if you may have more faith in it to offer explanations of illness and disaster than you do in magic or religion – but it is *faith*, rather than knowledge, in many cases!

Even practising scientists are aware of the mysteries that remain to be explained, and the extent to which they make assumptions that may later prove to be unfounded. Much of their learning is of 'theories', which are based on the best available understanding of a phenomenon at the time they were made, but which may well be disproved as further knowledge comes to light. Medical doctors are aware too of the enormous psychological value of their prescriptions, and they are not averse to offering what is known as a *placebo*, which has no specific pharmaceutical value, if they feel their patients will benefit. Practitioners of East Asian medicine tend to allow more time and attention to their patients than Western doctors do, because they see this as an important part of the healing process. Indeed, indigenous knowledge from most societies offers a whole range of efficacious healing mechanisms which lack the kinds of explanations that Western experimental scientists would accept.

The most frightening diseases are those which appear to have no cure, or worse, no understanding, such as AIDS and certain forms of cancer. Once diagnosed by 'scientific' rationale as a hopeless case, sufferers and their families anywhere are often open to suggestions about alternative healers, and they may travel long distances if they feel there is a chance that they could be 'magically' cured. A friend of mine who was told she was suffering from terminal cancer travelled from Oxford to Mexico to learn about a special diet, which held her symptoms at bay for several years. The strength of public support for this kind of venture may be seen when communities raise the funds to send a local child halfway around the world to be treated at a clinic of special renown. Functional explanations work rather well with this kind of faith that somewhere there may be an effective way of dealing with a life-threatening problem.

A Structural Approach

Another influential approach, which differs quite fundamentally from the structural functional, as it was called (which examined the **functional** role of components of a particular society for maintaining the social **structure**), is the **structural analysis** of the French anthropologist Claude Lévi-Strauss, who was more interested in a universal organisational capacity of the human mind. We have mentioned that he applied this method to the subject of **totemism**, but he developed his ideas most successfully in the analysis of **mythology**, including nursery rhymes, just-so stories and other collectively owned materials, when he noticed amazing similarities in the structure of stories from widely separated parts of the world.

> Mythology confronts the student with a situation which at first sight appears contradictory. On the one hand it would seem that in the course of a myth anything is likely to happen. There is no logic, no continuity. Any characteristic can be attributed to any subject; every conceivable relation can be found. With myth, everything becomes possible. But on the other hand, this apparent arbitrariness is belied by the astounding similarity between myths collected in widely different regions. Therefore the problem: If the content of a myth is contingent, how are we going to explain the fact that myths throughout the world are so similar?   (Lévi-Strauss 1963: 08)

Lévi-Strauss collected huge volumes of stories, including several different versions of the same tale, divided them up into what he perceived as their smallest elements, and analysed the structure which he felt was common to all, by looking at the relations between these elements. He concluded that they act as devices for apparently mediating important and usually impossible oppositions such as those between life and death, man and god, nature and culture. The analyses are often long, complicated and not always immediately convincing, but to give a flavour of the idea let us examine part of his attempt to explain why the role of a *trickster* is so often played by a raven or a coyote in many native American myths.

> If we keep in mind that mythical thought always progresses from the awareness of oppositions towards their resolution, the reason ... becomes clearer. We need only assume that two opposite terms with no intermediary always tend to be replaced by two equivalent terms which admit of a third one as a mediator; then one of the polar terms and the mediator become replaced by a new triad, and so on.   (Ibid. 224)

Through this process, Lévi-Strauss identifies a mediating structure in the Native American myths in which the initial pair *life* and *death* is replaced by a triad of agriculture (on the life side), warfare on the death side, and hunting in the middle (as having qualities of each). This is in its turn replaced by a further triad, where herbivorous animals replace agriculture, beasts of prey replace warfare, and carrion-eating animals, such as the ubiquitous raven and coyote, appear in the mediating position, again as having some qualities of each of the others. A story centred around one of these ambiguous characters thus usually appears to mediate the actually irreconcilable opposition between life and death.

Further details of this analysis, and other aspects of Lévi-Strauss's work, may be pursued in his book *Structural Anthropology* (1963), which serves as a good preliminary to the more difficult tomes of mythological analysis which he has also published, with intriguing titles such as *The Raw and the Cooked* and *From*

Honey to Ashes. Another good and relatively accessible analysis of myth is to be found in his essay, the 'Myth of Asdiwal' (Lévi-Strauss 1967). Because the oppositions he considers are usually impossible actually to mediate, characters who appear in the myths tend to be the same anomalous or abnormal beings such as monsters, incarnate deities or virgin mothers, which, we noted in Chapter 2, provide the focus for taboos and ritual observance.

Edmund Leach, who introduced those ideas in a consideration of language, also put forward an interesting structural analysis in his *Genesis as Myth* (1969), mentioned in passing in Chapter 5, where he sets out to resolve the paradox that Christians, who forbid incest, are all descended from Adam and Eve. He argues that a series of stories which offer a number of examples of incest, some worse than others, place the tribal neighbours of the Israelites in varying degrees of inferior status. By comparison, the marriage of Abraham to his paternal half-sister seems almost virtuous, he argues. This, and indeed some of Lévi-Strauss's analysis, actually confirms a functional role, as Malinowski suggested, justifying the status quo in a particular social configuration.

The structural approach to religion may actually supplement the functional explanations discussed above, which have also been called *instrumental* explanations. As well as looking at the function of certain rites, the idea is to look for *meaning* which may be described as *expressive*, which may tell us something about the delineation of the important categories of society, or, as Radcliffe-Brown put it, 'express ... their fundamental notions of life and nature' (1964: 330). In a more formal structural mode, however, we are back to the identification of systems of classification, and the association of anomalous and abnormal beings with mediation of impossible oppositions is another way to identify the liminal middle ground between these categories.

In the case of **rites of passage** people are moved from one category to another – an *instrumental* aspect of the rite, creating new adults, or members of a particular group, or moving people safely from one area or time zone to another, but the rites themselves divide up life into meaningful chunks, just as they divide up space and time for that particular people. This is the *expressive* aspect. Looking at religious activities in a structural way therefore also means looking for what they can tell us about the dividing up of people and their world. In a very readable ethnography about how the Zapotec people of Oaxaca, Mexico, categorise and celebrate the dead members of their society (Haley and Fukuda 2004), we can also learn how the teachings of the Catholic Church have been adapted and accommodated to strong expressive and instrumental ideas that pre-dated their arrival.

Many other studies demonstrate the structural role of religious activities in any one case. My own work in Mexico revealed a neat parallel between the Holy Family emphasised by Mexican Catholics, which places the Virgin of Guadalupe (see First-hand Account 3.2 on pp. 60–1) in a position of greater importance than God, or even Jesus, and the actual Mexican family, where the mother very often plays the dominant role in holding things together. Mexican men sometimes have two or three different nuclear families they have fathered, and they are peripheral in the maintenance of even one. The real source of stability in any particular case is the mother who must find a way to provide for her children, so it is small wonder that Mexicans of both sexes prefer to bring their important prayers to a female source of divine power.

John Middleton's book *Lugbara Religion* (1960), based on fieldwork in the Uganda/Belgian Congo borders in the 1950s, is an excellent example of an ethnography organised to present the expressive role of religious activities, which centre around ancestor worship held at shrines associated with the lineage groups important in everyday life:

> The cult of the dead is intimately connected with the maintenance of lineage authority. The exercise and acknowledgement of this authority are bound up with the cycle of lineage development. Senior men attempt to sustain their authority against their juniors' claim to independence, and the consequent conflict is conceived largely in mystical and ritual terms ... I show how the men of a single lineage group manipulate the cult of the dead as a means to the acquisition and retention of authority. (Middleton 1960: v)

The chapters of the book are organised in such a way that the background information about Lugbara social and political life is presented first, then the details of the cults of the dead, both material and conceptual, after which the chief focus of the book – the ritual action – may be understood in its proper context. Finally, Middleton addresses the effect of the religious ideas on the moral community. The overall picture is one in which religious ideas reflect the social life of the Lugbara people, which is physically mapped out in the arrangement of shrines within the village compound.

Religion as a Moral System

Clearly, in considering large world religions such as Christianity, Islam, Judaism and the Indian religions, an important aspect of their role in society is to lay out the moral order by which people are expected to live. They are associated with books and teaching, much of which is concerned with spelling out these ethical codes. As mentioned briefly in Chapter 3, giving freely is usually a part of these codes, and it is their basis in soteriology or salvation of one sort or another which allows the principles of reciprocity to be applied to this apparent generosity, though it may not be seen in exactly that way. In these cases explanations of this world and the next will be inextricably linked to ideas of behaviour acceptable to the wider society.

soteriology – a term used to refer to ideas about salvation in any particular system of cosmology, notably in the religious traditions that are based on written scriptures, where they form part of a broad moral system.

In most Western countries, the legal system is influenced by Judaeo-Christian ideas, though now often tempered with a fair degree of 'humanism', and in the Islamic world much legislation is rooted in the Qur'an. Punishment meted out to criminals and others who break the law is often justified in moral terms, and those who escape the earthly justice system may fear retribution in heaven, or 'the other place'. The idea of 'burning in hell' is still part of common parlance, or at least it was until early 1996 when the Church of England declared hell a much less fiery place, perhaps in recognition of the fact that people are probably less worried that this will be their fate than they used to be.

Not all religious traditions include such a clear connection with laying out a moral code. Indeed, in small-scale societies, moral values and the ideas that may be termed religious pervade social life so completely that neither can be clearly separated from the rest of social interaction. Ancestors may be seen as the repositories of moral order, and illness and other misfortunes may be interpreted as an expression of their wrath, incurred almost immediately because of contraventions of moral or social rules. However, there may be no notion of sacredness associated with the activities of these former human beings. Explanations of misfortune may also manifest themselves in other ways, as we will see in Chapter 8. A more detailed consideration of social rules and the various mechanisms for their enforcement will be the subject matter of Chapter 9, on social control.

Cults: The Persistence of Religious Movements

Contrary to the evolutionary expectations mentioned at the beginning of this chapter, and despite the predictions of sociologists and others that modernisation would bring with it secularisation in the world at large, religion does not seem to be giving way to more 'rational' ways of explaining the world. Indeed, new religious sects are appearing abundantly around the world – and there is quite a variety to choose from. In Japan, some people turn from one to another, seeking solutions to problems they may be experiencing, and in several countries around the world Japanese new religious groups are quite active. The neighbour in Japan mentioned in Chapter 3, who introduced me to the niceties of meeting further neighbours, became a Christian shortly after I left, and I came back to find two or three Japanese Buddhists among my students.

New religious movements have often appeared in times of great social change and upheaval, according to another variety of anthropological explanation, and some special *cults* demonstrate an interesting expression of cultural confusion. Typically where the lives of one people have been profoundly affected by the invasion, however peaceful, of another, religious reactions can be shown to express efforts to adjust in one way or another to the new situation. In North America, for example, there was widespread practice of a 'ghost dance' amongst the Plains Indians whose land and livelihood had been devastated by the arrival of Europeans. The aim of the dance was to rid the ancestral land of these cruel and destructive invaders and bring about a return of the native bison they had hunted. The medium was prayer to the ancestors through dance.

Native Americans, called First Nations in Canada, have in fact made some considerable progress in renewing their association with their lands and their ancestors, though they may not have succeeded in expelling the 'invaders', and there are now even new herds of bison being bred. The Red Power movement of the 1960s was perhaps the turning point, with the occupation of the Island of Alcatraz and the site of their massacre at Wounded Knee. A first-hand description of this period, and its religious associations, is graphically portrayed in the book *Lakota Woman* by Mary Crow Dog (1991), who gave birth to her first son during their siege at Wounded Knee. Local activities of a spiritual or 'religious' nature are practised all over the Americas, but there is an interesting Pan-Indian movement that has emerged, and the annual Sundance gathering that takes place at Pipestone, Minnesota is one event that expresses this new form of identity.

Even more spectacular examples of religious reaction to the arrival of outsiders sometimes took place at considerable distance from the new settlement so that knowledge of the invaders was largely second-hand. Cults would grow up whose aim was to achieve the greater standard of living which had been observed, possibly only by one or a few prophet-like figures, and the aim was again a kind of moral regeneration of society. Usually, there would be a charismatic leader, and the results were sometimes devastating. In one part of South America, for example, a whole congregation of indigenous people jumped off a cliff, believing that they would subsequently be reborn white, with all the advantages they had heard that would bring.

In Melanesia, cults arose which have become known as 'cargo cults', for their practices were aimed at attracting the goods to which they saw white people had access. Some of these have been brought to the attention of the public in film and on stage. A Jacques Tati film showed a group of people building an airport in the hope that they could attract the enormous birds they saw delivering all manner of good things to the white people who had settled nearby. A stage play entitled *Sergeant Ola and His Followers* illustrated even in its title the role of the charismatic leader. In this production, local people dressed up as whites and spent their time trying to replicate their activities, reading newspapers and tapping away at a typewriter, although they were in fact still illiterate.

Peter Worsley's book *The Trumpet Shall Sound* (1970) includes a comprehensive survey of these cults, which were found in various parts of New Guinea as well as in Fiji, the Solomon Islands and the New Hebrides. He also calls them millenarian movements because of their similarity to movements found all over the world that are characterised by a belief in the imminence of the end of the world, some of which occurred in Europe in the run up to the year 1000. The expectation is that a cataclysm will destroy everything, but that the ancestors, or some prior god, will return and liberate the people from their new oppressors, incidentally making available all the goods these same oppressors seem to own. Hence the preparations.

These movements are, of course, not peculiar to Melanesia, as Worsley himself points out, nor are they only to be discovered in the anthropological fieldnotes of the past, especially as another new millennium has now been entered. The shocking release of poisonous gas in the Tokyo underground in 1995, and the mass suicide/murder of members of the Branch Dravidian cult in Waco, Texas, two years before that, may both be seen as examples of the continuing power of people preaching about the end of the world. The tale of the Japanese group Aum Shinrikyo, which has been blamed for the deaths and injuries in Tokyo, is a textbook example of a millennium cult. In a well-informed study of the group, Ian Reader writes of its leader, Asahara Shōko:

> He … achieved prominence because of his frequent, drastic prophecies, which stated that an apocalypse would occur before the end of the century to engulf the vast majority of humanity and sweep away the corrupt material world and destroy Japanese society. He proclaimed that he was a messiah who had come to save his followers from the apocalypse and lead them forward to form a new, ideal spiritual universe that would emerge from the ruins of the old. (1996: 2)

Worsley's survey concludes by putting the Melanesian material in a broader anthropological and historical context, where he identifies common features in a wide range of different movements. Resistance to oppression is a common theme, as is the drawing together of a new, and possibly powerful amalgamation of smaller groups. The promise of a better life is of course another powerful characteristic, and the charismatic leader is a virtual *sine qua non*. These cults allow a kind of generalisation, which is rare in anthropological literature, and Worsley's book is an accessible example of how this may be done.

Conclusion

This chapter has been concerned with several ways in which anthropologists have dealt with categories like religion, cults, magic and mythology, but largely in their own terms, or applying their own terms across the board to draw up theories that hold good in a comparative context. Many of these theories were short-lived and floundered on the ethnographic evidence, although one or two, like our last example, have stood better the test of time, and the arrival of new phenomena. In the next chapter we turn again to an examination of the more culturally specific, which allows a more informed interpretation of the 'magico-religious' phenomena found in any one place.

Discussion Questions

1   What does the word 'religion' mean to you? Compare your idea with those of some of your friends. Do you have a collective view?

2   Remember the functionalist questions at the end of the Introduction to this book? Consider the extent to which religions may respond to those basic needs? What are the limitations to this approach?

3 Consider the idea that 'science' is a world view, like a faith or a belief system. For example, how much 'science' do you take on trust? Can you think of occasions when 'scientists' have been discredited? Does this undermine your faith in 'science', and if not, why not?

References and Further Research

Books

Bowie, Fiona (2005) *The Anthropology of Religion*, 2nd edn (Oxford: Blackwell Publishing).

Boyer, Pascal (2001) *Religion Explained: The Human Instincts That Fashion Spirits and Ancestors* (London: Heinemann).

Burridge, Kenelm (1960) *Mambu: A Melanesian Millennium* (London: Methuen).

Durkheim, Emile (1915) *The Elementary Forms of the Religious Life*, translated J. W. Swain (London: George Allen & Unwin).

Evans-Pritchard, E. E. (1965) *Theories of Primitive Religion* (Oxford: Clarendon Press).

Frazer, Sir James George (1922) *The Golden Bough: A Study in Magic and Religion*, abridged edition (London: Macmillan).

Gombrich, Richard (1971) *Precept and Practice: Traditional Buddhism in the Rural Highlands of Ceylon* (Oxford: Clarendon Press).

Haley, Shawn D. and Fukuda, Curt (2004) *Day of the Dead: When Two Worlds Meet in Oaxaca* (Oxford: Berghahn).

Hendry, Joy (2005) *Reclaiming Culture: Indigenous People and Self-Representation* (Basingstoke: Palgrave Macmillan).

Jenkins, Timothy (1999) *Religion in English Everyday Life: An Ethnographic Approach* (Oxford: Berghahn).

Jenkins, Timothy (2006) *An Experiment in Providence: How Faith Engages with the World* (London: Society for Promoting Christian Knowledge).

Leach, Edmund (1969) *Genesis as Myth and Other Essays* (London: Cape Editions).

Lévi-Strauss, Claude (1963) *Structural Anthropology* (Harmondsworth: Penguin Books).

Lindstrom, Lamont (1993) *Cargo Cult: Strange Stories of Desire from Melanesia and Beyond* (Honolulu: University of Hawaii Press).

Malinowski, Bronislaw (1974) *Magic, Science and Religion* (London: The Free Press).

Middleton, John (1960) *Lugbara Religion: Ritual and Authority among an East African People* (London: Oxford University Press for the International African Institute).

Morris, Brian (1987) *Anthropological Studies of Religion: An Introductory Text* (Cambridge: Cambridge University Press).

Ohnuki-Tierney, Emiko (1984) *Illness and Culture in Contemporary Japan* (Cambridge: Cambridge University Press).

Radcliffe-Brown, A. R. (1984) *The Andaman Islanders* (New York: Free Press).

Reader, Ian (1996) *A Poisonous Cocktail: Aum Shinrikyo's Path to Violence* (Copenhagen: Nordic Institute for Asian Studies).

Tambiah, Stanley Jeyaraja (1990) *Magic, Science, Religion, and the Scope of Rationality* (Cambridge: Cambridge University Press).

Tylor, Edward B. (1913) *Primitive Culture*, vol. 2 (London: John Murray).

Whitehouse, H. (2004) *Modes of Religiosity: A Cognitive Theory of Religious Transmission* (Walnut Creek, Cal.: AltaMira Press).

Worsley, Peter (1970) *The Trumpet Shall Sound: A Study of 'Cargo' Cults in Melanesia* (London: Paladin).

Articles

Caplan, Lionel (1985) 'Fundamentalism Pursued', *Anthropology Today*, 1(4): 18–19.

Engelke, Matthew (2002) 'The Problem of Belief: Evans-Pritchard and Victor Turner on "the Inner Life"', *Anthropology Today*, 18(6): 3–6.

Leach, Edmund (1969) 'Genesis as Myth', in *Genesis as Myth and Other Essays* (London: Cape Editions).

Lévi-Strauss, Claude (1963) 'The Structural Study of Myth', in *Structural Anthropology* (Harmondsworth: Penguin Books, 1963).

Lévi-Strauss, Claude (1967) 'The Myth of Asdiwal' in Edmund Leach (ed.), *The Structural Study of Myth and Totemism* (London: Tavistock).

Webber, Jonathan (1985) 'Religions in the Holy Land: Conflicts of Interpretation', *Anthropology Today*, 1(2): pp. 3–10.

Novels and Other Works of Interest

Crow Dog, Mary (1991) *Lakota Woman* (New York: Harper Perennial) is the moving first-person account of the wife of a medicine man during the Native American revival movement.

Eco, Umberto (1983) *The Name of the Rose* (London: Vintage Classics) is a murder mystery set in an Italian monastery in 1327.

Endo, Shusaku (1976) *Silence* (London: Peter Owen) tells the story of two European missionaries whose less than successful work in Japan finds them seeking some sign from God that their work is not in vain.

Hillerman, Tony (1993) *Sacred Clowns* (Harmondsworth: Penguin) is a murder mystery involving two Native American detectives and a sacred festival.

Kneale, Matthew (2001) *English Passengers* (London: Penguin) is a novel set in the nineteenth century about a fanatically religious traveller and his encounters with people of different origins, notably Manx and Tasmanian.

Trollope, Joanna (1992) *The Choir* (London: Black Swan) takes the reader into a fictional world of politics, scandal and social relations in a Church of England community.

Films

The Dervishes of Kurdistan (Brian Moser, André Singer and Ali Bulookbashi, 1973) illustrates some of the extraordinary feats people with strong faith are able to perform.

The Kalasha: Rites of Spring (John Sheppard and Peter Parkes, 1990) is another very good 'Disappearing World' film about a minority people living in the mountains of Pakistan who resist the surrounding Islamic influence.

Koriam's Law, or the Death Who Governs (Gary Kildea and Andrea Simon, 110 minutes, 2005). Australian anthropologist Andrew Lattas and Peter Avarea of Pomio, New Britain, Papua New Guinea explore the Pomio Kivung movement and the phenomenon of the Melanesian cargo cult.

Native Spirit and the Sun Dance Way (World Wisdom, 2007). Thomas Yellowtail, a revered Crow Medicine Man and Sun Dance Chief for over 30 years, describes and explains the ancient ceremony that is sacred to the Crow tribe.

Tantra of Gyuto: Sacred Rituals of Tibet (1985), a documentary, introduced by the Dalai Lama and directed by S. Rochlin *et al.*, about the lives and spiritualism of Tibetan tantric monks, with coverage of various historical events.

Websites

http://www.isca.ox.ac.uk/research/cognitive_research.shtml – the site for the Centre for Anthropology and Mind.

http://www.qub.ac.uk/schools/InstituteofCognitionCulture/ – the site for the Institute of Cognition and Culture.

http://66.249.93.104/search?q=cache:Xm3xEWhGSDEJ:www.routledge-ny.com/ref/modfrenchthought/levistrauss.PDF+%27levi-strauss+anthropology%27&hl=en&client=firefox-a – a general overview and introduction to Lévi-Strauss and other anthropologists.

http://varenne.tc.columbia.edu/bib/info/tax00sol53appranth.html – a discussion between Lévi-Strauss and other anthropologists

http://varenne.tc.columbia.edu/bib/auth/levstcld0.html – a list of some of Lévi-Strauss' works and links to extracts from various texts

http://www.geocities.com/axeopoafonja/ – a site with information about Candomblé, an Afro-Brazilian spiritualist movement.

8

Cosmology II: Witchcraft, Shamanism and Syncretism

Indigenous Categories of Cosmology

In this chapter, we will turn to examine in detail some important categories which have interested anthropologists over the years, and in which they have sometimes engaged in interesting dialogue with historians. The first subjects are witchcraft and sorcery, which are not without intriguing meaning in the English language, but we will turn for our initial definitions to an African people studied by one of the better-known British anthropologists introduced in the last chapter, namely Edward Evans-Pritchard. The people are the Azande, a tribe of the Southern Sudan, for whom the word *mangu*, translated as 'witchcraft', was perhaps the most commonly used in their language when Evans-Pritchard lived among them. It was a matter of daily discussion, irritating rather than frightening, and, as an ethnographer, he could hardly ignore it.

Evans-Pritchard chose this subject for his study because it clearly pervaded the thinking of the Zande people and he realised that an understanding of their social life depended upon an understanding of their ideas about witchcraft. He became aware that their moral universe was not constructed around a Supreme Being, or the ghosts of ancestors, but around their ideas about witchcraft. The practice of witchcraft he found was almost synonymous with bad character, with greed and jealousy:

> witches tend to be those whose behaviour is least in accordance with social demands. Those whom we would call good citizens – and, of course, the richer and more powerful members of society are such – are seldom accused of witchcraft, while those who make themselves a nuisance to their neighbours and those who are weak are most likely to be accused. (1976: 52)

The study of witchcraft thus provided an essential key to understanding Zande systems of thought and paved the way to deciphering many related aspects of their social and political life.

Evans-Pritchard's work among the Azande also allowed him to devise theory about witchcraft which proved highly influential amongst ethnographers making observations in a wide range of other societies. His analysis has thus provided a basis for comparison with almost all the further studies which have been made. Some of these agree with his ideas, providing further examples of the general principles, others offer modifications or alternative types of analysis. None ignore his work, and even if only for this reason, it seems essential to start with his study and the theory it engendered. It is also a fascinating case, written in an extremely accessible style, so it is an excellent introduction for the student of witchcraft phenomena.

It is not everywhere that notions of witchcraft were found to be important, however, and other indigenous categories are thought better translated as spirit possession, shamanism, and so forth. These phenomena are discussed in the second part of the chapter, again with an emphasis on local understanding. In the last part of the chapter some attention is paid to places where ideas and beliefs from more than one religious tradition appear to coexist quite happily, a phenomenon again quite difficult to comprehend from the perspective of Europe and the Middle East, where history would be decimated if it ignored the many times people and places have been ravaged by religious wars. This is another area in which the knowledge acquired by anthropologists might be put to good use, were people convinced to listen.

Terminology

The terms witchcraft and sorcery were, until Evans-Pritchard's time, used rather unsystematically to describe a wide variety of ideas held in different parts of the world about mystical powers which people may possess. This power may have been thought to be a psychic one, with which a person is born, or a skill which can be learned, and perhaps passed on through an initiation ceremony. It may have been thought to emanate from the body, perhaps even unconsciously, or to be manipulated con-

witchcraft – ideas about psychic powers thought to be held by certain people, and the associated practices held to harness them, or sometimes to oppose them.

sorcery – ideas about the use of medicines and other occult powers, usually for evil ends, and the ways in which these are passed on from one practitioner to another.

sciously through the use of spells. Evans-Pritchard, in his classic book *Witchcraft, Oracles and Magic among the Azande* (1976), made clear a distinction between witchcraft and sorcery, which he saw as an evil form of magic, based on these sorts of characteristics. The distinction includes the following elements:

Witchcraft
- a psychic power
- often hereditary
- may be unconscious

Sorcery
- use of medicines for evil ends
- anyone can learn it
- conscious

This distinction was based initially on the Azande case, where witchcraft was said to be inherited in the male or female line, i.e. passed from father to son, or mother to daughter, although Evans-Pritchard did notice that this was not always the most important criterion when people were trying to identify a possible witch to accuse. The power was thought to reside in a substance in the belly, but this power could lie dormant or 'cool' indefinitely, and would only be activated if its owner became angry or jealous. People could also be entirely unaware of their power and it was held to be something of an individual quality for it to become active. If the witch died, an autopsy was said to confirm whether or not the substance had been present; however, the colonial government banned these operations, so Evans-Pritchard was not able to observe them.

Sorcery, on the other hand, was held to be a skill which could be learned, and passed on through conscious study. It was defined as the evil use of medicines, a practice also known as black magic, thereby seen as parallel to white magic used for positive purposes. Anyone with an interest could learn these skills and put them into practice, whereas the activation of witchcraft power was held often to be unconscious as well as limited to those with the substance in their bodies. The distinction is also held to distinguish kings and princes in Zande society from commoners, for the former are said to be both incapable of and immune to witchcraft, whereas they may be subject to the evil effects of sorcery.

Evans-Pritchard's distinction holds up rather well cross-culturally, but it is not possible to make in every society, and other efforts have been made to delineate the same sort of subject matter. For example, in their book *Witchcraft and Sorcery in East Africa* (1963) the authors John Middleton and E. H. Winter suggest the term wizardry to cover all such mystical activities. Another suggestion, made by I. M. Lewis in an article he contributed to the collection edited by Mary Douglas, entitled *Witchcraft: Confessions and Accusations* (1970) was that spirit possession be included together with witchcraft and sorcery in a notion of *mystical attack*, which could

wizardry – beliefs which people have about the capabilities and activities of others and the action which they take to avoid attacks or to counter them when they believe they have occurred (Middleton).

spirit possession – an engagement with the spirit world distinguished from others (by Raymond Firth) as largely involuntary, though some (like Lewis) interpret possession as invited – either way, a spirit is thought to express itself through a human being, causing the latter to engage in extraordinary behaviour.

be classified as *oblique* or *direct*, depending on the perceived motives of the accuser, rather than the accused. Lewis pointed out that it is after all the accuser who initiates the attack of public opinion against the witch, who in the end is the victim of social action, and this is parallel to some of his ideas about spirit possession. We will return to the subject of possession later in the chapter. In the meantime, however, let us turn to examine further the ideas of Evans-Pritchard, gleaned from the Azande.

Roles of Witchcraft and Sorcery Beliefs

The most influential aspects of the theory about witchcraft which Evans-Pritchard drew up were his considerations of the roles ideas about witchcraft played in relation to norms of good behaviour in Zande society. His discussion about these roles can be laid out under four headings, and in the pages that follow we can draw also on comparisons from other studies of witchcraft and sorcery. Perhaps most widespread of all is the way witchcraft could provide an explanation of misfortune.

(1) Witchcraft as an Explanation of Misfortune

Amongst the Azande people, witchcraft would be blamed for all kinds of unfortunate events which occurred in everyday life. Crop failure, illness, or simply a lack of fish could all be put down to witchcraft, although Evans-Pritchard emphasises that the Azande were not unaware of natural causes, such as adverse weather conditions, as well. Perhaps his most famous illustration of this principle is when he describes the Zande explanation of the collapse of a granary on a group of people eating their lunch. They know that the granary supports had been eaten by termites, he asserts, and they knew that the people sitting under the granary were doing it to take advantage of the shade it offered. It is witchcraft, however, which explains why the granary fell down at that particular time on those particular people.

In Evans-Pritchard's view, witchcraft carries an explanation to its logical conclusion. It explains why misfortune happens to certain people at a certain time, and in this way, explanations are carried one stage further than they may be elsewhere. A common view for someone involved in a car crash, for example, may be to ponder whether if they'd left home a few minutes later they would not have been hit by that person jumping a light. Someone missing a plane or bus that crashed might feel strangely lucky or protected. They may wonder about 'fate', 'destiny', 'luck' or 'acts of god', but with less immediate confidence than the Azande have, who are quite sure about why particular people are in the path of misfortune at a particular time – it's due to witchcraft.

Other belief systems have a similar confidence, however. For example, a Muslim's view of misfortune may see it immediately as an act of God. Indeed, an expression commonly used in Islamic circles allows for this intervention when a person modifies an arrangement by adding *insh'Allah*, meaning 'God-willing', to their proposed plans. In Western countries there seems to be a need to find a human cause for misfortune, so that a disaster will be followed by a court of inquiry to see where the blame lies. In an air crash, it is always important to seek the 'black box', for example, and ferry disasters have led to considerable modification to the design and execution of the journey. A disaster seems somehow less destructive in the long run if some action may be taken, and this is another role which notions of witchcraft allow.

(2) Witchcraft Provides Some Action which May Be Taken

The second role played by witchcraft is that ideas about it offer clear steps which may be taken to alleviate the misfortune. Just as one feels better about illness if someone knows what it is and how to treat it, the Azande can take action to find out who is bewitching them and why. They turn to oracles for this purpose. The most famous of these is known as the chicken oracle, when a series of chickens are fed doses of strychnine which are on the borderline of being lethal. Questions are presented as each chicken is given the dose, and the answer is provided by the death or otherwise of the chicken. Less expensive oracles involve putting sticks in a termite mound to see which is eaten faster, and the use of a 'rubbing board'. This last is described, by Evans-Pritchard, as:

> a miniature table-like construction ... carved out of the wood of various trees. They have two parts, the 'female', or the flat surface of the table supported by two legs and its tail, and the 'male', or the piece which fits the surface of the table like a lid.
>
> When the operator jerks the lid over the table it generally either moves smoothly backwards and forwards or it sticks to the board so firmly that no jerking will further move it, and it has to be pulled upwards with considerable force to detach it from the table. These two actions – smooth sliding and firm sticking – are the two ways in which the oracle answers questions. They correspond to the slaying or sparing of fowls by the poison, the eating or refusing of the branches by the termites.   (1976: 168–70)

(3) Witchcraft Brings Social Tensions out into the Open

Questions put to the oracles are usually in a form which requires a yes/no answer, and Evans-Pritchard noticed that those conducting the investigation consider not who is a known witch, but who might bear malice against the afflicted person. Witchcraft among the Azande is supposed to occur spontaneously if a person with the innate power is angry with or jealous of another, so that considering who might feel that way is thought likely to elicit a positive answer from the oracles. There is then a procedure to approach the person, most formally by presenting the wing of the dead chicken. The accused is likely to deny malice, but will probably go through a rite of blowing water on the wing to cool the witchcraft and exorcise any ill-feeling. This procedure serves a simultaneous purpose of bringing underlying tensions between people into the open, Evans-Pritchard argues, and deals with them in a way acceptable to both parties.

(4) Witchcraft has a Normative Effect on Society

These beliefs about witchcraft may serve as 'corrective to uncharitable impulses', argued Evans-Pritchard, 'because a show of spleen or meanness or hostility may bring serious consequences in its train' (1976: 54–5). In other words, people will try to curb their jealousy and other forms of unpleasantness for two important reasons:

- to avoid being accused of witchcraft, and
- to avoid incurring the wrath of a witch.

Accusations are usually made to those who are rude, dirty, and jealous, he notes, those with a generally bad character, so the whole system is a discouragement to people to behave in an unpleasant manner. 'Since Azande do not know who are and who are not witches, they assume that all their neighbours may be witches, and are therefore careful not to offend any of them without good cause' (ibid.).

Reactions and other Theories of Witchcraft

Most people who have discussed witchcraft since Evans-Pritchard wrote his classic book have reacted in one way or another to his work, many reinforcing his ideas about the roles played, particularly about the way it provides an explanation of misfortune. An interesting article by the historian Keith Thomas (1970), for example, describes the situation in sixteenth- and seventeenth-century England. He points out that misfortune could also be explained by the wrath of God, but witchcraft offered people more scope for action (see (2) above) than the new Protestant church did.

> A man who decided that God was responsible for his illness could do little about it. He could pray that he might be cured, but with no very certain prospect of success, for God's ways were mysterious, and, though he could be supplicated, he could not be coerced. Protestant theologians taught that Christians should suffer stoically like Job, but this doctrine was not a comfortable one. The attraction of witchcraft beliefs, by contrast, was that they held out precisely that certainty of redress which the theologians denied. A man who feared that a witch might attack him could invoke a number of magical preservatives in order to ensure his self-protection. If the witch had already struck, it was still open to him to practise counter magic ... Best of all, the victim could have the witch prosecuted and executed. For the point of such witch trials was not merely that they afforded the gratification of revenge, but that, according to contemporary belief, they positively relieved the victim.   (Thomas 1970: 57)

The Roman Catholic Church had had clearer procedures to be followed, and this difference could account to some extent for the rise in witchcraft trials after the Reformation, Thomas argued. He also offers support for (3) above by suggesting that accusations of witchcraft may well have followed feelings of guilt at having offended a neighbour, or refusing a person asking for alms, and that these ideas might therefore have encouraged neighbourly behaviour and generally reinforced moral standards. As in (4) above, people would try to avoid behaviour which might lead to accusations of witchcraft or the curses of a witch.

Both Keith Thomas and Evans-Pritchard point out, however, that it can sometimes be advantageous to have a reputation for power. In England, old ladies begging for alms could benefit from the fear that their potential benefactors might have of their bewitching capabilities. Among the Azande, those with a reputation for witchcraft were often offered extra meat when the spoils of a hunt were being divided up. This was thought to protect against possible interference during a further hunt, indeed it would be an incentive for the witch to ensure good hunting fortune, they argued.

Writing of the Amba of Uganda (Middleton and Winter 1963), Winter argues that witchcraft is not always beneficial to society, however. Indeed, he shows how notions of witchcraft tend to disrupt the social cohesion of the village. Witches in an Amba view exhibit an inversion of physical and moral qualities of human beings. They hang upside down, eat human flesh, quench their thirst with salt, go about naked and, unlike the situation in the case of feuds, they take their victims from their own villages and share them with witches in other villages.

> Thus if witches in a particular village kill a person they invite the witches from another village to share the ensuing feast. At a later date, the witches of the second village must reciprocate by inviting their previous hosts to a feast at which they will serve the corpse of a victim from their own village. (1963: 292).

The behaviour of witches is thus precisely the opposite of that expected of ordinary people, who abhor the idea of eating human flesh, and always go about with clothes on their bodies. The notions of witchcraft should be examined in the context of the whole moral universe, Winter argues, when they can be seen as a *structural inversion* of the social order. This argument is thus an example of an *expressive* role of witchcraft, in the same sense as we used the idea in the previous chapter, in that it tells us something about important categories in society. It thereby goes beyond, and complements the *instrumental* or functional role presented by Evans-Pritchard and others, when they identify the normative effect witchcraft has on society.

Other structural interpretations are found in the analyses of sorcery accusations made in South America. Peter Rivière's chapter in *Witchcraft: Confessions and Accusations* (1970) describes the way lines of sorcery accusation reflect the sociopolitical structure of the Trio Indians of Surinam in helping to demarcate divisions between villages. In the case of the Akwe Shavante of southern Brazil, they reflect lines of division between political factions. In both cases, the groups are somewhat fluid. Allegiances can alter, and people move to rearrange their neighbourly links. Confirmation of a new division is clear when sorcery accusations are made, for these do not occur amongst people who share a village, or a faction.

In the introduction to the same book, Douglas describes witchcraft as 'essentially a means of clarifying and affirming social definitions' (1970: xxv). If the witch is an outsider, there is a reconfirmation of the inside, whatever that may be. If the witch is an insider, witchcraft may have the function of controlling deviants in the name of community values, it may promote factional rivalry, or it may redefine a hierarchy. In *Purity and Danger* (1966) she argued that uncontrolled witchcraft is attributed to people in dangerously ambiguous roles, people who may be potential sources of disorder. They may have their own niche in one group, but be an intruder from the point of view of another. 'Witches are the social equivalents of beetles and spiders who live in the cracks of the walls and the wainscoting' (1966: 24). An example she gives is Joan of Arc, 'a peasant at court, a woman in armour, an outsider in the councils of war' (ibid.) – small wonder she was accused of witchcraft.

Peter Brown, in another chapter in the Douglas collection (1970) points to so-called flashpoints of sorcery accusation at times of crisis and social change, suggesting an increase when areas of the social structure are ill-defined. Some of his examples are the fourth-century remains of the Roman Empire, sixteenth- and seventeenth-century England, which he relates to the undefined position of the poor until the passing of the Poor Law, and a rise of witchcraft in Africa with colonisation and missionary work.

It is difficult to say whether current witchcraft practices in England are related to any kind of crisis or social change, or, indeed, whether they have ever really abated over the intervening years. It is certainly true, however, that magic and witchcraft continue to intrigue members of the wider society, and practising witches are found amongst the most apparently staid and middle-class of professions. These subjects have occasionally attracted undergraduate students at Oxford Brookes, and those who have gained access to local covens have written very interesting dissertations. A Cambridge PhD thesis which became an excellent ethnography of British Witchcraft – *Persuasions of the Witch's Craft* (Luhrmann 1989) – is a good introduction to the subject, which also addresses the thorny question of rationality.

Another good book to follow up links the ideas about witchcraft that we have discussed in this chapter with the powers of rumour and gossip that we will discuss in the next. *Witchcraft, Sorcery, Rumors and Gossip* (2004), by Pamela Stewart and Andrew Strathern, ranges across Africa, India, New Guinea and Europe, and from the Middle Ages to the present day, in looking at the way that rumours and gossip lead to accusations of witchcraft and sorcery. They investigate the relationship of all these things with situations of conflict and violence, and examine how the latter is justified in the interests of some greater social good that also happens to bring benefits to powerful people in that society.

Possession and Shamanism

Explanations of misfortune form part of the **cosmology** of a society, and in industrialised societies, science is very often invoked for this purpose. Thus, people visit a doctor when they are ill, ask a forensic expert to help solve a murder, examine fingerprints in the case of theft, and seek the 'black box' to explain a plane crash. In many societies people also turn to spirits for explanations of all these kinds of eventualities, usually by asking a specialist such as a shaman, a diviner, or a witch-doctor to intervene in communicating with the spirit world. Communication with the spirits may take place on behalf of an individual or it may take place at a large gathering, often with much ribaldry and enjoyment, and ethnographers have commented on the entertainment value of these occasions.

shaman – a person thought to have the power to communicate with the spirit world, perhaps by travelling there or receiving a spirit into his or her body, and also sometimes to influence and control the activities of those spirits.

The different words used for these practitioners tend to be associated with particular regions. 'Shaman', for example, is a word taken from the Tungus tribe of Siberia, although it is used elsewhere, particularly to describe practitioners who claim to have a soul which can leave their body and travel to a heaven or an underworld. People of South America often have practitioners such as these, although of course with their own local names, who may train to go into trances, perhaps by drinking tobacco juice or taking hallucinogens, and then claim to go on trips to visit the spirit world. They may also learn a technique for receiving spirits into their

diviner – a person thought to have powers to explain the past, anticipate the future and to advise about related decisions, such as causes of illness, marriage partners and travel plans.

own bodies, which will then speak to the assembled company (in any number of different voices!) about their problems and requests.

Audrey Colson, who worked amongst the Akawaio people of British Guyana, describes such occasions in lively detail (Colson 1977). Indeed, one of my strongest memories as a student learning anthropology was listening to Audrey's tape of an Akawaio seance, because the audience is extremely participative and the whole thing sounds immensely exciting. The visiting spirits are asked to deal with misfortune, to help find lost articles, including determining who may have stolen them in case it was a matter of theft, and to identify the causes of sickness, and recommend ways to bring it to an end. People in the audience join in with their own suggestions throughout the procedure, and Colson argues that the shaman, or the spirits who are possessing the shaman, make decisions which reflect public opinion.

In this way, the Akawaio seance plays some of the same roles as described by Evans-Pritchard for witchcraft beliefs. It provides an opportunity for underlying tensions to be expressed in a legitimate fashion, for people in a contained situation to throw out accusations against others whose behaviour could have brought about the misfortunes – perhaps by upsetting the spirits who would bring about illness, for example. Because names of possible transgressors are brought to the visiting spirits, Colson argues that this is a strong disincentive to people to behave in an antisocial way, and the whole procedure again has a normative effect on Akawaio society.

'Diviner' refers to a broader category of people who may address themselves to similar problems. In Japan and other parts of the Far East their roles include divining the causes of illness (perhaps by claiming to enter the body of the afflicted), assessing the suitability of a marriage or a proposed alteration to a house, and determining auspicious days for a venture of any sort. A complicated calendar may be consulted for these purposes, and this is drawn up according to astrological ideas, in association with ideas about the division of the world into *yin* and *yang*. The classification of time, discussed in Chapter 1, is influential here too, so the work of a diviner is not only concerned with communication with spirits.

However, Japanese diviners may also be consulted to explain misfortune, and some of their explanations may involve dissatisfied ghosts and ancestral spirits. Memorials for the dead should be carried out on certain death days, for example, and forgetting these could cause trouble. A relatively recent reaction to misfortune has been to attribute it to the souls of aborted babies, and Buddhist temples have set aside areas for small memorial statues, as well as running monthly rituals to appease these lonely souls. New temples have even opened which cater exclusively to the souls of aborted babies (see Lafleur 1992 for more detail). Japanese people anyway think nothing of consulting a variety of diviners *and* doctors about the same ailment, as was mentioned in the last chapter.

Practitioners of this sort in Africa are more commonly described as spirit mediums or witch-doctors, though their roles may be very similar, that is divining the cause of illness, and finding out how to appease an offended spirit. In talking of communication with spirits in different societies, Raymond Firth suggested that a distinction be made between:

spirit mediumship – an engagement with the spirit world where communication is thought to be voluntary so that the medium makes deliberate efforts to call spirits into the presence of gathered company, although he/or she may have limited control.

- **spirit possession**, which is largely involuntary
- **spirit mediumship**, where communication is voluntary, and
- **shamanism**, which involves some control over spirits.

There have been many different approaches to this subject, and I. M. Lewis (1971) discussed some of them in *Ecstatic Religion*. As was mentioned in the last section, Lewis (1970) compares the interpretation of spirit possession with that of witchcraft. He considers possession as a strategy employed by a person seeking an outlet for distress. Amongst the BaVenda of Southern Africa, for example, the treatment for a woman's possession involves the husband and family according the afflicted person special respect and kindness, and, perhaps not unexpectedly, this kind of possession is said to recur rather frequently. A similar form of spirit possession occurs elsewhere amongst men of low status, who thereby have their position at least temporarily enhanced. Persistence of the 'affliction' may lead to suspicion of witchcraft and *direct* rather than *oblique* mystical attack, in Lewis's terms.

There are several ethnographies that give pride of place to the practice of spirit possession, and some of these are listed below. A useful article which examines Lewis's broader theories about spirit possession in the context of the particular case of the Newar people of the Kathmandu Valley is that by David Gellner (1994), entitled 'Priests, healers, mediums and witches'. A classic collection is that by Beattie and Middleton, which focuses on the role of spirit mediumship in Africa, and a nice introduction to interaction with spirits in Japan is the book by Carmen Blacker entitled *The Catalpa Bow* (1975).

Syncretism

In complex multicultural worlds, different cosmologies must needs coexist. Tolerance of different faiths is one way of seeking a peaceful life, and people of varying backgrounds do manage to live alongside one another in many cities of the world. In urban schools, these days, children may learn a veritable medley of ideas about the faiths which the teachers find amongst their charges. They may encourage children to share their notions of this world and any other they have been taught to believe in, and the school may play host to all manner of different festivals and rites. The aim is to teach tolerance, but it may also engender a degree of confusion, and some of my students who have been brought up in this climate of opinion are only devout when they talk of environmental issues.

Those who become most serious on this subject may turn to a form of nature worship known as Paganism, which has become quite influential in Northern European countries. Although there are many forms of this movement, which has adopted as a name the word used to describe pre-Christian religious ideas, there is in Britain an overarching organisation which aims to keep different groups in touch with one another (http://www.paganfed.org/). One of the common themes seems, appropriately, to be the revival of ideas which were prevalent in Europe before Christianity, but there is also a common concern with the conservation and protection of the environment. Anthropologist Charlotte Hardman, writes:

> the state of Paganism in the UK has been changing ... Ecologically, although Paganism has always had behind it a romantic view of the land and has always been 'green' philosophically, it has now also become more clearly an activist movement in this area .... Respect for Nature, being 'green', is no longer just part of the philosophy; the eco-magic of Pagan ritual can be activated towards environmental, social and spiritual change. (1996: xiv – xv)

There is some overlap here with Luhrman's witches, but she also had informants who did not classify themselves as Pagans, and some even practised Christianity (Luhrman 1989: 5).

People who turn to paganism and witchcraft in Europe are revitalising old categories into new systems of cosmology. They draw on an abundant fund of ancient ideas to create a new way to impose order on an increasingly confusing world. Sometimes in despair at the way scientific discovery appears to ignore the fragility of natural resources, people look back to times which seem idyllic from the perspective of nuclear power and mass destruction. Like the art collectors mentioned in Chapter 6, who seek solace in aboriginal paintings, these people look for wisdom in ancient or disappearing worlds. They reject the excesses of a scientific world view, and seek to find a spiritual life which reflects the concerns of the world in which they find themselves.

Drawing elements of different cosmological systems into a new world view is a practice as ancient as cultural exchange, and the results are sometimes called syncretism, literally the coexistence of beliefs, although in practice one set may virtually subsume another, when it may be called synthesis. As Christianity has spread around the world, it has often incorporated elements of previous belief systems into its range of varying ideas and practices. The timing of the celebration of the birth of Christ to coincide with mid-winter conveniently replaced previous northern European festivals, for example, as mentioned in Chapter 4, and the celebration of Hallowe'en, now a 'religious' practice only in Pagan circles, is not by chance

syncretism – the coexistence of cosmological systems which can still be identified as distinct, although in practice may become quite intermingled.

Photograph 8.1 Offerings to departed relatives in Mexico, made on the days of All Saints and All Souls in the Christian calendar, also reflect pre-Christian customs for what is known as el Dia de los Muertos, or the Day of the Dead (photograph: Raquel Hernandez-White).

held on days known in the Christian calendar as celebrations of All Saints and All Souls.

In Mexico, these days are amongst the most important in the calendar, when people remember their departed loved ones and visit their graves. Principally known as the Day of the Dead (see also First-hand Account 3.2 on pp. 60–1 and Photograph 8.1), the period is marked by the construction and sale of an abundance of goods and sweets with ghoulish themes, such as rubber skeletons and chocolate skulls. In the book referred to in the last chapter by Haley and Fukuda (2004), it is clearly shown how the pre-Christian Zapotec ideas have been interwoven with the Roman Catholic ones in contemporary practice. It is several centuries since Christianity was introduced to the Mexican people, but there is evidence in the writings of the missionaries of the time that efforts were made to incorporate indigenous practices, and it is interesting that the Virgin of Guadalupe made her first appearance on a hill sacred to Tonantzin, an important Aztec Earth Mother.

The 'Disappearing World' film *Witchcraft among the Azande* noted below, also gives a demonstration of how the ideas described above have found ways to coexist with the more newly introduced Christianity.

Photograph 8.2 Three Buddhist *chityas* (cult objects) outside the Bhimsen Temple, Kathmandu. The *chitya* in the foreground is of the style popular in the 17th and 18th centuries, the other two are the syncretic form which became popular in Kathmandu in the later 19th and early 20th centuries, a time of intensive Hinduisation. They incorporate as part of the base a water course that is copied from the most common Hindu cult object, namely the *shivalinga* (photograph courtesy of David Gellner).

When I was about 10 years old, I was given a paper in school that asked what religion I was. As I didn't know, I went back home and asked my grandfather. He said, 'We are Udays. Our caste is Tuladhar and we are Buddhists'.

Almost all the Udays live in the densely populated ancient city of Kathmandu. I grew up living in two houses: one in the mountain town of Pharping and the other in Kathmandu. My grandparents taught me how to act like a Tuladhar and how to speak according to my audience. I learned that within the Udays there are lots of castes, but Tuladhars are the highest. I was told that Bajracharyas and Shakyas come before the Udays, so the language I should use with them, especially with those Bajracharyas that are acting as our Buddhist priests, has to be very polite. It is almost a different language.

First-hand account 8:

Bhawana Tuladhar-Douglas, Newar – on Syncretism in Nepal

We do our morning worship, or *puja*, before breakfast. There are various special days when we do *puja* for specific deities: our lineage deity (each caste branch has their own), the stupa at Svayambhu, the Avalokiteshvara of Jana Bahal, Akash Bhairav, Kal Bhairav and other deities. There are festivals where every Buddhist can walk in a procession called a *jatra*, like Mataya, the procession of lamps that remembers the recently dead. When we are someplace other than the Kathmandu house – such as the Pharping house, where I lived – we remember exactly where our (lineage) god is located, visualise them, and do the *puja* from our roof. To worship the lineage deity you must come from a family which has been accepted as part of the caste association, called a *guthi*. Almost every Newar family is part of a *guthi*.

People say that there used to be 10 Buddhist monasteries in Pharping, but none of them are there anymore, nor are there any proper old Buddhist families. There are two Bajracharya families, but just as we were really from Kathmandu, those families were from Lalitpur. The only son in one family married a Jyapu, a Newar farmer, so that family collapsed and became

Jyapus. After that they could no longer work as priests. The other family still stays at the Vajrayogini temple and they work as priests there. There had been another Uday family, Sthapits, but the son married a Jyapu, and his son married a Balami so that family lost their membership in their *guthi*, and now have no communication with their relatives.

During the Buddhist festival month of Gumla in Pharping people do Vajrayogini *pujas* all month and at the end of the month there is a big procession. In Kathmandu, during Gumla every town square has its own devotional music (*bhajans*). Usually a few musicians come to play early in the morning to wake people up. Everybody follows the musical group and we visit lots of Buddhist deities in a long procession that finishes back at our square. For the Buddha's birthday we usually go to Svayambhunath in Kathmandu. In Pharping, on the same day, there is a Buddha image on a cart that goes around to each of the seven town squares of Pharping. All Newars do annual *pujas* as part of their *guthis*. For Udays, this is a big *puja* done together with a Bajracharya priest, and we have a special feast afterwards.

My parents had a love marriage. My mother was born in a Parbatiya Brahmin family. Because she was a very high caste Brahmin, my grandparents and our *guthi* were prepared to accept her. However, one of my father's mother's cousins fell in love with a Shrestha girl, and they married. She was neither allowed in the kitchen nor in *guthi*. It was real luck that my mother – and so also us, her children – were allowed in our society.

I didn't visit my mother's family house until I was 13 years old. There was a fight about our religion and caste system, poor and rich, between two families. For Parbatiyas all the Newars are Jyapus, a farmer caste. They do not have any knowledge of the Newar caste system. In school my Parbatiya friends called me 'Jyapu'. When I visited my mother's family, in Palanchok, my grandmother was very happy to see me but she was upset by the fact that my mother had married a Jyapu. In her house I saw only Hindu deities but not Buddhist ones. I found their way of worshipping gods and the way I was taught were very different indeed. I did see a picture of the Buddha in my mother's brother's new house at Kathmandu, but only in the sitting room as a part of room decoration.

Until 2006 Nepal was a Hindu monarchy with a Parbatiya king. I remember reading in my school book that 'Nepal is a multi-religious and multi-lingual country'. All our course books are either in Nepali or in English. There are pronunciation differences

– Newari does not distinguish a retroflex 't'- so Newars get teased by Parbatiyas. As a result our language is dying. So far as religion goes, in school I read one small chapter about Buddha, his birth place and his enlightenment. There were lots of chapters about Hindu deities.

Every week we had Hindi Dharawahik show on NTV, about the Hindu epic, Ramayana, Mahabharata and then the Vishnupuran. These shows are still a constant feature of the national broadcast programme. Nepalese people wonder if the gods only speak in Hindi. Yet they do like watching Hindi films. In films if anything goes wrong the hero or their relative goes to pray in a Hindu temple, and then everything turns out okay. We all talked about these films in school with friends – it was a kind of pressure on people to worship some Shiva or Vishnu, directly or indirectly.

My great-grandmother became a Buddhist nun for a few years. She does not really know the differences between Theravada and Mahayana Buddhism. What she does know is Sakyamuni Buddha and his life, and about the secret initiations that she has been given, and how she will be treated after her death by the funeral *guthi*. Because she had secret initiations from the Bajracharya priests, she believes her dead body will be carried to the cremation ground with special Newari music.

In a proper Buddhist Newar family we are given secret mantras by the Bajracharya priest. Once you have the mantra you are not allowed to tell anyone. If you did tell another person then, according to the priest, your head would explode. I don't think any one would want to die like that – so the pure Buddhist mantras die with people. Hindu mantras, however, you can learn in a book or from a television programme where some Babaji says it clearly so you can pick it up. I know both Hindu and Buddhist mantras – though probably more Hindu mantras because they're so easy to find.

So far as I can tell, both for Newars and other groups, people don't make much of a distinction about going to Hindu or Buddhist shrines. Hinduism dominates Nepalese culture, though, for all the reasons I have given. I still believe of myself that I am Buddhist. My grandfather said that Buddha is the 'light of Asia'. I believe Buddha is the light of the world.

In Japan, the situation is rather different, and provides a better example of syncretism. The indigenous Shinto, which literally means 'path of the gods', was a set of rather miscellaneous ancient beliefs without a name, possibly related to Taoism, until they needed to be distinguished from other more established traditions which were introduced from the outside. These now coexist with ideas and practices from Buddhism, Confucianism and Christianity. These, of course, have their own dogma, teachings and ritual experts, but ordinary Japanese people seem to find little difficulty in drawing on anything available in turning to what might be called religion.

We have already noted that the Japanese language sometimes classed Shinto ideas 'superstition' in the postwar disapproval of its support for imperial expansion, but the word usually translated as religion (*shūkyō*) is also more appropriately used for the teachings introduced from outside than for these indigenous ideas. The word for 'believer' (*shinja*) is also applied rather to someone who chooses a special (often 'new') religious path than to the many Japanese people who incorporate various strands of religious influence into their life almost imperceptibly. Visits to Shinto shrines at birth, Buddhist funerals, Christian weddings, and the consultation of a (possibly Taoist) shaman may all be practised by the same person in Japan.

Analysis of the practices of the people who lived in the rural community where I carried out fieldwork (Hendry 1981) coincided with the findings of those who have specialised in looking at religious practises in Japan. On the whole, Shinto is found to be drawn upon in celebrations associated with life and health, Buddhism with death and memorials for the ancestors. The former are usually community celebrations, perhaps held at the community shrine, the latter are household ones which make use of the household altar. Clearly, these practices may again be seen as playing an *expressive* role, one which is reinforced when we notice that the consultation of the less well defined shaman takes place in times of illness, marriage and housebuilding, when the important categories are threatened or undergoing change.

Christianity in Japan has not made much progress, counting less than two per cent of Japanese as practitioners. Perhaps this is because the syncretic system, which now also includes a number of 'new' sects of Buddhism and Shinto, is not only at odds with the more exclusive nature of Christianity, but also still serves to accommodate the changing structures of Japanese society. Looking back over 1500 years of Japanese history, the two major strands of what are now called Shinto and Buddhism can be seen to have undergone much separation and assimilation, but certain elements have also continued to persist. Confucianism has been a long-term influence too, but largely in the underpinning of morals and ethics, a subject we will consider in more detail in the next chapter.

Some discussants (Stewart and Shaw 1995) of syncretism have argued that all religions have drawn on different traditions over the centuries, so little is to be gained by using the term, but the notion is useful for contrasting with the relatively ethnocentric nature of the idea that one religion should make an exclusive call on its adherents. David Gellner (1997), in a critique of the Stewart and Shaw book, considers different varieties of syncretism, and makes a comparison between the Buddhism found alongside Shinto and Confucianism in Japan and the case of the Newar people of the Kathmandu Valley, in Nepal, who continue to practise Tantric Buddhism in a predominantly Hindu state. His book *Monk, Householder and Tantric Priest* (1992) is a detailed ethnography of the Newar people who live in the Hindu Buddhist city of Lalitpur, and focuses on the religious activities which provide many good examples of syncretism in practice (see Photograph 8.2). First-hand Account 8 on pp. 163–5 includes an account of one person's life in this kind of syncretic situation.

Conclusion

This chapter has laid out a selection of the indigenous categories of cosmology that have been studied by anthropologists, and focused in on a few of the more influential, in order to give a feel for some of the different ideas held by people in what might be called their spiritual life. We have also considered some of the ways in which people communicate with worlds that are held to exist beyond the mundane. In the next chapter we draw again on ideas that may be termed religious or spiritual, but among many others that serve as constraints in everyday social life.

Discussion Questions

1 How do you explain misfortune in your own life? Do you call on a religious faith, or science, or the interference of spirits? Or do you use words like 'luck' or 'fate'? What do your explanations tell you about your own upbringing?

2 Do your explanations of misfortune relate to norms in your own society? Can you think of any 'structural' or 'expressive' roles they might play?

3 Consider the value of syncretic ideas in the contemporary world. How might they work to the long-term survival of our planet?

References and Further Research

Books
Beattie, John and Middleton, John (1969) *Spirit Mediumship and Society in Africa* (London: Routledge & Kegan Paul).

Blacker, Carmen (1975) *The Catalpa Bow: A Study of Shamanistic Practices in Japan* (London: Allen & Unwin).

Blain, Jenny, Ezzy, Douglas and Harvey, Graham (2004) *Researching Paganisms* (Oxford: Altamira Press).

Douglas, Mary (1966) *Purity and Danger* (Harmondsworth: Penguin).

Douglas, Mary (ed.) (1970) *Witchcraft: Confessions and Accusations* (London: Tavistock).

Eliade, Mircea (1964) *Shamanism: Archaic Techniques of Ecstacy* (Princeton: Princeton University Press).

Evans-Pritchard, E. E. (1976) *Witchcraft, Oracles and Magic among the Azande* (Oxford: Clarendon Press).

Gellner, David (1992) *Monk, Householder and Tantric Priest* (Cambridge: Cambridge University Press).

Haley, Sharon D. and Fukuda, Curt (2004) *Day of the Dead: When Two Worlds Meet in Oaxaca* (Oxford: Berghahn).

Hardman, Charlotte (1996) 'Introduction' in Graham Harvey, and Charlotte Hardman (eds), *Paganism Today: Wiccans, Druids, the Goddess and Ancient Earth Traditions for the Twenty-First Century* (London: Thorsons).

Hendry, J. (1981) *Marriage in Changing Japan: Community and Society*, (London: Croom Helm).

LaFleur, William R. (1992) *Liquid Life: Abortion and Buddhism in Japan* (Princeton, NJ: Princeton University Press).

Lewis, I. M. (1971) *Ecstatic Religion: An Anthropological Study of Spirit Possession and Shamanism* (Harmondsworth: Penguin).

Luhrmann, Tanya (1989) *Persuasions of the Witch's Craft* (Blackwell: Oxford).

Marwick, Max (ed.) (1982) *Penguin Readings on Witchcraft*, 2nd edn. (Harmondsworth: Penguin).

Middleton, John and Winter, E. H. (eds) (1963) *Witchcraft and Sorcery in East Africa* (London: Routledge & Kegan Paul, 1963.

Stewart, Charles and Shaw, Rosalind (eds) (1995) *Syncretism/Anti-Syncretism: The Politics of Religious Synthesis* (London: Routledge, 1995).

Stewart, Pamela J. and Strathern, Andrew (2004) *Witchcraft, Sorcery, Rumors and Gossip* (Cambridge: Cambridge University Press).

Articles

Boddy, Janice (1988) 'Spirits and Selves in Northern Sudan: The Cultural Therapeutics of Possession and Trance', *American Ethnologist*, 15(1): 4 – 27

Brown, Peter (1970) 'Sorcery, Demons and the Rise of Christianity from Late Antiquity into the Middle Ages', in Mary Douglas (ed.) *Witchcraft: Confessions and Accusations* (London: Tavistock), pp. 17–45.

Colson, Audrey (1977) 'The Akawaio Shaman', in ed. E. B. Basso (ed.) *Carib- Speaking Indians: Culture, Society and Language* (Tucson: University of Arizona Press).

Gellner, David (1994) 'Priests, Healers, Mediums and Witches: The Context of Possession in the Kathmandu Valley, Nepal', *Man*, 29: 27–48.

Gellner, David (1997) 'For Syncretism. The Position of Buddhism in Nepal and Japan Compared', *Social Anthropology*, 5(3): 277–91.

Humphrey, Caroline (1999) 'Shamans in the City', *Anthropology Today*, 15(3): 3–10.

Jencson, L. (1989) 'Neo-paganism and the Great Mother-Goddess: Anthropology as the Midwife to a New Religion', *Anthropology Today*, 5(2): 2–4.

Lewis, I. M. (1970) 'A Structural Approach to Witchcraft and Spirit Possession', in Mary Douglas (ed.), *Witchcraft: Confessions and Accusations* (London: Tavistock), pp.293–309.

Riches, David (1994) 'Shamanism: The Key to Religion', *Man*, 29: 381–405.

Rivière, Peter (1970) 'Factions and Exclusions in Two South American Village Systems', in Mary Douglas (ed.), pp. 245–55.

Thomas, Keith (1970) 'The Relevance of Social Anthropology to the Historical Study of English Witchcraft', in Mary Douglas (ed.), *Witchcraft: Confessions and Accusations* (London: Tavistock), pp. 47–79.

Willis, Roy (1994) 'New Shamanism', *Anthropology Today*, 10:(6): 16–18.

Novels

Lowry, Malcolm (1962) *Under the Volcano* (Harmondsworth: Penguin Books) is a novel about a disillusioned and alcoholic British consul living in Mexico, but it is of interest here because much of the action takes place on the Day of the Dead.

Mantel, Hilary (2005) *Beyond Black* (London: Fourth Estate) is a novel about the life of a spirit medium in suburban London.

Miller, Arthur (1996) *The Crucible* (London: Methuen) is a play about the Salem witch trials in seventeenth-century United States.

Okri, Ben (1991) *The Famished Road* (London: Cape) is a novel full of African spirits and mysticism.

Warner, Sylvia Townsend (1978 [1926]) *Lolly Willowes* (London: The Women's Press) is a comic novel about a spinster who joins a coven – an allegory for feminist subversiveness.

Films

Bridewealth of a Goddess (Chris Owen, 72 minutes, 2000) is a unique insight into a secret spirit cult among the Kawelka people in the western Highlands of Papua New Guinea.

Witchcraft among the Azande (André Singer and John Ryle, 1982), a 'Disappearing World' film that depicts the world of Azande witchcraft within the new context of widespread conversion to Christianity.

The Guardian of the Forces (Anne Laure Folly, 52 minutes, 1991) explores the significance of sacrifice and possession in communicating with spirits of ancestors and voodoo deities.

Kataragama, A God for All Seasons (Charlie Nairn and Gananath Obeyesekere, 1973) is another 'Disappearing World' film set in Sri Lanka (then, Ceylon) which, at least at first, illustrates the variety of ways a people may seek to understand the misfortune of losing an 11-year-old son.

Shamans of the Amazon, a documentary by Dean Jeffreys about a visit, with his family, to shamans on the Amazon in Ecuador.

The 'Strangers Abroad' film about Evans-Pritchard, entitled *Strange Beliefs* (see Chapter 1) includes an examination of Zande material too.

The Crucible, Nicholas Hytner's 1997 feature film of Arthur Miller's play.

Websites

http://personalwebs.oakland.edu/~dow/courses/an271/bswmr.html – James Dow's bibliography for witchcraft studies.

http://www.bbc.co.uk/religion/religions/paganism/ataglance/glance.shtml and http://www.paganfed.org/ – two websites about Paganism.

http://www.shamanism.org/ – homepage for The Foundation for Shamanic Studies.

http://www.drugnerd.com/archives/435/shamans-of-the-amazon-great-documentary/ – weblink to a film about Amazonian shamanism.

9

Law, Order and Social Control

Rules and Norms

In this chapter and the next we are again taking as a focus categories from the English language, and we will examine manifestations of behaviour observed in different parts of the world which conform approximately to the specifications these terms encompass. The terms in question – 'law' and 'politics' – overlap in any society. When a formal political system is distinguished from a legal system, it is still the politicians who design and discuss the laws, while a different set of professionals – lawyers and judges – put them into practice. In both cases we deal, on the one hand, with persons in positions of power – the subject matter of Chapter 10 – and, on the other, with the constraints imposed on members of the society at large by the mechanisms of control. In most societies, too, the people themselves constrain the acts of others amongst them in a variety of less formal ways.

In this chapter we will focus on the constraints. Any society needs mechanisms which ensure that its members behave for the most part in a reasonably ordered fashion. In countries at national level, there are laws, together with systems of policing and courts which execute the enforcement of these laws. There are also prisons and other institutions to exact punishment or rehabilitate offenders. And there are norms of behaviour, which may or may not coincide with these laws, that people learn as they grow up within social groups, and everywhere there is some kind of reaction on the part of most other people if these norms are transgressed. Details vary from one group to another – indeed, within one group – but some form of social control is found everywhere.

norms - aspects of expected behaviour that people learn as they grow up within social groups, and which provoke some kind of reaction from those groups if transgressed.

At a local level, and within specific communities, informal constraints on the behaviour of individuals are rather effective, sometimes more effective than the laws of the land, and in this chapter, we will concern ourselves particularly with these mechanisms for 'keeping order' in society. The experience of anthropologists, working for long periods amongst smallish groups of people, sometimes very isolated from any wider legal system, has given them a special insight into the workings of these informal methods of social control. They are able to observe the kinds of pres-

social control - mechanisms within a society that act to constrain members of that society to behave within a range of acceptable norms.

sures which induce people to conform to certain norms and standards, and they can identify incentives people cite for complying with the expectations of their friends and neighbours.

Actually, we have already considered several methods of social control in previous chapters. In the last one we looked at the shaman's seance, where we noticed that the likelihood of being picked out as a possible transgressor was thought to induce people to behave within accepted norms amongst the Akawaio of British Guyana. It was also suggested that ideas about witchcraft and spirit possession had a normative effect on the behaviour of the Azande of the Southern Sudan and the Bavanda of Uganda respectively. In Chapter 7, on religion, we talked of the prospect of salvation, or divine retribution, as well as the wrath of ancestors and fears of burning in hell, as incentives to conform to the behaviour expected by the moral system.

During my own first fieldwork in Japan, when I was focusing on patterns of marriage, I noticed an interesting mechanism of social control in the way people would check up on the families of prospective spouses. Meetings are often arranged by relatives so that young people can meet likely candidates for marriage, and if there is serious interest between them, each family will take steps to find out about the other. In the countryside this may involve a visit to the village where they live, and simple enquiries amongst neighbours and in the local shops. The owner of the general store in my village told me that she was regularly approached in this way. She also explained that she felt a moral obligation to tell the truth as she saw it. If a family were to set up a marriage with a family she knew to be difficult or unpleasant, she would forever feel responsible.

There was also an economic element at play here, since the shopkeeper would clearly lose custom if she protected people who turned out to make life miserable for a new housewife and potential customer. For the existing village families, well aware of the system, it was a powerful incentive to keep on good terms with the shopkeeper, again bringing her custom, especially as one's children approached marriageable age. Amongst neighbours too it could be very difficult if one were to acquire a bad reputation, and two families in the village had had to set up a marriage between themselves, although marrying out of the village was usually preferred, because of their reputation for rudeness and bad temper. There is clearly an element of social control at play here.

There have been several attempts to make general statements about social control, and in this chapter we will examine two of these in some detail and make reference to a third. In all three cases, the anthropologists have drawn heavily on material from small-scale societies, but their findings may also be usefully applied to segments of more complex societies. First, we will look at the approach of Radcliffe-Brown, who sought an understanding of this subject by looking at *social sanctions,* which he defines as follows:

> A sanction is a reaction on the part of a society or of a considerable number of its members to a mode of behaviour which is thereby approved (positive sanctions) or disapproved (negative sanctions).   (1952: 205)

The standards of behaviour by which people judge one another are based on the norms of that society, ideas of right and wrong, which are learned early, as we discussed in Chapter 2. These may be highly complicated, however, and quite situationally specific. Indeed in some societies the situation may be a more important consideration than any absolute rules, as is sometimes argued for Japan. To take an example which will be recognisable in most societies, there is usually a rule or law against killing another human being. However, under certain circumstances this rule may be broken. In most societies, war is a sufficient excuse, though its definition may vary; in some societies, vengeance, 'honour killings' or the legal retribution of capital punishment is accepted; and in Japan – as well as certain fundamentalist religious groups – people are sometimes admired ... for, and helped in ... taking their own lives.

In any society it is possible to learn about the norms which people share by observing the sanctions which come into play to encourage some kinds of behaviour and discourage others, and Radcliffe-Brown drew up a system for classifying these, which we will shortly consider. It must also be remembered, however, that different members of any one society will have somewhat differing views, and the degree to which variation is tolerated is another aspect of this subject of social control. In some societies, it is possible to live quite an idiosyncratic life; in others the leeway is far less broad. The examination of sanctions is not so good at identifying this kind of range of acceptance, or, indeed, the possibility of contested norms within one society.

The second approach we will consider can be more effective in this respect. Laid out in detail by Simon Roberts in his book *Order and Dispute* (1979), there are some areas of overlap with looking at sanctions, as we will see, but Roberts decided to focus on the resolution of disputes. He starts with the assumption we made above, that there must be order in any society, and he also takes as given that disputes are inevitable. His interest is in the variety of methods which come into play to resolve them, and we will examine these in some detail. In our third example, we will turn to a collection of papers which considers actual disputes from a detailed ethnographic perspective (Caplan 1995), and here we will encounter the ability to detect contested norms in a specific case.

Sanctions

Radcliffe-Brown drew up a very useful list of different types of sanctions which come into play as part of the regulation of social behaviour. He first made an important distinction between *positive* and *negative* sanctions, helping us to identify some of the positive forces for action which are present in any society, but particularly in places like Japan and Melanesia where a strong emphasis on harmony discourages open disputes. These positive sanctions include

sanction - a reaction on the part of a society or of a considerable number of its members to a mode of behaviour which is thereby approved (positive sanctions) or disapproved (negative sanctions).

material rewards such as prizes, titles and decorations, but they also include things less easy to define such as the good opinion of neighbours and workmates, prestige and status within the community, and general support and success in social activities.

Negative sanctions are those which form some kind of penalty for stepping out of line, for behaving in a way which is unacceptable to members of the wider society. These include definite, regulated punishments such as the fines and prison sentences meted out by courts of law, and those of other constituted organisations such as the Church, which may defrock a priest, or excommunicate a parishioner, and professional bodies which may strike off a medical or legal practitioner. They also include more spontaneous expressions of disapproval through gossip, avoidance and ridicule within the local community. Radcliffe-Brown's second distinction, between *organised* and *diffuse* sanctions, corresponds to these two extreme sets of examples, as well as to the different types of positive sanctions mentioned above.

Organised sanctions are characteristic of large-scale, anonymous societies, but diffuse ones are found amongst any group of people who live in face-to-face contact. They are particularly effective in small-scale societies where it is difficult for people to move away if they fall out with their neighbours, for these are people whom one must meet constantly. In an agricultural or horticultural society, where a good deal of time and effort has been invested in the cultivation of land, they are strong, but they work effectively amongst the employees of large companies in industrial society too, if people want to keep their positions. In practice, sanctions may fall on a continuum between the highly organised at one end and the totally spontaneous at the other in almost any situation. Let us look at a few examples.

Japanese people discussing their own society often turn to the cultivation of rice as an explanation for the strong emphasis on harmony and cooperation, for much mutual support is necessary for a successful crop. The fields must be flooded when the rice seedlings are planted out, and complicated irrigation networks have been built up over the years to ensure this process. However, the water supply must be shared out, so villages work to a rota, and families used to help one another to do the planting, and later the harvesting, to gain maximum advantage from the period when they are allocated sufficient water, on the one hand, and when the ears ripen, on the other. Now that there are machines to do many of the tasks, it is not so vital to share out these roles, but people still turn to this process to explain the cooperative nature of Japanese society.

The most severe sanction which could be brought into play in a Japanese village, especially during the premodern period when it was forbidden to move from one part of the country to another, was called *mura-hachibu*. This means 'village eighth-part' and it restricts neighbourly cooperation to the bare minimum required for the family to survive, which is seen as one-eighth of the usual level. Otherwise, members of the whole household could be totally ostracised. No one was to speak to anyone concerned, not even the children, and no one was to invite members of the family to participate in village meetings, celebrations or festivals. Personal events such as birth, marriage and death would receive none of the usual support; indeed arranging a marriage with such a family would be well-nigh impossible. This was a highly organised sanction, arranged by the village assembly and limited to a specific period, after which the offending behaviour would supposedly be curtailed, although the only case I know personally involved the expression of disapproval about the building of a factory, which is in fact still in place.

Ostracism may also be a much more diffuse sanction, of course, and the avoidance of a person who has offended in some way is a common occurrence in many societies. In English, there is an expression, 'sending to Coventry', which is a relatively organised arrangement made by some people to cut off communication with another. The expression probably dates back to the historical decision of the people of Coventry (in Warwickshire) to pull their curtains and look away when the unpopular King of Mercia's wife, Lady Godiva, was forced to ride around the streets naked to achieve the pardon she had sought for some local prisoners. In the Irish film *Ryan's Daughter*, there are impressive scenes where a family was ostracised because of the association of their daughter with a British soldier.

House-burning is another sanction which may be more or less organised. In the Highlands and Islands of Scotland, where it was for long the custom to close down all forms of business on Sundays, including cafés, restaurants and even bed-and-breakfast establishments, to all those who were not booked in on the Saturday, a few places were mysteriously burnt to the ground when they began to try and alter the custom. No one was arrested, and the police could find no witnesses. Word had it that the fires were clearly 'an act of God'. Opposition to the opening of businesses on a Sunday is still strong in the Island of Lewis, and an article that appeared in the *Stornaway Gazette* in August 2006 reported that a man who had planned to open a convenience store on Sunday in the community of Bragar on the west coast of the island changed his mind on receiving a message direct from the Almighty (see website below).

In the almost abandoned village of Hampton Gay, just outside Oxford, a ruined house is said to stand witness to a similar occurrence (see Photograph 9.1). Local people say that the nineteenth-century occupants were extremely angry when their peace was shattered by the coming of the railway, which ran very close to the house. When an accident took place nearby, and nine railway carriages fell into the river, it is said that they refused to open their doors to help the injured, and they would lend no blankets to keep them warm. The house burnt down some time later. Historical records show that the fire actually happened several years after the accident, so the stories relating the events may be apocryphal, but their existence can in itself be seen as a potential form of social control, expressing shock at such selfish and unsympathetic behaviour.

A third kind of more-or-less diffuse sanction is of a type described by Radcliffe-Brown as *satirical*, usually involving some kind of public mockery. In the same film, *Ryan's Daughter*, the British soldier's woman has her beautiful hair cut off in a manner reminiscent of the 'tarring and feathering' practised in earlier times. A custom known in part of Spain as the *vito* brings neighbours round to sing abuse outside the house of a person of whom they disapprove, typically for a transgression of a sexual nature, such as adultery (see Pitt-Rivers 1971: 169–77). A similar custom in rural England is known as 'loud-shouting' or 'rough music'

Photograph 9.1 The ruined house at Hampton Gay, near Oxford (photograph: Joy Hendry).

(Thompson 1991: 467–533) – and some evening-class students I taught in rural Oxfordshire described singing repeatedly: 'We know you're in there' outside the house of an adulterous couple of whom they all roundly disapproved. Under these circumstances, in an English village, the recalcitrant(s) may see such a display as unreasonable, but if they want to stay together, their only option would probably be to move out of the community.

Fear of such unpleasant sanctions is an even more powerful force for social control in countries where the avoidance of ridicule and laughter is tied up with strong values of honour and shame. An excellent ethnographic example of this situation is to be found in an article by Juliet du Boulay (1976), about rural Greece, where she analysed in some detail the relationship between mockery as a force for social control and the use of lies to conceal misdemeanour in the maintenance of family honour in the community where she worked.

Social relations in the community were characterised by competition between different families over wealth and reputation, and people constantly sought faults in others apparently in order to maintain their own relative superiority:

> On discovery of some offence, the discoverer immediately relates it to his or her friends and relations, and in no time at all the story is all round the village and everyone is, as they say, 'laughing' (velame). The more serious or ludicrous the offence is, the more people mock the principals of it. The more they laugh, the more the victims of the laughter are humiliated, because the chief ingredient of laughter is lack of respect, and it is this above all that is the enemy of reputation and self-esteem ... Mockery, therefore, may be said to work through shame to preserve honour.
> (1976: 394–5)

Clearly nobody can be perfect at all times, however, and as a form of defence in this hostile environment, the local people used lies in a systematic way to protect their reputations. Du Boulay identified no fewer than eight different kinds of lies, and she makes very clear that some forms of lying are not only tacitly accepted, but almost expected, especially when they become opposed to betraying another family member. Others are quite taboo, however, and understanding the system is evidently an important aspect of the maintenance of honour. As du Boulay puts it:

> Because the reputation for which everyone strives is something which is given by the community, this reputation, and, in the last extreme, honour itself, in a very literal sense only has reality if the rest of the community grants it that reality ... it is [thus] more important to be thought to be in the right than it is actually to be in the right, and ... deceit comes to be regarded as an indispensable element in social relations ... Deceit, therefore, and the avoidance of public mockery, appear as phenomena ultimately connected with the structure of the value system and as part of the legitimate means by which the honour of a family is preserved and the prosperity of a house maintained.   (Ibid. 405–6)

This value system may be quite difficult to understand for those brought up in a society where frankness and honesty are granted high value, though they may think nothing of telling a 'white lie' in a social situation where 'politeness' is called for. 'Lies' are assigned negative value in many societies which have a high regard for diplomacy, but most peoples have acceptable forms of indirect communication which could also be described as a type of deceit. We will return to this subject in the next chapter, but du Boulay's paper is an interesting examination of these issues as well as providing a good example of mockery as a form of social control. Some other ethnography from Mediterranean societies illustrates more broadly how these kinds of values play out in everyday life (see, for example, Pitt Rivers 1971; Herzfeld 1985; Cowan 1990; Sutton, 1998; Just 2000).

Radcliffe-Brown also talked of *religious and ritual sanctions* which depend on a system of belief. Some people avoid certain types of behaviour because of the fear that ancestral ghosts will take retribution, others may regulate their lives in a way conducive to a favourable position in a life after death. The terrible threats of hell preached in Christian, Muslim and Buddhist faiths alike are certainly strong forces for social control, as are the positive images of heaven and 'nirvana', and here a further distinction is made between 'immediate' and 'delayed' sanctions. In many societies, illness and other misfortunes are put down to the wrath of god(s), spirits or ancestors, as we saw in the last chapter, and it is the role of priests, shamans and other mediums to intercede and find ways to make retribution.

The reciprocal principle which may underpin such recourse is also to be found in economic sanctions, which were picked out by Malinowski as particularly important because they were often related to survival. In the Trobriand Islands, people are careful to get on with their neighbours because they are involved in the exchange of goods essential to their diet, he argued, and this must be the most important sanction of all. The 'do as you would be done by' principle is part of many forms of religious and moral dogma, although it may not always be practised. Nor are economic sanctions always effective, as we see from time to time when countries express disapproval of one another by cutting off certain supplies, or by boycotting goods. A worldwide avoidance of French wine and other goods had no effect whatsoever on nuclear testing in the Pacific, but its avoidance again in the USA when France refused to support the invasion of Iraq apparently caused some hardship (McCartney 2003).

Reciprocal principles may be useful in bringing about a neutralisation of the infringement of rules and norms of society. The payment of compensation may go some way towards appeasing an angry customer, or a person hurt by another, although in litigious cultures monetary demands for every small misfortune has also been described as more of an act of opportunism on the part of eager lawyers. In some societies a recognised form of 'blood-money' is paid in the case of murder, and there are also all sorts of ritual ways of cleansing people and bringing them back into the fold, as it were. Many peoples have some way or other of giving their recalcitrants a second chance, as long as they appear to be sorry for what they have done, and in Japan, judges try to bring about reconciliation between parties to a dispute, rather than deciding clearly who is right and wrong. This undoubtedly again reflects the emphasis on maintaining, where possible, a harmonious front for social relations.

Order and Dispute

Simon Robert (1979) takes a slightly different approach to the subject of social control, as we outlined above, and his focus is on possible reactions to *dispute*. He assumes it to be inevitable that disputes will arise in any society, and he identifies different types of reaction which come into play. Of course, the expression of dispute will vary from one society to another too, but this is something we will leave until the last section of the chapter. Here, Roberts is concerned with 'legal anthropology', or the reactions he sees as in some way equivalent to or comparable with the exercise of law. However, he is at pains to point out that there may be quite different ways of keeping order, which involve nothing like the application of law, and his aim is to seek these mechanisms.

The first he discusses is the permitted exercise of *interpersonal violence*. Here, the principle is very often the reciprocal one, discussed above, where a limited amount of interpersonal violence is seen as an appropriate response to the suffering of the same. Thus, vengeance is approved in some societies, although usually only up to the limit of the hurt received, as in an 'eye for an eye, a tooth for a tooth'. Of course, in practice, the side suffering the vengeance may perceive things quite differently from the side meting it out, and the continuation of such disputes into a long-term feud between groups is not at all uncommon. Indeed it forms the stuff of well-known dramas such as *Romeo and Juliet* and *West Side Story*, and it may underpin a wider political system, as we will see in the next chapter when we consider the Nuer people of the Southern Sudan.

In some cases, an organised arrangement of interpersonal violence may divert attention from the original object of the dispute and bring about a resolution. In New Guinea, among the Minj-Wahgi people, for example, Roberts describes an institution known as the *tagba boz*, which involves men from two opposing sides lining up, clasping their hands behind their backs, and kicking at each other's shins until one side withdraws. Another example was reported to be found among several Inuit groups (still called Eskimo in the Roberts text, but see the website listed below for a more recent Inuit comment, and Photograph 9.2), who would either sit opposite one another and engage in head-butting, or stand up and deliver straight-arm blows to each other's heads. In either case, the battle continues until one side falls over.

In case this sounds uncivilised behaviour, the reader might like to consider the dawn duel between gentlemen, or the trenches of The First World War, as ways of resolving quarrels in Europe. In the cases cited by Roberts, on the other hand:

An essential feature of controlled conflict of this kind is that there are recognised conventions which delimit the struggle, and ideally have the effect of preventing death or serious injury on either side ... thus making continuous and escalating violence unlikely. (1979: 59)

There is an element of ritualisation of the dispute in these cases, but a complete representation of the violence forms a second type of reaction which Roberts calls *channelling conflict into ritual*. Another good example he gives is also taken from Inuit societies, where a song contest allows both sides to enunciate their grievances at a public gathering, but only through the medium of song and dance. After each side has exhausted itself in hurling as much melodious abuse as it can at the other, one party apparently usually emerges in receipt of greater public acclaim, but in any case each has had plenty of opportunity to get the problem off their chests. A similar practice is reportedly found amongst the Tiv people of Nigeria.

The practice of sport may be seen to some extent as a ritual form of channelling conflict, for it allows in the same way representatives of two opposing groups to exercise skills in the enactment of a battle. People living in neighbouring towns and villages very often build up resentment against each other, and a weekly sporting event allows the expression of competition between them usually

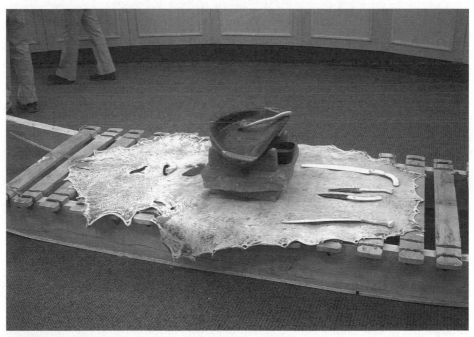

Photograph 9.2 The new Canadian province of Nunavut has a large majority of Inuit population, and the Legislative Assembly likewise was 85% Inuit control in 2005, and rising. Decisions about dispute resolution are therefore now in a state of flux again. The objects in this photograph – all essential to Inuit life in the past – have pride of place in the centre of the Assembly hall.

to be carried out in a controlled fashion. Of course, *interpersonal violence* may still break out, and it could be argued that the sporting event incites this violence, but such a breakdown of control is then subject to considerable censure on the part of the wider society. When the popular footballer Eric Cantona crossed 'the magic line' dividing the field and the fans to kick a member of the audience who shouted abuse at him in 1995, he was punished severely and roundly condemned, even by his own supporters (see website).

A side-effect of the Inuit-type song contest is that it makes public all the aspects of a misdemeanour, which may well shame the guilty party into future compliance, and it is this *shaming* which forms Roberts's third type of reaction to dispute. He cites various examples, but one of them, the public harangue, will illustrate the point. In parts of New Guinea, a person who feels he has been mistreated will stand at his door, usually in the middle of the night or very early in the morning, and simply deliver a harangue against the person or persons he believes responsible. The villages are compact enough, and the night sufficiently silent, for all to hear clearly what is said. The response is typically absolute silence, the guilty party to be found 'with his head bowed under the imagined stare of the whole community' (Roberts 1979: 62, quoting from Young 1971: 125).

The next two types of response discussed by Roberts are very similar to examples of sanctions cited by Radcliffe-Brown, namely the appeal to *supernatural agencies*, and *ostracism*. The latter we have already discussed in some detail, and Roberts gives further examples of the principles involved. The former includes consideration of societies which hold ideas about **witchcraft** and **sorcery**, which were the subject matter of our last chapter. Where misfortune of one sort or another is put down to witchcraft or sorcery, the response either involves identifying the witch or practising retaliatory sorcery. Various ordeals may be administered to suspected witches, as they were in Europe, and very often the ordeal itself becomes a punishment if the person accused is proved guilty. In West Africa, for example, an accused person is made to drink a concoction prepared with the poisonous bark of the Sasswood tree. If they vomit and survive, they are pronounced innocent. If they die, they were clearly guilty.

The last type of dispute resolution discussed by Roberts is *talking*, and this common form of response he considers under three further headings, namely *bilateral negotiation*, *mediation*, and *umpires*. In the first case, the two parties concerned address one another directly, to air and try to iron out their differences; in the second case a third party becomes involved, perhaps to carry the grievances to and fro between them, or to set up a meeting. The role of the mediator is to ease communication and to advise, but if a third party is engaged to make a decision about the dispute, this Roberts classifies as being an *umpire*. He also distinguishes two types of umpire, the first an *arbitrator*, who is someone the disputants ask to make a decision on their behalf; the second an *adjudicator*, a person who already holds authority in the society concerned.

The last case will, of course, cover most systems of courts, where the judge and jury play the roles of umpire, but we should remember that the punishment they mete out for a misdemeanour may represent forms of the other types of response discussed above. Imprisonment is an example of formal ostracism, for example, and capital and corporal punishment are clearly examples of interpersonal violence, though this time removed from the disputants themselves and carried out by the wider, impersonal state. Nor are courts confined to industrial societies. In small-scale communities, there may be formal trials for those accused of misdemeanour, and the classic work of Max Gluckman (1955) is an excellent illustration of such a case.

In a monograph entitled *The Judicial Process among the Barotse of Northern Rhodesia* (now Zimbabwe), Gluckman analysed the processes used by this Indigenous people, identifying and illustrating concepts parallel to English notions invoked in legal situations, and describing methods used in the examination of crimes, the interviewing of witnesses, and the application of the notion of 'a reasonable man'. Another classic work is that of Paul Bohannan (1957), in his book *Justice and Judgement among the Tiv*, about a Nigerian people, which emphasises the motives and rationale of the individuals involved rather than the overall structure of the system which comes into play. A recent issue among Indigenous peoples in different parts of the world is that they resent having their own legal systems, which they regard as perfectly fair, sidelined by a national system which they feel (probably with some justice) treats them unfairly.

Contested Norms and Social Control in a Context

A collection of papers, entitled *Understanding Disputes: The Politics of Argument* (ed. Caplan 1995), examines in various contexts the work of a man, Philip Gulliver, who spent much of his life observing *disputes*. The papers move from national disputes over access to water sources, through 'gentlemanly values' in two sets of political circles, to family wrangles over failed marriages, intra-family strife about death and funerals, and concepts of passion and compassion. The contexts considered are also extremely various, and the reader is introduced to discrepant values in locations as far apart as nineteenth- and twentieth-century Ireland, rural Nepal, London, Lagos, and more specific African locations in Kenya, Tanzania and Uganda.

Some of the broader themes covered include discussion of a move from judicial institutions to negotiation as the more 'civilised' means of dispute resolution, including a realisation that both these systems still favour the more powerful partner, despite ostensible efforts to incorporate approaches previously more characteristic of weaker peoples. There are also examples of resistance, and some of these illustrate the ways different parties draw on different values and methods of approach, just like the situation of colonised Indigenous peoples mentioned above.

An excellent example is a paper by Stephen Gaetz about disputes between the leaders and members of an Irish youth club, where the latter resort to violence because they feel excluded from decision making. The leaders respond to this plea by setting up committee meetings, and then can't understand why the youths don't turn up, or fail to air their views. From the point of view of the youths, who have no experience of committees and little confidence that they would make a difference, these are just another way for the leaders to exert their authority. Here the important point is illustrated that the disputing *process* may be more significant than any resolution.

Most of the papers follow Gulliver's emphasis on understanding the political and historical context of any dispute and 'categories of meaning by which the participants themselves comprehend their experience'. Sometimes the parties to a dispute do not even share these categories of meaning, and each seeks to manipulate the situation to suit their own understanding. In another case, the same people under different circumstances may invoke different sets of norms. Pat Caplan shows how the three sets of Islamic law, Tanzanian law and local custom available in Mafia Island, Tanzania, where she did her fieldwork, make possible a continual negotiation of rules and behaviour, allowing a situation of contested norms to be counterpoised to relations of unequal power. Those who are at ease with the three possibilities have a distinct advantage over those who know only one.

In this detailed discussion of a specific long-term dispute, Pat Caplan, who is also the editor of the papers, illustrates her contention at the start of the book that the study of disputes leads us:

> straight to the key issues in anthropology – norms and ideology, power, rhetoric and oratory, personhood and agency, morality, meaning and interpretation – and enables us not only to see social relations in action but also to understand cultural systems. (1995: 1)

What her paper also illustrates very nicely is the fluidity of norms, and their manipulative possibilities, an issue we raised in the introduction to this chapter.

Attempts to classify responses to dispute, and sanctions which come into play, are extremely useful in the understanding of methods of social control which people exercise upon one another in different parts of the world. The work of anthropologists is particularly valuable for a deep understanding of the constraints which inform the organisation of undisputed life, for it is only with long-term observations that strongly held, underlying forces of influence may be identified and evaluated. It is a pity that the governments of politically powerful countries do not take into account the work of their own anthropological experts in particular parts of the world, alongside that of their economists, before they make decisions about dealing with, and especially invading, other countries. As I wrote the second edition of this book, the situation in Iraq and other war-torn countries of the Middle East was clear testament to decades of misunderstanding of local issues on the part of the leaders of the big economies who think they should make decisions on behalf of the world.

In my own study of Japan, a focus on child-rearing methods revealed some of the complicated mechanisms of peer pressure which profoundly affect the lives of Japanese adults and the decisions they make about how to behave. One of the overt aims of kindergarten education, for example, is to inculcate an understanding of the way that subordinating self-interest to the needs of a wider group will have long-term benefits for all involved. Teachers use various means to encourage children to discipline one another in this endeavour, thus imparting a principle which underpins the success of the whole education system and later working life. Two books by the Japanese anthropologist Emiko Ohnuki-Tierney (2002, 2006) reveal a lot about the way this kind of upbringing filtered through into the behaviour of the so-called *kamikaze* pilots of the Second World War, revealed by their diaries to be frightened but compliant young lads, intelligent but obedient – in fact, the cream of a generation.

The present good relations between Japan and the powerful countries of the West are of course related to the country's postwar economic success, but I would like to think that the work Ruth Benedict carried out in the internment camps where Japanese citizens of the Allied countries were held during the Second World War – mentioned in the Introduction to this volume – might have influenced the Occupation policies and hence laid the foundations for them. Likewise, I suggest that the work of some of the anthropologists who have studied in Japan, both insiders and outsiders, contributes to continuing cooperation. Certainly, one of my former students has established an organisation with the specific aim of helping to 'defuse and prevent ethnic and religious conflict' (see www.oicd.net for further details).

We end this chapter by looking at a book that focuses on social control in a particular society, and which approaches it from an angle which might not at first have been anticipated. In *Power and Persuasion*, subtitled *Fiestas and Social Control in Rural Mexico*, Stanley Brandes (1988) examines in minute detail the events and processes leading up to annual festivals which find the villagers relaxing in a frenzy of fun and fireworks. The villagers almost certainly enjoy themselves, for each fiesta is a culmination of months of arrangements and planning, financing, purchasing and allocation of tasks, and the successful accomplishment of the various elements of the event demonstrate that things in the village are operating in an orderly fashion.

Various aspects of the moral universe are played out during the course of a festival, and power relationships are expressed in the relative financial contributions made by each household in the village to the huge pyrotechnic displays of material wealth and influence. Masked figures in a dance performance known as 'La Danza' portray in symbolic form the system of religious and moral values which underpin social life. They break normal social rules in the way they dance, but the figures they portray, like Death and the Devil, are so abhorrent that Brandes argues that they actually exert and demonstrate a strong force for social control.

Fiestas in general are expected to find people reversing the expectations of normal everyday life, and turning upside down the moral system. This they do, but their production offers an excellent window on the workings of social and political relations within the village. In Brandes' words:

> To be successful, fiestas of all types depend on two predictable circumstances: cooperation among leaders and order among the participants. When a fiesta is over, and both order and cooperation have prevailed, villagers know that their society is intact. Perhaps the constant threat of disorder and uncooperativeness ... actually keeps the whole fiesta cycle in motion, as people demand periodic affirmation of cooperation and social control. (1988:165)

Conclusion

In another location, the details might be different. We have now seen several examples of approaches identified by anthropologists as important for understanding systems of social control. We have looked at witchcraft among the Azande, shamanism among the Akawaio, marriage in Japan and fiestas in Mexico. The anthropologists concerned could possibly have chosen a different focus and come up with something equally interesting, but they could not easily have anticipated all that they would find before they got to the field. Unearthing a system of social control is a long-term endeavour, but it is a satisfying one, and it is one which demonstrates the value of the kind of qualitative research anthropologists engage in.

Discussion Questions

1 Think about constraints again. What or who makes you adjust your behaviour, or avoid certain activities? What are the positive influences in your life? Can you relate these to general norms and values in your society?

2 Under what circumstances would you consider it acceptable to tell a lie? What would be your motivation? Would your peers approve of your actions? What about other members of your society?

3 Think about Roberts's various methods of solving disputes. What would work best in situations in your own life? Have you any others to add to his list?

Reference and Further Research

Books:

Alia, Valerie (2007) *Naming and Nunavut: Culture and Identity in Arctic Canada* (Oxford: Berghahn).

Bohannan, Paul (1989[1957]) *Justice and Judgement among the Tiv* (Prospect Heights: Waveland Press.

Brandes, Stanley (1988) *Power and Persuasion: Fiestas and Social Control in Rural Mexico* (Philadelphia: University of Pennsylvania Press).

Caplan, Pat (ed.) (1995) *Understanding Disputes: The Politics of Argument* (Oxford: Berg).

Cowan, Jane K. (1990) *Dance and the Body Politic in Northern Greece* (Princeton, NJ: Princeton University Press).

Desjarlais, R. (1997) *Shelter Blues* (Pittsburgh: University of Pennsylvania Press).

Gluckman, Max (1955) *The Judicial Process among the Barotse of Northern Rhodesia* (Manchester: Manchester University Press).

Herzfeld, Michael (1985) *The Poetics of Manhood: Contest and Identity in a Cretan Mountain Village* (Princeton, NJ: Princeton University Press).

Just, Roger (2000) *A Greek Island Cosmos: Kinship Community on Meganisi* (Oxford: James Currey Publishers).

Moore, Sally Falk (1978) *Law as Process: An Anthropological Approach* (London: Routledge & Kegan Paul).

Nader, Laura and Todd, Harry F. (1978) *The Disputing Process: Law in Ten Societies* (New York: Columbia University Press).

Ohnuki-Tierney, Emiko (2002) *Kamikaze, Cherry Blossoms and Nationalisms: The Militarization of Aesthetics in Japanese History* (Chicago: University of Chicago Press).

Ohnuki-Tierney, Emiko (2006) *Kamikaze Diaries: Reflections of Japanese Student Soldiers* (Chicago: University of Chicago Press).

Pitt-Rivers, Julian A. (1971) *The People of the Sierra* (Chicago: University of Chicago Press).

Roberts, Simon (1979) *Order and Dispute* (Harmondsworth: Pelican Books).

Sutton, David (1998) *Memories Cast in Stone* (Oxford and New York: Berg).

Thompson, E. P. (1991) *Customs in Common* (London: Penguin Books).

Young, Michael (1971) *Fighting with Food* (Cambridge: Cambridge University Press).

Articles

Bazin, Laurent, Gibb, Robert, Neveu, Catherine and Selim, Monique (2006) 'The Broken Myth: Popular Unrest and the "Republican Model of Integration" in France', *Anthropology Today*, 22(2).

Bergsma, Harold M. (1970) 'Tiv Proverbs as a Means of Social Control', *Africa: Journal of the International African Institute*, 40(2) 151–63.

du Boulay, Juliet (1976) 'Lies, Mockery and Family Integrity', in J. G. Peristiany (ed.), *Mediterranean Family Structures* (Cambridge: Cambridge University Press).

Cohen, Abner (1980) 'Drama and Politics in the Development of the London Carnival', *Man* 15: 65–87.

Gaetz, Stephen (1995) ' "Youth Development" : Conflict and Negotiation in an Urban Irish Youth Club', in Pat Caplan (ed.), *Understanding Disputes* (Oxford: Berg), pp. 181–201.

Goldschmidt, Walter, Foster, Mary Lecron, Rubenstein, Robert A. and Silverberg, James (1986) 'Anthropology and Conflict', *Anthropology Today* (special issue on Anthropology and Conflict), 2(1).

Gulliver, P. (1969) 'Dispute Settlement without Court: The Ndendeuli of Southern Tanzania' in L. Nader (ed.), *Law in Culture and Society* (Chicago: Aldine).

McCartney, Robert J. (2003) 'US Boycott being felt, French say', *Washington Post*, 16 April, p. A32.

McNamara, Sean Cush (1986) 'Learning How to Bribe a Policeman', *Anthropology Today*, 2(2): 2–3.

Radcliffe-Brown, A. R. (1952) 'Social Sanctions', in *Structure and Function* (London: Cohen & West).

Roberts, Simon (1994) 'Law and Dispute Processes', in T. Ingold (ed.), *Humanity, Culture and Social Life* (London: Routledge & Kegan Paul).

Novels

Blythe, Ronald (1972) *Akenfield* (Harmondsworth: Penguin Books) is a detailed historical account of life in a medieval English village.

Gulik, Robert van (1989) *The Chinese Maze Murders* (London: Sphere Books) is a series of detective stories which demonstrate the value of an understanding of indirect and non-verbal cues, rather in the manner of Sherlock Holmes, but in a more openly culturally specific mode.

Kafka, Frank (2004[1925]) *The Trial* (London: Vintage Classics) is a story about a man who is arrested and tried, although he is not told what his crime is. It is about the power of bureaucracy.

Mo, Timothy (1990) *Sour Sweet* (London: Hodder & Stoughton) is a novel about a Chinese family that settles in Britain, and the social constraints they experience, more from the Chinese community than the wider British one.

Nafisi, Azar (2004) *Reading Lolita in Tehran* (London: Fourth Estate).

Orwell, George (2000[1949]) *1984* (London: Penguin Classics) is a novel about a totalitarian state, seen as the future when it was written in 1949.

Ouzo, Mario (1969) *The Godfather* (Greenwich, Conn.: Fawcett Publications) is a classic novel about the social control exercised among members of Sicilian/American mafia groups.

Films

Atanarjuat: The Fast Runner is a 2002 Inuit-produced film, directed by Zacharias Kanuk, which depicts a legend that at the same time illustrates Inuit mechanisms of social control.

Divorce Iranian Style (Kim Longinotto and Ziba Mir-Hosseini, 80 minutes, 1998). This documentary film, set in the Family Law Courts in central Tehran, concentrates on ordinary women who come to this court to try and transform their lives.

The Lives of Others (*Das Leben der Anderen*) is an originally German feature film (by Henckel von Donnersmarck, Florian), which illustrates state control of East Germany through secret service observation of the detail of its citizens' lives.

The two 'Disappearing World' films, *The Mehinacu* (Carlos Pasini and Thomas Gregor, 1974), about a people of the Brazilian rain forest, and *The Kirghiz of Afghanistan* (Charlie Nairn and Nazif Shahrani, 1976), about a people virtually imprisoned on a mountain top between Russia and China, which they may not legally enter, both illustrate aspects of social control discussed in this chapter.

Romeo and Juliet and *West Side Story*.

Ryan's Daughter is David Lean's 1970 film which tells the story of an Irish girl who has an affair with a British soldier during the First World War.

Sisters in Law is a 2005 Cameroonian documentary film, directed by Kim Longinotto and Florence Ayisi, about the everyday work of a female judge dispensing justice in her own way in a small town in Cameroon.

Websites

http://www.stornowaygazette.co.uk/ViewArticle.aspx?SectionID=2629&articleid=1668591 – an article in the local newspaper on the Island of Lewis about Sunday trading.

http://www.erudit.org/revue/etudinuit/2002/v26/n1/009271ar.pdf – a detailed discussion about a workshop held with Inuit Elders on the subject of social problems and social control.

http://news.bbc.co.uk/onthisday/hi/dates/stories/january/27/newsid_2506000/2506237. stm – reports on the severity of the reaction to Eric Cantona's crossing of the line.

10

The Art of Politics

Political Possibilities

It was pointed out in the introduction to the last chapter that it is not always possible to make a clear distinction between the concepts of 'law' and 'politics', but our discussions there fell more into the realms of 'law' than politics. However, we took pains to broaden our approach to include mechanisms of social control which could hardly be described as legal, even in the broadest sense of the word, although our approach was certainly not confined to societies which have no overarching legal system. In this chapter we will turn to areas more usually associated with what the English language might term 'politics', though again the reader must be prepared to have a broad and flexible mind. We will start with the internationally familiar, however, but we will move gradually into examples of societies whose political systems, if we may call them such, were at first quite impenetrable to observers from outside nations.

Much of the early work in the area of political anthropology was carried out by anthropologists in a colonial situation, itself a prime example of the ruthless exercise of power, which is still a topic of concern in the field, especially in former colonies where Indigenous people are now trying to reclaim their lands. Ethnographers were inevitably caught up with helping their own governments to maintain order in unfamiliar circumstances, although they may also have found themselves acting as advocates for the people they came to know better than any other outsider, and even taking a critical stance towards the colonial rule. At the time, they were dependent on the goodwill of the local administrators for their continued presence in a fieldwork location, however, and their positions were at best ambiguous.

The influential early British examples of local political systems were African, and they were classified under two main headings, namely *centralised* and acephalus (Fortes and Evans-Pritchard 1940). The first were known as kingships, with relatively stable hierarchical units, and the second were 'headless', the Greek meaning of the term. Two famous anthropological studies which are cited to illustrate these types are again by Evans-Pritchard, both of peoples of the Sudan. The first, the Shilluk, exemplify a kingship, and the Nuer people of Southern Sudan have been held up as a model for the second, acephalus type. We will discuss both cases so that the reader will become aware of the base line in this area of the field.

acephalus (literally, 'headless') **political system** – a system without any easily recognisable head or system of hierarchy.

kingship – a centralised system of hierarchy, not necessarily responsible for political activity, in which the holders of high rank have a status and authority that were compared by European anthropologists with their own systems of monarchy.

As ethnographic material became available from different parts of the world, however, it became clear that these two approaches were actually better described as opposing ends of a continuum of types of political system, with interesting and sometimes rather recognisable cases in the middle. We will consider some cases from the Latin American rain forest as an example of the middle ground, in a section entitled 'leadership', but we could have chosen to look at people from any number of other locations for all these sections. It is a good exercise to read a complete ethnography to get a feel for the intricacies of a particular political system, and the books at the end of the chapter by Ahmed, Barth, Maybury-Lewis, Leach and Strathern are a few excellent examples.

This chapter is named 'the art of politics' in deference to the stunning ingenuity of human beings in creating and manipulating relations of *power* and authority in a rich variety of ways in different parts of the world, so after the examination of classic political 'types' we turn to consider some of this variety and ingenuity at the level of human interaction. The importance is noted again of guarding against carrying assumptions about behaviour from one political system to another, particularly where the unspoken is almost as important as the spoken word. By its very nature politics often involves disputed ideas of the type we discussed towards the end of the last chapter, and anthropologists are well placed to contribute to this arena too (see, for example, Shore 1990).

In the end this chapter must be a cursory glance at a huge subject, for political science forms an academic discipline in its own right, and anthropologists themselves devote whole books to the political branch of their subject (for example, Balandier 1967; Bloch 1975; Godelier 1986; Gledhill 1994; Vincent 2004; Vincent and Nugent 2006), but it is useful to examine some of the findings of anthropologists in this sphere for three reasons. First, in the classic works we can identify an interesting range of ideas about the distribution of *power* in society, which may now be interpreted within the context of colonial endeavour (Gledhill is particularly good on this subject). Secondly, we can identify in all the variety some persistent themes which run through the gamut of political life, which can inform for anyone the familiar exercise of power, but with unusual twists. Thirdly, the chapter will demonstrate the importance of anthropology for seeing beyond the social science concepts of political science, which were developed along European lines and which cannot take account of the range of variety to be found in the world.

Types of Political System

Centralised systems

The political system which was most familiar to European nations setting up colonies was a centralised one with various forms of hierarchical arrangements. There are clearly a great number of possibilities for how such a system may work, but we can identify some characteristic features. First, in its most organised form, a centralised system will have a *head* at the top and layers of lesser positions with degrees of authority and dependence below that. The position of the head may be *hereditary*, and it may even have some divine qualities, or it may be filled by a person elected by the people at large. These two possibilities may seem quite different within conventional approaches to politics, but they are both part of centrally organised systems. Several countries, including Belgium, Britain, the Netherlands, Norway, Sweden and Thailand, manage to maintain both types of centralised system, as indeed does Japan, and the two types play different roles, but they are both *centralised*.

In both cases, the people indicate submission to the system, willingly or unwillingly, by paying tribute or tax, and this makes available public funds that allow for certain other possibilities, for example:

tribute – goods or other forms of wealth paid to a central person or body, which shows recognition of that body, and enables the central body to administer the public funds made available on their behalf.

- a *ruling class* with officials to carry out activities on behalf of the group;
- *protection* in times of dispute;
- *courts* for dealing with disputes;
- buildings and other *facilities* for public use;
- *feasts* and *aid* for the needy;
- *ritual* support, perhaps in dealing with spirits.

A classic example from the anthropological literature is provided by the case of the Shilluk people, who have a hereditary *kingship*, legitimated by the idea that the spirit of their god, Nyikang, passes from one king to another. The king symbolises the people and the changeless moral order, but his role is sacerdotal rather than governmental. He reigns, and others do the ruling. The Shilluk nation is divided into settlements, each with a chief and council, and further subdivided into hamlets, each with a head, usually of a lineage. Myths validate the overall hierarchy, as all can trace their descent from characters in a saga which tells of Nyikang dividing up the land on conquest. Lineage heads have ritual duties to the king, who is a mediator between man and god. He must keep ritually pure and healthy to avoid natural disaster. If he falls ill or senile, he should be killed for the sake of the people.

sacerdotal, a term meaning 'priestly', used by anthropologists to refer to the role of communicating with higher powers, such as gods and spirits, often played alongside the more mundane **governmental** role in a system of dual leadership or authority.

When colonists encountered a society such as this, they had relatively little difficulty in understanding the political arrangements, and they were able to incorporate the system under their own overarching umbrella. By respecting the king, and his entourage, for something akin to their own, they could communicate in a relatively trouble-free manner, from their point of view, though things did not always proceed smoothly, as history has taught us. The case of India is a particularly good example of where things at first fell neatly into place to provide 'the jewel in the crown' of the British Empire, but then became more complicated, as Paul Scott's 'Raj Quartet' novels made clear in an anthropologically interesting manner.

In some cases potential colonists were understandably opposed in their efforts to impose a new order, but a centralised system was relatively easy to defeat. If the head is deposed, and the new rulers observe most of the niceties of social life as far as keeping the underlying hierarchy in place, they can simply rely on existing mechanisms to impose their new regime, and this happened for centuries within Europe. This is also what happened in many cases of centralised systems elsewhere, and the pre-existing culture became gradually eroded. One well-known example is the case of the Aztec empire in precolonial Mexico, a highly organised centralised system, under the rule of the Emperor Montezuma. However, it espoused a set of beliefs which happened to see the arrival on their shores of the Spanish conquistadors as fulfilling a legend that one of their gods would return.

It was therefore relatively easy for Hernando Cortez to step into the position of supreme ruler in the Aztec court, and he and his party could set about colonising Mexico for Spain. It was not long before Aztec culture was destroyed, although many other Indigenous people remained, and there is now even a revival of Aztec customs such as dancing. This is the society we mentioned in Chapter 1 where the curtailment of the practice of human sacrifice, seen as a way to keep the gods content and the society prosperous, coincided as predicted with the end of the period of cultural supremacy. The other example of a centralised system in South America was the Inca empire and this suffered a similar fate in the country which became Peru; however, not all of South America was so easy to colonise, as we will see in the next section.

Meanwhile, the centralised case of Japan may be cited to illustrate some of the complications of the too-easy application of a 'political type' for understanding the locus of power in any situation. Although Japan has never been a colony to another power, it was occupied after defeat in the Second World War, when the Allied Forces insisted on 'democratising' the political system, already modelled on European prototypes when Japan set out to 'modernise' in the latter half of the nineteenth-century. Japan's system thus has recognisable elements such as a parliament, political parties and constituencies, as well as full adult franchise and free and fair elections. According to political observers from the outside world, this is a system they can analyse and understand.

In practice, however, in a large part Japan's system still works according to principles which pre-date even the first modernisation process. The confrontational nature of the chambers of the parliament is not a mode of communication in which decisions are easily reached in Japanese discourse; large political parties tend to operate at a factional level more reminiscent of social relations found elsewhere in Japan; and voting is not always an individual decision in a society where reciprocity and loyalty to local benefactors counts highly. This is a good example of why it is useful to examine politics in the context of a wider social system, rather than making assumptions about categories such as 'centralised', and we will return to consider some strategies for the exercise of power in the last part of this chapter.

Leadership

Amongst the peoples who inhabit the tropical rain forests of Latin America, politics is much less clear cut than the centralised systems we have sketched above. Nevertheless, their leaders have recognisable qualities and their arrangements are still open to comparison with the politics of the industrialised world. Some people become *leaders* and others are content to follow them. There are many societies we could consider here, but the work carried out by anthropologists on the Yanomamö people of Venezuela and Brazil, encountered in Chapter 3 (see also Ferguson 1995), and the Akwe Shavante, also of the Brazilian rain forest (Maybury-Lewis 1974, see website also), provide good cases for examination. The following characteristics are generally common to the area.

No Central Administration
Here is the first major difference to the societies we have been considering so far, because these peoples have no formal system of authority, and they have therefore posed many problems to the governments of the countries where they are found.

Typically, such governments will try to appoint a local chief amongst Indigenous people and work through that chief to maintain communication. They will offer remuneration to such a chief, and possibly a uniform or some other badge of office. Those who accepted such an incentive to represent their people to outside bodies very often found themselves the laughing stock of the community, however, and any pretensions to leadership they may have held before such an arrangement would soon disappear. In some areas only a person regarded locally as an idiot would contemplate such a role.

Village Autonomy

One of the reasons for this situation is the strong value placed on village autonomy in this part of the world. Leaders can come and go, and if there happened to be two in conflict within one community, the community itself might well split and redefine itself. We referred in Chapter 8 to Peter Rivière's argument about how, amongst the Trio of Surinam and the Akwe Shavante, these divisions may be initiated through sorcery accusations. Ultimately, the villagers follow a leader only as long as they see it to be in their interest, and they are not inclined at all to be dictated to by outsiders, even if the latter do try to work through their own people.

The Leaders Lead

As the word implies, leaders in this area have none of the coercive power or accepted authority of the 'chiefs' discussed in the previous section. They simply lead, and if others approve, they follow. Thus, if the leader thinks it time to clean up the central square he will start doing it, perhaps calling to his companions to join him. He has no power to instruct others to carry out such tasks for him, and if others fail to see the sense of his plan, he will be left unsupported. It is even said amongst the Akwe Shavante that they are likely to kill bossy leaders! Putting on airs would also clearly be unacceptable, and this would explain why the provision of a uniform and a salary might disrupt an otherwise effective relationship.

Environmental factors

These are undoubtedly important in the political life of these communities. This is an area where slash-and-burn cultivation is the norm among many peoples, requiring commitment to a particular patch of land for only a few years at a time. A smallish area of the forest is cleared for cultivation (see Photograph 10.1 and the First-hand Account 10 overleaf for an illustration from the Trio people of Surinam) but its nutritional value is limited so communities are small and where possible people move on regularly. The diet is supplemented with sporadic hunting and fishing, but none of these economic activities requires much managerial organisation, as was pointed out by Anthony Leeds in a consideration of the Yaruro people of south-central Venezuela:

> Given the techniques and tools of the Yaruro, all the subsistence activities ... can conveniently be done by one person. ... the logic of tools and

Photograph 10.1 Trio Indians in Surinam clear the rainforest for planting in the slash-and-burn cultivation style (photograph taken from a print in the Rivière Collection, Pitt Rivers Museum, University of Oxford, PRM 2001.33.262.4).

techniques concerned demands utilization by single persons. Activities of all sorts may be done by aggregates of persons, each utilizing his own tools and techniques individually but neither the activity, the tools nor the techniques entail the aggregation of individuals. Thus, from the point of view of human organization, the technology, by itself, entails no managerial functions, no coordination of tasks which must be overseen by someone occupying an appropriately defined status.   (1969: 383)

The major cooperative venture is choosing and clearing land and setting up a village to administer it. Decisions must be made about when and where to move, and a potential leader is able to judge his support by the response he gets to an initiative to seek a new site. The length of a longhouse, which is shared by the men in the group, is a spatial indication of a leader's support, for it will be tailored to suit the size of the community, although people can of course leave if they grow tired of a particular leader, and moving is a time for realignment, as we have seen.

The qualities required by an aspiring leader in these rain forest communities are interesting to observe, for they are mostly quite recognisable. First of all, a leader is usually an example of a successful person by local standards, so an *athletic, well-built* person who is good at hunting would be an appropriate type. A leader needs to display *generosity* with goods, and a good hunter is well placed to share his spoils as well as to attract several wives so that he can maintain a surplus of cooked food. *Oratorical skills* are admired here as elsewhere, and they are

We have a field, we have an older field and right now we are preparing a new one. We still have some cassava and cotton and sweet potatoes and bananas and sugar cane and pineapples on our oldest field. Right now we are making a new field, because it is sun time [1 November 2006] and we always plant before the rain begins to come back. We only plant once a year, then we have enough food. Pananakiri [strangers, white people] say one can plant more than once a year, but we have plenty when we do it when our field is ready.

First-hand account 10:

Merinto Taje, Tarëno (also known as Trio) – on Slash-and-Burn Cultivation in Surinam

Everybody grows cassava [i.e. bitter cassava] and corn and watermelons and bananas and different sorts of sweet potatoes and also cotton for hammocks. Close to our houses we have peppers and sometimes papayas and other fruit trees. No, we don't grow green vegetables, we are not like caterpillars [most Trio are scared to death of caterpillars]. Some people grow more watermelons or corn than others do. I always grow lots of sweet cassava, but hardly any corn.

Cutting a field is much easier for the Trio men than it used to be in the past, when the men had to cut a field in the forest with axes. Now they have chain saws and moreover they don't even need to cut the tall trees. Why? Well, since we have been living at Tepu for so many years now [since 1970], we are cutting our new fields in areas where the forest has not become real forest yet [i.e. in long-deserted fields].

This year the rainy season was very bad. Many fields were flooded for more than six days. When the flood was over, a great deal of our food was spoiled, in particular our bread [i.e. cassava]. It smelled very, very bad, because of all the dead worms that had come out of the earth and than drowned. At first the children had a lot of fun playing in the flooded village, but afterwards many of us had terrible stomach problems. Nobody died, but we were very sick indeed. There was no famine, because the higher fields came out all right and the soldiers [government, WHO] brought us lots of rice. We like rice, but we did not really need it. But when they ask: 'Are you hungry? Do you need rice?' our village leader says on our behalf: 'Yes, our cassava is spoiled and we don't have rice. So send us many bags of rice.' And that is what happened. We got many bags of rice. Rice is nice.

Some people lost all their cassava, others still had plenty. In those cases we always help others who are in need without asking for payment. And we always plant larger fields than we really need, because we know that floods may ruin part of the crops and it is not only heavy rains. Sometimes there may be enormous numbers of caterpillars that eat all the leaves of all our young cassava plants. However, the worst threats are the many, many ants that cut the cassava leaves and carry those leaves all underground.

Merinto Taje is living at Tepu, Upper-Tapanahoni (river), in the Sipaliwini District of Surinam. This text was translated and annotated [using square brackets] by Cees Koelewijn.

sometimes used in formal negotiations between villages known as ceremonial dialogue, for resolving potential disputes, as well as for trade, to arrange marriages, and so forth. These skills are also important to resolve disputes within the local group, and the skills of a *moderator, mediator* and *peace-maker* are highly regarded. Amongst the Nambikwara, for example, the word for leader is, literally, 'one who unites'.

Amongst the Akwe Shavante, who are a large enough group to be split into factions, their leaders are permanently in a state of competition over minor disputes, and their skills need to be flexible. The leader of the dominant faction at any one time may emphasise his skills of impartiality, tolerance and wisdom to maintain peace and harmony within the wider community. If threatened, he needs to be ready to become more assertive and aggressive. As Maybury-Lewis notes (using the term 'chief' for the most dominant Akwe Shavante leaders):

ceremonial dialogue – a way of transacting formal negotiations between villages for many peoples in the rain forests of Latin America, used for resolving disputes and potential disputes, as well as for trade and to arrange marriages.

> A chief is therefore in a difficult position. The qualities ideally required of him and the behaviour expected of him while he is in office are diametrically opposed to those of which he had to make use when he aspired to the chieftancy. Indeed, in a community where the dominant faction is not firmly established, they are opposed to the talents he must display in order to maintain himself in office at all ... chiefs [therefore] tend to veer from one type of behaviour to its opposite. Sometimes they handle seemingly intractable situations with great patience and forensic skill. At others they deal summarily and ruthlessly with only incipient opposition. (1974: 204)

Finally, some leaders may need to have **shamanistic** qualities, although this may be a separate but influential role. This split between the *sacerdotal* and the *governmental*, also noted above for the Shilluk, is actually found in many societies. A system found in ancient Japan, for example, held a brother and a sister at the top of the hierarchy. The sister was a religious figure in constant touch with the deities, while the brother took care of everyday political matters. The twin imperial/ governmental system still in practice in Japan evidently has ancient roots. Other contemporary monarchies become quite commonplace too in view of these examples, although the role of the monarch is usually more symbolic than religious for most people.

Other examples of leadership and how it may be acquired abound in the ethnography, but the Latin American case gives a good example of the importance of placing a particular political system in its local environmental, ecological and demographic context. This is also an area where anthropologists can hardly fail to get involved in helping the people with whom they work to represent themselves to the outside world. The rain forest habitat is constantly threatened by developers, now seeking oil as well as timber and pharmaceutical products, and anthropologists need to address questions of compatibility between the different political strategies involved in the negotiations. According to Laura Rival, an anthropologist specialising in this area:

> We need to study ethnographically how, when communities encounter the oil transnationals, they come to think in a new way and to take decisions about their futures; and how they come to abandon their self-reliant marginality as they envisage their sustainable integration into wider spheres ... We need to understand how, in the course of unequal negotiations, emerging forms of political agency are built up through the strategic use of particular rhetorical styles. Under what conditions can the abstract notion of 'equal partnership' become a reality?   (1997: 3)

The film cited below about the Kayapo people of the Altamira region of the Xingu valley, is an excellent illustration of such negotiations. Thanks to the help of an anthropologist who had worked in the area, and the film crew who helped the Kayapo to record their deals with the Brazilian authorities, the outcome was relatively positive. Others have not been so fortunate, and there is still much work to be done, according to Rival. However, there has been a successful resurgence of indigenous political power in several South American nations, most notably Bolivia, where the president Evo Morales is a member of the Aymara, a local indigenous people, so it will be interesting to see how this works out in the future.

Acephalus societies

Segmentary systems

Anthropologists from states with highly centralised political systems for a while found it difficult to understand how some African societies were organised at all.

They seemed to have very little in the way of political organisation, and yet retained order in everyday life. Detailed field research eventually revealed some of the principles underlying this order, and Evans-Pritchard made a breakthrough in describing the segmentary system of the Nuer of Southern Sudan, a people who 'hate authority', and who 'strut about like lords of the earth .... equals who regard themselves as God's noblest creation' (1940: 182). It is important in reading the description that follows to distinguish between the *ideal* system and that which operated in practice. Bear in mind also that the lives of the Nuer have been badly affected since the time of Evans-Pritchard by the continuing war in Sudan (see website below).

segmentary system – An abstraction of a social and political system, first described by Evans-Pritchard for the Nuer people of the Southern Sudan, as a 'set of structural relations between territorial segments'.

The Nuer are a cattle-keeping people who live a transhumant life, spending the dry season in camps by the rivers, when they also fish, and moving away to villages on high land, where they also grow millet, during the wet season when the river floods. They thus spend part of the year in territorially defined communities separated from each other by flooded land, and part in larger, more fluid

transhumant – a type of lifestyle spent between two distinct locations, usually related to annual changes in the climate, such as dry and wet, or hot and cold seasons.

settlements when people can move amongst each other. The basic economic unit is conceptually, or *ideally*, a group of relations who move to and fro together, but each move is also an opportunity for *political* realignment, and some members of a village may thus be together for political reasons and not in fact be related. This *territorial* unit is therefore described by Evans-Pritchard as the smallest *political segment*, which in turn belongs to larger *segments* occupying a particular region.

The whole tribe or clan is made up of people related in this way. However, Nuer men *think of themselves* very much in terms of belonging to a group which shares descent from a common ancestor. They *ideally* share living arrangements with close relatives, described by Evans-Pritchard as a minimal lineage, and carry out economic and ritual activities of various sorts with larger groups of relatives, which he describes as minor, major or maximal lineages. The largest group defined in this way is a *clan* of people ultimately descended from one founding ancestor, who is described as related to the founding ancestors of the other clans in a way that binds the whole Nuer people.

descent – unilineal descent groups – groups of people related on the basis of lineal descent from a common ancestor.

This *ideal* model is distinguished in Evans-Pritchard's description from groups which align themselves in practice into what he calls *political segments*. The smallest, the villages, belong to *tribes*, which correspond approximately to

lineage – a group of relatives based on lineal connections.

the *clans*, but they may also align themselves for particular political issues with *segments* of varying sizes, which Evans-Pritchard calls primary, secondary and

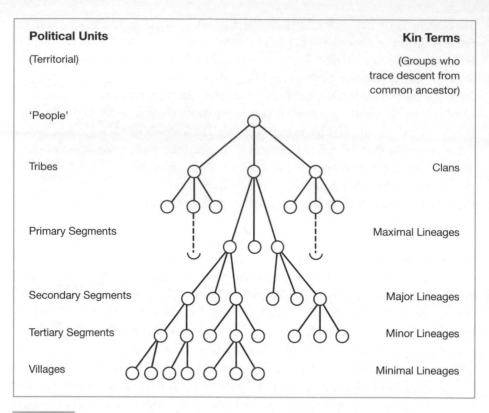

Political Units		Kin Terms
(Territorial)		(Groups who trace descent from common ancestor)

'People'

Tribes — Clans

Primary Segments — Maximal Lineages

Secondary Segments — Major Lineages

Tertiary Segments — Minor Lineages

Villages — Minimal Lineages

Figure 10.1 A representation of the social and political organisation of the Nuer

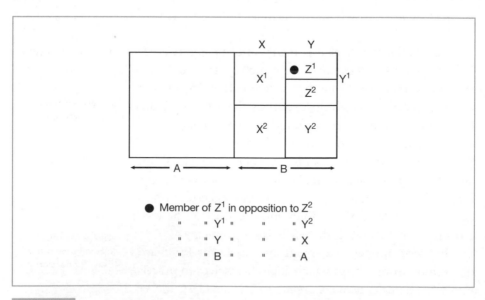

Member of Z^1 in opposition to Z^2
"   " Y^1 "   "   " Y^2
"   " Y "   "   " X
"   " B "   "   " A

Figure 10.2 The segmentary system

Source: E. E. Evans-Pritchard, *The Nuer* (1940), p. 144, by permission of Oxford University Press.

tertiary (see Figure 10.1). The moral universe varies depending on a specific issue which may arise, and people may only conceive of themselves as members of a particular segment in opposition to others in a different one.

To give an example, if a dispute arises between members of two different villages, their relatives will support them according to principles of common ancestry, which in practice is translated into common territorial segments. Thus, in reference to Figure 10.2, if a member of Z^1 fights with a member of Z^2, the quarrel is between the two Z groups. If a member of Z^1 fights with a member of Y^1, then the differences between the two Z groups will be put aside as the two align in opposition to Y^1 as Y^2. Similarly if a member of Y^1 quarrels with a member of X^1, the whole of Y will align in opposition to X, overriding their previous differences. A common political phenomenon in Nuerland is the feud, and it is more difficult to resolve the larger the groups involved. A feud may be between camps, or villages, or any larger group up to the whole tribe, versus neighbouring people like the Dinka.

This description forms the basis of what has been described as a segmentary system. Evans-Pritchard described such a political system as a 'set of structural relations between territorial segments'. A man is a member of a group by virtue of opposition to another group, and thus group membership is relative to the situation:

> political values are relative and ... the political system is an equilibrium between opposed tendencies towards fission and fusion, between the tendency of all groups to segment, and the tendency of all groups to combine with segments of the same order. The tendency towards fusion is inherent in the segmentary character of Nuer political structure, for although any group tends to split into opposed parts these parts must tend to fuse in relation to other groups, since they form part of a segmentary system. Hence fission and fusion in political groups are two aspects of the same segmentary principle, and the Nuer tribe and its divisions are to be understood as an equilibrium between these two contradictory, yet complementary tendencies ... the tendency towards segmentation must be defined as a fundamental principle of their social structure (1940: 48)

Similar principles were found amongst other African peoples, after Evans-Pritchard had published his study, but these principles can be used in other parts of the world too. Consider the case of sporting activities, where people alter their allegiances depending on the magnitude of the occasion. Thus supporters of a local town team in any country would oppose another town in a match between the two, but would join forces to support a larger team drawn from both towns to represent a wider area. In an international event, supporters of all these teams would become supporters of their national team against another country. A very readable ethnography that draws heavily on the ideas of the segmentary system is *The Social Order of the Slum*, a fascinating account of 1960s life in the poorer areas of Chicago (Suttles 1968). Herzfeld's *Poetics of Manhood* (1985), to which we referred in the last chapter, demonstrates its value in a Greek society as well.

Age sets and age grades

The Nuer also divide themselves up into **age sets** and **age grades**, but Evans-Pritchard didn't think that these had much political importance. In other African societies, it is the system of age grades which is seen as the basis of the political system. Examples are to be found in the books cited below by Paul Spencer (1973) and Monica Wilson (1963). Typically, all men in the society participate in such a system, women less often. All those born during a particular period of time are automatically members of a particular *age set*, and they share this membership with their *age mates* throughout life, moving gradually through *age grades* as they get older. Typically, these will include:

age grade – divisions of society through which people pass, and which may determine various roles, particularly ritual and perhaps political, during the course of a lifetime. They are found quite commonly in Africa, but also to a lesser extent in Japan and other Asian countries.

- *youths* – who will be learning the ways of their people;
- *warriors* – who will be responsible for defence and protection; and
- *elders* who – will be responsible for political decisions and dispute resolution.

In some larger tribes, the members of age sets will co-operate with their contemporaries in other groups to form *age regiments*. The Southern African Zulu people had such a system.

Examples of people with an age grade political system are the Nandi and the Maasai people of East Africa. The Nandi, for example, have no fewer than seven age grades, and each age set recruits for about 15 years, so there is some overlap in practice with the functional roles they are able to play. The youngest group is *small children*; the next one is *initiates* who have some free sexual access between the girls' and boys' groups; the next are *warriors*, who are expected to get married; and there are four groups of elders, each of whom is expected to defer to and obey those above them. Members of the same age set are seen as equals and should help one another, even to the extent of sharing spouses. The names of the age sets circulate so that each new group takes the name of the last oldest group, who would by then usually have died out. Important political roles may thus be allocated throughout the society on the basis of age.

Again, this system uses a principle of social order which is found in any society, whether or not it is part of the political system. A cohort of young men may be called upon anywhere to take part in the defence of a nation, or smaller group, although the extent to which age brings greater respect is more variable, especially in the industrialised areas, where people are expected to retire from active work at a certain age. In some parts of Japan there are *age grades,* just as in Africa, with functions that operate in a rather similar way at a local level, and this provides an opportunity to keep even the oldest members of the community valued. These comprise:

- *children's groups* – which meet for sports activities, entertainment, and to play a ritual role in festivals;

- *youth groups* – which also have ritual roles at festivals, meet each other for sports tournaments, and go on trips together, sometimes as a kind of *ordeal;*
- *fire brigades* – which are groups of young married men who are responsible for *protection* in times of danger or local disaster;
- *adults in the prime of life* – who make *decisions* about community affairs, resolve *disputes* and plan *festivals;*
- *old peope* – who also meet for sports, travel together, and carry out tasks in the local community.

   In some parts of Japan there are also age sets who meet regularly for social events. They may collect money regularly, help out in times of need, and make journeys together. These groups have little to do with the political system, but they are important for interpersonal relations in everyday life. In general, in Japan, people are expected to defer to their elders, using polite language to address them, and they can only be really relaxed with members of their own age group, hence the importance of age sets and other age-related groups such as old class mates. This is a factor which feeds indirectly into political life in Japan, as the implicit hierarchical difference in relations between those of different ages impinges on the way that they can treat one another, at least in public.

Acquiring and Achieving Political Power and Status

Age is in fact a universal way of measuring *status*, and determining people's *roles* in social life. This is an *ascribed* status, which we cannot choose, like gender and inherited qualities such as membership in a lineage or a royal family. *Achieved* status is that gained through one's occupation, skills and success in other fields. In democratic societies, this latter is generally regarded as the more important and acceptable type of status, although acquired characteristics may in practice be vital to achieving success in political circles. In age-set and lineage societies, formal status is *ascribed*, though informal status may be acquired through oratory and other interpersonal skills.

   In any society people interested in the acquisition and manipulation of power will need to negotiate the system as they find it, and anthropologists have adopted different approaches in understanding the rich variety of material they encounter in the field. Evans-Pritchard's studies, cited above, set out an abstract 'structural' system only really accessible to someone who is not caught up within it. He is trying to make clear the way in which the world is classified by the people involved, and thus help a reader to understand the social background within which the behaviour of the individuals he observed may be interpreted.

   Others have focused directly on the point of view of the individual members of a society in practice in everyday life, seeking through analysing their personal and interested behaviour to work out how social patterns emerge. The protagonist in this field was Fredrik Barth, a Norwegian anthropologist who worked in several locations, but who made his name writing about the political leaders of the Swat Pathan with an approach he termed transactionalism. This emphasises looking at the way individuals make choices, usually in their own self-interest, in order to *achieve* status and power (Barth 1965). This approach has been highly influential, but has also been criticised for failing to lay out the important categories within which the Pathans were working, and Ahmed's (1976) subsequent work sets out to rectify some of this by placing the Swat Pathan material within the context of the state.

transactionalism – a theory about political behaviour, developed by Frederick Barth, which focuses on the negotiations of individuals and the choices they make in order to achieve political power.

Another ground-breaking study that emphasised again the importance of looking at people in the wider context in which they found themselves was carried out by Edmund Leach (1970). His book *Political Systems of Highland Burma* involves members of several different language groups, and he lays out the formal possibilities for political action by presenting important categories of a system of classification shared across the area in all the languages. This is a structural overview again, and Leach has been criticised for presenting the situation as if it were static, but he argues that he is describing *ideal* systems. As we saw above, it is important to distinguish these from practice, and since this case involves marriage alliances as a vital part of the system, we shall discuss it further in the next chapter.

Opposing principles of equality and hierarchy underpin much of Leach's study, as we shall see, and these also form the focus of a collection of papers, edited by Brenneis and Myers (1984), which examines the situation in a variety of Pacific communities. Entitled *Dangerous Words*, this study approaches the subject of politics through the use of language (cf. Bloch 1975), and indeed, through the suppression of language, or the use of non-verbal and other indirect means of communication in the pursuit of political power. Many of the communities under consideration place a high value on harmonious interaction, as discussed in the previous chapter, and great pains are taken to avoid direct and open confrontation. Such an avenue to political power is quite unfamiliar to people who have been brought up in a society where government is carried out through debate between a party in power and others in open opposition, but it is precisely an anthropological approach which can reveal the mechanisms of political interaction in societies that do not prize the dialectical means of resolving issues.

In my book *Wrapping Culture*, referred to in Chapter 3, I set out to demonstrate some of the layers of indirect communication which could enter into a struggle for power, and although Japan was the main ethnographic focus, and gifts and their wrapping the prototype, there are many other examples. We considered cases of the power of 'wrapping the body' in Chapters 5 and 6, when we looked at the adornment of the Wahgi people of New Guinea and the political implications of the body tattoo. The use of castles and palaces to express authority as well as demonstrating physical power is an example of the 'wrapping of space', and I have also suggested a notion of 'wrapping time' in the subtle forms of organisation and presentation which may be used in meetings.

In all these cases there is political advantage to be gained by those who can exploit these indirect forms of communication. In a society such as Japan which apparently has a rather fixed set of principles ordering people into hierarchical frames, the skilful use of various forms of 'wrapping' allows considerable manipulation of the *status quo* by people who understand the system. In Japan, these different layers of operation are clearly recognised, and in any formal situation there is a 'front' and 'rear' or inside activities, going on. It was my view, in using the notion of 'wrapping', that an understanding of the Japanese case might help people to see parallel cases in other societies, especially those which value harmony and avoid direct confrontation.

In approaching the subject through a consideration of polite and formal language in order to address the question of hierarchy and how it is perceived in Japan, it might be thought beneficial to be from an eminently hierarchical society such as Britain, which also has a complicated set of rules about politeness and etiquette. There may be some truth in this, as there are historical and practical parallels between the two systems, but there is also a danger of expecting things to operate in a recognisable way, as we shall also see in the next chapter. Children in Japan learn about the responsibilities attached to being older, and the advantages of being younger, before they learn about the reverse, which I contend is commoner in many Western countries. This sets up values and expectations that colour future relationships in quite a different way, though direct translation may reveal little of this discrepancy. Much of my research was also carried out amongst women, who demonstrated clearly the power attached to skill in the manipulation of different forms of language, and it is here, too, that perceptions of outsiders about the 'meek and demure' Japanese housewife can be shown in practice to be quite false.

There are many societies in which women carry more power than was recognised by anthropologists who came from a male-dominated political background. Even if the researchers were women, they tended to look to the men they worked with to understand the political system, whereas more recent work–like that of Annette Weiner, which we discussed in Chapter 3, and Lynn Stephen's (2005) work with Zapotec women – has revealed different forms of power that reside with the female members of a society. The Six Nations of the Haudenosaunee people have a confederacy of chiefs, a system which is supposed to have influenced Benjamin Franklin and others when they drew up the American constitution (see website below), but less well known is their system of clan mothers, who choose those chiefs, and wield much power behind the scenes (see website).

Conclusion

We have identified several examples where looking at a political system in its wider social context is vital to a deep understanding of where power is located and how it is used. This theme will persist into the next chapter, where we consider the importance of seeing kinship and marriage in their social context, and again warn of the dangers of making assumptions too quickly when we find something similar to the system with which we have been brought up.

Discussion Questions

1 Do you think democracy is the only acceptable way to run a country? Why? Does it actually fulfil those reasons in practice?

2 What qualities would you admire in a leader in your society? How do they reflect the wider system of values? Are 'managers' leaders?

3 Do you consider economic power to be ultimately the most effective? What other forms of power do you use in your own life? How about others around you?

References and Further Research

Books

Ahmed, Akbar S. (1976) *Millennium and Charisma among the Pathans* (London: Routledge and Kegan Paul).

Balandier, Georges (1967) *Political Anthropology* (London: Allen Lane).

Barth, Fredrik (1965) *Political Leadership among the Swat Pathans* (London: Athlone Press).

Bloch, Maurice (ed.) (1975) *Political Language and Oratory in Traditional Societies* (London: Academic Press).

Brenneis, Donald Lawrence and Myers, Fred R. (1984) *Dangerous Words: Language and Politics in the Pacific* (New York: New York University Press).

Evans-Pritchard, E. E. (1940) *The Nuer* (Oxford: Oxford University Press).

Evans-Pritchard, E. E.(1948) *The Divine Kingship of the Shilluk of the Nilotic Sudan* (Cambridge: Cambridge University Press).

Ferguson, R. B. (1995) *Yanomami Warfare: A Political History* (Santa Fe, NM: School of American Research Press).

Fortes, M. and Evans-Pritchard, E. E. (1940) *African Political Systems* (Oxford: Oxford University Press).

Gledhill, John (1994) *Power and Its Disguises: Anthropological Perspectives on Politics* (London: Pluto Press).

Godelier, Maurice (1986) *The Making of Great Men* (Cambridge: Cambridge University Press).

Gupta, A. and Ferguson, J. (eds) (1997) *Culture, Power, Place: Explorations in Critical Anthropology* (Durham, NC: Duke University Press).

Hendry, Joy (1993) *Wrapping Culture* (Oxford: Clarendon Press).

Herzfeld, Michael (1985) *The Poetics of Manhood: Contest and Identity in a Cretan Mountain Village* (Princeton, NJ: Princeton University Press).

Leach, E. R. (1970) *Political Systems of Highland Burma* (London: Athlone Press).

Maybury-Lewis, David (1974) *The Akwe Shavante* (Oxford: Oxford University Press).

Shore, Cris (1990) *Italian Communism: The Escape from Leninism* (London: Pluto Press).

Spencer, Paul (1973) *Nomads in Alliance* (London: Oxford University Press).

Stephen, Lynn (2005) *Zapotec Women: Gender, Class and Ethnicity in Globalized Oaxaca* (Durham, NC: Duke University Press).

Strathern, Andrew (1971) *The Rope of Moka: Big Men and Ceremonial Exchange in Mount Hagen, New Guinea* (London: Cambridge University Press).

Suttles, Gerald D. (1968) *The Social Order of the Slum: Ethnicity and Territory in the Inner City* (Chicago and London: University of Chicago Press).

Vincent, Joan (2004) *The Anthropology of Politics: A Reader in Ethnography, Theory and Critique* (Oxford and Malden, Mass.: Blackwell Publishing).

Vincent, Joan, and Nugent David (2006) *A Companion to the Anthropology of Politics* (Oxford: Blackwell Publishing).

Weiner, Annette B. (1992) *Inalienable Possessions* (Berkeley: University of California Press).

Wilson, Monica (1963) *Good Company: A Study of Nyakyusa Age-Villages* (Boston, Mass.: Beacon Press).

Articles

Anthropology Today (2005) Special Issue on Policy and Islam, 21(1).

Jakubowska, Longina (1990) 'Political Drama in Poland: The Use of National Symbols', *Anthropology Today*, 6(4): 10–13.

Keenan, Jeremy (2006) 'Conspiracy Theories and "Terrorists": How the "War on Terror" is Placing New Responsibilities on Anthropology', *Anthropology Today*, 22(6): 4–9.

Khazanov, Anatoly M. (1996) 'Anthropologists in the Midst of Ethnic Conflicts', *Anthropology Today*, 12(2): 5–8.

Lecomte-Tilouine, Marie (2004) 'Regicide and Maoist Revolutionary Warfare in Nepal: Modern Intricacies of a Warrior Kingdom', *Anthropology Today*, 20(1): 13–19.

Leeds, Anthony (1969) 'Ecological Determinants of Chieftanship among the Yaruro Indians of Venezuela', in Andrew P. Vayda (ed.), *Environment and Cultural Behaviour* (Austin and London: University of Texas Press).

Rival, Laura (1997) 'Oil and Sustainable Development in the Latin American Humid Tropics', *Anthropology Today*, 13(6): 1–3.

Seneviratne, H. L. (2001) 'Buddhist Monks and Ethnic Politics: A War Zone in an Island Paradise', *Anthropology Today*, 17(2): 15–21.

Novels

Clavell, James (1975) *Shōgun* (London: Hodder & Stoughton) is a well known-novel, subsequently filmed for television in a less anthropologically interesting way, about the encounter between a British sailor–explorer and the Japanese power structure during a period in the sixteenth century when Japan was relatively open to outsiders.

Heller, Joseph (1994[1961]) *Catch-22* (London: Vintage). A general critique of bureaucratic operation and reasoning.

Mishima Yukio (1967) *After the Banquet* (Tokyo and Rutland, Vt.: Tuttle) is a novel which portrays life behind the scenes of early twentieth-century Japanese politicians, showing also the potential power of women close to the men with big names.

Primary Colors (London: Vintage, 1996) was first published anonymously, but was later revealed to be by the journalist Joe Klein and based on Clinton's first presidential campaign.

Rand, Ayn (2007[1959]) *Atlas Shrugged* (London: Penguin Modern Classics) sets out to portray any form of state intervention in society as systemically flawed. Rand claimed that the politics portrayed in the novel are a result of her attempt to display her image of the ideal person and the individual mind's position and value in society.

Scott, Paul (1996) *The Jewel in the Crown* (London: Mandarin) and the subsequent three novels in the *Raj Quartet* portray life in the closing years of British rule in India.

Films

Gandhi (Richard Attenborough, 1982) tells the story of Mahatma Gandhi's leadership through his philosophy of non-violent but direct-action protest.

The Kawelka: Ongka's Big Moka (see Chapter 3).

The Kayapo: Out of the Forest (Michael Beckham and Terence Turner, 1988), another excellent 'Disappearing World' film discussing the resistance and reunification of peoples of Altamira against a huge hydroelectric dam project on the Xingu River, a large tributary of the Amazon.

The Masai (see Chapter 4).

Metropolis (Fritz Lang, 1927) is a silent futuristic film depicting an urban dystopia of 2027 and is about a society brutally divided into 'thinkers' and 'workers'.

The Mursi: War with the Bodi: Decision-making and *Relations with the Kwegu* (Leslie Woodhead, 1985) are anthropological films about a cattle-keeping people of South-West Ethiopia who have no formal chiefs or leaders.

Nixon (Oliver Stone, 1995) tells the story of American president Richard Nixon's political and personal life.

The Shilluk of Southern Sudan (Chris Curling, Paul Howell, Walter Kunijwok and André Singer, 52 minutes, 'Disappearing World' series) is a compelling analysis of Shilluk kingship in 1975. See the website below for a more recent update on the situation.

Websites

http://www.centrelink.org/ANTH423/bibliography.htm – a bibliography of political anthropology.

http://www.sudan101.com/nur.htm – an evangelical website about the Nuer in war-torn Sudan.

http://www.paxchristi.nl/files/Documenten/afrika/soedan/040505_report_shilluk_kingdom.pdf – a report from Nairobi about the current situation of the Shilluk people.

http://www.ratical.org/many_worlds/6Nations/ – an account of the history and politics of the Iroquoian (Haudenosaunee) people.

http://www.peace4turtleisland.org/pages/womensbelt.htm – concerned with women of the Haudenosaunee.

http://www.mnsu.edu/emuseum/cultural/southamerica/shavante.html – a website about the Shavante people of Mato Grosso, Brazil.

Family, Kinship and Marriage

Varieties of Kinship

Within the subject of social anthropology, *kinship* and *marriage* are amongst the oldest and most debated topics. It is within a family group of some sort that most of us are reared, and therefore where most of us learn about social relationships. As we discussed briefly in Chapter 1, it is here that we learn to classify other human beings, and how we should behave towards them. Because these distinctions are learned so early, they are hard to dislodge, and, as we shall see, they tend to colour our views of other peoples, and their relations. We may or may not see much of our close relatives, but it is with these that we celebrate important life crises such as birth, marriage and death, and it is to these people that we may well turn in times of need.

In different societies, people have different ideas about how to classify their relatives, and how to calculate their degrees of relatedness. They even have different ideas about how people become related in the first place. Ideas of genealogy are found in all societies, but ideas about conception and the development of a new human being are rather varied, and with the advent of *new reproductive technologies*, virulent debates have emerged. Not everyone is exclusively concerned with 'blood ties', as the

English language would suggest: some attach as much importance to relatives according to the nurturing roles of parents who might be described as 'adopted' in English; others derive relationships through a common bond with the land.

The sharing of a household is often an important factor to consider, and in several systems of kinship, this will override relationships which may be described as 'natural' or 'biological'. The film *Secrets and Lies* illustrated in a bitter-sweet way the social and emotional problems that can arise when people reared in an adoptive family take steps to make contact with their parents of birth, compounded here when details of an interracial union had been concealed from even those closest to the parties involved.

The immediate family group varies from one society to another, too, and there are numerous possibilities for residential arrangements. In Western societies, the familiar nuclear family has undergone a great deal of change in recent years, and the 'single-parent family' has become a common phrase, though the actual form, where it comprises a mother and her children, is not unusual in the world at large although that of a father and children is rarer. The terminology implies the lack of another parent, however, and expresses

> **nuclear family** – a basic unit of parents and children, as defined by English language usage.

an ideological preference for two parents to be involved with the rearing of children, even if they are not both related to the children, and the children may have 'parents' in more than one home. Another recent addition to Western societies can be found in same-sex marriages and parentage (see First-hand Account 11.1 overleaf), and we will see that this is not unheard of elsewhere as well. In any case, so-called 'natural' features have become complicated. When a child is conceived in a test-tube, now called *in vitro* fertilisation or IVF, and possibly carried to the point of birth by a *surrogate* mother (who has not donated the genetic material), the maternal biological link is confused, and if the paternity is assisted, too, the child's parenthood becomes very unclear. In an early anthropological comment on the Warnock Report, the first official British response to scientific developments which made possible 'human-assisted reproduction', Peter Rivière's article 'Unscrambling Parenthood' (1985) argued for the role social anthropology might play in helping to sort out some of the confusion.

Two of the important points he made were, first, that any construct of genealogy and parenthood is cultural, and secondly, that examples from societies anthropologists have studied may help to disentangle the issues involved. For one thing, in considering the problems of artificial insemination, we already have the vocabulary to distinguish between a child's genetic father and a man who has taken on a social role with regard to that child. Based on work with African people like the Nuer, for whom we saw in the last chapter that lineal relations are politically very important, anthropologists devised a distinction between a genitor, for the genetic father, and a pater for the social role.

> **genitor** – a term devised by anthropologists to describe the genetic father of a child, when this might be distinguished from a social parent, who would be named **pater**.

In cases already considered by anthropologists, some of which we will encounter in this chapter, the genitor could be a person who made it possible for another man, known as the pater, to have a child to carry on his line, so there were in fact precedents for the issues which arose in considering the legal, ethical and social issues surrounding the donation of sperm for artificial insemination. The distinction has been useful in understanding arrangements in many socie-

pater – a term devised by anthropologists to describe a man who plays the social role of father to a child when this needs to be distinguished from a genetic parent, who would be named **genitor**.

ties, and, where genealogy is a vital element of social and political life, there are various forms of social construction to overcome problems such as infertility or premature death.

It is not conceptually difficult for this distinction to be modified to apply to the case of the donation of an egg for an infertile mother to carry, when she might be termed *mater* and the donor *genetrix* but, as Rivière pointed out, there was no precedent for the separation of roles of conception and gestation which technology has made possible. In some systems of thought, the period of gestation has been regarded as more important than the moment of conception for the development of the new human being, and the father may be expected to keep 'feeding' the foetus with further sexual encounters. This may sound a little bizarre, but one of the concerns of the British public, and therefore the Warnock Committee, was certainly about how a child should be treated once it is born if it is to develop into a well-balanced member of the society in which it lives, as mentioned above in the case of the 'single-parent family'.

Rivière discussed the further complications which arise if all three roles – provision of an egg (the role of the *genetrix*), the carrying of the child, and the subsequent rearing of that child – are separated. The need to use Latin words for these roles already indicates the linguistic problems which arise in English, but there are all sorts of other issues related to cultural constructions of the family, legal ideas about legitimacy and inheritance, religious, scientific and social ideas about the nature of a human being, and the rights of men and women to be in control of their bodies.

There has been much debate amongst anthropologists on this subject since that time (see, for example, Franklin 1997; Shore 1992; Strathern 1992; Carsten 2004) but Rivière wrote rather cautiously:

> I am not advocating ... that we should therefore adopt the ideas and practices of other people. I am merely suggesting that it might help if we removed our cultural blinkers and saw our problems in a wider perspective. If we did this, the surrogate mothers might not appear to be the threat to civilization that some people make them out to be. (1985: 6)

In a sense, this is a plea which could apply to many social issues, and the article expresses a concern at the time of writing which has dissipated over the years, but as we have already seen in our examination of the work of anthropologists, we too find it hard to escape those 'cultural blinkers'.

Same-sex relationships are not new in the United States, as is evidenced in calling them 'Boston marriages' in Victorian days. This phrase was used to describe two women living together, while discreetly avoiding the true nature of the relationship. It has only been in modern times that same-sex relationships between women, and men for that matter, have been openly discussed and, to some degree, regarded as an acceptable coupling. When you throw children into the mix, it becomes more controversial. As a lesbian couple living in San Francisco, California (which is known for its liberal attitudes), we do not face the prejudice and misunderstanding that may exist in other parts of the United States.

First-hand account 11.1:
Mary Martha Beaton, American – on Same-Sex Parentage

Having two adopted girls (Jesse and Sara – five years' age difference – both two and a half years old at adoption), we felt it was important to give them the support they needed and an exposure to an accepting society. We did not want to subject them to name calling and other prejudicial labels that might have been applied, so we moved from Boston to the liberal West Coast. In reality, I think we could live anywhere, but I wanted it to be easier on the girls.

Not having been in a traditional marriage, I cannot draw direct comparisons, but I can say that I feel our family was (and still is) as normal and healthy and functional as any traditional parent–child relationship. We laughed together, cried together, grew together, had the usual mother–daughter conflicts and, while there were two mothers, the girls always seemed to know exactly who they could get what they wanted from, and how. They soon learned how to work each parent to their advantage, and learned to avoid asking 'that mother' when they knew the answer would be 'no'. To them, having two mothers was natural, and because they were brought up to be proud of their family, and knew they were loved, and in a supportive school system, for the most part, their having two mothers was not an issue. This is not to say there were not real struggles in raising Jesse and Sara.

USA

California

There were the usual parent–child fights and arguments about curfews, boyfriends, slumber parties, party attendance, school grades, cleaning their rooms, choirs, and the usual conflicts parents all have. Speaking specifically about same-sex parents, I would say when adolescence hit, our younger daughter, Sara, was less secure about telling people she had two parents of the same sex than her older sister, Jesse. Sara struggled with that and we let her come to terms with it in her own time. Eventually, as she matured, she found that her friends thought it was 'fun' to have two mothers, and even labelled her as lucky, so she came to appreciate her family configuration.

Our girls are now 21 and 25 years old, with intact self-esteems, living on their own and both in healthy relationships with men. We raised them with the same values that any family would: respect for others, acceptance of others, tolerance for differences, and knowing the importance of spirituality, love of family, and tradition. I feel we made the same sacrifices, the same commitments, the same decisions, and had the same devotion to family as any parents would.

Some anthropologists have tried over the years to draw up typologies of 'kinship systems' which would eventually encompass all possible varieties; others have concentrated on developing often very complex theories about logical possibilities for kin relations. In the 1970s, as part of a 'rethinking' vogue within anthropology, a book entitled *Rethinking Kinship and Marriage* (Needham 1971) focused on basic difficulties, first about defining something universal which could be called kinship, and then about isolating such a thing from wider aspects of the social system in which it was found. The authors suggested that early anthropologists were somewhat blinded by their own expectations of kinship, based on deeply ingrained ideas about biological links, and later ones followed their lead without enough reflection about what they were doing and how they might be taking some aspects of social life out of their context.

The editor, Rodney Needham, wrote:

> kinship – a term used by anthropologists to describe sets of relationships considered primary in any society, also called *family* and *relations*, but demonstrating huge variety in different societies in practice.

> There has been a fair amount of discussion about what 'kinship' really is. My own view is that much of this debate is pretty scholastic and inconsequential ... Let me simply adopt the minimal premiss that kinship has to do with the allocation of rights and their transmission from one generation to the next. These rights are not of any specific kind but are exceedingly various: they include most prominently rights of group

membership, succession to office, inheritance of property, locality of residence, type of occupation, and a great deal else. They are all, however, transmissible by modes which have nothing to do with sex or genealogical states of transmitter or recipient. (1971: 3-4)

In Britain, kin relations are often relatively isolated from the rest of social life, and an overlap of family loyalty into economic and political life may be perceived negatively as *nepotism*, or regarded with suspicion. The rise to wealth of Mark Thatcher, son of the former British Prime Minister, is a good case to illustrate this point, especially in view of his later dubious African affairs. Becoming wealthy in his own right by taking advantage of his mother's name is one less than admirable thing, but a hint of overlap with political decision making was totally unacceptable to the British press. A similar reaction can be found among some Americans about politicians and their families, and there is some resentment about access to Hollywood (see website below). In fact, most people expect to help their kin to get on in the world, but there is sometimes quite a sharp dividing line between acceptable family support and confusing the needs and desires of one's relatives with one's wider public duty.

In the previous chapter we began to discern an example of a situation where kin relations were entirely bound up with political life – indeed it would have been impossible to understand one without an idea of the other. Although actual neighbourly relations amongst the Nuer may be more important than kin when people work out who to support in a particular political situation, they use the genealogical vocabulary to classify one another. **Lineage** membership is a most important principle for calculating relationships, so if a man dies without issue, a ghost marriage may be arranged between him and a woman who takes a living man as genitor, providing children to continue the line through the dead man (known as the pater). In this case the child inherits group membership without a 'biological' relationship.

ghost marriage – a marriage arranged posthumously to ensure lineal continuity and thus perhaps care of the soul of the dead in the afterlife.

In the world at large, there is a huge variety in the way in which people classify others around them, and relations whom we might at first think of as *kin* may actually have little to do with genealogical connections. They may also be inextricably tied up with economic transactions, the political system and the religious beliefs of the people concerned. It is thus very important to understand how people's *relations* fit into the wider society in which they are found before trying to isolate them. It is for this reason that the whole subject of kinship has been left until we have covered other areas, and in this chapter we will consider a specific case to illustrate this point, but first we need introduce some of the terminology.

Within multicultural societies, people from specific ethnic backgrounds still grow up within their own families, and it is here that they learn to look out at the social life within which their family is lodged. The great variety mentioned above is not confined to certain locations, then, it is scattered throughout the world. It is thus not only possible for a wide range of people to broaden the assumptions and expectations associated with relatives by simply taking an interest in those around them; it can also be crucial to good neighbourly understanding. The material presented here is not only curious and interesting, then; it may be an important part of everyday life across the globe.

To introduce some of the conventions adopted by anthropologists for describing kin relations, we examine first what we will call a *standard English family*, a kind of model of how people using the English language classify one another as relatives, wherever the language is used. We will then place this system in a wider context by turning to look at unilineal descent groups, which offer a completely contrasting way of classifying relatives, found in various forms in different parts of the world. We will then give a concrete example of how relatives may be perceived in a multicultural situation by focusing on the Pakistani community in Oxford. This case study will lead us into the last part of the chapter, where the focus will be marriage.

Classifying Kin Relations

In order to discuss family relationships at all, various conventions have been adopted. Some of these are familiar to those who take an interest in family trees, others are understood readily only by the professional anthropologist. If we start with the so-called 'standard English family', we can draw a diagram which depicts people in terms of their nearest relations, namely parents and siblings, and, by extension, to their more distant aunts, uncles and cousins. We can place marriages on this diagram, and there is a convention for depicting serial marriage in the case of death or divorce and remarriage.

Figure 11.1 is a representation of this 'standard English family'. It uses a small circle (○) to represent a woman and a triangle (△) to represent a man. An equals sign (=) represents a marriage or an informal union which results in offspring, and a line joining a circle and a triangle from above stands for a brother–sister relationship. It is important to remember that this is not a representation of an actual situation, but a set of logical possibilities. Thus, there is only one brother and sister in each unit, because these stand for the two possible positions that children may occupy terminologically. This becomes significant in the next generation when the pair would take on new roles to each other's children.

By examining the diagram that results we can work out a number of implications which can be drawn from the English-language system of designating relatives. The terms used separate off units of parents and children from more distant relatives by having unique terms for each category of member–mother, father, son, daughter – as opposed to blanket terms like uncle, aunt and cousins which cover a wide range of people outside that unit. All of the latter may have special characteristics for their actual relations, and the terms may even be used for friends, but the terms themselves make no such distinctions. The marked

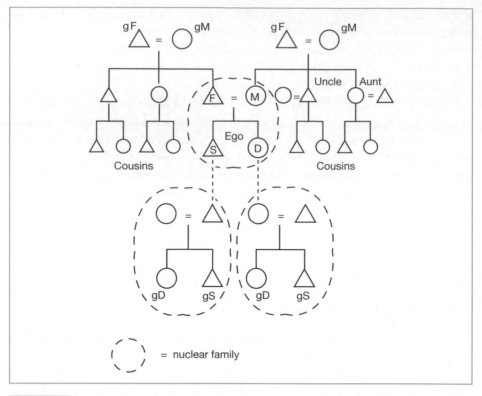

Figure 11.1 A standard English family

family units, comprising people who do have distinct terms, are technically called *nuclear families*, and in many English-speaking and other countries people live in units that express degrees of closeness in a similar way.

Up and down the diagram, the terms used in the nuclear unit are qualified for the people outside it by adding the prefix *grand* to the four distinct terms (as in grandmother, grandson, and so forth) or a number of *greats* to indicate further generational distance (as in great-grandmother, and so on). These terms distinguish the lineal relatives, named after the line which can be traced through the generations, from uncles, aunts and cousins, essentially related through siblings, which are termed lateral, after the Latin for 'out to the side'. This use of terminology suggests another marking which may have practical implications too.

Rights and obligations concerned with inheritance rules are one example, and these are usually determined by family relationships in any particular legal system, which

lineal relatives – individuals related along a line which can be traced through the generations; see also **patrilineal** and **matrilineal** relatives.

lateral relations – the term used to describe relatives who are connected through siblings, distinguished in many languages in the next generation (i.e. for the children of siblings) as **matrilateral** or **patrilateral** in order to mark important kin divisions in a society.

inheritance – rules for passing on status, roles, goods and membership in particular social groups from one generation to the next.

will distinguish different degrees of proximity, though the details vary from one country to another. In some cases, there is a system of primogeniture, for example, which indicates a special role for an eldest son. In Japanese, where terminology makes distinctions otherwise rather similar to the English case, there are terms to mark the birth order among the children, especially marking the eldest son, and in Nahuatl, an indigenous Mexican language, it is the youngest son who may be denoted in this way.

primogeniture – indicates a special role of inheritance for an eldest son.

Terminology does not always indicate practice, however, and an interesting aspect of our 'English' diagram is the lack of a distinction based on gender, let alone birth order. From the point of view of a child in the middle nuclear family, a reference point often termed *ego* by anthropologists, no terminological distinctions are made between relatives on the mother's or father's side. In practice, however, children's surnames are usually taken from the father in English-speaking societies, and women may well turn to their mothers for help with their own children, for example, and perhaps to pass on certain material objects, such as porcelain and jewellery.

Inheritance is of course important in all societies, and in many other languages distinctions of this sort are made. Anthropologists therefore decided to use Latin terms to devise a system of talking about inheritance in cases where the English language is lacking in appropriate distinctions. Thus, when something is passed through the male line, as is usually the case for English names, it is said to be passed patrilineally. When it is passed through the female line, the term used is matrilineal inheritance (see Figure 11.2 for a way of depicting these lines).

In some societies matrilineal inheritance may still be passed from man to man, that is, a man receives his share of his inheritance from his *mother's brother* (rather than from his father, as in a patriline), and, likewise, a man passes it on to his *sister's son* (in Figure 11.2, the share would then pass between the triangles

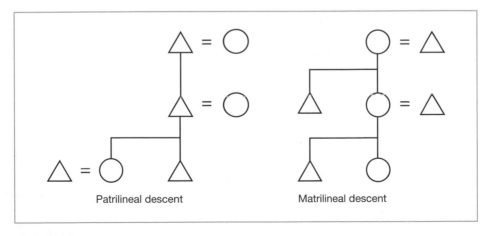

Patrilineal descent   Matrilineal descent

on the left-hand side of the second diagram). Where this latter preference predominates, the whole society has sometimes been termed a **matrilineal** society. It is important to consider *property*, *status*, *titles* and *group membership* separately, however, as these may not be the same. In the following section the last will be the focus of attention.

Unilineal Descent Groups

Principles of **descent** are particularly important in societies where they lead to the formation of groups descended from one common ancestor. In Figure 11.3 the situation is depicted of a *patrilineal descent* group, where the shaded brother and sister pair at the bottom are again in the position of *ego*. This time their rela-

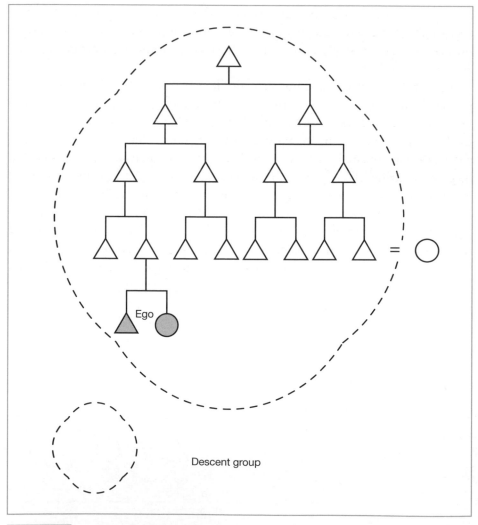

Figure 11.3 A unilineal descent group

tives are worked out by virtue of membership in a group traced through men, as shown in the diagram. Women who are born into the group, like the female *ego*, usually marry out, so they are not shown. Wives of the males are members of other groups, as shown in the case of the example of a wife at the right hand side of the diagram.

Groups of this sort may be *clans* such as those of the Ancient Romans, Hebrews and Scots, or they may form a complicated lineage system like that seen amongst the Nuer and discussed in the previous chapter. Membership in such a group may determine residence possibilities, as well as economic partners such as companions for herding, hunting and agriculture, and it may define political allegiances and obligations in case of war, although the latter may also be affected by one's membership in an age grade. It is also very likely to affect possibilities for marriage, since people are usually expected to marry out of their own group.

Ancestors who preceded the present incumbents as members of unilineal descent groups may appear as important characters in local legend and mythology, and they may also play a part in religious and ritual life. These may be the beings to be blamed and consulted in the case of misfortune, as we have seen, and their help may also be sought in times of need. Association with particular ancestors may bring rights and/or obligations, and they will certainly play a part in the identity of a living being in their social world. In return, the living will perform rites for the care of their ancestors in the afterlife, and arrangements are very often made for a person with no issue to have descendants through some kind of social adoption, or ghost marriage, as described above for the Nuer.

In some relatively closed societies everybody may be classified as a member of a lineage, and the relationship with everyone else in the society determined by relationships between these groups. Naming terminology will reflect these allegiances, and appropriate behaviour follows depending on the type of relationship involved. Members of one's own lineage would be in a more intimate relationship than those of the lineage into which one had, or expected to be, married, and in-laws may be treated with special respect or even avoidance. Anthropologists approaching such people found it necessary to be adopted into a group of relatives in order to communicate in a meaningful fashion at all. Once they had found a niche, everyone was able to work out the appropriate behaviour.

Such arrangements make it quite difficult to translate kin terms into the English language. For example, the term which might be translated as *brother* refers in some societies to all male members of one generation in the same lineage, and *father* to all those of the senior generation. Earlier anthropologists called such usages *classificatory terminology*, to distinguish them from terms which applied more exclusively to categories they recognised, which they called *descriptive terminology*. However, if the range of people denoted by the term is understood, the terms are *descriptive* in each situation, and they may indicate some important social categories, so seeking to identify the *descriptive* significance of a term is a good way to proceed.

Terms of address may also carry further significance in making sense of the system of classification in a particular society. For example, in a society where group membership is inherited matrilineally, but passed from man to man, as discussed above, there may be a lineage term for *father's sister* which literally means *female father*, and similarly *mother's brother* may mean *male mother*. Here the terms for father and mother will be less concerned with gender than with group affiliation. The 'male mother' will simply be a male of the senior generation in one's own lineage, and the 'female father' a representative of the group to which a father owes his allegiance and inheritance. To the first a young person may owe obedience and respect, to the second, deference and distance.

matrilateral relatives – those in the same generation related through the mother's family.

Siblings usually form a unit related to others in the same way, and many people make terminological distinctions between matrilateral (related through one's mother) and patrilateral (related through one's father) relatives, sometimes because these are automatically members of different clans, and one might have to marry out of one's own clan. Cross-cousins (related through siblings of the opposite sex) are also very often distinguished from parallel-cousins (related through siblings of the same sex). These distinctions are illustrated in Figure 11.4, where the sibling pair in the centre of the diagram take the position of *ego*, and their matrilateral and patrilateral cousins, on the right and left of the diagram respectively, are marked as parallel or cross, depending of their parents' relationships.

patrilateral relatives – those in the same generation, but related through the father.

cross-cousins – are the offspring of siblings of opposite sex.

parallel-cousins – are the offspring of siblings of the same sex, male or female.

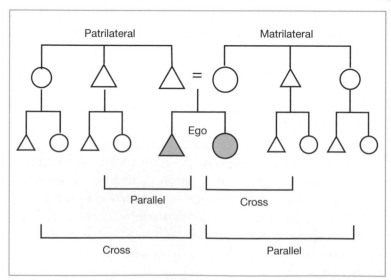

Figure 11.4

Cross-cousins and parallel-cousins

Kinship in a Multicultural Context: A Case Study

To pick up the point made earlier by Rodney Needham about the advisability of looking at 'kinship' in its social context, this section of the chapter will be devoted to a detailed examination of one particular case. The example has been chosen to illustrate another, earlier point about the multiplicity of systems now found in many parts of the world, and the need to understand our neighbours. The case is the Pakistani community in Oxford, and the section is largely based on the ethnography of Alison Shaw (1988, 2000), with some personal insights from second-generation members of the community. Photograph 11.1 illustrates the mosque built by members of this community to which neighbours and other faith groups were invited as it was being built.

Throughout her books, Shaw makes comparisons with the situation of continuing relations in Pakistan and elsewhere, and argues that the similarities between the old and new communities outweigh the differences brought about by coexistence of the new one with the wider community in England. She is also keen to break down prejudices and assumptions which are commonly made by the wider community about the Pakistanis in Britain, and sometimes vice versa, and her study takes pains to present the point of view of the people with whom she worked.

Most members of this community come from the Punjabi district of Pakistan, many from the Jhelum area, south-east of Islamabad, and they maintain contact with their forebears through visits, by sending money and other resources, and by arranging marriages and funerals back in Pakistan. Many families also feel it important to send their British-born children to spend time with their Pakistani

Photograph 11.1 The mosque in Oxford built by members of the Pakistani community described in this chapter (photograph: Bob Pomfret).

relatives. Within Britain, the group which would seem to be most significant for members of this community is known as the *birādarī*, commonly translated as 'relations'. This group is not clearly defined as a group of kin, although it may comprise a set of brothers or cousins and their offspring, but it is the most immediate circle of people on whom a member may depend, and to whom a person feels obliged.

The limits of the group are contextual, somewhat in the spirit of the segmentary system of the previous chapter, and the whole Pakistani community in Oxford could be described *birādarī* in contrast with the wider cosmopolitan citizenship. In other situations, the *birādarī* is conceived to include members of the family who have remained behind in Pakistan, on whom one can call to put up one's children, and to whom one may well be expected to send goods and money (a situation we will raise again in Chapter 14). In practice, in everyday life, this group will consist of a set of people who live together, or in close proximity, and it is the women of the group who seek to preserve the strength of the immediate set of close relations through the explicit exchange of gifts.

The composition of a Pakistani household in Oxford sometimes confuses their non-Pakistani neighbours, as may their arrangement of rooms, and Alison Shaw works from the plan of a typical house in Pakistan to explain the modifications of more traditional British use to the often Victorian houses. The most important distinction is between the male and female worlds, for these are Muslim families who seek to preserve Islamic ideals:

> A notable feature of all east Oxford Pakistani houses is that despite the different physical layout of the houses considerations of *purdah* are very important. This is best illustrated by the arrival of visitors. If male visitors arrive and a male family member is at home, the visitors may first be detained at the door while the women of the household, modestly adjusting their *dupattās* over their heads, leave the front room and retreat to the backroom or kitchen. For as long as unrelated men are present, the women of the household will not usually enter the front room; instead the men of the household will go or send children to the backroom with requests for food and tea for the guests. The men may themselves carry the food or drinks from the kitchen to the front room, though sometimes the women will do this, without speaking to the male visitors. (Shaw 1988: 63)

The children of a house come under the guidance of the women, but young married couples very often live with the parents of the husband, and the grandmother is sometimes addressed with the same term as 'mother' in Urdu and Punjabi, namely '*ammi*', which can be confusing when the children begin to translate things into English. Similarly, they may use the same Urdu/Punjabi terms for brother and sister in reference to their cousins, especially if they are co-resident, because the strict terms are simply 'aunt/uncle-born brother/sister', with distinctions for matrilaterality and patrilaterality. On the male side, too, the term for father may also be used for grandfather, and the term for father's brother is appropriate for father's cousins and may also be used for friends' fathers and fathers' friends, as a sign of respect to the senior generation.

Clearly, the view of a child growing up in this community will be somewhat different from that of a child whose first language defines the 'standard English family' detailed above, although that was of course only a model. When a small child from the Pakistani community goes to school and is asked about his or her relatives, the response of an unsympathetic teacher could be withering, but it could also be creative and helpful – a good reason for welcoming students of education on anthropology courses. In practice, the Pakistani children living in Oxford have adapted some of their relationships to make more sense when they speak in English, and a local young informant gave me the terms which fitted a 'standard English' view as well as his own indigenous one.

Expectations of behaviour within the Pakistani family are sometimes quite shocking to outsiders in British communities, especially on the touchy subject of gender. Men are in a position to order their female relatives to attend to their needs, it seems, and the same informant reported gleefully that his sister is obliged to bring him things in the home. He also noted that this expectation only starts as the girls grow up, however, and if he tries to get his youngest sisters to wait on him he is given short shrift. This expectation is part of a wider view still maintained in the more conservative families that men are the ones to earn the money and women to take care of the home, but a stronger constraint on all family members is usually to play an appropriate part in contributing to the wider needs of the *birādarī*.

Alison Shaw started her first book with an example of her own initial misunderstanding of the decision of a promising member of the community she had studied to turn down a place at university. She goes on to present his rationale in terms of the expectations of the wider Pakistani community, and compares this with her own reasons for being disappointed on his behalf. She uses this example to illustrate the difficulties of undoing one's own preconceptions in looking at those of people brought up with a different set, but also to introduce the value of belonging to a wider group such as the Pakistani *birādarī*.

Later in the book, Shaw details several cases of real material help people have received from their relatives – for house purchase, building, education, marriage and so forth – and this is of course the positive side of the commitment which imposes the constraints that she had initially interpreted negatively. Being part of a large social group such as we have described here clearly involves fitting in at least to some extent with the wider expectations of the group. Those who wish to receive the benefits must also make a contribution. They will be continually involved in the exchange of gifts, and they will participate in the perpetuation of the society through marriage as well as in maintaining economic security.

Within the family, youngsters are expected to defer to the wishes of their elders, and it is the elders who make arrangements for the marriages of their children, both boys and girls. Some children have rebelled and made their own marriages outside the community, occasionally successful, but all can also site cases where a new, second marriage has had to be arranged for such tearaways when the first one broke down. Whether an outside spouse is accepted depends partly on the extent to which they are prepared to adopt and contribute to the social life of the community.

Marriages are usually arranged between members of the same *birādarī*, very often between first cousins, and one important criterion is that the families should be compatible.

> In most cases the question of caste status in marriage does not arise explicitly because of the traditional Pakistani Muslim preference for marriage with first cousins. This stated preference is sometimes justified with reference to the Qur'ān, which permits first-cousin marriage, and the life of the Prophet Mohammed whose daughter Fatima was married to her cousin, the Prophet's nephew. It is also justified in terms of maintaining 'purity of the blood' and in this context the particular qualities of the family or caste are emphasised. In a society in which a dowry must be given by the girl's family when a daughter is married, the preference for first-cousin marriage is also important as a means of keeping property within the family. (Shaw 1988: 98)

Alison Shaw investigated the extent to which younger members of the community, particularly those of the second generation, resented having their marriages arranged for them, and she found only a small amount of real dissent. In most cases, people felt that the system was good for them, and they preferred being part of the community which they seem to see as more caring and meaningful than the 'free' outside world. It seems from the more recent work of Fozia Tenvir, and Shaw herself, that this situation continues into the third generation, and families are less worried than they used to be about letting their daughters go to mixed schools. Girls whose outside marriages failed have proved a strong negative example, and although Pakistani boys sometimes have relationships with white girls from the wider community, they see these as playful, and argue that the girls don't mind, as their own sisters might.

This is one case of a relatively strong, well-defined ethnic community in a wider society, and it was chosen largely for the rich ethnography relating to the subject matter of this chapter. The First-hand Account 11.2 (overleaf) by a Jain student studying in the same city in 2006 presents a very different view, though compare this with Reynell's (1991) article listed below, and briefly referred to in the next section. For an alternative insight into the lives of some British families of immigrant origins, the novels by Zadie Smith (2000) and Monica Ali (2003 – see end of Chapter 14) are hard to beat!

Marriage

One of the reasons that Pakistani girls in Oxford prefer to marry within their own community is because they will be able to continue to count on the support of the wider *birādarī*. Marriage for them is more than a relationship between two people, and there may be reasons for making a match which goes beyond personal choice. They also observe the fragility of some of the unions made in wider British society, as divorce rates increase and remarriages complicate the lives of the children involved (see Simpson 1994). There are also religious differences, of course. Perhaps these alternative marriages don't seem very impressive.

It must be part of this chapter, then, to consider what exactly we mean when we talk about *marriage*. Let us start again by looking at the word in the English language, as an element in the *standard English family* we used as a model above. Something called marriage clearly played an important part in the construction of the *nuclear* unit, and it is 'marriage' which moves people from the family of their birth to a new one for procreation and continuing the lines of descent. However, what do people need to do in order to make this transition? And is it actually necessary for people to marry at all, if they simply give birth to children of their own?

First of all, there is a legal definition of marriage, and this will vary from one system to another, affecting the way that people are permitted to behave within any particular society. Inheritance rules are affected by the legal situation, and so may be the status of children. In some systems of legislation, it is only possible to have one legal spouse at a time, whereas in others polygamy is not only possible but sometimes a preferred arrangement. The laws with regard to divorce will indicate the possibilities for breaking a union once formed, and arrangements for children will also be part of the legal framework.

Polygamy – marriage involving more than one spouse, male or female

There are also often strong religious ideas about the state of marriage, and these may even be at odds with the evolving legal system. In a Christian church, for example, a couple makes a solemn undertaking to spend the rest of their lives together, through thick and through thin – 'in sickness and in health, until death us do part'. Not everyone gets married in church, but many of the couples getting divorced have done so, and even seek to do it again, an act which is actually permitted in some churches. Clearly there is a difference between the ideals expressed in the ceremony and the practice of real life. In other societies marriage may have little to do with religion, but it is not uncommon to find a discrepancy between ideals and practice.

This brings us to a third definition of marriage, namely the customary one. Here we enter the area of social control again. A couple wishing to marry is expected to comply with legal regulations, and they may choose to formalise their union with a religious ceremony, but it is also quite possible to set up a family without doing either of these things. It may not be the preferred arrangement of the parents of the couple concerned, but neighbours may well treat them in much the same way as they would people with a more conventional union. The term 'partner' has gained common currency in the English language for the relationship formed in such a situation, and it is also used for long-term homosexual relationships, although it is now possible in several countries for homosexuals to formalise their union with a marriage.

Marriage within Jain communities has traditionally been arranged with religious – and, often group – endogamy strongly being adhered to. That is, parents would not only prefer someone from the same sect, they would likely also choose someone from certain family lines that had shared origins and would be recognised as being part of the same 'group' (also known as caste, although without any hierarchical connotations). Marriage with kin or within a lineage would generally not be permitted and matches would usually be made between two families of similar socioeconomic standing.

First-hand account 11.2:
Ashini Kothari, Jain – on Marriage

You now find more of a mixture of approaches to marriage both from young people and their parents, which varies according to individuals, families, groups and communities! For instance, while arranged marriages and endogamy are still the norm in India, it is now more common to hear of cases to the contrary, especially in metropolitan cities such as Mumbai. Jain communities outside India are generally considered to be slowly changing their practices and attitudes although it varies greatly from one community to another. For example, the small Jain community in Antwerp, Belgium largely consists of first-generation migrants that originated from one town in Gujarat and who still regularly travel back to India. As a result, arranged and/or endogamous marriage is more common there than in England, for instance. In the case of the latter, not only is there a greater mix of different Jain groups and interaction with the host population, but many families spent a generation in Africa before moving to England, which could explain the greater changes and variances in their practices. Jain communities outside India often have a sense of shared identity, which may assume greater importance than the aforementioned 'groups' defined by family origins. Youth in overseas communities often share outlooks and backgrounds, which sometimes makes matches within them – arranged or otherwise – easier. Even the way in which marriages are 'arranged' varies.

Belgium

Communities in India mostly have instances where the couple only meets for a handful of occasions before the engagement. But, in England, and even in communities in the USA, an 'arrangement' usually just entails families introducing a couple, and it is then largely the couple's prerogative as to how and whether they wish to pursue the relationship. It is often followed by dating for an extended period as the couple gets to know each other.

I think most young people in England view marriage as something which should be their choice and while most identify themselves as being part of the Jain community, decreasing numbers feel as though endogamy is vital. Both parents and young Jains tend to express a preference for spouses to have similar backgrounds (e.g. a preference for a Jain or Hindu over other religious groups), although this is stronger in the case of the former. Reasons for this preference among young Jains vary from parental or social pressure to personal choice. Of course, different families and individuals also differ in the extent of their preferences and there are plenty of cases where families' and individuals' wishes and views clash, which I think is greater now than ever before due to an uncomfortable blend of traditional and 'Westernised' ideas.

Ashini Kothari wrote this piece in 2006 while a student at Oxford University; she is a resident of Antwerp, Belgium.

Marriage for many people may be considered to be a union that should be entered into freely by a couple wishing to share a major part of their lives together, but this idea is by no means universal, and it is necessary to think carefully about what the institution means. It may, for example, be seen as something much closer to a political or an economic alliance, enabling the uniting of potentially hostile groups, or the consolidation of a vital means to trade. In rural Japan, the character used for a bride (or wife) is a combination of one for 'woman' and one for *ie*, or 'house', suggesting that the bride is seen as married to the house as a whole, not just to the young husband with whom she shares a bed. In some societies unions between ghosts, or between two women, are also quite possible, and it may certainly be thought less necessary for the couple to make choices than for social expectations to be fulfilled.

As was the case with kinship, *marriage* means different things in different societies, and in an article about the problems of defining marriage in *Rethinking Kinship and Marriage*, Peter Rivière even went so far as to write that 'marriage as an isolable phenomenon of study is a misleading illusion' (1971: 57). Again, he recommends, we must look at marriage as part of the wider society where it is found, at how it fits into wider systems of exchange and political allegiance, and then we can understand the role it plays in a particular case. Anthropologists have developed theory around the term *alliance* to examine some of the examples found in a way which does not imply underlying notions associated with the term *marriage*. In this final section, however, we will simply introduce and explain terms which have been used in describing arrangements in various societies, and try to give some idea of the variety that is possible. This will lay the groundwork for readers to understand any more specific ethnography they might find.

Endogamy, Exogamy and Incest

In most societies there are some limits, broadly agreed, about whom one may or may not marry. Rules of exogamy define groups *out of which* one should marry, and rules of endogamy define those *within which* one should marry. Rules of exogamy sometimes, but not always, coincide with rules of incest, in other words those who are prohibited for marriage are usually the same people with whom it would be inappropriate to have sexual relations. These groups vary from one society to another: they may include only the nuclear family, they may comprise a lineage to a certain distance, or even a whole clan sharing a name. The Chinese character for incest literally means 'confusion of relationships', and this is a nice expression of the way rules of incest and exogamy often actually help to define important groups in any particular society. However, they must be separated as concerned with sexual relations and marriage respectively.

exogamy – rules relating to marriage outside a particular group.

endogamy – rules relating to marriage within a particular group.

incest – sexual relations which are forbidden in any society because the partners are too closely related.

Anthropologists have pointed out that *marrying out* creates *alliances* between groups that may not otherwise have a great deal of contact, or whose contact may be hostile. Tylor even went so far as to suggest that people 'marry out or die out'. Others have written that in Africa people 'marry our enemies' in order to create peaceful ties, although in the tropical forest of South America, marriage is no insurance of peace and there are even people whose word for 'brother-in-law' is synonymous with that for 'enemy'. However, as was pointed out in the section on exchange, marriage is one means of maintaining *communication* between peoples, whether it be friendly or hostile.

Rules of endogamy, on the other hand, put an outer limit on the range of marriage partners. Even where there are few explicit rules, marriages may provoke disapproval if they cross lines of class, race, religion or nationality. We saw that members of the Pakistani community in Britain choose to arrange marriages with their own people, preferably cousins of a similar caste background. In the India subcontinent, there may be more explicit *caste endogamy* since members of different castes are often regarded as different kinds of people. At the same time there may be *village exogamy*, so the two categories are by no means mutually exclusive.

Marriage as Exchange – Dowry and Bridewealth

Another phenomenon found in India is hypergamy, which refers to the fact that those who receive a wife, the *wifetakers*, are regarded as superior to the *wifegivers*. This system must be seen in the context of the payment of dowry, which is wealth that travels with a bride to her new family. The Jains of Jaipur (northern India), a religious community concentrated mainly among business and trading castes, provide an example. According to Josephine Reynell (1991), the dowry here includes furniture, kitchen utensils and electrical goods to equip the bride's new home, as well as clothes and jewellery for the bride, and money for the bride's new-parents-in-law. The practice of religious and caste endogamy, as a way of maintaining control over economic resources, limits

hypergamy – a system of marriage in which a bride moves into a family that occupies a higher position in some locally accepted form of hierarchy.

dowry – wealth which travels with a bride to her new family.

Photograph 11.2 A Jain marriage ceremony, in Jaipur, northern India. The father of the bride (right) has formally handed his daughter over into the safekeeping of the groom and his family. The bride holds her hands over the right hand of the groom. Their right hands will be bound, symbolising their lifelong union (photograph courtesy of Josephine Reynell).

overall hierarchical difference, but a bride's parents would not eat with her new family after the marriage (Photograph 11.2 was taken at a Jain marriage ceremony; however see First-hand Account 11.2 on pp. 224–5 for a personal Jain view).

In other societies this system is reversed and *wife givers* will be seen as superior to *wife takers*, when the situation is described as hypogamy. In this case, it is more likely that goods called bridewealth, or brideprice, will be travelling in the opposite direction. Whenever imbalances of this sort occur, exchange must be *indirect*, or *generalised*, to use Lévi-Strauss's terms mentioned in Chapter 3; in other words, there must be at least three groups involved as people can't be seen as superior and inferior at the same time. A more straightforward exchange, where women move on a regular basis between two different groups (see below), was called by Lévi-Strauss *direct exchange*, and this can also refer to a situation where women are apparently being exchanged for *labour* or for bridewealth.

hypogamy – a system in which the bride's family is regarded as superior to that of the groom.

bridewealth (or **brideprice**) – goods or wealth travelling from a groom's family to that of his bride as part of the establishment and formalisation of continuing relations between their peoples.

Missionaries and other visitors from outside societies where such systems operated condemned these arrangements because they appeared to represent the purchase of women or, perhaps worse, the persuasion by the use of wealth to have women taken away. A deeper examination reveals much more significance, however, and bridewealth in different locations may also play one or more of several important roles. It is, for example, very likely to initiate or continue a series of exchanges which ensures long-term *communication* between the groups involved, who will of course both be related, as kin, to the children of any union set up.

Bridewealth may also play the important role of *validating* the marriage. In the absence of any other kind of legal contract, a couple setting up home without prior payments could well be seen to have an improper, illegitimate union. The payments also act as a kind of *security*. If a husband and his family treat the wife badly and she returns home, they will lose the payments they have made. Conversely, if the wife behaves badly, her husband may ask for a return of his payments. Since the bride's family may already have handed on the bridewealth to marry one of their menfolk, it is likely that they would put pressure on the woman to fit into her new home.

In Japan, there is no term for 'bridewealth', as such, but wealth in various forms is paid over by the groom's family in betrothal gifts which the bride uses in turn to prepare her *trousseau*, usually worth much more than the payments received. She receives goods from her own family and, like some cases of *dowry*, she takes these away again if the marriage breaks up, for they also represent a share of her family's inheritance. In families with no inheriting son, the initial payments may be made from the bride's family to that of the groom, who will join the house as potential successor. In both cases, as in situations in societies where a substantial dowry is paid over with a bride, the goods become part of the security of the new family.

Particularly in Africa, where bridewealth is often paid in cattle, the movement of animals may be seen as marking out a kind of map of human relationships. Bridewealth received for a daughter will be used for the wives of sons, and many relatives will make contributions to each other's weddings when they have livestock available in the knowledge that they will be able to draw on reciprocal support when they need it. Writing of the Nyakyusa of Malawi and Tanzania, Monica Wilson (1963) thus noted that cattle are continually driven down the paths of human relationships. Beattie suggested going a step further when he said, 'they tread out these paths' (1964: 125). The movement of wealth made in connection with marriage can clearly play roles which go way beyond the nuptial link being made.

Direct sister exchange (see Figure 11.5) is another type of marriage discussed by anthropologists as a way of describing long-term arrangements of *alliance* between two groups in which men who think of themselves as 'brothers' set up reciprocal links through their wives and sisters. In practice, the men involved probably share a lineage group, as described above, where the category 'brother' includes all males of the same generation. As the relationships continue through

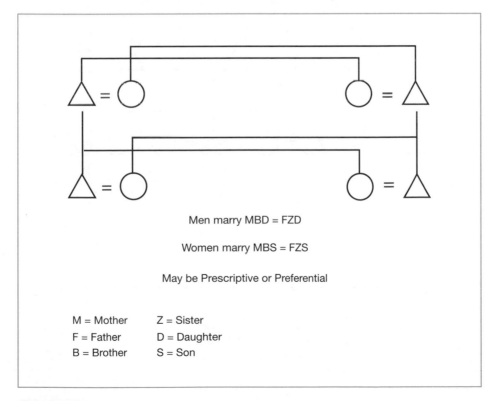

Men marry MBD = FZD

Women marry MBS = FZS

May be Prescriptive or Preferential

M = Mother   Z = Sister
F = Father   D = Daughter
B = Brother   S = Son

Figure 11.5   Direct (sister) exchange (for example, the Amba of Uganda)

the generations, a girl from a man's mother's lineage, a mother's 'brother's' daughter (MBD in the diagram) would be an appropriate partner, who would also be classified as a 'father's' sister's daughter (FZD).

Such a situation would be compatible with the system of exogamy which ensures communication between different groups of people, but it is a very male-oriented view and allows the women involved less say in the matter than they may in practice exercise. In Figure 11.5 I have also shown the relationships from the point of view of the wives. *Direct exchange* is found in situations where this type of alliance is *preferred*, perhaps to keep goods within a family group, but not necessarily *prescribed*, as would need to be the case for an interesting form of *indirect* exchange known as *matrilateral cross-cousin marriage*, where men *must* marry their mother's brother's daughters to make the system work (see Figure 11.6).

It is important again to remember that the triangles and circles here represent categories of people in particular relationships to one another. It will be noted that men in such a system move in one direction and women in the other, so direct exchange of sisters would not be possible. There may also be an element of hypergamy or hypogamy here, where the wife givers are considered superior or inferior to the wife takers, and this may have ramifications for the political sys-

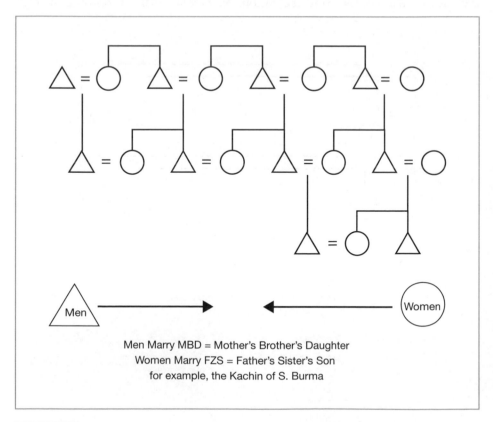

Men Marry MBD = Mother's Brother's Daughter
Women Marry FZS = Father's Sister's Son
for example, the Kachin of S. Burma

Figure 11.6 Matrilateral cross-cousin marriage (example of prescriptive system)

tem. An interesting example of this is the case of the Kachin people of southern Burma, described by Edmund Leach in *Political Systems of Highland Burma*. He writes:

> Much the most important set of relationships in any Kachin community are those which establish the mutual status relations between the various *htinggaw* groups that exist in that community. From the individual's point of view every *htinggaw* group within the community falls into one or other of four categories:
> (i)   ... lineages which are treated as being of the same clan as Ego's own and are near enough related to form an exogamous group with Ego's ...
> (ii)   *mayu ni* are lineages from which males of Ego's lineage have recently taken brides.
> (iii)   *dama ni* are lineages into which females of Ego's lineage have recently married.
> (iv)   .... lineages which are recognised as relatives .. but with which the relationship is distant or indefinite ...
> The essential feature of the system is that the [first] three categories ... are distinct. A man may not marry into his *dama*, a woman may not marry into her *mayu*. From an analytical point of view the system is one of matrilateral cross cousin marriage, but it needs to be stressed that a Kachin, in marrying a girl from his *mayu ni*, does not normally marry a true matrilateral cross cousin but only a classificatory cross cousin.
> (1954: 73–4)

The practicalities of such a system are discussed in great detail by Leach, who demonstrates in this now classic study an example both of the ingenious possibilities of structural analysis to make sense of social and political behaviour, and the way that such an abstract construct works in the practice of real-life relationships. Another extract, this time laying out more clearly the political elements of this system, also illustrates this point:

> This account of Laga village has brought out the fact that within the village the more permanent *mayu-dama* links serve to display the formal political status relations between different *htinggaw* lineage groups. In this formal system it is assumed that the *dama* are the political subordinates of the *mayu*; but let it be stressed that even within the village this subordination may be theoretical rather than actual. Any nominal inferiority can, in practice, be largely compensated by strategic marriages outside the village. (1954: 81)

Locality of Marriage Residence

Decisions about where a couple will live after they are married are very often decided by custom, or by a practical economic or political consideration, in a particular society. Anthropologists have terms to describe various arrangements. For example, where a man moves in with his wife's family, or into his wife's community, the marriage is said to be *matrilocal* (from the point of view of the next generation) or *uxorilocal* (from the Latin for 'wife'). If the woman moves to the man's former residence, the marriage is said to be *patrilocal* or *virilocal*. A completely new residence would be *neolocal*.

Factors like this may have very important ramifications for future relations, and again may play a part in the political system of the people concerned. In a society with patrilineal descent and patrilocal marriage, strong stable descent groups are likely to result, and these can form the basis of the political system, as is found among the Nuer. In Japan, during a period between the ninth and thirteenth centuries, there was a family known as the Fujiwaras who dominated the political scene through a continual series of matrilocal marriages with the imperial family, which for generations ensured that the child emperors grew up in a Fujiwara household. They were thus subject to the influence of their Fujiwara grandparents from an early age, and usually married into another Fujiwara household where they would be close to Fujiwara in-laws as they came to the throne. The Fujiwaras occupied a series of positions in the court, but the influence they exerted through marriage is widely acknowledged by historians of the period today.

Monogamy and Polygamy

So far we have talked little about forms of marriage that involve more than two partners. A system involving *one* person marrying *one* other is known as *monogamy*, where *mono* stands for 'one'. In a society where this is the law, if one of those partners wishes to marry someone else, they must first divorce their existing spouse. If a person thereby takes several spouses over a period of time, this is called serial monogamy. In some societies, however, it is perfectly acceptable for a man to maintain marriage to more than one wife (polygyny) or a woman to have more than one husband (polyandry). In either case, the system is described as *polygamy*, or multiple marriage.

polygyny – marriage involving one man and more than one woman.

In some ostensibly monogamous societies, where it is illegal for people to have more than one spouse, it is nevertheless fairly institutionalised that a man may maintain more than one household, one with a legal wife, others with his mistresses. The *casa chica*, or 'small house' is a phenomenon of this sort found in Latin America, and the situation has also been well known in Japan. A man's wealth will determine his ability to do this, of course, as it would in

polyandry – marriage involving one woman and more than one man.

a society that accepts polygamy, and his status will also be affected. In the case of the leaders of the tropical rain forest, discussed in the politics section, an abundance of wives were mentioned as a distinct advantage. The living arrangments for women in polygamous marriages, often in separate units with their children, may thus be rather similar to the 'single-parent families' we mentioned at the start of the chapter.

The Nayar and the Anderi, of India, are examples of peoples who practise polyandry. In the first case, women grow up and continue to live with their brothers, receiving visits from one 'husband' at a time. He leaves a spear at the door to deter any other who might think of calling while he is there. In the second case, one woman may be expected to take care of a whole group of brothers single-handedly, as a mechanism to avoid dividing up the family land. This will also have the effect of limiting the number of children they might collectively produce. Small wonder that polygyny is much more common!

Conclusion

This chapter has brushed rather cursorily over some of the abundance of work anthropologists have produced on the subject they call *kinship*, and the related one of *marriage* – it is probably one of the most widely studied fields in anthropology, and a selection of books on the subject have been listed below, both theoretical and ethnographic. David Schneider's (1980) influential symbolic analysis of American families conflicted with that proposed by Needham (outlined above), although both reacted to the important work of Lévi-Strauss that we mentioned briefly in Chapter 3. Carsten (2004) revisits some of the issues in a readable recent publication. Otherwise, the volume has abated somewhat, attention turning instead to the consequences of new forms of technology on family and reproduction. We have therefore focused on equipping the reader with a conceptual framework to make sense of other studies they may find. The textbook by Parkin (1997) and the reader he edited with Stone (2004) offer good sources of further depth for those who wish to pursue the subject.

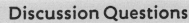

Discussion Questions

1   If you draw up a family tree, anthropological style, of all your known relatives, how far back can you go? And with how many degrees of collateral relatives do you keep in touch? Does it matter where they live?

2   Do you have different ways of behaving with people in different positions of relationships to you? Can you identify categories here, or is this just a personal thing?

3   Are there any groups of people with whom you would be unhappy to marry, or to find your son or daughter marrying? Why? What are the boundaries of your social world?

References and Further Research

Books
Beattie, John (1964) *Other Cultures* (London: Routledge & Kegan Paul).
Carrithers, Michael and Humphrey, Caroline (eds), *The Assembly of Listeners: Jains in Society* (Cambridge: Cambridge University Press).

Carsten, J. (1997) *The Heat of the Hearth: The Process of Kinship in a Malay Fishing Community* (New York: Oxford University Press).

Carsten, Janet (2004) *After Kinship* (Cambridge: Cambridge University Press).

Edwards, Jeanette (2000) *Born and Bred: Idioms of Kinship and the New Reproductive Technologies in England* (Oxford: Oxford University Press).

Franklin, Sarah (1997) *Embodied Progress: A Cultural Account of Assisted Conception* (London: Routledge).

Goody, Jack and Tambiah, S. J. (1973) *Bridewealth and Dowry* (Cambridge: Cambridge University Press).

Holy, Ladislav (1996) *Anthropological Perspectives on Kinship* (London and Chicago: Pluto Press).

Howell, Signe (2006) *The Kinning of Foreigners: Transnational Adoption in a Global Perspective* (Oxford: Berghahn Books).

Leach, E. R. (1954) *Political Systems of Highland Burma* (London: Athlone).

Needham, Rodney (ed.) (1971) *Rethinking Kinship and Marriage* (London: Tavistock).

Parkin, Robert (1997) *Kinship: An Introduction to the Basic Concepts* (Oxford: Blackwell).

Parkin, Robert and Stone, Linda (2004) *Kinship and Family: An Anthropological Reader* (Oxford: Blackwell).

Scheper-Hughes, Nancy (1993) *Death without Weeping: The Violence of Everyday Life in Brazil* (Berkeley: University of California Press).

Schneider, David (1980) *American Kinship: A Cultural Account* (Chicago and London: University of Chicago Press).

Shaw, Alison (1988) *A Pakistani Community in Britain* (Oxford: Blackwell).

Shaw, Alison (2000) *Kinship and Continuity: Pakistani Families in Britain* (London: Routledge).

Strathern, Marilyn (1992) *Reproducing the Future: Anthropology, Kinship and the New Reproductive Technologies* (Manchester: Manchester University Press).

Wilson, Monica (1963) *Good Company: A Study of Nyakyusa Age-Villages* (Boston, Mass.: Beacon Press).

Articles

Abrahams, Ray (1986) 'Anthropology among One's Affines', *Anthropology Today*, 2(2): pp. 18–20.

Clarke, Morgan (2006) 'Islam, Kinship, and Reproductive Technology', *Anthropology Today*, 22(5): 17–21.

Keenan, Jeremy (2000) 'The Father's Friend: Returning to the Tuareg as an "Elder"'. *Anthropology Today*, 16(4): 7–11.

Reynell, Josephine (1991) 'Women and the Reproduction of the Jain Community', in Michael Carrithers and Caroline Humphrey (eds), *The Assembly of Listeners: Jains in Society* (Cambridge: Cambridge University Press).

Rivière, P. G. (1971) 'Marriage: A Reassessment', in Rodney Needham, *Rethinking Kinship and Marriage* (London: Tavistock) pp. 57–74.

Rivière, P. G. (1985) 'Unscrambling Parenthood: The Warnock Report', *Anthropology Today* 1(4): 2–7.

Sherif, Bahir (1999) 'Gender Contradictions in Families: Official v. Practical Representations among Upper Middle-Class Muslim Egyptians', *Anthropology Today*, 15(4): pp. 9–13.

Shore, Cris (1992) 'Virgin Births and Sterile Debates: Anthropology and the New Reproductive Technologies', *Current Anthropology*, 33: 295–314 (including comments).

Simpson, Bob (1994) 'Bringing the "Unclear" Family into Focus: Divorce and Re-marriage in Contemporary Britain', *Man*, 29: 831–51.

Simpson, Bob (2006) 'Scrambling Parenthood: English Kinship and the Prohibited Degrees of Affinity', *Anthropology Today*, 22(3): 3–6.

van Bremen, Jan (1998) 'Death Rites in Japan in the Twentieth Century', in Joy Hendry (ed.), *Interpreting Japanese Society*, 2nd edition (London: Routledge) pp. 131–44.

Novels

Achebe, Chinua (1962) *Things Fall Apart* (London: Heinemann) is a best-selling story of an Igbo family trying, but largely failing, to adapt to a British Nigeria.

Ariyoshi Sawako (1981) *The River Ki* (trans. by Mildred Tahara; Tokyo: Kodansha, 1981) is a moving tale about several generations of a Japanese family.

Ishiguro Kazuo (2005) *Never Let Me Go* (London: Faber & Faber) is a gripping, bitter-sweet story about growing up in the age of new technologies, which addresses the whole question of what it means to be human.

Jung Chang (1991) *Wild Swans* (London: HarperCollins) is the much-celebrated account of three generations of Chinese women who lived most actively through the tremendous changes of the Cultural Revolution.

Mistry, Rohinton (2002) *Family Matters* (London: Faber & Faber) is a moving tale of a Parsi family dealing with matters that touch on universal themes.

Smith, Zadie (2001) *White Teeth* (London: Hamish Hamilton) weaves a complicated tale of relations between families of a variety of origins living in North London.

Tanizaki, Junichiro (1993) *The Makioka Sisters* (London: Mandarin) is a novel which details the problems that arise for a Japanese family trying to arrange appropriate marriages for a group of four sisters.

Films

Secrets and Lies (directed by Mike Leigh, 1996) is a feature film illustrating problems which can arise when people reared in an adoptive family take steps to make contact with their parents of birth.

Strangers Abroad: Everything is Relatives (André Singer, 1985) is a film about the anthropologist W. H. R. Rivers, whose work we discussed in Chapter 1, focusing on his study of kinship and genealogy among the various people with whom he worked.

Under the Sun: The Dragon Bride (Joanna Head, 1993) depicts the preparations and marriage of a 16-year-old girl of the Nyinba people of Nepal to four brothers from another village. Personal interviews flesh out and illustrate this unusual example of fraternal polyandry.

*Without Fathers or Husbands (*Hua Cai, 26 minutes, 1995) tells of the Na, an ethnic group in south-east China, where all the members of each household are consanguineous relatives, their social organisation is matrilineal and their sexual life mainly takes the form of nocturnal visits of men to women.

Websites

http://www.geocities.com/Hollywood/Theater/2404/nepotism.htm – a long list of actors who have made it into 'showbiz' because of their famous parents.

http://www.umanitoba.ca/faculties/arts/anthropology/kintitle.html – an online interactive tutorial on kinship from the University of Manitoba, Canada.

http://www.preacherssons.com – a website about a male couple and their five sons adopted from foster care.

12

Economics and the Environment

Introduction

In the last two chapters we dipped our toes into some of the deeper issues anthropologists address, but we also glimpsed a little of the way an anthropological approach can contribute to an understanding of subjects of wider interest. In this chapter we take up this theme in reference to the contribution anthropologists can make, and have made, to the study of economics and the environment. While doing this, we will draw together elements of anthropological work that we have considered in previous chapters of the book, and demonstrate how a good understanding of economic life depends on an understanding of the systems of classification and notions of exchange that we introduced in Chapters 1 and 3.

environment – a broad term referring to surrounding conditions and circumstances that influence the life of a people, but that the people classify and use in different ways.

We will start with a very basic part of the study of any society, and draw up a fairly crude classification of social groups according to the means of subsistence. Most classic anthropological studies actually start out by describing the economic base of a particular people and the environment in which they live, for this is usually a highly influential part of social life. Even at the most basic level, the environment is socially constructed, however, and it is important for anthropology students to be aware that the big 'global' discourses about threats to the natural world reflect levels of technological achievement. We will return to that specific theme in Chapter 14, when we look at global issues more broadly, but in this chapter we will lay out some of the variety of possibilities.

Over the years anthropologists have learned a lot about social life by focusing on small groups, and those who live at a basic economic level provide interesting information which is not irrelevant in a more complex, multicultural world. In the end, one person can only operate socially within a limited number of family, friends and associates, and there are certain rules of behaviour which pervade life in these micro-level groups, wherever they are found. In Chapter 3 we discussed Sahlins' ideas about forms of generalised reciprocity, which he argued operate within the closest circles; in Chapter 9 we examined methods of social control effective in such groups; and in the last chapter, we looked at the specific example of the Pakistani *birādarī*. There we glimpsed the important idea, continually aided by developments in information technology, that groups geographically separate can also easily keep in touch.

Subsistence and Survival

Economics is first of all concerned with the means of *survival* and how this is achieved. It is concerned with the way food is produced, shelter is provided, and with other everyday activities essential to life. Exchange, and specifically that of a market, is a further development of economic life, made possible when subsistence is secure. Small-scale societies were divided into three types by early anthropologists making sense of the world they observed (for example, Forde 1934), and these divisions are still used to describe forms of basic economy of both isolated contemporary peoples and earlier forms of social life described by archaeologists, though evolutionary schemes and generalisations about social interaction have been severely challenged. The three types are: hunter–gatherers, pastoralists and agriculturalists.

Hunter-gatherers or 'gatherer-hunters'

People described in this way collect food from their immediate environment, and they have been characterised as picking or catching only as much as they could eat at any one time to avoid problems of storage or transport. They were said to be usually nomadic, since they must move about to avoid exhausting their supplies, and to seek foods when they are in season and abundant. They were also said to have little role specialisation, the chief division of labour being made along lines of age and gender, so that the healthy and capa-

nomadic - a term used to describe people who move about in the course of making a living rather than settling in one place.

ble collect for the very young and the very old and infirm, and, typically, men hunt, while women gather.

Economists had described this life as hard and difficult, but ethnographic material indicated that many such people only 'worked' for long enough to provide themselves with sustenance, leaving the rest of their lives to relax and enjoy each other's company. Marshall Sahlins thus described hunter–gatherers as the 'original affluent society':

> Hunters and gatherers have by force of circumstances an objectively low standard of living. But taken as their *objective*, and given their adequate means of production, all the people's material wants usually can easily be satisfied [a common understanding of 'affluence', Sahlins 1974: 1] ... The world's most primitive people have few possessions, *but they are not poor*. Poverty is not a certain small amount of goods, nor is it just a relation between means and ends; above all it is a relation between people. Poverty is a social status. As such it is an invention of civilization. (Sahlins 1974: 36–7)

Sahlins' argument is worth following up, for he makes the interesting point that if people want no more than their food, and that is available, then they have all they desire. In other words, they have not been corrupted by the addictive and competitive traps of property ownership and capitalism. This idea became somewhat romanticised, however, using as a classic example the Ju/'hoan (also known as San Bushmen, see Barnard 2007 for a discussion of names) of the Kalahari Desert, whose warm and abundant surroundings made life comparatively rather easy. The feature film *The Gods Must Be Crazy*, cited below, illustrates this view when it tracks the events following the arrival of an empty Coca-Cola bottle into a Ju/'hoan camp, thrown carelessly out of the window of a small plane, but forthwith corrupting the otherwise innocent lives of these formerly apparently idyllically happy people. The subsequent fate of the Ju/'hoan people is something we will return to in the next chapter.

In practice, there are many and varied peoples in different parts of the world who have sustained themselves largely through hunting and gathering techniques, or 'gathering and hunting', as some feminists have argued they should be called, in deference to the female provision of gathering as the basis of their economy, with hunting supplementing the diet only for special or sporadic occasions. Some own property and store food, and others live very tough and difficult lives in regions much less hospitable than that of the continual African sunshine. They have a range of interesting sets of power relations and ideologies, and they also produce some highly skilled art and material culture.

Anthropologists of peoples who fall under the category of 'hunter–gathering', or 'gatherer–hunting', tend to meet and compare their findings, despite this diversity, and a very useful two-part collection (Ingold et al. 1988) justified this practice, as follows:

> In some ways hunter-gatherer societies have developed independently of other branches of social anthropology. Yet we believe that they are

not simply in tune with social anthropology more generally: they are the backbone of the discipline. They are often much more in touch with the essence of what it is to be human than are trends in virtually any other branch of the subject. (Barnard and Woodburn 1988)

Examples of surviving hunters and gatherers, apart from the rather well known Ju/'hoan Bushmen and Mbuti Pygmy peoples of southern Africa, include several groups of Australian Aborigines, such as the Yolngu people whose art was discussed in Chapter 6, rain forest peoples, for example in Malaysia, and like those of South America whose politics we discussed in Chapter 10, and peoples like the Inuit and Cree who still make at least a part of their living by hunting in the harsh snowy climes of the extreme northern hemisphere. Some groups on the West Coast of North America used to challenge the original definition by having settlements as well as leading a largely hunter–gatherer life, and they also made beautiful artefacts. Among these are the Kwakwaka'wakw (formerly described as Kwakiutl), Tlingit and Haida, whom we considered in Chapter 3 as practising exchanges described as *potlatch*.

Many more people lived from hunting and gathering in the distant past, and they used to be seen as technologically the most primitive people (as Sahlins suggests above), but anthropologists who specialise in contemporary hunter–gathering peoples are keen to point out the social and cultural complexities that may go along with this means of subsistence, and argue that it is not necessarily possible to learn about ancient societies by looking at the modern ones. Few of the latter are now completely out of contact with the wider world, and they have anyway changed themselves over time, apart from adapting to technological change. A good collection about hunter–gatherers is to be found in Ingold et al. (1988).

Pastoralists

Pastoralist is the term used for people who live off the produce of herds of cattle, sheep, goats and so forth. They also generally need to move about to find fresh grazing for their animals, so they may be nomadic, but they could also be **transhumant**, that is, moving between fixed locations, as we saw in the case of the Nuer. The splendid tents (known as *yurts*) constructed and occupied by various nomadic peoples of Central Asia, and displayed in many ethnographic museums around the world, demonstrate the extent to which 'mobile homes' may be substantial and highly decorative. Some people in this part of the world now own houses in the towns, but at certain times of the year prefer to live in their *yurts*, even erecting them in their back yards when they are not in the desert because they prefer to sleep outside.

Some pastoralists satisfy almost all their requirements – food, shelter, clothes and fuel – from their animals, as well as finding aesthetic appreciation in them, as we saw in Coote's discussion of the Nilotic peoples, such as the Nuer and Dinka, in Chapter 6. They may also create semi-permanent relationships of exchange with their neighbours, for example giving cheese to secure grazing rights. An example of this type of situation is described in an excellent ethnography by John Campbell (1964) about the Sarakatsani, Greek shepherds whose view of the world also demonstrates a system of classification based on different degrees of trust, a scheme of relations rather similar to that outlined by Sahlins for his cycles of reciprocity (discussed in Chapter 3).

The greatest trust is with the family, but lesser degrees of trust are established with 'patrons' on whom the Sarakatsani depend for grazing, both sets distinguished from other outsiders. Campbell writes:

> Sarakatsani are deeply concerned about three things; sheep, children (particularly sons), and honour. It is a common feature of many pastoral peoples with simple material cultures that they are highly dependent on their physical environment and that the care of herds, the structure of the community, and its social values, form a coherent pattern of activities and sentiments which present few inconsistencies. The three concerns of the Sarakatsani are mutually implicated. The sheep support the life and prestige of the family, the sons serve the flocks and protect the honour of their parents and sisters, and the notion of honour presupposes physical and moral capacities that fit the shepherds for the hard and sometimes dangerous work of following and protecting their animals. (1964: 9)

Campbell goes on to present the social and spiritual life of these shepherds, within the wider Greek community, as totally constructed around the sheep who form the economic base of their lives. It is also an excellent example of another society where the values of honour and shame underpin the system of social control so that fear of gossip and ridicule are strong sanctions for compliant behaviour, as we saw in Chapter 9.

Agriculturalists

The earlier evolutionary economic arguments turned to the development of agriculture and horticulture as requiring a more sedentary lifestyle, and a longer-term investment in the land, which could then support larger populations. This, they argued, allowed a greater division of labour, specialisation became feasible, and a complex political system could be sustained, freeing some people from the needs of survival to rule, fight, judge and so forth. Differences may still be based on age and gender, but there could develop further possibilities for gaining status and more ways to develop an aptitude, for example for oratory, or divination.

A sedentary population is in a better position to accumulate surpluses, which allows the greater development of systems of *exchange*, it was argued, and as the extent of these spreads out from the immediate surrounding community, the beginnings of a *market economy* may be observed. As a society becomes more and more complex, any one individual is less likely to provide for his own survival directly, and more likely to be engaged in exchange and specialisation. Food is mostly purchased, and the wherewithal to purchase it is earned through specialist employment. It was from this point of perceived complexity that it seemed appropriate to apply and develop economic theory, and a branch of anthropology developed called Economic Anthropology (see, for example, Firth 1967).

In fact, people who grow crops may also move about, as we have seen in shifting agriculture, such as the *slash-and-burn* type of cultivation found in the tropical rain forest of South America, and the millet growing of the transhumant, predominantly pastoral, Nuer, and we have looked at some of the social implications of these systems in Chapters 8 and 10. We have also seen that property and exchange may characterise the lives of peoples in simpler economic circumstances, such as hunter–gathering and pastoralism. Thus the evolutionary economic argument is not particularly helpful, though we did see in Chapter 9 the greater effectiveness of certain social sanctions in a cooperative rice-growing community, than where people could easily move in and out. In the next two sections we will consider some of the contributions ethnographic studies have made and can still make to an understanding of economic ideas.

Property and Tenure

Important aspects of economic life are related to notions of *property* and *land tenure*, and anthropologists have gathered interesting material on these subjects. Ideas about the ownership of land have been variable throughout the world, with subtle differences eventually causing horrendous long-term problems between neighbouring and colonising peoples. Hunters and gatherers are dependent on using land as they need it, which is fine as long as there is abundant land available. Pastoralists, too, need to seek pasture for their animals and, if this is scarce, they may have to seek grazing rights. Even agriculturalists, such as those who cultivate by the slash-and-burn method, may just have expected to move around as they needed to, but such freedom has become rare in the modern world.

A scarcity of land for the people trying to use it leads to the development of rules, which may become more and more complex as the pressure increases. In some parts of Africa and North America, there was a concept described by anthropologists as usufruct, which granted rights to use land, but without overall ownership. The land may have been perceived of as belonging to a tribe, a lineage, to 'the Creator' or to a king, perhaps, and if it were not in use it would revert to a central pool. So long as a family used it, they could pass it on through the generations, but it was not seen as theirs in perpetuity. This was one of the areas of greatest misunderstanding and conflict between Europeans and Native Peoples in North America, where the latter granted rights to use land, which the former then thought they had purchased (see First-hand Account 12 overleaf).

usufruct – a term to describe ideas certain peoples hold about land which gives them the right to use it, but without implying outright ownership of it.

Throughout the colonised world, and particularly since the raising of local awareness during the United Nations' Year of Indigenous Peoples in 1993, problems such as these have become hot political issues. Anthropologists have had a

Indigenous peoples of Turtle Island (The Americas) value the sacredness of every rock, every tree, every river, and every blade of grass as imbued with life; with breath. When I was growing up in the Northern Boreal forests as a young Cree girl, I was always mindful of the aliveness of the ecosystem around us. Our parents, aunties and uncles taught us much about the interconnections we needed to sustain us and to keep us healthy and well. The plant life, from their roots to their leaves, provided much wealth for our food and medicinal and wellness needs. The animals gave their lives for

First-hand account 12:
Laara Fitznor, Cree First Nation with German/Scots ancestry – on Space-Place-Location and Sacredness

our needs. We honoured them by offering Tobacco to the Creator as a sacred transaction. Our Elders tell us that the Tobacco is a sacred plant given by the Creator to our people to use for giving thanks and gratitude for the bounties of the Earth and Land. It was not meant to be misused like it is today by smoking as an addiction. When I was an adult learning about our ways I realised that this practice of using Tobacco as an offering was unique to our indigenous lifeways, and it was one of the practices threatened by the colonial experience so that many of our people no longer practise this activity. I learned that by engaging in this practice it reminds us to be ecologically minded and thankful for the health and wealth of the Earth/land.

I learned that engaging relationships that energise an eco-balance of all life forms across all space–place–location is an important goal for sustainability now and in the future. Our Elders tell us that everything was placed on earth by the Creator and that our Sacred Places are blueprints left by our wisdom keepers to engage our present living and to work to care for the earth for the mutual benefits of future generations to come. We were given a responsibility to 'look after' what was left for us to use in our daily lives. We are to be sustainable engagers of everything alive. A respected Indigenous American scholar, Greg Cajete, tells us that 'the land and the place we lived were in a perfect state... the real test of living was to establish a harmonious relationship with that perfect state was Nature – to understand it, to see it as the source of one's life and livelihood, and the source of one's essential well-being … this nature-centred orientation helped individuals come to terms with the environment where they lived in a holistic way' (1994: 75). This ecological thinking calls us to give attention to space–place–location and the holistic engagement of people as an aspect of understanding our respective responsibilities to respect the spaces we use for our families and communities.

Our Elders tell us that people must recognise that we are primarily receivers of the gifts given by our Mother the Earth and there is a tenuous relationship that currently exists because of the colonial agenda of our recent past wherein the onslaught of land appropriation has damaged ongoing relationships between people and the land. Perhaps, how much has been robbed from our indigenous understanding of space-place-location of our lands might be measured by the minimal use of our lands as sacred places today. Much of our land has become a playground for use by people not from that place. The sense of spirituality and sacredness of lands tend to get lost in the translation of using the land for other uses, spurred by the 'the rapid transformation of the Earth by science and technology, and the ecological crises that has begun to unfold…' (ibid. 81).

For example, during the past few centuries the consequences of misusing and appropriating our sacred lands are showing their devastating effects on the environment. If tourism is a way for our indigenous populations to continue to sustain local economies our responsibility becomes clear to ensure that space–place–location finds its ecological centre and a 'spiritually integrated perception of Nature' (ibid). This kind of ecological thinking then moves us to become an integral part of sustaining the places where we live without adding more damage to the environment.

Reference
Cajete, Greg (1994) *Look to the Mountain: An Ecology of Indigenous Education* (Kivaki Press, 1994).

Laara Fitznor, originally from Wabowden, Manitoba, Canada, has a Doctor of Education Degree from the University of Toronto, and now teaches Aboriginal education at the University of Manitoba. Laara received an award recognizing her 'Environmental Education and Aboriginal Cultural Studies'.

role to play in helping Indigenous people translate their point of view into terms which could be understood by the wider authorities, and the Kayapo Indians of the Xingu Valley in Brazil were aided in this way, as we saw in Chapter 10. However, the rights of Indigenous peoples have become a global issue now, and the support of the United Nations in setting up standing committees has enabled considerable mutual support for people helping themselves to reclaim their lands. Hugh Brody's film *Time Immemorial* addresses these issues for the Nishga'a First Nation in the interior of British Columbia in Canada.

Important rules have developed about the inheritance of land, as we have already glimpsed in the section on kinship in the last chapter, and about keeping land within a family, as may be a consideration in the setting up of a marriage. If land is constantly divided between children, the area will become smaller and smaller, so there are usually institutionalised ways of avoiding this. The solution of the Anderi, where a group of brothers work together, marrying one wife between them, is rather unusual. In Japan, the *ie*, or 'house', was until postwar legal changes seen as owning the land, but only one person inherited the position of head of the house, with the right to cultivate the household property. Other children left to set up their own houses, or to marry into pre-existing ones. In Mexico, there is a dual system, with owned land, known as *huerta*, and village land which is leased to families to use, known as *ejido*. The latter reverts to the common pool if it is not cultivated.

Moveable property, on the other hand, may be exchanged, and passed on, and there may be separate inheritance rules for this, as was mentioned in the section on kinship. It may also be given as **tribute** to a leader, which helps to perpetuate a centralised political system, as we saw in Chapter 10. In societies without money or recognised currency, people would give away perishable goods as a kind of insurance for future needs. They trust that those who receive the goods will return the favour when they have a surplus. Similarly, the payment of tribute to a chief may be seen as a kind of investment, and chiefs have even been described as primitive bankers. Some of this form of exchange has economic aspects, then, but much of it is social, and it is difficult to draw a hard and fast line.

Market Economics

We discussed the social aspects of some simple market economies in Chapter 3, where we talked of the villages in Mexico and Guatemala which specialise in the production of specific goods, such as bread, pots, woollen garments, flowers and fireworks, and we suggested that the markets serve to maintain communication over a wide area and offer entertainment as well as providing for basic needs. This system works because people marry **endogamously** within their communities, passing on the skills required for their trade through the generations. The economic aspects of these markets are thus best understood within the context of social arrangements through time.

These endogamous villages were contrasted with those in Africa and elsewhere where rules of **exogamy** can be seen to ensure communication over particular cultural areas. In this case, women seem to become commodified as objects of exchange, at least according to some interpretations, but this idea was modified in the last chapter, where we saw that outsiders such as missionaries and colonial administrators misunderstood bridewealth transactions. In practice, they embodied important social elements like the validating of the union, the legitimising of offspring and the provision of security.

Anthropological studies of markets and exchange usually throw up social factors which economists are inclined to overlook, and this emphasis affects the principles of analysis too. The concept of value, related to their cherished laws of *supply and demand*, is an interesting aspect of economic theory to consider. It is usually associated with scarcity, and very often related to the degree of access to resources. It is no good offering gold to someone dying for lack of water in a desert, for example, but in global terms water is much more abundant than gold, and the latter has acquired a widely recognised exchange value. Once subsistence is secure, food too is assigned differential value. The avocado, a relatively luxurious fruit in British supermarkets, lies rotting in superabundance in Mexico. Apples, which often do the same in Britain, are highly prized in Japan, where an aubergine, or eggplant, again a less usual and therefore more valued part of the British diet, is regarded as a poor food.

Serving a 'high value' food, is a way to gain status and even a contemporary visit to palaces built and decorated by European monarchs during the periods of discovery and exploration of the New World (as far as they were concerned) illustrates some of the social reasons why they were prepared to make enormous investments of their resources in ships and sailors. The example of gold also demonstrates the idea of aesthetic value, and a consideration of the use of gold for the production of jewellery can lead us into its symbolic value. Wedding rings denote a social relationship which, as we have seen, may have a variety of particular connotations, and gold and silver are commonly used for gifts to mark rites of passage. The loss of such objects means more than a reduction in wealth.

The conversion of wealth into status was demonstrated forcibly in Chapter 3 by the case of the potlatch feasts, but another Mexican example illustrates a different element of constraint in this type of transfer. Here, fiestas are financed by one person known as a *mayordomo* who pays for the whole event, thus winning a position of respect and power within the community. So unpopular are those who gain wealth but fail to do this that people will bankrupt themselves for several years to put on a good show when their turn comes. George Foster's (1965) 'Theory of Limited Good' relates this practice to a collective idea that if one family gets too rich others believe they are being deprived. Financing a festival not only redistributes wealth, then, but also offers a means to avoid jealousy and bitterness.

We briefly discussed social ideas about money in Chapter 3, where we gave examples of how cash may be converted into a gift. The use of any type of currency requires a certain agreement about its value, and the locally symbolic nature of this value is immediately evident when we return from travelling abroad with a pocketful of foreign coins. Out of the country where they are recognised, they might as well be pebbles for all the use they are. A credit card, likewise, has little intrinsic value, but it has acquired a very useful global symbolic status. In the end, the global value of 'money' is determined in international markets in a system which looks remarkably like the barter that economists called 'primitive'. We also showed in Chapter 3 that barter may be imbued with morality, and the lack of a shared system of morality at a global level may be another factor that bothers critics of the contemporary capitalist world order.

In Sahlins' cycles of reciprocity, the generalised end of the continuum is the area of most social and moral implication, and thus another problem for Western economic theory when it assumes that people are always trying to *maximise their gains*. Even if the gains of prestige, power, status and divine benefits are added to material gains, there still remain the personal ties of that closest group, expressed in culturally specific notions like love, friendship and loyalty, even just a shared system of classification. At all levels of economics social factors play a part, and one of the reasons why foreigners doing business in Japan find themselves so well wined and dined is because their Japanese counterparts assign great value to making a business relationship a social one.

Anthropologists have now ploughed several ragged edges into the universalist furrows economists had previously presented as so straight and clear, and the use of words such as **commodity** and **consumption** abound in *their* recent discourse. An influential work entitled *The Social Life of Things: Commodities in Cultural Perspective* (Appadurai 1986) sought to shift attention from the forms of exchange and reciprocity, such as gift-giving, barter and trade, to the objects themselves, and how they are understood and appropriated in different ways, with different values and interpretations in the different situations in which they find themselves. We saw examples of this type of approach in the last section of Chapter 3.

An earlier influence was *The World of Goods: Towards an Anthropology of Consumption* (Douglas and Isherwood 1979), where an anthropologist and an economist together focused similar questions on the reasons behind the purchasing and acquisition of goods. The focus on consumption as a means to understanding social behaviour has since become popular amongst anthropologists, including not only the behaviour of shoppers in supermarkets and other retail outlets, but subjects formerly seen as ritual and symbolic, such as weddings. In Japan, a wedding package may be purchased in its entirety, including every detail of dress and bridal coiffure, ceremony and feast, through to the arrangement of a suitable honeymoon location – the consumption of all of which Ofra Goldstein-Gidoni has interpreted in the global marketplace as an expression of Japaneseness (1997).

Social Views of the Environment

We come back here to thinking about classification. In the early chapters we discussed anthropologists who classified themselves at the pinnacle of the developed world. At the time of this writing, the whole world's 'natural environment' is thought to be under threat from too much development, and the same people whom our forebears thought primitive are admired for their care and techniques of conservation. In practice, problems arise in thinking about the *environment* because of apparently incompatible views, and an anthropological approach can help to formulate less fiercely opposed alternatives. This, in turn, can help decision-making bodies to take account of all the people involved when they devise plans to make economically advantageous developments.

In a book entitled *Environmentalism: The View from Anthropology*, Kay Milton has collected together a series of articles which offer various contributions to the debate. She points out, in the introduction, that concerns with the preservation of the environment are by no means new in small-scale societies:

> The Australian Aborigine who avoids hunting animals on sacred sites, and performs ceremonies to ensure the continued existence of edible species, is, like the Greenpeace campaigner, implementing environmental responsibilities. The rubber-tappers of Amazonia, the Penan of Borneo, the subsistence farmers of northern India and many other communities have attempted to defend their traditional patterns of resource-use against what they see as the destructive consequences of large-scale commercial exploitation. (1993: 3)

Milton considers the advantages some local discussion and interpretation could have when governments and international NGOs (non-governmental organisations) formulate their environmental policies. An understanding of each other's motives and expectations would go a long way towards easing in changes perceived as globally important at a local level, but a greater understanding of local views might even offer an opportunity for a better system of conservation to be put into place. As Milton explains, ideas about the environment are constituted through discourse, and this draws on all kinds of ammunition depending on the point of view being advocated. Aboriginal people may be credited quite falsely with environmental concerns if it suits an argument for them to be so cited. On another occasion, the same people may be painted in a negative light for the same set of practices. Before we pursue this line of discussion, it is important that we try and see how complicated the issues may be.

In industrialised countries, for the most part, people are able to transcend environmental limitations, except in extremes of weather, such as snow, floods and excessively high wind, and even then they get upset when the forecasters don't warn about the problems in time, or the authorities don't react swiftly enough. Damage caused by environmental phenomena is something that appears on television, and the *tsunami* that caused havoc in South East Asia in late 2004 was particularly shocking to people in the rest of the world who watched chaos hit a normally idyllic holiday zone. Equally shocking was hurricane Katrina, which devastated New Orleans, a place with an international reputation for music and easy living in the heartland of the richest country in the world. Another shock was the stark contrast between technological achievement and the indiscriminate damage caused by the mighty earthquake which hit Kobe, Japan, in January 1995.

People in less highly industrialised regions live in much closer contact with the physical environment, and their view of the world may well reflect this intimacy. The various Inuit groups have a multitude of ways of dealing with the snow and ice in which they spend so much of the year, reflected in their words for different forms of it, and the Bedouin of the Sahara desert have a similar understanding of the sand. An anthropologist living amongst such people must consider environmental factors as a prime feature of their study, but novelists and film-makers have sometimes better captured the feel of a way of life so alien to a cosseted twentieth century city dweller. The novel by the Danish writer Peter Høeg, *Miss Smilla's Feeling for Snow*, presents a Greenlander's view of the snow, for example, and some passages of Michael Ondaatje's book *The English Patient* forcibly illustrate the importance in the desert of understanding different types of wind. Both of these works have now been made into films that well illustrate the environmental exigencies of life in these extreme circumstances, and an early anthropological film known as *Nanook of the North* makes clear the stark daily life of a traditional Inuit family.

Anthropologists must look at environmental conditions wherever they work, but they realise that the world view of the people they live with may involve quite different perceptions to those which they themselves classify as 'the environment'. The anthropologist must aim to unearth this view, and in Chapter 6, where we showed how perceptions of the landscape could be unlike anything familiar to proponents of Western, or even Eastern art, we began to approach the potential complexity of the problem. Another aspect of the subject is the way in which people place themselves in the context of their surroundings and, in this environmentally conscious contemporary world, the extent to which their ideology is reflected in practice.

In the opening of the book *Japanese Images of Nature*, the authors write:

> It is often claimed that the Japanese have a particular love for nature, a love often reflected in their art and material culture. But today equal notice is being given to the environmental degradation caused by the Japanese at home as well as abroad. How can these phenomena be reconciled? The aim of this volume is to address this question through an in-depth analysis of the human–nature relationship in Japan.   (Asquith and Kalland 1997: 1)

In the book, much attention is devoted to Japanese ideas which are translated as 'nature', demonstrating again the problems of definition, as well as conceptions of human interaction with the rest of the world.

In another article in Milton's book, developed further in a fascinating collection of his own essays entitled *The Perception of the Environment* (2000), Tim Ingold makes a point very apt in this context about our whole notion of the environment as a *global* phenomenon. To think of the world we live in as a *globe* implies a view taken from the outside, as opposed to an earlier (European) view of humankind being part of a series of spheres which surrounded as well as included human activity. We learn of the world at school in global terms, although few of us have actually seen more than a photograph of this version of our environment, and we also study maps which colour the land masses in nation states which represent a history of colonialism and voyages of discovery and exploration.

Ingold refers to an idea that this view represents a triumph of technology over cosmology which, in contrast,

> places the person at the centre of an ordered universe of meaningful relations.... and enjoins an understanding of these relations as a foundation for proper conduct towards the environment. (1993: 41)

Seeing the world as a globe puts human society '*outside* what is residually construed as the "physical world" and furnishes the means for the former's control over the latter' (ibid.). Ingold concedes, however, that each view contains the seeds of the other, and this is the basis of the approach taken up by some of the contributors to the Asquith and Kalland volume, mentioned above. Japanese often argue that they think of themselves as 'one with nature', an idea which they oppose to a Western desire to control it, although, in practice, the Japanese clearly make efforts to control natural forces too.

In an indigenous system of Indian thought, too, a person is seen as integrally connected with the cosmos. According to Tambiah:

> The Ayurvedic system we have in mind postulates that the constituents of nature and of man are the same, and that processes such as the ingestion of food and medicine and the excretion of bodily waste products are part and parcel of the flow of energies and potencies between man and nature. Physical illness is the result of imbalances that can be corrected by exchanges at various levels – by ingestion of the right substances and diet, by exposure to or protection from climatic conditions, by maintaining proper relations with other persons – family, kin, and the gods. (1990: 34)

It is important not to fall into the temptation of explaining the whole of social and political life in environmental terms, however. Several explanations of Japanese idiosyncratic 'character' seek causes in the rugged mountainous scenery, or the predominance of rice cultivation. There are mountains elsewhere, however, and plenty of people grow rice. It is important to avoid a *determinist* view. The physical environment undoubtedly limits the social arrangements a people are able to make, but it cannot be said to *determine* them. If it could, there would always be the same social system in the same environment and this is by no means the case. A glance at the variety of Mexican ethnography will illustrate the point, for there have been highly centralised, artistically and technologically advanced peoples living in precisely the area now populated with societies much more diffuse in political organisation, and much less developed in technological terms.

To take one environmental factor, one 'problem' for a people to solve, usually reveals a variety of solutions, and these will depend on cultural differences. Everyone needs water to live, and a shortage of water can be a serious issue. The hunter–gatherer and pastoralist people discussed in the previous section generally solve the problem by moving around, by seeking water sources to resolve their needs immediately. Their response to the 'problem' is the nomadic way of life, and the transhumance of people like the Nuer is a more stable possibility. Elsewhere, a long-term response to the same 'problem' may be achieved through the building of irrigation systems, which in turn involves a social organisation capable of maintaining and administering them, as well as sharing out the supplies. Rules of land ownership are then likely to characterise economic life, and access to water will very likely be regulated. Edmund Leach's book *Pul Eliya* (1961) is about the system of land ownership in a community in Sri Lanka, and it gives an abundance of detail about the social consequences of such a system.

The environment cannot be said to *determine* the social system because the environment is no objective reality. It is always categorised by the people who live in it and make use of it, according to their view of the world. One last example of different views, which has become a highly contentious international issue, involves the varying perceptions of the problems of *whale conservation* found in Japan and among members of different Western nations. According to a Japanese view, based on their own independent research – a view which is shared by Norwegians and Icelanders – there are enough whales to be harvested for consumption; indeed, if they are not harvested they will eat up food supplies for fish which could otherwise also have been caught to feed the Japanese population. Whale meat is a valuable source of protein, and the catching and preparation of whales are specialist occupations, which have been passed down through generations.

The predominant Western view, however, is that the whale population is threatened with extinction, and if the Japanese (and others) keep catching them, they will soon be no more. Many of the people who take this view have been brought up on stories about affable whales such as Moby Dick, and the tale of Jonah, and very few of them regard whale meat as part of their diet. Japanese commentators remark that if the whales were called 'cows' there would be no problem, and criticise the Western world for being sentimental. A very similar, but measured, anthropological view is presented by Niels Einarsson (in Milton's collection), who set out the case of Icelandic fisherman who were losing their entire livelihood for reasons seen locally as quite indefensible. A Norwegian anthropologist, Arne Kalland, even took a place on the International Whaling Commission to try and present a more objective viewpoint.

I have no idea whose scientific figures are more accurate, and this is not the place to take up the issue. A demonstration of differing perceptions is the aim at this point. The whaling issue emphasises the importance of seeing how the environment is classified by those who live in it, and also how views of the environment may be created through discourse about it. Greenpeace can be commended for its commitment to many important issues, but it can hardly be denied that it has made use of – nay, even exploited – the romanticism of the 'intelligent, singing' whale in attracting support. If these words are making the reader angry, then turn to consider the plight of the people around the world who rely on whales and other sea animals for their livelihood (see, for example, Barnes 1996 and Photograph 12.1).

Photograph 12.1 Villagers in Lamalera, Indonesia, divide up a whale they have hunted – a good source of protein (photograph courtesy of R.H. and R. Barnes).

Environmental Influence in Social Life

The environment does of course influence economic, political and ritual life in most parts of the world, although in industrial societies this relationship may very often be neglected, especially from the reciprocal point of view. However, as we have seen in the case of the whale, all apparently economic resources may not be regarded in the same way, and when a whale became trapped in the Thames estuary in 2006, no one mentioned its previous value as a huge source of food, oil and whale-boned corsets. Amongst Hindus, the cow is regarded as a sacred animal, and though perfectly edible in objective terms, it is forbidden for consumption by local custom. Cows wander rather freely in some parts of India, damaging crops and impeding traffic, possibly even competing with human beings for the limited resources available.

Map 12.1 A view of the world from the Southern hemisphere

As we have seen elsewhere in this book, it is also possible to point to relationships between the environment and political arrangements. In the first section of this chapter we saw that the choice of economic activity affects the possibilities for political development. Hunter–gatherers and pastoralists live in groups limited in size by the availability of food for themselves and, in the second case, their cattle, whereas sedentary agriculturalists are better able to develop larger populations and more complex political systems. The case of Nuer politics, sometimes called *fission/fusion politics*, is clearly influenced by the transhumance of their lives, since allegiances can be adjusted twice a year.

Environmental features also undoubtedly influence ritual and religious activity. Festivals are often associated with changes of seasons, planting and harvest, or the depths of winter and summer. Even where the agricultural cycle has been superseded by the wonders of technology for bringing goods to the supermarket, seasonal goods such as pumpkins, strawberries and sprouts are still drawn upon for celebrations. In Japan, where the land area is 90 per cent mountainous, mountains are the sites of religious shrines and pilgrimages, as well as often being regarded as mystical in particular ways. In a land where irrigation is important, water festivals are to be expected, and long spells of dry weather may still be punctuated with rain-making dances.

The very cosmology a people hold is often quite unintelligible without an understanding of attitudes to the environment, its limitations, and associations that have been created with it. Christmas in Europe and North America is inevitably associated with snow, for example, whereas the same feast in Australia is held in mid-summer. It is interesting the way that some of the symbolic associations have persisted through this inconvenient climatic difficulty, and in parts of Australia there is a 'seasonal Christmas' festival, probably largely a commercial venture, but allowing the use of northern symbols such as blazing fires and snowmen at the appropriate time of year.

A visit to the opposite hemisphere, or a completely different climate, is a good way to realise how environmentally orientated one's language is. For those of European stock who have grown up in Australia, New Zealand, or other southern climes, daily language contains some wonderful anomalies imported from a completely different ecosystem. The four seasons used in Australia are sometimes only illustrated by the deciduous trees planted by the colonisers and the agricultural cycles imposed by their farmers. Australian indigenous trees flower in the winter and the climate is very often rather warm, especially in the north. Map 12.1 illustrates a view of the world, from an Australian point of view.

Conclusion

In global parlance, too, we have adopted some originally directional words to take on meanings now quite inappropriate in orientation. The 'Far East', like the 'Middle East', was measured from the point of view of Europe, actually west from America, and north from Australia and New Zealand. 'The West' is an expression used to describe an amorphous collection of non-Eastern countries, now rather different from each other, but sharing the language which perpetuates these directional idiosyncrasies. I hope that this book, though it emanates from the original source of these misnomers, will have made way for a more equal and open sharing of different possibilities for seeing that world. In the next chapter we consider the increased likelihood of intercultural encounters that might offer an opportunity to express that awareness.

Discussion Questions

1 Consider what proportion of your life is spent securing your survival. How do you achieve this? On whom do you depend, and what do you offer in return? Now consider how much more time you spend working, and for what, or whom, are the extra benefits?

2 Under what circumstances would you give away your last food, when you yourself were still hungry? Would this be economically rational behaviour? If not, how would you explain it?

3 What for you is the epitome of 'nature'? Consider how much of this vision has actually been influenced by the intervention of human beings. Did they improve the vision you hold?

References and Further Research

Books
Appadurai Arjun (1986) *The Social Life of Things: Commodities in Cultural Perspective* (Cambridge: Cambridge University Press).
Asquith, Pamela and Kalland, Arne (1997) *Japanese Images of Nature: Cultural Perspectives* (London: Curzon Press).

Barnard, Alan (2007) *Anthropology and the Bushman* (Oxford and New York: Berg).

Barnes, R. H. (1996) *Sea Hunters of Indonesia: Fishers and Weavers of Lamalera* (Oxford: Clarendon Press).

Biesele, Megan, Hitchcock, Robert K. and Schweitzer, Peter P. (2000) *Hunters and Gatherers in the Modern World: Conflict, Resistance, and Self-Determination* (Oxford: Berghahn).

Campbell, J. K. (1964) *Honour, Family and Patronage* (Oxford: Clarendon Press).

Douglas, Mary and Isherwood, Baron (1979) *The World of Goods: Towards an Anthropology of Consumption* (London and New York: Routledge).

Firth, Raymond (ed.) (1967) *Themes in Economic Anthropology* (London: Tavistock Press).

Forde, Daryll (1934) *Habitat, Economy and Society* (London: Methuen).

Goldstein-Gidoni, Ofra (1997) *Packaged Japaneseness: Weddings, Business and Brides* (London: Curzon).

Humphrey, Caroline and Hugh-Jones, Stephen (1992) *Barter, Exchange and Value: An Anthropological Approach* (Cambridge: Cambridge University Press).

Ingold, Tim (2000) *The Perception of the Environment: Essays in Livelihood, Dwelling and Skill* (London: Routledge).

Ingold Tim, Riches, David and Woodburn, James (eds) (1988) *Hunter–Gatherers* (Oxford: Berg).

Koelewijn, Cees and Rivière, Peter (1987) *Oral Literature of the Trio Indians of Surinam* (Leiden: KITLV).

Leach, Edmund (1961) *Pul Eliya* (Cambridge: Cambridge University Press).

Mauss, Marcel (1979) *Seasonal Variations of the Eskimo* (London: Routledge & Kegan Paul).

Milton, Kay (ed.) (1993) *Environmentalism: The View from Anthropology* (London: Routledge).

Sahlins, Marshall (1974) *Stone Age Economics* (London: Tavistock).

Strang, Veronica (2004) *The Meaning of Water* (Oxford and New York: Berg).

Tambiah, Stanley Jeyaraja (1990) *Magic, Science, Religion, and the Scope of Rationality* (Cambridge: Cambridge University Press).

Articles

Barnard, Alan and Woodburn, James (1988) 'Property, Power and Ideology in Hunter–gathering Societies: An Introduction', in Tim Ingold et al., *Hunter–Gatherers* (Oxford: Berg), pp. 4–31.

Crook, Tony (2000) 'Length Matters: a Note on the GM Debate', *Anthropology Today*, 16(1): pp. 8–11.

Foster, George (1965) 'Peasant Society and the Image of Limited Good', *American Anthropologist* 67: 293–315.

Hill, Polly (1985) 'The Gullibility of Development Economists', *Anthropology Today*, 1(2): pp. 10–12.

Ingold, Tim (1993) 'Globes and Spheres: the Topology of Environmentalism', in Kay Milton (ed.), *Environmentalism: The View from Anthropology* (London: Routledge) pp. 31–42.

Kalland, Arne (1993) 'Whale Politics and Green Legitimacy: A Critique of the Anti-Whaling Campaign', *Anthropology Today*, 9(6): 3–7.

Richards, Caspian (2004) 'Grouse Shooting and Its Landscape', *Anthropology Today*, 20(4): 10–15.

Novels

Høeg, Peter (1994) *Miss Smilla's Feeling for Snow* (London: Fontana) is a novel that is set in the context of a Greenlander's immensely deep and detailed understanding of the qualities and characteristics that snow may have to tell a story.

Ondaatje, Michael (1992) *The English Patient* (London: Picador) contains passages that illustrate the importance for those who dwell in the desert of understanding the wind and its effects on their environment.

Sobel, Dava (1999) *Galileo's Daughter: A Drama of Science, Faith and Love* (London: Fourth Estate) brings to life the family story of the great astronomer and the force of resistance he encountered in early seventeenth-century views of the environment.

Films

Depending on Heaven (Peter Entell, 56 minutes, 1988), a film focusing on the Mongols living in the Inner Mongolia Autonomous Region of China.

The Emerald Forest (John Boorman, 1986) is a feature film about industrial threats to the life of an imaginary Indigenous people of the Amazonian tropical rain forest in which the young son of the chief engineer is captured and reared by the Indians.

Garden Days: A Village in Papua New Guinea (Ariane Lewis, Jon Jerstad and Gilbert Lewis, 25 minutes, 1988) shows domestic life in the Sepik area of Papua New Guinea, mainly from the women's point of view. It describes their everyday activities in the 'gardens' in order to produce the staple food (sago). The different stages of the preparation and cooking of sago are shown. The film closes with the puberty rite of a young girl.

The Gods Must Be Crazy (James Uys, 1980) is a somewhat overly dramatic feature film about the San Bushmen, now more properly known as the Ju/'hoan, of the Kalahari and the encounter of one of them with life in a neighbouring African war.

A Kalahari Family (John Marshall, 2002) is a five-part, six-hour series documenting 50 years in the lives of the Ju/'hoansi of southern Africa, from 1951 to 2000. These once independent hunter–gatherers experience dispossession, confinement to a homeland, and the chaos of war.

Medicine Man (John McTiernon, 1992) is a feature film, which stars Sean Connery as a researcher looking for pharmaceuticals in the Amazon rain forest, where he comes under the threat of loggers and rival researchers, all working to the detriment of the local Indigenous people.

Nanook of the North (Robert Flaherty, 1922), one of the earliest ethnographic films, depicts the life of an Inuit man and his family.

Ten Canoes (Rolf de Heer and the People of Ramingning), 2004 – a storytelling film set in Aboriginal Arnhemland, Australia, during a hunt for goose eggs.

Time Immemorial (Hugh Brody, 1991) is a moving film about the land claim of the Nishga'a people of British Columbia, Canada.

The Whale Hunters of Lamalera, Indonesia (John Blake and Robert Barnes, 51 minutes, 1988, 'Disappearing World Series'). The film vividly and carefully records the technical process involved in catching cetaceans and large fish, culminating in the catch itself.

Website

http://www.fieldtofactory.lse.ac.uk/ – film and ethnography of industrialisation in Chattisgarah, Central India.

http://www.drugnerd.com/archives/435/shamans-of-the-amazon-great-documentary/ – link to a film about environmental destruction in Amazonian Equador.

13

Tourism and the Intercultural Encounter

Cultural Difference for Recreation

An interesting thing has happened to cultural difference over the last few decades, for it has become part of the battery of interests and activities available for people to pursue during their leisure hours, and large numbers of individuals around the world, way beyond anthropologists, become involved. No longer is the intercultural encounter reserved for the intrepid explorer, the economic migrant or the curious anthropologist; it is now much more likely to be an expected part of normal life. This is the case whether you hail from a country that hosts a myriad of 'ethnic' restaurants, and sends out vast numbers of tourists to inspect the rest of the world, or whether you happen to live in one of the formerly relatively isolated places that the same tourists have 'discovered'. In this chapter we will examine both ends of the process, and some of the consequences that have emerged.

An early example of people exploring cultural difference for recreation was the use of food: going out to eat in Chinese, Indian, Mexican and Italian restaurants (and plenty more) has in many countries other than the host ones become a regular option for everyday as well as special occasions. It is often a relatively cheap way to engage in an experience that may seem quite exotic – though an Indian dish that has become one of the most popular 'British' foods in the country, chicken *tikka masala*, is said to have been designed to please the local British population. For residents of the source countries, for whom some of the foreign versions of their food may actually be quite strange, it is likely that the locals will also have the opportunity to enjoy exotic food, even if it is only the ubiquitous American fast fare with the Scottish name. There are local adaptations, even to the McDonalds menu and ethos, however, as an interesting anthropological collection on this subject soon made clear (Watson 1998).

With several days of free time to spend, those with the resources may choose to go further afield for their foreign experience, and a huge global industry has made it possible for such a venture to come quite cheap as well, certainly within Europe. It is now economically possible for large numbers of people to travel abroad, even if only for sunshine and sea air, but their arrival necessarily impacts on the experience of the local people, and this impact may be positive or negative. Visitors usually take an interest in some aspect of the cultural difference they encounter, and many local people benefit from the extra income that derives from the tourists enjoying their holidays, but there can also be problems. An area of interest to anthropologists, and others, is how locals react to being *on display*, and how far their presentations may be considered to be *authentic*.

Young travellers, who pack their worldly goods on their backs and set off to spend a year or more travelling around the world, may be surprised to know that this 'gap year' has become institutionalised only rather recently. When I took off in the late 1960s to try out life in a few other countries, even some of my peers were rather shocked, and my parents were worried that I would never settle down. Australians and New Zealanders I met on the way were ahead of the game, for visiting 'the continent' (of Europe) was already a popular thing for young people to do, and several were already spending time working abroad to finance their trips. Some of my contemporaries joined the 'hippie trail' through the now war-torn countries of Persia and Afghanistan, among others, and they probably contributed to the trend.

Now, according to returning students, backpackers vie with one another to find unusual locations to visit, and there to encounter 'real' people in their 'real homes', an experience which may not be as welcome to the local people as they might have imagined. At a conference I attended on international tourism in Indonesia, the nation that includes the so-called paradise island of Bali, several speakers mentioned the intrusion to local people of strangers tramping through their fields and villages, often inappropriately dressed, and behaving in a manner locally quite unacceptable (Nuryanti 1997). The backpacking visitors may be having a great experience, but thinking about how they appear to local people is another matter, and these informal encounters provide grist to the new anthropological mill of analysis.

An intriguing spin-off to the recreational interest in cultural difference that has been growing around the world is to be found in the use of culture as a theme for entertainment parks, and my own research for a while took this subject as a focus. Delving into the variety of possibilities to be found around the world, I came to the conclusion that museums, or at least the new, interactive versions of them, could be discussed in the same category as the more sophisticated theme parks I encountered. The museum is a product of the colonial world, housing collections of usually foreign material culture for research and posterity, but, like the findings of anthropologists, their treasures now attract an interest way beyond the educational. The implications of this popularisation of material culture provide another field of study, and another opportunity for a (relatively contained) intercultural encounter.

A last example of the popularisation of interest in travel and cultural difference is to be found in the television programmes that have been attracting large audiences. The first edition of this book included a list of films at the end of each chapter, mostly made by anthropologists, or at least with their help and consultation, and many had appeared on television. They were educational films for the most part, and some started their broadcasting lives as schools' programmes, but there was a wonderful period when anthropology reached prime-time viewing. Reality TV and house and garden makeovers now occupy many of these slots, but there has been a small resurgence of interest in cultural difference, though this time with more of an entertainment slant. *Tribe*, which documents the visits of one young British man to the homes of various isolated peoples, would seem to be a BBC version of foreign food and ethnic travel, and anthropologists are as yet not quite sure what to make of it (see the discussion in various issues of *Anthropology Today* following Caplan 2005). Michael Palin's encounters with local people where he wanders may be seen in the same vein and the globally distributed Discovery Channel is another example, which does use anthropological consultation. Film references are still to be found in this edition, but this is an explanation of why some may seem rather old.

The Study of Travel and Tourism

Travelling for pleasure is, of course, not new at all (see First-hand Account 13.1, on pp. 260–2, for example), and it is quite likely that all people everywhere have found ways of enjoying journeys that they might make, alongside any more practical reasons for their trips. They may well have enjoyed meeting new people along the way as well, for tales of journeys pepper the literature from most historical periods, and in the stories of many pre-literate peoples as well. Chaucer's *Canterbury Tales* is an example that we study in England, and *The Long Narrow Road to the Far North* is a classic work of the Japanese poet Basho. Polynesian peoples tell wonderful tales of the long, arduous boat journeys that they made across vast swathes of the Pacific Ocean, and the Six Nations of the Iroquoian peoples was founded upon the travels of a prophet they call the Peacemaker.

The increase in sheer numbers of tourists makes it quite difficult to move around in some of the more popular tourist resorts as can be seen here at the Ponte della Paglia in Venice (photograph: Robert Davis and Garry Marvin).

[Three major things have changed in the last couple of generations, however. First, it has become possible to travel large distances in a relatively short period of time, so visits to the other side of the world may be completed within a fortnight's summer holiday. Secondly, journeys such as these are within the economic means of increasingly large numbers of people, so the sheer volume of human bodies on the move has grown out of all proportion to those who travelled in the past (see Photograph 13.1). Thirdly, the propensity for people to make journeys simply in order to have fun and enjoy themselves has been met with an equally avid provision of entertainment for their edification–at least at first. The result of all this activity has attracted the attention of scholars in several fields–geography, economics, sociology, and, of course, anthropology. Indeed, a huge new disciplinary field of tourism has opened up, often to be found in Departments of Business and Marketing, to reflect the growing size of this huge global industry, as well as the economic possibilities for host communities.]

Anthropologists were not the first to comment on this propensity for leisure travel; indeed, they were sometimes a little put out to find places where they had worked being 'invaded' by less well informed travellers. We have spoken of the way that anthropologists arriving in a relatively isolated area would be taken in, fed and accommodated, by no means unusual treatment for strangers anywhere–when they were few and far between. An anthropologist also expected to adapt to the ways of the people he or she encountered, and would gradually find ways to reciprocate the hospitality received. Tourists, on the other hand, very often expect to find at least some of the facilities they enjoy at home, even though they have travelled halfway round the world.

The title of an early anthropology book on the subject – *Hosts and Guests* (Smith 1977) – alludes to the relationship between peoples thrown into contact by this tourist phenomenon, at the same time as highlighting the old expectation broken. Tourists may bring the resources to pay for their expectations, but the often huge differential access to income between the visitors and the local people adds political and ethical dimensions to the relationship that has formed an

The investigation of tourism and intercultural encounter in Egypt has a long history which goes beyond recent decades. The unique features of Egypt encouraged a wide spectrum of people to visit and explore the country. One of these features, inter alia, is that Egypt hosts the oldest university in the world, Al-Azhar University (see www.alazhar.org), which allowed students from all over the world – since the tenth century – to visit, settle in and travel around the country.

By the end of the eighteenth century, the discovery of the Rosetta Stone opened the door, even more, for further exploration, tourism activities and cultural encounters – in particular, for archaeologists. However, more recently, in the mid-1970s, the political stability in the Middle East in general and in Egypt in particular witnessed the beginning of a new era for the tourism industry in Egypt.

First-hand account 13.1:
Ashraf Tageldeen, Egyptian – on Tourism and the Case of Cultural Encounter

Another perspective for looking at the cultural encounter in Egypt requires not only an exploration of Egyptian history but also Egypt's location and topography. Situated at the conjunction of three continents, Africa, Asia and Europe, Egypt has always been a passage and commercial route, more recently via the Suez Canal. This location created a sort of familiarity with foreigners being around, at least at the major cities and ports.

The landscape of Egypt influences and reflects the culture of the population and their readiness for cultural encounters and tourism because it dictates the economic patterns and activities of life. For instance, the west of the country is mainly desert with some oases and valleys, limited population and few historical sites. The east is mainly high land, with some unique seashore and natural sights but once again with very limited population. Lastly, the most populated area is the strip around the Nile Valley that used to be the land of pharaohs, where the ancient Egyptian civilisation thrived. Therefore, it should be stated that the Nile Valley strip was more open and more ready for cultural encounters with foreigners and tourists, in particular the north and the south of this strip.

Since the late 1970s, the focus of tourism activities in Egypt has mainly been on cultural tourism, i.e. visiting historical sites. In late 1980s, more opportunities were explored, including recreational types of tourism (in areas like Sharm El Sheikh and Hurghada) and adventure travel (such as mountain climbing in Sinai and safaris in the Western Desert), attracting a new kind of tourist. This opened the door for change in the local culture of the western and eastern population as a new economic opportunity became apparent.

In addition, the introduction of the new types of tourism created a sort of local migration of some professionals working in the tourism industry, which enhanced understanding and the cultural encounter between the local population and tourists. In the past, it was common to meet only tourists in historical sites and accommodation premises but nowadays it has become ordinary to meet tourists in the underground or in other venues of normal life. In 2006, Egypt had a record of 9.81 million visitors, with the ambition of reaching 14 million by 2011.

The sensitivity to local people and local culture has been tackled early on by travel agents organising tours and travel plans to Egypt. I can recall from my experience while working in the hotel industry that tourists (visiting Egypt via organised tours) used to have a short briefing from their tour guides about the local culture and other spiritual issues, for instance, the fasting month (Ramadan).

It can also be claimed that indigenous people in many places around the country were able to recognise the benefits of providing tourism-related services and products. In popular areas for tourism, a large number of families have inherited tourism-related professions and crafts. In line with this view, the Egyptian Ministry of Tourism is embarking on an awareness campaign to demonstrate the importance of tourism to local people, as tourism is related to almost 70 other industries in Egypt.

A reflection on how Egyptians provide their own account of cultural encounters can be found in various formats. For instance, the sound and light at the Pyramids, Salah Eddin Castle, and the Temple of Karnak in Luxor aim to reflect the identity and authenticity of Egypt, and the Pharaonic Village on the Nile provides a living museum for ancient Egypt, the objective being to provide a link and confirm the identity of the Egyptian civilisation.

Confirming the identity and the authenticity of the Egyptian civilisation to tourists can be seen as an impossible task to achieve, considering the changes in lifestyle and similarity of daily routine between local people in Egypt and tourists in their own countries. However, exploring local culture and enjoying contact and culture difference is an experience that tourists look forward to – something that can only be witnessed by sharing rather than by material culture in its traditional form.

Dr Ashraf Tageldeen is Lecturer in Tourism and Hotel Management at Alexandria University, Alexandria, Egypt

important focus of the study. When Smith's edited volume came out, in 1977, she reported that tourism was already one of the world's largest industries, pumping an estimated 80 billion US dollars into the world economy; economists and geographers were already busy analysing the effects.

The first edition of *Hosts and Guests* contains a wealth of small studies that examined the way that tourism was changing the lives of the people with whom the authors had been working, and a range of issues were raised about the impacts of the intercultural encounters that resulted. Some talked of the breakdown of the previous economy, others of the revitalisation of the local production of arts and crafts. Some presented the views of the local people affected, others sought to analyse the motives of the visitors. A second edition, some 20 years later (Smith 1989), was able to follow up with a longer-term evaluation, and place the earlier material in a broader, global context; and there is now a new book called *Hosts and Guests Revisited*, which set out to examine tourism in the twenty-first century (Smith and Brent 2001).

In the meantime, the field has become much more widely studied in anthropology, and there have been several books that focus on particular regions. *Coping with Tourists*, for example, is a volume to which Jeremy Boissevain (1996) invited contributions from anthropologists working in European tourist destinations. His own long-term work in Malta would have been incomplete without taking account of the burgeoning tourist trade there:

> The Maltese Islands had developed from a poor, insular backwater to a thriving, modern tourist destination whose inhabitants were themselves increasingly becoming tourists. If in the 1960s tourists were welcomed with pride and native hospitality, by the beginning of the 1990s the welcome seemed less enthusiastic. (1996: vii)

There is a detailed analysis of the Maltese case by Annabel Black (1996) in the same volume. Tourism is not new in Europe, of course, and the visitors are very often people who themselves receive tourists in their own home locations, but the sheer increase in numbers has brought about many changes, and Boissevain's book addresses the strategies used in Europe to cope with these changes.

Earlier anthropological studies tended to focus on the more stark interferences that the arrival of large numbers of strangers brought about in the areas where they had worked. Michael Hitchcock, for example, published a number of articles about tourism in South East Asia, addressing how this affected local ideas about ethnicity and identity (Hitchcock et al. 1993 and Hitchcock and Teague 2000 contain many references to this work). Numerous and well-organised tourist groups from Japan have become a common sight around the world, and Japanese anthropologist Shinji Yamashita has published in both Japanese and English, notably about the effects of tourism in Bali, but broadening his approach comparatively as well (e.g. Yamashita 2003).

Various theoretical approaches had actually already been advanced by sociologists and students of tourism, but it is interesting that some of these classical writers have gradually come around to realising things about travel and tourism that anthropologists were probably aware of earlier by force of their own experiences. For example, there is recently a resistance by scholars of tourism to dividing participants into visitors and those who are visited, looking instead at the mobile nature of the whole touristic venture (Rojek and Urry 1997; Sheller and Urry 2004). *Authenticity* has been a thorny subject, too, with early writers discussing how tourists were inadvertently destroying the very cultural authenticity they were seeking to visit, or encouraging people to reinvent themselves along the lines of tourist expectations and enjoyment. In the next sections of this chapter, we will examine some contributions anthropologists have made to these debates.

Play and Rites of Passage

An important early anthropological contributor to the subject was Nelson Graburn, whose work in both the Inuit Arctic and in Japan has raised an interesting range of issues over the years. A classic article of his (Graburn 1977, 1989, 2001) that appeared in all three editions of *Hosts and Guests* puts the activities of a tourist – or simply a traveller – in the broader context of anthropological theories about rites of passage. Thus travel is seen as marking a break in normal routines, a separation of the play of tourism from the usual life of work. This division he shows as parallel to that between the sacred aspects of festivals and the profane ones of the everyday life, therefore celebrated in some way by all people everywhere, as we saw in Chapter 4 (pp. 77ff.).

It is clearly possible to compare the travel associated with tourism with van Gennep's territorial rites of passage, as we intimated in discussing the routines associated with air travel. Before setting off, tourists also often make quite elaborate preparations, such as:

- buying special clothes
- preparing a selection of protective products

During their time away they:

- eat different food

- send back postcards
- buy presents to bring back, for friends and relatives,
- buy souvenirs for themselves.

The activities are thus marked in the same ways that were noted for ritual activities in Chapter 4, and some travellers even seek physical ordeals, such as:

- sleeping rough
- climbing mountains
- bungee-jumping etc.

Graburn also discusses the way that touristic breaks mark variations in the passage of time (referring to the Leach article we discussed in Chapter 4), as well as different stages in life, so that the 'gap year' may in this way be seen as another part of the attainment of adulthood, just as a period in the bush is for the Maasai and others.

Some aspects of tourism are specifically associated with the sacred, indeed pilgrimage journeys have many of the same qualities, and before the advent of cheap holidays a spiritual quest of this sort was a common goal of travel. In Japan, for example, whole communities would save up collectively to send small groups of members, in turn, to visit important shrines such as the site of remembrance of the founding ancestor Amaterasu in Ise; these trips were rare opportunities to enjoy travel during periods when other movement was forbidden. The Hajj, the pilgrimage journey made by Muslims to Mecca, is one of Islam's five essential pillars, said to have been taking place annually for over 1400 years. Preparations for, and the activities of, this journey bear many of the characteristics of a rite of passage, and a person who has completed it is said to be transformed for life (see Hammoudi 2005 for the personal account of a Moroccan anthropologist).

Graburn goes further, however, arguing:

> For Westerners who value individualism, self-reliance and the work ethic, tourism is the *best* kind of life for it is sacred in the sense of being exciting, renewing and inherently self-fulfilling. The tourist journey is a segment of our lives over which we have maximum control, and it is no wonder that tourists are disappointed when their chosen, self-indulgent fantasies don't turn out as planned. (1977: 23)

This is not a new phenomenon, Graburn notes, for by the seventeenth-century, Europeans with the financial means were regularly travelling to visit historical sites, as well as for activities such as hunting and health, and in eighteenth-century Britain a Grand Tour of Europe became an essential rite of passage for aristocrats and other potential leaders. The provision of breaks for spiritual and physical renewal began to be provided more generally during the Industrial Revolution in England by philanthropic (and often religious) employers, and Thomas Cook, now a name well associated with mass tourism, was actually a Baptist minister whose first 'package' tour was part of a programme of social reform – taking a party to a temperance meeting (ibid. 25).

Now it is commonplace for tourists to seek refreshment and renewal–in a nutshell 're-creation' – when they travel, whether they choose history and culture as a focus, total relaxation in the sun, or 'natural' activities, like hunting and fishing, which might well have been the means of livelihood of their forebears, or of the local people in the places they visit. North Americans and other former colonials also sometimes display a yen for outback living as a way of bonding – perhaps between father and son, or a group of young people, even alone – and this experience can again take on the qualities of a rite of passage. It is ironic, and sometimes more seriously invasive, if there are local people whose land is taken over by the tourist industry so that outsiders can make a living off their traditional lands, and the case of the San Bushmen in Botswana is a notorious example of this problem, also found in the so-called wildernesses of America and Australia, for example.

We will return to the impact on local people of tourism in the next section, but in the meantime, the aim of our travellers can often simply be translated as *play* of one sort or another. Victor Turner drew up some parallels with the analysis of ritual activities in small-scale societies by identifying playful periods in the lives of members of larger, complex societies as liminoid, a development of the term *liminal*, used for the transition period in a rite of passage. He also used this term for theatrical performances, suggesting a sense of make-believe or fantasy, but he tended to continue with the idea of associating such a period with the sacred, and a good development of his argument is to be found in the book about pilgrimage published with his wife, Edith (Turner and Turner 1978).

liminoid – a term proposed by Victor and Edith Turner to describe periods of play and other activities that have qualities of rites of passage and the **liminal**, but which may be less ritually (and religiously) important than many of the classic ones discussed.

For many other commentators, *play* is a quite secular activity, but it can nevertheless be separated rather clearly from the ordinary workaday life, and the characteristics of the liminal, or transition period of a rite of passage may well apply to people during play, especially when they are away from home. Tourists are outside of their usual social milieu, and therefore unconstrained by their normal rules of conduct, so they might well experience a sense of freedom and escape. Even on a trip to the seaside, people wear clothes that they would never don in the office, and in some European resorts, wild groups of noisy tourists have been known to create havoc among the local facilities – drinking too much, taking illegal drugs, and seeking to satisfy their sexual urges in any convenient location, however public it might be. These examples might be extremes, but in the next section, we will examine a variety of consequences for local people of the arrival of tourists.

Ecotourism and Sacred Places

While tourists are seeking renewal and perhaps spiritual fortification by 'playing', the story may be very different for residents of the locations where those tourists make their fun, as we have already mentioned in connection with groups whose lands have been designated as recreational parks. In some cases, local people may be hired for their knowledge of terrain or tracking and hunting techniques; in others, they have been barred from their own lands so that tourists can be more easily guided to observe and photograph the non-human animals that live there. In Africa and parts of South East Asia, especially, animals are often given priority over humans in conservation programmes, and the people who collect money from the tourists and other visitors are only rarely local residents, though the latter may be given some minor benefits to keep them from making too much fuss.

Two examples will serve to illustrate the point, and the first was partly recounted to me by a student taking the anthropology course at Oxford Brookes. He had grown up as a white resident of Botswana, where he had been employed during his school holidays as a guide for people he described as 'rich tourists' seeking to hunt big game. The land they used had previously been the source of all livelihood for the San Bushmen, who had been excluded by the Botswana government, in theory for the conservation of big animals, but in practice for tourism and, if the price is right, for hunting with guns. Survival International regularly publicised information about the plight of these San people, quite a number of whom had died in the resettlement camps in which the government had housed them. As this book goes to press, the high court in Botswana ruled that the government's eviction of the Bushmen was 'unlawful and unconstitutional', and that they have the right to live on their ancestral lands ... so it will be interesting to see what happens next.

The second example is of a large park in Malaysia which was opened a few years ago precisely to display the natural resources the country can boast, as well as various forms of cultivation that have been developed and practised there. Visitors are encouraged to wander over a substantial area of land, or they may take a park bus from one to another of the special features that have been laid out for them. Monkeys swing freely in and out of the trees on either side of the pathways, occasionally swooping down to rob passing visitors neglectful of their sandwiches. It seems fun, unless a visitor takes enough interest in the section of the park map marked *Orang Asli* – or **Aboriginal** people – for those who used to occupy and live off this area of land are now confined to a cramped village in one small corner of it.

These examples may represent extreme-sounding cases, but the problem becomes more subtly controversial when the tourists' so-called spiritual experience of communing with nature and wildlife comes directly or indirectly into conflict with the spiritual life of people in the areas where they travel. In a book entitled *Is the Sacred for Sale?*, Alison Johnston (2006) examines the concept of ecotourism, which in theory has a positive ring to it because of its association

ecotourism – a term that has been used by tour operators to induce travellers to feel comfortable about activities that otherwise might seem to be compromising aspects of the environment, which indeed they still may, especially for local people whose lives are affected by the arrival of tourists.

with sustainability and respect, but in practice often literally destroys the lands and lives of the Indigenous people who are featured as part of it:

> Testimonies from Indigenous Peoples confirm that ecotourism is highly oversold as a concept. Most say that ecotourism proposals look little different in character than other industry ventures in their midst. Their experience is that the ecotourism industry profiteers off indigenous cultures, behind a mask of doing good. (Johnston 2006: 15)

Bristling with examples from locations around the world, the book examines a range of issues from the policies and directives of big international bodies such as the United Nations and NGOs to the desperate attempts of local people to confine and contain the interests of tourists that also bring much-needed income.

One famous sacred site discussed in some detail is Machu Picchu, still a sacred place to the Quechua-speaking peoples of Peru but now also designated as a World Heritage site by the United Nations and an archaeological Inca ruin by the Peruvian government. The annual gate receipts of some six million dollars constitute only a fraction of the overall benefit to Peru of the industry brought by this tourist magnet, but most Quechua people cannot even afford the 20 dollar entrance fee, and on Sunday, when they can enter free, they have no chance of maintaining the silence that used to mark their respect for the ancestral presence there (Johnston 2006: 127). The other famous site that gets attention is Uluru – or Ayers Rock – in Australia, advertised as a site sacred to the Anangu people, who have occupied that land for some 60,000 years, and who now do officially share in the running of this designated World Heritage Area. Unfortunately their message – that the rock should not be climbed – is ignored by a large percentage of the visitors (ibid. 129–30).

This kind of exploitation is being gradually turned around in some parts of the world, and during my own research in North America and the Pacific, I was able to witness and talk to people who were reclaiming their own representations alongside a renewed use of their lands (Hendry 2005). In New Zealand, for example, there are several places where the representations of Māori culture are entirely in the hands of Māori people, and they make the rules (see First-hand account 13.2. Indeed, there are some Māori entrepreneurs who have started to make a good living out of their tours for tourists, who seem to appreciate first-hand attention, and are quite willing to go along with requests to make Māori greetings, and respect requests to stay off certain parts of the land (see Photograph 13.2). In Vanuatu, as well, an independent country that banned outside anthropologists for a period, and where local fieldworkers are employed to record customary practices, some tours have been created especially so that tourists may learn what ni-Vanuatu people wish to present.

It is quite rare to find places where the actual Indigenous people are making much of a living out of tourism, however, for their priority to respect and protect their own land and sacred sites conflicts with what seems to appeal to outsiders, namely to find out about precisely what the Indigenous people are trying to con-

Māori cultural tourism offers individuals an understanding of 'the unique set of values and behaviours of Māori through which they seek to foster a sense of oneness and unity with the world' (Royal 2002: 30). This is particularly important given the view of many Māori and others that 'the world and humanity as a whole has to make some kind of quantum paradigm shift towards a fundamental unity' (ibid. 44). This shift is required to address the social and environmental challenges the world needs to face in order to overcome the 'crisis of sustainability' (Cajete 2005). Tourism, as the largest vehicle for human connectedness, can participate in achieving sustainability – and Māori cultural tourism can be at the forefront of this as a global leader.

First-hand account 13.2:

Chellie Spiller, Māori – on Principles that Help Guide the Actions of Sustainable Māori Cultural Tourism Businesses

Many Māori entrepreneurs draw upon *mātauranga* and *mōhiotanga* (which is rendered as *knowledge* and *wisdom* and the insights contained therein) to develop sustainable models of business. Thus, Māori cultural tourism businesses are guided by principles such as: *Whakapapa* – an ordering principle that encompasses human genealogies and the evolution of the Universe; *Wairuatanga* – spiritual knowledge; *Kotahitanga* – respect for individual differences and the desire to reach consensus, unity and solidarity; *Kaitiakitanga* – setting a high value on stewardship or guardianship of the environment; *Manaakitanga* – demonstrating caring, sharing and hospitality; *Whanaungatanga* – acknowledging the importance of bonds of kinship that exist within and between *whanau* (family), *hapu* (clan) and *iwi* (tribe) and building and encouraging a wide range of stakeholder relationships; and *Tau utuutu*, often referred to as the principle of reciprocity – giving back or replacing what is received. Several of these principles are expanded upon below with references from field research.

Māori businesses can incorporate *wairuatanga* (spirituality) as a guiding principle. Henare (2001) describes this as a respect for life and the physical, intellectual, emotional and spiritual well-being of things and people. It is to remember, at all times, the 'spirit'

Aotearoa
New Zealand

of people, and of the endeavour in which they participate with others and it is also to acknowledge the forces that are greater than human endeavours. A leading tour guide sees the principle of spirituality as being at the heart of the experience offered to cultural tourists:

> I make it a spiritual experience, I make it a memorable experience, I make them feel at home, I make them feel part of my family. The spirituality part of their experience starts from the beginning... with a prayer, grace, karakia... from there – once we enter into the forest, it just entwines it in a different atmosphere ... you just get more ... it just gets stronger ...

Manaakitanga (hospitality) guides Kaupapa Māori cultural tourism organisations to welcome visitors and show them fitting hospitality: in *manaakitanga* 'to be is to give' (Shirres 1997: 119). *Manaakitanga* is to care for the *mana* of others and the 'real sign of a person's *mana* and *tapu* is not that person's power to destroy other people, but that person's power to *manaaki*, to protect and look after people' (ibid. 47). The CEO of a case-company explains this:

> It's about, once again, the authentic experience. I keep using that word but it's about people being committed to serving someone else, *tangata whenua* (Maori) serving *manuhiri* (visitors). Genuinely. Hospitality. That they really want another person to enter their world to be entertained, to be informed. We want them to see what their life is like in that connection to the land, in their *Whakapapa* (genealogy), in their role in the history of this place.

The concept of 'sacred ecology' (Cajete in Royal 2002: 29) represents 'unification of the human community with the natural world' and is of uppermost concern for Māori. 'I believe', says Marsden (in Royal 2002: 3), 'that whilst colonisation is a reality for so-called "indigenous" peoples, the ontological and epistemological concern of unification with the world is a better place for us to meet'. This is reflected in a CEO's aspiration for their clients:

> [what I want people to leave with is to] take back that Māori people are a gift to the world, really that we still have what some cultures have lost in terms of oneness, a linking together, a feeling of belonging to each other and the world.

Following on from this is the principle of *Kaitiakitanga* that indicates stewardship or guardianship of the environment. Many Māori cultural tourism enterprises realise they are in a unique position to 'teach' visitors about living in harmony with the environment, and in doing so they are contributing to global awareness of living with respect for the environment. This principle is described by Henare (2001) as caring for and nurturing all aspects of the environment, physical, intellectual, emotional and spiritual. It is also to act as, and be seen to act as, guardians of the resources that Māori are entrusted to care for. Henare observes that this need not be impossibly altruistic but can act as a guideline for organisational development and activity. A research participant CEO highlighted this imperative and the opportunity for its achievement:

> [we want to] send people in touch with themselves and their environment, you can't help not being aware of the environment when you are here.

Chellie wrote this piece in 2007 while a PhD student at the University of Auckland Business School. See the end of this chapter for full references for Cajete (2005), Royal (2002) and Shirres (1997), and Chapter 3 for Henare (2001).

serve. A wonderful show of dinner, dancing and story-telling put on by Coast Salish people at the top of Grouse Mountain in Vancouver, Canada, was poorly attended when I was there, and later I heard it had closed down. In Brantford, Ontario, the Aboriginal tourist office works with the local Ontario office to publicise their attractions, but an Aboriginal person I met who was working in the tourist industry there had given up that job because she was unable to make a decent living.

Photograph 13.2

Greeting for visitors at the Māori Arts and Crafts Institute in Thermal Valley, Rotorua, New Zealand (photograph, Joy Hendry, courtesy New Zealand Māori Arts and Crafts Institute).

Elsewhere, Indigenous people have more or less closed off their sacred sites, and especially their events, because large numbers of tourists with cameras completely devalue the occasion. The Hopi, for example, whose well-known Kachina dolls represent spiritual beings powerful in their world view, may allow visitors to watch the dances when the spirits appear, but they have banned photography. In Johnston's book there is a sign reproduced that clearly bans 'outside white visitors' altogether from a Hopi village 'because of your failure to obey the laws of our tribe' (Johnston 2006: 251). As Johnston points out, among many Indigenous Peoples the word 'sacred' is fundamentally synonymous with the idea of 'sustainability', for the way to sustain the Earth is through respecting its Creator and its spiritual power (ibid. 250).

Performance, Identity and Authenticity

How then to proceed? So far, we have assumed that there can be people called tourists, and those formerly called hosts, who received them in their territory. However, these terms are far from clear-cut, and another good collection of papers by anthropologists (Abram et al. 1997) sets out to examine and discuss some of the variations, and their implications. So-called tourists, for example, may be residents, even if temporary, in a place foreign to them, others may even have chosen to live there, or anyway be there primarily for work. On the other hand, some of the contributors to their book examine the 'community' that the tourists are visiting, and discuss ways in which local people perform cultural difference, often specifically for the benefit of visitors (see also Coleman and Crang 2002). In both cases, the editors argue, an important issue is one of identity, and how this is constructed and differentiated from another such identity.

I mentioned in the last section that tourists to Vanuatu may learn what ni-Vanuatu people wish to present, and a short description of one example will raise the various themes of this section. In Port Vila, visitors may buy a ticket to visit a place called Ekasup Cultural Village. At the appointed time, they board a bus that transports them to the edge of a nearby forest, where they are asked to continue on foot. As they approach the place of the presentation, a man dressed in the very skimpy garments that used to be worn in this land jumps out and challenges the party to identify itself, just as he would have done in precolonial times when strangers passed close by. The leader of the tour knows how to respond, and once they have been 'approved' the visitors continue to a reconstituted 'village', where details of life in the bush are explained and demonstrated.

identity – ideas about oneself and one's social allegiances that usually reflect birth and upbringing, but may also include an element of choice, especially in response to the global dissemination of goods and cultural ideas, and the increased movement of people within this globalised world.

As well as the guide, there are people recreating the life of the past, just as if they had had no contact with the industrialised world of electricity and mobile phones, and families with children simultaneously pass on their heritage as they entertain the tourists. On one level, this situation may be compared with displays of *heritage* around the world, as we will see shortly. For the tourists, their visit to Vanuatu has been enhanced by a display of life as it was before they had access to such a situation, and they may or may not find this recreation 'authentic', especially if they catch sight of some of the 'villagers' in town later, dressed like everyone else in jeans and T-shirts. On another level, however, these people are reconfirming their own identity as ni-Vanuatu people by recreating life as it used to be before outsiders – not unlike many of the tourists who now come to look– came and colonised their lands.

In the situation we have described, people in Vanuatu are *performing* their past for the benefit of the tourists, and, at the same time, they are confirming their own identity by putting on this performance. It may not be the pristine past those tourists may seek, but without change they would know nothing of it, and the crucial fact is that the people who are performing it have chosen to do it themselves. In many other situations around the world, big multinational enterprises build the hotels and other tourist facilities and expect to pick up the profits. If local people are engaged to display aspects of their culture – dancing shows are a popular example, or stalls of local handicrafts laid out in the hotel lobbies – they receive only a small proportion of the takings, and they may be strictly limited in what they can present. The tourists, on the other hand, can relax in comfortable, relatively safe surroundings, so they may prefer this kind of arrangement if they have the resources.

Abram's own article, in the book we referred to above (Abram et al. 1997), examines the *performance* of history in the Auverne in rural France in various situations and in the presence of varying degrees of outsider. Again, music and dancing are common activities, and the choice of clothes now not often seen in everyday life may mark an occasion for representation of characteristics of the locality. Abram argues that there is a difference between presentations to total touristic outsiders, who need 'explicit labelling and framing of events', and those which draw in local people, or visitors from nearby communities, for whom some of the knowledge and experience is shared. In either case, the performance is also an opportunity for the expression of identity, and the making and selling of postcards and souvenirs to tourists and other visitors is a means to maintain valued practices and continuity with the past.

In these cases, then, the presence of visitors actually encourages the definition and redefinition of local identity, rather than destroying it, as others had previously argued. Another article (by Kohn 1997) in the same book looks at the way that visitors themselves may absorb more and more local identity by participating over a period of years in the activities of an island in the Inner Hebrides of Scotland, even if they only spend their summers there, and some of those with the strongest 'natural' claims to local identity – like birth and language – may work away for many years in the city. A parallel case, set in a magical spot in Mallorca now marketed as the place where Chopin and Georges Sand stayed, though actually only for a few months, is analysed by Waldren, both in this volume (Abram et al. 1997), and in a book entitled *Insiders and Outsiders – Paradise and Reality in Mallorca* (Waldren 1996), a great ethnography on the subject.

All these examples illustrate the flexible and dynamic nature of identity, always defined through difference and in contrast to something else, here embodied – even if unconsciously – in the presence of tourists and other relative outsiders taking an interest in it. For visitors to imagine some pristine 'authentic' situation that existed before they arrived and 'discovered' another people, however, is an arrogant way of thinking about cultural difference. It also irritates the people who are accused of inauthenticity because they have changed over the years. Of course they have changed, they have undoubtedly always been changing, and that these new arrivals should expect the world to change only when they arrive, albeit with a wealth of high-tech tools and toys, sadly misunderstands and undervalues millennia of local knowledge and experience.

Theme Parks, Museums and Material Culture

Sharon Macdonald (1997) extrapolates some of these ideas a little further by recounting the tale of a pair of young Gaelic speakers who set up a heritage centre called Aros in the island of Skye, just off the coast of Scotland. This, they say, is for local people, to conserve *their cultural heritage*, as well as to present it to tourists. Such an idea seems only to develop those we have been discussing already, but the venture is not necessarily popular within the community, and it has encountered some opposition. Crucially, however, Macdonald argues that the work it brings allows these young people to stay there, rather than needing to go off and seek work in the city, so in this case the possibility of bringing visitors is actually enabling them to conserve and continue their own heritage.

The idea of putting cultural heritage on display is not a new one, and museums have been doing it for a long time, if only by using collections of objects from far-flung places as evidence of travel, and of the extent of imperial power. In countries that became part of such an empire, it was an important exercise to erect a museum which laid out examples of the material culture of the people who had formerly lived there. This was partly an exercise in *conservation*, for as the fruits of the Industrial Revolution were dispersed throughout the world, the wherewithal for preindustrial craft production often became redundant, but it was also a kind of record of peoples who were either eliminated, or thought to be dying out. For the same reasons, examples of such materials were carried home and stored, or displayed in ethnographic museums.

In fact, many of the descendants of those people have survived and are now choosing to emphasise and represent (by themselves) those earlier identities, so for them museums may still carry the negative connotations of such untimely and unpleasant predictions. Probably partly in response to this, many more lively and active forms of cultural display have appeared around the world, some still called museums, but perhaps with modern work alongside the older objects, or houses laid out in the open air. Others have contrasting names such as culture or heritage centres – one is the Box of Treasures we discussed in Chapter 3 – serving the purpose of enabling local people to retrieve and celebrate a selected identity for themselves, at the same time as offering a contained version of their cultural features for their visitors. Some sites of cultural display – often in this case of others, rather than selves – may even be called theme parks.

In the book *The Orient Strikes Back: A Global View of Cultural Display* (2000) I examined examples of cultural display found in different parts of the world, from the ethnographic and other museums found in Europe, through the development of World Fairs and Exhibitions that spread around the world, to Disneyland and other kinds of theme parks that became popular, first in America, and then beyond. My initial interest had been aroused by an abundance of such so-called theme parks in Japan, which chose to build replicas and representations of the major attractions of several foreign countries, thus enabling visitors to spend a day or more imagining themselves abroad without all the hassle and inconvenience of actually going there! Investigating beyond Japan, but still in East Asia, I found many other kinds of impressive displays of cultural difference, much more sophisticated than American-style theme parks, but engaging forms of representation, such as replica and reconstruction, that are not usually approved of in museums.

In a book that has become a classic in tourism studies, sociologist Dean McCannell (1976) suggested that the separation of cultural artefacts from their original context, and the interest of others in visiting such representations, was an important characteristic of *modernity*. The artificial conservation and reconstruction of the premodern is a characteristic of the modern, he argued, and the interest of those who feel they have lost their traditional cultural forms in others who they think still have them is a search for *authenticity* in a world that was rapidly losing it. For those who became bothered by such interest in their 'backstage' lives, it was necessary to create a way to satisfy the visitors, and preferably benefit from their interest, so, McCannell argues, tourist spaces began to 'stage authenticity'.

The creation of copies of things, or the reconstruction of trips that might be dangerous in real life (such as the Jungle Cruise in Disneyland), have in fact been interpreted as *postmodern*, and McCannell himself argues in a later edition of his book that the social arrangements he described in the 1970s became out of date as his book went to press – if the founding claims of postmodernism are taken seriously (1999: 1). In the same way that I commented above about authenticity, however, I suggest that it is another form of Western arrogance to classify the behaviour of people around the world according to our divisions of recent time and 'development' towards our ways of doing things as signs of 'modernity', or 'postmodernity'. I predict that these descriptions will enter the historical list of expressing ways of thinking – such as 'primitive' and 'pre-logical – that we began to draw up as characteristic of the early anthropologists in Chapter 1 of this book.

Conclusion

As anthropologists, I suggest that we still need to look at local situations in their own context, and within their own systems of rationality, and my interpretation of the Japanese theme parks included not only the global picture – which clearly influenced the Japanese choice of words to describe their *tema paku* (or theme parks) – but also prior Japanese ideas about display and learning. These include a very positive attitude to copying, as a good way to learn and pass on skills, and also as a way to ensure the continuity of things which might otherwise eventually disappear. The idea of reconstructing something from the past is also seen positively, and several parks in Japan represent historical periods of importance, just as they now do elsewhere, in fact. A reconstruction of Shakespeare's birthplace is found in one Japanese park (see Photograph 13.3), which admits that it is a 'copy' of the 'real place' in Stratford-upon-Avon, but claims greater *authenticity* as it is more like it would have been when the Bard himself lived in it!

This Japanese version of the 'New Place', Shakespeare's later home in Maruyama, Japan, has been built according to historical accounts of building techniques in England at the time.

Museums and collections of material culture, even humble souvenirs (see Hitchcock and Teague 2000 for an interesting set of articles on this subject), have for some centuries marked the interest of travellers, explorers and colonial settlers – and of course anthropologists – in the unusual 'other' people they encountered in parts of the world they visited. More recently, craft centres have provided places where people may sit and make their characteristic materials for the visiting tourists, and miles and miles of shops, street markets – even emporia – offer goods for sale to the growing numbers of curious visitors, though often with overheads collected by entrepreneurial outsiders. The newer culture centres, where local people are able to design and present themselves as they see fit, and even use methods that might shock some of the foreign visitors, are a relatively new way that culture may be *shared* rather than *consumed*, and here I suggest that a more satisfactory intercultural encounter may be secured wherever one may travel.

Discussion Questions

1   Have you spent time travelling abroad? How much do you think your visits impacted on the lives of the local people? Did they benefit from your visit, or do you think your behaviour could have been annoying, at least to some of them? If the latter, do you have any ideas about how the situation could be rectified?

2   Have you had the experience of tourists, or other foreigners arriving in your place of residence, or in a place that you regard as special or sacred? If so, how well do you think they behaved? If not, try to imagine a scenario where the visitors are quite noisy and numerous. What are the limits of toleration in a situation such as this?

3   Now consider how you behave when foreign visitors come to stay in your home. Do you change anything about your usual way of life? If you are asked to show the visitors around, where would you take them and what would you show them? Would the visitors get an 'authentic' experience?

References and Future Research

Books

Abram, Simone, Waldren, Jacqueline and Macleod, Donald V. L. (1997) *Tourists and Tourism: Identifying with People and Places* (Oxford and New York: Berg).

Boissevain, Jeremy (1996) *Coping with Tourists: European Reactions to Mass Tourism* (Oxford: Berghahn).

Coleman, Simon and Crang, Mike (2002) *Tourism: Between Place and Performance* (Oxford: Berghahn).

Crick, Malcolm (1994) *Resplendent Sites, Discordant Voices: Sri Lankans and International Tourism* (Switzerland: Harwood).

Davis, Robert and Marvin, Garry (2004) *Venice, the Tourist Maze* (Berkeley, Los Angeles and London: University of California Press).

Harrison, Julia (2003) *Being a Tourist: Finding Meaning in Pleasure Travel* (Vancouver: University of British Columbia Press).

Hendry, Joy (2000) *The Orient Strikes Back: A Global View of Cultural Display* (Oxford: Berg).

Hendry, Joy (2005) *Reclaiming Culture: Indigenous People and Self Representation* (New York: Palgrave).

Hitchcock, Michael, King, Victor T. and Parnwell, Michael J. G. (eds) (1993) *Tourism in South-east Asia* (London: Routledge).

Hitchcock, Michael and Teague, Ken (eds) (2000) *Souvenirs: The Material Culture of Tourism* (Aldershot: Ashgate).

Johnston, Alison M. (2006) *Is the Sacred for Sale? Tourism and Indigenous Peoples* (London: Earthscan).

MacClancy, Jeremy (1992) *Consuming Culture* (London: Chapmans).

MacDonald, Sharon (1997) *Reimagining Culture: Histories, Identities, and the Gaelic Renaissance* (Oxford: Berg).

McCannell, Dean (1976) *The Tourist* (New York: Schocken Books; 2nd edn Berkeley, Los Angeles and London: University of California Press, 1999).

Nuryanti, Wiendu (1997) *Tourism and Heritage Management* (Yogyakarta: Gadjah Mada University Press).

Rojek, Chris and Urry, John (eds) (1997) *Touring Cultures: Transformations of Travel and Theory* (London and New York: Routledge).

Royal, C. (2002) *Indigenous Worldviews – A Comparative Study*, a Report on Research in Progress, prepared 21 February 2002.

Sheller, Mimi and Urry, John (eds) (2004) *Tourism Mobilities: Places to Play, Places in Play* (London and New York: Routledge).

Shirres, M. (1997) *Te Tangata: The Human Person* (Auckland: Accent Publications).

Smith, Valene L. (ed.) (1977) *Hosts and Guests: The Anthropology of Tourism* (Philadelphia: University of Pennsylvania Press; also Oxford: Blackwell, 1978; and 2nd edn, Philadelphia: University of Pennsylvania Press, 1989)

Smith, Valene L. and Brent, Maryann (eds) (2001) *Hosts and Guests Revisited: Tourism Issues of the 21st Century* (New York: Cognizant Communication).

Turner, Victor and Turner, Edith (1978) *Image and Pilgrimage in Christian Culture: Anthropological Perspectives* (Oxford: Basil Blackwell).

Urry, John (1990) *The Tourist Gaze: Leisure and Travel in Contemporary Societies* (London: Sage).

Waldren, Jacqueline (1996) *Insiders and Outsiders: Paradise and Reality in Mallorca* (Oxford: Berghahn Books).

Watson, James L. (ed.) (1998) *Golden Arches East: McDonalds in East Asia* (Stanford, Calif.: Stanford University Press).

Yamashita, Shinji (2003) *Bali and Beyond: Explorations in the Anthropology of Tourism* (Oxford: Berg).

Articles

Adler, Judith (1985) 'Youth on the Road: Reflections on the History of Tramping', *Annals of Tourism Research*, 12: 335–54.

Anthropology and Tourism Special Issue (2004) *Anthropology Today*, 20(3).

Black, Annabel (1996) 'Negotiating the Tourist Gaze: the Example of Malta', in Jeremy Boissevain, *Coping with Tourists* (Oxford: Berghahn), pp. 112–42.

Cajete, G. (2005) *Indigenous Science: A Foundational Paradigm for Sustainable Economic Development*, in 'Te Ara Matariki: Pathway to New Beginnings' Conference, 20–1 June 2005, Centre for Māori Innovation and Development, Rotorua.

Caplan, Pat (2005) 'In Search of the Exotic: a Discussion of the BBC2 Series *Tribe*', *Anthropology Today*,. 21(2): 3–7, and discussion in several subsequent issues of *Anthropology Today*, including 22(4) and 23(2).

Eindhoven, Myrna, Bakker, Laurens and Persoon, Gerard A. (2007) 'Intruders in Sacred Territory: How Dutch Anthropologists Deal with Popular Mediation of Their Science'. *Anthropology Today*, 23(1): 8–12.

Fish, Adam and Evershed, Sarah (2006) 'Anthropologist Responding to Anthropological Television: A Response to Caplan, Hughes-Freeland and Singer', *Anthropology Today*, 22(4): 22–5. .

Graburn, Nelson (2001) 'Tourism: The Sacred Journey', in V. Smith, *Hosts and Guests* (1977, 1989) and V. Smith and M. Brent, *Hosts and Guests Revisited* (2001).

Holtorf, Cornelius (2007) 'What Does What I'm Doing Mean To You: a Response to the Recent Discussion on Tribe', *Anthropology Today*, 23(2): 18–20.

Kohn, Tamara (1997) 'Island Involvement and the Evolving Tourist', in Abram, Simone, Jacqueline Waldren and Donald V. L. Macleod, *Tourists and Tourism* (Oxford: Berg), pp. 13–28.

Macdonald, Sharon (1997) 'A People's Story: Heritage, Identity and Authenticity', in Chris Rojek and John Urry, *Touring Cultures* (London and New York: Routledge), pp. 155–75.

Moore, Alexander (1980) 'Walt Disney World: Bounded Ritual, Space and the Playful Pilgrimage Center', in *Anthropological Quarterly*, 53(4): 207–18.

Pellow, Deborah (1986) 'An American Teachers' Strike in China: Misreading Cultural Codes', *Anthropology Today*, 2(4): 3–5.

Russell, Andrew (1997 'Miss World Comes to India', *Anthropology Today*, 13(4): 12–14.

Selwyn, Tom (2001) 'Bosnia-Hercegovina, Tourists, Anthropologists', *Anthropology Today*, 17(5): 1–2.

Russell, Andrew (1997 'Miss World Comes to India', *Anthropology Today*, 13 (4): 12–14.

Selwyn, Tom (2001) 'Bosnia-Hercegovina, Tourists, Anthropologists', *Anthropology Today*, 17 5: 1–2.

Novels and Other Books of Interest

Garland, Alex (1997) *The Beach* (London: Penguin Books, 1997) is a page-turning mystery novel set among young travellers in Thailand.

Hammoudi, Abdellah (2006) *A Season in Mecca: Narrative of a Pilgrimage* (translated from the French by Pascale Ghazaleh, Cambridge: Polity Press), recounts the decision and journey of a young Moroccan anthropologist to join the Muslim Hajj.

Heldke, Lisa (2003) *Exotic Appetites: ruminations of a food adventurer* (New York and London: Routledge) is an amusing account of the huge variety of food the cosmopolitan world now has available to enjoy and consume.

Films

The Beach, a feature film starring Leonardo DiCaprio, based on Alex Garland's novel about backpackers, listed above.

Cannibal Tours (Dennis O'Rourke, 1988). The film follows a number of Europeans and Americans as they travel from village to village throughout the Sepik River area in Papua New Guinea, driving hard bargains for local handcrafted items, paying to view formerly sacred ceremonies and taking photographs of every aspect of 'primitive' life. The tourists unwittingly reveal an unattractive and pervasive ethnocentrism to O'Rourke's cameras.

Condors and Bulls Brought on Stage (Andre Affentranger, 41 minutes, 2003, student film). A bull-fight, in which a condor is tied on the back of a bull, in the South-Peruvian Andes is visited year by year by photographers and film teams from all over the world in order to document this event for a foreign audience. This film, shot during two years of anthropological fieldwork, focuses on these visitors from abroad and argues that the idealisation of other cultures as a kind of market strategy, can well be interpreted as a form of visual colonisation.

Culture Show (Rong Li, 36 minutes, 2003). In a remote Sani village, local leaders and ordinary people interact with anthropologists, television journalists and other Sani groups to create a picture of a traditional life that tourists find attractive.

80 Days, *Pole to Pole*, *Himalaya*, *Sahara* and *Full Circle* document Michael Palin's intercultural encounters with people around the world (see website below).

Global Villages (Tamar Gordon, USA, 61 mins) Global villages are theme parks in China and Japan that show imagined cultures. (RAI Festival 2005 submission.)

Harpoons and Heartache (Bessie Morris, 1998, 30 minutes, student film, Granada Centre for Visual Anthropology). An exploration of the relationships between female tourists and local Greek men, focusing on the personal story of Vassilis, a young bartender in the tourist resort of Hania, Crete. These relationships are often said to be exploitative, but who is exploiting whom?

Hippie Massala (Damaris Luethi and Ulrich Grossenbacher, 2006, 93 minutes). From the mid-1960s onwards thousands of Western hippies and 'flower children' moved to India in search of an alternative lifestyle, spiritual enlightenment and drug experimentation. Most returned after a few months or years, but some stayed forever.

Holy Man and Fools (Michael Yorke, 2005, 61 minutes). Uma Giri, a Swedish woman, has become a Hindi nun. She is one of the few Western women to be accepted into the most radical order of wandering Hindu ascetics. The film follows her and 29-year-old yogi Vasidhit giri on an 18-day pilgrimage into the High Himalaya.

A Kalahari Family: Part 5, Death by Myth (John Marshall). Shows the impact of a tourism project on Kalahari Bushmen in Namibia.

Lost in Translation (Sofia Coppola, 2003) is a feature film set in Tokyo about two Americans who are there for different reasons but find themselves doing things together. It appealed to foreigners, but went down very badly in Japan – a useful exercise would be to try and work out why this was the case.

Tribe is a somewhat controversial BBC film series, which employs anthropological researchers, but focuses as much on the presenter Bruce Parry as on the people he visits in each film (see website below).

Walking Pilgrims: Arukihenro (Tommi Mendel, 2006, 73 minutes – student film). For over a thousand years, the Shikoku Henro pilgrimage has connected 88 sacred places along a circular route of 875 miles around Shikoku, Japan's fourth largest island. Shot over a period of nine months and based on ethnographic survey methods, this film reveals in an intimate manner the motives, aims and desires of modern Japanese people as they follow this Buddhist pilgrimage.

Websites

http://coombs.anu.edu.au/Biblio/biblio_tourism1.html – a bibliography for the anthropology of tourism.

http://www.anthrobase.com/Txt/M/Mollerup_Paulsen_Simonsen_01.htm – online paper on interactions between tourists and salespeople in Egypt.

http://www.bbc.co.uk/tribe/ – the website for the BBC series *Tribe*, provides access to further information about the peoples concerned, as well as an opportunity to see the films.

http://www.palinstravels.co.uk/ – lists Michael Palin's various films and provides links to further detail, new programmes, etc.

14

Transnationalism, Globalisation and Beyond

Anthropology for the Future

The subject we set out to describe at the start of this book has been transformed in several ways over the century or so of its existence, and in this last chapter we look towards the future. The first twelve chapters of this book demonstrated the way that understanding the different subjects that anthropologists study is ultimately dependent on seeing links between them in any one society, wherever that society might be. In the last chapter and this one, however, we are examining ways in which new technologies have enlarged our perspectives, our methods and our potential roles, though not our basic approach to that deeper understanding we have always sought among people with whom we work.

transnationalism – a word used in the social sciences to refer to the phenomenon, made possible by advances in technology, of large numbers of people whose family and other close connections transcend national boundaries.

The conditions described in the last chapter to account for the huge tourism industry and related aspects of the recreational interest in cultural difference have brought about many other consequences in the contemporary world. First, fast and relatively cheap transport attracts many movers beyond the tourists, and as large numbers of people travel around the world, anthropologists have followed them to gain an understanding of what they are doing and why. Some of the movers are part of the huge development of multinational corporations which have permeated the world at large with an apparently shared culture of Coca-Cola, sushi and brand-name trainers, to name but a few of the material objects that have travelled in their wake. In local contexts, however, this 'global culture' of *consumption* is interpreted and used in quite different ways, despite the apparent similarities, as we began to see in Chapter 13 and will consider further below.

Another big change has been in the opportunities for people who move to keep in touch with those who stay behind, indeed, for instantaneous and quite cheap communication between people in widely separated places. Internet and mobile telephone technology have introduced completely new forms of communication and cultural sharing that have also provided grist to the anthropological mill. To keep abreast of the social and cultural consequences of these technological developments, anthropologists have had to devise and discuss new forms of research that allow them adequately to follow up their new interests, and in another section of this chapter, we will take a look at some of the ways they have been doing this.

Thirdly, and most importantly for the future of our subject and the global world, anthropologists have potentially helpful roles to play in this new arena. As intercultural encounters become commonplace, but are still often troublesome, those who can understand and explain cultural difference could be out there using their training and knowledge to alert people in positions of power about how to avoid problems that may arise. This kind of work is needed at the local level to enable people of different origins to live side by side, but at the global level too, where another aspect of the new technologies that have been developed is that they have the potential to destroy us all. More slowly, but evidently quite surely, this is happening already, and some of the Indigenous people with whom we have long worked have also been aware at the local level of big problems that the so-called 'developed' world has been blindly ignoring. In the last section of this chapter we will examine some of the ways in which anthropologists can and do make positive contributions to the intercultural understanding that the global world so sorely needs, and we will look ahead to how these contributions could develop in the future.

People on the Move and Transnational Connections

In this new world of heightened people movement, there are many reasons for setting out that go beyond the pleasure trips we examined in the last chapter. For example, a large number of movers are economic migrants – people who seek to improve their standard of living, or their general lifestyle, by finding a new home away from their place of birth. This phenomenon is not new in itself, indeed people have been moving around in this way since time immemorial, but in the last couple of decades it has become much easier for migrants to maintain links with their home base. Thus young people will set off to find more lucrative work than they can gain at home, possibly only for a temporary period in the first instance, and they will send much of the new-found wealth – which may be relatively little in the places they settle – back to their families. Others may settle down and start a new life.

Another set of people on the move are those who have been forced out of their homelands because of invasions, wars, famine, and other natural disasters such as earthquakes and *tsunami*. These kinds of events have also always scattered migrants, and refugees have been a subject of anthropological study for some time. A growing phenomenon in Europe has been the sheer number of people who are choosing to settle in the countries that had formerly colonised their own. Thus the focus of an anthropological study about a particular people may now quite easily be moved from Africa to France, from India to England, or from Indonesia to Holland, and residents of my own home town of Oxford include Dinka people whom we discussed in Chapters 1, 6 and 10 as living in (the now war-torn) Southern Sudan (see websites).

Again, technology has made it possible for people on the move to keep in touch with each other, and also for people who have built separate, new communities in lands far from those of their heritage to re-establish contact with their homelands. The resulting movement of goods and capital is of interest to economists, of course, but for anthropologists the transnational connections that have been set up have formed a whole new area of study. A good introduction to the subject is a book by Ulf Hannerz (1996), which is actually a collection of essays and lectures he gave as he worked on and developed the study of this subject. His style is easy to follow, and he recounts cases around the world that will be recognisable and understandable to a wide range of readers. He writes:

transnational connections – links between families and other social and ethnic groups that are scattered across different nations but which, with modern technology, may be maintained at quite a high level of frequency and intensity.

diaspora – a term, taken from the Greek, for a group of people scattered geographically but still sharing a common identity, usually ethnic or perhaps religious.

> this is a time when transnational connections are becoming increasingly varied and pervasive, with large or small implications for human life and culture. People move about across national boundary lines, for different reasons: in the Swedish village, because for someone an earlier way of life elsewhere has been destroyed, in a part of Germany no longer German, or for someone else because the pay in Canada is better. The technologies of mobility have changed and a growing range of media reach across borders to make claims on our senses. (1996: 4)

Another phenomenon that has formed a focus of anthropological attention has been the increased development among scattered peoples of a kind of shared cultural identity, known after the Greek as diaspora, but also used to refer to groups bound by other criteria, such as religion. The Jewish situation was an early example of this. Now many people around the world grow up in one country, but maintain an important part of their identity as part of another one, or at least as part of another people who in turn form part of another one, and it is interesting to see how much is conserved, and how much changes in the new locations. Steven Vertovec (2000) examines the different meanings that have been assigned to this word, as well as presenting a detailed case, in a book that focuses on another long-standing example, namely the Hindu diaspora.

More locally – and, ironically, often quite tragically – people are nowadays sometimes displaced in the interests of large global policies like the conservation of biodiversity. A book edited by Dawn Chatty and Marcus Colchester (2002) brings together a wealth of research on this subject; in a nutshell, ideas about wildlife conservation and the general protection of the environment have led to the setting aside of lands which were formerly the means of livelihood for mobile Indigenous people, as illustrated by the cases mentioned in the last chapter in the context of so-called ecotourism. Always marginalised, these peoples are often now excluded from their own ancestral lands, and this subject of human–wildlife conflict has become another focus for anthropologists, bringing together primatologists, as well as biological and social anthropologists.

Another interesting set of travellers are the Indigenous people themselves, however, for there is a huge, global movement of people reclaiming their lands and various other rights, with the help of NGOs and international bodies like the United Nations, which has several standing committees to discuss their issues. They find all sorts of reasons for visiting each other, offering support, comparing situations, and doing something they call 'cultural exchanges' (Hendry 2005, especially chapter 5). Thus, members of many First Nations I worked with in Canada knew more about the Ainu – as fellow Indigenous People – than they knew about the rest of Japan. This is ironic, because the Japanese government does not officially recognise that status for Ainu people, though the financial support it offers for 'cultural preservation' enables many Ainu to travel abroad as dancers or artists.

First Nations – an expression chosen by Native peoples of Canada to express their prior status within that nation; it is now officially accepted in various contexts such as the First Nations Assembly, the First Nations University, First Nations' art and so forth.

Globalisation of Business, Objects and Ideas

Technology has actually made communication between widely separated parts of the world so quick and easy that people do not even need to meet each other in order to carry out quite productive relationships. My last book, for example, was commissioned and marketed in New York, where the cover was also designed, but with art work made in Canada. It was mostly written in Scotland, but based on fieldwork carried out in Canada, Japan, and a number of other countries. The copy-editing and book production were very skilfully carried out in India. Finally, the finished book was distributed from Virginia, USA. A minor glitch occurred when a set of proofs was temporarily diverted by being sent to Scotland, USA, but even that was quickly remedied. During the whole procedure I met none of the people involved in the production process!

This kind of scattered business forms the economic base of a phenomenon now described as globalisation, and the constant movement of people, things, ideas and encoded messages around the globe provides the impetus for the title. The notion is ultimately a by-product of the way of thinking described by Tim Ingold (explained in Chapter 12), and those who think globally can make a lot of money, largely because of the huge differential in costs and local wages, as we saw for tourism. This phenomenon is not new either, of course, except for the speed of the transport and communication, and European colonial expansion into all corners of the earth built a framework for what has ensued – often upon or against prior colonial endeavours. A preliminary definition of 'globalisation', proposed in a very useful anthropological reader on the subject, is 'the intensification of global interconnectedness' (Inda and Rosaldo 2002).

globalisation – a term used in different ways in different disciplines to describe the consequences and increased global connectedness associated with the new intensified movement of people, things, ideas and encoded messages around the globe in a way made possible by a huge surge in technological competence.

Inda and Rosaldo go on to discuss some of the deeper implications, because this intensification of communication is largely brought about by the possibilities for speedy contact, and the subsequent 'shrinking' of our social constructions of the world whether we move about in it or not.

> Yes, space is shrinking. The pace of life is speeding up. The time taken to do things is becoming progressively shorter. The world, in short, is witnessing the intensification of the compression of time and space. (2002:7)

In other words, our notions of time and space have been profoundly affected by the fact that we can maintain those previously named 'face-to-face' relationships with people in geographically distant locations, and even perhaps see their faces as we speak through computers or into our mobile phones. Not everyone is moving in this new global world, but those who stay put are increasingly affected by the movements of others, and their worlds invaded at the very least by the consumer goods that are also available a thousand miles away.

It is a mistake to assume that the same things found in different places will operate, or be understood, in the same way, however, as we found for theme parks in the last chapter. In other disciplines, scholars who have taken a broad overview of this phenomenon of globalisation have been predicting a decline in cultural difference and a general Americanisation of the world, noting that America is now the big spreading colonial power because of its economic wealth. Anthropologists, on the other hand, are particularly good at demonstrating the importance of understanding local differences, and their reports may be very different. It is important to remember that the focus of anthropological study is ultimately people, and how they think and behave, even in this world of technological wizardry, still varies greatly.

My colleague Mitch Sedgwick, for example, has focused for many years on the organisation of Japanese companies, but he has carried out extensive field-work in Thailand and France, as well as in Japan. His findings demonstrate two major departures from the theories of Americanisation, for he is able to describe detailed ways in which Japanese companies have developed quite distinctive work patterns, though they may have followed America's lead in expanding into a global market, and at the same time, he can show how those Japanese work patterns have had to be adapted to local differences in Thailand and France. The reactions of the Thai and French employees of these Japanese companies have also greatly informed his understanding of global business (Sedgwick 2000, 2007).

Japan has also been playing a leading role in disseminating popular culture, as well as the means to consume it, and young people around the world share the experience of enjoying *manga* (comics) and *anime* (cartoons) created by Miyazaki Hayao and his team, as well as a great variety of video games and the exploits of their characters. The now almost taken-for-granted portability of entertainment, information, and the ability to communicate with friends, family and business, was largely pioneered in Japan and, according to a former PhD student of mine, builds rather well on historical aspects of Japanese material culture. Phil Sawkins (2007) examined mobile phone use for his thesis, and identified several significant differences in the way people use these instruments in different cultural groups.

Photograph 14.1

Mobile phone use in Japan is much more likely to be text-based than spoken, especially on trains. This sign politely asks users to refrain from speaking on them (photograph Phil Sawkins).

携帯電話の通話はご遠慮ください

To give just one example, there is a notable difference in different countries in the extent to which people use the speaking facility on their phones in public, some being quite happy to air all sorts of business, and even personal anguish, in front of the whole restaurant or train carriage, others being more reticent. In Japan, a lot of people use their mobile machines on the train, but they are doing it silently, sending and receiving text messages and e-mails rather than speaking out loud, and an incoming phone call usually has the recipient rushing to the end of the carriage to avoid the irritated stares of fellow passengers (Photograph 14.1). Sawkins has argued that this cultural difference affects the technological development, so that Japan was years ahead in prioritising the use of the 'phone's' screen, and he links the clever use of text-messaging in Japan to the influence of short, pithy poetry such as *haiku* and *tanka* (ibid.).

Nevertheless, the spread of popular culture still gives a superficial feeling of sameness in cities around the world, as large advertisements announce the presence of familiar brand names, and music emerging from loudspeakers in hotels and restaurants may often be quite recognisable. Indeed, travellers can quite easily strike up companionship, possibly leading to longer-term friendships, through shared interests in fashion, world music, sports, and perhaps dancing styles. As we discussed in Chapter 5, people symbolise things about themselves in the clothes they wear, and the way they behave, and global cultural forms are emerging all the time, especially amongst young people travelling around before they decide to settle down somewhere. Indeed, this travelling may be influential in the way they ultimately form an identity for themselves.

Identity formation is another area of interest to anthropologists, and ease of travel and communication offers new opportunities for people to choose an identity that differs from that of their parents, already a phenomenon common in the UK, as we also discussed in Chapter 5 of this book (see First-hand Account 14.1 opposite for an example of the possibilities for one person). There is evidence to suggest that when people are sent to work abroad, especially if the period is limited, their use of markers of cultural identity from their own background may actually increase in daily life, but an interesting aspect of the global dissemination of goods, people and ideas seems to be a general resurgence of efforts by people at all levels to consider their identity, and very often to seek cultural associations to help mark their place in this world of shifting boundaries. A book by Gordon Mathews (2000) entitled *Global Culture, Individual Identity: Searching for Home in the Cultural Supermarket* examines precisely this issue, and one set of examples is taken from a group of jazz musicians, born and usually resident in Japan, but making different choices about whether to emphasise their identity as Japanese, or go for the influence of the music they perform.

My work with Indigenous people offers another example of this phenomenon, as many of them have faced choices about whether to express themselves as Ainu, Mohawks or whatever First Nation they can lay claim to through a parent, or even just a grandparent, or whether to try to assimilate to the wider society. Often

My name is Wong Si Lam. 'Wong' is my family name and 'Si Lam' are my given names. 'Wong Si Lam' is my Chinese name in Portuguese. I have been better known as 'Selina' instead of 'Si Lam' since I entered a Catholic English secondary school when I was 12 years old.

I was born in Macau, a former Portuguese colony. I am not pure Chinese because my grandmother was Indonesian. When I finished my junior secondary education in 1996, my family immigrated to Vancouver, Canada, because of the fear of the Chinese government. Soon after I received my Canadian citizenship, my brother and I came to England to study. I just received my MA award in the Social Anthropology of Japan this year.

First-hand account 14.1:
Wong Si Lam – on Transnational Identity

I always find it difficult to tell people who I am. Macanese? Definitely. Chinese? Yes, I think so. Portuguese? That is my nationality. Canadian? That is my nationality too. In fact, mine is not a special case at all in Macau and Hong Kong because we all went through similar situations. However, it is quite interesting to the people who 'have a country' or directly belong to a country. To me, and many people of both of these former colonies, the cities are where we belong – not Portugal, England or China.

We, the Macanese, have our own unique culture, which is not Chinese or Portuguese, but a combination of both. Because of the modern technology that makes communication between peoples from around the world possible, there are other cultural infusions that have taken place in Macau as well, such as Japanese and Korean culture. Such cultural infusions, however, have not weakened the cultural uniqueness of Macau. Although the Chinese are ashamed of their political weakness in the past and the Portuguese are so ashamed of their aggressiveness that they have removed some of the historical architecture in Macau, many of the beautiful buildings and sites still remain to remind us, the Macanese, the reasons why we have such a unique culture that makes us Macanese. In 2005, many such architectures have become World Heritage sites.

they, or their forebears, have experienced considerable discrimination, so giving in to the policies of assimilation imposed by many colonial, or formerly colonial, governments was an easy option that they may well have thought preferable for their children to grow up in. However, these days there is considerable support for Indigenous people in the world at large, and artists in particular may find that their careers are helped by emphasising Native origins, as I discuss in *Reclaiming Culture* (Hendry 2005).

In Canada, especially, some of the young people I talked to found the choice of a First Nation identity much more fulfilling than the broader Canadian one. Their determination to learn about their ancestors, and perhaps to learn a language that their parents have lost, seems to give them a real purpose in life, and sometimes they would criticise their age mates in the general high schools they attend for lacking any serious intentions in their studies. At a conference on language revival that I attended, I was deeply impressed by the speeches made – in English – by several school leavers (aged around 17 years) who had chosen to learn their native languages, virtually from scratch. They had also done well in the English medium, and they were extremely articulate, pronouncing that they 'knew who they were' and what they wanted to pass on to their children. I found similar sentiments expressed in several other countries by those who claim 'first' status there.

For these people, as well as for ethnic groups that have been struggling as minorities in the nations which, through circumstances beyond their control, virtually swallowed them up, globalisation has been a very positive phenomenon. The rapid dissemination of knowledge from beyond their own localities has brought awareness of shared situations that has, in turn, led to cooperation and mutual support, which has been enabled by the greater travel possibilities for visits and meetings. Mobile phone technology has reached more areas than land lines in some parts of the world (see the photograph in 'First-hand Account 6' for rural Tanzania), and the internet has been made available very widely among peoples formerly rather isolated. Type any tribal name into a search engine, and there will usually be a wealth of information, often written by the people themselves, though anthropologists may feature as well.

Indigenous political movements have also sometimes been quite dramatic, and the Zapatista movement that came to a head in Chiapas, Mexico, on New Year's Eve of 1994 has been reported widely in the world press. An excellent anthropological account of this movement and its place in the wider scheme of things has been published by June Nash, an anthropologist with long-term experience in Mexico and elsewhere. Her book, entitled *Mayan Visions: The Quest for Autonomy in an Age of Globalisation* (2001) looks to a future she calls 'pluricultural' in which a 'transnational civil society … cultivates multicultural coexistence' (ibid. 254). The election in early 2006 of an Indigenous president for Bolivia added a valuable plank to this vision for the renewal of some of the ancient peoples whose worlds were threatened.

New Themes and Methods for Anthropology

In this new world of movement, communication and self-representation, the field has also opened up considerably for anthropologists, who have been rethinking their approach. It has already been mentioned that our **informants** have now become **collaborators**, and the first-person voices in this book acknowledge the authority of people speaking for themselves. Although it is still as important as ever that anthropologists seek to gain a deep understanding of how others think, we must acknowledge that the people we work with may already know a lot more about the rest of the world than they did in the past. In my own first long-term fieldwork location, in rural Japan in 1975–6, I was the only foreigner that many local people had seen, but a student of mine who worked in the same area 20 years later had several foreign friends, and he has met people he worked with in the area in several other countries.

field – the site of research for an anthropologist, very often a single bounded location for a lengthy period of time, but recently also involving multiple sites, or movement alongside people or other themes of interest.

The kind of anthropological research required to make the studies described above – and for many of those referred to in the last chapter – has by its very nature to be carried out in ways that differ from those we described in the first, introductory chapter of this book. Researchers have to be much more mobile than they used to be in order to observe global movements and to follow people on the move, and a new type of anthropological research has become known as multi-sited ethnography. George Marcus (1995), who proposed the phrase, talked of following connections and associations, and he discussed various ways of structuring the process: for example by following the people, following the thing, following the metaphor, the plot or story, the life or biography, or perhaps following a conflict:

multi-sited ethnography – a term proposed by George Marcus to discuss anthropological research that involves more than one **field** site, possibly because people are moving, but also to follow objects, events and themes that move between and occupy distinct locations in a world linked by easy travel and instantaneous communication across the globe.

> Multi-sited research is designed around chains, paths, threads, conjunctions, or juxtapositions of locations in which the ethnographer establishes some form of literal, physical presence, with an explicit, posited logic of association or connection among sites that in fact defines the argument of the ethnography. (1995: 05)

Following people has probably been the most abundant in terms of research projects, and the transnational connections we talked of above would offer just such paths for anthropologists to pursue. In the global world, many people's lives are literally divided between their places and countries of birth and origin, and other places where they choose to work, and as they and their families travel between at least two sites in this way, an anthropologist wishing to understand how they are living would also need to move. An early example, mentioned by

Marcus, was the study of Mexicans moving regularly across the US border and back, and in Oaxaca a few years ago I was told that half the income of the state came from California, so it would be very incomplete to carry out a study there that did not take these movements into account.

Following a 'thing' has been another interesting line of research, as objects made in one place for one purpose may be acquired by someone quite unexpected and taken to another place where they are given a completely different value. Museums are full of such things, and some of them are now being requested for repatriation by people who claim they were stolen, or obtained under false pretences. Laura Peers (2003), at the Pitt Rivers Museum in Oxford, regularly works with people in Canada on just such a mission. I also have a PhD student, Leonor Leiria, who carried out fieldwork in museums in Europe looking at the way that precious lacquer boxes brought from Japan in the sixteenth century have been cherished, but reassigned roles and values over the centuries (see Photograph 14.2). Some came back with human relics inside them which have apparently been dusted away as though worthless (Leiria 2006). A good anthropological book on this subject is entitled *The Social Life of Things* by Arjun Appadurai (1986).

In my research on parks that represent cultural difference, I was literally following a theme, trying to work out possible influences on my main focus of Japanese parks, but at the same time looking to see what the local meaning would be. I also thought quite a bit about how and whether the work I was doing, running from one place to another in a full circumlocution of the world, could still be called anthropology (Hendry 2003). I decided that our strength as anthropologists lies precisely in pursuing a serious depth in the different ways that similar things are perceived and understood locally – something along the lines of the handkerchiefs we discussed in Chapter 1, when thinking about souvenirs and systems of classification. This is impossible unless we can draw on good relationships with people who know well the different locations we visit, so our network of collaborators also needs to be broadened.

The papers included in Eriksen's (2003) edited volume on *Globalisation* together illustrate a variety of ways in which anthropologists have adjusted to

Photograph 14.2

A lacquerware chest brought from Japan in the sixteenth century and now in the Mosteiro de Arouca in Portugal (photograph: Leonor Leiria, with permission of Arouca Monastery).

doing research in this new world of easy, speedy contact. First, as Eriksen himself points out in the introduction, anthropologists may simply be caught up with movement because the people they have chosen to work with move:

> when Karen Fog Olwig describes the creation of place among migrants from Nevis in far flung places in the USA and Europe, it is not necessarily because she is interested in movement as such, but because she is committed to a long-term ethnographic project dealing with Nevisians, whose social worlds cannot be physically encircled by the shores of Nevis itself. (2003: 5)

Hannerz (2003), on the other hand, points out in the same volume that one may well do multi-sited ethnography in the same physical location, say a city, where representatives of a number of different groups or networks may be located, or may simply meet as both parties pass through. His own work with foreign correspondents is his chief example here, but he cites several other cases of work which he describes as beyond place, or *translocal*.

Another interesting paper in Eriksen's volume reports on research which was very local, in that it was carried out in Trinidad, but that made its focus the use of the internet, a subject matter that could hardly be more global in extent. Miller and Slater (2004) again raise the idea of research beyond place: 'Where is one going – literally – in internet research?' they ask. 'Is sitting in one place and surfing to sites constructed on the other side of the planet a form of single-sited research or a form of multi-sited research?' Either way, their report of internet communication between people from Trinidad – or Trinis – in 40 different countries brings clear evidence that the internet allows people to express and exchange ideas in a way that they understand because of that shared heritage, and which actually enables the continuation of that heritage across the global stage!

My student Phil Sawkins, mentioned above for his work on the use of mobile phones in Japan, agonised for some time about his methodology, and about which aspects of living in the phone-infested country that Japan has become could be regarded as fieldwork. The answer was actually that almost anywhere could be fieldwork, as people were using phones around him wherever he went, and he could – as the name of the Japanese company DoCoMo literally suggests – be contacted anywhere, and, if he kept his phone switched on 24/7 in the Japanese way, anytime! Indeed, his fieldwork continued well into the thesis writing period, for communication no longer stops when the anthropologist returns home, and some of his best ideas have been suggested by Japanese living in Europe.

An interesting new theme arising in anthropology that has been made possible by computers and other technological advances paradoxically takes us back in time to follow up interests that were held by some of our anthropological ancestors. This is the work of Harvey Whitehouse and others that I referred to in Chapter 7, but see the First-hand Account 14.2 overleaf for a more detailed explanation of how this has come about, and how it brings us back into contact with other disciplines from which we had grown apart.

The future of anthropology may lie in the contributions it can make to answering major questions about the causes, origins and potential of human nature, society, history and cultural innovation. What features of human thinking and behaviour are universal and why? What are the causes of cultural variation? Why does history sometimes seem to repeat itself?

Many such questions were posed by the intellectual founders of the discipline: Frazer, Tylor, Spencer, Marx, Durkheim and Freud, among others. Enchanted by the idea that societies evolve, they nevertheless lacked the tools to build up a plausible account of those evolutionary processes and were subsequently castigated by generations of anthropologists for producing theories that were either unverifiable or, if rendered in a testable form, patently false. The apparent failure of early explanatory ambitions in the field, together with growing anxiety about the association between those ambitions and imperial colonial projects, brought grand theoretical aspirations almost to the brink of extinction. This lamentable descent began with a shift away from why-type questions towards how-type questions. Instead of asking about causes and origins (why societies and cultures are the way they are), anthropologists increasingly restricted themselves to problems of function and structure (how sociocultural systems fit together).

First-hand account 14.2:
Harvey Whitehouse – on the Future

Almost unobserved, however, some of anthropology's neighbours had been making some startling discoveries. After a long period in the theoretical wilderness, owing to the dominance of behaviourism (a largely sterile view of humanity that on principle ignored mental activity and focused exclusively on its outcomes), scientific psychology suddenly underwent a revolution. The invention of computers led, by the middle of the twentieth century, to radically new models of information processing which, taken together with advances in biology and the neurosciences, opened up a new window on the human mind and brain and its evolutionary history. The emerging cognitive sciences suddenly made it possible to address more persuasively than ever before the big questions that had led to the establishment of anthropology in the first place.

By now, unfortunately, relatively few anthropologists were listening any more. For several decades those pursuing big questions about human nature have been working in such fields as developmental psychology, primatology, experimental economics, cognitive archaeology, and co-evolutionary theory, largely without the help of their (at times grumbling) neighbours in anthropology. The implications of this work for the findings of social anthropology, and (equally importantly) the implications of ethnography for the cognitive sciences, have (on the whole, though not entirely) been somewhat neglected. The future, I suspect, may be rather different.

What is increasingly hard to ignore is that there are now a multitude of well-supported hypotheses in the cognitive sciences concerning the naturalness of many features of human thinking and behaviour. These features are natural in the sense that they emerge in much the same way in all normal human beings (barring pathology – itself often a valuable source of insight into natural cognition), irrespective of differing cultural contexts, and without the need for deliberate instruction or training. Natural cognition shapes and constrains sociocultural systems even if, reciprocally, at least some of those features of cognition are also 'tuned' by cultural environments. It is no longer intellectually defensible, for instance, to claim that the basic psychological differences between men and women are exclusively the effects of varying sociocultural, political or economic institutions. Many of the contrasts we observe in male and female psychology are rooted in biology (e.g. testosterone levels during foetal brain development) and patterns of gender difference arising from this are similarly apparent in all human populations. A key question for the anthropological study of gender must now be not whether but *how* historically constituted sociocultural environments impact on (and are in turn shaped and constrained by) the expression of natural gender differences. Just as feminist scholarship has begun seriously to grapple with and contribute to the discoveries of evolutionary sciences and experimental psychology, so too must anthropology. And this is true across all the traditional domains of anthropological research.

In my own area of specialist interest, the anthropology of religion, there can be little doubt that natural features of cognition contribute to the content and salience of beliefs in the afterlife, in supernatural beings, in the efficacy and meaning of ritual, in patterns of deference, myth-making, and notions of the sacred. Religious thinking and behaviour is underwritten by a mass of complex evolved psychology producing striking continuities across time and space despite the presence also of interesting differences. It so happens that my own research focuses most heavily on the causes of religious *variation*, in particular the differences obtaining between small cohesive cults and much larger (regional and global) religious traditions. But understanding variation also requires a firm grasp of natural cognition; in this case (I would argue) it requires knowledge of creative and analogical thinking, on the one hand, and systems of learning and memory, on the other. The nature of human minds is similarly vital for an understanding of economic behaviour, the world of politics, and patterns of kinship, marriage and descent (to take some of anthropology's traditional heartland subject areas) as well as more fashionable areas of research, for instance the study of performance, art and display or of intellectual property rights.

Over the course of the twentieth century, anthropology became 'mindblind' but more generally the discipline developed a kind of biological myopia. The future of anthropology lies in the development of much sharper vision in these areas. Anthropology not only needs to be informed by major discoveries in neighbouring fields but it can and should be a major player in making those discoveries. It remains one of the broadest of all the human sciences and its emphasis on cross-cultural comparison based on long-term ethnographic research makes it also the most informed discipline on questions of cross-cultural recurrence and variability. These are valuable traits, our discipline's abiding legacy to future generations.

Harvey Whitehouse is Professor of Social Anthropology at Oxford University.

The Value of Anthropology in our Future World

Anthropologists have many valuable roles to play in this world of increased intercultural encounter and rapid communication; indeed I would argue that the subject is crucial if the world is to be rebuilt in a peaceful and sustainable fashion. However, although governments around the world seek advice from economists on a regular basis, anthropologists who influence big policy decisions are still rather few and far between. At the time of the destruction of the twin towers of the World Trade Center in New York, for example, many of us were wringing our hands at the lack of understanding that underpinned the action and subsequent reactions, but it seems that few were invited officially to comment. A little book of essays, which came out a few years later, gives a taste of some of the deeper issues (Kapferer 2004).

There would, however, seem to be a gradual realisation that detailed advice about cultural difference is becoming essential in many spheres, and anthropologists are at last making some impact in some of them. The arenas of big business and finance, for example, until recently resisted our insistence on **cultural relativism** in the mistaken belief that the world was converging towards the kind of global homogenisation mentioned above. The so-called 'tiger economies' have illustrated forcibly that it is possible to contribute successfully to world markets, however, with many of their cultural differences still firmly in place, as Sedgwick and others have shown. Likewise, the oil barons of the Middle East retain their own distinctive views of the world. Anthropologists are now called upon not only to help companies set up outlets in foreign countries, but also to understand their own corporate culture from a social point of view.

Another important role that anthropologists have played for some time is to help the people with whom they have worked to defend their territories against the incursions of businesses, large and small, whose industries plunder the land and its produce that have sustained them for centuries. In the last chapter we considered the case of tourism, in Chapter 10 that of oil prospecting in the rain forests of South America. The rise of indigenous political movements mentioned above is often related to land issues, but also sometimes to intellectual property rights and protecting valuable indigenous knowledge that is sought, without proper recompense, by pharmaceutical companies. In some cases, anthropologists are standing aside now to let people represent themselves, but an anthropologist who did a lot of work in this area was Darrell Posey (see Posey 2004 for a selection of his work).

A growing role for those with anthropological training is a direct by-product of the phenomenon of globalisation, where increasing numbers of people travel outside their own home territories, individuals grow up in one place and settle in another, and children are born and raised in a mixture of cultural arenas. Schools around the world are realising the advantages of employing teachers who understand the plurality of backgrounds of the members of their multicultural classes, and a degree that includes combination of education and anthropology prepares students well for this role. At a local level, anthropologists can help schools reach the children of isolated or itinerant groups – even in Oxford, some of my ex-students play such roles in building good relations with Travellers/Gypsies, for example.

Health workers, carers and counsellors are also taking time and trouble to find out about the variety of attitudes and beliefs which exist amongst their patients and other clients, so that these may be taken into consideration in the treatment and advice they offer. Medical anthropology is a thriving branch of the subject, and many universities now offer one-year courses to train health professionals in the contribution the subject may make to their work, as well as opening their eyes to the values of indigenous methods of coping with ill health. Anthropologists have also had an important contribution to make to world health programmes, especially, for example, where the administration of inoculations may offend local cultural values, or there is local resistance to the treatment of sexually transmitted diseases like HIV/AIDS. For some of the possible complexity in communication in such a situation see Lambert (2001).

Anthropologists are also employed to advise on the realisation of development projects, whose administrators have gradually come to appreciate the advantages of taking into consideration the views of the people they are aiming to help before imposing expensive projects on recipients whose unwillingness has rendered them useless and wasteful. There have been some classic cases of misunderstanding, dotting the underdeveloped 'third' world with crumbling constructions, rusting machinery, and local boycotting of perfectly good health measures, simply because the people they were designed for were neither consulted, nor their views taken into consideration. Indeed, a series of books have been published recently about the advisability of incorporating local or indigenous knowledge into the so-called development plans, especially where practice that worked prior to colonisation may actually have been more successful in resisting the vagaries of local conditions. Bicker et al. (2004) is an accessible collection of essays on the subject.

The application of anthropology is not new, but sometimes the subject has become associated with endeavour which is now politically unacceptable at a local level. Some early anthropologists were expected to help colonial administrators rule the peoples in their charge, for example, so they set out to understand the customs, language and political systems of Aboriginal or tribal people in order that their compatriots could subdue them. Anthropologists also adopted a role of advocacy, helping the people they knew so well to represent their own interests comprehensibly to the outside world, but local people have also complained about feeling patronised and diminished by such help, so the aid situation is not without complications.

A very useful book on the subject of applied anthropology, including the reservations that people may have about it at both an academic level and in practice on the ground, is a volume edited by Sarah Pink (2006), which includes essays by a number of practitioners, some quite long-term. It opens with a section on the history and development of applied anthropology, attends to the applications of anthropology in industry, and examines the relationships between anthropology and the public sector. The final section includes an assessment of the role of anthropology in the media, including changes in its presence on television, and its usefulness in law. Roles in these last two arenas have been played by many of us over the years, when we are asked to advise people making television programmes where we have worked, or to act as expert advisees in legal cases involving people from our fieldwork zones.

Nevertheless, and despite all these contributions, there are those who argue that anthropologists need to make more effort to put ourselves and our knowledge into the public arena. Thomas Hylland Eriksen (2006) takes an uncompromising stand in his book *Engaging Anthropology: The Case for a Public Presence*, which he opens as follows:

> Anthropology should have changed the world, yet the subject is almost invisible in the public sphere outside the academy. This is puzzling, since a wide range of urgent issues of great social importance are being raised by anthropologists in original and authoritative ways. Anthropologists should have been at the forefront of public debate about multiculturalism and nationalism, the human aspects of information technology, poverty and economic globalization, human rights issues and questions of collective and individual identification in the Western world.
>
> But somehow the anthropologists fail to get their message across.
> (2006:1)

Eriksen writes from Norway, where anthropologists are assigned a role of high value among intellectuals, something we still need to assert in Britain, although our colleagues in Japan do better, I think. In general, he is right, though; we could and should make more of an impact, especially in situations where interethnic relations have broken down, and politicians without enough briefing about local ways of thinking make disastrous decisions that lead to the tearing apart of countries with a rich, proud history. We are not in a position to wave a magic wand, of course, and there is a limit to the value of mutual understanding in resolving disputes, but some of the roles we examined in Chapter 9 could be usefully applied in helping those who involve themselves in resolving such difficulties.

Conclusion

Some of the indigenous people with whom we have worked over the years claim that they were living in harmony with the land before European colonisers arrived and began telling them what to do (see First-hand Account 12 on pp. 242–3, for example). These ideas resonate quite well with those of activists in movements that are described – in Western ways of thinking – as 'environmental' and 'conservationist'. If we, the anthropologists, have become tarred with the brushwork of those of our forebears who took over the lands of such people and destroyed their means of livelihood, then maybe we need not only to listen to what they have to say, but to share that knowledge more broadly. That would be another good future for anthropology … perhaps you, the reader, can carry it forward?

Discussion Questions

1   Do you think about your own identity? How do you define it? Is it based on your parentage, your birthplace or where you live? Is it based on your occupation, or your taste in music? And does it vary depending on where you are and who you are talking to? Try comparing your ideas with those of your parents or grandparents.

2   If you look at the First-hand Accounts in this chapter you will see that they have no ethnic identity alongside the name of the writer. This is unlike those of all the other chapters, and there is a reason for this. Can you work out what it is, and also think about problems that might arise with the others? See first-hand account 12, for a hint ... look at the heading, and then compare it with the way the writer describes her upbringing. The book edited by Cohen (1982) on the reading list for Chapter 5 might help.

3   OK, so now you've finished the book ... how are you going to put your anthropological knowledge into practice? Have a look at the 'discover anthropology' website below for some ideas!

References and Further Research

Books

Appadurai, Arjun (1986) *The Social Life of Things: Commodities in Cultural Perspective* (Cambridge: Cambridge University Press).

Bicker, Alan, Sillitoe, Paul and Pottier, Johan (2004) *Development and Local Knowledge* (London and New York: Routledge).

Chatty, Dawn and Colchester, Marcus (eds) (2002) *Conservation and Mobile Indigenous People* (Oxford: Berghahn).

Collier, J. and Ong, A. (2004) *Global Assemblages: Technology, Politics and Ethics as Anthropological Problems* (Berkley, Calif.: University of California Press).

Edelman, Marc and Hangerud, Angelique (2005) *The Anthropology of Development and Globalization* (Oxford: Blackwell).

Eriksen, Thomas Hylland (ed.) (2003) *Globalisation: Studies in Anthropology* (London and Sterling, Vir.: Pluto Press).

Eriksen, Thomas Hylland (2006) *Engaging Anthropology: The Case for a Public Presence* (Oxford & New York: Berg, 2006).

Friedman, Jonathan (1994) *Cultural Identity and Global Process* (London: Sage).

Friedman, Kajsa Ekholm and Friedman, Jonathan (2005) *Global Anthropology* (Oxford: Altamira Press).

Hannerz, Ulf (1996) *Transnational Connections: Culture, People, Places* (London and New York: Routledge).

Hendry, Joy (2005) *Reclaiming Culture: Indigenous People and Self Representation* (New York: Palgrave).

Howes, David (ed.) (1996) *Cross-Cultural Consumption: Global Markets, Local Realities* (London: Routledge).

Inda, Jonathan Xavier and Rosaldo, Renato (eds) (2002) *The Anthropology of Globalisation: A Reader* (Oxford: Blackwell Publishing).

Kapferer, Bruce (2004) *The World Trade Center and Global Crisis* (Oxford: Berghahn).

Mathews, Gordon (2000) *Global Culture, Individual Identity: Searching for Home in the Cultural Supermarket* (London and New York: Routledge).

Miller, Daniel and Slater, Don (2004) *The Internet: An Ethnographic Approach* (Oxford: Berg, 2004)

Nash, June (2001) *Mayan Visions: The Quest for Autonomy in an Age of Globalisation* (London and New York: Routledge).

Peers, Laura (2003) *Museums and Source Communities: A Reader* (London: Routledge).

Pink, Sarah (ed.) (2006) *Applications of Anthropology: Professional Anthropology in the Twenty-first Century* (Oxford: Berghahn Books).

Posey, Darrell (2004) *Indigenous Knowledge and Ethics: A Darrell Posey Reader*, edited by Kristina Plenderleith (New York and London: Routledge).

Rapport, N. and Dawson, A.(1998) *Migrants of Identity: Perceptions of Home in World of Movement* (Oxford: Berg).

Sawkins, Phil. (2007) '(Not) only Connect – Investigating the Place of the Mobile Phone in Japanese Lives', PhD Oxford Brookes University.

Sedgwick, Mitchell W. (2007) *Globalisation and Japanese Organisational Culture: An Ethnography of a Japanese Corporation in France* (London: Routledge Curzon).

Vertovec, Steven (2007) *The Hindu Diaspora: Comparative Patterns* (London: Routledge).

Wilk, Richard (2006) *Home Cooking in the Global Village: Caribbean Food from Buccaneers to Ecotourists* (Oxford: Berg).

van Willigen, John (1993) *Applied Anthropology: An Introduction* (Westport, Conn. and London: Bergin and Garvey).

Yamashita, S. and Eades, J. S. (2002) *Globalization in Southeast Asia: Local, National and Transnational Perspectives* (Oxford: Berghahn).

Zolberg, Aristide R. and Benda, Peter M. (2001) *Global Migrants, Global Refugees* (Oxford: Berghahn).

Articles

Hendry, Joy (2003) 'An Ethnographer in the Global Arena: Globography Perhaps?', *Global Networks*, 3 (4).

Hannerz, Ulf (2003) 'Several Sites in One', in T. H. Eriksen, *Globalisation* (London and Sterling, VA: Pluto Press), pp. 18–38.

Lambert, Helen (2001) 'Not Talking about Sex in India: Indirection and the Communication of Bodily Intention', in Joy Hendry and C. W. Watson (eds), *An Anthropology of Indirect Communication* (London and New York: Routledge).

Leiria, Leonor (2006) 'Time Signature in *Namban* Lacquerware: Tangible Forms of Storing Remembrance', *Bulletin of Portuguese/Japanese Studies* 12: 21–38.

Marcus, George E. (1995) 'Ethnography in/of the World System: the Emergence of Multi-sited Ethnography', *Annual Review of Anthropology*, 24: 95–117.

Sedgwick, Mitchell W. (2000) 'The Globalizations of Japanese Managers', in H. Befu, J. S. Eades and T. Gill (eds), *Globalization and Social Change in Contemporary Japan* (Melbourne: TransPacific Press).

Novels and other Books of Interest

Ali, Monica (2003) *Brick Lane* (London: Doubleday) is a compelling novel set in a Bangladeshi community living in the East End of London through the world shocks of the 9/11 destruction of the towers of the World Trade Center.

Bryson, Bill (1996) *Notes from a Small Island* (London: Black Swan) – an amusing and affectionate account of the American writer on his travels around the UK.

Films

Amir (John Baily, 52 minutes, 1986) in which Amir, an Afghan refugee in Pakistan, tells his story through music. His work with other musicians and his precarious existence as a refugee are at the centre of the film.

A Kabul Music Diary (John Baily, 52 minutes 2003) in which ethnomusicologist John Baily returns to Kabul to see what is happening in the world of music one year after the defeat of the Taliban. Implicitly, the film identifies some of the dilemmas facing those seeking to help Afghans rebuild their music culture.

Calcutta Calling (Andre Hörmann, 16 minutes, 2006) is a film about Indian call centres, which at the time of making employed approximately 350,000 people to maintain contact between Western companies and their customers.

Reclaiming the Forest (Paul Henley and George Drion, 39 minutes, 1987) shows the potential conflict between the interests of Aboriginal peoples and the responsibility of nation states to implement ecologically sound policies in tropical forest areas.

Scenes of Resistance (Alejandra Navarro-Smith, 30 minutes, 2000), a student film from the Granada Centre for Visual Anthropology that presents a series of portraits of life in a Zapatista community in Chiapas, southern Mexico, and presents their own views of the fight against misrepresentation and oppression.

The Most Admired Man (Julia Berg, 29 minutes, 2002, a student film from the Granada Centre for Visual Anthropology), mythologised as the Daoist physician from the Jade Dragon Mountain, Dr Ho receives hundreds of visitors and tourists in search of the 'Real China' every year. But what lies behind the doctor and his fame?

Websites

http://www.courses.fas.harvard.edu/~anth1610/articles/escobar.pdf – Harvard University. Chapter by Arturo Escobar on anthropology and cyberculture.

http://www.discoveranthropology.org.uk/ – a great website full of ideas and information put out by the Royal Anthropological Institute in London, UK.

http://www.anthropologistabouttown.blogspot.com/ – a good website for residents and visitors to the UK about doing things with anthropological interest to them.

http://news.myspace.com/science/anthropology – lists recent anthropological news stories and blogs.

www.sil.si.edu/SILPublications/Anthropology-K12/ is designed specifically for US primary and secondary students/teachers.

http://www.exiledwriters.co.uk/projects.shtml

http://freddymacha.blogspot.com/2007/08/and-now_13.html – links to a website that features a performance about Darfur of the Sudanese ethnomusicologist Ahmed Rahman, when he was invited to perform at the Human Rights Centre in East London in 2007. As this book goes to press, Rahman is in the process of completing an interactive DVD about the peoples of Sudan and their music and culture. Look out for it!

Map of Peoples and Places

GREENLAND

ICELAND

Tlingit

NUNAVUT

Inuit (Eskimo)

Nishga'a

Cree

Haida
Kwakwaka'wakw
Haida Gwaii
Coast Salish
Vancouver
Crow
Pipestone
Brantford
Crow
Haudenosaunee
Chicago

ATLANTIC
OCEAN

Plains

Alcatraz

Zuni
Navajo
Waco
Hopi

Bermuda

Aztecs

Maya

Zapotec

Hawaii

Guatemala

Nevis

Trinidad
Yaruro
Akawaio
Trio

Piro
Yanomamo

Kayapo
Mehinacu

Samoa

Polynesia

Machu Picchu
Inca
Quechua
Aymara
Akwe Shavante
Nambikwara

Rio de Janeiro

World Map   Peoples and places mentioned in this book

302   Map of Peoples and Places

Lewis
Skye
Manx
Antwerp
Auverne
Mallorca
Venice
Sarakatsani
Kalasha
Tungus
Dervishes
MONGOLIA
Ainu
Beijing
Marrakesh
Malta
Cyprus
Swat Pathans
Kabul
Na
Jerusalem
Islamabad
Tokyo
Alexandria
Kirghis
Gujar
Newar
Bedouin
Jhelum
Nyinba
Yakha
Mecca
Anderi
Sani
Mumbai
Kachin
Macao
PACIFIC
OCEAN
Nuer
Fulani
Nuba
Nayar
Tiv
Bodi
Tamil Nadu
Andaman
Mende
Wodaabe
Dinka
Kerala
Is.
Bella
Kwegu
Pul Eliya
MALAYSIA
Shilluk
Mursi
Azande
Amba
Penan
Abelam
Lugbara
Mini-Wahgi
Nandi
Rendille
Kwoma
Pygmy
Kawelka
Lau
Masai
Mafia Is.
Bali
Flores
Solomon Is.
Nyakyusa
TORRES
STRAITS
Ndembu
INDIAN
Trobriand Is.
Vanuatu
Barotse
OCEAN
Malagasy
Yolngu
Fiji
KALAHARI
Arunta
DESERT
BaVenda
Anangu
Ju/'hoan
Uluru
Zulu
(Ayers Rock)
Cape Town
Maori
Tasmanians

©MAPS IN MINUTES™ 2008

Glossary

Aboriginal refers to the first status of **Indigenous** peoples around the world, used by explorers and travellers who arrived in their lands. Its negative connotations in the English language made it an unacceptable term in many countries for years, though it was still used in Australia. Now it has become a preferred term again by some of the people themselves (e.g. Aboriginal Peoples Television Network in Canada).

acephalus (literally, 'headless') **political system** – a system without any easily recognisable head or system of hierarchy. See Chapter 10 for various types.

aesthetics – strictly speaking, a branch of philosophy concerned with beauty and the physical ability to recognise it.

age grade – divisions of society through which people pass, and which may determine various roles, particularly ritual and perhaps political, during the course of a lifetime. They are found quite commonly in Africa, but also to a lesser extent in Japan and other Asian countries.

age set – a term used to describe a group of people who share a social position that cuts across kin ties. It is based on their birth within a particular period and they are therefore approximately the same age. Members of such a group share certain obligations to one another, and usually pass through age grades together.

animism – the attribution of souls or a spiritual existence to animals, plants and other natural objects, such as mountains and rocks, thought by early anthropologists to be an early stage of religion, a theory now shown to have no supporting evidence.

applied anthropology – using knowledge gained through the academic study of anthropology out in the public arena, usually to the benefit of people there.

bridewealth (or **brideprice**) – goods or wealth travelling from a groom's family to that of his bride as part of the establishment and formalisation of continuing relations between their peoples.

ceremonial dialogue – a way of transacting formal negotiations between villages for many peoples in the rain forests of Latin America, used for resolving disputes and potential disputes, as well as for trade and to arrange marriages.

classification – a system of organisation of people, places and things shared by all human beings, but in ways that differ in different societies, which therefore forms a subject of interest to anthropologists.

collaborators – a term used recently in anthropology to describe those with whom we work, who collaborate in our research, to replace the less equal-sounding term **informant**.

collective representations – symbols understood and used for communication between members of a particular social group (after Durkheim).

commodity – this word is used to describe articles designated an economic value, usually for the purpose of trade, and it may be applied to people and inanimate objects as well, if such an economic value is assigned.

conspicuous consumption – the ostentatious consuming of food, drink or other goods interpreted (initially by Veblen) as a way of demonstrating wealth, or laying claim to a wealthy group or society.

cosmology – broad ideas and explanations that people have about the world in which they live and their place in that world

couvade – a practice in some societies in South America where the father of a baby goes through a series of rites parallel to those undergone by the mother as a way of expressing and confirming his paternity.

cross-cousins – are the offspring of siblings of opposite sex.

cultural relativism – a term devised by Franz Boas to explain that as cultures are based on different ideas about the world, they can only be properly understood in terms of their own standards and values. The phrase has been misunderstood to deny human universals, and to suggest that cultures cannot change.

descent – **unilineal descent groups** – groups of people related on the basis of lineal descent from a common ancestor. See also **lineage**.

diaspora – a term, taken from the Greek, for a group of people scattered geographically but still sharing a common identity, usually ethnic or perhaps religious.

diviner – a person thought to have powers to explain the past, anticipate the future and to advise about related decisions, such as causes of illness, marriage partners and travel plans.

dowry – wealth which travels with a bride to her new family.

ecotourism – a term that has been used by tour operators to induce travellers to feel comfortable about activities that otherwise might seem to be compromising aspects of the environment, which indeed they still may, especially for local people whose lives are affected by the arrival of tourists.

endogamy – rules relating to marriage within a particular group.

environment – a broad term referring to surrounding conditions and circumstances that influence the life of a people, but that the people classify and use in different ways.

ephebism – displaying and admiring nubile bodies in their physical and sexual prime, although how the ideal body is conceptualised will vary from culture to culture.

ethnography – literally, writings about a particular 'ethnic' group of people, the descriptive part of what anthropologists provide in their reports of fieldwork. The term is also used in other disciplines to describe research methods that resemble those of anthropologists.

exchange, direct/ indirect, restricted/ generalised – words used to describe types of social interaction between individuals or groups, ranging from gift giving to marriage.

exogamy – rules relating to marriage outside a particular group.

field – the site of research for an anthropologist, very often a single bounded location for a lengthy period of time, but recently also involving multiple sites, or movement alongside people or other themes of interest.

fieldwork – carrying out practical investigations necessary to a particular study chosen by an anthropologist.

First Nations – an expression chosen by Native peoples of Canada to express their prior status within that nation; it is now officially accepted in various contexts such as the First Nations Assembly, the First Nations University, First Nations' art and so forth.

functionalism – a word used to describe theories that explain social behaviour in terms of the way it appears to respond to the needs of members of that society, as advocated by Bronislaw Malinowski and his followers.

gender – a term of classification used to refer to conceptions of male and female, or masculinity and femininity in any society, and 'gender studies' refers to research and teaching that makes this distinction its primary focus.

genitor – a term devised by anthropologists to describe the genetic father of a child, when this might be distinguished from a social parent, who would be named **pater**.

ghost marriage – a marriage arranged posthumously to ensure lineal continuity and thus perhaps care of the soul of the dead in the afterlife.

globalisation – a term used in different ways in different disciplines to describe the consequences and increased global connectedness associated with the new intensified movement of people, things, ideas and encoded messages around the globe in a way made possible by a huge surge in technological competence.

hypergamy – a system of marriage in which a bride moves into a family that occupies a higher position in some locally accepted form of hierarchy.

hypogamy – a system in which the bride's family is regarded as superior to that of the groom.

identity – ideas about oneself and one's social allegiances that usually reflect birth and upbringing, but may also include an element of choice, especially in response to the global dissemination of goods and cultural ideas, and the increased movement of people within this globalised world.

incest – sexual relations which are forbidden in any society because the partners are too closely related.

Indigenous People – a term adopted collectively by those, also called **Aboriginal** or **First Nations**, whose territories have become subsumed into nations built around them, and who are seeking various 'rights' through international bodies like the United Nations.

informants – the word used for members of the society under study by anthropologists.

inheritance – rules for passing on status, roles, goods and membership in particular social groups from one generation to the next.

initiate – a person joining a new stage of life, typically learning in order to be an effective member, sometimes through certain trials and ordeals.

kingship – a centralised system of hierarchy, not necessarily responsible for political activity, in which the holders of high rank have a status and authority that were compared by European anthropologists with their own systems of monarchy.

kinship – a term used by anthropologists to describe sets of relationships considered primary in any society, also called *family* and *relations*, but demonstrating huge variety in different societies in practice.

lateral relations – the term used to describe relatives who are connected through siblings, distinguished in many languages in the next generation (i.e. for the children of siblings) as **matrilateral** or **patrilateral** in order to mark important kin divisions in a society.

liminality – a term used by anthropologists to describe something separate from, or on the periphery of the wider society; thus used to describe those set apart during the period of transition in a rite of passage, or a people marginalised in a particular social situation.

liminoid – a term proposed by Victor and Edith Turner to describe periods of play and other activities that have qualities of rites of passage and the **liminal**, but which may be less ritually (and religiously) important than many of the classic ones discussed.

lineage – a group of relatives based on **lineal** connections.

lineal relatives – individuals related along a line which can be traced through the generations; see also **patrilineal** and **matrilineal** relatives.

matrilateral relatives – those in the same generation related through the mother's family.

monotheism – a belief system that holds that there is only one God.

multi-sited ethnography – a term proposed by George Marcus to discuss anthropological research that involves more than one **field** site, possibly because people are moving, but also to follow objects, events and themes that move between and occupy distinct locations in a world linked by easy travel and instantaneous communication across the globe.

mythology – a term used by anthropologists to describe the study of myths, bodies of stories held by a people about themselves and their origins, described by Malinowski as a codification of belief, which acted as a charter for ritual, justifying rites, ceremonies and social and moral rules.

nomadic – a term used to describe people who move about in the course of making a living rather than settling in one place.

norms – aspects of expected behaviour that people learn as they grow up within social groups, and which provoke some kind of reaction from those groups if transgressed.

nuclear family – a basic unit of parents and children, as defined by English language usage.

objets d'art – literally, an object with artistic value, but used here in French to suggest the way that people in the world of very expensive art create a language of their own to make decisions about what (and who) may and may not qualify for inclusion.

parallel-cousins – are the offspring of siblings of the same sex, male or female.

participant observation – a method used by anthropologists to learn about a people and their activities by observing at the same time as participating in their lives.

pater – a term devised by anthropologists to describe a man who plays the social role of father to a child when this needs to be distinguished from a genetic parent, who would be named **genitor**.

patrilateral relatives – those in the same generation, but related through the father.

pollution/ purity – a pair of terms used by anthropologists to describe institutionalised ideas about dirt and cleanliness in any particular society, especially where these have connotations with notions of spiritual power.

polyandry – marriage involving one woman and more than one man.

Polygamy – marriage involving more than one spouse, male or female

polygyny – marriage involving one man and more than one woman.

polytheism – a belief system that holds that there are multiple gods.

primogeniture – indicates a special role of inheritance for an eldest son.

profane – see under **sacred/profane**.

public symbols – are those shared by members of a particular social group, usually meaningful to all members of that group, though possibly in different ways.

reciprocity – a return for something given, often part of a continuing arrangement expressing social relations, and analysed by Marshall Sahlins into three types: generalised, balanced and negative.

rites of passage – rites that celebrate and protect the move of an individual or a social group from one 'class' or social category to another.

ritual – behaviour prescribed by society in which individuals have little choice about their actions; sometimes having reference to beliefs in mystical beings or powers.

sacerdotal, a term meaning 'priestly', used by anthropologists to refer to the role of communicating with higher powers, such as gods and spirits, often played alongside the more mundane **governmental** role in a system of dual leadership or authority.

sacred/ profane – this dichotomy is used by anthropologists to describe a variety of distinctions made between things, people and events that are set apart (sacred) from everyday life (profane), though the deeper meanings vary between societies, some of which have no such distinction, and they always require further study.

sanction – a reaction on the part of a society or of a considerable number of its members to a mode of behaviour which is thereby approved (positive sanctions) or disapproved (negative sanctions).

segmentary system – An abstraction of a social and political system, first described by Evans-Pritchard for the Nuer people of the Southern Sudan, as a 'set of structural relations between territorial segments'.

shaman – a person thought to have the power to communicate with the spirit world, perhaps by travelling there or receiving a spirit into his or her body, and also sometimes to influence and control the activities of those spirits.

social control – mechanisms within a society that act to constrain members of that society to behave within a range of acceptable norms.

social facts – the proper materials, which 'exist outside the individual and exercise constraint', to be collected by sociologists and anthropologists, as advocated by Emile Durkheim.

Social structure – a way of describing the make-up of the features of a society in order to devise general theories that could be applied to specific cases, but also allow cross-cultural comparison.

socialisation – the inculcation into a child of a society's systems of classification and ways of behaving so that it is converted from a biological being into a social one. The term may also be used for adults acquiring a new set of social rules and mores.

sorcery – ideas about the use of medicines and other occult powers, usually for evil ends, and the ways in which these are passed on from one practitioner to another.

soteriology – a term used to refer to ideas about salvation in any particular system of cosmology, notably in the religious traditions that are based on written scriptures, where they form part of a broad moral system.

spirit mediumship – an engagement with the spirit world where communication is thought to be voluntary so that the medium makes deliberate efforts to call spirits into the presence of gathered company, although he/or she may have limited control.

spirit possession – an engagement with the spirit world distinguished from others (by Raymond Firth) as largely involuntary, though some (like Lewis) interpret possession as invited – either way, a spirit is thought to express itself through a human being, causing the latter to engage in extraordinary behaviour.

structural functionalism – a theory of explanation of social behaviour which examines the way that components of a particular society functioned to maintain the **social structure**. It was developed by Radcliffe-Brown and applied for a while by his followers.

structuralism – a method, originally developed in linguistics, of analysing elements of social phenomena for their meaning in displaying the framework of society as a set of structural relations which express a universal human capacity to classify and construct such systems of thought.

symbol – a thing regarded as typifying, representing or recalling something else by possession of analogous qualities or by association in fact or in thought (*Concise Oxford Dictionary*, 1958). Symbols are particularly significant in the interpretation of rituals, but also as the visible features of invisible aspects of social organisation.

syncretism – the coexistence of cosmological systems which can still be identified as distinct, although in practice may become quite intermingled.

taboo – something prohibited, usually for reasons associated with a wider system of classification, perhaps related to ideas of pollution, or with notions of the **sacred** in any society.

total phenomenon – a social phenomenon that is found to involve all areas of life in a particular society. The term was chosen by Marcel Mauss in the case of *le don* – translated as gift or 'prestation' – which he saw involving simultaneous expressions of a 'religious, legal, moral and economic' nature.

totem – thought by some early anthropologists to be a sacred symbol, which represented a specific part of society known as a clan, but eventually discovered to have more complex meanings, which were different in Australia and in North America.

totemism – a term used by Emile Durkheim to describe what he thought was the earliest form of religion, which brought together the worship of ancestors with the notion of a **totem** to represent the clan to which they belonged.

transhumant – a type of lifestyle spent between two distinct locations, usually related to annual changes in the climate, such as dry and wet, or hot and cold seasons.

translation – for anthropologists, this practice involves much more than finding an equivalent word in a different language; gaining an understanding behind the meaning of words and phrases, is an important part of anthropological work.

transnational connections – links between families and other social and ethnic groups that are scattered across different nations but which, with modern technology, may be maintained at quite a high level of frequency and intensity.

transnationalism – a word used in the social sciences to refer to the phenomenon, made possible by advances in technology, of large numbers of people whose family and other close connections transcend national boundaries.

tribute – goods or other forms of wealth paid to a central person or body, which shows recognition of that body, and enables the central body to administer the public funds made available on their behalf.

usufruct – a term to describe ideas certain peoples hold about land which gives them the right to use it, but without implying outright ownership of it.

witchcraft – ideas about psychic powers thought to be held by certain people, and the associated practices held to harness them, or sometimes to oppose them.

wizardry – beliefs which people have about the capabilities and activities of others and the action which they take to avoid attacks or to counter them when they believe they have occurred (Middleton).

Index of Authors and Film-Makers

Abrahams, Ray, 234
Abram, Simone, 271, 272–3, 276
Achebe, Chinua, 235
Adler, Judith, 277
Affentranger, Andre, 278
Ahmed, Akbar S., 188, 202, 204
Ali, Monica, 224
Alia, Valerie 184
Altaf, Fatima, 49
Anderson, R.L., 118, 119, 127
Aoki, Tamotsu, 11, 15
Appadurai, Arjun, 246, 253, 290, 298
Ardener, Edwin, 26–7, 33
Ardener, Shirley, 31, 33
Ariyoshi, Sawako, 235
Asch, Patsy, 109
Asch, Timothy, 72, 109
Asquith, Pamela, 248, 253
Attenborough, Richard, 206
Avarea, Peter, 148

Baily, John, 299, 300
Baizerman, Suzanne, 97, 109
Bakker, Laurens, 277
Balandier, Georges, 189, 204
Banks, Marcus, 6, 7
Barbash, Ilisa, 128
Barker, Pat, 34
Barley, Nigel, 33
Barnard, Alan, 238–9, 254
Barnes, R., 251

Barnes, R.H., 251 254
Barth, Fredrik, 188, 201–2, 204
Basho, Matsuo, 258
Basso, Keith, 108
Baumann, Gerd, 53
Bazin, Laurent, 299
Beaton, Mary Martha, 210–11
Beattie, John, 106, 160, 167, 229, 234
Beauvoir, Simone de, 31
Benda, Peter, 299
Benedict, Ruth, 11, 14, 183
Benthall, Jonathan, 71
Berg, Julia, 300
Bergsma, Harold M., 185
Best, Elsdon, 56–7, 58, 72
Bicker, Alan, 296, 298
Biesele, Megan, 254
Black, Annabel, 262, 277
Blacker, Carmen, 160, 167
Blain, Jenny, 167
Bloch, Maurice, 67, 189, 202, 204
Blythe, Ronald, 186
Boas, Franz, 11, 58
Boddy, Janice, 168
Bohannen, Paul, 181, 184
Boorman, John, 255
Boulay, Juliet du, 176–7, 185
Bourdieu, Pierre 123
Bouissevain, Jeremy, 262
Bowden, Ross, 115–16, 127
Bowen, E. Smith, 34
Bowie, Fiona, 147
Boyer, Pascal, 147
Brandes, Stanley, 183–4

Brenneis, Donald van, 202–3
Brent, Maryann, 262, 277
Brody, Hugh, 255
Brown, Peter, 157
Bryson, Bill, 299
Burridge, Kenelm, 147

Cajete, Gregory, 268, 269, 277
Callaway, Helen, 29
Campbell, John, 240, 254
Cannadine, David, 91
Caplan, Lionel, 148
Caplan, Pat, 31, 33, 173,
    181–2, 185, 258, 277
Carey, Peter, 128
Carsten, Janet, 233
Chagnon, Napoleon, 64, 72
Charsley, Simon, 107-8
Chatty, Dawn, 283, 298
Chaucer, Geoffrey, 258
Chevalier, Tracy, 128
Clarke, Morgan, 234
Clavell, James, 205
Clifford, James, 29, 33
Cohen, Abner, 185
Cohen, Anthony, 104–5, 108
Colchester, Marcus, 283, 298
Coleman, Simon, 271, 276
Collier, J., 298
Colson, Audrey, 158–9, 168
Comte, Auguste, 9
Condorcet, M.J.A.N.C.,
    Marquis de, 9
Cook, Captain, 38, 111
Cooper, Matthew, 3
Coote, Jeremy, 112–13, 115,
    121, 123, 127, 239
Coppet, Daniel de, 53, 75, 91
Coppola, Sofia, 279
Cornwall, Andrea, 32, 33
Cowan, Jane K., 177
Crang, Mike, 271, 276
Crick, Malcolm, 276
Crook, Tony, 254
Crow Dog, Mary, 145, 148
Curling, Chris, 92, 206
Cushing, Frank Hamilton, 25

D'Alisera, JoAnn, 91
Darwin, Charles, 10, 137
Davies, Charlotte, 14
Davis, Robert, 45
Dawson, A., 299
de Heer, Rolf, 255
Deliege, R., 42
Desjarlais, R., 185
Diamant, Anita, 41, 49
Douglas, Mary, 12, 42–4, 152,
    157, 167, 246, 254

Drion, George, 300
Dumont, Louis, 42, 59
Dunbar, Robin, 136
Durkheim, Emile, 11–12, 21,
    24–8, 30, 33, 133–7, 147,
    292
Durrell, Lawrence, 34

Eades, J.S., 299
Eco, Umberto, 148
Edelman, Marc, 298
Edwards, Jeanette, 109
Edwards, Walter, 86, 91
Einarsson, Niels, 250
Eindhoven, Myrna, 277
Eliade, Mircea, 168
Endo, Shusaku, 148
Engelke, Matthew, 148
Entell, Peter, 255
Erikson, Thomas Hyland, 290,
    297
Escobar, Arturo, 300
Evans-Pritchard, Edward, 12,
    133–4, 147, 150–5, 169,
    188, 197–200, 201, 204
Evershed, Sarah, 277
Ezzy, Douglas, 167

Faris, J.C., 112, 127
Fassin, Didier, 49
Ferguson, Adam, 9
Ferguson, R.B., 191, 204
Firth, Raymond, 56, 57, 99,
    159, 241, 254
Fish, Adam, 277
Fitznor, Laara, 242–3
Flaherty, Robert, 255
Folly, Anne Laure, 169
Ford, Hiroko, 82–3
Forde, Daryll, 237, 254
Forge, Anthony, 117, 128
Forster, E.M., 15
Fortes, M., 188, 204
Foster, Robert J., 71
Foster, George, 245, 254
Franklin, Sarah, 209, 234
Frazer, Sir James, 131–2, 292
Freud, Sigmund, 292
Friedman, Jonathan, 298
Friedman, Kajsa Ekholm, 298
Fruzzetti, Lina, 128
Fukuda, Curt, 45, 140, 162
Fukuzawa, Yukichi, 44

Gaborieau, Marc, 49
Gaetz, Stephen, 181–2, 185
Ganly, Mick, 46
Gardner, Robert, 109
Garland, Alex, 278

Geissler, Wenzel, 91
Gell, Alfred, 33, 98, 108, 115,
    123, 127
Gellner, David, 160, 167
Gennep, Arnold van, 77–90
    passim
Gibb, Robert, 185
Glass, Aaron, 72
Gledhill, John, 189, 204
Gluckman, Max, 181, 185
Godelier, Maurice, 189, 204
Goldschmidt, Walter Foster,
    185
Goldstein-Gidoni, Ofra, 5,
    246, 254
Gombrich, Richard, 130, 147
Goody, Jack, 234
Gordon, Tamar 278
Gow, Peter, 114, 127
Graburn, Nelson, 263–4, 277
Greer, Germaine, 31
Gregor, Thomas, 186
Grossenbacker, Ulrich, 278
Gulik, Robert van, 186
Gullestad, Marianne, 32
Gulliver, Philip, 181–2

Haley, Shawn D., 140, 162
Halverson, J., 48
Hammermesh, Mira, 49
Hammoudi, Abdellah, 148
Hangerud, Angelique, 298
Hannerz, Ulf, 282, 291, 298,
    299
Hardman, Charlotte, 160, 168
Hardy, Robin, 92
Harrison, Julia, 276
Hart, Keith, 15
Hawkins, Richard, 92
Hayne, Katie, 125
Head, Joanna, 92, 235
Heald, Suzette, 92
Heldke, Lisa, 278
Heller, Joseph, 205
Henare, Manuka, 56, 268, 270
Henckel von Donnersmarek,
    Florian, 186
Hendry, Joy, 15, 49, 69, 70, 91,
    166, 168, 175, 267, 274,
    276, 288, 298, 299
Henley, Paul, 300
Hernandez White, Maria
    Guadalupe, 60–1, 161
Hertz, R., 33
Herzfeld, Michael, 177, 199
Hiatt, Les, 92
Hill, Polly, 254
Hillerman, Tony, 148
Hirsch, Eric, 114, 127

Hirschon, Renée, 31, 33
Hitchcock, Michael, 263, 275, 276
Hitchcock, Robert K., 254
Hoeg, Peter, 248, 254
Holtorf, Cornelius, 277
Holy, Ladislav, 234
Hörmann, André, 300
Howell, Paul, 206
Hua, Cai, 235
Hugh-Jones, Stephen, 254
Hughes-Freeland, Felicia, 91
Hugo, Victor, 49
Hume, David, 9
Humphrey, Caroline, 254
Huntingdon, Richard, 91
Husmann, Rolf, 15
Hytner, Nicholas, 169

Inda, Jonathan Javier, 284, 298
Ingold, Tim, 238–9, 249, 254, 284
Isherwood, Baron, 246, 254
Ishiguro, Kazuo, 128, 235
Itami, Juzo, 92

Jeffreys, Dean, 169
Jencson, L., 168
Jenkins, Timothy, 138–9
Jerstad, John, 255
Johnston, Alison, 266–7, 271, 276
Jonaitis, Aldona, 58
Jung, Carl G., 94, 108
Jung, Chang, 235
Just, Roger, 177

Kafka, Frank, 186
Kalland, Anne, 248, 250, 254
Kanuk, Zacharias, 186
Kapferer, Bruce, 295, 298
Keenan, Jeremy, 205
Khazanov, Anatoly, 205
Kildea, Gary, 72, 148
King, Victor, 276
Kneale, Matthew, 148
Koelewijin, Cees, 195
Kohn, Tamara, 39, 272
Kothari, Ashini, 222-3
Kumar, Hari, 42

La Fontaine, Jean, 91
Lambert, Helen, 296, 299
Lamphere, Louise, 31, 34
Lang, Fritz, 206
Lattas, Andrew, 148
Layton, Robert, 127
Leach, Edmund, 45–7, 76, 89–90, 106, 140, 147, 202,

204, 231, 234, 250, 254
Leach, Jerry, 72
Lean, David, 186
Lecomte-Tilouine, Marie, 205
Lecron, Mary, 185
Leeds, Anthony, 192, 205
Leigh, Mike, 235
Leiria, Leonor, 290, 299
Letham, Jonathan, 109
Lévi-Strauss, Claude, 12, 56, 57, 63–4, 135, 138–40, 228, 233
Lévy-Bruhl, Lucien, 21, 23
Lewis, Ariane, 255
Lewis, E. Douglas, 10
Lewis, Gilbert, 75, 91, 255
Lewis, I.M., 152–3, 159, 168
Lewis, Oscar, 29
Lewycka, Marina, 15
Li, Rong, 278
Liep, John, 171
Lindisfarne, Nancy, 32
Llewelyn-Davies, Melissa, 50, 92
Lodge, David, 15
Loizos, Peter, 235
Longinotto, Kim, 191, 186
Lowry, Malcolm, 169
Luethi, Damaris, 278
Luhrmann, Tania, 157, 160, 169

McCannell, Dean, 274, 276
McCartney, Robert, 177
MacClancey, Jeremy, 6, 40, 49
McCullers, Carsten, 71
MacDonald, Sharon, 273, 276
McDougall, David, 92
McDougall, Judith, 92
McKenzie, Kim, 92
McLennan, J.F., 10
MacLeod, Donald V.L., 276
McNamara, Sean Cush, 185
McTiernon, John, 255
Mageo, Jeanette, M., 102, 109
Mahfouz, Naguib, 34
Maine, Henry, 10
Malinowski, Bronislaw, 10, 54, 67, 71, 132–3, 137–8, 140, 147, 177
Mann, Thomas, 109
Mantel, Hilary, 169
Maranda, Pierre, 49
Marcus, George, 29, 34, 289
Marshall, John, 255, 279
Martin, Diana, 40–1, 49
Martin, JoAnn, 29
Marvin, Garry, 45
Marwick, Max, 168

Marx, Karl, 292
Masquelier, Adeline, 49
Mathews, Gordon, 286, 299
Mauss, Marcel, 12, 21, 24–8, 53–9, 62, 64, 67, 91, 254
Maybury-Lewis, David, 188, 191, 195, 205
Mead, Margaret, 11
Mendel, Tommi, 279
Middleton, John, 141, 152, 156, 160, 168
Miller, Arthur, 169
Miller, Daniel, 291, 299
Millet, Kate, 31
Mills, David, 15
Milton, Kay, 247–8, 254
Mir-Hosseini, Ziba, 186
Mishima, Yukio, 205
Mistry, Rohinton, 235
Miyazaki, Hayao, 285
Mo, Timothy, 186
Montesquieu, M. de Secondat, Baron de, 9
Moore, Alexander, 278
Moore, Sally Falk, 185
Moretti, Daniele, 109
Morphy, Howard, 114, 124–5
Morris, Bessie, 278
Morris, Brian, 147
Myers, Fred R., 202–3

Nader, Laura, 185
Nafisi, Azar 186
Nairn, Charlie, 72, 169, 186
Nash, June, 288, 299
Navarro-Smith, Alejandra, 300
Needam, Rodney, 12, 21, 211–12, 219, 233
Neilson, Finn Sivert, 14
Neveu, Catherine, 185
Newton, Isaac, 25
Nugent, David, 189
Nukada, Iwao, 120, 127
Nuryanti, Wiendu, 257, 277

Obeyesekere, Gananath, 169
Ödtör, Ákos, 128
O'Hanlon, Michael, 98, 109, 114, 121, 128
Ohnuki-Tierney, Emiko, 137, 147, 183
Okely, Judith, 29, 44, 49
Okri, Ben, 169
Ole Ngila, Lesikar, 100–1
Olwig, Karen Fog, 291
Ondaatje, Michael, 248, 255
Ong, A., 298
O'Rourke, Dennis, 278
Orwell, George, 186

Ouzo, Mario, 186
Owen, Chris, 169

Pamuk, Orhan, 34
Parkin, Robert, 233
Parnwell, Michael J.G., 276
Parry, Jonathan, 57, 59, 67
Pasini, Carlos, 186
Peers, Laura, 290, 299
Pellow, Deborah, 277
Pink, Sarah, 8, 296
Pitt-Rivers, Julian, 175, 177, 185
Posey, Daryll, 295, 299
Pottier, Johan, 298
Price, Simon, 91
Prince, Ruth, 91

Quigley, Declan, 42, 49

Radcliffe-Brown, 10–11, 12, 49, 137, 142, 147, 172–7, 180, 185
Raheja, Gloria Goodwin, 59, 71
Ranapiri, Tamati, 56
Rand, Ayn, 205
Rapport, N., 299
Raymattja Marika, 124–5
Reader, Ian, 146
Redfield, Robert, 29
Reynell, Josephine, 224, 227–8, 234
Richards, Caspian, 254
Riches, David, 168, 239, 254
Rival, Laura, 196, 205
Rivers, W.H.R., 22–3, 34
Rivière, Peter, 156, 168, 208, 209, 225–6, 334
Roberts, Simon, 172–3, 178–80, 185
Rochlin, S., 148
Rojek, Chris, 263, 277
Rosaldo, Michelle Z., 31, 34
Rosaldo, Renato, 284, 298
Royal, C., 268–9, 277
Rubenstein, Robert, 185
Russell, Andrew, 278
Ryle, John, 169

Sahlins, Marshall, 56, 57, 64–6, 71, 237, 238, 240, 246, 254
Saint-Simon, C.H. de R., Comte de, 9
Sawkins, Phil, 285–6, 291, 299
Scheper-Hughes, Nancy, 128
Schnedier, Arnd, 128
Schneider, David, 233, 234
Schrift, Alan D., 57

Schweitzer, Peter, 254
Sedgwick, Mitchell, 285, 295, 299
Selim, Monique, 185
Selwyn, Tom, 278
Seneviratne, H.I., 205
Shahrani, Nazif, 186
Shaw, Alison, 219–24, 234
Shaw, Rosalind, 166, 167
Sheller, Mimi, 263, 277
Shelton, Anthony, 112, 115, 121, 123, 127
Sherif, Bahira, 234
Shinoda, Masahiro, 109
Shirres, M., 269–70, 277
Shore, Bradd, 38, 49
Shore, Cris, 188, 205, 209, 235
Sillitoe, Paul, 298
Silverberg, James, 185
Simon, Andrea, 148
Simpson, Anthony, 109
Simpson, Bob, 224, 235
Singer, André, 148, 169, 235
Slater, Don, 291, 299
Smith, Adam, 9
Smith, Valene, 259, 262, 277
Smith, Zadie, 224, 235
Sobel, Dava, 255
Solomons, Natasha, 34
Spencer, Herbert, 10, 133–4, 292
Spencer, Paul, 200, 205
Sperscheinder, Werner, 15
Spiller, Chellie, 268–9
Sprenger, Guido, 91
Steinbeck, John, 72
Steiner, Franz, 38, 49
Stephen, Lynn, 203
Stewart, Charles, 166, 167, 168
Stewart, Pamela, 157
Stone, Oliver, 206
Strang, Veronica, 254
Strathern, Andrew, 72, 157, 185, 205
Strathern, Marilyn, 209, 234
Suttles, Gerald D., 199
Sutton, David, 177
Sykes, Karen, 7

Tageldeen, Ashraf, 260–2
Taje, Merinto, 194–5
Tambiah, S.J., 131, 147, 234, 249, 254
Tan, Amy, 15
Tanizaki, Junichiro, 235
Tartt, Donna, 91
Tati, Jacques, 143
Tayler, Donald, 2, 15
Taylor, Drew Hayden, 15

Taylor, Lucien, 128
Teague, Ken, 263, 275, 276
Tenvir, Fozia, 224
Thomas, Keith, 155–6, 168
Thomas, Nicholas, 67–8, 71
Thompson, E.P., 176, 185
Todd, Harry, 185
Trollope, Joanna, 148
Tuchtenhagen, Ruth, 91
Tuladhar-Douglas, Bhawana, 163–5
Turner, Edith, 265, 277
Turner, Terence, 206
Turner, Victor, 76, 91, 105–6, 109, 265
Tylor, Edward, 12, 119, 130, 131, 133–4, 147, 226, 292

Urry, John, 263, 277

van Willigen, John, 299
Vertovec, Steven, 283
Vincent, Joan, 189

Waldren, Jacqueline, 273, 276, 277
Warner, Sylvia Townsend, 169
Wasan, David, 72
Watson, C.W., 299
Watson, James L., 257, 277
Webber, Jonathan, 148
Weiner, Annette, 57, 67, 71, 203
Wendt, Albert, 72
Whisson, Michael G., 15
Whitehouse, Harvey, 136, 291–4
Wilk, Richard, 299
Willis, Roy, 168
Williamson, Margaret H., 116,128
Wilson, Monica, 200, 205, 229, 234
Winter, E.H., 152, 156, 168
Wong Si Lam, 28–9, 287
Woodburn, James, 239, 254
Woodhead, Leslie, 49–50, 206
Worsley, Peter, 143–6

Yamashita, Shinji, 263, 277
Yellowtail, Thomas, 148
Yorke, Michael, 279
Young, Michael, 180, 185

Zolberg, Aristide R., 299

Index of Peoples and Places

This list is made up of categories that may be used to identify groups of people who share ideas by virtue of membership in those groups. The **world map**, on pp.302–3 gives the approximate locations of **peoples** and **places** which may be defined geographically, but national boundaries, anyway less relevant sometimes than a notion of shared identity, have not been marked. However, further geographical information is included below.

Abelam (Papua New Guinea), 117
Aborigines (Australia), 24, 111, 114, 126, 135, 239, 247
Afghanistan, 257, 300
Africa, 22, 83, 118, 157, 159, 188, 196, 200, 208, 226, 229, 241, 266, 282; East, 200; West, 97, 180
Afro-Caribbeans, 87
Ainu, 283, 286
Akawaio (British Guyana), 158–9, 171, 184
Akwe Shavante (Brazil) 156, 191–2, 195
Alcatraz Island, 143
Alexandria, 262
Amazonia, 114, 206, 247, 255
Amba (Uganda), 156, 229

America, 253; Latin, 188, 191, 196, 232; North, 90, 96, 118, 135, 145, 239, 241, 252, 265, 267; South, 3, 81, 156–7, 191, 226, 241, 295; United States of, 11, 44, 84, 104
Americans, Native, 11, 55, 119, 139, 142–3, 241
Amsterdam, 16
Anangu (Australia), 267
Andaman Islands (Bay of Bengal), 10, 137
Anderi (India), 233, 244
Andes (Peru), 2
Antwerp, 224–5
Aotearoa (New Zealand), 56, 268
Apache, 108
Arctic, 263
Arnhem Land, 92
Arunta (Australia), 135
Auckland (New Zealand), 66
Australia, 10, 84, 90, 111, 113–14, 123, 253, 257, 265
Auverne, France, 272
Ayers Rock see Uluru
Aymara (Bolivia), 196
Azande (Southern Sudan), 150–5, 169, 171, 184
Aztecs (Mexico), 22, 190

Bali, 257, 263
Bangkok, 2
Barotse (Zimbabwe), 181
Battersea (London), 105
BaVenda (Southern Africa), 159–60, 171

Bedouin (Sahara Desert), 248
Beijing, 19
Belgium, 189
Bella (West Africa – Liberia), 97
Bermuda, 2
Birmingham, 2
Bodi (Ethiopia), 206
Bolivia, 196, 288
Boston, 210
Botswana, 265, 266
Bragar, 175
Brahmins, 42
Brantford, Ontario, 270
Brazil, 156, 186, 191, 196, 244
Brighton, 2
Britain, 2, 10–11, 19, 36–7, 42, 44–6, 53, 55, 84, 89, 99, 103, 104, 144, 160, 189, 203, 212, 226, 245, 297
British, 96, 106, 108, 125, 174–5, 209, 224, 257
British Columbia, 58
Bruges (Belgium), 60
Brussels, 19
Buddhists, 144
Bushmen see Ju/'hoan

California, 290
Cameroon, 186
Canada, 55, 84, 90, 103, 135, 178, 283, 287, 288
Cape Town, 10
Cape York Peninsula, 92
Central Asia, 239
Chiapas (Mexico), 288, 300
Chicago, 11, 199
China, 27, 28, 90, 113, 120, 186, 278
Chinese, 40, 186, 235
Chinook, 55
Christians, 80, 89, 106, 142, 145, 155; Armenian, 96; Protestants, 96, 105, 106; Roman Catholics, 87, 105, 107, 133, 142
Church Hanborough, 8
Coast Salish, 270
Colonial Williamsburg, 90
Cree, 239
Crow, 148
Cyprus, 235
Czech Republic, 8

Dervishes (Kurdistan), 148
Devon (England), 105
Dinka (Southern Sudan), 23, 112–13, 199, 239, 298

East Asia, 274
Egypt, 260–2
Ekasup Cultural Village, 271
England, 42, 88–9, 96–7, 106, 155–6, 157, 175–6, 219, 258, 282
English, 23, 88
Equador, 169
Eskimo see Inuit
Europe, 10, 37, 43, 87, 95, 103, 113, 114, 120, 135, 145, 151, 161, 180, 253, 282
Europeans, 21, 53, 67, 104, 125, 144, 188, 189, 241, 245, 249, 264, 278, 284

Fiji, 38, 143
First Nations, 283, 286, 288, 283
Flores (Indonesia), 109
Florida, 248
France, 9, 11, 36, 87, 103, 177, 282, 285
Fulani, Bororo (West Africa), 97, 128

Germany, 90
Gisu, 92
Glasgow (Scotland), 105, 107
Göttingen, 16
Greece, 31, 32, 176, 199
Greeks, 126, 240
Greek Cypriots, 235
Greenland, 248
Grouse Mountain, Vancouver, 270
Guatemala, 62–3, 244
Gujars (North India), 59

Haida, 55, 120
Haida Gwaii, 119, 120
Hampton Gay (Oxford), 175
Haudenosaunee, Six Nations of the, 203, 206
Hawaii, 90
Hebrews, 217
Hindus, 39–40, 88, 251, 279, 283
Holland, 90; see also Netherlands
Hong Kong, 28–9, 40–1
Hopi, 271

Iceland, 250
Inca, 267
India, 36–7, 42, 58–9, 190, 226, 233, 247, 249, 251, 282, 300
Indian sub-continent, 226–7

Indonesia, 251, 282
Inner Hebrides (Scotland), 272
Inuit (Eskimo), 178, 179–80, 239, 248, 255, 263
Iraq, 177, 182
Ireland, 181–2; Northern, 105
Irish, 175, 181
Iroquoian, 206, 258; see also Haudenosaunee
Ise, 264
Islamabad, 219
Israel, 103
Israelites, 140
Italy, 87
Ivory Coast, 128

Jain, 222–3, 224, 227
Jakarta, 90
Japan, 4, 18, 19, 25, 44, 51–2, 68–70, 82–3, 85–7, 89–90, 98–9, 102, 120–1, 137, 166, 171–4, 177–8, 183–4, 191–2, 200–3, 232, 244, 246, 252, 264, 274, 275, 278, 283, 285, 286, 289, 291; historical, 37, 101, 103–4, 107, 166, 174, 196
Japanese, 11, 22, 27, 41–2, 62, 79–80, 111, 112, 113, 120–1, 142–3, 159, 160, 173–4, 249, 250
Jerusalem, 96
Jews, 11, 40, 81, 84, 88, 96–7, 283
Jhelum (Pakistan), 148
Ju/'hoan (Southern Africa), 238, 255

Kabul (Afghanistan), 300
Kathmandu, 162, 163–4, 167
Kawelka (New Guinea), 72, 206
Kayapo (Xingu, Brazil), 196, 206, 244
Kenya, 83, 97, 181
Kerala, 109
Kobe, Japan, 248
Kurdistan, 148
Kwakiutl (British Columbia), 55, 118, 239; see also Kwakwa̲ka'wakw
Kwakwa̲ka'wakw, 58
Kwegu (Ethiopia), 206
Kwoma (Sepik River, Papua New Guinea), 115–18, 126

Lagos (Nigeria), 181
Lalitpur, 167

Lamalera (Indonesia), 251
Laos, 91
Lau (of Malaita – Solomon
    Islands), 49–50
Lewis (Outer Hebrides), 105,
    174–5
Liverpool, xvii
London (England), 10, 12, 37,
    66, 118, 126, 181, 299
Long Island (USA), 128
Lugbara (Uganda and Belgian
    Congo), 141
Luo, 91
Luxor, 261

Macao, 28
Machu Picchu, 267
Mafia Island, Tanzania, 182
Malagasy (Madagascar), 38
Malaysia, 266
Mallorca, 272–3
Malta, 262
Mambudiri Brahmins, 109
Manx, 148
Māori (New Zealand), 54–5,
    56–8, 67, 268–70
Marrakesh (Morocco), 50
Masai/Maasai (Kenya/
    Tanzania), 83, 92, 99,
    100–1, 200, 206, 264
Mayan (Mexico), 162
Mbuti Pygmy (Southern
    Africa), 239
Mecca, 264
Mediterranean, 177, 185
Melanesia, 22–4, 143, 173
Mende (Sierra Leone), 123
Mexico, 4, 12, 29, 60–1, 62–3,
    69, 85, 95–6, 138, 140–1,
    161, 162, 184, 244–5,
    249–50, 288, 300
Middle East, 37, 103, 151, 253,
    295
Minj-Wahgi (Papua New
    Guinea), 179
Mohawks, 286
Mongolia, 255
Monserrat, 248
Mumbai, 224
Muslims, 40, 153, 219–23, 264

Na (China), 235
Nambikwara (Brazil), 195
Namibia, 279
Nandi (East Africa), 200
Nayar (India), 233
Ndembu (Zambia, Central
    Africa), 83, 106
Nepal, 39, 160, 163–5, 167,

181
Netherlands, the, 189
Nevisians, 291
New Hebrides (Vanuatu –
    Melanesia), 143
New Zealand, 66, 253, 257,
    267, 270; see also Aotearoa
Newar (Kathmandu Valley,
    Nepal), 160, 163–5, 167
Ni-Vanuatu, 267
Niger, 128
Nigeria, 34
Nile River, 260–1
Nishga'a (British Columbia,
    Canada), 255
Norway, 189, 250
Nuba (Southern Sudan), 112
Nuer (Southern Sudan), 112,
    179, 188, 197–200, 208,
    212, 217, 232, 239–40, 250,
    252
Nunavut, 178
Nyakyusa (S.W. Tanzania and
    Malawi), 229
Nyinba (Nepal), 235

Oaxaca, 140, 290
Oceania, 67
Oxford, 7, 12, 37, 119, 138,
    213, 219–24, 282, 295
Oxfordshire, 176

Pacific: communities, 202;
    Islanders, 67–8
Pakistan, 219, 299
Pakistani, 213, 219–24
Papua New Guinea, 11, 97–8,
    114–17, 121, 143, 179, 180,
    202, 255, 278
Paraiyars, 49
Parsi, 235
Patua (of West Bengal), 128
Penan (Borneo), 247
Persia, 257
Peru, 191, 267
Pharping, 163–4
Pipestone, Minnesota, 143
Piro (Amazonian Peru), 114
Plains Indians (North
    America), 142
Poland, 103
Polynesia, 38–9, 54–5, 90, 98,
    99–100, 102, 258
Pomio (New Britain), 148
Port Vila, Vanuatu, 271
Pueblo Indians, 25
Pul Eliya (Sri Lanka), 250
Punjab (Pakistan and Oxford
    community), 219

Quechua, 267
Queen Charlotte Islands see
    Haida Gwaii

Ramingning (Aboriginal
    Arnhemland, Australia),
    255
Rendille (Kenya), 97
Rio de Janeiro, 16
Romans, Ancient, 40, 157, 217
Russia, 186

Samoa (Polynesia), 11, 54, 67,
    102
San Francisco, 210
Sani (South China), 278
Santa Cruz de Arriba
    (Mexico), 63
Sarakatsani (Greece), 240
Scotland, 9, 37, 107, 273, 283;
    Highlands of, 174–5
Scots, 88–9, 96, 217
Sheffield (England), 32
Shenzhen (China), 90
Shilluk (Sudan), 188, 190, 196
Siberia, 158
Sierra Leoneans, 123
Singapore, 90
Skansen (Sweden), 90
Skye (Scotland), 273
Solomon Islands, 22, 50, 143
South Asia, 49
South East Asia, 263, 266
Southall (West London), 53
Sovereign Hill (Australia), 90
Spain, 90, 175, 190
Spaniards, 22
Spanish conquistadors, 190
Sri Lanka, 130–1, 169, 250
Stratford upon Avon, 275
Sudan, 22–3, 112, 150, 179,
    188, 282
Swat Pathan (Afghanistan),
    202
Sweden, 90, 120, 189
Sydney, 10

Taiwan, 90
Taliban, 300
Tamil Nadu, 49
Tanzania, 83, 181, 229
Tarëno (also Trio), 194–5
Tasmanian, 148
Tehran, 186
Texcoco, Mexico, 63
Thailand, 285
Tibet, 148
Tikopia (Solomon Islands), 99,
    102

Tiv (Nigeria), 179, 181
Tlingit (Alaska, USA), 55, 118, 239
Tokyo, 146, 279
Torres Straits, 92
Traveller Gypsies, 44–5, 46–7, 295
Trinis (Trinidad), 291
Trio (Surinam), 156, 192–5
Trobriand Islands, 54, 67, 69, 121, 132, 177
Tungus (Siberia), 158
Turkey, 120
Turtle Island, 206, 242

Uganda, 141, 156, 171, 181
UK, 81

Uluru, 267
'Untouchables', 49

Vanuatu 267, 271–2
Venezuela, 191, 192
Venice (Italy), 17, 259
Virginia (USA), 284

Wabowden, 243
Waco (Texas), 146
Wahgi (Highlands of Papua New Guinea), 97–8, 121, 123, 202
Welsh, 26
Wodaabe (Nigeria), 128
Wounded Knee, 145

Yakha (East Nepal), 39
Yanomamö (Brazil and Venezuela), 64, 191
Yaruro (Venezuela), 192
Yolngu (Northern Australia), 123, 124–5, 239
Yorkshire (UK), 105

Zambia, 83
Zapotec, 140, 203
Zimbabwe, 181
Zulu (Lesotho, Southern Africa), 200
Zuni, 25

General Index

Note: Anthropological and other technical terms that appear in **bold** in the index are discussed particularly at the page numbers that appear in bold

Aang Serian, 101, 109
Abraham, 140
abuse, 45, 175, 179
accuracy, 6, 56–7
accusations, 155–9, 192
Adam and Eve, 142
addiction, 242
address, terms of, 217
adjudication, 180–1
adolescence, 3, 105
adoption, 208, 217
adornment, 54, 73, 95–102, 121, 122
adultery, 175–6
adulthood, 47, 83–4, 105, 135, 142, 183, 201; attainment of, 85–6
advertisements, 286
advocacy, 111, 188, 247
aesthetics, 110–27 *passim*, 240, 245
affection, 50
affluence, 238
afterlife, 22, 59, 87, 130, 177, 217
age, 4, 22, 29, 31, 84, 203, 237, 240; **grades, 200–1; mates**, 86, **200**; regiments, 200; **sets, 81, 200–1**
agency, 114, 118, 131, 182, 196
Ages of Magic, Religion and Science, 132

aggression, 117, 195
agricultural cycle, 253
agriculturalists, 87, 139, 173, 217; shifting, 240
All Saints Day, 161, 162
All Souls Day, 161, 162, 226, 228–30
alliance, 65, **228–30; theory, 226**
alms, 65, 156
almanacs, 27
Amaterasu, 264
ambiguity, 4, 47, 156
analysis, 25, 43, 52, 59, 93, 130, 137–42, 150, 157, 166, 219, 244; ancestors, 85, 114, 117, 126, 144–6, 150, 159, 166, 171, 217, 248; common, 197; wrath of, 177
ancestral: land, 266; presence, 267
ancestry, 199, 242
Anglicanism, 138–9
animal(s), 25, 27, 97, 99, 118, 124, 134, 141, 145, 228, 239, 247, 251, 266; categories, 45–6; as food, 24, 39–40, 3; human distinction, 94; markings, 112; *see also* cattle; sheep
anime (cartoons), 285
animism, 134, 136
anomaly, 43, 142, 252
anthropology, 202; applied, 7, 196, 296; of art, 110–27 *passim*; biological, 283; cognitive, 56; cultural, 11; economic, 241; of landscape, 114; legal, 178; political, 187–8; qualitative research in, 184; 'rethinking', 209; value of, 294–7

Arafat, Yasser, 103
arbitration, 180
archaeology, 1, 237
architecture, 115
arrest, 104, 175
art, 12, 68, 94, 111–27 *passim*, 239; bodily, 112; collectors, 161; and craft, 125; corporate, 119, 121, 'folk', 111, 125; historians, 111, 112, 126; living, 112–15; practical, 119; 'primitive', 111, 125; Western/Eastern, 248
artificial insemination, 209
artists, 113–14; intent of, 125; tattoo, 112
Asahara Shoko, 146
ascetics, 133
assimilation policies, 288
assumptions, 2, 29, 131, 140, 172, 188, 203, 213, 219, 225, 246
astrology, 27, 159
'Auld Lang Syne', 88
Aum Shinrikyo, 146
auspiciousness, 58–9, 159
authenticity, staging 263, 271–3, 274
authority, 38–9, 117, 118, 180, 182, 189, 191–2, 196, 202
avoidance, 43, 80, 173, 217
Ayurvedic system, 249
Aztec Earth Mother, 162

babies, 20–1, 41, 45, 47, 80–1; aborted, 159; cutting cord of, 80
baby-sitting circles, 66
backpackers, 257, 278
bar mitzvah, 77, 84
barter, 54, 65, 66–7
bathing, 37, 41, 52
beatniks, 99
beauty, 18, 68, 110–11, 112, 120–1, 123, 124, 126
belief, 76, 130, 133, 135, 152, 155, 159, 161, 190, 245; codification of, 137; systems, 153, 160, 177
betrothal, 78, 85; gifts, 86, 228
bias, 23–9 *passim*; male, 30, 67
Bible, the, 43, 88, 137
'biological' relationships, 207–12
biology, 30
birâdari, 22–4, 237
birth, 41, 77–8, 80–1, 88, 166, 174, 208, 224; order, 214; rate, 27; symbolic re-, 78,

84; ante-natal classes, 81
birthing partner, 81
blame, 154
blasphemy, 45
blood: money, 177; ties, 207
body, 22, 40–1, 90, 107, 152, 158, 181; control of, 209; decoration, 97–9, 112, 121–2; exudations of, 18, 42, 47, 249–50; idealization of, 112; interaction, 37; piercing, 84–5; mutilations of, 83
boundaries, 45, 104, 122, 125–6
bowing, 75, 79, 103–4
brand names, 281, 286
breast milk, 106
bribery, 61
bride, 61, 85, 225, 227–8; and groom, 107, 227
brideprice, **228**
bridewealth, **227–9**, 245
British: government, 152; prime minister, 212
Buddhism, 107, 130–1, 133, 150, 162-7, 177, 297; Tantric, 167; Thravada, 165; Mahayana, 165
burial, 21–3, 105
business: dealing, 67; international, 70; partners, 66; people, 17; relationship, 246

cakes, 31, 75, 107; cutting, 107
calendar, 63, 89, 159, 161
call centres, 300
canoes, 54; boards, 123
capitalism, 66–7, 238
cards, 62, 75, 93
carnival, 89; Mardi Gras, 89
casa chica, 232
caste, 40, 42, 58–9; business and trading, 226–7
cattle, 112–13, 121, 197, 229, 240, 251
celebration, 52, 55, 68, 80–1, 87, 88, 166, 174, 252
ceremonial dialogue, **195**
ceremony, 2, 54, 75, 78, 86, 89, 111, 137, 225, 246–7; naming, 80
Chancellor of the Exchequer, 39
change, 30–1, 160, 207, 239, 247
character, Japanese, 249
chi (life force), 28–9

chieftainship, 38, 53, 55, 102, 190, 192, 195, 244, 252
child-rearing, 183, 208–9
childbirth, 30, 40–2, 80–1, 117
children, 20, 30–1, 44, 47, 52–3, 63, 75–6, 81–4, 101, 108, 137, 143, 166, 185, 203, 212, 228, 233, 240, 241, 245
children's groups, 200
Chinese: calendar, 80; ceramics, 120; characters, 229
chityas, 162
choice, 89, 96, 122, 193, 201
christening, 76–7, 80
Christianity, 73, 87, 102, 106–7, 130, 140, 147, 138–9, 160–2, 166, 177
Christmas, 88, 89, 95, 252
church, 20, 73, 79, 133, 225; confirmation, 173; denominations, 138; excommunication from, 155–6; Protestant/Roman Catholic, 155–6
Church of England, 76, 80, 142, 225
'churching', 80
circumcision, 81, 83, 100–1
civilization, 120, 125, 181, 209, 238
clans, 24, 117, 124, 197, 217, 218, 226, 231; hierarchy, 137; totem, 116, 135
class, 3, **18–19**, 77–8, 105, 122, 226; distinctions, 20, 31, 40, 42; mates, 201; priestly, 22–3, 59; ruling, 189
classification, **20–33**, 52, 83, 136, 201, 247; colour, 25–8; of environment, 248, 250; of human beings, 24, 207; of kin relations, 213–18; of social groups, 236; of space, 25, 27, 88; of time, 26–7, 88, 159; systems of, 36–7, 41–8, 73, 93, 107, 114–15, 142, 172, 202, 217, 237, 240, 246
cleanliness, 20, 37, 41, 43–5, 46–7, 48
clitoridectomy, 83
clot, 68
clothing, 44, 69, 76, 87, 94–9, 104, 107, 120, 156, 174, 227, 239, 265, 286; *see also* dress
club membership, 55, 96

Coca-Cola, 238
cognition, 293–4
coins, 89
collaborators, 5, 7, 289
collective representations, 30, 108, **115**, 245
colonial: administrators, 190, 244; authorities, 196, 288; endeavour, 68, 188; influence, 102; rule, 187–8
colonies, 39, 190
colonization, 22, 158, 190, 241, 252
colour(s), 25–8; animals, 112; of clothes, 76, 87, 94–5, 107; of skin, 42
'coming of age', 84
commerce, 59, 247, 252
commodity, **110**, **246**; women as, 244
communication, 20, 25, 51–2, 54, **62–4**, 102, 108, 120, 122, 180, 191, 226, 228–9, 244, 281, 284; cheap, 281; cut off, 174; indirect, 177, 203; intensification of, 284; intercultural, 69; new forms of, 281; non-verbal, 69, 202; subtlety of, 120; with spiritual world, 41, 157–9; symbolic, 94–5
community, 52, 54, 64, 80, 86, 96–8, 105, 115, 117, 137–8, 172, 173, 176, 180, 192–3, 197, 271; Aboriginal, 111; affairs, 201; British, 221; Chinese, 186; Greek, 240; isolated, 237; Mexican, 245; moral, 133, 142; Pakistani, 219–24; performing, 271; religious, 226; socioeconomic, 62; Sri Lankan, 250; structure of, 240; values, 156
companies, 118, 173; pharmaceutical, 295; transnational, 196
comparison, 129, 151–2, 178, 191, 220
compensation payments, 65, 177
competition, 29, 55, 106, 121, 176, 179, 238, 251
computers, 291, 292
copying, 275
conception, 208–10
Concise Oxford Dictionary, 94
condolence, 68, 87
confinement, 80, 83

conflict, 29, 137, 142; ritualization of, 179–80
confrontation, 191, 202–3
Confucianism, 18, 166, 167
confusion, 145, 160, 208, 220
consciousness, 152
conservation, 160, 247
consumption, 111, **246**, 250–1, 281; **conspicuous**, 55
contest, 68, 102; Inuit song, 180
context, 68, 106–7, 111, 136, 143, 146, 181–2, 188, 191, 195, 203, 233, 249
cooking, 31, 51
co-operation, 29, 136, 173–4, 183, 193, 200
corruption, 61
Cortez, Hernando, 190
cosmology, 111, **130**, 138, 150–1, **158**, 160–2, 249, 250, 252
cosmopolitan society, 110, 111, 120, 170
court, 156, 170, 189, 232; Aztec, 190; of inquiry, 154; of law, 173, 180–1
courtesy, 120
couvade, **81**
Coventry, sending to, 174
coxcomb, 97, 99
craft centres, revitalization of, 273, 275
creativity, 113, 126, 220
Creator, the, 271
credit, 64; card, 246
crime, 5–6, 144, 181
cross-cousins, **218**
cults, **142–6**; Branch Davidian, 146; 'cargo', 143; of the dead, 141
cultural: blinkers, 209; difference, 256–8, 273; encounter, 260–1; exchange, 283; preservation, 283; reciprocity, 113; **relativism**, 11, 23–32 *passim*, 36, 70, 93, 110, 295; systems, 182
culture, 112, 135, 137, 141, 273–4; centres, 275; end of, 190; global, 90; heroes, 117; material, 258, 262, 273–5; popular, 285–6; shock, 42; as theme for leisure, 98–0
currency, 19, 67, 244
custom(s), 2, 19, 22, 30, 36–7, 41, 51–2, 75–6, 86, 89, 98,

99, 103, 174–5, 182, 225, 231, 251

dân (or *dana*), 58
dance, 53, 88–9, 106, 179, 183, 272; 'La Danza', 183
danger, 6, 21, 42–3, 47, 73, 79–80, 105, 132, 137, 156, 200, 203, 239
data, 105–6
Day of the Dead, 161, 162
death, 21–3, 41–2, 47, 52, 77, 92, 94, 141–2, 146, 166, 174, 179, 181, 183, 207, 213, 225; brain, 22; days, 159; of a king, 84; premature, 208; symbolic, 78, 86
debt, 155
deception, 53, 177; social, 69
decision-making, 181–2, 191, 193, 200, 212, 221, 231, 247
decorations, 173, 240
defence, 200
deference, 218
definition, 35–6, 93, 123, 130–3, 135, 150, 157, 224, 239, 248
democratization, 191
demography, 29, 196
dependence, 59, 188, 189, 219
descent, 189, **197**, **216–18**, 225; groups, 216–17, 232
desert, 239, 245, 248
destiny, 153; *karmic*, 59
destruction, 55, 190, 247
determinism, 250
development, 21; hyper-, 23; threat of, 247
Devil, the, 183
diaspora, **282–3**
diet, 140, 177, 192, 238, 249–50
diffusion theory, 12
diplomacy, 177
dirt, 21, 38, 43–6, 155
disaster, 140, 154, 190, 201, 248; natural, 282
discipline, 183
discourse, 191, 246–7, 250; universe of, 122
disgust, 18, 36–45, 99, 112
displacement of people, 283
display, 86, 99, 112, 115, 117–19, 121, 123, 125, 176, 183; cultural, 273–4; heritage, 273; people on, 19
dispute, 92, 112–15, 172–3, **178**, 181, 197; resolution,

172, 178–81, 195, 200
disputing process, 182
divination, 26, 137, **158–60**, 240
divorce, 85, 115, 213, 224–5
doctors, 137–8, 158, 159, 173, 232
dogma, 107, 162, 177
dogs, 45, 46
domination, 67–8, 113
Downs syndrome, 46
dowry, 224, **227–8**, 228–9
drama, 179
dreams, 94, 134
dress, 19, 37, 74–5, 86, 88, 95, 99, 246, 271; battle, 97, 100, 104;up-, 78, 86, 89; *see also* clothing
drinking, 62, 79, 85, 88
drugs: hallucinogenic, 2, 158; illegal, 265
duel, 104, 179

Easter, 89
eating, 20, 24, 36, 52, 62, 85
ecology, 195–6, 252; sacred, 269
economic(s), **236–53**; activities, 53, 62–3, 192, 197; alliance, 197, 217, 226; base, 241; benefit, 111, 171, 231; groups, 123; life, 212, 250, 252; power, 118; resources, 29, 228, 251; security, 221; self-interest, 53, 59; theory, 240, 245–6; transactions, 69, 212
economies: 'third world', 66; tiger, 295
economists, 238, 245–6
ecosystem, 242, 253
ecotourism, **265–71**, 283
education, 11, 40, 42, 55, 83–4, 122, 183, 221; kindergarten, 19, 37, 183; students, 220
Eightsome Reel, 88–9
Ejido, 244
elders, 200–1, 221
clements, 25–7
elections, 191
emotion, 94, 126, 134, 137, 181, 207
emperor, 84, 77; child, 232; divinity of, 107; Montezuma, 190
empire: Aztec, 190; British, 190; Inca, 190
employment, 240

endogamy, 62, **226**, **224**; **caste**, 226–7; religious, 227
English Channel, 154
Enlightenment, the, 9
enmity, 99, 104, 226
entertainment, 53, 89, 158, 200, 244
enthronement, 84
environment, 19, 45, 114, 160, 192–3, 196, 237, **247–53**, 283; stewardship of, 268, 270
environmental destruction, 267–8
ephebism, 112
equality, 200, 202; in-, 107
eroticism, 103
ethics, 144, 166, 209
ethnic origins, 43
ethnicity, 6, 31
ethnographer, 25, 30, 51–3, 150–1, 188
ethnography, **6**, 9, 30, 32, 48, 67, 112, 135, 137, 141, 158, 160, 177, 188, 196, 226, 238, 240–1, 249, multi-sited, **289–90**
etiquette, 107–8, 203
etymology, 38
Eucharist, 106–7
exchange, 52–8, **62–4**, 67–8, 86, 103, 117, 121, 123, 177, 239–41, 244–6, 250; accounting of, 62; direct (sister), 229–31; generalised, 64, 228; indirect, 228, 230; marriage as, 63–4, **227–31**; 'primitive', 64; restricted, 63–4; systems of, 226
exclusion, 111, 115, 181
exogamy, 217, **226**, 230, 231, 245; village, 227
exorcism, 133, 155
explanation, 133–7, 143–4, 153, 158–9, 249
exploitation, 267, 278
exploration, 245, 249
everyday life, 26, 51, 195, 248
evolution, theories of, 9–12, 131, 144, 137, 237, 240

'face', 55
face-to-face relations, **5**, 173, 284
faith, 124, 131, 138, 160; *see also* religion
family, 4–5, 22, 24, 30–1, 41, 52, 65, 87, 103, 145, 171,

173–4, **207–16**, 228, 237, 240, 241–5, 249; cultural constructions, 209; Fujiwara, 232; group, 208, 230; Holy, 142; Imperial, 232; honour, 176–7; land, 233; loyalty, 212; Muslim, 220–4; **nuclear**, 81, 143, **208**, **214**, 224, 226; Pakistani, 219–24; royal, 38, 201; 'single-parent', 208, 233; standard English, 213–15, 220–1, 224; wrangles, 181
fantasy, 89
Far East, 37, 113, 159, 253
fashion, 94, 118
fasting, 88
fate, 144, 153
Fatima, 222
Favours, 62, 102
fear, 176
feasts, 53, 55, 69, 156, 189, 246
feminists, 31, 37, 238
Feng Shui, 28–9
ferocity, 92
fertility, 102, 116, 117, 121, 123; in, 208–9
festival, 41, 52, 62, 87, 90, 98, 160, 161, 174, 183, 201, 252; Dasain, 39; Diwali, 88; financing, 245; Gumla, 164; Hallowe'en, 161–2; Hanukah, 88; harvest, 87, 232; water, 252
feuds, 156, 179, 199
field, 289
fieldnotes, 146
fieldwork, 2–3, 6, 10, 29, 41, 51, 67, 69, 75, 85, 99, 138, 166, 171, 182, 188, 196, 201, 289, 297
fiesta, 184, 345
film(s), 13–14, 145, 174, 196, 238, 258; makers, 248
financial: contributions, 183; systems, 11
fire, 174–5; brigades, 201; works, 183
'first-footing', 88
first hand accounts, 28–9, 46–7, 56–7, 60–1, 82–3, 100–1, 124–5, 138–9, 163–4, 194–5, 210–11, 224–5, 242–3, 260–2, 268–70, 287, 292–4,
fishing, 41, 153, 192, 196, 239, 250
fission/fusion, 199, 252

flags, 95, 104
flowers, 244
folk tales, 22, 118
food, 3, 5, 22, 31, 37, 44, 78–80, 93, 106, 117, 120, 177, 220, 240, 252, 263; collecting, 237; cooked, 195; differential value of, 245; exotic, 257; sacred, 107, 133; ingestion of, 249; perishable, 103, 244; production, 237; taboos, 40–3
forensic: experts, 158; skill, 195
forest: rain see tropical rainforest
forgery, 126
formal pretence, 53
formality, 68, 76, 89, 104, 225
franchise, 190
frankness, 177
freedom, 241
French: Revolution, 135; wine, 177
friends, 17, 20, 52, 79, 86, 88, 107, 171, 176, 220
friendship, 45, 51, 62, 246
function, 62, 123, 126, 135
functional: explanation, 142; role, 142, 156, 200
functionalism, 10, 136–8
funerals, 23, 73, 76, 78, 87, 166, 181, 219
future, 280–1, 288, 292–7

galleries, 112, 121, 125, 126
gap year, 257, 264
garden(s), 113, 116, 117; of Eden, 111; gloves, 125–6
gathering, 238–9; see also hunter-gatherers
gender, 4, 19, 30–2, 37, 40, 45, 89, 92, 106, 115, 122, 142–3, 201, 216, 217, 220–1, 237–8, 241
genealogical: links, 24, 212; vocabulary, 212
genealogy, 208, 212
Genesis, Book of, 43, 106, 137, 142
generation, 3, 19, 23, 30, 64, 101, 106, 128, 133, 212, 214–15, 217–24, 244
generosity, 62, 143, 193
genetrix, 209
genetic material, 209
genitor, 208–9, 212
geomancy, 27

gestation, period of, 208
ghost(s), 134, 150, 159, 177; dance, 142
gift(s), 3, 18–19, 51–61, 69–70, 73, 77–8, 4, 102–3, 121, 246; exchange, 75, 93, 102, 219, 221; 'free', 59; of money, 86; wrapping of, 121, 202
global, 110, 246; community, 66; discourse, 237, 253; homogenisation, 295; interconnectedness, 284; market place, 69, 246; phenomenon, 249
globalization, 283–8, 290–1, 295
God, 40, 43, 76, 80, 134–5, 143, 156; acts of, 153, 174; creation of, 197; wrath of, 155, 174, 177
godparents, 80
gods, 47, 76, 131, 134, 141, 146, 161–2, 190–1, 195, 238, 249
gold, 245
gossip, 173, 240
government, 191, 202, 241, 247
Grand Tour, 264
graves, 87, 162
Greenpeace, 247, 251
greetings, 37, 52, 62, 64, 69–70, 75, 88, 94, 103–4
group membership, 212, 216, 217
Guadalupe, Lady/Virgin of, 60, 142, 162

hair, 82, 95, 97–102, 131, 175; style, 99, 121–2, 246
Hajj, 264
hand-binding ceremony, 86
handbags, 96
handkerchiefs, 17–19
handshakes, 79, 88, 103
harmony, 173, 195, 202–3
hau, 56, 57
head, 102, 189; butting, 179; gear, 96–7, 104; painting, 83; shaving, 99, 100; skin-, 99
headdress, 97–8, 121
healing, 140, 159
health, 112, 123, 166, 189, 225, 295–6
heaven, 142, 158, 177
hegemony, 68; Western, 125
Heisenberg uncertainty

principle, 29
hell, 142, 171, 177
herding, 112, 217, 239
heritage, 68, 118, 272, 273; centres, 273, 274; World sites, 267, 287
hermeneutics, 56–7
hierarchical: difference, 228; order, 55, 118, 157; organisation, 112, 117, 188
hierarchy, 190, 196, 202–3
Hinduism, 131, 164–5
Hippie trail, 257
historians, 150, 155, 232
historical records, 175
historical sites, 260–1, 262, 264
history, 8–13, 22, 53, 62, 89, 112, 146, 151, 155–6, 166–7, 174; colonial, 113, 190, 249; influence of, 43; of thought, 132
HIV/AIDS, 140, 296
htinggaw group, 231
Hogmanay, 88–9
holidays, 52, 87, 90, 248
holiness, 43
home, 30–2, 45, 65, 80, 115, 120, 221; mobile, 239
honeymoon, 86, 246
honour, 54, 176, 240; killings, 172
horoscopes, 28
horticulture, 173
hospital, 81
hospitality, 79
hostility, 155, 176, 225–6
hotel industry, 261, 272
house(s), 41–2, 4, 47, 66, 69, 74, 80, 86, 105, 166, 175–6, 183; building, 159, 166, 221; burning, 174–5; ceremonial men's, 115–17, 126; Japanese, 74, 79, 87, 174, 225, 244; Jewish, 79; long-, 193; plan, 220; Victorian, 220; warming, 52; work, 30–1, 221, 223
household, 208, 232; altar, 86, 106; property, 244
huerta, 244
human: mind, 140; nature of, 209; organization, 193; relations with nature, 249; rights, 297
humanism, 135, 141
humanity, 268
hunter-gatherers, 237–9, 241, 249–50, 252

hunting, 25, 141, 156, 193, 217, 239
hygiene, 43–4, 46
hypergamy, 227, 231
hypogamy, 228, 231

iconography, 119
identity, 89, 217, **271–3;** formation, 286, 288; transnational, 287
ideal, 195–7, 102; and practice, 225
ideology, 59, 94, 95, 104, 106, 182, 208, 239, 249
idiosyncrasy, 2, 70, 172
illness, 22–3, 40, 54, 138, 144, 154, 156, 157–7, 166, 177, 190, 225, 249
imperial/governmental system, 196
in vitro fertilization, 208
incense, 87
incest, 140, **226**
Indian religions, 143
indigenous: art, 111; categories, 150–1; ideas, 130, 133; knowledge, 266, 273; law, 188; people, 4, 68, 95, 111, 143, 181, 191, 241, 261, 267, 281, 283, 270–1, 286, 288, 297; political movements, 285, 295; practice, 162
individual, 2, 52, 62, 75, 82, 89, 104–5, 134–6, 154, 171, 191, 193, 201, 231
individualism, 95
individuality, 96, 99, 105
Industrial Revolution, 264, 273
industrialized: society, 158, 173, 181, 248, 251; world, 191, 200, 213
influence, 68, 183, 246
informants, 4, 7, 28, 106, 115, 160, 220, 289
inheritance, 151, 211–12, **214–16,** 218, 228, 244
inhibitions, 47
initiate, 200
initiation, 77, 81–5, 88–9, 92, 99, 117, 151
injury, 146, 175, 179
insurance, 244
intercultural encounter, 68, 70
international NGOs, 247
International Whaling Commission, 250
internet, the, 14, 281, 288

interpretation, 2, 8, 42, 59, 67–8, 69, 77, 93–5, 103–8, 111, 115, 118, 123, 135, 145, 146, 159, 182, 188, 201, 244, 246–7
interregnum, 74
insh'Allah, 154
inside/outside distinction, 44, 156–7
Irish Queen, 95
irrigation, 249–50, 252
Islam, 130, 141, 153–4, 177, 220–4, 264

Japanese Garden Society, 13
Japaneseness, 246
jealousy, 151, 152, 154–5, 245
Jesus Christ, 40, 88, 107, 133, 142
jewellery, 97, 215, 218, 245
Joan of Arc, 157
Job, 155
Jonah, 250
'joy-riding', 84
Judaism, 130, 141
judgement, 117, 122, 172, 181
judges, 170, 177–8, 180–1
jury, 180–1
justice system, 143–4, 180–1

Kachina dolls, 271
Kataragama, 169
kidnapping, 86
kin, 42, 198, 211, 220, 228, 249; diagrams, 213–14; terms, 217
king, 39, 77, 85, 152, 190, 244; -ship, **188,** 190; of Mercia, 174
kinship, 31, 66, 114, 204, **207–23,** 225, 233, 244; systems, typologies of, 211
kissing, 37, 79, 88, 103
knowledge, 2, 8, 53, 70, 107, 117, 118, 123, 124, 130, 132, 140; local, 266, 273; second-hand, 130; types of, 13
kosher, 40
kula, 54–5, 123

labour, 55; division of, 62, 81, 238, 240
Lady Godiva, 174
land, 55, 173, 193, 295; ancestral, 144; appropriation, 265–6; claims, 9; investment in, 241; ownership, 59, 250–1; scarcity of, 244; tenure,

244–5
landscape, 113–14, 248
language, 3–5, 10, 20–1, 52, 93, 95, 104, 112, 120, 221, 252–3, 288; British English, 48; Dinka, 112; English, 3, 20, 25–6, 38, 80, 95, 133, 137, 150, 170, 174, 207, 209, 213, 217, 224; formal, 203; groups, 202; Japanese, 26, 62, 166, 225; Kachin, 48; manipulation of, 203; Nahuatl, 215; Nuer, 112; Punjabi, 220; revival, 288; Sinhala, 131; taboos, 45, 47; unspoken, 188, 202; Urdu, 220; Welsh, 26; Zande, 150
laughter, 176, 191
law(s), 9, 30, 37, 38, 143, 170–84 *passim,* 187, 225, 232; dietary, 40, 43; Islamic, 182; of nature, 132; poor, 157; of social life, 8–10; Tanzanian, 182; tribal, 83
lawyers, 170, 173
leaders, 181–3, **191–6,** 232, 244; charismatic, 145; cultural, 56; qualities of, 193–4
leadership, 62, 188, 191–6, 252
learning, 2, 7, 19–20, 45–6, 126, 170, 172, 200, 207, 249
legal: changes, 241; contract, 228; definition, 234–5; ideas, 209; system, 84, 141, 170, 187, 208, 215
legend, 54, 190, 217
legitimacy, 209, 244
leisure parks, 258
Lent, 89
letters, 62
Leviticus, Book of, 43
lies, 4, 176–7, 207; white, 177
life, 21–3, 32, 47, 104, 139–40; crises, 207; explanations of, 130; stages of, 52, 81, 99; support machines, 22
liminality, 78, 79, 80, 86, 89, 142
liminoid, 265
lineage, 65–6, 82, 106, 190, **197–8,** 201, 217, 231, 241; authority, 143; groups, 143, 226, 230; membership, 212
linguistics *see* language
listening, 5
logic, 21–4, 132, 141, 153, 192, 209, 213
London School of Economics,

10

long-term study, 183–4
'loud shouting', 176
love, 5–6, 225, 246, 249
loyalty, 59, 191, 246
luck, 153

magic, 25, 55, 121, **131–3**, 138,
    157, 162; black, 152;
    counter, 155; eco-, 155;
    types of, 131
magico-religious beliefs, 78,
    131
make-up, 112
mana, 38, 54–5, 67, 102
manga, 285
managerial organization,
    192–3
mangu, 150
manipulation, 111, 151, 182,
    188, 202
mantras, 165
maps, 114, 228, 249
marginality, 115, 196
mariachis, 60
market, 63, 66, 95, 237, 245;
    day, 63; economy, 240, 245;
    super, 64, 245-6, 252;
    world, 246
marketing strategy, 70
marriage, 30, 52, 76–7, 115,
    142, 166–7, 184, 201,
    221–32, 244; alliance, 202;
    arranged, 5–6, 64, 195, 219,
    222, 224, 226; arrange-
    ments, 55, 65, 174; Boston,
    210; breakdown, 86, 181;
    classes, 24; cousin, 223,
    226; **ghost**, **212**, 217, 225;
    homosexual, 225; **locality**,
    232–3; love, 5–6; matrilat-
    eral cross cousin, 230–1;
    preferential/ prescriptive,
    230; predicition, 106; rites,
    85–7; and social control,
    171; strategic, 231; suit-
    ability for, 27, 159; validat-
    ing, 228, 244
masculinity, 32
masks, 117–18, 183
masquerade, 89
mate/toa, 22–3
mater, 209
material, 67; artefacts, 67–8;
    culture, 23, 58, 68, 120,
    239, 249; gains, 246; goods,
    5, 17, 53, 55, 65, 67, 145–6,
    162, 177, 219, 228, 230,
    238, 244, 246; help, 221;

raw, 14; rewards, 173;
    wants, 238; *see also* objects
matrilaterality, **218**, 220
matrilineality, **214**, 217
mayordomia, 245
mayu-dama, 231
meaning, 3, 12, 17, 20, 68,
    69–70, 94, 102, 105, 107,
    112, 117–18, 121–2, 140,
    182, 229, 253
media, 87, 89, 103, 105, 248
mediation, 141, 180, 195
medicine, 4, 25, 173, 249; East
    Asian, 140; evil use of,
    151–2
memorials, 158, 166, 217
menstruation, 40–1, 46
mentality, 21, 23–4
metaphysics, 56–7
meteorological phenomena,
    24
methodology, 291
Mezuzah, 79
migration, 281–3
military: assistance, 53; might,
    99
millenarian movements,
    143–4
ministry, 138
misdemeanor, 155, 179–81
misfortune, 27, 142, 159, 177,
    180, 217; explanations of,
    142, 153–4, 158
missionaries, 23, 157, 162, 28,
    244
misunderstanding, 221, 241
mobile (cell) phones, 285–6,
    288, 291
mobility, 282
Moby Dick, 250
Mockerdy, 46
'mods' and 'rockers', 99
models, 66, 80, 213, 221, 253
modernity, 274
modernization, 144, 191, 241
moieties, 24
monarchy, 196, 245
money, 66–7, 86, 201, 219;
    earning, 221
monogamy, **232–3**; serial, 232
monotheism, 9, 135
monsters, 142
moral: capacities, 240;
    condition, 99; dogma, 177;
    implications, 64–5, 246;
    regeneration, 145; system,
    67, 94, 136, 141–2, 150,
    156–7, 171, 183, 189
morality, 117, 166, 182, 246

Mother Earth, 243
mothers' day, 60
motherhood, 80–1, 106, 208
mourning, 87, 137
mudyi tree, 106
multi-cited ethnography,
    289–90
multicultural worlds, 160,
    212–13, 218
mura hachibu, 174
murder, 146, 157, 177
museums, 68, 104, 115, 119,
    125; 258, 273–4, 275;
    ethnographic, 239; negative
    attitudes to, 273–4;
    Western, 126
music, 123
mwali, 54
mystical: attack, 153, 159;
    beings, 76
mysticism, 106–7, 140, 169
myth, 23, 116, 117, 123, 190;
    of Asdiwal, 142
mythology, 99, 112, 123,
    137–40, 217

name(s), 126, 132, 158, 200,
    215, 217, 226
national: anthem, 104;
    costume, 96–7
nationalism, 297
nationality, 95, 226
'natural', 20, 45, 208; causes,
    153; disaster, 282;
    resources, 160
nature, 25, 31, 131, 141–2, 248;
    control of, 249; harmony
    with, 266; worship, 160
negotiation, 120, 180–1, 195–6
neighbours, 70, 85, 103, 145,
    171, 225; operation of, 51,
    174, 212, 240; good
    opinion of, 155–6, 173;
    problems with, 21, 151,
    175, 244; understanding,
    29, 213, 220–1
nepotism, 212
networks, 291
neurosciences, 292
new reproductive
    technologies, **207–10**
New Year, 77, 88
NGOs, 267, 283
nirvana, 133, 177
noble savage, 111
nomads, **237**, 239, 249
normative effect, 171; of
    shamanism, 158; of
    witchcraft, 155, 157

norms, 68, 106, 153, **170–2**, 177, 192, 172, 181–2; fluidity of, 182
novelists, 248
nuclear testing, 177
nurturing, 208
Nyikang, 190

obedience, 218
obi, 82–3
objectivity, 107
objects, 17, 54, 56, 102, 215, 245–6, 290; *d'art*, 110–11, 118; classifying, 18, 26, 32; entangled, 67–8; inalienable, 67; inanimate, 134; interpretation of, 52, 93, 111, 117, 124, 126; marketable, 111; ritual, 117, of study, 94, 115; women as, 245
obligation, 62, 64, 69–70, 53–8, 215, 217, 219, 221
obscenity, 45
observation, 106, 114, 131
occupation, 4, 5, 201, 212; specialist, 50
offerings, 134
office, 39; badge of, 191; succession to, 212
oil prospecting, 295
opposition, 142, 196, 197–9, 202
oracles, 152, 154, 166; chicken, 154; 'rubbing board', 154
oratory, 182, 193, 195, 201, 240
ordeals, 78, 83–4, 99, 112, 180, 200
order, 43, 170–84 *passim*; God's, 43
originality, 126
origins, 174, 180–1
ostracism, 174, 180–1
outside view, 249
outsiders, 17, 68, 69, 88, 105–6, 111, 122, 145, 187, 203, 221, 228
ownership, 54, 67, 118, 123, 238, 241
Oxford Centre for Cross Cultural Research on Women, 31

Pacific Ocean, 177, 258, 267
Paganism, 107, 160–1
pain, 99, 112
painting, 95, 111, 114, 116, 117–18, 123, 124;

aboriginal, 161
palaces, 245
Palestinian Liberation Organization, 103
Palin, Michael, 258, 278
pantomime, 89
paradise, 111
parallel cousins, **218**
parenthood, 208–9, 25; same-sex, 210–11
parliament, 191
Parry, Bruce, 279
participant observation, **2**, 51
parties, 62, 78, 80; birthday, 75–6, 81, 83; *despedida de soltera*, 85; farewell, 79, 85; Hogmanay, 88; 'shower', 85; stag, 85
pastoralists, 237, 239–40, 250, 252
pater, **209**, 212
paternity, 81, 208
patrilaterality, **218**, 220
patrilineality, **216–17**, 232
patriotism, 135
patronage, 240
patterns, 78, 81, 87, 112, 114
peer pressure, 183
perception, 30, 126, 203, 248, 250
performance, 23, 89, 93, 106, 271–3
personality, 95
personhood, 41, 182
philosophy, 9, 22; Greek, 126
photographs, 103, 123, 249
peace, 25, 175; -maker, 195
phenomenology, 57
pilgrimage, 252, 264, 265, 279
Pitt Rivers Museum 98, 121, 193, 290
placebo, 138
planting, 252
plants, 242
play, 87, 224, 263–5
pleasure, 52, 69
pleasure, 52, 69
poetry, 286
police, 84, 104, 170, 175
politeness, 70, 177, 201, 203
political, 69; allegiances, 217, 226; authority, 38; behaviour, 231; benefit, 110, 113; change, 123; correctness, 123; factions, 156, 191, 195; hierarchy, 55; institutions, 9; issues, 241; life, 142, 150, 188, 192, 208, 212, 249, 251; might, 88,

121; movements, 288, 295; organization, 198, 251–2; parties, 191; realignment, 197; role, 67, 192, 200; science, 188–9; strategies, 196; status relations, 231; systems, 131, 170, 178, 187, 196–204, 212, 232, 240, 242; value, 115, 199
politicians, 170
politics, 68, 148, 170, **187–204**, 233; of argument, 181; art of, 188; fusion, 252; international, 62
pollution, **37–45**, 58, 73, 79, 87, 131
polyandry, **232–3**
polygamy, **225**, **232**
polygony, **232–3**
Polynesian Cultural Centre, 90
polytheism, 9, 135
popular culture, 285–6
portability, 285
postmodernity, 274
potlatch, 55, 58, 239, 245
poverty, 29, 238
power, 39, 47, 61, 67, 69, 99, 118, 123, 146, 150–2, 183, 188, 190–2, 203, 246; acquisition of, 201–3, 245; divine, 143; innate, 155; manipulation of, 201; mystical, 76, 131, 151; physical, 202; positions of, 170, 181; psychic, 151; relations, 183, 188, 239; struggle for, 202–3; unequal, **182**
prayer, 86, 143, 15, 156
preconceptions, 29, 221
pregnancy, 40, 78, 80–1, 82–3, 101, 117
prejudice, 37, 131, 219
presentation, 52–3, 54, 69, 70, 120, 121, 202
prestation, 59; total 53
prestige, 54, 193, 240, 246
priesthood, 84, 95, 123, 133, 159, 166, 175, 177
primatology, 293
primitive/civilized distinction, 9, 21, 23–4, 30, 43, 53, 77, 99, 133, 179, 238, 247
primogeniture, **215**
prison, 104, 170, 181; sentences, 173
prisoners, 174
prizes, 103, 173
procreation, 225

profane, 38, 79
prohibition, 38, 41
property, 53, 55, 212, 215, 224,
    241–4; intellectual, 294,
    295; moveable, 244
prophesies, 146
Prophet Mohammed, 223
prosperity, 121, 177, 190
protection, 41, 59, 78, 80, 122,
    156, 160, 189, 201, 250;
    self, 156
psychiatry, 94
psychology, 9, 94, 133–4, 138
puberty, 81, 83; rites, 106
public: duty, 212; funds, 189;
    harangue, 179–80; life, 30;
    mockery, 175–6, 177;
    opinion, 152, 159; place, 37
puja, 163–4
punishment, 143–4, 170, 173,
    181
punks, 99, 101, 122
purdah, 220
purification, 41
purity, 38, 41–8, 58, 190; of
    blood, 223

quarrel, 103, 179
Qur'an, 137, 141, 233

Rabin, Yitzhak, 103
race, 31, 226
racial discrimination, 36
radio programmes, 28-9
rain-making dances, 252
Raj Quartet, 42, 190
rank, 39, 55, 65, 104
rationality, 119, 144, 158, 181
reciprocity, 59, 64–7, 102,
    143, 156, 177–8, 191, 229,
    240, 246, 251; **balanced,
    65–6; generalized, 65, 66;
    negative, 64, 65–7**
reconstruction, 274, 275
Reformation, 156
regulations, 37; legal, 11, 30,
    53; moral, 11, 30, 53
rehabilitation, 170
relationships, 5, 6, 41, 231;
    adaption of, 220;
    expression of, 52–3, 54, 62;
    map of, 228–9; rejection of,
    62; representation of, 107;
    symbolizing, 102–4
relatives, 21, 23, 24, 43, 52, 79,
    88, 108, 176, 208-9,
    219–24, 237
religion, 25, 41, 47, 55, 94, 99,
    106, 123, 125, 126, 161,

227, 283, 293–4; **definition
of, 130–2**; explanations of,
136–46; as a moral system,
141–2, 177; origin of, 9,
133–6; world, 59, 141
religious: activities, 143, 166,
195, 252; beliefs, 9, 59, 76,
154, 212; differences, 224;
faiths, 12, 40, 107, 136;
groups, 95; ideas, 209, 225;
life, 217; movements, 144;
orders, 95; practice, 133,
166; rites, 70, 136; service,
76; systems, 127, 183
remarriage, 213, 221–2
Renaissance, 114
renewal, 274, 265
repatriation, 290
replication, 126
representation, 32, 94, 107,
111, 114, 123, 126, 179,
196, 198; self, 276
reproduction, 208, 233
reputation, 68, 156, 172, 176
residence, 66, 207, 212, 216,
231–2
resistance, 181; to oppression,
146
resources, 55, 105, 112, 219;
access to, 245; investment
of, 245; scarcity of, 22, 245,
251; use, 247; waste of, 73
respect, 76, 122, 160, 176, 200,
218, 220, 245
responsibility, 41, 203, 247
restaurants, 256
retribution, 172, 177
revenge, 156
rhetoric, 182, 196
rice, 173, 240, 249
ridicule, 173, 176, 240
rights, 38, 59, 84, 209–10,
214–15, 217; grazing, 239,
241
rites, 2, 76, 135, 137, 155, 160,
217; **expressive, 140**; of
passage, 77–90, 93, 106,
140, 245, 263–5;
instrumental, 140
ritual, 23, 26, 48, 53, **73–90**,
93, 106–7, 122–3, 140, 159,
197, 200, 217, 246, 252;
bureaucratic, 79; behaviour,
75–6; charter for, 137;
cleansing, 177; of crossing
threshold, 79–80, 87;
experts, 162; precautions,
132; of purification, 41, 43;
support, 189; symbols, 106

rivalry, 99; factional, 157
role(s), 117, 121, 133, 159, 174,
180, 201, 213, 225, 228,
241; expressive, 142, 156,
166; gender, 30–1, 115;
instrumental, 156; reversal,
89, 183; specialization, 238;
symbolic, 196
Romeo and Juliet, 179
Rosetta Stone, 260
'rough music', 176
routine, 73, 87, 248; break
from, 87–90; technological,
132
Royal Anthropological
Institute, 300
rubbish, 44, 51
ruler, 190
rules, 37, 43–5, 52, 66, 76, 137,
172, 182; dietary, 24, 40; of
etiquette, 203;
infringement of, 144, 177;
inheritance, 214, 225,
241–2; lack of, 84, 86; of
land ownership, 241, 250;
marriage, 226

sacerdotal, 190, 196
sacred, 38, 43–4, 79, 120, 133,
135, 144, 264; cow, 40, 42,
47, 251; sites, 247
sacredness, 242–3
sacrifice, 43, 134; human, 22,
190–1
saint's day, 161, 162
Sakyamuni Buddha, 165
salvation, 143; personal, 133
same-sex parentage, 210–11
samurai, 101, 104, 108
sanctions, 37, 53, 64, 83,
172–8, 180, 182, 241
sanctity, 41
scarring, 83, 116
school, 52, 77, 160, 220, 249,
295; mates, 66
science, 130–3, 134, 137–8,
158; indigenous, 277
scientific: developments, 208;
discovery, 160; figures, 250;
ideas, 209; technology, 252
sculpture, 158–9, 171; Yena,
117–20
séance, 158–9, 171
seasonal goods, 252–3
seasons, 25, 88; change of, 77,
87, 252; cycle of, 89
seclusion, 80–1
secrecy, 84, 111, 207
secret societies, 84

secular activities, 75, 106–7
secularization, 144
security, 79, 228, 244
segment, **197–9**
segmentary system, **196–9**, 220
self: dual, 134; esteem, 176, 211; interest, 183, 201; reliance, 196
serenatas, 60–1
sexual: access, 200; 'feeding', 209; maturity, 83, 117; potency, 116; prime, 112; relations, 226; transgression, 175; urges, 265
sexuality, 31, 89, 99–100
sexually transmitted diseases, 296
shamanism, 151, **158–60**, 171, 177, 184, 196
shame, 176, 180, 240
sheep, 240
shelter, 240
shepherds, 240
Sherlock Holmes, 186
shining, 112, 121, 123
Sinto, 86, 107, 131, 166, 167
shoes, 44, 73–5, 79
shopping, 246
shrine, 123, 137, 143, 252; visit, 80, 86, 166
siblings, 218, 240, 242
sign, 79, **94–5**
silence, 5, 62
sin, 58
singing, 104, 175, 179, 250
skills, 55, 63, 97, 117, 125–6, 151–2, 179, 195, 201, 203, 244
slash and burn cultivation, 192–5, 241
slavery, 39, 55, 98
social: anti, 83–4; behaviour, 134, 231; change, 136, 145, 157, 160, 162; cohesions, 136, 156; constraint, 12, 30, 136, 171, 182, 221; construct, 207–8; context, 203; **control**, 144, **170–84**, 187, 225, 237, 241; differentiation, 32, 39; distance, 64–6; **facts**, **11**, 30, **136**, **137–8**; integrity, 137; organization, 95, 142, 198, 249–50; reform, 264; relations, 41, 48, 52, 62, 114, 176, 182–3, 191, 207; rules, 14, 183; **structure**, 10, 136, 157, 199; tensions,

154–5, 159
socialization, **20**, 136
society, 6; anonymous, 173; complex, 20, 137, 159, 172; creation of, 134; democratic, 201; small-scale, 53, 77–8, 127, 144, 171, 173, 181, 237, 247; state, 62; Zande, 152–3
sociologists, 144
sociology, 9–12, 134–6
songs, 104, 123, 124
sorcery, **150–3**, 157, 180, 191
soteriology, **141**
soul, 22, 41, 87, 134, 158
soulava, 54
sounds, 114
Southern hemisphere, 252–3
souvenirs, 17–19, 110–11, 275
space: division of, 25–6, 142; notions of, 114; shrinking of, 284; *see also* classification
specialization, 62, 64, 70, 105, 133, 240
speculation, 134, 136
spells, 131, 151
spirit(s), 117, 158, 169, 189; control over, 159; favour with, 55; **medium**, **159**, 176; **possession**, **152–3**, **159–60**, 171; world, 41, 117, 126, 157; wrath of, 177
spiritual: beings, 130, 266; forces, 54–5; healing, 111; life, 160, 240; meaning, 111; notions of, 113, 134; quests, 264; value, 115, 134
spirituality, 56, 269
sports, 63, 179–80, 199
standard: of behaviour, 172, 221; of living, 145, 238
statistical surveys, 6
status, 19, 39, 54, 58–60, 66, 82, 99–104, 117, 118–22, 160, 173, 193, 213, 232, 238, 240, 245–6; **ascribed and achieved**, **201–2**; caste, 224; change of, 52, 77; level of, 95, 142; relations, 231; symbol, 120
stories, 116–17, 118, 124, 139, 175–6
strangers, 15, 20–1, 37, 62, 70, 79
strategy, 160
streakers, 37
structural: **analysis**, **136–41**, 156, 231; **functionalism**,

10, **137**; inversion, 156; overview, 202; system, 201
structuralism, **12**, **140–3**
structure, 56, 106, 115–16, 117, 166, 181
students, 8, 29, 37, 83, 99, 143, 145, 150, 158, 160, 176
subsistence, 192, 237, 239, 245; farmers, 247
success, 173, 193, 201
succession, 84, 228
Suez Canal, 260
suicide, 99, 146, 172
suit of armour, 104, 157
supernatural, 118, 134; agencies, 180
superstition, 107, 131, 166
Supreme Being, 150
surrogacy, **208**
survival, 174, 177, 237, 240
Survival International, 266
suspicion, 37, 42, 212
sustainability, 267, 268, 271
symbolism, 90, **93–108**, 115, 121, 123, 183, 246, 252
symbols, 109; ban-the-bomb, 104; bodily, 95–102, 110; group, 104–5; manipulating, 102, 105; private/public, 94–5, 102; sacred, 135
syncretism, **160–7**

taboo, **38–41**, 43, 73, 106, 131, 142, 176
tabu, 38, 55
tagba boz, 179
Taman Mini Indonesia Indah, 90
Taoism, 26, 166
taonga, 55, 57, 67
'tarring and feathering', 175
taste, 11, 19, 96, 122–4
tattooing, 84, 97–9, 112, 202
tax, 189; return, 30
teaching, 144, 19, 144, 161, 183, 219–20
technological: achievement, 25, 27, 248; change, 239; development, 21, 122, 249; routine, 76; superstate, 26
technology, 135, 192–3, 208, 233, 282; information, 237
telephone calls, 62, 79
television, 248, 258; anthropology on, 296; taboo on watching, 41
temple, 41, 43, 79, 137, 159
terminology, 108, 112, 151–3,

213–15, 217–18
text messaging, 286
theatre, 89, 123, 145
theft, 55, 65, 84, 157–8
theme parks, 89–90, 273–5, 290
theory, 79, 29, 42, 59, 67, 77, 79, 88, 102, 131–2, 133–40, 151, 153; of kinship, 209; of witchcraft, 155–7
Theory of Limited Good, 245
Thomas Cook, 264
thought: modes of, 115; mythical, 141; scientific, 132; systems of, 29, 150; theories of, 132
time, 23, 26–7, 30, 64–5, 89, 142; divisions of, 26; investment of, 112, 173; notions of, 114; passage of, 77, 87–90; and space, 284, 294; waste of, 73
titles, 173, 214
tobacco, 242
tolerance, 160, 172, 195
Tonantzin, 162
tools, 192–3
total phenomenon, 53
totem, 118, 135; poles, 118–19, 121, 135
totemism, **135,** 139
tour: guides, 261, 269; package, 264
tourism, 17, 90, 95, 111, 257, 258–76, 280–1, 295; cultural, 261, 268–70; industry, 260, 267; see also ecotourism
trade, 57, 121, 64–6, 195, 226, 244, 246
tradition: European, 114; Judaeo-Christian, 130,143
training, 84, 133, 158; anthropological, 203; child, 74
trances, 134, 158
transactionalism, 202
transcendental experience, 130
transhumance, 239–40, 250, 253
transition, 78–9, 84, 88
translation, 6, 20, 21, 24, 129, 203, 217, 220, **280–98;** dictionary, 3
translocal, 291
transnational connections, 282, 289
transnationalism, 287, 280

travel, 17, 21, 36, 54, 70, 200–1, **258-63,** 286, 295; agents, 261; ethnic, 258; railway, 175
travellers, 23, 68, 111, 126; tales, 9
treaties, 65, 103; peace, 25
trials, 181; witch, 155–6, 169
tribe, 23, 54, 65–6, 83, 197–201
tribute, 189, 244; as investment, 244
trickster, 141
tropical rain forest, 114, 186, 188, 192–6, 226, 232, 240, 252, 255
trousseau, 228
trust, 67, 244
Turkish carpets, 120

umpires, 180–1
uniform, 104, 191–2
unilineal descent groups, 216–17
underworld, 158
United Nations: standing committees, 244; Year of Indigenous Peoples, 241
universality, 124, 245
university, 52, 221; degree conferment, 103; of Oxford, 130; Oxford Brookes, 157; 'rag week', 83
upbringing, 19, 21, 124
Upper Canada Village, 90
usufruct, 241

value(s), 10–11, 56, 69–70, 106, 110–11, 122–3, 181–3, 203, 240, 261, 268, 268, 280, 290, 296; concepts of, 245; contested, 123, 181; economic, 17, 72; esoteric, 111; 'gentlemanly', 181; moral, 144; nutritional, 192; socioeconomic, 22; symbolic, 245–6; system, 5, 176–7
variation, 264, 271
vengeance, 172, 179
victim, 152, 156, 176
Victoria and Albert Museum, 118
video games, 285
village, 63, 65–6, 86, 115, 156, 173, 176, 179, 183, 197–9, 231; autonomy, 192; meetings, 174
violence, 65, 99, 104, 181;

interpersonal, 178–80, 181
virginity, 107
vito, 175

wake, 87
war, 53, 64, 104, 116, 141, 157, 172, 217; First World, 179; religious, 151; Second World, 107, 131, 191
Warnock report, 208-9
warriors, 200
water: shortage, 250; supply, 173–4, 181, 245
wealth, 53–5, 61, 65–6, 97, 112, 118, 121, 176, 183, 212, 229, 232
wedding(s), 27, 37, 73, 76, 85–7, 107–8, 166, 228-9, 246; cake, 107–8; rings, 245
West Side Story, 179
Western society, 27, 30–2, 62, 96, 103, 115, 123, 154, 208, 250, 253
whale, 251; conservation, 250
'wilderness', 265
Windows of the World, 90
winter solstice, 88
witchcraft, 131, **150-7,** 161, 169, 180, 184; coven, 157; roles of, 153–7, 171
witchdoctor, 159
wizardry, 152
women's: liberation, 30, 32; studies, 31
work, 30, 52, 88, 183, 238; mates, 42, 173; patterns, 285; retirement from, 200
world: ancient, 160; creation of, 88, 130; as globe, 249; high-tech, 112; New, 245; views, 115, 137, 160, 248, 250, 253
World Trade Centre, 295, 299
worship, 43, 106, 137; ancestor, 134, 143; nature, 160; rites of, 135
wrapping, 67–70, 73, 75, 102, 120–2; of the body, 202; paper, 69; social, 69; of space and time, 202–3
writing, 29

yin and *yang,* 26, 159
Yirritja and *Dhuwa,* 124–5
youth, 88, 99, 112, 182, 200; club, 181; groups, 201
yurts, 239

Zapatista movement, 288, 300

Ethnicity and Causal Mechanisms

MICHAEL RUTTER

Institute of Psychiatry
King's College London

MARTA TIENDA

Office of Population Research,
Department of Sociology and
Woodrow Wilson School of
Public and International Affairs
Princeton University, Princeton

CAMBRIDGE
UNIVERSITY PRESS

CAMBRIDGE UNIVERSITY PRESS
Cambridge, New York, Melbourne, Madrid, Cape Town, Singapore, São Paulo

Cambridge University Press
40 West 20th Street, New York, NY 10011-4211, USA

www.cambridge.org
Information on this title: www.cambridge.org/9780521849937

First published 2005

Printed in the United States of America

A catalog record for this publication is available from the British Library.

Library of Congress Cataloging in Publication Data

Ethnicity and causal mechanisms / edited by Michael Rutter, Marta Tienda.
   p.   cm. – (The Jacobs Foundation series on adolescence)
Includes bibliographical references and index.
ISBN 0-521-84993-4 (hardcover) – ISBN 0-521-61510-0 (pbk.)
1. Minority teenagers – Research.   2. Minority teenagers – United States.   3. Minority
teenagers – Great Britain.   4. Ethnicity – United States – Psychological aspects.
5. Ethnicity – Great Britain – Psychological aspects.   6. Ethnopsychology.
I. Rutter, Michael, 1933–   II. Tienda, Marta.   III. Series.
HQ796.E73   2005
305.235'089 – dc22   2004030540

ISBN-13   978-0-521-84993-7 hardback
ISBN-10   0-521-84993-4 hardback

ISBN-13   978-0-521-61510-5 paperback
ISBN-10   0-521-61510-0 paperback

Contents

List of Contributors   *page* ix

Foreword   xi

Preface   xiii

1 Natural Experiments, Causal Influences, and Policy
   Development   1
   Michael Rutter

2 Growing Up Ethnic in the United Kingdom and the United
   States: Comparative Contexts for Youth Development   21
   Marta Tienda

3 The Multiple Facets of Ethnicity   50
   Michael Rutter and Marta Tienda

4 Educational Attainments: Ethnic Differences in
   the United Kingdom   80
   Barbara Maughan

5 Race and Ethnic Inequality in Educational Attainment in the
   United States   107
   Charles Hirschman and Jennifer C. Lee

6 Racial and Ethnic Disparities in Crime and Delinquency in
   the United States   139
   Jeffrey D. Morenoff

7 Explaining Ethnic Variations in Crime and Antisocial
   Behavior in the United Kingdom   174
   David J. Smith

8 Cultural Differences in the Effects of Physical Punishment   204
   Kirby Deater-Deckard, Kenneth A. Dodge, and Emma Sorbring

9   Ethnicity and Mental Health: The Example of Schizophrenia
    in the African-Caribbean Population in Europe   227
    Peter B. Jones and Wai Lun Alan Fung

10 Ethnic Variations in Youth Suicide   262
    Jewelle Taylor Gibbs

11 Ethnicity and Intergenerational Identities and Adaptations in
    Britain: The Socio-Political Context   281
    Tariq Modood

12 Assimilation, Dissimilation, and Ethnic Identities: The
    Experience of Children of Immigrants in the United States   301
    Rubén G. Rumbaut

13 Deciphering Ethnicity: Reflections on Research Opportunities   335
    Marta Tienda and Michael Rutter

Author Index   351
Subject Index   364

Contributors

Kirby Deater-Deckard, Associate Professor of Psychology, University of Oregon, Eugene, OR (U.S.A.).

Kenneth A. Dodge, William McDougall Professor of Public Policy Studies in the Terry Sanford Institute of Public Policy, Duke University, Durham, NC (U.S.A.).

W. L. Alan Fung, University of Toronto Faculty of Medicine, Toronto, Ontario, Canada.

Jewelle Taylor Gibbs, Zellerbach Family Fund Professor Emerita, School of Social Welfare, University of California at Berkeley, Berkeley, CA (U.S.A.).

Charles Hirschman, Boeing International Professor, Department of Sociology, University of Washington, Seattle, WA (U.S.A.), and Fellow of the American Academy of Arts and Sciences and the American Association for the Advancement of Sciences.

Peter B. Jones, Professor of Psychiatry and Head of Department, University of Cambridge (UK), Consultant Psychiatrist at Addenbrooke's NHS Trust.

Jennifer C. Lee, Assistant Professor, Department of Sociology, University of California, Irvine, CA (U.S.A.), and Fellow at the Center for Advanced Study in the Behavioral Sciences.

Barbara Maughan, Reader in Developmental Psychopathology, Institute of Psychiatry, King's College London (UK), and member of the UK Medical Research Council's External Scientific Staff.

Tariq Modood, Professor of Sociology, Politics and Public Policy, Founding Director of the Centre for the Study of Ethnicity and Citizenship, University of Bristol, Bristol (UK).

Jeffrey D. Morenoff, Assistant Professor of Sociology and Faculty Associate, Population Studies Center and the Survey Research Center, University of Michigan, Ann Arbor, MI (U.S.A.).

Rubén G. Rumbaut, Professor of Sociology, University of California, Irvine, CA (U.S.A.), and Co-Director of UCI's Center for Research on Immigration, Population and Public Policy, Founding Chair of the Section on International Migration of the American Sociological Association.

Michael Rutter, Professor of Developmental Psychopathology, Institute of Psychiatry, King's College London (UK).

David J. Smith, Professor of Criminology, University of Edinburgh, Scotland.

Emma Sorbring, Lecturer in the Department for Studies of the Individual and Society, University of Trollhättan-Uddevalla, Vänersborg, Sweden.

Marta Tienda, Maurice P. During '22 Professor in Demographic Studies, and Professor of Sociology and Public Affairs at Princeton University, Princeton, NJ (U.S.A.).

Foreword

Christian Jacobs, Chairman
Jacobs Foundation

Over the years, ethnic minority groups have often been viewed by both the media and the general population as "problems." For some this has been because they have been viewed as representing social disadvantage, and for others because they have been seen as genetically inferior. Currently, many countries are in the midst of intense political debate about the supposed way in which immigrant groups are undermining the host culture and asylum seekers are constituting a burden on the state. The Jacobs Foundation has been concerned with the reality that some ethnic minority groups do indeed experience difficulties and, equally, with the fact that the prevailing stereotypes are usually misleading in several rather different ways. Accordingly, we were very pleased to initiate and sponsor the international, interdisciplinary conference that provided the basis for this edited volume.

The Foundation was keen that both the conference and the book would provide an incisive, insightful new look at ethnicity, and the contributors to this book have done this in admirable fashion. Three main themes constitute the basis for this truly fresh approach to ethnicity. First, there is discussion of the many facets of ethnicity. It is not an objective "thing." Rather it is a complex amalgam of cultural traditions, religion, geography, skin color, facial appearance, self-identification, host labeling, political decisions and genetic background. Each of these facets may be crucially important in different circumstances, but often they pull in different directions. Moreover, some of the facets are dimensional and some are categorical. Furthermore, research has shown that it is common for people to have more than one ethnic identification. Any meaningful consideration of ethnicity has to take this complexity into account.

Second, research findings, as well as experiences, emphasize that ethnic groups are far from homogeneous. Some tend, on average, to be unusually disadvantaged, but also some are advantaged relative to the total population of which they form a part. In addition, all groups are very heterogeneous within themselves. In most circumstances, the variation within ethnic groups is as great, or greater, than that between groups.

Third, there is the most distinctive feature of this volume which differentiates it from all others examining ethnicity. That is, these variations within and among groups, with respect to a range of psychological features, are used to test competing hypotheses about possible mediating causal mechanisms. It is evident that this important research approach has already led to a better understanding of some key issues. It is also clear, however, that much more needs to be done if we are to have a firm knowledge about causal processes. Each of the chapters seeks to provide some look ahead to the challenges remaining to be met.

Finally, in keeping with the Jacobs Foundation commitment to the need to make research inform policy and practice, the last chapter seeks to draw the threads together, insofar as that is possible, to conclude what remains to be done. The result is not the simple, universally applicable solution that some politicians look for, but it does constitute a thoughtfully constructive discussion of priorities.

All too often, discussions about ethnicity are. All too often, discussions about ethnicity are viewed as too complex to be productive because they are so prone to degenerate into expressions of prejudice and stereotype. The Jacobs Foundation prides itself on its willingness to take on controversial areas so long as it is convinced that to do so will be useful for policy and practice and that the discussions can be undertaken in a fair, well-informed, and balanced manner. In our view, this volume well illustrates both the need to take on politically tricky topics and the fact that this can be done in an honest and transparent fashion.

Preface

Ethnic groups differ on a wide range of features – spanning health, education, mental disorder, and crime, to mention but a few. These differences have given rise to a substantial literature on supposed cultural influences. In recent years, interest in cultural differences has been associated with a major paradigm shift from cross-cultural to within-culture studies (Shweder et al., 1998). For the most part, this shift reflects a concern that the concepts and measures derived in any one culture cannot be assumed to cover the universe of features that operate in other cultures. We share that concern and accept the value of qualitative, in-depth studies of a single culture.

However, the aim of this book is not to understand how any one particular culture functions. Because ethnic groups differ appreciably with respect to both their own characteristics and the patterns of psychological and social functioning with which they are associated, we sought to use variations across ethnic groups as a means of examining and, where possible, testing competing hypotheses about the mediating causal mechanisms. Accordingly, to somewhat oversimplify, the research strategy involves determining which risk or protective factors are significantly associated with particular psychosocial outcomes *within* each ethnic group. We reasoned that if specific factors mediate an observed *between-group* difference, then the prevalence of the risk/protective factor will differ between the ethnic groups; moreover, when the factor is introduced into a multivariate analysis, it will obliterate (or, at least, bring about a major reduction in) the difference between groups.

Because this analytic approach involves both within-group and between-group differences, the identification of the mediating mechanism for the one should throw light on the other. Moreover, the approach considers both good functioning and impairment; hence it makes no assumption that any one group sets the "norm." Also, by making comparisons across several ethnic groups, rather than merely between the majority group in any one country and some selected minority group, the generalizability of inferences is enhanced.

Rutter's opening chapter sets the scene by discussing some of the conceptual, research strategy, and methodological issues involved in using "natural experiments" of this kind to test causal hypotheses. Examples from a range of topics are used to illustrate the approach, with particular attention being paid to migration designs because of their power to "pull apart" different aspects of ethnicity.

We could have chosen to examine the effects of ethnicity across many different countries, but this would have compounded difficulties in interpretation because the patterns of ethnic differences are highly variable across nations, and because many countries lack appropriate statistics to implement our strategy. Accordingly, we chose to focus, for the most part, on just two countries – the United States and the United Kingdom. They have an interesting, and potentially informative, mix of similarities and differences that help in testing causal hypotheses. In the second chapter, Tienda pulls together the evidence on the social and demographic indicators across ethnic groups in the two countries and, drawing on a broader research literature, considers the possible implications of selected differences and similarities.

Because consideration of ethnicity is necessarily shaped by people's concepts of what it means, in the third chapter we discuss the diverse meanings that have been ascribed to ethnicity and the analytical challenges posed for identifying causal mechanisms. At one and the same time, it is a personal construct that gives rise to a self-description, it is a social construction imposed by society, it is a legal category, and it reflects genetically determined racial differences. Each of these constructs involves multiple contrasting facets. That many people consider themselves as belonging to several different groups, defined in different ways, further complicates the study and understanding of ethnicity.

The next two chapters constitute a pair in which Maughan considers ethnic differences in educational attainments in the United Kingdom, and Hirschman and Lee do the same for the United States, albeit using rather different kinds of data. Maughan notes the large differences among ethnic groups, with attainments highest for African Asians and Indians (also Chinese, but the sample size was small), intermediate for Pakistanis and Whites, somewhat lower for Black Caribbeans, and lowest of all in Bangladeshis. All ethnic groups showed educational gains in relation to their immigrant parents, but these were greatest for African Asians and least for Bangladeshis. Black Caribbeans experienced the highest rate of exclusion from school, and also the highest level of teacher–child conflict. Black Africans also exhibited a moderately high rate of exclusion from school, but the rate for Bangladeshis was very low. Although the rate of single-parent households was exceptionally high among the children of Caribbean immigrants, and although White children in single-parent households tended to have lower scholastic attainments, this was not so for children of Caribbean origin. Maughan explains that whereas White single mothers tended to be poorly qualified, single Caribbean mothers were better qualified than their married counterparts. On the basis of the frequency of racial harassment of both Blacks and Asians, one might suppose that this would have impeded the educational performance of both groups, but the educational performance of the Indians was generally higher than that of Whites. The findings to date do not allow any ready inferences on mediating mechanisms; indeed they present some apparent paradoxes that provide fertile ground for future research.

In their discussion of findings for the United States, Hirschman and Lee mainly focus on the transition from high school to college, making major use of their own study of college plans among high school students in a metropolitan school district in the Pacific Northwest. Asian Americans are the group most likely to attend college – a rate of about 80 percent compared with the mid-1960s for Whites, with lower rates for other ethnic groups. As in the United Kingdom, over time, college attendance rates rose for all ethnic groups. Hirschman and Lee show a similar pattern for college plans. The proportion of East Asians who intended to attend college was particularly high, whereas relatively few Hispanics had college plans and Whites were intermediate between these extremes. In many ways, the most striking finding (as in the United Kingdom) is that family structure predicted the educational ambitions of Whites and Asians, but it did not do so for Blacks. Parental education was also a more significant predictor of college intentions for Whites than for Black and Asian students. Interestingly, too, insofar as parental schooling influenced college plans, maternal rather than paternal education appeared more influential for Black students, whereas the opposite applied among Asian Americans. As in the United Kingdom, although hypotheses can be proposed to account for the observed patterns, the results do not suggest clear mediating mechanisms.

The next pair of chapters (6 and 7) deals with antisocial behavior in a parallel fashion. Morenoff considers the findings in the United States and Smith does the same for the United Kingdom. In both countries, previous reviewers have drawn attention to the striking disparity between the huge ethnic differences shown in official statistics and the much smaller ethnic variation found in self-report studies. Morenoff provides a thoughtful critique of what this difference might mean – pointing out the likely effects of the groups that tend to be missed out in the self-report studies, the greater focus on minor delinquency in questionnaires, and the evidence of some ethnic bias in self-reports (as shown by reverse record checks). He notes that methodological improvements should help to make future self-reports more valid. Subsequently, Morenoff systematically considers possible mediators of the ethnic differences in crime. He notes that although IQ has a robust association with crime in all ethnic groups, its meaning appears to differ among groups. For Blacks, but not Whites, the effect of IQ on crime is almost entirely attributable to school achievement. Both African Americans and Hispanics tend to be socially disadvantaged in comparison with Whites, but this seems an unlikely key mediator of the IQ–crime association because crime rates are high for African Americans but not for Hispanics. The socioeconomic context of the neighborhood is more strongly associated with the crime rate of Whites compared with Blacks. Morenoff suggests that this may be due to a ceiling effect because of the much greater deprivation experienced by African Americans compared with any other US ethnic group. Finally, Morenoff presents important new findings from the Chicago Neighborhoods Study. Crime rates (as self-reported) were highest, especially for high-frequency violent crime, among African Americans and lowest among Mexican Americans. Multivariate analyses showed that neighborhood disadvantage was the single most important mediator of the violent crime difference between African Americans and Whites; neither family structure nor SES was influential. The low rate of violent crime among Mexican Americans was traced to a combination of factors, including living with married parents and in a neighborhood with a high concentration of immigrants, as well as foreign birth. The different findings for African Americans and Mexican Americans suggest that neighborhoods can provide either risk or protection. Evidence that crime rates seem to be rising among third-generation immigrant Mexican Americans cautions against inferences that protective factors maintain their influence over generations.

Smith's analysis of UK crime data provides many parallels, but also several differences. He notes the lack of a consistent association between ethnic patterns of social disadvantage and ethnic patterns of crime rates. Offending rates tend to be low among both Pakistanis and Bangladeshis, who are among the most deprived ethnic groups. However, Indians and African Asians, who are among the least deprived ethnics, also exhibit low crime rates. Crime is particularly high among African Caribbeans, who are intermediate in social circumstances. Much the same applies with respect to educational achievement. Racial discrimination against both African Caribbeans and subcontinental Asians is high, yet the crime rate of the former is high while that of the latter is low. Bangladeshis and Pakistanis are the most geographically concentrated of the ethnic groups, and African Caribbeans the least so. Smith suggests that such concentration, depending on what goes with it, could constitute either a risk or a protective factor. He notes the very high rate of single parenthood among African-Caribbean families, but also the lack of data on whether it constitutes a risk factor for this group to the degree that it does for Whites.

Deater-Deckard et al., in Chapter 8, focus on the finding that physical punishment is a risk factor for antisocial behavior among European Americans, but not for African Americans. Yet, physical abuse is a risk factor for both groups. They present further research findings that seek to test competing hypotheses about the meaning of these findings, with results that are somewhat inconclusive. Children's attitudes toward punishment moderated the physical punishment effect among European Americans, but not African Americans. It may be that the risk effect derives not from the physical punishment as such, but from the uncontrolled anger that sometimes accompanies it; moreover, the extent to which this is the case varies by ethnicity. The finding of ethnic difference highlights the importance of always probing the meaning of variables, and differentiating between risk indicators and risk mechanisms.

In Chapter 9, which deals with schizophrenia, Jones and Fung present the findings of a systematic, well-designed study that investigates why the rate of schizophrenia is so much higher among African Caribbeans living in the United Kingdom than in either African Caribbeans living in the Caribbean or Whites living in the United Kingdom. On the one hand, they show that the ethnic difference is not an artifact of diagnostic practice or referral pattern, and that it similarly obtains in the Netherlands. On the other hand, the elevated rate is not confined to schizophrenia because, to a lesser degree, it also applies to mania. Interestingly, however, there is no differential in minor psychiatric morbidity. The differential is also not entirely restricted to African Caribbeans because it applies to some other ethnic minorities to a lesser degree, but not to Turks. The findings to date suggest that the higher rates of psychoses among African Caribbeans are not due to differential migration or to early brain injury; they also appear not to be attributable to the use of cannabis. Rather, the strong inference is that there is something psychotogenic about living in the United Kingdom for African Caribbeans, but the remaining challenge is to determine just what is involved.

In Chapter 10, Gibbs discusses the curious paradox of the finding that, despite their greater exposure to psychosocial adversities, both Black and Hispanic youth in the United States have rates of suicide that are lower than that of their more advantaged White counterparts. Interestingly, however, the patterns in Blacks and Hispanics differ. The findings for Blacks indicate that their rates of depressive disorder and of suicidal ideation, as well as their rate of suicide, are low in comparison with Whites. The main issue, therefore, is why all of these rates are relatively low. The situation with Hispanics is different in that their rates of depression and of suicidal ideation are *not* low, despite their low rate of suicide. Accordingly, the query is why their relatively high rate of depression does not result in a correspondingly high rate of suicide. Gibbs's review of risk and protective factors that might be relevant to ethnic variations in suicide raises more questions than it answers, but it shows that the questions could be tackled by appropriate research, and that such research should be undertaken.

The next pair of chapters (11 and 12) concerns aspects of ethnic identity; Modood discusses the UK situation and Rumbaut that in the US. Modood bases his account primarily on the large-scale study undertaken by the Policy Studies Institute. He notes that for South Asians, religion constituted the most important identifier of group, and "Blackness" was most important for about one third to one half of African Caribbeans, but scarcely so for any South Asians. There were marked differences among ethnic groups in rates of intermarriage, which were very high for African Caribbeans, but very low among Bangladeshis. Linguistic community was important for some, as was country of origin; however, ethnic minorities were more likely to identify with being English than with being British. Jobs also provided a source of identity for some people. Multiple ethnic identities were the rule rather than the exception, even if one identity was particularly salient. Modood notes that African Caribbeans have a leading-edge presence in youth culture. Possibly as a result, African-Caribbean ethnicity has brought considerable social dividends despite the rather limited economic benefits, but the pattern for Indians is precisely the reverse. He comments that prejudice against Asians is particularly high at present – probably as a result of the public association of Muslims with suicide bombers (although most Muslims do not support terrorists).

Rumbaut, in discussing the situation in the United States, primarily relies on findings from the Children of Immigrants Study undertaken in Southern California and South Florida. Based on a survey of youth at 14 to 15 years of age, with a follow-up interview at 17 to 18 years, he documents the extent to which self-reported ethnic identities remained constant over time. Nearly half maintained the same identity, but more than half shifted, the changes going in several different directions. Although society tends to expect one ethnic label (such as Hispanic or Asian) to subsume all facets of identity, youth were quite plural in their ethnic self-identifications. Their individual choices were shaped by a range of factors spanning personal experiences of discrimination, family influences, and the societal context. In addition, there are some striking intergenerational differences. For example, apart from the Mexicans, most parents who came to the United States from Latin America identified their race as "White," whereas their children were more likely to opt for "Hispanic" or "Latino." Rumbaut emphasizes the need to view ethnicity as a fluid, multifaceted concept.

In the final chapter, we seek to draw the threads together and to note policy implications. It is concluded that ethnicity is not a homogeneous concept; it is multifaceted rather than unidimensional, it is quantitative rather than qualitative, and it tends to be viewed differently by the various ethnic groups. Because of these features, ethnicity as such cannot be considered to be a mediator for any group difference in social, emotional, or behavioral functioning. On the other hand, some aspect of ethnicity must mediate the ethnic differences in these features, and the challenge is to identify which the mediators are likely to be. The answer is likely to be very informative as to the causal processes involved in producing differentiation more generally, and not solely ethnic variations.

Because many ethnic minorities suffer social disadvantage, some writers have tended to imply that the two are synonymous. Clearly, they are not. Ethnic groups compared in the foregoing chapters differ appreciably in their educational performance, some outperforming Whites and some lagging behind in scholastic achievement. Huge heterogeneity within all ethnic groups renders stereotypical images of the "typical" African American or Asian analytically useless and substantively meaningless. Societal influences are clearly operative with respect to both racial discrimination and housing policy, but discrimination as such may play less of a role in individual functioning than ordinarily supposed. Ethnic concentration in communities will have different consequences according to whether it brings social cohesion and mutual support, or social disorganization.

Because the differences among ethnic groups on single parenthood are so great, it is tempting to view this aspect of family structure as a likely key mediator, but there are indications that it may not be so. Probably researchers need to shift from a focus on family structure to a focus on family functioning. In parallel fashion, it is tempting to emphasize "cultural" influences to explain ethnic differences in psychosocial outcomes, but it is necessary not only to identify these, but also to determine their origins and the mechanisms that maintain or weaken them.

Until these matters are resolved, there are few straightforward policy implications with respect to prevention or intervention. Nevertheless, one crucial implication is the need to reject stereotyping, to acknowledge the multifaceted nature of most people's multiple ethnic identities, to appreciate the existence of intergenerational differences, and to recognize the fluidity of ethnicity. In addition, the extensive heterogeneity within ethnic groups is a powerful reminder that efforts to frame policies based on the specific needs of individual ethnic groups would most likely be misguided. Although that may occasionally be useful, prevention strategies need to be targeted on those who could profit from them, regardless of ethnicity. Thus, these should include strategies concerned with parenting, education, and employment skills and opportunities – to mention but a few examples. With respect to societal policies, the key need is to focus on inequities and inequalities brought about by social order and organization. Diversity and individual differences are both inevitable and acceptable; it is injustice and social constraints imposed by society that should not be tolerated.

Michael Rutter and Marta Tienda

Reference

Shweder, R. A., Goodnow, J., Hatano, G., LeVine, R. A., Markus, H., & Miller, P. (1998). The cultural psychology of development: One mind, many mentalities. In W. Damon & R. M. Lerner (Eds.), *Handbook of child psychology: Vol. 1. Theoretical models of human development* (5th ed., pp. 865–937). New York: Wiley.

1

Natural Experiments, Causal Influences, and Policy Development

Michael Rutter

Policy makers, like practitioners and members of the general public, are constantly faced with the need to decide when to take action on the basis of research findings supposedly showing that a particular individual characteristic or environmental circumstance is associated with a markedly increased risk for some negative outcome. Thus, over the years, campaigners have argued for the apparent need to prevent mothers from taking jobs outside the home, or to stop unmarried mothers from having children, or to restrict immigration, or to avoid immunization on the grounds that each of these carried serious risks for the children. But do they? How can we decide which research findings should lead to action and which should not?

In part, that issue involves asking which findings we should believe (is the claimed association real?); in part, it requires consideration of whether the causal inferences are justified; in part, it means questioning whether the proposed risk mechanisms are truly the ones that carry the risk; and, finally, it means considering whether the risks operate generally or only in certain circumstances. These questions constitute *the* major challenge for the whole field of social and behavioral sciences, and my purpose in this chapter is to discuss how they may be tackled. My messages are to caution against uncritical acceptance of claims regarding causal influences but to recognize that good research strategies are available to test causal inferences and to appreciate that these have led to some reasonably solid conclusions.

Hypotheses about possible risk factors that might contribute to the causal mechanisms involved in the origins of some maladaptive, or otherwise undesirable, psychosocial outcome are usually based on some form of group comparison showing that there is a statistically significant association between the putative risk factor and the outcome of interest. Thus, the origin might be evidence that males are more likely than females to engage in antisocial behavior (Moffitt, Caspi, Rutter, & Silva, 2001); or that children experiencing prolonged early group day care outside the family home are more likely than those receiving home care to be aggressive (Belsky, 2001); or that schizophrenia is more frequent in those of African-Caribbean background than in Caucasians living in the United Kingdom (Rutter, Pickles, Murray, & Eaves, 2001). As already noted, the four crucial questions in relation to any such evidence are (a) is the association valid?; (b) if valid, does it represent a causal effect?; (c) if there is a causal influence, what element in the experience or circumstance provides the risk and by what mechanism does it operate?; and (d) does the risk operate in all people in all circumstances or is it contingent on either particular individual characteristics or a particular social context? These issues constitute the subject matter of this chapter.

Validity of the Association

Although there are numerous methodological points that have to be considered with respect to the validity of the association between any putative risk factor and the adverse outcome being considered, the two most basic concern representativeness of sampling and comparability of measurement across the groups being contrasted (Moffitt et al., 2001; Rutter, Pickles, et al., 2001a; Rutter & Nikapota, 2002; Rutter, Caspi, & Moffitt, 2003).

Sampling
With respect to sampling, the key need is for representative general population epidemiological samples with a low attrition or nonparticipation rate (Berk, 1983; Sher & Trull, 1996; Thornberry, Bjerregard, & Miles, 1993). Clinic groups or volunteer samples are highly likely to be biased in ways that matter, and individuals who are untraceable or decline to participate in a study tend to be systematically different from those who take part.

Measurement
Comparability of measurement is fundamental for all epidemiological studies. Traditionally, the approach used to be to take some majority group, select the measures that worked best in that group, and then apply those measures to the supposed risk population. However, it has long been obvious that that is potentially biasing. Thus, questions had to be raised as to whether insecure attachment has the same meaning in children experiencing group day care as in those looked after at home by their parents (NICHD Early Child Care Research Network, 1997) or in children suffering severe institutional deprivation (O'Connor et al., 2003) or in children from cultures with very different patterns of parenting (van IJzendoorn & Sagi, 1999). Similarly, there were queries on whether males and females showed their antisocial behavior in the same ways (Moffitt et al., 2001) and on whether cultural and ethnic groups vary in the manner in

which they expressed their psychopathology (Rutter & Nikapota, 2002). When the measurement of adverse outcomes is dependent on police practice and judicial processing (as is the case with crime statistics – Rutter, Giller, & Hagell, 1998; Williams, Ayers, Abbott, Hawkins, & Catalano, 1996) or on psychiatric diagnosis (see, for example, Hickling, McKenzie, Mullen, & Murray, 1999, regarding schizophrenia in ethnic minorities) it is also necessary to determine whether these procedures operate in the same way across the groups to be compared. In each instance, what is required is systematic validity testing of the measures in *each* of the groups to be studied, and use of the same set of measures across groups, with the set inclusive of what is optimal with respect to sensitivity and specificity for each group.

Statistical Analyses

Given appropriate sampling and measurement, the further need is to undertake suitable statistical analyses. In that connection, the two most basic hazards are (a) the danger of false positives if a large number of possible risk factors are studied in the style of an unfocussed fishing expedition; and (b) the error of concluding that if an association is statistically significant in one group and not in a second group, there is a significant difference among the groups in the association found (see Cohen, Cohen, & Brook, 1995). It does not. The most fundamental point, however, is that (regardless of the level of statistical significance) the only true test in science of the validity of a finding is independent replication of the result in a separate sample by a different group of researchers. Until that happens, policy makers and practitioners should be hesitant about accepting any finding as valid.

Noncausal Alternatives

Before discussing the range of research strategies available to test causal inferences, we need to consider the alternatives to causation once it has been established that there is a replicated valid association to explain. Five main possibilities have to be considered: (a) that the association reflects some form of social selection; (b) that the causal arrow runs in the reverse direction; (c) that there is a causal effect but it is genetically, rather than environmentally, mediated; (d) that it is due to some third variable with which the putative risk factor happens to be associated; and (e) that the risk element has been mis-specified.

Social Selection

The underlying point with respect to social selection is that environments are not randomly distributed (Rutter, Champion, Quinton, Maughan, & Pickles, 1995). For example, being born to a teenage parent is well

established as an important risk factor for children's psychological disturbance (Moffitt & the E-Risk Study Team, 2002), but it is known that young
people who become parents as adolescents are very likely to have shown
disturbed behavior or low educational attainments themselves, and it is
necessary to ask whether the risks derive from being reared by a teenage
parent or from the genetic and environmental risks (for the offspring) associated with the types of teenager who become a parent at an unusually
early age. It is evident that similar questions need to be asked with respect
to the effects on children of parental divorce, or being brought up by a
single parent, or indeed with respect to almost all aspects of child rearing.

In not quite so obvious a fashion, it also applied to studies of ethnicity.
Thus, immigrants may represent an atypical sample of the inhabitants of
the country from which they have come (Odegaard, 1932), and the operation of housing and job discrimination may mean that ethnic minority
families have an increased likelihood of social disadvantage that reflects
the response of the host culture to immigrants or ethnic minorities, rather
than anything about the immigrants or ethnic minorities themselves.

Person Effects on the Environment

When the putative risk factor concerns any kind of socialization experience, it is always necessary to consider whether the association between
that experience and some adverse outcome represents the causal effect of
socialization on the child's functioning, or whether, instead, it is due to the
child's effect on his/her social environment (Bell, 1968; Bell & Chapman,
1986). There is good evidence that how children behave influences the reactions of other people to them and thereby shapes their environment. Of
course, too, to an important extent, children can select the environments
they enter. This is most obviously the case with respect to their choice
of peer groups (Kandel, 1978; Rowe, Woulbroun, & Gulley, 1994), but the
point applies more broadly. This alternative explanation does not apply
directly in the case of risks supposedly associated with an individual characteristic such as gender or ethnicity, but it is certainly relevant with respect
to many of possible mediating mechanisms associated with the individual
characteristic.

Genetic Mediation

The next alternative in relation to any socialization experience is that the
risk is mediated genetically rather than environmentally (Plomin, 1994,
1995). This possibility arises because genes affect individual variation in
all forms of behavior. This means that any experience that can be influenced
by how people behave involves the possibility that the risks are (at least in
part) genetically, rather than environmentally, mediated. This applies, for
example, to any aspect of parenting, to divorce or single parenthood, and
to many types of life stress. The mere fact that a variable is conceptualized

as "environmental" does not necessarily mean that the associated risks are environmentally mediated.

The same consideration, but the other way round, applies to individual characteristics. Thus, whether a person is male or female is determined genetically, but that does not necessarily mean that any associated risks for psychopathology involve a proximal risk process that is genetically mediated (see Rutter, Caspi & Moffitt, 2003, 2004). Even more so, the same applies to ethnicity. Ethnicity is a complex concept that may be based on religion, history, or geography rather than biology (Rutter & Nikapota, 2002; see also Chapter 3 in this volume). Nevertheless, some identifying ethnic features (such as skin pigmentation) are genetically determined, or at least strongly genetically influenced. But that certainly does not mean that any risks associated with skin color are genetically mediated. Thus, racial discrimination concerns an environmental influence from other people, and not a genetic effect within the individual. The need, as always, is to avoid inferring either genetic or environmental mediation, but instead to use research strategies to test which it is.

Third-Variable Effects

An ever-present consideration in any study of risk and protective factors is whether the demonstrated association in reality reflects some third variable with which the risk factor happens to be associated. Thus, for example, with respect to ethnicity or immigrant status it is essential to consider whether any association might have arisen because the immigrant group tends to be much younger than the population as a whole, or because the ethnic minority sample includes a disproportionate number of individuals without work or living in poverty or in poor-quality housing (Wilson, 1987). In other words, is the association between ethnicity and some adverse outcome really due to a risk effect deriving from one of these other variables? The need in all cases is to consider what these third-variable effects might be, and then to undertake studies of populations that differ in their associations with the other variables. Internal analyses of a single sample can perform much the same task but, for a variety of reasons, they are less satisfactory (see Rutter, Pickles, et al., 2001). Causal inferences become convincing only when it has been shown that the associations are maintained across a diverse range of samples and circumstances.

Mis-specification of the Risk

A closely related possibility is that the risk factor may have been mis-specified. For example, with respect to the notion that "broken homes" caused an increased risk of crime, depression, and other forms of psychopathology, it was necessary to undertake epidemiological studies to determine whether the risk was due to parental loss, or to the family discord that led to the breakup of the marriage, or to the adverse effects of the breakup on the parenting provided to the children (see Fergusson, Horwood, & Lynskey, 1992; Harris, Brown, & Bifulco, 1986; Rutter, 1971). In these circumstances, it may often be helpful to conceptualize and specify the situations in which there should not be a risk effect if the risk has been correctly specified (Rutter, 1974).

In the case of immigrant status or ethnicity, the possible mis-specifications include features such as preimmigration experiences, religion, experience of racial discrimination, educational/occupational level, family structure, and economic circumstances – to mention just a few possibilities. It should be noted, however, that such mis-specification does not mean that ethnicity is unimportant; rather it points to the need to break down ethnicity according to the differing meanings and different facets (see Chapter 3 of this volume).

Overview: Individual Characteristic Risks and Risk Alternatives
With respect to the risks associated with relatively fixed individual characteristics, such as gender or ethnicity, the alternative of person effects on the environment is nonoperative, but otherwise the alternatives apply. The main difference from the testing of variable individual characteristics (such as intelligence or personality features or pubertal status), or from the testing of environmental risks, stems from the supposedly fixed nature of the characteristic. That has two key implications. First, it is not possible to use the test of a "dose-response" relationship when the risk factor is categorical and fixed. Ordinarily, unless there is a reason to suppose a threshold effect, if there is a true causal effect, it may be expected that the greater strength of a risk factor, the greater the effect on the adverse (or beneficial) outcome. That cannot apply to a fixed categorical feature. However, it needs to be emphasized that the apparently fixed nature of a characteristic is entirely dependent on the risk or protective mechanism that is operative. Thus, in the case of sex, clearly chromosomal sex is fixed and, short of major surgery, so is genital sex. By contrast, sex hormone levels are not fixed and are, in any case, dimensional rather than categorical. This is even more the case with respect to sex roles and societal expectations. Exactly the same applies to ethnicity. Skin pigmentation is fixed and so are the genetic aspects of race (see Chapter 3 of this volume). On the other hand, personal ethnic identification is not fixed and neither is racial discrimination or societal constructions regarding the meaning of ethnicity.

Second, it makes no sense to conceptualize the risk effects of fixed characteristics as operating as a direct proximal risk mechanism. Instead, it is necessary to consider different levels of risk mechanism (Rutter, Caspi, & Moffitt, 2003). Thus, in the case of sex (gender), the basic distal starting point has to be the genetic determination of the biological sex as male or female, because it is that that defines the fixed risk characteristic. The second level comprises the varied consequences of being male or female. These consequences are quite diverse – spanning prenatal hormonal effects; hormonal changes in later life; biological effects on physical vulnerability and life expectancy; biologically determined, sex-limited, experiences such as childbirth; and a wide range of culturally influenced experiences that differ between the two sexes (such as the nature of peer groups, living with a male partner, sexual discrimination, and the likelihood of being sexually abused or suffering a head injury). These second-level consequences get one closer to the actual process that leads to psychopathology (or whatever outcome is being considered), but are unlikely to constitute the direct proximal causal risk mechanism. That requires some third-level process that arises out of the second-level consequences. Again, the possibilities are many and various. Thus, with respect to psychopathology, they span personality features such as neuroticism or sensation-seeking, cognitive sets or styles such as a bias towards the attribution of hostile intent or self-blame, or a high susceptibility to certain psychosocial stressors.

It is obvious that parallel considerations will apply to risk or protective features described in terms of ethnicity or immigrant status. The distal starting point will, of course, vary according to the particular concept – be it skin color, religion, geography, or history. Genetic influences will be major for some aspects of ethnicity but much less so for others. Similarly, the second-level consequences will vary according to the concept, but it is necessary to appreciate the diversity of the possibilities. Thus, there are genetic liabilities associated with some ethnic groups (but different from the genes implicated in the definition of ethnicity). For example, there is the genetic propensity to develop an unpleasant flushing response after the ingestion of alcohol that occurs in about a quarter of Japanese individuals but not Caucasians (Ball & Collier, 2002; Heath et al., 2003). The abnormal response derives from a single gene mutation that leads to an inactive enzyme; its psychopathological importance lies in the considerable protective effect against alcoholism that it provides. It is a second-level consequence and not a first-level one because it does not define Japanese ethnicity and because it is present in only some Japanese people. It is a second, not third proximal, level feature because the flushing response is not itself directly involved in the causal process. Rather, it is the affective correlates that are closer to the key mechanisms. The apparently lesser risk of Alzheimer's disease associated with the apoE4 gene in those of African racial background constitutes another example (Hendrie, Hall, et al., 1995; Hendrie, Osuntokun, et al., 1995; Rubinsztein, 1995), as does the sickle-cell trait and its protective effect against malaria (Davies & Brozovic, 1989; Weatherall & Clegg, 2001).

Of course, the genetic consequences of ethnicity constitute but one possibility. In addition, and often of greater importance, are the responses of other people, as evident in racial or religious discriminations, and life-style effects, such as those that may involve constraints on females. None of these directly cause psychopathology or even individual differences in psychological traits, but they may make them more likely because of the connections with proximal risk factors. The proximal risk factors are likely to be similar to those found in other groups, so that the key question is why and how they are linked with ethnicity.

Unfortunately, genetic considerations in relation to ethnicity bring forth all sorts of prejudicial responses in many people. In view of the historical abuses associated with eugenics (see Devlin, Fienberg, Resnick, & Roeder, 1997) it is understandable that these attitudes exist. Nevertheless, it is crucial to seek to get the balance right (see Chapter 3 of this volume). In that connection, we need to note that, biologically speaking, "races" are not categorically distinct, and that the genetic similarities among ethnic groups far outweigh the differences. Even so, in particular instances, as the examples given illustrate, the differences may be crucially important (see Risch et al., 2002). We all recognize the severe dangers of inferring a genetic basis for psychological differences among ethnic groups on the evidence of genetic influences on individual differences within ethnic groups (Tizard, 1975). On the other hand, it is quite possible that genetic factors may play a role in some differences among ethnic groups with respect to biologically influenced traits.

For example, just conceivably, that possibility might apply to our findings on height in London children of African-Caribbean origin some 30 years ago (Yule, Berger, Rutter, & Yule, 1975). The children were some 4 cm taller than their Caucasian peers of the same age but, within the children of West Indian parentage, those born in the United Kingdom were some 2 cm taller than those born in the West Indies. The latter finding was probably a function of nutritional differences, but the former might reflect genetic influences on either height or rate of physical maturation. We did not follow up the finding because it was not the focus of our research, but the point is that the combination of within- and between-group differences may suggest possible modes of mediation worth investigating further.

Research Strategies to Test Possible Causal Mechanisms

It has been argued that there are five essential design features (in addition to multiple methods of measurement, the use of longitudinal data, and good statistical methods) that characterize the research strategies needed to put causal hypotheses on mediating mechanisms to the test (Rutter, Pickles, et al., 2001). They are, first, the selection of samples that serve to pull apart variables that ordinarily go together; adoptee strategies, twin designs, natural experiments of different kinds, migration designs, time-series analyses and intervention experiments all serve to do this. Because of the importance of interaction effects, as discussed hereafter, there is particular value in designs that can simultaneously "pull apart" and "put together" risk and protective variables. Second, it is necessary to consider the processes that lead to risk exposure. The main problem in causal inferences is the nonrandom assignment of risks, rather than the operation of multiple causes. Third, it is vital to compare and contrast alternative causal mechanisms, rather than test just one favored possibility. Fourth, it is crucial to identify the key assumptions in the chosen design and test whether these assumptions are actually met. Finally, it is helpful to combine consideration of causal influences with respect to both individual differences in liability and group differences in rates or level of the outcome being studied. In the remainder of this section of the chapter, the prime focus, however, will be on the testing of causal inferences on the mechanisms that might be operative in group differences in the level of some psychological trait or disorder. The examples chosen all concern "negative" outcomes of one sort or another, because those are what have been the main subject of research. However, it is crucial to note that ethnic variations concern positive, as well as negative, outcomes (see Chapter 3 of this volume). Indeed, maximum research leverage is obtained by considering both together. The same principles apply. Six different approaches will be used to illustrate the range of the main considerations that need to guide the choice and use of research designs.

Sex Difference in Antisocial Behavior

The first example concerns the use of the Dunedin longitudinal study to investigate the mechanisms that might mediate the well-established tendency for males to be more likely to engage in antisocial behavior (Moffitt et al., 2001). In this case it was necessary to start by checking whether the difference might be an artifact of the two sexes showing their antisocial behavior in different ways or of the need to use a different threshold in males and females. Predictive validity in relation to adult functioning constituted the main test. The findings showed that, although there were some interesting differences in pattern, comparabilities far outweighed differences. But, it was also found that the sex difference largely applied to lifecourse-persistent antisocial behavior, was much less evident for such behavior when it was largely confined to the adolescent years, and was least evident for domestic violence. The focus, therefore, needed to be particularly on the marked male excess for antisocial behavior beginning early in childhood and continuing into adult life. The next research questions concerned the possibilities that the risk factors differed in males and females, that males experienced more (or more severe) risk factors, or that they were more susceptible to the same stressors. In brief, it was found that the key difference was that males were more likely to show early-onset hyperactivity, cognitive impairment, and temperamental difficulty; these were risk factors in both sexes but they were more likely to be

experienced by boys. When these variables were introduced into a causal
model, they eliminated most (but not all) of the sex difference. The research
focus now needs to shift to the question of why these risks more often occur in males. In addition, the findings emphasize the likely importance of
these risk factors for antisocial behavior more generally in both sexes.

Language Impairment in Twins
The next example concerns the investigation of the causes of the, on average, impaired language development in twins as compared with singletons
(Rutter, Thorpe, Greenwood, Northstone, & Golding, 2003; Thorpe, Rutter,
& Greenwood, 2003). Three main alternative explanations had to be
considered: (a) that the difference was a function of the higher rate of
obstetric and perinatal complications in twins; (b) that it was due to some
risk factor (such as the transfusion syndrome or an overcrowded womb)
that was specific to twins; or (c) that it was a consequence of some altered
pattern of family interaction brought about by having to deal with two babies at roughly the same developmental level at the same time. In this case,
the comparability issue particularly concerned the fact that twins tend to
be born biologically less mature than singletons. This meant that the language outcome had to be adjusted to be in line with the children's age since
conception rather than since birth. Also, obstetric risk analysis had to recognize that the optimum gestation period for twin is 37 weeks, rather than
40 weeks as for singletons. Accordingly, it was necessary to standardize
within groups in order to examine the effects of unusually short or long
gestation.

Having dealt with these measurement issues, four requirements were
set for the criteria for a valid inference on causation (with respect to the
twin–singleton difference in language): (a) the putative risk variables had to
differ significantly in frequency or severity between twins and singletons;
(b) the variables had to be significantly associated with language outcome
at 3 years within both the twin and singleton samples; (c) this association
had to be maintained after taking account of the children's language level at
20 months (this requirement that language progress constitute the outcome
was necessary to rule out the possibility that the risk variables were brought
about by the language impairment, rather than the other way round); and
(d) when introduced into a causal model, the risk variables that met the first
three criteria obliterated (or greatly reduced) the twin–singleton difference
in language performance.

As it turned out, the only variable that met these four criteria were the
indices of mother–child interaction and communication. The finding not
only accounted for the twin–singleton difference but also indicated that
variations in socialization experiences within the normal range (and not
just at an abnormal extreme) could affect psychological outcomes. As with
the sex difference in antisocial behavior example, the findings on the group

difference were particularly important with respect to their implications for causal mechanisms more generally.

Family Care Versus Group Day Care
The third example, dealing with the question of whether family care or group day care carried greater risks for physical aggression in young children, brings out the further crucial point that effects may apply only in particular circumstances. Borge et al. (2004) used the large Canadian general population epidemiological data set on 2- and 3-year-olds to tackle this issue. The first relevant finding was that there was a very strong social selection effect; less well-educated parents with many children were most likely to be looking after their young children at home. The second key finding was that physical aggression was significantly more frequent in children receiving family care at home, but that this effect was seen *only* in children in the families at highest risk. In short, the finding indicated that the risk associated with home care applied only when it occurred in the context of family risk. The implication was that it was not home care as such that was risky but rather some aspect of the parenting provided by high-risk families. Because the home care had been provided from the time the children were born, longitudinal data could not be used directly to test the hypothesis that home care was causing an increased risk of aggression. In that respect home care was a relatively fixed-risk variable like sex, being a twin, or being a member of an ethnic minority. However, as with all these fixed variables, it is essential to translate the difference in risk into some form of risk mechanism or process that is not fixed. Thus, in this case, it may be suggested that the risk comes from some type of maladaptive parenting rather than from whether the parenting is provided in or outside the home of the biological parents. The testing of that possibility will constitute the essential next research step. When that is done, longitudinal data will come into their own, as do the variety of quasi-experimental research designs considered here.

Residential Care
The need to take social selection into account arises similarly with respect to the effects of group residential care. There is a wealth of evidence that children being reared in residential nurseries or group homes have an unusually high rate of emotional/behavioral disturbance, but the question is whether this is because the children receiving residential care come from backgrounds of exceptionally high risk (for either genetic or environmental reasons) or because of the adverse effects of residential care. Because the residential care for many children begins in infancy, it is not possible to study any changes that occur over the period of entry into residential care. Accordingly, it was necessary to use the strategy of choosing a sample of infants whose parenting had broken down in order to compare the outcomes

at 5 to 7 years of those receiving residential group care and those reared in foster families (Roy, Rutter, & Pickles, 2000), having first determined that the two groups were comparable with respect to family adversity before being taken into care. The finding that the rate of hyperactivity/inattention was markedly raised in the residential care children compared with both foster-care children and classroom controls strongly suggested that the residential care had had a causal influence (in a high-risk sample). When there is strong social selection, the most effective research strategy may be to equate for selection, rather than match outcome groups.

Institutional Deprivation and Adoption

We used a somewhat similar strategy to examine the effects of profound institutional deprivation in Romanian children adopted into well-functioning UK families (O'Connor et al., 2000; Rutter, Kreppner, & O'Connor, 2001; Rutter and the ERA Study Team, 1998; Rutter et al., 2004). The design involved two features that could be used to test the causal inference. First, we determined whether the radical change of environment (from extremely poor to somewhat above average) was associated with cognitive catch-up. It was, the rise being equivalent to about 40 IQ points. Second, insofar as the catch-up was incomplete, the key question was whether the likelihood of a persisting cognitive deficit showed a significant dose-response relationship with the direction of institutional deprivation. We found that it did; the effect was quite large – some 20 IQ points' difference between those with less than 6 months institutional deprivation and those with at least 2 years. With this example of extremely severe deprivation, the main risk predictor of outcome concerned the duration of deprivation and the main protective predictor concerned the fact of adoption. Within the relatively narrow range of (generally high) quality in the adoptive homes, the educational level of the adoptive parents was not influential. However, for less severely deprived children it has been shown to be important – using the rigorous test of within-individual change (Duyme, Dumaret, & Tomkiewicz, 1999).

Migration Designs

Because people take their genes with them when they move from one country to another, but may change their life style in radical ways, migration provides a useful natural experiment that pulls apart variables that ordinarily go together. At the crudest level, it provides a means of testing whether genetic or environmental differences are most likely to account for ethnic differences in the outcome of interest. Thus, one early study showed that the rate of coronary artery disease was very low in Japan but much higher in men of Japanese ancestry living in California, and that variation within the Californian sample was associated with degree of acculturation – pointing to the likelihood of dietary and lifestyle factors

(Marmot & Syme, 1976). A crucial element in the quasi-experiment concerns identification of the within-group risk factors and testing of whether these operate in similar ways across groups. Thus, Fang, Madhavan, and Alderman (1996) found that mortality from cardiovascular disease was higher among "Blacks" than "Whites" living in New York City, but also showed that this excess was largely a function of birthplace, being greater in those born in the southern states of America and least in those born in either the north-eastern states or in the Caribbean area. Cooper, Forrester, et al (1997) found that non-insulin-dependent diabetes had a very low rate (2%) among "Blacks" living in West Africa, but a high rate (9–11%) among those living in the Caribbean or the United Kingdom or the United States. Somewhat parallel findings applied to hypertension (Cooper, Rotimi, et al., 1997). Of course, this could reflect different gene distributions, but this explanation seems unlikely in view of the finding that across all these populations, there was the same relationship between body mass index and risk of diabetes. In other words, in all populations, obesity and lack of exercise constituted the main risk factors for diabetes; the geographical difference arose because life circumstances made both risks uncommon in West Africa. Nevertheless, puzzles remain. African Caribbeans in the United Kingdom have a relatively low rate of coronary heart disease despite their high rate of diabetes and of hypertension, these diseases being closely associated in most other populations (Chaturvedi, McKeigue, & Marmot, 1994; Wild & McKeigue, 1997). The low rate of coronary artery disease in African Caribbeans also stands in contrast with the unusually high rate in people of South African origin (McKeigue, Shah, & Marmot, 1991). This has been thought to be related to metabolic disturbances associated with insulin resistance, but the origins of this syndrome appear to be multifactorial. In that connection, although all South Asian groups seem to share the important risk factors of obesity and lack of experience, they differ in other risk factors (such as smoking, lack of fruit/vegetables, and abstinence from alcohol), with Indians least and Bangladeshis most disadvantaged (Bhopal et al., 1999).

Application of Migration Designs to Psychological Outcomes

Three points need emphasis with respect to migration designs as applied to psychological outcomes. First, we need to note the essential features of the research strategy. The designs rely on the combination of comparing indices of some trait in three populations (the migrant population, the ethnically similar population in the migrants' country of origin, and the ethnically different indigenous population in the host country in which the migrants have settled), together with a systematic comparison of the rate of risk factors and the strength of risk associations with the trait in each of these three populations. The test then becomes one of determining which risks, when introduced into a causal model, obliterate the ethnic differences in outcome being considered (see Baron & Kenny, 1986; Moffitt et al., 2001; Rutter, Pickles, et al., 2001; Rutter, Thorpe, et al., 2003; Thorpe et al., 2003).

The second point is that genetic and environmental mediation should not be seen as mutually exclusive alternatives. There is growing evidence of the importance of gene–environment interactions (Rutter & Silberg, 2002). For example, obesity and diabetes are much more frequent in Pima Indians than in other ethnic groups living in the United States, but this difference does not apply to those living in Mexico (Ravussin, Valencia, Esparza, Bennet, & Schulz, 1994). The inference is that there is a genetic susceptibility to obesity but that this requires particular dietary and life-style conditions to be clinically manifest to a major degree. Similarly, Bhatnagar et al. (1995) found that both Indian immigrants from the Punjab living in London and their nonmigrant siblings in the Punjab had raised serum lipoprotein concentrations and greater insulin resistance than the Caucasian non-Indian population in the United Kingdom. Presumably, this reflected their common genetic or early rearing background, but the ill-health consequences were much more common in the Indians living in the United Kingdom than in their siblings living in the Punjab. An interaction with dietary and life-style risk factors associated with living in the United Kingdom may be inferred.

In the psychological arena, just as in the somatic arena, gene–environment correlations and interactions are likely to be operative (see Rutter & Silberg, 2000; Caspi et al., 2002, 2003; Eaves, Silberg, & Erkanli, 2003; Jaffee et al., in press). In the absence of knowledge on the relevant susceptibility genes, the testing for gene–environment correlations and interactions is inevitably somewhat indirect, but that situation is likely to change greatly during the next decade or so as such genes become identified as a result of advances in molecular genetics (Moffitt, Caspi & Rutter, in press). Meanwhile, there is a need to rely on indirect indices such as familial loading for the trait, or pattern of twin correlations/concordances.

The third point is that the environmental influences that are relevant may be ones that only become operative during adult life. In the somatic arena this is evident, for example, in the effects of smoking, obesity, lack of exercise, and life style. In the psychological area, the adult experiences with strong replicated effects include a harmonious marriage, Army service, unemployment, and heavy use of alcohol (Laub, Nagin, & Sampson, 1998; Laub & Sampson, 2003; Rutter, 1996; Rutter, Giller, et al., 1998; Sampson & Laub, 1996). With respect to influences on psychological functioning, it is also important to recognize that effects may be shaped by social context (Rutter, 1999). Among other things, this implies that it may be necessary to use qualitative life-history biographical data to derive the relevant meaning of experiences as well as to assess the role of personal agency (meaning what the individuals themselves do to respond to challenges and difficulties) (see Laub & Sampson, 2003). Quantitative analyses will always be necessary to test the hypotheses that stem from qualitative research methods, but the greatest leverage will often come from their combination (Rutter, 2001).

Conclusions

Studies of ethnic variations in psychological and social features have tended to remain rather separate from both the psychological literature on the use of quasi-experimental research designs that may be employed to test genetic and environmental mediation hypotheses, and the medical literature on the use of migration designs for the same purpose. There is abundant evidence of differences in psychological features among ethnic groups but, on their own, these have no theoretical relevance and have no policy or practice implications. The need is for research that can determine the causal mechanisms that may be operative. The situation is closely comparable to that which applies to other risk indices that involve relatively fixed individual characteristics – such as sex (gender). It is of no use to say that male sex causes an increased risk for some trait or disorder unless it is possible to go on to indicate the mediating mechanisms that bring about that risk. Exactly the same applies to all concepts of ethnic status. There is a considerable array of research designs that may be used to test mediation hypotheses and there is reasonable evidence that these can be effective (Rutter, Pickles, et al., 2001; Rutter, 2000 & 2005). It is necessary that greater use be made of these designs. Most crucially of all, it is essential to move from the sterile and unproductive position of viewing ethnic differences as an explanation (which they cannot be until the mediating mechanism is identified) to the constructive position of regarding ethnic differences as a starting point that indicates something to be investigated. It is not just that we need to know the explanation of why and how ethnic variations come about (although we do if we are to take any action on findings), but also that such variations provide a most valuable research lever for the investigation of causal mechanisms. It may be expected that the findings will prove illuminating with respect to the causal processes involved in both group differences in level and individual differences in frequency more generally. As discussed, the relevant features in the causal processes may involve either individual characteristics/experiences or societal influences or, more likely, some interplay between the two. Also, the causal model will almost certainly involve considerations of several different levels of causal effect. The research agenda is a most exciting one, and the rewards from its successful completion should have most important theoretical and policy consequences.

References

Ball, D., & Collier, D. (2002). Substance misuse. In P. McGuffin, M. J. Owen, & I. I. Gottesman (Eds.), *Psychiatric genetics and genomics* (pp. 267–302). Oxford: Oxford University Press.

Baron, R. M., & Kenny, D. A. (1986). The moderator-mediator variable distinction in social psychological research: Conceptual, strategic, and statistical considerations. *Journal of Personality and Social Psychology, 51,* 1173–1182.

Bell, R. Q. (1968). A reinterpretation of the direction of effects in studies of socialization. *Psychological Review, 75,* 81–95.

Bell, R. Q., & Chapman, M. (1986). Child effects in studies using experimental or brief longitudinal approaches to socialization. *Developmental Psychology, 22,* 595–603.

Belsky, J. (2001). Developmental risks (still) associated with early child care [Emanuel Miller Lecture]. *Journal of Child Psychology and Psychiatry, 42,* 845–859.

Berk, R. A. (1983). An introduction to sample selection bias in sociological data. *American Sociological Review, 48,* 386–398.

Bhatnagar, D., Anand, I. S., Durrington, P. N., Patel, D. J., Warder, G. S., Mackness, M. I., et al. (1995). Coronary risk factors in people from the Indian subcontinent living in West London and their siblings in India. *Lancet, 345,* 405–409.

Bhopal, R., Unwin, N., White, M., Yallop, J., Walker, L., Alberti, K. G., et al. (1999). Heterogeneity of coronary heart disease risk factors in Indian, Pakistani, Bangladeshi, and European origin populations: Cross sectional study. *British Medical Journal, 319,* 215–220.

Borge, A. I. H., Rutter, M., Côté, S., & Tremblay, R. E. (2004). Early childcare and physical aggression: Differentiating social selection and social causation. *Journal of Child Psychology and Psychiatry, 45,* 367–376.

Caspi, A., McClay, J., Moffitt, T. E., Mill, J., Martin, J., Craig, I. W., et al. (2002). Role of genotype in the cycle of violence in maltreated children. *Science, 297,* 851–854.

Caspi, A., Sugden, K., Moffitt, T. E., Taylor, A., Craig, I. W., Harrington, H. L., et al. (2003). Influence of life stress on depression: Moderation by a polymorphism in the 5-HTT gene. *Science, 301,* 386–389.

Chaturvedi, N., McKeigue, P. M., & Marmot, M. G. (1994). Relationship of glucose intolerance to coronary risk in African-Caribbeans compared with Europeans. *Diabetologia, 37,* 765–772.

Cohen, P., Cohen, J., & Brook, J. S. (1995). Bringing in the sheaves, or just gleaning? A methodological warning. *International Journal of Methods in Psychiatric Research, 5,* 263–266.

Cooper, R. S., Forrester, T., Rotimi, C. N., Wilks, R., Kaufman, J. S., Riste, L. K., et al. (1997). Prevalence of NIDDM among populations of the African diaspora. *Diabetes Care, 20,* 343–348.

Cooper, R., Rotimi, C., Ataman, S., McGee, D., Osotimehin, B., Kadiri, S., et al. (1997). The prevalence of hypertension in seven populations of West African origin. *American Journal of Public Health, 87,* 160–168.

Davies, S. C., & Brozovic, M. (1989). The presentation, management and prophylaxis of sickle cell disease. *Blood Reviews, 3,* 29–44.

Devlin, B., Fienberg, S., Resnick, D., & Roeder, K. (Eds.). (1997). *Intelligence, genes and success: Scientists respond to The Bell Curve.* New York: Copernicus.

Duyme, M., Dumaret, A.-C., & Tomkiewicz, S. (1999). How can we boost IQs of "dull children"?: A late adoption study. *Proceedings of the National Academy of Sciences of the United States of America, 96,* 8790–8794.

Eaves, L., Silberg, J., & Erkanli, A. (2003). Resolving multiple epigenetic pathways to adolescent depression. *Journal of Child Psychology and Psychiatry, 44,* 1006–1014.

Fang, J., Madhavan, S., & Alderman, M. H. (1996). The association between birthplace and mortality from cardiovascular causes among Black and White residents of New York City. *New England Journal of Medicine, 335,* 1545–1551.

Fergusson, D. M., Horwood, L. J., & Lynskey, M. T. (1992). Family change, parental discord and early offending. *Journal of Child Psychology and Psychiatry, 33,* 1059–1075.

Harris, T., Brown, G. W., & Bifulco, A. (1986). Loss of parent in childhood and adult psychiatric disorder: The role of lack of adequate parental care. *Psychological Medicine, 16,* 641–659.

Heath, A. C., Madden, P. A. F., Bucholz, K. K., Nelson, E. C., Todorov, A., Price, R. K., et al. (2003). Genetic and environmental risks of dependence on alcohol, tobacco, and other drugs. In R. Plomin, J. C. DeFries, I. W. Craig, & P. McGuffin (Eds.), *Behavioral genetics in the postgenomic era* (pp. 309–334). Washington, DC: American Psychological Association.

Hendrie, H. C., Hall, K. S., Hui, S. L., Unverzagt, F. W., Yu, C. E., Lahiri, D. K., et al. (1995). Apolipoprotein E genotypes and Alzheimer disease in a community study of elderly African-Americans. *Annals of Neurology, 37,* 118–120.

Hendrie, H. C., Osuntokun, B. O., Hall, K. S., Ogunniyi, A. O., Hui, S. L., Unverzagt, F. W., et al. (1995). Prevalence of Alzheimer's disease and dementia in two communities; Nigerian Africans and African Americans. *American Journal of Psychiatry, 152,* 1485–1492.

Hickling, F. W., McKenzie, K., Mullen, R., & Murray, R. M. (1999). A Jamaican psychiatrist evaluates diagnoses at a London psychiatric hospital. *British Journal of Psychiatry, 175,* 283–285.

Jaffee, S. R., Caspi, A., Moffitt, T. E., Dodge, K. A., Rutter, M., Taylor, A., et al. (in press). Nature x Nurture: Genetic vulnerabilities interact with child maltreatment to promote behavior problems. *Development and Psychopathology.*

Kandel, D. B. (1978). Homophily, selection and socialization in adolescent friendships. *American Journal of Sociology, 4,* 427–436.

Laub, J. H., & Sampson, R. J. (2003). *Shared beginnings, divergent lives: Delinquent boys to age 70.* Cambridge, MA: Harvard University Press.

Laub, J. H., Nagin, D. S., & Sampson, R. J. (1998). Trajectories of change in criminal offending: Good marriages and the desistance process. *American Sociological Review, 63,* 225–238.

Marmot, M. G., & Syme, S. L. (1976). Acculturation and coronary heart disease in Japanese-Americans. *American Journal of Epidemiology, 104,* 225–247.

McKeigue, P. M., Shah, B., & Marmot, M. G. (1991). Relation of central obesity and insulin resistance with high diabetes prevalence and cardiovascular risk in South Asians. *Lancet, 337,* 382–386.

Moffitt, T. E., Caspi, A., Rutter, M., & Silva, P. A. (2001). *Sex differences in antisocial behavior: Conduct disorder, delinquency, and violence in the Dunedin Longitudinal Study.* Cambridge: Cambridge University Press.

Moffitt, T. E., Caspi, A., & Rutter, M. (in press). Interaction between measured genes and measured environments: A research strategy. *Archives of General Psychiatry.*

Moffitt, T. E., & the E-Risk Study Team (2002). Teen-aged mothers in contemporary Britain. *Journal of Child Psychology and Psychiatry, 43,* 727–742.

NICHD Early Child Care Research Network (1997). The effects of infant child care on infant-mother attachment security: Results of the NICHD study of early child care. *Child Development, 68,* 860–879.

O'Connor, T. G., Marvin, S., Rutter, M., Olrick, J. T., Britner, P. A., & the English and Romanian Adoptees Study Team (2003). Child-parent attachment following early institutional deprivation. *Development and Psychopathology, 15,* 19–38.

O'Connor, T., Rutter, M., Beckett, C., Keaveney, L., Kreppner, J. M., & the English and Romanian Adoptees (ERA) Study Team (2000). The effects of global severe privation on cognitive competence: Extension and longitudinal follow-up. *Child Development, 71,* 376–390.

Odegaard, O. (1932). Emigration and insanity: A study of mental disease among Norwegian born population in Minnesota. *Acta Psychiatrica et Neurologica Scandinavica, 7,* 1–206.

Plomin, R. (1994). *Genetics and experience: The interplay between nature and nurture.* Thousand Oaks, CA: Sage.

Plomin, R. (1995). Genetics and children's experiences in the family. *Journal of Child Psychology and Psychiatry, 36,* 33–68.

Ravussin, E., Valencia, M. E., Esparza, J., Bennet, P., & Schulz, L. (1994). Effects of a traditional lifestyle on obesity in Pima Indians. *Diabetes Care, 17,* 1067–1074.

Reed, T. E. (1985). Ethnic differences in alcohol use, abuse, and sensitivity: A review with genetic interpretation. *Social Biology, 32,* 195–209.

Risch, N., Burchard, E., Ziv, E., & Tang, H. (2002). Categorization of humans in biomedical research: Genes, race and disease. *Genome Biology, 3,* 2007.1–2007.12.

Rowe, D. C., Woulbroun, E. J., & Gulley, B. L. (1994). Peers and friends as nonshared environmental influences. In E. M. Hetherington, D. Reiss, & R. Plomin (Eds.), *Separate social worlds of siblings: Impact of nonshared environment on development* (pp. 159–173). Hillsdale, NJ: Erlbaum.

Roy, P., Rutter, M., & Pickles, A. (2000). Institutional care: Risk from family background or pattern of rearing? *Journal of Child Psychology and Psychiatry, 41,* 139–149.

Rubinsztein, D. C. (1995). Apolipoprotein E: A review of its roles in lipoprotein metabolism, neuronal growth and repair and as a risk factor for Alzheimer's disease [Editorial]. *Psychological Medicine, 25,* 223–229.

Rutter, M. (1971). Parent-child separation: Psychological effects on the children. *Journal of Child Psychology and Psychiatry, 12,* 233–260.

Rutter, M. (1974). Epidemiological strategies and psychiatric concepts in research on the vulnerable child. In E. Anthony & C. Koupernik (Eds.), *The child in his family: Children at psychiatric risk* (pp. 167–179). New York: Wiley.

Rutter, M. (1996). Transitions and turning points in developmental psychopathology: As applied to the age span between childhood and mid-adulthood. *International Journal of Behavioural Development, 19,* 603–626.

Rutter, M. (1999). Social context: meanings, measures and mechanisms? *European Review, 7*, 139–149.

Rutter, M. (2000). Psychosocial influences: Critiques, findings, and research needs. *Development and Psychopathology, 12*, 375–405.

Rutter, M. (2001). Family influences on behavior and development: Challenges for the future. In J. P. McHale & W. S. Grolnick (Eds.), *Retrospect and prospect in the psychological study of families* (pp. 321–351). Mahwah, NJ: Erlbaum.

Rutter, M. (2005). Environmentally mediated risks for psychopathology: Research strategies and findings. *Journal of the American Academy of Child and Adolescent Psychiatry, 44*, 3–18.

Rutter, M., Caspi, A., & Moffitt, T. E. (2003). Using sex differences in psychopathology to study causal mechanisms: Unifying issues and research strategies. *Journal of Child Psychology and Psychiatry, 44*, 1092–1115.

Rutter, M., Champion, L., Quinton, D., Maughan, B., & Pickles, A. (1995). Understanding individual differences in environmental risk exposure. In P. Moen, G. H. Elder, & K. Lüscher (Eds.), *Examining lives in context: Perspectives on the ecology of human development* (pp. 61–93). Washington, DC: American Psychological Association.

Rutter, M., & and the English and Romanian Adoptees (E.R.A.) Study Team (1998). Developmental catch-up, and deficit, following adoption after severe global early privation. *Journal of Child Psychology and Psychiatry, 39*, 465–476.

Rutter, M., Giller, H., & Hagell, A. (1998). *Antisocial behavior by young people.* New York: Cambridge University Press.

Rutter, M., Kreppner, J., O'Connor, T. G. on behalf of the English and Romanian Adoptees (ERA) Study Team (2001). Specificity and heterogeneity in children's responses to profound institutional privation. *British Journal of Psychiatry, 179*, 97–103.

Rutter, M., & Nikapota, A. (2002). Culture, ethnicity, society and psychopathology. In M. Rutter & E. Taylor (Eds.), *Child and adolescent psychiatry* (4th ed., pp. 277–298). Oxford: Blackwell Scientific.

Rutter, M., O'Connor, T. G., & the ERA Research Team (2004). Are there biological programming effects for psychological development? Findings from a study of Romanian adoptees. *Developmental Psychology, 40*, 81–94.

Rutter, M., Pickles, A., Murray, R., & Eaves, L. (2001). Testing hypotheses on specific environmental causal effects on behavior. *Psychological Bulletin, 127*, 291–324.

Rutter, M., & Silberg, J. (2002). Gene-environment interplay in relation to emotional and behavioral disturbance. *Annual Review of Psychology, 53*, 463–490.

Rutter, M., Thorpe, K., Greenwood, R., Northstone, K., & Golding, J. (2003). Twins as a natural experiment to study the causes of mild language delay: I. Design; twin-singleton differences in language, and obstetric risks. *Journal of Child Psychology and Psychiatry, 44*, 326–341.

Sampson, R. J., & Laub, J. H. (1996). Socioeconomic achievement in the life course of disadvantaged men: Military service as a turning point, circa 1940–1965. *American Sociological Review, 61*, 347–367.

Sher, K., & Trull, T. (1996). Methodological issues in psychopathology research. *Annual Review of Psychology, 47*, 371–400.

Thornberry, T. P., Bjerregard, B., & Miles, W. (1993). The consequences of respondent attrition in panel studies: A simulation based on the Rochester Youth Development Study. *Journal of Quantitative Criminology, 9,* 127–158.

Thorpe, K., Rutter, M., & Greenwood, R. (2003). Twins as a natural experiment to study the causes of mild language delay: II. Family interaction risk factors. *Journal of Child Psychology and Psychiatry, 44,* 342–355.

Tizard, J. (1975). Race and IQ: The limits of probability. *New Behaviour, 1,* 6–9.

van IJzendoorn, M. H., & Sagi, A. (1999). Cross-cultural patterns of attachment: universal and contextual dimensions. In J. Cassidy & P. R. Shaver (Eds.), *Handbook of attachment: Theory, research, and clinical applications* (pp. 713–734). New York: The Guilford Press.

Weatherall, D. J., & Clegg, J. B. (2001). *The thalassaemia syndromes* (4th ed.). Oxford: Blackwell Scientific.

Wild, S., & McKeigue, P. (1997). Cross sectional analysis of mortality by country of birth in England and Wales, 1970–92. *British Medical Journal, 314,* 705–710.

Williams, J. H., Ayers, C. D., Abbott, R. D., Hawkins, J. D., & Catalano, R. F. (1996). Structural equivalence of involvement in problem behavior by adolescents using multiple group confirmatory factor analysis. *Social Work Research, 20,* 168–177.

Wilson, W. J. (1987). *The truly disadvantaged: The inner city, the underclass, and public policy.* Chicago, IL: University of Chicago Press.

Yule, W., Berger, M., Rutter, M., & Yule, B. A. (1975). Children of West Indian immigrants – II. Intellectual performance and reading attainment. *Journal of Child Psychology and Psychiatry, 16,* 1–17.

2

Growing Up Ethnic in the United Kingdom and the United States

Comparative Contexts for Youth Development

Marta Tienda

Introduction

Understanding whether and how group membership influences adolescent behavior and a myriad of outcomes requires an appreciation of the social and economic arrangements in which youth forge their transition to adulthood. Because several chapters that follow involve paired comparisons of youth experiences in the United Kingdom and the United States, this chapter situates them in context by sketching a socio-demographic overview of youth in both countries. First, I provide the demographic sketch of both countries, focusing on how migration altered their ethnoracial landscapes. Subsequently, I characterize the current social and economic conditions of immigrant and minority youth, offering temporal perspectives as data permit.

This enterprise presumes the availability of comparable data over time, but this mere condition is seldom met. Not only do official classification systems evolve, but so also do the methods for collecting migration status and ethno-racial group membership. I briefly acknowledge these limitations and, perforce, limit cross-country comparisons to general overviews based on social and demographic indicators. To capitalize on the nuances of country-specific data, the social conditions of immigrant and minority youth are profiled separately, reserving for the conclusion a synthesis of key differences and similarities. My use of the phrase *immigrant and minority youth* is deliberate, to acknowledge that not all immigrant youth are members of minority populations and that groups designated as minorities are not necessarily foreign-born (although their parents or distant ancestors may be immigrants). It is desirable to distinguish between immigrant and native-born ethnic minorities to understand how ethnic differences are produced and maintained. Nevertheless, this distinction is both helpful and problematic because of uneven paths of assimilation, and differences in modes of incorporation complicate intergenerational comparisons.

A distinction between U.S. African Americans as minorities and Hispanics as immigrants illustrates this point, not only because growing Caribbean immigration has greatly diversified the generational composition of the Black population, but also because the majority of Hispanic youth are not immigrants. Instead, as members of the burgeoning second generation, some become identified as ethnic minorities (e.g., Mexicans and Guatemalans) and others as ethnics (e.g., Cubans and Argentineans), whereas for others (e.g., Puerto Ricans and Dominicans), pigmentation assumes the salient status for classification by others. Similar difficulties are present in the United Kingdom, which are, moreover, compounded by religious differences. My reliance on official data for the profiles precludes further refinement of groups beyond national origin.

The Demographic Context: Contemporary United Kingdom and United States

The most recent decennial censuses enumerated close to 59 million residents of the United Kingdom compared with over 281 million U.S. residents (see Table 2.1). Thus in terms of sheer size, the United States is more than four and a half times larger than the United Kingdom, and it is growing at a slightly faster rate, although fertility is declining in both countries. Both the United Kingdom and United States registered below-replacement fertility rates, which in 2001 stood at 1.7 and 2.0, respectively.

TABLE 2.1. *Selected Demographic and Social Characteristics: United Kingdom and United States, 1980–2001*[a]

	United Kingdom	United States
2001/2000 Population (millions)	58.8	281.4
Total Fertility Rate, 1991	1.8	2.1
Total Fertility Rate, 2001	1.7	2.0
% Population Ages 15–19, 1981/1980	8.2	9.2
% Population Ages 15–19, 1998	6.1	6.8
Migrants/1000 Population, 1991	1.3	3.8
Migrants/1000 Population, 2001	2.2	3.7
% Foreign-Born Population, 1981/1980	6.3	6.2
% Foreign-Born Population, 1991/1990	6.9	7.9
% Foreign-Born Population, 2001/2000	8.0	10.4

[a] UK census taken in years ending in 01; U.S. census taken in years ending 00.

Sources: Coleman and Salt, 1996: Table 4.10; Columbia University, 2001: Table 40; UK Office of National Statistics, 2003b: Table 1.1; 2003c: Table KS05; UK Office of Population Censuses and Surveys, 1983: Table D; U.S. Census Bureau, 2000: Table P1; 2001: Figure 1.1; 2002a: Tables 8 and 28.

The higher U.S. fertility rate implies a slightly younger population. In 1980, just over 8 percent of the UK population was ages 15–19, compared with 9 percent for the United States. Twenty years later, this age group comprised 6.1 and 6.8 percent of the UK and U.S. populations, respectively. During a period of declining fertility, migration has permitted populations of both countries to grow, but particularly in the United States, where immigrant admissions accounted for one third to one half of population growth since 1970.

Much starker country differences obtain for the migration component of population change. For example, the 1990 U.S. crude migration rate of 3.9 immigrants per thousand population was more than four times the comparable rate for the United Kingdom (U.S. Census Bureau, 2002a). A decade later the United Kingdom's crude migration rate rose 70 percent, largely because of the openness of its border to residents of European Union (EU) member countries. For the most part, EU migrants are not classified as immigrants or ethnic minorities. The strong tradition of international migration to the United States also continued throughout the 1990s, but the crude migration rate remained unchanged. In both countries, high migration rates increased the foreign-born population share – from 6 to 10 percent in the United States, and from 6 to 8 percent in the United Kingdom. By 2002, the U.S. foreign-born population exceeded 32 million, representing 11.5 percent of all persons (Schmidley, 2003: Figure 1).

In addition to differences in the timing and volume of migration, the migrant source countries destined to the United Kingdom and the United States differ. Two sets of circumstances undergird the volume and composition of migration to the United Kingdom. First, the "settlement system" draws on traditional colonial ties; second, the "refugee" system offers asylum to persons from troubled countries (Coleman and Salt, 1992). Once in the queue, selections are made based on labor needs and individual skill levels of applicants. Increases in the migration rate notwithstanding, the general tenor over the past quarter of a century has been toward greater restriction on United Kingdom–destined migrants, except those who move freely within Europe after the creation of the EU. For example, the 1962 Commonwealth Immigration Act strove to limit the arrival of Commonwealth citizens; its sequel, the 1968 Commonwealth Immigration Act, further tightened immigration controls to restrict the numbers of migrants from newly independent African nations. Moreover, as Parliament made UK immigration legislation more restrictive, it also created penalties for fraudulent refugee entries (Coleman & Salt, 1992).

The impact of the settlement system is clearly evident in the source country composition of migrants to the United Kingdom. Since the end of World War II, the majority of UK immigrants from New Commonwealth and Pakistan (NCWP) have been non-White. Caribbean migrants began arriving after WWII, followed by Indians and Bangladeshis during the 1970s

TABLE 2.2. *Regional Origin of Immigrants Admitted to the United Kingdom and United States, 1997 and 2001*

| | United Kingdom | | | | United States | | | |
| | 1997 | | 2001 | | 1997 | | 2001 | |
	'000	%	'000	%	'000	%	'000	%
Asia	25.6	43.6	43.3	40.5	265.8	33.3	349.8	32.9
Africa	13.2	22.5	31.4	29.4	47.8	6.0	53.9	5.1
Europe	7.7[a]	13.1	13.8	12.9	119.9	15.0	175.4	16.5
Americas	7.8	13.3	11.9	11.1	360.4	45.1	476.8	44.8
Oceania	3.1	5.3	5.5	5.2	4.3	0.5	6.1	0.6
Other	1.3	2.2	0.9	0.8	0.2	0.0	2.3	0.2
All Regions[b]	58.7	100.0	106.8	99.9	798.4	99.9	1064.3	100.1

[a] Includes EEA nationals who choose to seek settlement, but EEA residents are not obliged to report themselves as foreign-born.
[b] Sums of percentages may not equal 100% due to rounding.
Sources: UK Office of National Statistics, 2003b: Table 9.5; U.S. INS, 2001: Table 3.

and 1980s, and, most recently, Black Africans. In a country where the host population is predominantly (more than 90 percent) White, the NCWP population is identified by color and unified in the popular mind (Coleman & Salt, 1992: 448). Although many United Kingdom–bound migrants lack formal educational qualifications, the foreign-born population exhibits considerable diversity in skills and social background according to country of origin and time of migration (Modood & Berthoud, 1997). Similarly, the composition of U.S. immigrants reflects the impact of past political alliances and restrictionist policies. Following the 1965 Amendments to the Immigration and Nationality Act, the source countries of United States–bound migrants shifted from predominantly European to Asian and Latin American nations (Smith & Edmonston, 1997; Tienda, 2002). Currently, more than half (52.2 percent) of the U.S. foreign-born population is from Central and South America, with Mexico the largest single source of all U.S. immigrants (Smith & Edmonston, 1997).

Table 2.2 provides more specific regional breakdowns of the source origin countries and volume of immigrants admitted to the United Kingdom and United States in the recent past. Both countries have witnessed an increase in the volume of immigrants from all regions: 82 percent versus 33 percent for the United Kingdom and United States, respectively. However, in 2001, the absolute number of immigrants admitted to the United States was roughly ten times the number admitted to the United Kingdom. That the U.S. population is not ten times larger than that of the United Kingdom signals a greater social and demographic impact of immigration in the former (Smith & Edmonston, 1997). Of course, the social impact depends on the ways migrants differ from the host population and their mode of reception (Portes & Rumbaut, 1996). The United Kingdom receives about 40 percent of its migrants from Asia, but only about one-third of U.S. migrants are of Asian origin. By contrast, nearly half (45 percent) of recent U.S. immigrants were from the Americas, compared with only 11–13 percent of UK immigrants. Finally, only between 5 and 6 percent of U.S. migrants originate in African nations compared to 23–29 percent of migrants destined for the United Kingdom. For historical reasons, about 5 percent of UK migrants originate in Oceania, but few U.S. migrants trace their origins to Australia or New Zealand.

The evolution of source countries sending migrants both to the United Kingdom and United States has direct implications not only for the integration prospects of new arrivals, but also for the emergence and construction of ethnicity among immigrant and minority youth (Portes & Rumbaut, 1996). As chapters by Modood (this volume) and Rumbaut (this volume) illustrate, for youth whose race, ancestry, or religion differs from that of the host society, the process of social integration is intertwined with the process of identity construction, and both are associated with these life chances. How these associations emerge and confer unequal social standing along racial and ethnic lines is the subject of the chapters that follow.

These different migration histories have altered the ethno-racial composition of the UK and U.S. populations. As Table 2.3 shows, just under 8 percent of the total UK population was classified as minority compared with 28 percent for the United States. This means that *in relative terms*, the

TABLE 2.3. *Ethno-Racial Composition of UK and U.S. Population, 2000: Total and Young People (percentages)*

	United Kingdom		United States	
	Total	<16	Total	<18
White	92.1	88.0	71.5	64.0
Black	2.0	3.0	12.2	14.5
Hispanic	–	–	11.8	16.2
Asian	4.0	6.0	3.8	4.3
Mixed	1.2	3.0	–	–
Other[a]	0.8	1.0	0.7	1.0
TOTAL[c]	100.1	101.0	100.0	100.0

[a] For United Kingdom, Asian includes Indian, Pakistani, Bangladeshi, and other Asian, but not Chinese.
[b] Other includes Chinese and those who did not state ethnicity.
[c] Sums of percentages may not equal 100% due to rounding.
Sources: UK Office of National Statistics, 2003d: Table 273; 2003e: Table 5701; U.S. Census Bureau, 2002b: Table 15; U.S. DOE, 2003: 9.

U.S. minority population is 3.5 times that of the United Kingdom, and this share is even greater for young people. In the United Kingdom, 12 percent of persons aged 16 and under are minority, compared with the United States, where almost one in three young persons belongs to one of the largest racial and ethnic groups. Asians comprise about half of the United Kingdom's minority young people, with Blacks and persons of mixed race or ancestry accounting for the remainder.

In the United States, Black and Hispanic youth comprise the largest minority groups, each representing about 15 percent of the total population, whereas Asians and other races combined represent a scant 5 percent. Recently, the Hispanic population surpassed Blacks as the largest minority group (U.S. Census Bureau, 2003). The national origin composition of the Asian and Black populations also differs across settings. In the United Kingdom, the major Asian nationalities include Indians, Pakistanis, Bangladeshis, and others, but exclude Chinese, who are allocated to the residual *other* category in published tabulations. The Black population of the United Kingdom is divided into groups hailing from Caribbean nations, African nations, and a residual. In the United States, Hispanics are disaggregated along national origin lines, but the major divisions are among Mexicans, Puerto Ricans, Cubans, and Central/South Americans. The last group has grown rapidly at the expense of the Cuban population in recent decades because the long-standing U.S. embargo against Cuba officially restricts the flow of persons as well as goods. The majority of U.S. Blacks are native-born; therefore, origin countries are seldom specified for them. However, in recent years immigration from the Caribbean has expanded. Black immigrants to the United States trace their origins to Jamaica, the West Indies, and Haiti.

Because immigration and high fertility of foreign-born women are the two forces driving the diversification of the UK and U.S. populations, minority populations are younger, on average, than the majority White population, as Figure 2.1 illustrates. Chinese in the United Kingdom and Asians in the United States are notable exceptions. The age cut-offs reported in Figure 2.1 differ by two years for the United Kingdom and United States, but the age structures of racial and ethnic populations vary in similar ways. In the United Kingdom, the youngest age structures correspond to Southeast Asian and African origin groups. Compared with the White majority, among whom one in five persons is under age 16, over one third of Pakistanis, Bangladeshis, and Blacks are 15 years old or younger. Persons of mixed ancestry are the youngest of all, with more than half under age 16.

In the United States, about one in four persons classified as White or Asian is aged 17 and under, compared to more than one in three Hispanics and Native Americans and just fewer than one in three African Americans. As in the United Kingdom, the multirace population is the youngest of all minority groups, with 42 percent under 18 years of age. This suggests several possible explanations: that interracial marriage has been increasing;

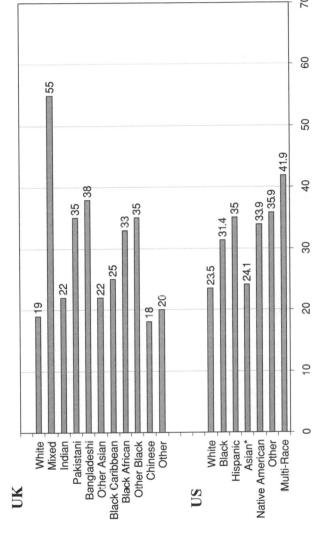

FIGURE 2.1. Age composition of minority groups: United Kingdom (percent ages 15 and under, 2001–2) and United States (percent ages 17 and under, 2000). Asian category excludes Pacific Islander and Native Hawaiian. *Sources*: UK Office of National Statistics, 2002b, Table D6206; Meyer, 2001. Figure 4.

that younger couples are more likely to identify themselves and their off-spring as multiracial; that immigrants of dark pigmentation do not easily classify themselves into the discrete racial categories; or some combination of the above (Goldstein & Morning, 2000; Morning, 2000). Although the foreign-born population is older, on average, than the native-born, with 9 versus 28 percent, respectively, under 18 years of age, the higher fertility of migrants has diversified the school-age population, particularly for Asians and Hispanics. Consequently, almost three of four Hispanic youth are either foreign-born or children of immigrants compared with 62 percent of Asian youth. By contrast, only 10 percent of Black school-aged youth are either foreign-born or children of immigrants, and an even smaller share of White youth so qualify (Lloyd, Tienda, & Zajacova, 2001: Figure 2).

How the U.S. and UK immigration scenarios play themselves out socially and culturally for youth depends on several circumstances, including the residential settlement patterns of the migrant and ethnic populations and the socioeconomic resources of their parents. For immigrant minority populations, residential concentration permits cultural differences to flourish in the face of the homogenizing influences of public education; for native-born ethnic minorities, residential segregation often limits social and economic integration and diminishes life chances to varying degrees and in myriad ways. In particular, growing up amid concentrated poverty thwarts opportunities for normative development in the absence of functional substitutes for healthy and nurturing adult role models (Tienda & Wilson, 2002).

More than two thirds of Britain's ethnic minorities reside in its 88 most fiscally deprived districts, compared with 40 percent of the general population (UK Cabinet Office, 2003:94). London houses the largest share of people from minority ethnic groups, but specific nationalities also tend to concentrate in particular cities and within boroughs of the larger cities. For example, according to the census of 2001, 2 percent of the population of England and Wales is Indian, with nearly one in four residing in Leicester. Black Caribbeans are concentrated within a few London boroughs, including Lewisham, Lambeth, Brent, and Hackney, where they comprise 10 percent of the residents. Although Bangladeshis represent less than 1 percent of the population of England and Wales, one in three residents of London's borough of Tower Hamlets is of Bangladeshi origin (UK Office of National Statistics, 2003a).

Similarly, in the United States, minority and immigrant populations are disproportionately concentrated in the poorest neighborhoods of the large central cities (Lloyd et al., 2001; Wilson, 1987). Compared with Blacks and Hispanics, Asians are more residentially dispersed (Massey & Denton, 1993). For example, nearly half of school-aged Blacks reside in a central-city school district compared with only 14 percent of all White students. Similarly, the vast majority of Native Americans attend rural schools rather than higher-performing suburban schools, which are disproportionately populated by White youth. These differences in the geographic distribution of youth would be inconsequential if the social and economic opportunities afforded in central city, suburban, and rural areas were roughly comparable. Unfortunately, minority students are more likely than majority White students to attend highly segregated and low performing schools where educational opportunities are limited (Orfield, Eaton, & The Harvard Project on School Desegregation, 1996).

Because the statistical reporting of socioeconomic outcomes differs between the United Kingdom and the United States, the remainder of this chapter portrays the social and economic contours of well-being for immigrant and minority youth using the country-specific classifications organized around the broad themes of income and poverty status and educational inequality. In keeping with the migration paradigm set forth in this introduction, several chapters that follow consider whether racial and ethnic differences in youth outcomes reflect group-specific predispositions to engage in particular behaviors, such as premature school withdrawal, or whether other factors, such as unequal opportunities or weaker social supports, are largely responsible for observed group differences. Country-specific comparisons of racial and ethnic differences in socioeconomic status, as portrayed by parental education and income status, serve as a backdrop for understanding the mechanisms that produce unequal psychosocial outcomes among minority and immigrant youth. The concluding section will, in addition to synthesizing broad generalizations, highlight important similarities and differences that bear on the psychosocial functioning of immigrant and minority youth in the United Kingdom and the United States.

Socioeconomic Differentiation of Minority and Immigrant Youth

A voluminous literature testifies that parental socioeconomic status is one of the most powerful correlates of youth outcomes because it serves as a proxy for a vast array of material and social resources on which young people draw in their transition to adulthood. Family income has substantial impacts on child and adolescent academic achievement (Brooks-Gunn & Duncan, 1997). Children reared in poverty are at much greater risk of school failure than their counterparts who are better off materially. In particular, parental education shapes youth expectations about their possible selves and determines financial, material, and intellectual resources deployed to promote these goals. Variation in parental socioeconomic status is crucial for understanding racial and ethnic differences in a myriad of youth outcomes, including scholastic performance, the timing of school departure, labor force entry, and health status. Because data for the United Kingdom and the United States are not strictly

comparable, the following sections characterize the socioeconomic circumstances of immigrants and minorities residing in each context separately.

Poverty and Educational Differentials in the United Kingdom
Recent social indicators reveal that immigrant and minority households
were more likely than White households to live on low incomes, but Pakistanis and Bangladeshis were far more likely than other groups to be poor
(White, 2002:11). In the United Kingdom, low income is defined as having less than 60 percent of the median disposable income, adjusted for
household size and composition. Before housing costs, nearly 60 percent
of Pakistani and Bangladeshi households were classified as low income,
but this share exceeded 65 percent after housing costs were considered.
Almost half of Black non-Caribbean households were classified as low income once housing costs were taken into account, compared with about
30 percent of Black Caribbean units. White households were least likely to
be classified as poor – 16 and 20 percent, respectively, without and with
housing costs considered (White, 2002, p. 11). These differences in household poverty imply large economic disparities among immigrant and minority youth.

  Table 2.4 presents the quintile distribution of household income to portray racial and ethnic disparities in the economic circumstances of youth.
With this metric, relative equality implies that approximately 20 percent of
each group would be represented in each quintile. As the bottom panel reveals, the overall distribution is weighted toward the lower tiers, with only
13 percent of all youth residing in households classified in the top quintile
of the income distribution. Overall, and because Whites represent more

TABLE 2.4. *Quintile Distribution of Income for Youth Under 16 Years of Age by Race/Ethnicity of Household Head: United Kingdom, 2000/01[a]*

	Bottom Quintile	Second Quintile	Third Quintile	Fourth Quintile	Top Quintile	All Youth (Millions)
Ethnic Group of Head of Household						
White	23	24	22	18	14	10.1
Black Caribbean	28	30	16	14	12	0.2
Black Non-Caribbean	42	25	12	13	9	0.2
Indian	37	22	16	14	11	0.2
Pakistani/ Bangladeshi	70	22	5	2	2	0.4
Other	41	17	13	13	16	0.2
All Youth	25	24	21	17	13	11.3

[a] Net income before housing costs, adjusted for household composition and size.
Source: UK DWP, 2002: Table 4.1.

than 90 percent of Britain's population, the household income distribution for White youth mirrors the national average, with a slight advantage toward the upper quintiles.

Although minority youth are considerably more disadvantaged than their White counterparts, there are appreciable differences in the economic circumstances of the major nationality groups. Nearly three of four Pakistani and Bangladeshi youth reside in households classified in the lowest quintile of the income distribution, compared with fewer than one quarter of White youth and just barely more than one quarter of Black Caribbean youth. Nationally, about one in four youth resides in households with income in the lowest quintile. However, two of five non-Caribbean Black youth – mainly African Blacks – are situated at the lowest quintile of the income distribution, as are more than one in three Indians. Focusing on the upper end of the income distribution, only 2 percent of Pakistani youth reside in households classified in the top quintile of the income distribution, compared to between 9 (non-Caribbean) and 12 (Caribbean) percent of Black youth. White youth are more privileged: Roughly 14 percent reside in households that enjoy incomes in the top quintile of the distribution.

Educational attainment does not perfectly predict income status, particularly for immigrants who often experience a period of downward mobility as they adjust to a new labor market. Even so, aggregate racial and ethnic income inequality mirrors educational differences of the UK adult population (Table 2.5). The average distribution of school attainment, represented by the category that pools all groups, reveals that at the low end of the education distribution, between 15 (men) and 18 (women) percent of adults have no formal educational qualifications whatsoever. At the opposite extreme, between 17 (men) and 14 (women) percent held formal degrees according to the latest figures prepared by the Department of Education and Skills (UK Office of National Statistics, 2002a: Table 3.17). Between these extremes there is significant variation in attainment among Britain's minority populations.

Not surprisingly, the White share of degree holders is similar to the national average, but among men, the share of non-Black minority degree holders actually exceeds the national average. This would appear to bode well for their offspring, except that minority parents are also overrepresented among those lacking any formal qualifications. Between the extremes of formal college degree holders and those with no educational qualification, there is further differentiation in qualification levels, with below-average shares of the Asian nationalities reporting some higher education, GCE A-level attainment. Concomitantly, above-average shares of minority parents report nonacademic qualifications, presumably vocational skills or a vocational certification.

Fairly similar patterns obtain for women, with two notable differences. First, the share of Asian origin women reporting no qualifications is

TABLE 2.5. *Racial and Ethnic Differences in Qualification Levels of Adults: Great Britain, 1999–2000[a] (percentages)*

	Degree or Equivalent	Higher Education[b]	GCE A Level or Equivalent	GCSE Grades A* to C or Equivalent	Other Qualification	No Qualifications	All[e]
Males[c]							
White	17	8	31	18	13	14	101
Black	16	9	20	17	22	16	100
Indian/Pakistani/Bangladeshi	20	4	16	15	24	20	99
Other Groups[d]	23	5	18	12	30	12	100
All Groups	17	7	30	18	13	15	100
Females[c]							
White	13	10	17	28	14	18	100
Black	14	11	18	22	21	15	101
Indian/Pakistani/Bangladeshi	13	5	14	16	23	29	100
Other groups[d]	18	10	14	13	30	15	100
All groups	14	9	17	27	14	18	100

[a] Combined quarters: Spring 2000 to Winter 2000–1.
[b] Below degree level.
[c] Males aged 16 to 64, females aged 16 to 59.
[d] Includes those who did not state their ethnic group.
[e] Sums of percentages may not equal 100% due to rounding.

Source: UK Office of National Statistics, 2002a: Table 3.17.

TABLE 2.6. *Racial and Ethnic Differences in Attainment of 5 or More GSCE Grades A*-C in Year 11: England and Wales, 1992 and 2000 (percentages)*

	1992	2000
White	37	50
Black	23	37
Indian	38	62
Pakistani	26	30
Bangladeshi	14	30
Chinese/Other Asian	46	70
Other	NA	43

Source: UK Cabinet Office, 2001: Table 1.

significantly higher than the national average for all women. Furthermore, and by contrast to men, the share with higher education degrees does not reach, much less exceed, the national average. Another noteworthy difference vis-à-vis men is that the share of Black women lacking any qualifications is several percentage points below the national average of 18 percent. However, these classification schemes are quite heterogeneous because, for example, among the Asian nationalities, Indians tend to complete higher levels of education whereas the Pakistanis and Bangladeshis do not. Dale, Fieldhouse, Shaheen, and Virinder (2002) found that language barriers prevent minority women both from upgrading their educational credentials and from earning money outside of the household – challenges that are compounded by their domestic responsibilities.

Intergenerational educational mobility notwithstanding, differences in parental socioeconomic resources are mirrored in minority and immigrant youth. Persisting inequities spawned several government sponsored school and local initiatives to close educational gaps along racial, ethnic, and gender lines (Gillborn & Mirza, 2000; Pathak, 2000). Table 2.6 reveals that youth of all racial and ethnic groups have witnessed significant improvement in their educational attainment of 5 or more GSCE grades A*-C by year 11 of their schooling curriculum, but the rate of improvement was very uneven. Consequently, rather large differences in the achievement of this important educational benchmark remain (Gillborn & Mirza, 2000). Between 1992 and 2000, White youth showed a 13 percentage point increase in the share who attained five or more GSCE Grades A*-C by the end of their compulsory education. Although a comparable improvement was registered for Black youth, their lower starting level implies that the relative education gap changed very little.

Asian youth also made significant strides in their educational attainment during this period, but their uneven gains widened the education gaps for some while narrowing them for others. For example, Indian pupils made the greatest gains in the past decade and they overtook their White peers as a group, but Pakistani and Bangladeshi youth remain well behind White youth (Gillborn & Mirza, 2000, p. 14). Chinese and other Asian youth report the highest educational attainment, with nearly 70 percent attaining 5 or more GSCE grades of A*-C by the end of compulsory schooling, up from 46 percent in 1992. Bangladeshi pupils also improved their educational attainment; yet because the educational achievements of White youth also continued to rise, their attainment vis-à-vis White youth remained unchanged. Even more disturbing, the gap between African-Caribbean and Pakistani students and their White peers is substantially larger now than a decade ago (Gillborn & Mirza, 2000, p. 14).

Pathak (2000) and others noted that lack of fluency in English is responsible for early underachievement of Pakistani and Bangladeshi youth, but that it can not account for their performance throughout their schooling careers. According to a 1999 report by UK OFSTED (1999), once these youth become proficient in English, their attainment matches or surpasses that of English-speaking students in similar socioeconomic circumstances. However, their generally lower attainment in higher grades at GCSE remains problematic. Even more worrisome is the eroding progress of Black Caribbean students as they progress to the secondary level – a circumstance that cannot easily be traced to the educational resources of their parents or to linguistic impediments.

Performance in the lower and secondary school grades determines the representation of immigrant minority and White students in higher education. Although there is evidence of underachievement in the lower grades, particularly for Black Caribbean youth, Pathak (2000) claimed that immigrant and minority youth also are overrepresented in higher education compared with their White counterparts. In light of the high educational achievement of Chinese and Indian students in the lower grades, their disproportionate representation in higher education is not surprising. However, the erosion of educational attainment that appears to characterize Black immigrant youth remains a puzzle that warrants further research, as the chapter by Barbara Maughan (this volume) discusses.

Poverty and Educational Differentials in the United States

As a long-standing concern of U.S. policy makers, child poverty and economic well-being assumed center stage in the late 1990s because various academic and political constituencies were concerned about the potentially deleterious effects of welfare reform on children and youth. Brooks-Gunn and Duncan (1997) identified several pathways through which the harmful effects of poverty operate. Noting that the timing, duration, and depth of poverty have variable impacts on specific outcomes, they conclude that family income status influences scholastic outcomes more than emotional ones.

U.S. child poverty trends, while showing some progress during the 1990s, reveal large gaps between Asian and White youth on the one hand, and Black and Hispanic youth on the other hand (Figure 2.2). In light of mounting evidence that children reared in economic disadvantage, and especially extreme and protracted poverty, are also more prone to scholastic underperformance and low educational attainment than youth reared in affluent families, trends in poverty are both troubling and promising. On the optimistic side, the Black–White poverty ratio, which hovered around 3 throughout the 1980s and early 1990s, finally dropped to around 2.4 in 1997 – following several years of impressive economic growth. Although this provides strong grounds for optimism, the slow economic growth and job contraction after 2001 do not bode well for reducing poverty among Blacks and young people. Yet, according to recent government statistics, it appears that progress in reducing child poverty, although slowed by the economic recession, has not yet been reversed (U.S. DHHS, 2002: Table ES 1.2.A).

Although the Hispanic–White youth poverty ratio is lower than that of Blacks for most of the period displayed, this ratio proved rather resistant to change until after the mid-1990s. The falling Black youth poverty rate in the face of persistent Hispanic youth poverty resulted in some convergence of their rates. This trend also is worrisome because the population of Hispanics is growing much more rapidly than that of Blacks and currently represents a much larger share of all youth. Furthermore, Hispanic poverty is largely associated with low-wage work, which has proven more difficult to modify through policy interventions than nonworking poverty. Finally, the Asian–White youth poverty ratio has hovered around 1 throughout most of the 1990s, and despite initial convergence with Whites, began to rise during the latter part of the 1990s for reasons that are not well understood but may be related to immigration.

Because child poverty reflects parental earning capacity, it is closely associated with parental educational attainment. Despite the secular increase in U.S. education levels (Mare, 1995), unequal increases along racial and ethnic lines imply larger rather than smaller gaps for some groups. According to the National Center for Education Statistics (U.S. DOE, 2001), rising educational attainment of Black parents narrowed the race gap in parental schooling between 1974 and 1999, but the comparable schooling gap between Hispanic and White parents remained relatively constant. Changes in the volume and composition of immigration since 1970 further accentuated racial and ethnic educational inequality. This is because immigrants from Central and South America – the dominant share of recent arrivals – have education levels well below the national average, whereas

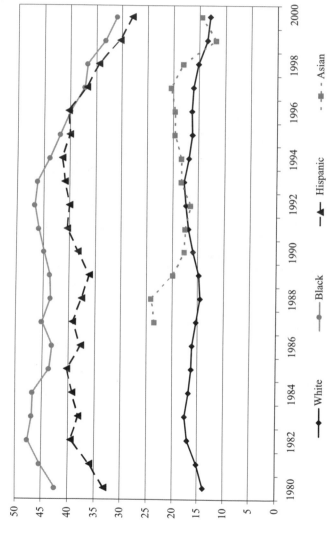

FIGURE 2.2. Percentage of youth aged 18 and under living in poverty by race and Hispanic origin: 1980–2000. *Source:* U.S. Census Bureau, 2002c, Table 3.

Asians are positively selected educationally vis-à-vis the U.S. population (Smith & Edmonston, 1997; Tienda, 2002).

As Figure 2.3 shows, the gap in the percentage of Hispanic and Black youth with college-educated parents actually rose over the 25 years between 1974 and 1999. This larger parental education gap reflects changes in Hispanic and Black mothers' and Hispanic fathers' college attainment because the gap between fathers of Black and White children remained constant (U.S. DOE, 2001: Table 2.4–1). Only 10 percent of Hispanic youth have college-educated fathers, and despite the rapid growth of the Hispanic population since 1974, this share increased only 2 percentage points over the 25 years between 1974 and 1999. By contrast, in 1999 one in three White youth had college-educated fathers, and this share had risen 14 percentage points since 1974. Only half as many Black as White youth had college-educated fathers, but over the 25 years, the share of Black youth reared by fathers holding college degrees rose from a meager 4 percent to 17 percent (Lloyd et al., 2001). The significance of these differentials cannot be overstated because of their implications for the transmission of socioeconomic disadvantages over generations and, thereby, the manifestation of racial and ethnic gaps in educational outcomes.

In large measure, the sizeable education deficit of Hispanic parents' vis-à-vis Whites reflects the impact of recent immigration of persons with low levels of education. There are small nativity differences in the percentages of adults with college degrees because migrants who gain admission under the occupational preferences are highly selected toward advanced degrees. However, the nativity differential in high school graduation is appreciable: 87 percent of native-born persons ages 25 and over are high school graduates, compared with 67 percent of the foreign-born (Tienda, 2002). These differentials reflect the comparatively low educational levels of recent immigrants from Central and South America, but especially Mexico.

Inequities in educational attainment of U.S. immigrant and minority youth are most starkly illustrated by the percentages who fail to complete high school. Because high school graduation no longer guarantees access to jobs that pay a living wage, the astoundingly high rates of premature withdrawal among Hispanic, but especially Mexican, youth bode ill for their life chances. Between 1967 and 2000, the White high school dropout rate was cut in half – from 15.5 to 7.7 percent. During that period, the Black dropout rate also was reduced by more than half, although it remains 5 percentage points above that of Whites. However, the Hispanic dropout rate, which has hovered around 28 to 30 percent throughout the 1980s and 1990s, after falling from 35 percent in the early 1970s, has proven quite resistant to change (Lloyd et al., 2001).

Figure 2.4 demonstrates how immigration has exacerbated racial and ethnic differences in educational attainment because for Hispanics, and Mexicans in particular, the high average dropout rates are pushed up by the

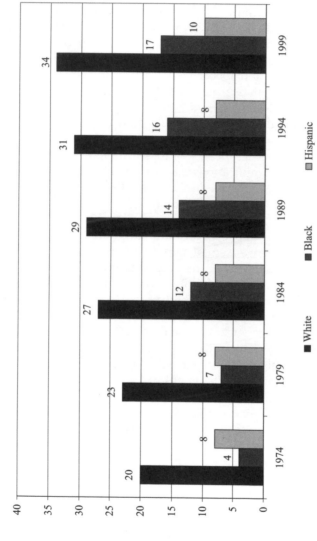

FIGURE 2.3. Racial and ethnic differences in percentages of youth ages 6–18 with college-educated fathers: 1974–1999. *Source:* U.S. DOE, 2000b, Table 5–1.

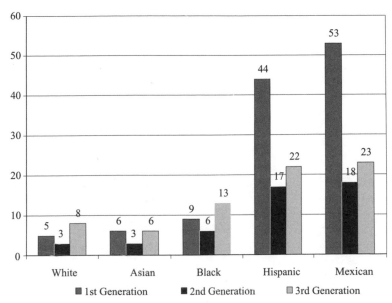

FIGURE 2.4. Racial and ethnic differences in percentages of youth ages 16–24 withdrawn from high school, by immigrant generation. Source: U.S. DOE, 1998, p. 84.

first generation. Almost half of Mexican immigrant youth and more than 40 percent of all Hispanic immigrant youth fail to complete high school. This compares with fewer than 10 percent of Black, Asian, and White immigrant youth. That dropout rates of second- and third-generation Hispanics also are substantially higher than their Asian, White, and Black foreign-born counterparts implicates other factors besides foreign birth in accounting for the pronounced educational underachievement of Latino youth.

Two such factors are proficiency in English and school readiness. Both indicators are correlated with parental education, but the underlying mechanisms are rather complex. Linguistic diversity is relatively trivial for Blacks and Whites, including the foreign-born, because the majority of Black and White immigrant youth hail from English-speaking countries. However, linguistic differences are quite salient for Asians, and especially Hispanic youth, among whom the foreign-born population shares have been rising for the last quarter century. Table 2.7 reveals that more than seven in ten Hispanic youth live in homes where a language other than English is spoken, compared with 51 percent of Asians and Others. Only trivial proportions of White and Black youth report that a non-English language is spoken at home. Furthermore, nearly one in four school-age Hispanics report having difficulty speaking English, compared with only 11.7 percent of Asian and Other youth. These linguistic indicators are important

TABLE 2.7. *Racial and Ethnic Differences in Language and Early Educational Proficiency*

	White	Black	Hispanic	Asian and Other
% Youth, Ages 5–17 Who Speak Non-English Language at Home[a]	3.9	4.5	70.9	51.0
% Youth, Ages 5–17 Who Have Difficulty With English[a]	1.0	1.0	23.4	11.7
% Kindergarteners in Top Quartile of:				
Math Proficiency[b]	32.0	10.0	14.0	38.0
Reading Proficiency[b]	30.0	15.0	15.0	39.0

[a] Data for 1999.
[b] Data for 1998.
Source: Federal Interagency Forum on Child and Family Statistics, 2002: Table POP4; U.S. DOE, 2000a: Tables 12–1 and 12–2.

because they signal difficulties not only in the ability of youth to comprehend and master academic material, but also in their parents' efficacy in navigating the school system to strengthen the support between the family and the institutional setting. Parents with limited English communication skills are less able to engage with the school system and to broker on behalf of their children, or to provide help with homework and to participate in various school activities.

If linguistic diversity were the main reason for scholastic underperformance of Black and Hispanic youth, Asians would score lower than both Whites and Blacks on standardized tests. However, as revealed in the lower panel of Table 2.7, White, Black, Hispanic, and Asian youth enter the school system at very uneven starting lines. The underpinnings of educational inequality begin at very early ages and widen during the primary school years (Reardon, 2003). This is clearly evident in the large differences in math and reading scores of minority and nonminority children upon arrival at the schoolhouse. Even before entering first grade, Asians outperform White children, but especially outperform Blacks and Hispanics. These differences are not about linguistic diversity; mostly they reflect the social class composition of immigrant and minority groups, especially the educational attainment of parents.

That large shares of Black and Hispanic youth fail to complete high school narrows their educational pipeline to college. Although college enrollment rates have been rising gradually for all groups, the gap between Hispanics on the one hand, and Blacks and Whites on the other hand, has widened over time. College enrollment rates have risen by about 14 percentage points for Blacks and Whites since the early 1970s, but by only

TABLE 2.8. *Racial and Ethnic Differentials in College Enrollment*[a]

	White	Black	Hispanic	Asian
% First Generation College Attendance	11	15	23	17
% Ever Enrolled in College by Age 20:				
Low SES	30	43	40	77
Middle SES	64	57	59	75
High SES	90	66	90	93
% Ages 18–24 Enrolled in College by Generation:				
First	45	37	12	49
Second	51	58	28	56
Third	38	29	22	57

[a] Data for 1994.

Source: U.S. DOE, 1996: Table 21; Unpublished data calculations from the U.S. DOE *National Education Longitudinal Study* (NELS) of 1988 Eighth Graders.

7 percentage points for Hispanics. Temporal data for Asians are less complete, but all sources show that their college enrollment rates remain well above those of Whites by a substantial margin (Lloyd et al., 2001). To some extent, differentials in college enrollment rates reflect socioeconomic differences – mainly disparities in parental education – but also values that make educational attainment a priority for both parents and their children. As Table 2.8 shows, even among low-SES families, almost 80 percent of Asian youth enroll in college, compared with about 30 to 40 percent of others. At the other extreme of the SES distribution, college enrollment is not differentiated among Whites, Hispanics, and Asians. However, high-SES Blacks are significantly less likely to enroll in college than their high-status White, Black, or Asian counterparts, which appears to parallel the experience of Caribbean youth residing in the United Kingdom.

That Hispanic youth are significantly more likely than Asians, Blacks, or Whites to be first-generation college-goers also lowers their likelihood of college attendance because the norms and expectations about post-secondary schooling are largely, though not exclusively, set by parental experiences. As the base of college-educated Hispanic parents continues to rise, greater numbers of college-educated youth will be socialized into the norms and expectations of post-secondary schooling. However, if unskilled immigration continues to increase the share of parents with less than high school diplomas, the prospects of narrowing the Hispanic–White education gap will be dimmed into the foreseeable future. This is partly why group differences in immigrant composition manifest themselves in racial and ethnic inequities in college enrollment, and why the association between generational status and college enrollment varies among demographic group. Only 12 percent of first-generation Hispanic youth enrolled in college compared with nearly half of all first-generation Asian youth, and more than one third of Black immigrant youth. For all groups except Asians, the highest college enrollment rates correspond to second-generation youth, yet Hispanics still lag far behind Blacks and Whites on this score.

The reasons for these inequities lie partly in social class differences, but not exclusively; equally important are the group differences in access to quality primary- and secondary-level education and the unequal propensity of youth to leave school early in order to secure a job. Ahituv and his associates (Ahituv, Tienda, & Hotz, 2000) identified these modalities of school-leaving that correspond roughly to racial and ethnic groups. Hispanic youth enter the workforce early, but do so at the expense of their schooling, whereas Black youth enter the workforce at later ages but prolong their education. White youth combine the most advantageous of both circumstances by entering the labor force early, and thereby acquiring valuable work experience, and also prolonging their education, acquiring more formal skills, on average, than either Blacks or Hispanics. Although Hispanic youth's decision to enter the workforce at younger ages may provide short-term relief for economic disadvantages, it implies lifelong consequences for those who enter the workforce at the expense of continuing their education (Ahituv & Tienda, in press; Schoenhals, Tienda, & Schneider, 1998). However, the apparent group modalities in the transition from school to work reflect differences in family background more than racial and ethnic differences in predispositions toward employment or education.

Summary and Implications

Immigration has diversified the populations of both the United Kingdom and the United States during the past three or so decades, and this trend is expected to continue well into the future. With a population of just under 60 million in 2000, the United Kingdom is expected to grow to 65 million by 2025. The minority share of the total population is expected to rise because around two thirds of the projected population growth assumes a net annual increase of 135,000 migrants (Barham, 2002). Similarly, based on recent trends, U.S. population projections indicate that over the next 10 years, minority ethnic groups will be responsible for more than half of the increase in the U.S. working-age population (Mosisa, 2002). This portends even greater ethno-racial diversification well into the future. According to Prewitt (2002), whether diversity is defined linguistically, culturally, religiously, or ethnically, the United States is the most demographically complex nation in world history.

Obviously, the characteristics of future migrants will continue to shape the socioeconomic contours of racial and ethnic inequality in both countries. Ethnic minorities in the United Kingdom are younger, live in larger households, and generally live on lower incomes compared with the native White population (Pathak, 2000; UK DWP, 2002; White, 2002). Likewise, U.S. Black and Hispanic minority populations are younger, less well educated, and of lower socioeconomic status than their nonminority White counterparts, although as a group, Asians are more similar to the White majority and they fare better educationally. That both the U.S. Asian and Hispanic populations are quite heterogeneous in their socioeconomic composition renders these generalizations based on pan-ethnic groups somewhat tenuous for specific nationalities. Similarly, in the United Kingdom, there are great differences in life chances of Asian minority groups, as Indians exhibit the highest status, whereas Pakistani and Bangladeshi youth rank last in almost all socioeconomic indicators.

In both countries, parental socioeconomic profiles signal bleaker life chances and opportunities for minority and immigrant youth compared with their White counterparts. Moreover, many immigrant parents lack proficiency in English when they migrate, and this hinders their integration prospects in addition to the social exclusion on the basis of phenotype. For example, a recent study conducted by Alba and colleagues (Alba, Logan, Lutz, & Stults, 2002) argued that for Asian and European immigrants, English is adopted at nearly the same rate, whereas for descendents of Spanish-speaking immigrants, the process is slower. This implies that the socioeconomic divide between Hispanic and Asian minorities could continue to widen in the future. Although many migrants to the United Kingdom are from Commonwealth countries where English is spoken, proficiency levels are sufficiently varied that labor market and scholastic performance are affected.

Of course, the prevalence of child poverty remains a critical risk factor for negative psychosocial outcomes of all youth, but particularly minorities, whose chances of being poor are considerably higher than native Whites. According to Dickens and Ellwood (2003) social policies in the United Kingdom are more effective in reducing child poverty compared with those pursued in the United States. Their comparative social policy analysis focuses on the welfare policies implemented by the Blair and Clinton administrations. The UK strategy sought to reduce child poverty through redistribution of wealth, whereas the U.S. approach focused on moving welfare recipients into paid employment. Both governments cast their child welfare policies within the broad rubric of eliminating social exclusion, but according to Brewer, Clark, and Goodman (2003), a redistributive agenda "necessarily implies a bolder and more redistributive programme than would a focus on absolute poverty" (p. F256). Given the relatively smaller size of the UK minority population, their redistributive approach likely will be more effective in reducing racial and ethnic differences in economic well-being.

One important puzzle that emerges from a comparison of minority and immigrant youth in the United States and United Kingdom concerns the plight of Caribbean Blacks, who in relative terms fare poorly in the United Kingdom but not in the United States, where Jamaican youth outperform their native-born African American counterparts in many social and economic outcomes. This is troubling because Caribbean Black youth are *not* the most economically disadvantaged immigrant minority on their arrival to the United Kingdom, and their parents are not the most educationally disadvantaged. Perceptions of their underachievement may serve to contribute to their low performance in the education and employment arenas, but the triggering mechanisms are not obvious (Gillborn, 1996). Prejudice and discrimination are strong contenders for the educational underperformance of Caribbean Black youth, as 62 percent of the young men interviewed by Fitzgerald and colleagues (Fitzgerald, Finch, & Nove, 2000) felt they had been treated unfairly because of their skin color. Caribbean Blacks ages 18 to 30 were more likely than Whites to experience protracted unemployment, and despite their acknowledgment of the importance of a good education for securing a well-paying job when interviewed, educational underperformance remains the norm.

By contrast, U.S. Caribbean immigrants have fared better than native African Americans. Kasinitz and associates (Kasinitz, Battle, & Miyares, 2001) report that children of Anglophone Caribbean immigrants are relatively well-off, particularly compared to other second-generation immigrant minority youth. According to Waters (1999), Caribbean immigrants are more apt to abide by the immigrant work ethic, and many employers are more positively predisposed to hiring recent immigrants who are perceived as hard working than unskilled natives. Another purported reason for the relative success of U.S. Caribbean immigrants is that they exhibit less animosity toward the country's White majority (Foner, 1985). However, as the social distinctions between Caribbean Blacks and African Americans blur, particularly among second-generation adolescents, their relatively advantaged status in the eyes of Whites erodes. A less sanguine view of the apparent advantage of U.S. Caribbean Blacks compared with their UK counterparts derives from social comparison theory. Simply stated, in the United States, Caribbean Blacks are compared with the lowest standing group created by the legacy of slavery and reified by decades of discrimination and social exclusion. Moreover, analyses of the experience of Caribbean Blacks residing in the United Kingdom have focused on their downward trajectory, which is shared by other U.S. immigrant groups.

Kasinitz and his colleagues (2001) maintained that race, rather than national origin, is the more salient attribute shaping the life chances of immigrant children from the Anglophone Caribbean. Moreover, it is not clear that other Caribbean groups, such as Haitians, ever enjoyed the protections of being a Black immigrant in the United States, however short-lived this privileged status may be. For example, based on 20 years of fieldwork, Stepick and his colleagues (2001) claim that Miami Haitians experience prejudice and discrimination from teachers, administrators, and students. That Haitian youth's experiences with discrimination differ from those of Jamaicans suggests that Caribbean origin per se is not a consistent protective factor for Black immigrant minorities residing in the United States. Therefore, a systematic comparison of the Caribbean Black experience in the United States and the United Kingdom could provide analytical leverage for teasing out the context- and group-specific experiences that produce such clearly divergent outcomes for these ethnic groups.

The comparison of the early fates of Caribbean-origin Black youth in the United States and United Kingdom illustrates the difficulty of attributing social exclusion and economic disadvantage to a single indicator, such as membership of a racial or ethnic group. Circumstances such as the timing of migration, reception factors in the host community, resettlement patterns, and the cultural differences between origin and destination all contribute to the socioeconomic integration of immigrant youth and their construction of ethnic identities. Minority youth, particularly those from third and higher generations, cannot directly trace their disadvantaged statuses to the migration experience, although these vestiges persist to varying degrees beyond the immigrant generation. That minority and immigrant youth are more likely to be poor and to have parents with low education poses formidable analytic challenges in unraveling group differences in psychosocial outcomes, such as criminal activity, schizophrenia, and school achievement, from their association with low social standing. The immigration experience itself can produce social dislocations with variable individual and group-specific consequences. As the following chapters illustrate, the migration paradigm outlined in the introductory chapter to this volume provides important analytical leverage to begin the task of separating racial and ethnic variation in psychosocial outcomes from social class and the intergenerational continuities that are perpetuated as a result. A remaining challenge is that of explaining the persistence of widened racial and ethnic inequities among third- and higher-order generations. The migration paradigm may be helpful for this purpose, but is clearly insufficient to explain the persisting significance of race among nonimmigrant minority groups.

References

Ahituv, A., & Tienda, M. (in press). Employment activity and school continuation decisions of young women. *Journal of Labor Economics, 22*(1): 115–158.
Ahituv, A., Tienda, M., & Hotz, V. J. (2000). The transition from school to work: Black, Hispanic and White men in the 1980's. In R. Marshall (Ed.), *Back to Shared Prosperity.* Armonk, NY: M. E. Sharpe.

Alba, R., Logan, J., Lutz, A., & Stults, B. (2002). Only English by the third generation? Loss and preservation of the mother tongue among the grandchildren of contemporary immigrants. *Demography, 39*(3), 467–484.

Barham, C. (2002). Labour market and demography project. *Labour Market Trends, 110*(3), 151–158.

Brewer, M., Clark, T., & Goodman, A. (2003). What really happened to child poverty in the UK under Labour's first term? *The Economic Journal, 113* (June), F240–F257.

Brooks-Gunn, J., & Duncan, G. J. (1997). The effects of poverty on children. *The Future of Children, 7*(2), 55–71.

Coleman, D., & Salt, J. (1992). *The British Population: Patterns, Trends, and Processes.* Oxford: Oxford University Press.

Coleman, D., & Salt, J. (Eds.) (1996). *Ethnicity in the 1991 Census* (Vol. 1). London: HMSO.

Columbia University. (2001). *Summary table of demographic, labor market and educational data.* The Clearinghouse on International Developments in Child, Youth and Family Policies at Columbia University. Retrieved April 15, 2003, from http://www.childpolicyintl.org/youthpoliciestables/schooltowork/table40.pdf

Dale, A., Fieldhouse, E., Shaheen, N., & Virinder, K. (2002). The labour market prospects for Pakistani and Bangladeshi women. *Work, Employment and Society, 16*(1), 5–25.

Dickens, R., & Ellwood, D. (2003). Child poverty in Britain and the United States. *The Economic Journal, 113*(June), F219–F239.

Federal Interagency Forum on Child and Family Statistics. (2002). *America's Children: Key National Indicators of Well-Being, 2002.* Washington, DC: U.S. Government Printing Office.

Fitzgerald, R., Finch, S., & Nove, A. (2000). *Black Caribbean young men's experiences of education and employment.* Research Brief 186. Department for Education and Employment, UK Government. Retrieved April 15, 2003, from http://www.dfes.gov.uk/research/data/uploadfiles/RB186.doc

Foner, N. (1985). Race and color: Jamaican migrants in London and New York City. *International Migration Review, 19*(4), 708–27.

Gillborn, D. (1996). Exclusions from school. *University of London Institute for Education Viewpoint* (No. 5).

Gillborn, D., & Mirza, H. S. (2000). *Educational Inequality: Mapping race, class and gender.* London: Office for Standards in Education Institute of Education. Retrieved April 6, 2002, from http://www.OFSTED.gov.uk/publications/docs/447.pdf

Goldstein, J., & Morning, A. (2000). The multiple-race population of the United States: Issues and estimates. *Proceedings of the National Academy of Sciences of the United States of America, 97*(11), 6230–6235.

Goldstein, J., & Morning, A. (2002). Back in the box: Allocating multiple-race responses back to single races. In J. Perlmann & M. Waters (Eds.), *Mixed results.* New York: Russell Sage Foundation.

Kasinitz, P., Battle, J., & Miyares, I. (2001). Fade to Black? The children of West Indian immigrants in southern Florida. In R. Rumbaut and A. Portes (Eds.), *Ethnicities: Children of immigrants in America.* Berkeley: University of California Press.

Lloyd, K., Tienda, M., & Zajacova, A. (2001). Trends in educational achievement of minority students since *Brown v. Board of Education.* In T. Ready, C. Edley, & C. Snow (Eds.), *Achieving High Educational Standards for All: Conference summary.* Washington, DC: National Academy Press.

Mare, R. D. (1995). Changes in educational attainment and school enrollment. In R. Farley (Ed.), *State of the Union: America in the 1990s*. New York: Russell Sage Foundation.

Massey, D. S., & Denton, N. A. (1993). *American apartheid: Segregation and the making of the underclass*. Cambridge, MA: Harvard University Press.

Meyer, J. (2001). Percent of population by selected age groups, race, and Hispanic or Latino origin: 2000, *U.S. Census Bureau Brief* C2KBR/01–12.

Modood, T., & Berthoud, R. (Eds.) (1997). *Ethnic minorities in Britain: Diversity and disadvantage (The fourth national survey of ethnic minorities)*. London: Policy Studies Institute.

Morning, A. (2000). Who is multiracial? Definitions and decisions. *Sociological Imagination, 37*, 209–229.

Mosisa, A. T. (2002). The role of foreign-born workers in the U.S. economy. *Monthly Labor Review, 125*, 3–14.

Orfield, G., Eaton, S. E., & The Harvard Project on School Desegregation. (1996). *Dismantling desegregation: The quiet reversal of Brown v. Board of Education*. New York: New Press.

Pathak, S. (2000). Race research for the future ethnicity in education, training and the labour market. *Department of Education and Employment Research Topic Paper*, 01, March. Retrieved March 2, 2003, from http://www.dfes.gov.uk/research/data/uploadfiles/Rtp01.pdf

Portes, A., & Rumbaut, R. G. (1996). *Immigrant America* (2nd ed.). Berkeley: University of California Press.

Prewitt, K. (2002). Demography, diversity and democracy: The 2000 Census story. *The Brookings Review, 20*, 6–9.

Reardon, S. F. (2003). *Sources of educational inequality: The growth of racial/ethnic and socioeconomic test score gaps in kindergarten and first grade*. Working Paper 03–05R, University Park, PA: Population Research Institute at Penn State University.

Schmidley, D. (2003). "The foreign-born population in the United States: March 2002," *Current Population Reports*, P20–359. Washington, DC: U.S. Census Bureau.

Schoenhals, M., Tienda, M., & Schneider, B. (1998). Educational consequences of adolescent employment. *Social Forces, 77*, 723–761.

Smith, J. P., & Edmonston, B. (1997). *The New Americans*. Washington, DC: National Academy Press.

Stepick, A., Stepick, C. D., Eugene, L., Teed, D., & Labissiere, Y. (2001). Shifting identities and intergenerational conflict: Growing up Haitian in Miami. In R. Rumbaut & A. Portes (Eds.), *Ethnicities: Children of immigrants in America*. Berkeley: University of California Press.

Tienda, M. (2002). Demography and the social contract. *Demography, 39*, 587–616.

Tienda, M., & Wilson, W. J. (Eds.). (2002). *Youth in cities: A cross-national perspective*. Cambridge, UK: Cambridge University Press.

UK Cabinet Office. (2001). *Ethnic Minorities and the labour market*. Retrieved April 17, 2003, from http://www.cabinet-office.gov.uk/innovation/2001/ethnicity/scope2.htm

UK Cabinet Office. (2003). *Ethnic minorities and the labour market*. Retrieved April 15, 2003, from http://www.cabinet-office.gov.uk/innovation/2003/ethnic/report/report.pdf

UK DWP (UK Department for Work and Pensions). (2002). *Households below average income 2000/01.* Retrieved April 15, 2003, from http://www.dwp.gov.uk/asd/hbai/hbai2001/pdfs/ch4tabs/tab4_1.xls

UK Office of National Statistics. (2002a). Highest qualification held: by gender and ethnic group, 2000–01. *Social Trends,* 32. Retrieved April 24, 2003, from http://www.nationalstatistics.gov.uk/downloads/theme_social/Social_Trends32/Social_Trends32.pdf

UK Office of National Statistics. (2002b). *Annual local area labour force survey, 2001/02.* Retrieved April 16, 2003, from http://www.statistics.gov.uk/STATBASE/Expodata/Spreadsheets/D6206.xls

UK Office of National Statistics. (2003a). *Census 2001 – Ethnicity and religion in England and Wales.* Retrieved April 18, 2003, from http://www.statistics.gov.uk/census2001/profiles/commentaries/ethnicity.asp

UK Office of National Statistics. (2003b).*UK 2003: The official yearbook of the United Kingdom of Great Britain and Northern Ireland.* Retrieved April 17, 2003, from http://www.statistics.gov.uk/StatBase/Product.asp?vlnk=5703

UK Office of National Statistics. (2003c). *Country of birth: Census 2001, Key statistics for local authorities.* Retrieved April 17, 2003, from http://www.nationalstatistics.gov.uk/StatBase/Expodata/Spreadsheets/D6559.xls

UK Office of National Statistics. (2003d). *Population size.* Retrieved April 17, 2003, from http://www.statistics.gov.uk/CCI/nugget.asp?ID=273&Pos=5&ColRank=2&Rank=1000

UK Office of National Statistics. (2003e). Children under 16 by ethnic group, 2001–02. *Labour force survey.* Retrieved April 15, 2003, from http://www.statistics.gov.uk/STATBASE/Expodata/Spreadsheets/D5701.xls

UK Office of Population Censuses and Surveys. (1983). *Census 1981: National report. Part 1.* London: Her Majesty's Stationery Office.

UK OFSTED (UK Office for Standards and Education). (1999). *Raising the attainment of minority ethnic pupils: School and LEA responses* (Publication No. HMI 170). Retrieved April 6, 2003, from http://www.ofsted.gov.uk/publications/docs/771.pdf

UK SEU (UK Social Exclusion Unit). (2000). *National Strategy for Neighbourhood Renewal: Minority ethnic issues in social exclusion and neighbourhood renewal* (Chapter 2). Retrieved April 15, 2003, from http://www.socialexclusionunit.gov.uk/publications/reports/html/bmezip/02.htm

U.S. Census Bureau. (2000). *Total population from Census 2000 summary file 1, 100-Percent Data.* Washington, DC: U.S. Census Bureau.

U.S. Census Bureau. (2001). Profile of the foreign-born population in the United States: 2000. *Current Population Reports,* Series P–23, No. 206.

U.S. Census Bureau. (2002a). Entries for "United Kingdom" and "United States" in *International Database.* Retrieved December 12, 2002, from http://www.census.gov/ipc/www/idbnew.html

U.S. Census Bureau. (2002b). *Statistical Abstract of the United States of America.* Washington, DC: U.S. Government Printing Office.

U.S. Census Bureau. (2002c). *Poverty status of people, by age, race, and Hispanic origin:1959 to 2001.* Retrieved April 16, 2003, from http://www.census.gov/hhes/poverty/histpov/hstpov3.html

U.S. Census Bureau. (2003). *National population estimates – characteristics* (Table S-EST2001–ASRO-02). Retrieved April 17, 2003, from http://eire.census. gov/popest/data/national/tables/asro/US-EST2001–ASRO-02.php

U.S. DHHS (U.S. Department of Health and Human Services). (2002). *Trends in the well-being of America's children & youth, 2002.* Washington, DC: Office of the Assistant Secretary for Planning and Evaluation.

U.S. DOE (U.S. Department of Education). (1996). *Dropout rates in the United States.* National Center for Education Statistics report 96–663. Retrieved April 25, 2003, from http://nces.ed.gov/pubs96/96863.pdf

U.S. DOE (U.S. Department of Education). (1998). *The condition of education, 1998, Indicator 24.* Retrieved April 17, 2003, from http://nces.ed.gov/pubs98/ condition98/c98p24.pdf

U.S. DOE (U.S. Department of Education). (2000a). *The condition of education, 2000.* Retrieved April 17, 2003, from http://nces.ed.gov/pubsearch/pubsinfo.asp? pubid=2000062.

U.S. DOE (U.S. Department of Education). (2001). *The condition of education, 2001, Indicator 4.* National Center for Education Statistics. Retrieved April 6, 2003, from http://nces.ed.gov/pubs2001/2001/125.pdf

U.S. DOE (U.S. Department of Education). (2003). *Status and trends in the education of Hispanics.* National Center for Education Statistics Report 2003–008. Washington, DC: U.S. Government Printing Office.

U.S. INS (U.S. Immigration and Naturalization Service). (2001). *Statistical yearbook of the Immigration and Naturalization Service.* Washington, DC: U.S. Government Printing Office. Retrieved April 16, 2003, from http://www.immigration. gov/graphics/shared/aboutus/statistics/Yearbook2001.pdf

Waters, M. (1999). *Black identities: West Indian immigrant dreams and American realities.* New York: Russell Sage Foundation.

White, A. (2002). *Social focus in brief: Ethnicity 2002.* London: Office for National Statistics. Retrieved March 2, 2003, from http://www.statistics.gov.uk/ downloads/theme-social/social-focus-in-brief/ethnicity/ethnicity.pdf

Wilson, W. J. (1987). *The truly disadvantaged.* Chicago: University of Chicago Press.

3

The Multiple Facets of Ethnicity

Michael Rutter and Marta Tienda

Dictionary definitions of ethnicity clearly bring out the complexity of the concept. Thus, the fifth edition of the *Shorter Oxford English Dictionary* (OED 2002) notes that it refers to population groups "sharing a distinctive cultural and historical tradition, often associated with race, nationality, or religion, by which the group identifies itself and others recognize it." Ethnic minority is defined in terms of an "ethnic group differing physically or culturally from the rest of the community." Constituting part (but only one part) of the concept of ethnicity, race is defined rather differently in terms of "a tribe, nation or people, regarded as of common stock" – with the key feature being biological descent from a common ancestor. A racial group is, then, an ethnic group whose members are believed, by others if not by themselves, to be physiologically distinctive (Alba, 1992). Biologically, according to the definition, race means a genetically or morphologically distinct species or subspecies.

Obviously, these multiple facets complicate the conceptualization of ethnicity. Does it mean a cultural, religious, or national group; or rather does it refer to a genetically distinct subspecies of humankind with physical characteristics that make it recognizable? When these different facets pull in different directions, which should be given preference? And, who should decide how to weight and prioritize the multiple facets of ethnicity? Clearly, there is no single unambiguously "correct" answer to those questions; much depends on the purposes to which the concept is applied.

Accordingly, in what follows, we elaborate on these multiple facets and others that illustrate how ethnicity manifests itself over time and across settings. We begin by considering the implications of measuring ethnicity using self-identification. Following an overview of the social constructionist approach to ethnicity, we review the debate about racial differences in IQ, both to raise questions about how genetic factors operate (or not) in producing ethnic variation and to highlight methodological challenges for teasing apart ethnic differences. This provides the foundation to our third section about the genetic construction of ethnicity. The remainder of the chapter considers possible mediators of ethnic effects, which are framed as questions for further research in the concluding section.

Ethnicity as a Self-Description or Personal Construct

Ethnicity is one of the most difficult attributes for researchers to measure reliably and validly (Davis, 1991; Kertzer & Arel, 2002; Perlmann & Waters, 2002). It has become standard practice in both national statistics and research surveys to assign ethnicity solely on the basis of self-identification. Ethnically, each of us is whatever we decide. This approach is reasonable given the absence of any independent indicator of what the "true" designation "should" be. However, in practice, people lack a free choice because they are forced to select from a predetermined set of categories (which usually includes a residual "other"). But even when given consistent, predetermined categories, people respond inconsistently over half the time (Petersen, 1987). In addition, political (and other) regulations add further constraints. The United States operated under the "one-drop" rule for decades where census categories such as quadroon and octoroon reinforced "blackness" of mixed-race persons (Davis, 1991). Similarly, when apartheid operated in South Africa, any non-White "blood" in the biological lineage forced a classification of non-White. Nazi Germany used similar characterizations with respect to Jewish ancestry.

Although some explicit designations of multiracial categories are no longer used officially, racial divisions are still used in practice. For example, many countries prohibit adoption of mixed-race children by White parents because mixed race is treated as non-White. Yet, in countries such as the United Kingdom where mixed marriages between "Whites" and people of African-Caribbean background are extremely common (see Chapter 11 of this volume), the non-White segment of the population will increase simply because of such arbitrary ways of handling mixed-race parentage.

In the U.S., where cross-ethnic coupling and marriage is rising, multi-race reporting was allowed in the census of 2000, but all persons who report more than one race are allocated to the non-White group for reporting purposes. Even with the option of selecting multiple races, a growing share of Hispanics – in excess of forty percent – self-classify as "other" – rejecting the pre-established categories.

Laws are also full of arbitrary classification rules. Twenty years ago, UK citizenship for a child could only be claimed if the father had UK citizenship; the same rights did not apply if only the mother was British. Conversely, by Jewish law, being Jewish is transmitted by the mother and not the father. For a long while, U.S. law forced nationality according to place of birth (Petersen, 1987).[1]

Another classification issue complicating the study of ethnicity is that the categories used differ across countries; comparing the United States and United Kingdom, for illustration, prevailing categories reflect different historical traditions, migration patterns, and the resulting population composition. Before 1970, the U.S. census did not enumerate the Hispanic population as a national, pan-ethnic group. Rather, surname, birthplace, and parentage items were used to identify regional subgroups (Bean & Tienda, 1987). Currently, "Hispanics" constitute a very large, highly diverse, and rapidly growing segment of the U.S. population, but one so small in the United Kingdom that its existence is not even recognized. Conversely, there is a very large Asian community in the United Kingdom that is, moreover, further subdivided along religious lines. That has no direct parallel in the United States, yet the census enumerates several Asian nationalities as separate "races" – a practice begun in response to successful lobbying of public advisors that continued through the successive two censuses (Petersen, 1987).

Census categories are often rejected by subnational populations. Within the United Kingdom, the Welsh people clearly see themselves as a meaningfully distinct ethnic group on the grounds of both language and a different cultural heritage (and, in recent times, also a degree of self-government), but Welsh is seldom included in lists of ethnic categories. Much the same, albeit to a somewhat lesser degree, applies to the Scots, except that few people now speak Gaelic. In the United States, peoples from Central and South America reject the pan-ethnic labels, preferring instead labels that identify nationalities, such as Mexican, Colombian, or Peruvian (Brodie et al., 2002).

The salience of ethnicity and its constituent elements vary greatly according to social context. Thus, within England, religious affiliation as Catholic or Protestant is seldom consequential, whereas in Northern Ireland, it is the defining aspect of group membership. The significance of language also varies greatly across countries. In Canada, it matters greatly whether someone is Francophone or Anglophone; in Belgium, it matters whether someone is Flemish or French speaking; and in Spain, it matters whether someone speaks Catalán or Gallego. By contrast, within England, for most people it matters little (to the individuals themselves or to the broader community) whether a person's first language was French, German, Spanish, or English, and in large cosmopolitan cities such as London, New York, and Los Angeles, the diversity of languages spoken at

---

[1] When Rutter first lived in the United States, an act of Congress was required to allow his entry because the law there classified him as Lebanese despite the fact that, by both Lebanese law and British law, he was British.

home is enormous. Thus, at a local secondary school participating in a recent study by Rutter, the families of the student population represented 67 different languages. Although that mattered greatly with respect to communications between the school and the parents, it did not in most cases coincide with clearly demarcated ethnic groupings. In the United States, however, accented English often serves as a marker for racial group membership, and Spanish speakers are assumed to be Hispanic.

Presumably, the ethnic group membership young people choose for themselves is meaningful because it reflects cultural traditions or values or because it will identify the main peer group identity. However, because self-designated ethnicity is a highly fluid psychological self-concept, there are many exceptions. For example, an adolescent adoptee born to Gypsy parents insisted to both his friends and his school that he was African Caribbean. He explained to his counselor that he felt that this carried status (through associations with pop stars, footballers, and the like), whereas being Gypsy was a source of shame. However, in the area where he lived, there were scarcely any young people of African-Caribbean background; hence his professed ethnicity reflected neither family nor peer-group culture or values (about which he knew relatively little). An adolescent girl born and reared in London by Jamaican-born parents was told, with great pleasure, by her parents that the next doctor whom she would see at the clinic was Jamaican. She was very fed up being saddled with someone she termed a "foreigner"; she saw herself as primarily a Cockney Londoner; being "Black" was of some importance, but she did not feel any connection with her parents' birthplace. Two adolescent brothers born to the same mixed-race parents, but with one youth born in England and the other in Trinidad, differed in the ethnicity they professed when filling in school questionnaires. The first described himself as "English" and the second as "African Caribbean," although both were light brown in skin color and both were part of predominantly "White" (but ethnically mixed) peer groups.

Using a categorical self-descriptive approach to classify ethnicity poses three main problems. First, it assumes that a single term can encompass the most salient aspects of ethnic identity, which for many people makes little or no sense. Religion, skin color, nationality, language, country of origin, and cultural affiliation may differ in their importance and meanings, depending on social and political context as well as stage of individual development. Forcing a choice between these damages the validity of one's self-concept. Second, there is no evidence that a categorical approach is preferable to a dimensional one. A categorical approach to race is nonsensical because most people's biological heritage involves a mixture of races, whether recognized or not. A dimensional measure designating particular types of admixture would provide a more valid representation of race, but as the recent U.S. experience shows, there is no "natural limit" to the number and precision of categories, which might undermine their value (Prewitt, 2002). The same applies to other indices of ethnicity. Thus, for example, the importance of religious affiliations and engagement in religious practices are obviously dimensional. Third, the self-descriptive approach presupposes that it is each person's own self-concept that matters most, whereas, at least for some psychosocial features, it may be the response of others that is most decisive. That most data sources impose self-descriptions of ethnicity requires care both to acknowledge their limitations and to consider multiple facets of ethnicity whenever possible.

Social Construction of Ethnicity

The foregoing discussion underscores the fluid nature of ethnicity, illustrating myriad and arbitrary ways through which ethnic differences are produced, maintained, and transformed. For individuals to self-identify presumes the existence of categories that are both meaningful and practical for reporting purposes. Sometimes these emerge after demographic changes that lead to revised taxonomies. Government agencies play a direct role in the construction of ethnic classification schemes, partly for the purpose of bureaucratic accounting, partly in response to identity politics, and partly in direct response to new realities, such as those fostered by large waves of immigration (Kertzer & Arel, 2002; Petersen, 1987; Prewitt, 2002). Changes in classification schemes and enumeration practices can have dramatic effects on the size of ethnic and minority populations, as illustrated by the fourfold increase in the size of the U.S. Native American population over a 30-year period. Both changes in enumeration schedules that required listing a tribal affiliation and the expansion of social benefits tied to Native American heritage encouraged individuals to self-identify as American Indians (Goldscheider, 2002), but the changing social circumstances that reduce the penalties and stigma of self-identification also contribute to higher willingness of individuals to claim part-Indian heritage.

The social locations of ethnic groups depend on various social and political processes, such as assimilation, discrimination, subordination, stigmatization, and the resulting classification systems and social labels. Sociological perspectives on the construction of ethnicity emphasize how shared experiences and cultural traditions enable groups to develop collective identities and group boundaries in response to intergroup contact. Of particular importance are the historically specific circumstances that bring culturally distinct groups into contact (Lieberson, 1961; Noel, 1968); the spatial arrangements that shape the nature and intensity of intergroup contact (Heitmeyer, 2002); and the specific interactions around which meaning is constructed (Chapter 11 of this volume).

Sociologists studying immigration reported long ago that a common sense of nationality or ethnic identity emerges only after migration, which triggers self-awareness through cultural contrast. Beginning with the Chicago school of ethnic relations through the neoclassical statement of Milton Gordon (1964), conventional wisdom held that, over time, new-comers would "melt" into their host societies, producing either a new ethnic amalgam or a plural society, where ethnic differences were socially inconsequential, or symbolic at best. However, many groups proved to be unmeltable – including several lacking immigrant origins, such as African Americans and Native Americans. Moreover, under some circumstances, ethnic differences were accentuated over time rather than diminished – a phenomenon Portes and Rumbaut (1996, 2001) dubbed "reactive ethnicity." Presumably, when immigrant groups predisposed to assimilate encounter rejection from the host society, they respond by accentuating their differences, capitalizing on attributes that underscore apartness from their hostile hosts (Portes & Rumbaut, 2001).

Perhaps the most central concern in sociological approaches to ethnicity is how group membership acquires its social content, specifically with respect to location in the stratification system. That much ethnic variation in psychosocial outcomes can be traced to group differences in class membership makes this line of inquiry particularly important for understanding the causal mechanisms that undergird observed differences among groups. The dominant paradigm for understanding the association between group membership and socioeconomic status is Milton Gordon's (1964) assimilation typology, which begins with acculturation, proceeds to structural assimilation, and concludes with civic and identification assimilation (that is, unhyphenated American). It has been challenged for presuming a linear succession leading to ineluctable acceptance and absorption of immigrant and minority groups into the social mainstream, but a compelling alternative has not been proposed (Alba & Nee, 1999).

Numerous sociological studies show that the more that new immigrant minorities are similar to the dominant receiving society in terms of physical appearance, class background, religion, and language, the more favorable and swifter their integration into the host society (Portes & Rumbaut, 2001). However, evidence that not all groups assimilate completely; that some groups become integrated more easily than others; and that intercultural contact produces reciprocal adaptation processes warranted some revision of the assimilation paradigm, but not its total rejection (Gans, 1979). For example, comparing the immigrant and second generations, Portes and Rumbaut (2001) distinguish among dissonant acculturation, consonant acculturation, and selective acculturation – each with different implications for the tension between parents and children, as well as the social support parents are likely to receive from other members of the community.

The correspondence between national origin and economic disadvantage requires identifying the circumstances that eventuate into segmented assimilation for some, reifying ethnic minority status with disadvantage, while allowing for the emergence of symbolic ethnicity that carries relatively few socioeconomic consequences for others (see Gans, 1979). Portes' (1995) notion of segmented assimilation, which recognizes the possibility of immigrants' downward mobility, mirrors Joan Vincent's (1974) distinction between minority and ethnic groups – one used by Nelson and Tienda (1985) to explain the diverse socioeconomic trajectories of Mexican, Puerto Rican, and Cuban immigrants to the United States. Although both ethnic and minority groups are collectivities sharing common cultural norms, values, identities, and so forth, they differ in the extent to which they have access to the reward system of the dominant society and whether ethnic labels are a matter of individual choice. To wit, all minority groups are ethnic groups, but the reverse does not hold.

Just as individuals can alter their self-conceptions, so too can groups change their boundaries to become more or less inclusive. That ethnicity is partly constructed around outwardly visible physical and cultural attributes serves to maintain boundaries. "Racial" differences are the most obvious example, but language and dress also demarcate boundaries among groups. The rigidity of group boundaries to a large extent depends on the stigmatization of particular groups and the social institutions instituted to maintain apartness. Residential segregation of the Black population in the United States and in apartheid South Africa are perhaps the most blatant examples. The caste system operated to similar effect for many decades on the Indian subcontinent, and its vestiges still influence intergroup relations. In the United States, decades of exclusion from all facets of social and economic life reified "blackness" with inferior status positions, such that the African American population became "a self-conscious group with an ethnic identity" (Davis, 1991, p. 15).

Because people construct meaning through their social interaction, social labeling, which involves the social assignment of identity to others (or to self), also contributes to the social construction of ethnicity. Once accepted, ethnic labels acquire meanings from the contexts in which they emerge and evolve. Labeling theory gained prominence through its application to crime and delinquency, but it is helpful for understanding the social construction of ethnicity because labels are often stigmatizing and thereby serve as the basis for discriminatory treatment.[2] Labeling is crucial for understanding the social construction of ethnicity first because it demarcates group boundaries, which in turn acquire meanings based on shared

---

[2] Economists and sociologists refer to "statistical discrimination" when individuals are treated unequally by virtue of belonging to a low status group. That is, if employers believe that particular groups are poor workers, knowing an individual job applicant is a member of the devalued group will increase the chance that the applicant will be denied a job.

identities. Second, labeling reifies social categories, even when the initial foundations on which the groups were demarcated cease to exist. Third, social classification serves to channel positive and negative attributions, with the latter frequently leading to stigmatization. Fourth, labels create a foundation for individual identification, often fueling identity politics and, depending on group placement in the class structure, reactive ethnicity. The following section illustrates the power of labeling using medical examples.

Labeling as a Social Construction

The social construction perspective applies to features that are clearly objective and easily defined, as well as to those that are essentially "fuzzy" in concept. Thus, there is a straightforward legal reality as to whether a child has been born to two married parents living together. However, half a century or more ago, the implication would be that, when this was not the case, the birth had been unwanted and that the child was being reared by a single mother, usually in disadvantaged circumstances. Major social stigma was involved, and the derogatory term "bastard" summarized the negativity and shame. Currently, in both the United Kingdom and the United States, about one in three births involves parents who are not legally married (Kiernan, 2004; NCHS, 2003). However, in sharp contrast with the past, most are born to cohabiting couples in a stable relationship, with the birth registered in the name of both parents. The situation involves no stigma or shame, and most of the births were wanted and had been planned. The meaning and consequences of what used to be termed "illegitimacy" have changed out of all recognition.

There are also parallels in the medical field. Thus, from a medical perspective, it is crucial to differentiate among cerebral palsy (which is due to brain damage and involves little genetic influence), muscular dystrophy (which is an entirely genetic condition), and poliomyelitis (which is neither genetic nor due to brain damage). However, school children tend not to be concerned with such distinctions; the insulting term "spastic" is likely to be used for all, as well as for mentally retarded children or those with autism. The peer group construct will be vital when social stigma or discrimination is implicated, but the differentiation between conditions that do and do not involve organic brain dysfunction will be much more important than the social construction with respect to the risks for either cognitive impairment or psychiatric disorder (Goodman, 2002). The degree of physical impairment also does not contribute to these risks; rather, the presence or absence of brain abnormality matters (Rutter, Graham, & Yule, 1970; Seidel, Chadwick, & Rutter, 1975).

Somewhat similar issues arise with respect to congenital deafness. Deafness is readily susceptible to objective audiological measurement, and severe hearing impairment is usually attributable to either genetic causes or severe prematurity (Hindley & van Gent, 2002). Accordingly, medical doctors view it as an abnormal condition that merits treatment. By contrast, some individuals with deafness reject that view, preferring to see it as a difference rather than an abnormality. They emphasize the validity and reality of a deaf culture that is characterized by a primarily visual experience of the world, membership of an oppressed minority, and the use of sign language (Meadow-Orlans & Erting, 2000). The stigma arises from the attitudes of the hearing population, but the sense of a coherent deaf culture arises primarily from the constructs of the individuals with deafness. Which of these matters most depends upon circumstances, and whether either is more important than the medical differentiations, will depend on the consequences under consideration.

Similar considerations apply to ethnicity. Thus, for example, in the United Kingdom, society's designation of "Black" includes dark-skinned Asians as well as Africans, despite the fact that neither see themselves as similar; their historical and cultural backgrounds are as different as their genetic makeup. In the same way, the general population in the United Kingdom tends not to differentiate between those who came to the United Kingdom from Africa and those who originated in the Caribbean, although these two groups differ markedly in culture and in pattern of migration, and tend sometimes to be somewhat antagonistic toward each other. Similarly, in the United States, distinctions between African Americans and Caribbean Blacks are often blurred unless, and until, spoken English sets them apart (Stepick, Stepick, Eugene, & Teed, 2001; Waters, 1999). In parallel fashion, the insulting term "Paki" is applied to persons who originated in Bangladesh or India, just as much as those who came from Pakistan, thus ignoring a host of differences among these groups, not the least of which is religion.

Racism tends not to be concerned with the niceties of culture or history or community. Thus, it was of no concern in Nazi Germany whether people viewed themselves as Jewish or practiced the Jewish religion. Suspicion of having Jewish "blood" was quite sufficient for their confinement in a concentration camp or being sent to the gas chamber. As already noted, such attitudes remain all too prevalent today. It is necessary to conclude that both personal constructs and societal attitudes are important in the social construction of ethnicity, and labeling plays a large role in this form of constructionism.

Genetic Influences: Racial Differences in IQ

Just over 30 years ago, Jensen (1969) wrote a controversial article in which he argued that racial variations in IQ must be attributed, at least in part, to genetic differences. His views today remain the same (see Miele, 2002), and similar arguments have been put forward by other prominent reviewers (for example, Herrnstein & Murray, 1994). Among most social scientists, it has now become politically incorrect even to suggest that Jensen's views warrant serious scrutiny. It is necessary, therefore, to consider whether this blanket rejection of the possibility of genetic causes is justified. Both scientific and social considerations are relevant.

The main rationale for Jensen's argument was that the difference between African Americans and Caucasians, with respect to skin pigmentation and physiognomy, is obviously genetically determined (clearly, that is the case), that there are strong genetic influences on individual differences in IQ (this is also true), and, ergo, that it was reasonable to suggest that the genetic differences associated with race were also responsible for the observed mean difference between African Americans and Caucasians in IQ level. On the face of it, his logic appears persuasive, but there were two serious scientific objections (plus other lesser concerns). First, although there was good evidence from twin and adoptee studies that there was substantial heritability of IQ in Whites, there were no good data on whether or not that also applied for African Americans. The objection is nontrivial because estimates of heritability are population-specific and are likely to differ if environments vary (see, for example, Rowe et al., 1999; Turkheimer et al., 2003).

Second, and more problematic, it is not valid to extrapolate from within-group findings to between-group inferences. Tizard (1975) well illustrated the falsity of this extrapolation by reference to the evidence on height. Height is a human characteristic that is most strongly genetically influenced (with a heritability of about 90 percent). Despite this, there was a huge rise in the average height of individuals throughout the world over the course of the 20th century – a rise almost certainly due to improved nutrition (Fogel, 2000a, b). So far as it is known, height remained highly heritable over the whole of this time period, but genetic influences were not responsible for the group (that is, intergenerational) differences in mean height. Clearly, these objections do not mean that genes play no role in ethnic group differences in mean IQ, but they do mean that Jensen's argument was flawed.

The social concerns are different, but they do serve to explain why Jensen's views are treated with hostility, rather than simply ignored as scientifically mistaken. First, despite his claims to the contrary, he has not been even-handed in his handling of evidence. For example, he used the findings of the Minnesota Transracial Adoption Study (Weinberg, Scarr, & Waldman, 1992) to argue that the intermediate IQ position of the mixed-race children, together with the loss of advantage between 7 and 17 years of rearing in a White, middle-class home, supported a genetic explanation. (Levin, 1994, and Lynn, 1994, have argued similarly.)

However, it needs to be noted that the racial groups compared differed markedly in their preadoption experiences, and such differences were systematically associated with their IQ outcome (Waldman, Weinberg, & Scarr, 1994). The decline with age in the mean IQ of the Black and interracial adoption children was no greater than that for the White children. Scarr, Weinberg and Waldman (1993) showed that the heritability of IQ in these adopted children was similar to that found in other groups, but the environmental influence remained much the same, between 7 and 17 years (if anything, it marginally increased). Such environmental influences, of course, are likely to include racial discrimination as experienced outside the home, as well as influences within the family. In fact, the Transracial Adoption Study findings do not allow unambiguous conclusions on the possible role of genes with respect to ethnic group differences in intelligence. Transracial adoption constitutes a potentially useful research design, but care is essential to ensure that like is being compared with like.[3]

The second concern relates to the language used by Jensen. Races are described as "breeding populations," these being equated to animal subspecies. The rate of interracial marriage has tended to be quite low in the United States, but it is high in the United Kingdom between persons of African-Caribbean background and Caucasians. The rate of intermarriage is a function of societal attitudes, rather than genes. Moreover, the implication that ethnic groups are as categorically different as, say, Poodles, Cocker Spaniels, and Great Danes was offensive to many readers.

The third social concern has been Jensen's willingness to accept research funding from organizations widely regarded as racist in their aims, his admiration for slippery characters such as Burt and Eysenck, and his unwillingness now to accept that Burt's data involved fraud, or at least an unacceptable degree of data massaging (see Joynson, 2003). None of these social concerns mean that Jensen's claims of genetic or ethnic variations in IQ are necessarily wrong, but they inevitably raise concerns about his approach to the topic, and his objectivity in interpreting results. This is not helped, either, by his elevation of IQ to the human trait of overwhelming importance, and by his exclusive focus on the IQ deficit in African Americans.

Although this constitutes an essential background to the rejection by most social scientists of genetic explanations for ethnicity correlates, it is necessary to consider whether there is an acceptable face to genetic hypotheses. The issues are well brought together in two recent review articles (Burchard et al., 2003; Cooper, Kaufman, & Ward, 2003).

---

[3] These approaches need to be added to those employed in the research described in other chapters in this volume – see also Rowe and Cleveland (1996) for extension to mixed-race sibling designs.

Genetic Construction of Ethnicity

The ability to identify individual genes has clearly shown that the five major racial groups as identified in the U.S. Census (Black/African American; White; Asian; Native Hawaiian and other Pacific Islander; and American Indian/Alaskan Native) differ from each other in genetic makeup (Bowcock et al., 1994; Burchard et al., 2003; Cavalli-Sforza & Cavalli-Sforza, 1996; Rosenberg et al., 2002). For the most part, these differences coincide with geographical distance, reflecting its important effect on mating patterns. Modern genetic analyses can be remarkably successful in identifying the geographical origins of any individual's biological ancestors. However, there are important differences between these genetic patterns and ethnicity as a cultural construct. Thus, for example, South, Central, and West Asians cluster genetically with Europeans and not East Asians. Also, some ethnic groups – most notably Hispanics – are genetically admixed to a major degree, including White, Native American, and African ancestry (Hanis, Hewett-Emmett, Bertin, & Schull, 1991). Furthermore, some racial groups such as Africans are particularly variable genetically, despite being similar in skin pigmentation and some physiognomic characteristics.

The key question, however, is not whether there are genetic differences among racial groups (which clearly there are), but whether and how such differences influence outcomes that are manifested as differences along race and ethnic lines. So far as Mendelian, single-gene disorders are concerned, the relevance of race and ethnic background is obvious. Rare mutations are usually race-specific to a major degree, often specific to ethnic subgroups within races. Thus, there are numerous examples of mutations with a frequency below 2 percent that occur uniquely in Ashkenazi Jews, French Canadians, the Amish, or European Gypsies. In each case, this is because these groups descend from a relatively small number of founders and have remained largely endogamous (that is, marrying only within-group) for much of their history.

Less clear is the extent to which there are clinically important racial and ethnic differences in the frequencies of genetic allelic variations that are associated with susceptibility to complex multifactorial disorders, such as asthma or schizophrenia, or multifactorial traits, such as intelligence or antisocial behavior. Certainly, there are well-documented examples of susceptibility genes where this is the case (see Burchard et al., 2003), although their prevalence remains unknown. Also, not only is there huge overlap between races with respect to these common allelic variations, but there remain many puzzles about the mechanisms by which they operate. Alzheimer's disease, the commonest cause of dementia, provides the best-known example. It can be diagnosed with reasonable accuracy in developing countries (Prince et al., 2003), and there are puzzling variations across populations in its rate of occurrence (Kalaria, 2003), with rates low in Nigeria, China, and India as compared with those of African Americans. The apoE4 allele is known to carry a substantially increased risk for Alzheimer's disease, and the frequency of this allele varies across race, being substantially lower among Japanese than African Americans. Even more strikingly, however, the risk for Alzheimer's disease varies hugely across races, with the increased risk from homozygosity for the APOE-4 varying from a factor of 33 in Japanese to 15 in Whites, but only 6 in African Americans. The reason for this variation remains unknown, and the answer could lie in either the effects of other genes or environmental modifiers of the gene effects.

There is also some evidence of racial variations in the distribution of allelic variations of the serotonin transporter gene (Gelernter, Kranzler, Coccaro, Siever, & New, 1998; Lotrich, Pollock, & Ferrell, 2003). This is potentially important with respect to the apparently lower rates of lifetime depression in African Americans as compared with Hispanics and Whites (Kessler et al., 2003). Although the "short" version of the gene is associated with an increased risk of depression, the risk only operates when the susceptibility gene is combined with either acute or chronic stressful experiences (Caspi et al., 2003). In other words, the gene seems to be concerned with a vulnerability to stressors in relation to depression; it is not a direct determinant of depression. There is growing evidence of just this sort of gene-environment interplay (Caspi et al., 2002; Rutter & Silberg, 2002). As Ridley (2003) put it, nature frequently operates via nurture. The implication is that genes could well play some role in the ethnic variations found for certain psychological characteristics, but if so, the risk will likely be contingent on coaction with environmental adversities and stressors.

Such findings highlight the importance of understanding race and ethnicity as products of a marriage of social and biological influences – to use Cooper et al.'s (2003) phrase. Researchers should be concerned that the concept of race has been used not only to organize populations, but also to create a classification scheme that is purported to explain meaning in the social order, such as patterns of subordination. There is a legitimate concern that a focus on genetics could lead to a neglect of the huge ethnic variations in environmental risk exposure, but the main message from genetics runs counter to that tendency. There can be little understanding of the role of genes without studying the interplay with the environment. There is a parallel concern that race could come to serve as a surrogate for genetic constitution in the fields of medicine and public health, but this would clearly be nonsense, both because race needs to be viewed as a dimension rather than a category (because of admixture), and because of the major allelic variation within races. As Cooper et al. (2003) argue, if you want to know someone's genotype you have to test the DNA to find ut; the crude grouping of a racial category is a hopeless substitute. On

nd, from a research perspective, it is necessary to discover the
es (along with a broad range of personal and societal risk and
factors) in ethnic variations in the distribution of psychological
he crucial point is to treat possible genetic contributions as one of
ple hypotheses to be tested, rather than an inference to be drawn.

Possible Mediators of Ethnic Effects

For all the reasons discussed above, it is obvious that ethnicity as such cannot sensibly be viewed as an explanation for differences in psychological features or as a mediator of effects. Because ethnicity is such a multifaceted concept, without knowing which facet is operative, conclusions that there are ethnic effects cannot inform mechanisms. Therefore, ethnicity must be disaggregated into its multiple components in order to test for mediation – see Baron and Kenny (1986) for the general approach, and Thorpe, Rutter, and Greenwood (2003) and Moffitt, Caspi, Rutter, and Silva (2001) for applications to group differences. The following list of headings illustrates the diversity of facets that need to be considered, but it is not intended to be exhaustive.

Personal Group Identity

For most people, the ancestry or nationality group with which they mainly identify in official statistics or surveys is meaningful to them. However, the psychological reality often does not coincide with the categories on offer. In the United Kingdom, where the rate of intermarriage among some (but not all) ethnic groups is very high (see Chapter 11 of this volume), it is very frequent for the personal group identity to differ from official categories. This may not have been a major issue in the past for many African Americans because interracial marriage was relatively uncommon (Small, 1994) and because their personal identities often coincided with the broad groupings used in the census. However, that situation is changing and it has long been an issue with other groups in the United States. That is especially the case for Asians and Hispanics, for whom pan-ethnic labels incur a growing resistance from individuals whose racial and ethnic identity leads them to reject the official categories. For Hispanics, the share who identified with the residual "other" race has grown over the past 20 years. Moreover, many individuals have multiple group identifications. To some extent, that is also true for the children of immigrants in the United States (see Chapter 12 of this volume). In both the United Kingdom and the United States, it is crucial to seek information without forcing a choice among, say, race, religion, or geographical region, to mention just three alternatives.

Many people wish to identify themselves as Scots, Welsh, or English, rather than British. Also, some wish to narrow the group to Scouse

(Liverpool), Geordie (Newcastle), Black Country (a part of
Midlands), or Cockney (a particular part of London) – each of
distinctively different dialect as well as accent (plus their own
special types of jokes). Similarly, some people from an African-C
background who have grown up and attended school in these areas
the majority of their peer group non-African-Caribbean, also adopt l
tional identities. In the future, too, it may be that some people will prefer
a broader pan-ethnic identity, such as being European. Pan-ethnic identities are already used by some people, but with quite varied degrees of
acceptance. For example, a colleague from the Sudan with a Christian upbringing always referred to his ethnicity as Middle Eastern because he
did not feel part of the Muslim culture, did not maintain an active church
involvement, and did not wish to be identified with the Palestinian suicide bombers. He might at one time have referred to himself as an Arab
(Arabic was his first language), but that too, for him, involved both positive
and negative connotations. If the aim is truly to identify an individual's
group identity, it is crucial to allow free choice of multiple identities. In
addition, it is desirable to have some measure of the strength and impact
of such identities – as shown, for example, by the choice of close friends,
the composition of the peer group, and participation in the cultural (or
political) activities of the group with which they identify. Of course, these
complexities multiply the difficulties of drawing inferences about statistical
regularities without very large samples. Even then, analytical complexities
can become unwieldy, as occurred in the United States by allowing individuals to mark more than one race category (Perlmann & Waters, 2002;
Prewitt, 2002).

Religion
Religion is a main group of identification for many people of Asian background living in the United Kingdom, and for Whites in Northern Ireland.
It is also so for members of evangelical religions. Irrespective of whether
or not religion is used as the main personal classifier, it may be necessary to ask which religion people belong to and especially to inquire how
important it is to them. This may be measured, in part, by asking about
the peer group, involvement in church/mosque/synagogue functions,
adherence to religious "rules," and acceptance of religious beliefs. Thus, the
interest needs to be both on religiosity (that is, the importance of religion
as such) and on the particular religious denomination. In that connection,
however, it is crucial to appreciate that religious heritage continues to be
important to many people who have long ago rejected the religious beliefs of their upbringing, no longer attend church (or its equivalent), and
follow none of the religious "rules" (or rituals). Among social and behavioral scientists and practitioners in the United Kingdom today, there would
be few individuals who maintain a religious faith, but there would be
far more for whom their Jewish, Quaker, Catholic, or Muslim upbringing

continues to have major meaning in relation to their values. This, too, needs to be asked about. However, in the United States, such information can only be asked in special surveys, seldom with minors, and never in Census Bureau questionnaires, in which such questions are prohibited by law.

Language Spoken at Home and in the Peer Group

Similar issues apply with respect to the language used at home and in the peer group. According to Arel (2002), "language is a potent force in nationalist policies since it simultaneously acts as a symbol of identity, a privileged means of social, economic, and political mobility, and a claim to territory" (pp. 114–115). Unlike religion, language cannot be disassociated from the state, and for many, it is a core ingredient for regional claims to sovereignty. At a private level, language serves as a marker of ethnic transition, particularly between the first and second generations (Chapter 12 of this volume).

As already noted, the importance of language varies greatly by geography and social context. There are increasing numbers of children, too, in the United Kingdom being reared by two parents who differ in their first language. When that is so, it may be important to know which language the child uses with each parent and with siblings, and whether this is of any consequence in specific social domains such as schooling or extracurricular activities.

Social Community

Each of the groupings already discussed may provide an important social community for the individual. Thus, for many English people, the Church of England has little or no religious meaning, but rather provides a grounding in social life, and a source of social contacts, especially when moving into a new community. Much the same would apply to national groupings, sometimes organized around the church that is most characteristic of the country from which they have emigrated. But psychologically important social groups for young people may also be provided by youth organizations (such as Scouts) or sports organizations (for example, tennis club or football team) or political group or local community associations. Again, it is important to ask both about frequency of participation and the importance of the group to the individual.

Intergenerational Differences

Over the years, important changes in attitude and beliefs take place – partly as a result of people becoming older and partly as a consequence of altered social mores (Halpern, 1995). With respect to the children of immigrants, there is the additional feature that the parental culture is likely to be that of the country (and sociocultural group) from which they came, whereas for the offspring there are likely to be strong peer group influences that convey

multi
traits. Th
protectiv
role of gen
the other hai

The Multiple F

66   *Michael Rutter and Marta Tienda*

a quite different set of values and expectations. Thus, for some, this may involve the role of women and acceptance of their having an independent career, or the acceptability of arranged marriages, or attitudes to sexuality, drugs, and alcohol. As with any other intergenerational differences, all of this is managed harmoniously with mutually acceptable compromises in most families. However, in some, it may be the source of conflict, occasionally at a serious level. Accordingly, it is necessary to enquire about the extent of parent-offspring differences and the extent to which they matter to the individual young person. This information is necessary to evaluate Portes and Rumbaut's (2001) hypotheses about dissonant, consonant, and selective acculturation.

Social Position and Level of Affluence

It has been apparent for a long time that some ethnic groups are economically, as well as socially, disadvantaged in relation to society as a whole. Wilson (1987) has documented a rise among African Americans in both the proportion of well-educated professionals and the proportion living in poverty. He suggested that some of the effects usually attributed to race were in reality more a function of social class than group membership, but initially this view was widely contested. In practice, it has not been easy to determine the true causal effect of poverty on psychological functioning because of the difficulty of differentiating between social selection and social causation (Dohrenwend et al., 1992). Thus, it is necessary to question whether the statistical association between poverty and psychological functioning is a consequence of the sort of people who fail economically or, rather, the effects of lack of economic resources on people's emotions or behavior.

Very occasionally, natural experiments provide the means to test causal hypotheses in rigorous fashion (Rutter, Pickles, Murray, & Eaves, 2001). The examination of the effects on psychopathology of the opening of a casino on an American Indian reservation, which gave every American Indian an income supplement that increased annually, provides a good example (Costello, Compton, Keller, & Angold, 2003). By good fortune, this affected families involved in a prospective longitudinal study, and the astute investigators were quick to see the research opportunity so provided. The findings showed that the level of conduct disorder and oppositional-defiant symptoms fell significantly in those who rose out of poverty as a result of the income supplement (as compared with those who remained poor). However, there was no effect on anxiety or depression symptoms. Taken in conjunction with other evidence that mainly points in the same direction (Duncan & Magnuson, 2004), this suggests that poverty can and does have adverse effects on at least some aspects of psychological functioning. These effects of poverty may, therefore, be relevant for some ethnic differences.

Nevertheless, it is still necessary to ask what it is that, given external opportunities, enables some families to rise out of poverty whereas others seem unable to take advantage of what is on offer. The same applies to comparisons among ethnic groups: What is it that allows some to greatly improve their economic position over generations, whereas that occurs less often with others? Conceivably, part of the answer lies in societal discrimination. Thus the Policy Study Institute studies in the United Kingdom (Daniel, 1968; Smith, 1978) provide compelling experimental evidence of the reality of racial discrimination in both housing and employment. So also do housing and employment audit studies conducted in the United States (Fix & Struyk, 1993). Although illegal, and less prevalent than it was, it remains a problem (see Chapters 4 and 7 of this volume). The effects are evident in the higher rate of unemployment in young people from ethnic minorities, even after taking account of educational levels. Indeed, the differences are most marked among the better educated. However, the question remains as to why some people deal more successfully with these societal barriers than others.

Education
Similar issues apply to education, where there are major differences among ethnic groups, both in the United States and the United Kingdom, in levels of scholastic attainment at all levels in the system (primary, secondary, and tertiary), as discussed in some detail by Maughan (this volume) and Hirschman and Lee (this volume). Some of the differences are attributable to variations among the ethnic groups in the educational attainments of the parents. Thus, the African Asians thrown out of Uganda by Idi Amin who came to the United Kingdom lost their money and property, but they came with a background of both educational achievement and occupational success (indeed, that was why they were expelled). This parallels the experience of Cubans who immigrated to the United States, first as possible temporary refugees and eventually as permanent settlers. Such achievement and success were much more rare among UK immigrants from Pakistan and Bangladesh (see Chapter 4 of this volume). Differential patterns of migration may also partly explain the apparently greater success of African Caribbeans in the United States than in the United Kingdom. It appears that Jamaican migration to the United States was more selective than that destined to the United Kingdom, but unfortunately, adequate data to examine this possibility directly are lacking.

Education is also relevant as a possible mediator of ethnic differences with respect to other psychological features. For example, delinquents tend to have a mean IQ somewhat below that of nondelinquents (see Moffitt, 1990, 1993) and some have suggested that the lower mean IQ of African Americans might partially explain their higher crime rate (Wilson & Herrnstein, 1985). However, Lynam, Moffitt, and Stouthamer-Loeber

(1993) found that, although the effect of IQ on delinquency for Whites was not altered much by taking account of educational attainment, for African Americans school performance accounted for almost all of the IQ–crime association. Although the same risk factors may operate similarly in all groups (Rowe, Vazsonyi, & Flannery, 1994), they need not do so, as in this instance. The findings emphasize the ever-present need to go beyond statistical associations to a testing for mediating mechanisms.

Area Influences

One of the striking differences between the United States and the United Kingdom is the prevalence and character of ethnic ghettos (Peach, 1996). In the United States, a high proportion of African Americans live in areas where the majority of other residents are also African American, whereas in the United Kingdom that applies only to a small minority of ethnic groups, including African Caribbeans (Modood et al., 1997). Also, the ghettos tend to be more complete in the United States; that is, they incorporate schools, leisure facilities, and shops, and not just homes. On the other hand, although ethnic ghettos are less prevalent in the United Kingdom, about half of people from ethnic minorities live in socially disadvantaged areas (see Chapter 4 of this volume).

Area influences could work in either of two opposite directions. On the one hand, immigrants from ethnic minorities often choose to live in the same area because of the available social support. In the United Kingdom, this pattern is particularly relevant to Asian groups, and in the United States, most recent immigrants settle in areas where others like themselves reside – at least temporarily. Ethnic neighborhoods can provide a positive influence in terms of community cohesion and mutual support (see Reiss, 1995). On the other hand, socially disadvantaged communities also represent adverse influences if they *lack* social cohesion and social controls (Sampson, Raudenbush, & Earls, 1997), and they may retard ethnic integration of newcomers or foster selective acculturation (Portes & Rumbaut, 2001). Because both possibilities exist, it is necessary always to question the social meaning of area influences for individuals and to document the degree of cohesion and informal control as they operate for area residents.

Three further issues also warrant attention. First, what is the evidence that neighborhood effects on individual emotions and behavior exist that cannot be reduced to the under-the-roof influences of the families comprising those areas? That has been tackled using several sorts of designs, including multilevel analyses (Sampson et al., 1997), and the consequences of moving in or out of the area (Osborn, 1980; Rutter & Quinton, 1977). More recently, however, there has been a randomized controlled trial in which families from public housing located in high-poverty neighborhoods moved into private housing in poor or nonpoor neighborhoods, with a subset remaining in public housing (Leventhal & Brooks-Gunn, 2003). At a 3-year follow-up, boys who moved to less poor neighborhoods reported fewer emotional problems. The second new approach uses genetic designs to examine neighborhood effects (Caspi, Taylor, Moffitt, & Plomin, 2000; Cleveland, 2003), with results showing some environmental mediation. The data are too sparse for any overall conclusion about the magnitude of area effects on psychosocial outcomes, the circumstances under which neighborhood effects are most pronounced, or the psychological functions most affected. However, there is enough evidence to conclude that area effects are real.

The second issue concerns the interplay between individuals and the communities in which they live (Wilson, 1987, 1991). This is not just a question of possible negative synergism between personal/family disadvantage and area disadvantage with respect to both the creation and consequences of social disorganization (Schuerman & Kobrin, 1986; Skogan, 1990), but also of the possible role of positive cohesion within ethnic groups. Comparisons across ethnic groups with measurement of both positive and negative features could be most informative. It also remains to be determined whether area effects are greater or lesser in the case of individuals at risk for other reasons.

Third, there is the question of whether ethnic differences in crime apply in the case of youths living in nondisadvantaged areas. In their Pittsburgh study, Peeples and Loeber (1994) found that they did not. On the other hand, the overall effect on violence of living in a bad neighborhood, as defined by the census, on both Caucasians and African Americans, was weak and statistically nonsignificant (Farrington, Loeber, & Stouthamer Loeber, 2003). By contrast, the Chicago study (see Chapter 6 of this volume) found major neighborhood effects on violent offending behavior. Further research is needed to resolve these differences and to establish their meaning.

Social Context and Meaning
In considering ethnic differences with respect to any psychological feature, it is important to bear in mind that the influence of risk and protective factors may be affected by social context and meaning (see Rutter, 1999). Although many factors have broadly similar effects across societies, researchers cannot assume that this will always be the case (Rutter & Nikapota, 2002). For example, a half-century ago, Christensen (1960) showed marked differences among cultural groups in the effects of a premarital pregnancy on subsequent marriage; similarly, Stevenson et al. (1990) showed that families differed across countries in their response to variations in educational attainment; and the same probably applies to attitudes to obesity and to thinness (Richards, Boxer, Petersen, & Albrecht, 1990; Russell, 2000). Deater-Deckard and colleagues (in Chapter 8 of this volume) suggest similar conclusions with respect to physical punishment.

It is also notable that family structure and parental social class seem to differ across ethnic groups in their effects on children's psychological functioning (see chapters in this volume by Maughan, by Morenoff, by Smith, and by Hirschman and Lee). This may reflect differences in the socially ascribed meaning of these features, of their frequency in the ethnic group, of differences across groups in the level of the risk/protective factor, or possibly measurement or sampling considerations. Alternatively, it may mean that the supposed risk factor has been wrongly identified in all groups, and the true risk mediation derives from some correlate for which the frequency of the true risk factor varies across ethnic groups. Studies will need to be designed to allow testing of these different possibilities.

Life Styles and Family Structure

Race and ethnic differences in family structure are large in both the United States (Farrington et al., 2003; Lichter, McLaughlin, Kephart, & Landry, 1992) and the United Kingdom (Modood et al., 1997). Most strikingly, both African Americans in the United States and African Caribbeans in the United Kingdom are much more likely to be brought up by a single mother or to experience a "broken home" for other reasons. The Moynihan report (Moynihan, 1965) argued that the weakness of family structure constituted the prime reason for the intergenerational cycle of poverty and deprivation and for the high rate of crime. Matsueda and Heimer (1987) concluded that the adverse effects of broken homes (by virtue of their effects on parental supervision) were greater for African Americans than for Whites. More recent data raise queries, however. In the Pittsburgh study (Farrington et al., 2003), the effects of a broken family, of being on welfare, and of physical punishment were all greater for Caucasians than for African Americans, with the effects in the latter both weak and statistically significant. Similarly, Deater-Deckard et al. (Deater-Deckard & Dodge, 1997; Chapter 8 of this volume) found that although overt physical abuse had similar adverse effects in both ethnic groups, a high rate of physical punishment was a risk factor only in Whites and not African Americans.

The problem with positing family structure as a possible mediating variable is that structure per se is unlikely to produce observed ethnic differences (Rodgers & Pryor, 1998). Single parenthood, like teenage parenthood (also more frequent in African Americans and African Caribbeans than in Whites), is an important risk *indicator* (Moffitt et al., 2001) because it is associated with so many other adverse factors. However, it is more dubious whether single parenthood per se constitutes a risk *mechanism*. There is need for more detailed measures of parent–child interaction and of family functioning than those available in the main studies of ethnic variations. In investigating mediation effects, particular care is needed in identifying risk and protective variables that operate differently across ethnic groups.

However, the study of ethnic diversity could be very helpful in pinpointing just what is involved in risk and protective processes. It is unlikely that such processes will vary considerably among different ethnic groups (although that possibility will need to be considered). Rather, the apparent differences are likely to reflect differences either in meanings of the factors or in the contextual pattern in relation to other risk and protective factors.

Life-style differences cannot be confined to family structure and relationships. Both drugs and alcohol are strong correlates of antisocial behavior (Rutter, Giller, & Hagell, 1998; Silberg, Rutter, D'Onofrio, & Eaves, 2003), and their possible relationships with ethnic difference in both depression and crime need to be considered. The same applies to the propensity to carry guns or other offensive weapons.

In that connection, it will be important to consider patterns of psychological features when seeking to understand the mediating mechanisms for any outcome; for example, the rate of suicide in "Blacks" is lower than that of "Whites" in the United States, despite the fact that most of the key risk factors for suicide are more common in the former group (Oquendo et al., 2001). Interestingly, this does not seem to be explicable on the basis of ethnic differences in depressive disorder.

Immigration

The need to consider immigrant status in the study of ethnic variations arises for at least four different reasons. First, experiences prior to immigration may be influence-measured outcomes. Most obviously, this applies to refugees and asylum-seekers, but subnutrition and other health issues are likely to be more widespread risk factors. Second, both lack of knowledge of the English language and limited schooling accentuate initial educational difficulties, at least initially. Third, the experience of relocation to a new country will bring at least short-term stresses for some. Fourth, immigrants and nonimmigrants from the same ethnic group may differ markedly in their life styles. For example, this has been found to be the case with smoking in the United States (Baluja, Park, & Myers, 2003). Usually, immigrants had significantly lower smoking rates; this led to a plea for the need to disaggregate health statistics by race/ethnicity, immigrant status, and country of birth, which currently they are not. On the other hand, as discussed by Rutter (this volume) and well demonstrated by Jones and Fung (this volume), immigrant generational status provides a most useful framework for testing causal hypotheses with respect to risk and protective factors.

Minority Status

In much of the literature, ethnic groups are referred to as "ethnic minorities." In that connection, it is relevant to note that in the United States, many individuals from so-called ethnic minorities grow up and live in ethnically segregated communities. Whether someone is a member of a minority group may or may not matter. The comparison of communities that vary in this respect, but that are similar in social resources, would be informative. However, on the limited evidence available to date, it would seem that it is not so much a minority or majority group membership that matters, but rather the group's social standing. Clearly, that does vary by ethnicity.

External Stigmatization and Racial Discrimination

That issue obviously connects with the broader concerns of stigmatization and discrimination. This is likely to be influential in two somewhat different, albeit related, ways. First, it will affect entry to opportunities (with respect to housing, education, and careers). Individuals so affected may or may not be aware that the doors have been closed as a result of discrimination. Irrespective of their awareness, stigmatization and discrimination will affect the social order as applied to ethnic groups. Second, individuals may have personal experiences with stigmatization and group prejudice. This may take the form of racial taunting or insulting, negative targeting – as in police practices of stop-and-search (see Chapter 7 of this volume) or discriminatory behavior by teachers at school (see Chapter 4 of this volume). The existence of substantial racial discrimination is not in doubt (see earlier discussion) and most people would regard it as morally unacceptable (as well as illegal). However, as discussed in chapters throughout this volume, it has not been easy to determine the extent to which prejudice and discrimination actually constitute a risk factor for young people's psychological functioning. Unfortunately, very few studies have measured the experience of stigma and discrimination at an individual level, and, obviously, that is much needed to understand better the mechanisms responsible for group differences.

Genes

Finally, as discussed above, it is important to consider the possible role of genes as mediating variables in the observed ethnic differences in psychological outcomes. The unsubstantiated inference that unidentified genetic factors account for observed variations is not very helpful, and it has rightly received a critical press. So far, only a few identified genes are known to be relevant in relation to multifactorial psychological traits, but in the decades ahead many more are likely to be identified and, when they are, they need to be used in a thoughtful, critical fashion to test causal hypotheses on mediating mechanisms. Quite often, however, they will operate in conjunction with, or even via, environmental risk and protective factors so that the study of genes and environment must constitute a joint research enterprise.

Conclusions

No data set in the world provides adequate coverage of the range of possible mediators discussed here (not to mention others not included). Nevertheless, the chapters that follow all seek to take our understanding forward by pitting one possibility against others. In that connection, comparisons across ethnic groups and social contexts are vitally important. It is clearly apparent that ethnic groups are widely diverse on almost any feature selected for examination. Any notion that there is a unity to non-White groups can be rejected out of hand. They differ among themselves at least as much as they differ from "White" populations. It is also evident that ethnicity is multifaceted with many people feeling an identification with several groups. Therefore, researchers must accept the analytical challenges implied by these multiple identifications in order to avoid misinterpreting causal mechanisms. Because ethnicity is so extremely multifaceted, it can never be regarded as a mediator of anything. Thus, the need to break down ethnicity into its various components in order to determine which carry the mediating effects is essential. Also, socially, psychologically, and genetically, ethnicity needs to be seen as operating dimensionally at least as much as it does categorically.

Finally, the chapters that follow note several examples in which risk/protective factors appear to operate differently across ethnic groups. Extreme caution is necessary in the use of multiple regression analyses to test mediation hypotheses in such circumstances. If a factor constitutes a risk in one group but a protective feature (or a neutral one) in another group, equating the groups on that feature makes little conceptual or statistical sense. Ordinarily, the testing for mediation in relation to group differences requires that the variables operate in the same way in both groups, unless constraints are provided by distributional features or ceiling effects (Moffitt et al., 2001; Rutter, Thorpe, Greenwood, Northstone, & Golding, 2003; Thorpe et al., 2003). On the other hand, the very fact of differences in risk effects across groups will often provide an invaluable research lever for the conceptualization and testing of causal hypotheses.

References

Alba, R. (1992). Ethnicity. In E. F. Borgotta & M. L. Borgotta (Eds.), *Encyclopedia of sociology* (Vol. 2, pp. 575–584). New York: Macmillan.

Alba, R., & Nee, V. (1999). Rethinking assimilation theory for a new era of immigration. In C. Hirschman, P. Kasinitz, & J. DeWind (Eds.), *The handbook of international migration* (pp. 137–160). New York: Russell Sage.

Arel, D. (2002). Language categories in censuses: Backward- or forward-looking? In D. Kertzer & D. Arel (Eds.) *Census and identity: The politics of race, ethnicity, and language in national censuses.* Cambridge, UK: Cambridge University Press.

Baluja, K. F., Park, J., & Myers, D. (2003). Inclusion of immigrant status in smoking prevalence statistics. *American Journal of Public Health, 93*, 642–646.

Baron, R. M., & Kenny, D. A. (1986). The moderator-mediator variable distinction in social psychological research: Conceptual, strategic, and statistical considerations. *Journal of Personality and Social Psychology, 51*, 1173–1182.

Bean, F. D., & Tienda, M. (1987). *The Hispanic population of the United States.* New York: Russell Sage Foundation.

Bowcock, A. M., Ruiz-Linares, A., Tomfohrde, J., Minch, E., Kidd, J. R., & Cavalli-Sforza, L. L. (1994). High resolution of human evolutionary trees with polymorphic microsatellites. *Nature, 368*, 455–457.

Brodie, M., Suro, R., Brodie, M., Suro, R., Steffenson, A., Valdez, J., et al. (2002). *National survey of Latinos.* Washington, DC: Pew Hispanic Center and Kaiser Family Foundation.

Burchard, E. G., Ziv, E., Coyle, N., Gomez, S. L., Tang, H., Karter, A., et al. (2003). The importance of race and ethnic background in biomedical research and clinical practice. *New England Journal of Medicine, 348*, 1170–1175.

Caspi, A., McClay, J., Moffitt, T. E., Mill, J., Martin, J., Craig, I. W., et al. (2002). Role of genotype in the cycle of violence in maltreated children. *Science, 297*, 851–854.

Caspi, A., Sugden, K., Moffitt, T. E., Taylor, A., Craig, I. W., Harrington, H. L., et al. (2003). Influence of life stress on depression: Moderation by a polymorphism in the 5-HTT gene. *Science, 301*, 386–389.

Caspi, A., Taylor, A., Moffitt, T. E., & Plomin, R. (2000). Neighborhood deprivation affects children's mental health: Environmental risks identified in a genetic design. *Psychological Science, 11*, 338–342.

Cavalli-Sforza, L. L., & Cavalli-Sforza, F. (1996). *The great human diasporas: The history of diversity and evolution.* Reading, MA: Addison-Wesley.

Christensen, H. T. (1960). Cultural relativism and premarital sex norms. *American Sociological Review, 25*, 31–39.

Cleveland, H. H. (2003). Disadvantaged neighborhoods and adolescent aggression: Behavioral genetic evidence of contextual effects. *Journal of Research on Adolescence, 13*, 211–238.

Cooper, R. S., Kaufman, J. S., & Ward, R. (2003). Race and genomics. *New England Journal of Medicine, 348*, 1166–1170.

Costello, E. J., Compton, F. N., Keeler, G., & Angold, A. (2003). Relationships between poverty and psychopathology: A natural experiment. *Journal of American Medical Association, 290*, 2023–2029.

Daniel, W. W. (1968). *Racial discrimination in England.* London: Penguin.

Davis, F. J. (1991). *Who is Black? One nation's definition.* University Park, PA: The Pennsylvania State University Press.

Deater-Deckard, K., & Dodge, K. A. (1997). Externalizing behavior problems and discipline revisited: Nonlinear effects and variation by culture, context, and gender. *Psychological Inquiry, 8*, 161–175.

Dohrenwend, B. P., Levav, I., Shrout, P. E., Schwartz, S., Naveh, G., Link, B. G., et al. (1992). Socioeconomic status and psychiatric disorders: the causation-selection issue. *Science, 255*, 946–952.

Duncan, G. J., & Magnuson, K. (2004). Individual and parent-based intervention strategies for promoting human capital and positive behavior. In

P. L. Chase-Lansdale, K. Kiernan, & R. J. Friedman (Eds.), *Human development across lives and generations: The potential for change* (pp. 93–135). New York & Cambridge, UK: Cambridge University Press.

Farrington, D. P., Loeber, R., & Stouthamer-Loeber, M. (2003). How can the relationship between race and violence be explained? In D. J. Hawkins (Ed.), *Violent crimes: Assessing race and ethnic differences* (pp. 213–237). New York: Cambridge University Press.

Fix, M., & Struyk, R. J. (1993). *Clear and convincing evidence: Measurement of discrimination in America*. Washington, DC: Urban Institute Press.

Fogel, R. W. (2000a). The extension of life in developed countries and its implications for social policy. *Population and Development Review, 26*(Suppl), 291–317.

Fogel, R. W. (2000b). *The fourth Great Awakening & the future of egalitarianism.* Chicago: The University of Chicago Press.

Gans, H. J. (1979). Symbolic ethnicity: The future of ethnic groups and cultures in America. *Ethnic and Racial Studies, 2,* 1–19.

Gelernter, J., Kranzler, H., Coccaro, E. F., Siever, L. J., & New, M. (1998). Serotonin transporter protein gene polymorphism and personality measures in African American and European American subjects. *American Journal of Psychiatry, 155,* 1332–1338.

Goldscheider, C. (2002). Ethnic categorizations in censuses: Comparative observations from Israel, Canada, and the United States. In D. Kertzer & D. Arel (Eds.), *Census and identity: The politics of race, ethnicity, and language in national censuses.* Cambridge, UK: Cambridge University Press.

Goodman, R. (2002). Brain disorders. In M. Rutter & E. Taylor (Eds.), *Child and adolescent psychiatry* (4th ed., pp. 241–260). Oxford: Blackwell Scientific.

Gordon, M. (1964). *Assimilation in American life: The role of race, religion, and national origins.* New York: Oxford University Press.

Halpern, D. (1995). Values, morals and modernity. In M. Rutter & D. J. Smith (Eds.), *Psychological disorders in young people: Time trends and their causes* (pp. 324–387). Chichester, UK: Wiley.

Hanis, C. L., Hewett-Emmett, D., Bertin, T. K., & Schull, W. J. (1991). Origins of U.S. Hispanics: Implications for diabetes. *Diabetes Care, 14,* 618–627.

Heitmeyer, W. (2002). Have cities ceased to function as "Integration Machines" for young people? In M. Tienda & W. J. Wilson (Eds.), *Youth in cities: A cross-national perspective.* Cambridge, UK: Cambridge University Press.

Herrnstein, R. J., & Murray, C. (1994). *The bell curve: Intelligence and class structure in American life.* New York: Free Press.

Hindley, P., & van Gent, T. (2002). Psychiatric aspects of specific sensory impairments. In M. Rutter & E. Taylor (Eds.), *Child and adolescent psychiatry* (4th ed., pp. 842–857). Oxford: Blackwell Science.

Jensen, A. R. (1969). How much can we boost IQ and scholastic achievement? *Harvard Educational Review, 39,* 1–123.

Joynson, R. B. (2003). Selective interest and psychological practice: A new interpretation of the Burt affair. *British Journal of Psychology, 94,* 409–426.

Kalaria, R. N. (2003). Dementia comes of age in the developing world. *The Lancet, 361,* 888–889.

Kertzer, D. I., & Arel, D. (2002). Censuses, identity formation, and the struggle for political power. In D. Kertzer & D. Arel (Eds.), *Census and identity: The politics of race, ethnicity, and language in national censuses.* Cambridge, UK: Cambridge University Press.

Kessler, R. C., Berglund, P., Demler, O., Jin, R., Koretz, D., Merikangas, K. R., et al. (2003). The epidemiology of major depressive disorder: Results from the national comorbidity survey replication (NCS-R). *Journal of the American Medical Association, 289,* 3095–3105.

Kiernan, K. (2004). Cohabitation and divorce across nations and generations. In P. L. Chase-Lansdale, K. Kiernan, & R. J. Friedman (Eds.), *Human development across lives and generations: The potential for change* (pp. 139–170). New York & Cambridge, UK: Cambridge University Press.

Leventhal, T., & Brooks-Gunn, J. (2003). Moving to opportunity: An experimental study of neighborhood effects on mental health. *American Journal of Public Health, 93,* 1576–1582.

Levin, M. (1994). Comment on the Minnesota Transracial Adoption Study. *Intelligence, 19,* 13–20.

Lichter, D., McLaughlin, D. K., Kephart, G., & Landry, D. J. (1992). Race and the retreat from marriage: A shortage of marriageable men? *American Sociological Review, 57,* 781–799.

Lieberson, S. (1961). A societal theory of race and ethnic relations. *American Sociological Review, 26,* 902–910.

Lotrich, F., Pollock, B., & Ferrell, R. (2003). Serotonin transporter promoter polymorphism in African Americans: Allele frequencies and implications for treatment. *American Journal of Pharmacogenomics, 3,* 145–147.

Lynam, D., Moffitt, T. E., & Stouthamer-Loeber, M. (1993). Explaining the relation between IQ and delinquency: Class, race, test motivation, school failure, or self-control? *Journal of Abnormal Psychology, 102,* 187–196.

Lynn, R. (1994). Some reinterpretations of the Minnesota Transracial Adoption Study. *Intelligence, 19,* 21–27.

Matsueda, R. L., & Heimer, K. (1987). Race, family structure, and delinquency: A test of differential association and social control theories. *American Sociological Review, 52,* 826–840.

Meadow-Orlans, K. P., & Erting, C. (2000). Deaf people in society. In P. Hindley & N. Kitson (Eds.), *Mental health and deafness* (pp. 3–24). London: Whurr.

Miele, F. (2002). *Intelligence, race and genetics: Conversations with Arthur R. Jensen.* Cambridge, MA: Westview Press.

Modood, T., Berthoud, R., Lakey, J., Nazroo, J., Smith, P., Virdee, S., et al. (1997). *Ethnic minorities in Britain: Diversity and disadvantage.* London: Policy Studies Institute.

Moffitt, T. E. (1990). The neuropsychology of juvenile delinquency: A critical review. In M. Tonry & N. Morris (Eds.), *Crime and justice* (pp. 99–169). Chicago: University of Chicago Press.

Moffitt, T. E. (1993). The neuropsychology of conduct disorder. *Development and Psychopathology, 5,* 135–152.

Moffitt, T. E., Caspi, A., Rutter, M., & Silva, P. A. (2001). *Sex differences in antisocial behaviour: Conduct disorder, delinquency, and violence in the Dunedin Longitudinal Study.* Cambridge, UK: Cambridge University Press.

Moynihan, D. P. (1965). *The Negro family: The case for national action.* Washington, DC: Office of Policy Planning and Research, U.S. Department of Labor.

NCHS (2003, June 25). *Births: Preliminary data for 2002. National Vital Statistics Reports, 51*(11). Retrieved December 14, 2003, from http://www.cdc.gov/nchs/data/nvsr/NVSR51/NVSR51_11.pdf

Nelson, C., & Tienda, M. (1985). The structuring of Hispanic ethnicity: Historical and contemporary perspectives. *Ethnic and Racial Studies 8*(1), 49–74. Reprinted in *Ethnicity and race in the U.S.A.* Boston: Routledge and Kegan Paul, PLC. Reprinted in P. Hondagneu-Sotelo and V. Ortiz (Eds.), *The Latino experience in the United States*. Boston: Routledge (1997).

Noel, D. J. (1968). A theory of the origin of ethnic stratification. *Social Problems, 16,* 157–172.

Oquendo, M. A., Ellis, S. P., Greenwald, S., Malone, K. M., Weissman, M. M., & Mann, J. J. (2001). Ethnic and sex differences in suicide rates relative to major depression in the United States. *American Journal of Psychiatry, 158,* 1652–1658.

Osborn, S. G. (1980). Moving home, leaving London and delinquent trends. *British Journal of Criminology, 20,* 54–61.

Peach, C. (1996). Does Britain have ghettos? *Transactions of the Institute of British Geographers, 21,* 216–235.

Peeples, F., & Loeber, R. (1994). Do individual factors and neighbourhood context explain ethnic differences in juvenile delinquency? *Journal of Quantitative Criminology, 10,* 141–157.

Perlmann, J., & Waters, M. C. (2002). *The new race question: How the census counts multiracial individuals*. New York: Russell Sage Foundation.

Petersen, W. (1987). Politics and the measurement of ethnicity. In W. Alonso & P. Starr (Eds.), *The politics of numbers*. New York: Russell Sage Foundation.

Portes, A. (1995). Children of immigrants: Segmented assimilation and its determinants. In A. Portes (Ed.), *The economic sociology of immigration: Essays on networks, ethnicity, and entrepreneurship*. New York: Russell Sage Foundation.

Portes, A., & Rumbaut, R. G. (1996). *Immigrant America*. Berkeley: University of California Press.

Portes, A., & Rumbaut, R. G. (2001). *Legacies: The story of the immigrant second generation*. Berkeley and New York: University of California Press and Russell Sage Foundation.

Prewitt, K. (2002). Race in the 2000 Census: A turning point. In J. Perlmann & M. Waters (Eds.), *The new race question: How the census counts multiracial individuals* (pp. 354–361). New York: Russell Sage Foundation.

Prince, M., Acosta, D., Chiu, H., Scazufca, M., Varghese, M., & 10/66 Dementia Research Group (2003). Dementia diagnosis in developing countries: A cross-cultural validation study. *The Lancet, 361,* 909–917.

Reiss, A. J. (1995). Community influences on adolescent behavior. In M. Rutter (Ed.), *Psychosocial disturbances in young people: Challenges for prevention* (pp. 305–332). Cambridge, UK: Cambridge University Press.

Richards, M. H., Boxer, A. M., Petersen, A. C., & Albrecht, R. (1990). Relation of weight to body image in pubertal girls and boys from two communities. *Developmental Psychology, 26,* 313–321.

Ridley, M. (2003). *Nature via nurture: Genes, experience and what makes us human*. London: Fourth Estate.

Rodgers, B., & Pryor, J. (1998). *Divorce and separation: The outcomes for children*. York, UK: Joseph Rowntree Foundation.

Rosenberg, N. A., Pritchard, J. K., Weber, J. L., Cann, H. M., Kidd, K. K., Zhivotovsky, L. A., et al. (2002). Genetic structure of human populations. *Science, 298*, 2381–2385.

Rowe, D. C., & Cleveland, H. H. (1996). Academic achievement in Blacks and Whites: Are the developmental processes similar? *Intelligence, 23*, 205–228.

Rowe, D. C., Jacobson, K. C., & van den Oord, E. J. C. G. (1999). Genetic and environmental influences on vocabulary IQ: Parental education level as moderator. *Child Development, 70*, 1151–1162.

Rowe, D. C., Vazsonyi, A. T., & Flannery, D. J. (1994). No more than skin deep: Ethnic and racial similarity in developmental process. *Psychological Review, 101*, 296–413.

Russell, G. (2000). Anorexia nervosa. In M. G. Gelder, J. J. López-Ibor, & N. Andreasen (Eds.), *New Oxford textbook of psychiatry* (Vol. 1, pp. 835–855). Oxford: Oxford University Press.

Rutter, M. (1999). Social context: meanings, measures and mechanisms. *European Review, 7*, 139–149.

Rutter, M., Giller, H., & Hagell, A. (1998). *Antisocial behavior by young people.* New York: Cambridge University Press.

Rutter, M., Graham, P., & Yule, W. (1970). *A neuropsychiatric study in childhood.* London: SIMP/William Heinemann.

Rutter, M., & Nikapota, A. (2002). Culture, ethnicity, society and psychopathology. In M. Rutter & E. Taylor (Eds.), *Child and adolescent psychiatry* (4th ed., pp. 277–298). Oxford: Blackwell Scientific.

Rutter, M., Pickles, A., Murray, R., & Eaves, L. (2001). Testing hypotheses on specific environmental causal effects on behavior. *Psychological Bulletin, 127*, 291–324.

Rutter, M., & Quinton, D. (1977). Psychiatric disorder – Ecological factors and concepts of causation. In H. McGurk (Ed.), *Ecological factors in human development* (pp. 173–187). Amsterdam: North-Holland.

Rutter, M., & Silberg, J. (2002). Gene-environment interplay in relation to emotional and behavioral disturbance. *Annual Review of Psychology, 53*, 463–490.

Rutter, M., Thorpe, K., Greenwood, R., Northstone, K., & Golding, J. (2003). Twins as a natural experiment to study the causes of mild language delay: I. Design: twin-singleton differences in language, and obstetric risks. *Journal of Child Psychology and Psychiatry, 44*, 326–334.

Sampson, R. J., Raudenbush, S. W., & Earls, F. (1997). Neighborhoods and violent crime: A multilevel study of collective efficacy. *Science, 277*, 918–924.

Scarr, S., Weinberg, R. A., & Waldman, I. D. (1993). IQ correlations in transracial adoptive families. *Intelligence, 17*, 541–555.

Schuerman, L., & Kobrin, S. (1986). Community careers in crime. In A. J. Reiss & M. Tonry (Eds.), *Communities and crime* (pp. 67–100). Chicago: University of Chicago Press.

Seidel, U. P., Chadwick, O. F. D., & Rutter, M. (1975). Psychological disorders in crippled children: A comparative study of children with and without brain damage. *Developmental Medicine and Child Neurology, 17*, 563–573.

Silberg, J., Rutter, M., D'Onofrio, B., & Eaves, L. (2003). Genetic and environmental risk factors in adolescent substance use. *Journal of Child Psychology and Psychiatry, 44*, 664–676.

Skogan, W. G. (1990). *Disorder and decline: Crime and the spiral of decay in American neighbourhoods*. New York: Free Press.

Small, S. (1994). *Racialised barriers: The Black experience in the United States and England in the 1980s*. London/New York: Routledge.

Smith, D. J. (1978). *Racial disadvantage in Britain*. London: Penguin.

Stepick, A., Stepick, C. D., Eugene, E., & Teed, D. (2001). Shifting identities and intergenerational conflict: Growing up Haitian in Miami. In R. Rumbaut & A. Portes (Eds.), *Ethnicities: Children of immigrants in America*. Berkeley: University of California Press.

Stevenson, H. W., Lee, S.-Y., Chen, C., Stigler, J. W., Hsu, C.-C., & Kitamura, S. (1990). Contexts of achievement: A study of American, Chinese and Japanese children. *Monographs of the Society for Research in Child Development, 55*, 1–123.

Thorpe, K., Rutter, M., & Greenwood, R. (2003). Twins as a natural experiment to study the causes of mild language delay: II. Family interaction risk factors. *Journal of Child Psychology and Psychiatry, 44*, 342–355.

Tizard, J. (1975). Race and IQ: The limits of probability. *New Behaviour, 1*, 6–9.

Turkheimer, E., Haley, A., Waldron, M., D'Onofrio, B., & Gottesman, I. I. (2003). Socioeconomic status modifies heritability of IQ in young children. *Psychological Science, 14*, 623–628.

Vincent, J. (1974). The structuring of ethnicity. *Human Organization, 33*, 375–379.

Waldman, I. D., Weinberg, R. A., & Scarr, S. (1994). Racial-group differences in IQ in the Minnesota Transracial Adoption Study: A reply to Levin and Lynn. *Intelligence, 19*, 29–44.

Waters, M. (1999). *Black identities: West Indian immigrant dreams and American realities*. New York: Russell Sage Foundation.

Weinberg, R. A., Scarr, S., & Waldman, I. D. (1992). The Minnesota Transracial Adoption Study: A follow-up of IQ test performance at adolescence. *Intelligence, 16*, 117–135.

Wilson, J. Q., & Herrnstein, R. J. (1985). *Crime and human nature*. New York: Simon and Schuster.

Wilson, W. J. (1987). *The truly disadvantaged: The inner city, the underclass, and public policy*. Chicago, IL: University of Chicago Press.

Wilson, W. J. (1991). Studying inner-city social dislocations: The innercity, the underclass, and public policy research. *American Sociological Review, 56*, 1–14.

4

Educational Attainments

Ethnic Differences in the United Kingdom

Barbara Maughan

Introduction

Immigration of non-White ethnic minority groups to the United Kingdom is a largely post–World War II phenomenon. The first main waves of migrants arrived from the Caribbean in the late 1940s and 1950s; less than two decades later, African-Caribbean communities were expressing concern over their children's school achievements, and by 1979 an official Committee of Enquiry had been established to report on the educational needs and attainments of children of Caribbean origin. Subsequent waves of immigration, predominantly from south Asia and Africa, have been followed by further concerns, but also by awareness of the diversity in patterns of attainment that has emerged: most second-generation minority groups have made marked progress by comparison with the migrant generation, and by the mid-1990s some of the most, as well as the least, positive school achievements were recorded by young people from minority communities.

This chapter examines recent evidence on the attainments of ethnic minorities in the United Kingdom, and the factors thought likely to influence them. First, to set the empirical findings in context, it provides a brief overview of patterns of immigration to Britain in the second half of the twentieth century, and the geographical location and economic and social status of minority groups in the current population. Second, it reviews recent empirical evidence on the attainments of minority children and young people at different stages in the educational process, from entry to primary school to involvement in further and higher education. Finally it explores likely contributors to ethnic group differences in attainment, and their relevance to an understanding of intergenerational continuities and discontinuities.

Background

Immigration and Demographics: Minority Ethnic Populations in the United Kingdom

Tienda (this volume) provides a detailed picture of recent trends in migration to the United Kingdom and their impact on the current population structure. At the 2001 Census just under 8 percent of the total population, and more than 12 percent of those under 17 years old, classified themselves as non-White. Just under half are of South Asian origin (from India, Africa, Pakistan, and Bangladesh), 30 percent Black (of Caribbean, African, and other Black descent), and the remainder made up of people of Chinese, other Asian, and mixed ethnic backgrounds.

In examining educational attainments, we need to set these current trends in a longer term perspective. The various minority groups represented in the current UK population were drawn from widely differing cultural and educational backgrounds in their countries of origin and followed quite distinct patterns of migration to Britain. The first large-scale economic migration – predominantly of people from the Caribbean – began shortly after the Second World War and continued into the 1950s and 60s. This was followed by migration from India and Pakistan in the 1960s and early 1970s, from Bangladesh in the early 1980s, and from Africa in the 1980s and '90s. The most recent arrivals – now largely refugees and asylum seekers – have come from Vietnam, Somalia, the Middle East, and the former Yugoslavia.

These varied migration patterns are reflected in the differing age structures and generational statuses of individual minority groups in the UK population. By the late 1990s, for example, the great majority of school-aged children of South Asian descent were British-born, but only a small minority of their parents had been born and educated in the United Kingdom. Among Caribbeans, by contrast, most primary school aged children in the 1990s were second- or third-generation British born, but the cohorts represented in the most recent school-leaving statistics (those born in the 1980s) continued to include a substantial minority of first-generation British born young people (Modood et al., 1997). Even in the most recent education statistics, comparisons between minority groups are thus also often comparisons between young people of different generational status in the United Kingdom.

Social and Economic Status

Parents' educational levels and their socioeconomic standing constitute major influences on the educational attainments of children. For immigrants, however, these two indicators are often pulled apart: Migration frequently results in downward occupational mobility that is only redressed in later generations. It is abundantly clear that many early

immigrants faced severe social and economic disadvantage in the years immediately after their arrival in the United Kingdom. The postwar migration
from the Caribbean and South Asia was based on colonial ties, but its main
impetus was economic: Postwar reconstruction in Britain created demands
for labor in manufacturing, public transport, and the Health Service that
could not be met by the existing population. Although both qualified and
unqualified workers were recruited from abroad, racial discrimination in
the employment market was widespread. As a result, regardless of qualifications, early Caribbean and South Asian migrants were very largely
confined to low-paid manual jobs often well below their previous occupational levels, and quite discrepant from their educational backgrounds
(Daniel, 1968; Smith, 1977).

More recently, social and economic progress has been made by some
groups, though others are clearly still considerably disadvantaged. In the
late 1990s, for example, unemployment rates remained high among people from ethnic minority communities, and especially those of Pakistani
and Bangladeshi descent; at every level of educational qualifications Asian
people were more likely to be unemployed than White people, and Black
people more likely to be unemployed than Asians. Direct and indirect discrimination continue to play important parts in these trends (Modood et al.,
1997).

Considering specific minority groups, the fourth Policy Studies Institute
(PSI) survey (Modood et al., 1997) concluded that by 1994 Pakistanis and
Bangladeshis remained at severe and consistent disadvantage on a wide
range of indicators by comparison with the White majority, and often also
by comparison with other minority groups. The class position of these two
groups is compounded by their generally larger family size, and the fact
that married women are rarely in paid employment outside the home; as
a result, more than 80 percent of families of Pakistani and Bangladeshi
descent lived in poverty, with incomes less than half the national average. By contrast, African Asians had achieved broad parity with White
people, and people of Caribbean and Indian origin fell between these two
extremes, disadvantaged on some but not all indicators, and differing in
the specifics of their social circumstances. This complex mix of social and
material circumstances forms a key part of the backdrop to understanding
patterns of educational attainment.

Geographical Location

Minority ethnic groups continue to be heavily concentrated in the large
urban centres in the United Kingdom. In the late 1990s just under half
(49 percent) lived in Greater London (where they made up 28 percent of
all residents, and approaching 40 percent of the school-age population)
and the great majority of the remainder lived in metropolitan areas in
the midlands and the north of England (Scott, Pearce, & Goldblatt, 2001).

Unlike the situation in many U.S. cities, however, levels of segregation in the United Kingdom have not generally been high, and many people from minority communities live in local areas where the majority of the population is White. In the early 1990s Bangladeshis were the most likely to live in areas with a high concentration of their own ethnic group; even here, however, the representation of minorities rarely rose above 45 percent (Modood et al., 1997). Many of the areas with the largest minority populations are also among the most socially deprived. Recent data show, for example, that more than half of the ethnic minority population live in one of the 12 percent of local authority areas that are most deprived, and that those areas contain proportionately four times as many people from ethnic minority groups as other local authorities (Social Exclusion Unit, 2000). Educational achievements for all children are poorer in these deprived areas than in other parts of the United Kingdom.

Educational Attainments: Empirical Evidence

Data Sources: Strengths and Limitations

Rutter (this volume) highlights the basic methodological requirements needed to ensure the validity of group comparisons and to provide an appropriate basis for tests of causal influences on outcomes. Central to these are representative sampling and comparability of measurement. Although data on some aspects of the educational attainments of minority children in the United Kingdom clearly meet these requirements, others as yet do not. A range of official statistics are now published on children's school achievements, but only a limited number are recorded and reported by ethnic group. As a result, data on the attainments of minority groups largely derive from educational and social research studies that have included questioning on ethnicity, along with statistics published by individual local authorities with large minority populations.

A number of limitations are inherent in these various sources of information. First, approaches to ethnic group definition have varied over time in UK social research.[1] The most widely used classifications relate to family country of origin or nationality, and few take account of generational status in the United Kingdom, or of language, religious, or other cultural factors that may be equally salient for educational achievement. Second, with the exception of the Policy Studies Institute (PSI) surveys, few studies

---

[1] The Youth Cohort Study (2000), for example, combines together findings for all Black groups (of Caribbean, African, and other descent), whereas the Labour Force Survey, although reporting a category of Black Caribbean, categorizes respondents who classify themselves as Black British (the majority of whom are likely to be of Caribbean origin) as Black Other. Most sources other than the PSI surveys combine together findings for all groups of Indian origin; some 30 percent of these came to the United Kingdom from Africa and differ in important ways from those arriving directly from the subcontinent.

have purposively stratified samples by ethnic group. Given the size and geographical concentration of minority communities in the United Kingdom,
this means that even large-scale nationally representative samples often include only small numbers in specific minority groups. Third, much current
evidence on attainments in the early school years depends on statistics collected by local Education Authorities. In London – where, as we have seen,
approaching half the ethnic minority population lives – the dissolution of
the city-wide Education Authority in the early 1990s has meant that more
recent data relate to relatively small administrative districts, often serving
particular minority populations, and varying in the social composition of
the White groups used for comparison.

Taken together, these various factors mean that evidence on educational
attainments must be drawn from a patchwork of different – and often not
directly comparable – data sources. Most studies report on some combination (or subset) of the five largest minority groupings defined in the 1991
census – children and young people of Black African, Black Caribbean,
Indian, Pakistani and Bangladeshi descent – along with a broadly defined
"White" comparison group. There are few consistent data on small but
potentially informative groups such as the Chinese (who have positive
achievements in higher education, but are too geographically dispersed to
figure largely in local area statistics at the school stage), or Turkish Cypriots,
whose attainments have long given rise to concern in the local areas where
they live. Finally, despite widespread recognition of the need to consider
ethnic group differences in the context of social and economic variables,
few current data sources allow for statistical adjustments of this kind, and
checks on the comparability of measurements are rare. Where data on
factors such as SES background are available, they are often applied as
covariates in between-group comparisons with little consideration of their
implications for different ethnic groups. It is far from clear, however, that
such strategies will always be appropriate.

Intergenerational Trends: Overview
Cross-sectional data from the fourth PSI Survey (Modood et al., 1997) provide an initial picture of generational trends in school-leaving and post-
compulsory qualifications among minority groups in the early 1990s. The
survey was based on a nationally representative sample of 5,196 adults
(aged 16 and older) of Caribbean and Asian origin in England and Wales,
together with a comparison sample of 2,867 White people. Comparisons between respondents of different ages/lengths of stay in the United Kingdom
give a beginning picture of intergenerational continuities and discontinuities in patterns of achievement.

The Migrant Generation
As outlined by Tienda (this volume), the majority of immigrants entering the United Kingdom over the second half of the twentieth century

TABLE 4.1. *Highest Qualifications of Migrants to the United Kingdom Age 16 and older*

Qualifications	Black Caribbean %	Indian %	African Asian %	Pakistani %	Bangladeshi %	Chinese %
None, or below O level	71	52	45	63	75	48
O level or equivalent	8	12	21	20	11	9
A level or equivalent	19	12	18	8	5	19
Degree	2	28	16	9	9	23

Source: Fourth PSI Survey (Modood et al., 1997).

lacked formal educational qualifications. Within this broad pattern, however, more detailed qualification profiles varied both within and between migrant groups. Table 4.1 shows the qualification levels of members of the migrant generation interviewed for the PSI survey. As it suggests, the six migrant groups covered by the survey fell into two broader groupings. The first – including Black Caribbeans, Pakistanis, and Bangladeshis – were largely unqualified, with between 60 percent and 75 percent having no basic school-leaving qualifications. The second, including migrants from India, East Africa, and China, showed a quite different educational profile: Although around half were unqualified, substantial minorities in these groups came from professional backgrounds and had degree-level qualifications before their arrival in the United Kingdom. Degrees were much less common among migrants from Pakistan and Bangladesh (many of whom came from rural farming communities) and rare among those from the Caribbean. Gender differences modified the picture further. Women were more likely to be qualified than men among Caribbean immigrants, but the opposite was true for South Asians: Indeed, a substantial minority of women arriving in the United Kingdom from Pakistan and Bangladesh had had no formal schooling at all. In addition, a large proportion of Asian migrants – probably the majority – had very limited spoken English at the time of migration. By the early 1990s most men spoke English fluently or fairly well, but only around half of women from Pakistan and Bangladesh did so (Modood et al., 1997). Many migrants from the Caribbean spoke a Creole dialect of English, or in some cases of French.

The Second Generation
Table 4.2 shows a comparable breakdown for 25- to 44-year-olds in the second generation (i.e., those born in Britain, or aged 15 years or younger at migration). By contrast with the migrant generation, most groups had

TABLE 4.2. *Highest Qualifications of 25- to 44-Year-Olds Born in the United Kingdom, or Aged 15 Years or Younger at the Time of Migration*

Qualifications	White %	Black Caribbean %	Indian %	African Asian %	Pakistani %	Bangladeshi %	Chinese %
None, or below O level	30	26	31	24	54	74	[11][a]
O level or equivalent	22	30	24	17	18	14	[34]
A level or equivalent	37	38	30	36	15	8	[28]
Degree	12	7	15	23	11	4	[27]

[a] Based on small sample size.

Source: Fourth PSI Survey (Modood et al., 1997).

TABLE 4.3. *16- to 24-Year-Olds with No Qualifications/Less Than O Levels*

	White %	Black Caribbean %	Indian %	African Asian %	Pakistani %	Bangladeshi %	Chinese %
Men	22	31	27	23	44	42	[16][a]
Women	26	18	21	19	40	52	[10]

[a] Based on small sample size.
Source: Fourth PSI Survey (Modood et al., 1997).

made significant progress: The proportions with no qualifications had dropped markedly in most minority groups, and the proportions with "O" and "A" level equivalent qualifications had increased. As a result, the qualification profiles of second-generation Caribbeans and Indians broadly matched those of their White age peers, and those of African Asians and Chinese exceeded them. As Table 4.2 shows, however, two groups had not shared in these upward trends. First, although Pakistanis (especially women), had made some progress at degree level, the proportions with no qualifications/less than O levels remained high. Second, the figures for second-generation Bangladeshis showed little if any progress at any point in the qualification spectrum by comparison with those of the migrant generation.

The "New" Generation
Table 4.3 focuses on the "new generation," aged 16–24 in 1994, the huge majority of whom were United Kingdom–born. Because many of these young people were still in education at the time of the survey, overall qualification levels could not be assessed; instead, the table focuses on the proportions without a minimal level of school-leaving qualifications. Smaller proportions in all ethnic groups were without a qualification than in older generations, though the overall position of Caribbean men was not improved over 25- to 44-year-olds; in addition, twice as many Caribbean-origin men as women were without qualifications, a gender gap in this group noted in many other studies. Finally, though showing considerable improvement by contrast with earlier generations, Pakistanis and Bangladeshis continued to include the highest levels of unqualified or poorly qualified young people.

Recent Trends
Although more recent data do not generally allow for any direct assessment of intergenerational changes, they can provide a picture of evolving trends in the relative performance of different groups. Most studies report cross-sectional data, comparing performance at specific ages or stages of schooling. In a few instances longitudinal findings are also available, allowing

for some estimates of relative progress over time. As will be apparent, these two approaches highlight somewhat different patterns of effects.

Attainments During the School Years

In the early 1980s a review of the attainments of children of Caribbean origin undertaken for the Rampton/Swann Enquiry concluded that "research evidence shows a strong trend to under-achievement of pupils of West Indian origin on the main indicators of academic performance" (Taylor, 1986). In addition to poor test performance, children of Caribbean descent were more likely to be in the lower streams of mainstream schools, more likely to be placed in special educational settings, and more often seen by teachers as presenting discipline problems in the classroom.

Ten years later, a second review (Gillborn & Gipps, 1996) concluded that evidence covering the school years was limited and somewhat inconsistent; in particular, results from the National Curriculum assessments at ages 7 and 11 years often varied among metropolitan areas. On average, for example, pupils of Caribbean origin performed less well than their White peers – but that situation was reversed in one large urban authority, possibly reflecting differences in the social composition of the White comparison group. Low average attainments among Pakistani and Bangladeshi groups were more consistently reported. English language fluency seems likely to be an important contributory factor here, especially in the early stages of schooling. Figure 4.1 shows average reading levels of 5- to 15-year-olds drawn from a nationally representative sample assessed in 1999 in the course of the Office for National Statistics study of child mental health (British Child and Adolescent Mental Health Survey, 1999 [B-CAMHS99]; Meltzer & Gatwood with Goodman & Ford, 2000). Although the numbers of ethnic minority children and adolescents included in the study were

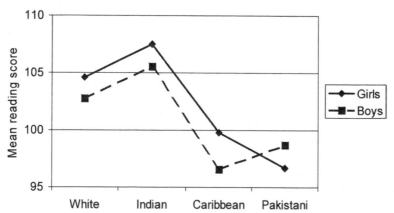

FIGURE 4.1. B-CAMHS99: Mean reading levels in 5- to 15-year-olds. *Source:* B-CAMHS99: unpublished analyses.

small (93 Caribbeans, 181 Indians, and 124 Pakistani/Bangladeshis, together with a White group of more than 9,000), the pattern of between-group differences reflects those reported elsewhere. Adjusted for effects of age and gender, children of Caribbean and Pakistani/Bangladeshi origin achieved less well than their White peers ($p = .008$ and $p < .001$ respectively), whereas children of Indian descent scored significantly better ($p = .018$).

Qualifications at Age 16

Examination attainments at age 16 are of particular importance in the United Kingdom, providing accreditation for entry to post-compulsory education and many sectors of the labor market. The Department for Education and Employment Youth Cohort Study (YCS) – a series of longitudinal surveys of school-leavers in England and Wales – provides the most extensive data on recent trends in the General Certificate of Secondary Education (GCSE) taken at age 16. Most initial samples have included between 20,000 and 25,000 young people, ensuring reasonably sizeable numbers in most minority groups. Figure 4.2 shows the proportions of White and Black (African and Caribbean) respondents achieving five or more higher graded GCSE passes in selected years between 1989 and 2000, and for young people of Indian, Pakistani, and Bangladeshi origin from 1992 onward.

Several important trends emerge from these data. First, the 1990s saw a marked increase in the overall proportions of young people completing their compulsory schooling with qualifications at these levels, from 30 percent in 1989 to 49 percent in 2000. Second, all ethnic groups shared in these improvements to some extent; indeed, judged against the baseline of their 1992 performance, all minority groups except Pakistanis made greater

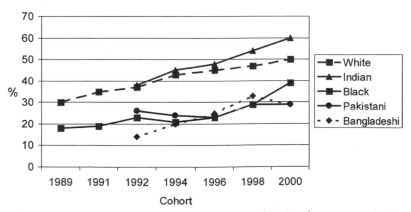

FIGURE 4.2. Youth Cohort Study percentages achieving five or more higher grade GCSE passes by ethnic origin. *Source: Youth Cohort Study, 2000.*

proportional gains than their White peers. Third, however, absolute levels of attainment clearly varied among ethnic groups and reflected two broad attainment "clusters," one composed of White pupils and those of Indian descent, the other of young people of Black, Pakistani, and Bangladeshi origin. Although the classifications used in the YCS differed somewhat from those in the PSI studies, these two clusters are clearly strongly reminiscent of the ethnic group variations in qualification levels found in the migrant generation.

More detailed analyses suggest that social class and gender differences (girls outperforming boys) were apparent within each ethnic group (Gillborn & Mirza, 2000). In general, the gender gap was of similar proportions across all ethnic groups, but social class gradients were least marked among young Black people, and analyses separated by class showed that Black pupils from middle-class families often achieved little better than their White working class peers. Multivariate analyses confirmed that ethnic group differences were maintained with social class and gender controlled (Gillborn & Mirza, 2000).

Progress During the School Years

Longitudinal data across the school years are more limited, but of interest in highlighting somewhat different patterns of relationships. First, a number of studies have suggested that children from some minority groups – especially those of Caribbean origin, and in some studies especially boys – show a relative decline in performance over the primary and early secondary school years (see, e.g., Sammons, 1995; Smith & Tomlinson, 1989; Tizard, Blatchford, Burke, Farquhar, & Plewis, 1988). Although these studies were all conducted in the 1980s, cross-sectional data for children of different ages in one local authority in the 1990s suggest a similar pattern (Gillborn & Mirza, 2000). Second, two of the available longitudinal studies showed that by age 16 the relative *progress* of minority groups – taking account of earlier attainment levels, and adjusting for SES background and other factors – was at least comparable with, and sometimes exceeded, that of their White peers. Once again, more recent longitudinal findings have confirmed a similar pattern in the 1990s (Hague & Bell, 2001), and cross-sectional data for ethnic minority children in mainly White schools (Cline et al., 2002) appear to reflect similar trends. At age 11, the proportions of minority children achieving expected levels in English and math in these schools were considerably lower than for White pupils; at age 16, the proportions gaining 5 or more A*-C grades were closely comparable. Although the reasons for these variations are unclear, Sammons (1995) speculated that they might reflect a variety of factors: In particular, differences in the types of assessment used at different ages seemed relevant (GCSEs covering a wider spread of subject areas, and involving a considerable element of course work), along with the possibility that

TABLE 4.4. *Participation in Post-Compulsory Schooling Ages 18–24*

	White %	Caribbean %	Indian %	Pakistani %	Chinese/Other Asian %
Men	15.2	11.5	38.1	36.4	45.7
Women	14.9	15.6	33.2	28.5	47.3

Source: Leslie & Drinkwater (1999).

minority pupils become more motivated during the later secondary years, as awareness of the need for qualifications increases with impending entry to further education or the labor market.

Post-Compulsory Education
Beyond the years of compulsory schooling further key changes emerge. The most central of these concerns participation in post-compulsory education. It has long been clear from UK statistics that young people from ethnic minorities are more likely to continue in post-compulsory education than their White peers. By the late 1990s, for example, four fifths of young people from ethnic minorities, by comparison with two thirds of Whites, remained in full-time education post-16 (Owen, Green, Pitcher, & Maguire, 2000); contrasts were especially striking in the case of those with the poorest examination performance at age 16 (71 percent vs 37 percent). Table 4.4 shows recent data for 18- to 24-year-olds derived from the Labour Force Surveys (Leslie & Drinkwater, 1999). With the exception of Black Caribbean males, all minority groups were more likely to be in some form of education at these ages than Whites; among young people of Caribbean origin, women were more likely to be studying than men, while gender ratios were reversed in the South Asian groups.

Data from the Higher Education Statistics Agency confirm that most minority groups are also well represented in higher education. In 1997/8 minority ethnic groups (just over 8 percent of 19- to 24-year-olds in the population as a whole) made up nearly 13 percent of first degree-level students (Owen et al., 2000), though in many instances they tended to be concentrated in the less prestigious "post-1992" universities. Success rates for applications to degree and Higher National Diploma (HND) courses have increased for all minority groups since the mid-1990s; in 1996, for example, 18 percent of all acceptances to degree courses and 27 percent of acceptances to HND courses were from ethnic minority groups. Net of earlier attainments, recent analyses of YCS data (Gayle, Berridge, & Davies, 2002) confirm that social class, gender, and ethnicity all have independent effects on participation in degree-level courses. For cohorts born in 1969 and 1970 young people of Indian descent had the highest participation rates, with

26 percent studying for degrees, by contrast with 14 percent of Whites and Pakistanis, and less than 10 percent of Bangladeshi, Caribbean, and African young people. Young Black people (of both African and Caribbean origin) are more likely than their White peers to enter higher education as mature students, and Caribbeans are more likely to enter vocationally oriented courses. Other evidence suggests that general social class patterns are confounded at this stage in the educational process: Although two thirds of White university entrants are from nonmanual backgrounds, this is true for only just over a third of Pakistanis and Bangladeshis (see Shiner & Modood, 2002). Few data are available on course completion rates, but attainments of graduates are known to vary by ethnic group. Recent data show, for example, that 53.1 percent of White graduates achieved a first or upper class degree, by contrast with only 37 percent for minority groups; Black African students were the least likely to obtain degrees at this level (25.1 percent) (Owen et al., 2000).

What are the overall implications of these increased participation rates for aggregate profiles of attainment in adulthood? Data on this issue are limited as yet, but recent analyses of cumulated data from the General Household Survey (Rothon, 2001) suggest that they could be considerable. Focusing on respondents aged 20 and over, this study, like the PSI survey, found a substantial narrowing of the qualifications gap between White and minority respondents in more recent generations. In multivariate analyses of data for the migrant generation, all the minority groups studied (Black Caribbean, Indian, and Pakistani) showed decrements by comparison with British-born Whites in higher secondary, college, and degree-level qualifications with effects of age, gender, and parental social class controlled. In the second generation, similar controls reduced all these between-group contrasts to nonsignificance. If confirmed in future studies, these findings suggest that minority groups' greater investment in post-compulsory education has been of major significance in reducing educational differentials.

Understanding Ethnic Diversity in Educational Attainments in the United Kingdom

Taken together, these findings present a complex picture of both continuity and change in the educational attainments of minority groups in the United Kingdom. On the one hand, recent generations in all the main minorities have clearly made progress in terms of formal educational qualifications by comparison with the migrant generation; importantly, these changes took place during a period when social class variations in attainment narrowed only slightly (Heath, 2000). On the other hand, considerable diversity remains: A gap between the school attainments of young people of Caribbean origin and their White peers has persisted into the second and third generations, and children of more recent South Asian migrants include both the most and the least successful in educational terms. The relative performance of different groups appears to vary at different stages in the educational process, and more detailed data frequently reveal systematic gender differences within ethnic groups.

This pattern of findings clearly argues against any unitary concept of "ethnic minority disadvantage" in education: Although some influences may be common to all minority groups, different factors – or more probably combinations of factors – seem likely to be key to understanding effects for individual groups. In principle the marked differences in attainments both within and between ethnic groups provide a rich basis for testing different explanatory models; in practice, these opportunities have barely been explored. In addition, few of the more general theoretical models advanced to explain ethnic group variations in attainment in U.S. samples (see, e.g., Portes & MacLeod, 1999) have been systematically tested using UK data – and indeed most commentators agree that the data available are woefully inadequate to that task.

Judged against Rutter's (this volume) requirements for teasing out causal influences, the current UK literature also falls short. Empirical tests of competing models are rare, and a major divide continues between quantitative studies, typically exploring social background factors, and qualitative research, typically addressing aspects of school experiences. Finally, as Modood (in press) points out, progress has almost certainly been hampered by the heavy emphasis in both research and policy discussions on attempts to understand why some groups – especially Caribbean males – achieve poorly in the UK education system, rather than why others – most notably Indian and other Asian groups – do well. Taken together, these various factors mean that discussion of possible explanatory factors must be largely speculative at this stage. The following sections consider a series of likely influences, grouped under two broad heads: first, aspects of the human capital that minority groups bring to the educational process, and second, aspects of their experiences within that system.

Human, Cultural, and Social Capital

As outlined earlier, many minority communities continue to be considerably socially and economically disadvantaged in current UK society. This is at its most severe – to the extent of being described as a "plight" (Modood et al., 1997) – for people of Bangladeshi origin, and least marked for Asian migrants from Africa. Given the strong and persistent generational patterning of educational attainments in the White community by social class, family income, and parental education, these factors form a natural starting point for considering influences on intergenerational transmission in minority groups.

As Heath and McMahon (2000) point out, however, we cannot be certain that social origins or parental qualifications will necessarily carry the same implications for ethnic minorities as they do for the White population. For children of migrants, for example, the human capital of parents may be relatively culture specific, whereas for later generations other factors may override family influences. We found evidence to support these concerns many years ago, in a study of the school achievements of a first generation sample of Caribbean children in inner London (Maughan & Dunn, 1988): Social background indicators that followed "expected" patterns of association with the attainments of White young people had much less consistent effects for their Black peers. Rather than assuming comparability, we need to test how far social indicators do indeed carry similar implications for educational outcomes in different ethnic groups. Because few UK studies have addressed this question explicitly to date, analyses of the B-CAMHS99 survey (Meltzer et al., 2000) have been used to supplement published findings here. B-CAMHS99 included data on parental occupation, household income, maternal education, family composition, and neighborhood deprivation. Although small sample sizes in the minority groups precluded multivariate analyses of this full range of factors, preliminary tests seemed likely to be informative.

Social Class and Family Income
The impact of family social class and markers of income poverty on ethnic group differences in school achievements has now been assessed in a range of studies and produced three relatively consistent findings. First, the proportions of variance attributable to class background is generally higher than that attributable to ethnic group; second, the inclusion of indicators of class background and/or material resources considerably reduces, but rarely eliminates, ethnic group differences in school achievements; and third, although SES variations in attainment are typically found within each ethnic group, they are sometimes less pronounced in minority than in White samples (Gillborn & Mirza, 2000). On this evidence, continuing disparities in the occupational and economic circumstances of ethnic minorities appear to play an important role in continuing variations in children's school achievements. As outlined earlier, at higher qualification levels these processes may be even more salient; among minority adults born or fully educated in the United Kingdom, controls for class origins reduced ethnic group differences in qualification levels to nonsignificance (Rothon, 2001).

There are also clear pointers, however, that conventional class-based analyses of attainment may fail to capture key features of minority group experiences. First, as we have seen, the downward occupational mobility faced by many members of the migrant generation makes it likely that measures of occupational status alone will not provide a satisfactory basis for group comparisons and may indeed lead to inappropriate adjustments in some instances. Second, class effects are clearly heavily qualified in some communities by gender norms and expectations. Third, the striking *lack* of social gradients for many minority groups' participation in further and higher educational provides strong signals that other important factors are involved. Irrespective of class, groups such as South Asians and the Chinese appear to show a strong academic orientation that can override occupation-based classifications. And finally, as Modood (2003) suggests, although systematic data on this issue are lacking, it seems likely that some minority groups spend considerably more of their disposable income on private education than is typical in the White community. Although preferences of this kind are clearly shaped by class influences, they also appear to have a significant ethnic dimension; Modood (2003) estimates, for example, that on a per capita basis children of Indian descent are 2.5 times more likely to be in fee-paying schools than their White counterparts, and those of Chinese origin five times more likely. Reliance on indicators of social prestige or social disadvantage alone clearly fails to capture these and other qualifying factors that may be of major importance in contributing to variations between ethnic groups.

Parental Education
A second source of influence derives from parents' own educational experiences. Parental education is often used as an index of cultural capital – familiarity with the dominant culture in a society that in turn is seen as central to success in its education system. For immigrants, of course, these processes may be interrupted; for subsequent generations, parents' awareness of their own educational success (or lack of it) may also moderate expected associations.

Perhaps surprisingly, the impact of parental education per se has received much less attention than social class variations in UK educational research. In their study of schools with large Bangladeshi intakes (where more than a quarter of mothers either had no formal schooling at all, or only primary levels of education) Hague and Bell (2001) found that maternal education added significantly to the prediction of attainment in models including parental occupation and further reduced (though did not eliminate) effects of ethnic group. Figure 4.3 shows maternal qualification levels for each of the main ethnic groups included in the B-CAMHS99 survey. As other studies have found, the majority of mothers of children of Pakistani/Bangladeshi origin were still without formal educational qualifications in the late 1990s, whereas the profiles of Caribbean and White mothers were relatively similar. Figure 4.4 shows mean reading levels for children in this study, broken down by maternal education and ethnic group. Three features are of note. First, reading scores were clearly associated with maternal education within the White, Caribbean, and Pakistani/Bangladeshi groups, though not for children of Indian origin; second, controls for maternal education reduced Pakistani/White differences to nonsignificance; and third, at each level of maternal education mean reading levels were rather

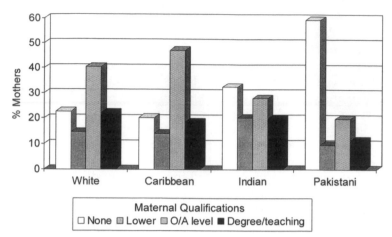

FIGURE 4.3. B-CAMHS99 Maternal qualifications and ethnic origin. *Source:* B-CAMHS99: unpublished analyses.

lower for Caribbean than for White children, so that in statistical models maternal education reduced, but failed to eliminate, Caribbean/White differences. If replicated, these findings suggest that the low achievement levels of many children of immigrants of Pakistani and Bangladeshi descent are strongly associated with the very limited educational experiences of their families of origin. For young people of Caribbean origin – most of whose parents are likely to have been educated in the United Kingdom – Black/White parity in maternal qualification levels does not yet appear to have translated into parity in children's reading skills.

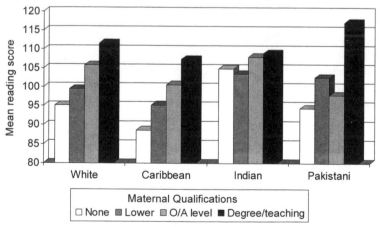

FIGURE 4.4. B-CAMHS99 Children's mean reading scores, maternal education, and ethnic origin. *Source:* B-CAMHS99: unpublished analyses.

English Language Fluency

For some minority groups – especially, in the context of the present discussion, those of Pakistani and Bangladeshi descent – English language fluency has clearly been a highly salient factor in influencing more general patterns of attainment. Average attainment levels rise systematically as English language fluency increases (see, e.g., Wandsworth Education Department, 2001), and local initiatives to identify and address the language needs of Bangladeshi pupils who speak languages other than or in addition to English have contributed to improved performance (see, e.g., Demie, 2001). One longitudinal study found that lack of full English fluency at age 7 continued to show a powerful impact on both reading and mathematics performance at age 10, but that differences between a broadly defined "Asian" subgroup and their White peers persisted with both English fluency and SES background controlled. By age 16, however, Asian young people as a group were outperforming their White counterparts, but the long-term implications of childhood lack of English fluency were still detectable in multivariate analyses (Sammons, 1995). Although early lack of English fluency clearly has a persisting impact on school achievements, other factors also appear to come into play at different stages of schooling.

Cultural Diversity and Cultural Capital

Over time, a variety of other factors have been proposed as influencing the cultural and social capital of ethnic minorities in the UK education system. Early studies of first-generation Caribbean families, for example, suggested that they lacked understanding of the developmental importance of play, toys, and parent–child interaction in the preschool years (see Taylor, 1986). More recently concerns have been expressed over the impact of Islamic values on attitudes to academic education, especially for girls, and the impact of Black youth culture on teacher–pupil relationships and attitudes to achievement, this time especially among boys (see, e.g., Sewell, 1997). Quantifying the effects of such influences is difficult. Early commentators also suggested that the Caribbean tradition of female-headed single-parent households might be salient for young Black people, the lack of authoritative father figures seen as contributing both to classroom disruptiveness and to patterns of attainment. Findings from the B-CAMHS99 study suggest that if processes of this kind were important for first-generation children of Caribbean migrants, they are less so today. Although rates of single-parent households in the Caribbean sample were high (66 percent, by contrast with 22 percent in the White sample and 6.5 percent among children of Indian origin), and family structure was associated with marked variations in the reading attainments of White children, it showed almost no effects on the attainments of children of Caribbean origin. More detailed tests suggested that this reflected quite different associations between single parenthood and maternal education for these two groups: Where White single mothers tended to be poorly qualified, single Caribbean mothers were, if anything, better qualified than their married counterparts.

Set against such potentially "inhibiting" influences on educational achievements, family attitudes and expectations are argued to play a key part in contributing to some of the positive outcomes observed. Though they may be less knowledgeable about the school system than their White peers, South Asian and Chinese parents do nonetheless appear to foster high expectations in their children, maintain clear discipline in relation to such issues as homework, and support their progress through encouraging attendance at extra classes out of school. Social capital of this rather different kind is expressed within the family and often supported and reinforced by attitudes in the wider community. As Modood (2003) comments: "In short, what they give is not a transfer of knowledge and skills but a sense that education is important, that teachers should be obeyed and that academic success takes priority over other pursuits, especially recreational youth culture."

Similar influences may also play a part in explaining the high rates of participation in post-compulsory education for all minority groups. A variety of factors, both positive and negative, underlie these trends: parental encouragement for continuance in education (Drew, Gray, & Sime, 1992); the value placed by economic migrants on qualifications as a means of social advance (Modood, 1998); awareness of the risks of unemployment, which might either function to postpone labor market entry, or to support the need for additional qualifications, or both (Drew, 1995); and awareness of discrimination and racism elsewhere (Leslie & Drinkwater, 1999). Given the importance of "school persistence" rates for the eventual qualification profiles of minority groups, the differing balance of these influences in specific ethnic groups clearly warrants further attention.

Family and Social Influences: Cumulative Impact

Considered separately, each of these aspects of family and social background appears to play some part in contributing to intergenerational continuities in ethnic group differences in attainment. In practice, of course, their impact will often cumulate. Table 4.5 shows distributions for each of the main ethnic groups in the B-CAMHS99 data on a simple index of three indicators of social disadvantage: household income in the bottom quartile, mothers with low/no qualifications, and social origins in classes IV or V. Ethnic groups differ markedly this combined measure: The cumulative disadvantage of children and young people of Pakistani/Bangladeshi origin becomes especially apparent, as does the general parity of social and family background circumstances between children of Indian origin and their White peers. Children of Caribbean origin fell between these two extremes:

TABLE 4.5. *Indicators of Cumulative Disadvantage: B-CAMHS99*

Indicators of Disadvantage[a]	White %	Indian %	Caribbean %	Pakistani %
0	57.9	52.2	32.5	18.5
1	24.2	29.2	41.1	38.2
2	12.4	13.5	18.4	29.4
3	5.6	5.1	8.0	13.9

[a] Social class IV/V, low household income, low/no maternal education.

Smaller shares than Pakistani/Bangladeshis faced multiple adversities, while smaller shares than Whites and Indians faced none. A multivariate analysis of children's reading scores controlling for these three factors (scored using their full range of categories, rather than as the dichotomies represented in Table 4.5) revealed significant differences between White and minority children only for children of Indian descent, who continued to outperform their White peers. The small numbers in each minority group in the B-CAMHS99 sample, along with the caveats previously expressed about comparability of measures, mean that these findings should be interpreted with considerable caution. If replicated using other samples, however, they suggest that taken together, the cumulative impact of a range of educational and social background influences may do much to account for continuing variations in achievement between ethnic groups.

The Education System and Educational Experiences
Alongside family and social influences, school system factors and the nature of young people's educational experiences are also likely to play a role in influencing patterns of attainment. Three broad groups of factors have been investigated here: first, variations in the nature of children's day-to-day experiences in the school setting, including the effects of teacher expectations and racial stereotyping; second, variations in access to resources and opportunities at different levels in the education system; and third, variations in the quality of schooling, and the possibility that some approaches to school organization may be differentially effective for ethnic minorities. Running through much of this literature is a concern with the effects of discrimination and institutional racism, and the impact these may have on the opportunities, attitudes, and motivation of ethnic minority students.

School Experiences
Though not always detected in larger scale surveys, qualitative studies (see Gillborn & Gipps, 1996, for a review) document variations in the patterns of school life for children from different ethnic groups. Probably the most widely reported is a relatively high degree of tension, often spilling into

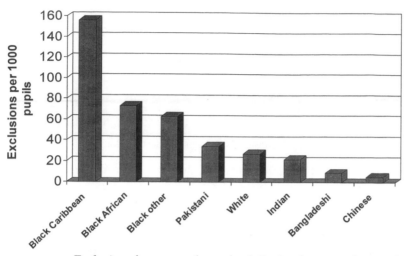

FIGURE 4.5. Exclusions from secondary school: England, 1993–4. *Source:* OFSTED, cited in Gillborn and Gipps, 1996.

conflict, in relationships between White teachers and pupils of Caribbean origin. Qualitative studies suggest that Caribbean pupils are often perceived as troublesome; that they are disciplined more frequently than other children; and that teachers often hold low expectations of their attainments. One quantifiable indicator of the most extreme form of difficulties of this kind is the marked excess of young people of Caribbean origin who are excluded from school. Figure 4.5 shows exclusion data for a variety of ethnic groups from 1993–4; although overall exclusion levels have fallen in more recent years, the higher risk for young people of Caribbean origin remains.

School exclusion affects only a tiny minority of pupils. Teacher–pupil conflicts arguably affect much larger groups and contribute in some instances to escalating processes whereby Black pupils (especially boys) are seen as challenging teachers' authority. Conceivably, these tensions may develop collectivist anti-school ideologies that further affect their chances of success (Sewell, 1997). It is impossible to know how far conclusions of this kind – usually based on observations in individual schools – are more widely generalizable (Pilkington, 1999). Similar accounts have, however, emerged in the 1970s, 1980s, and 1990s, making it likely that they do reflect salient features of the school experiences of some young Black people. To the extent that this is the case, they clearly need to be considered alongside other accounts as potential contributors to ongoing variations in patterns of attainment.

South Asian pupils, by contrast, are perceived as committed to classroom discipline and academic goals in ways that make them attractive to teachers, but vulnerable to racial harassment from peers (Gillborn &

Gipps, 1996). Although the incidence of bullying and violence in schools is difficult to quantify, numerous qualitative studies (along with a number of widely publicized examples of severe violence) attest to the reality of racial violence and harassment as elements in the school experiences of many ethnic minority pupils. Pupils of South Asian origin appear to be the most common victims of both verbal and physical attacks; qualitative studies suggest that they not infrequently experience a sense of threat associated with their schooling. It is unclear at this stage to what extent – if at all – this affects their patterns of attainment. Indeed, as Modood (2003) points out, there is an apparent paradox here: If the experience of racism contributes to young Black people being "turned off" schooling, why are no parallel effects observed for Asian youth, who are undoubtedly exposed to high rates of peer victimization? Although in general teachers' attitudes to South Asian pupils seem relatively positive, there are suggestions that the stereotype of the "docile" Asian girl, whose future may be restricted by early marriage, can nonetheless lead to lowered expectations for girls in particular, and to their being systematically forgotten or ignored in busy classrooms in ways that, over time, could contribute to undermining their performance.

Opportunity and Access

Despite legislation to restrict direct racial discrimination, "ethnic penalties" (Heath & McMahon, 1997) clearly persist in the UK labor market, and institutional racism remains a concern in many institutions (Macpherson of Cluny, 1999). Evidence of disadvantage in access to educational opportunities is scattered. Given the high levels of minority participation in post-compulsory education, it is perhaps ironic that some of the clearest evidence of disadvantage comes from particular sectors in the higher education field. Recent analyses suggest that although there is little evidence of ethnic disadvantage in overall rates of admission to universities – and indeed that the "new" universities may respond more positively to Chinese, Bangladeshi, and Indian applicants than they do to Whites – applicants from most minority groups do face an ethnic penalty in applying to the more prestigious "old" universities (Shiner & Modood, 2002). During the school years, evidence is more difficult to evaluate. The increasing "marketization" of schooling, with its emphasis on parental choice, is argued to have led to the development of local choice markets that operate to reinforce existing class and ethnic divisions, and qualitative studies suggest that the publication of "league tables" of results from individual schools has led to the diversion of resources within schools to focus disproportionately on high achievers (Gillborn & Youdell, 2000). Early versions of the National Curriculum introduced in the late 1980s were widely regarded as inadequately reflecting ethnic diversity, and there have been continuing concerns that Black Caribbean children have been inappropriately placed in low academic tracks on grounds of behaviour rather than academic skills.

Cumulatively, the effects of these various factors could undoubtedly have an impact on school achievements. That it is difficult to specify their degree of influence derives at least in part from the lack of systematic monitoring within the education system. By the late 1990s some local education authorities had still not begun monitoring key indicators of educational progress by ethnic origin, and the availability of such data continues to vary widely today. Without such monitoring, however, it is impossible for schools (or researchers) to gain any accurate picture of the extent to which variations in attainment are associated with inequalities of opportunity.

School Effectiveness

Alongside issues of access, questions of overall school effectiveness may also be relevant to variations in minority group attainment. Extensive evidence suggests that schools vary in their levels of pupil attainment (Rutter & Maughan, 2002); within this general framework there have been particular questions over the effectiveness of different styles of school organization for different subgroups of pupils, and of "compositional effects" in the intakes to schools.

Despite a growing number of quantitative studies in the school effectiveness field, few have focused specifically on ethnic group variations. Those that have (e.g., Mortimore, Sammons, Stoll, Lewis, & Ecob, 1988; Smith & Tomlinson, 1989) have generally concluded that although minority group children do indeed achieve better in some schools than in others, White children also fare well in those same schools; no particular factors were identified that were specific to minority achievement. Similar conclusions have emerged from case studies of individual schools identified by school inspectors as having especially successful results for minority pupils: "These successful schools have no recipe for the achievement of Black Caribbean pupils that is different from that for the rest of their pupils" (OFSTED, 2002). Descriptions of these successful case study schools resonate strongly with the wider school effectiveness literature: They displayed strong leadership and teamwork, had a positive, achievement-oriented ethos and high teacher expectations, built good contacts with parents and their local community, gave a clear priority to adequate resourcing for children with special educational needs, and took an unambiguous stand on racism and equality of opportunity.

If similar school policies benefit both White and minority children, it might still be the case that the achievements of minority young people are influenced by the ethnic composition of their schools, so that particular benefits accrue, for example, from being educated alongside larger or smaller numbers of peers of the same ethnic group. To date, however, little systematic evidence on this question is available in the United Kingdom. A recent study of minority children in mainly White schools in 35 nonurban local authorities (Cline et al., 2002) found that, like their White peers, minority children achieved more positively at age 16 than those in urban schools, though this advantage was not apparent at age 11. No other social background data were available in this study, however, making it difficult to assess how far these variations reflected other aspects of social background at the individual or school levels. In addition, it was clear that some difficulties might be more pronounced for minority children in mainly White schools: A substantial group of children, for example, reported race-related name calling or verbal abuse; policy approaches to ethnic diversity varied, as did provision for teaching English as an additional language; and many teachers felt poorly prepared by their initial and subsequent training to meet the needs of minority pupils in their schools.

Conclusions

As this brief overview suggests, current evidence on the educational achievements of ethnic minorities in the United Kingdom is both fragmentary and limited. At a descriptive level it is clear that ethnic group differences in attainments occur at all levels of the educational system; attempts to move to more explanatory models, however, are seriously hampered by a lack of appropriate data, and to an extent by the limited "explanatory" paradigms that dominate the literature. As a result, any interpretation of current findings must be speculative at best.

Three features emerge from the descriptive data as demanding explanation: first, the marked differences in both school and post-school attainments among young people of South Asian origin; second, the continuing gap between the attainments of young people of Caribbean origin – and especially young Caribbean men – and their White peers; and third, the apparently changing between-group profiles of attainment at different stages in the education system.

On the first of these issues – the strong contrasts between the performance of young people of Indian origin and their peers of Pakistani and Bangladeshi descent – it seems likely that variations in the human capital of the migrant generation, subsequently mirrored in their differing circumstances within British society, play key roles in accounting for these effects. Families of Bangladeshi origin, in particular, remain in a severely disadvantaged situation in the United Kingdom; many parents came to this country with very limited (in some cases no) experience of schooling, and a significant minority of children of Bangladeshi origin continue to enter school with limited knowledge of the English language. By contrast, immigrants from India (and especially those who came to the United Kingdom from East Africa) were generally much better qualified; as we have seen, their current UK social and economic circumstances now largely mirror those of the White population, and their investment in education appears to be especially strong. It is unclear at this stage how far religious or other cultural variations, or different modes of incorporation into UK society, contribute further to these effects (Portes & MacLeod, 1999). In the wider sociological literature there has been considerable interest in the concept of an "Asian trajectory," in which social mobility via education forms a key part. On this formulation, variations among South Asian groups are primarily a reflection of length of residency in the United Kingdom: Groups that are successful today were disadvantaged in the past, whereas those that are disadvantaged today will soon follow a more upwardly mobile trajectory. Data on the progress of the coming generations of school children will be central to assessing this claim.

Turning to young people of Caribbean origin, additional influences seem almost certain to be involved. Despite less disadvantaged social circumstances, average attainment levels among Black Caribbeans at age 16 differ little from those of Pakistanis and Bangladeshis; in addition, gender differences are marked at many stages in the educational process, and there are worrying suggestions that Caribbean children's performance may decline across the school years. If confirmed, these last findings almost certainly suggest that school-based influences are implicated. As we have seen, observational studies highlight perceptions of classroom disruptiveness, teacher–pupil tensions, low teacher expectations, and aspects of peer culture as possible influences here; awareness of discrimination in the wider society, and especially in the labor market, may also gain in importance as young people enter their teens. At present, however, no data sources allow for assessment of these factors alongside other effects. Given the apparently continuing disadvantages faced by young people of Caribbean origin in the UK education system, more systematic investigation of these issues is clearly a pressing need. In addition, as Tienda (this volume) notes, the very different educational trajectories of Caribbean migrants to the United States constitute a further challenge and suggest that more systematic use of international comparisons could prove illuminating in understanding key influences both within and between cultures.

Further data are also required to understand the apparently changing patterns of between-group differences in attainment highlighted at different stages in the educational process. To date, these findings derive almost exclusively from a patchwork of cross-sectional findings on children of different ages; without longitudinal data tracking the same individuals over time it is almost impossible to interpret what they might mean. Indeed, the dearth of longitudinal data emerges as a key lack at numerous points in this review. In time, the recently initiated Millennium cohort study, specifically designed to oversample ethnic minorities, should go some way to meet this need. More immediately, shorter term studies tracking children and young people across key transitions in the educational system, and including adequate data on both their family backgrounds and school experiences, would add greatly to our understanding of persisting variations in attainment.

References

Cline, T., de Abreu, G., Fihosy, C., Gray, H., Lanbert, H., & Neale, J. (2002). *Minority ethnic pupils in mainly white schools*. DfES Research Brief 365. Department for Education and Skills, London. Retrieved 05/08/2003 from www.dfes.gov.uk/research/data/uploadfiles/RB365.doc.

Daniel, W.W. (1968). *Racial discrimination in England*. London: Penguin.

Demie, F. (2001). Ethnic and gender differences in educational achievement and implications for school improvement strategies. *Educational Research, 43*, 91–106.

Drew, D. (1995). *'Race', education and work: The statistics of inequality*. Aldershot: Avebury.

Drew, D., Gray, J., & Sime, N. (1992). *Against the odds: The education and labour market experiences of Black young people*. England and Wales Youth Cohort Study, Report R&D No. 68. Sheffield: Employment Department.

Gayle, V., Berridge, D., & Davies, R. (2002). Young people's entry into higher education: quantifying influential factors. *Oxford Review of Education, 28*, 5–20.

Gillborn, D., & Gipps, C. (1996). *Recent research on the achievements of ethnic minority pupils*. London: HMSO.

Gillborn, D., & Mirza, H. S. (2000). *Educational inequality: Mapping race, class and gender*. London: OFSTED.

Gillborn, D., & Youdell, D. (2000). *Rationing education*. Buckingham: Open University Press.

Hague, Z., & Bell, J. F. (2001). Evaluating the performance of minority ethnic pupils in secondary schools. *Oxford Review of Education, 27*, 357–368.

Heath, A. (2000). The political arithmetic tradition in the sociology of education. *Oxford Review of Education, 26*, 313–331.

Heath, A., & McMahon, D. (1997). Education and occupational attainments: The impact of ethnic origins. In V. Karn (Ed.), *Ethnicity in the 1991 Census: Vol. 4. Education, employment and housing*. London: HMSO.

Heath, A., & McMahon, D. (2000). *Ethnic differences in the labour market: The role of education and social class origins*. Sociology Working Papers, Oxford University.

Leslie, D., & Drinkwater, S. (1999). Staying on in full-time education: Reasons for higher participation rates among ethnic minority males and females. *Economica* 66:63–77.

Macpherson of Cluny, Sir W. (1999). *The Stephen Lawrence Inquiry*. London: HMSO.

Maughan, B., & Dunn, G. (1988). Black pupils' progress in secondary school. In G. Verma and P. Pumfrey (Eds.), Educational attainments. *Issues and outcomes in multicultural education* (pp. 112–127). Lewes: Falmer Press.

Meltzer, H., & Gatwood, R., with Goodman, R., & Ford, T. (2000). *Mental health of children and adolescents in Great Britain*. London: HMSO.

Modood, T. (1998). Ethnic minorities' drive for qualifications. In T. Modood & T. Ackland (Eds.), *Race and higher education: experiences, challenges and policy implications*. London: Policy Studies Institute.

Modood, T. (2003). Ethnic differentials in educational performance. In D. Mason (Ed.), *Explaining ethnic differences*. Bristol: The Policy Press.

Modood, T., Berthoud, R., Lakey, J., Nazroo, J., Smith, P., Virdee, S., & Beishon, S. (1997). *Ethnic minorities in Britain: Diversity and disadvantage*. London: Policy Studies Institute.

Mortimore, P., Sammons, P., Stoll, L., Lewis, D., & Ecob, R. (1988). *School matters: The junior years*. Wells: Open Books.

Office for Standards in Education (OFSTED). (2002). *Achievement of Black Caribbean pupils: Three successful primary schools*. London: OFSTED.

Owen, D., Green, A., Pitcher, J., & Maguire, M. (2000). *Minority ethnic participation and achievements in education, training and the labour market*. Research Brief 225. London: Department for Education and Employment.

Pilkington, A. (1999). Racism in schools and ethnic differentials in educational achievement: A brief comment on a recent debate. *British Journal of Sociology of Education, 20*, 411–417.

Portes, A., & MacLeod, D. (1999). Educating the second generation: Determinants of achievement among children of immigrants in the United States. *Journal of Ethnic and Migration Studies, 25*, 373–396.

Rothon, C. (2001). *Explaining ethnic minority disadvantage in education*. Unpublished master's thesis, University of Oxford, Oxford, UK.

Rutter, M., & Maughan, B. (2002). School effectiveness findings 1979–2002. *Journal of School Psychology, 40*, 451–475.

Sammons, P. (1995). Gender, ethnic and socio-economic differences in attainment and progress: A longitudinal analysis of student achievement over 9 years. *British Educational Research Journal, 21*, 465–485.

Scott, A., Pearce, D., & Goldblatt, P. (2001). The sizes and characteristics of the minority ethnic populations of Great Britain – latest estimates. *Population Trends 105*. London: The Stationery Office.

Sewell, T. (1997). *Black masculinities and schooling*. Stoke on Trent: Trentham Books.

Shiner, M., & Modood, T. (2002). Help or hindrance? Higher education and the route to ethnic equality. *British Journal of Sociology of Education, 23*, 209–232.

Smith, D. J. (1977). *Racial disadvantage in Britain*. London: Penguin.

Smith, D. J., & Tomlinson, S. (1989). *The School Effect: A study of multi-racial comprehensives*. London: Policy Studies Institute.

Social Exclusion Unit. (2000). *Minority ethnic issues in social exclusion and neighbourhood renewal: A guide to the work of the Social Exclusion Unit and the Policy Action Teams so far*. London: Cabinet Office.

Taylor, M. (1986). *Caught between: A review of research into the education of pupils of West Indian origin*. Windsor: NFER-Nelson.

Tizard, B., Blatchford, P., Burke, J., Farquhar, C., & Plewis, I. (1988). Young children at school in the inner city. Mahwah, NJ: Lawrence Erlbaum.

Youth Cohort Study of England and Wales (2000). *Cohort Ten, Sweep One and Two*.

Wandsworth Education Department. (2001). *Annual statistics bulletin 2000–2001*. London Borough of Wandsworth.

5

Race and Ethnic Inequality in Educational Attainment in the United States

Charles Hirschman and Jennifer C. Lee

Introduction

In the United States, as in other modern industrial societies, education is the primary gateway to socioeconomic attainment. The single most important predictor of good jobs and high income is higher education. College graduates have average earnings 70 percent higher than those of high school graduates (Day & Newburger, 2002). With such wide differences in economic outcomes between the education haves and have-nots, most research on economic inequality and the process of social stratification must begin with the determinants of schooling, and in particular, on the transition from high school to college.

Equality of opportunity, which lies at the heart of the American dream of a meritocratic society, is still a distant goal. The fundamental, and inescapable, reality is that families work to subvert equality of opportunity. All parents, or at least most parents, want their children to do well and invest considerable resources and time to sponsor, prod, push, and cajole their offspring. Parents provide economic and social support as well as encouragement to further their children's schooling and subsequent occupational and economic attainment. Not all parents, however, have equal capacity and ability in this role. Inequalities of wealth, income, and other family resources certainly make a difference, and more subtle attributes, such as family cultures, child-rearing patterns, and social networks, may also influence the future career paths of children.

Families are not the only influence on the educational and socioeconomic attainment of children. The availability and quality of schooling can sometimes create opportunities, even in the absence of family support. For example, the extraordinarily high level of high school graduation in the United States; upwards of 85 to 90 percent of American adolescents graduate from high school (or receive a GED certification) is also a product of the availability of free public high schools and laws requiring attendance in school until age 16. In addition, the existence of college tuition poses constraints, especially to those from lower socioeconomic background. Thus, although there is a perceived opportunity for all to attain postsecondary education in the United States, those from a lower socioeconomic background are less able to afford it (Karen, 2002).

Another important dimension of social stratification in the United States is race and ethnicity. The American fabled commitment to freedom of opportunity for upward mobility has never been universal. American Indians and African Americans were denied basic rights by law for much of American history, and only in recent decades has there been the beginning of national efforts to right these historical injustices. Efforts to incorporate other minority groups, including immigrants from Europe, Asia, and Latin America (including those of Spanish heritage in annexed lands) have been uneven. There have been periods of hostility interspersed with indifference and occasional moments of welcome. The long-term progress of the descendants of immigrants is generally considered one of the great achievements of American social democracy, though the process has been slow, uneven, and incomplete.

In this chapter, we analyze the historical and contemporary patterns of race and ethnic inequality in education in the United States. After reviewing some of the major theories of race and ethnic influences on educational attainment, we describe some features of recent historical trends in educational attainment and transitions. The primary empirical focus of this study is an inquiry into the socioeconomic sources of race and ethnic differentials in educational ambitions, and in particular, the college plans and applications among high school seniors in a metropolitan school district in the Pacific Northwest. Although race and ethnic educational disparities are somewhat less in this region than for the country as a whole, the underlying structure mirrors national patterns. Differences in family socioeconomic background explain a significant share of the underachievement of historically disadvantaged groups. Although Asian American families are quite heterogeneous, several national-origin groups have very high educational ambitions even among families with modest socioeconomic resources.

Theories of Ethnic Inequality in Educational Attainment

Theories of race and ethnic stratification stress the impact of poor socioeconomic origins and discrimination on the lower attainments of minority groups. These factors are particularly important in explaining the lower educational and socioeconomic achievement of African Americans in American society (Duncan, 1969; Lieberson, 1980; Walters, 2001). For the first six decades of the twentieth century, African Americans had to confront state-sponsored segregation (including in public education) in the South and de facto segregation and informal color bars throughout the country.

Historically, other race and ethnic groups in the United States had also been handicapped by poverty, residential segregation, and discrimination, but the magnitudes of each have generally been less than those encountered by African Americans. Hispanics (Mexicans, in particular) and American Indians have had educational attainments even lower than those of African Americans (Mare, 1995). Asian Americans also experienced considerable political, social, and economic discrimination during the first half of the twentieth century, but were able to make important educational gains even under difficult circumstances (Hirschman & Wong, 1986). Immigrants from southern and eastern Europe who arrived in the early decades of the twentieth century started at the bottom of the urban labor market, but their children were able to reach educational and occupational parity with other White Americans by the middle decades of the twentieth century (Lieberson, 1980).

There has been considerable socioeconomic progress for all racial and ethnic groups during the second half of the twentieth century, but the pace of change has been much slower for Black Americans than for other groups (Hirschman & Snipp, 1999; Jaynes & Williams, 1989). In particular, African Americans continue to experience extraordinarily high levels of concentrated poverty and residential segregation in major metropolitan areas (Massey & Denton, 1993) and encounter prejudice on a regular basis (Correspondents of *The New York Times*, 2001). During the same period, race relations have become more complex with the renewal of large-scale immigration from Asia and Latin America during the last three decades (Tienda, 1999; Zhou, 1997). Most of these new immigrants are non-White, including many Black immigrants from the Caribbean. The absorption of the new immigrants has been uneven, but there are signs that the children of many new immigrants are doing well in schools, even in very poor circumstances (Caplan, Choy, & Whitmore, 1991; Waters, 1999; Zhou & Bankston, 1998).

The classical sociological theory proposed to account for race and ethnic inequality has been the assimilation model, which suggests that forces of modern societies, such as industrialization, competitive labor markets, and democratic institutions, will gradually erode the role of ascriptive characteristics, including race and ethnicity, in social stratification (Treiman, 1970). Although assimilation theory has many weaknesses, including the lack of a specific causal model and temporal boundaries, the theory is largely consistent with the historical absorption of the children and grandchildren of successive waves of immigration, largely from Europe, into American society (Alba & Nee, 1999).

A more complex theoretical account of how and why the new immigrants and their children may follow rather different paths of incorporation into American society than did earlier waves of immigrants is the segmented assimilation hypothesis of Portes and Zhou (1993; also see Portes & Rumbaut 1996, 2001). Segmented assimilation implies a diversity of outcomes within and between contemporary immigrant streams. According to the theory, some immigrant groups who have high levels of human capital and who receive a favorable reception may be quickly launched on a path of upward socioeconomic mobility and integration. Other groups with fewer resources may not be able to find stable employment or wages that allow them to successfully sponsor the education and upward mobility of their children. Indeed, the second generation may be exposed to the adolescent culture of inner city schools and communities that discourages education and aspirations for social mobility (Gibson & Ogbu, 1991; Suarez-Orozco & Suarez-Orozco, 1995). A third path is one of limited assimilation, where immigrant parents seek to sponsor the educational success of their children, but limit their acculturation into American youth society by reinforcing traditional cultural values.

The segmented assimilation hypothesis provides a lens to understanding the discrepant research findings on the educational enrollment of recent immigrants and the children of immigrants in the United States. Rather than expecting a similar process of successful adaptation with greater exposure to (longer duration of residence in) American society, the segmented assimilation hypothesis predicts that adaptation is contingent on geographical location, social class of family of origin, race, and place of birth (Hirschman, 2001). The segmented assimilation interpretation has been supported by case studies of particular immigrant/ethnic populations that have been able to utilize community resources to pursue a strategy of encouraging the socioeconomic mobility of their children, but only with selective acculturation to American society.

In their study of the Vietnamese community in New Orleans, Zhou and Bankston (1998) report that children who were able to retain their mother tongue and traditional values were more successful in schooling than those who were more integrated into American society. This outcome is consistent with research that found that Sikh immigrant children were successful precisely because they were able to accommodate to the American educational environment without losing their ethnic identity and assimilating to American society (Gibson, 1988). In another study, Mary Waters (1999) found that Caribbean immigrants are sometimes able to pass along an immigrant or ethnic identity to their children, which slows acculturation into the African American community. These findings suggest that the apparent differences among assimilation theory, segmented assimilation theory, and other theories of race and ethnic inequality in educational attainment may not be as great as suggested in some accounts. Socioeconomic origins and other attributes of families of origin are key explanatory variables in all theoretical perspectives.

To explain racial/ethnic inequality in education, Ogbu (1978) argues that involuntary minority groups – that is, those who have a history of oppression in the United States – are more likely to resist educational goals in opposition to the values of dominant society. Voluntary minorities – those that freely migrate to the United States – have more optimism and are more likely to internalize mainstream values and goals. His argument has been questioned in recent studies that find that Black students have high educational aspirations, and their poorer school performance is due to economic and social forces that limit the opportunities and material conditions for them to realize these goals (Ainsworth-Darnell & Downey, 1998).

Many other aspects of social and cultural contexts may influence race and ethnic difference in educational outcomes, including parenting styles and socialization, peer group influences, and encouragement from significant others. For example, because of their concentration in segregated inner-city schools, African American and immigrant children are most likely to encounter students and teachers with very low expectations for student attainment. Ferguson (1998) finds that teachers have lower expectations for Blacks than Whites and these perceptions have greater impact on Blacks than on Whites. In addition, Goyette and Xie (1999) argue that a socioeconomic explanation educational achievement is not adequate. They find that for some Asian groups that are well assimilated, socioeconomic factors play an important role, but not for others. However, for all groups, parental expectations are important factors in shaping educational expectations. Investigation of these topics is part of the future agenda of our research.

In this study, we present baseline models of the effects of family socioeconomic background and other social origin variables on plans for postsecondary schooling. We examine two dimensions of plans for college: one attitudinal and one behavioral. The attitudinal measure is plans for continued schooling right after high school, and the behavioral measure is whether the high school senior has actually completed an application for college. Neither of these measures may perfectly predict future educational careers. Some students may be overly optimistic and not be aware of potential academic and economic obstacles that lie ahead. On the other hand, some students may take a few years after high school to discover their latent educational ambitions and to begin college. Nonetheless, the disparities in planning for college among high school seniors provide an important baseline to evaluate the continuing role of race and ethnicity in shaping stratification outcomes in American society.

Race and Ethnic Inequality in Educational Attainment

Race and ethnic differentials in educational enrollment and attainment narrowed over the twentieth century, but remain significant (Jaynes and Williams, 1989; Lieberson, 1980; Mare, 1995). In addition to an expansion of formal schooling and an increasing emphasis on minimum educational credentials for many jobs, a variety of political and social changes have heightened the demand for increased schooling at all levels. The civil rights revolution and the demise of state-supported segregated schooling, if not of de facto segregation, reinforced popular claims for greater access and participation in schooling and other domains. Many colleges and universities, with intermittent support from government and foundations, have also encouraged greater representation of minorities in admissions and scholarships.

There remain, however, significant disparities in college attendance by socioeconomic origins and by race and ethnicity. African American and Hispanic youth are much less likely to enter and graduate from college than White youth. However, not all race and ethnic minorities are educationally disadvantaged. Asian American students are more likely to attend college than any other group, and many new immigrants (and the children of immigrants) have above-average levels of educational enrollment and attainment (Hirschman, 2001; Mare, 1995).

Based on the 1990 Population Census, Figures 5.1 though 5.4 show the history of race and ethnic disparities in educational attainment with a focus on four critical educational continuation ratios. (The source data are presented in Appendix Table 5.A1.) Educational continuation ratios are simply the conditional probabilities of advancement from one educational level to another (B. Duncan, 1968). The transitions highlighted here are: (1) the proportion of a birth cohort that completes ninth grade, (2) the proportion of those who completed ninth grade who go on to graduate from high school, (3) the proportion of high school graduates who enter college, and (4) the proportion of college entrants who complete college. In these graphs, continuation ratios are expressed per 1,000 eligible students.

The ten birth cohorts, ranging from 1916–1920 (age 70–74 in 1990) to 1961–1965 (age 25–29 in 1990), represent generations of students who were in the school-going age range from approximately the mid-1920s to the early 1980s. Across these generations, there has been increasing schooling for all race and ethnic groups, and educational disparities have generally been reduced, especially in graded schooling (from grade 1 through high school). The trends, however, have been uneven, and there are signs of widening race and ethnic disparities in access to and completion of higher education.

Among those who started school before World War II, there was a wide gap in the schooling of Whites and all minorities (Figure 5.1). More than

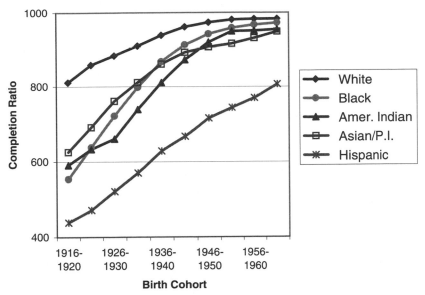

FIGURE 5.1. Educational transition ratio of persons completing 9th grade per 1000 persons by birth cohort and race and ethnicity.

80 percent of White (non-Hispanic) students in the pre–World War II generations reached high school or beyond. In contrast, only about 55–65 percent of racial minorities reached the ninth grade among cohorts who were attending school in the 1920s and 1930s, and only about 45 percent of

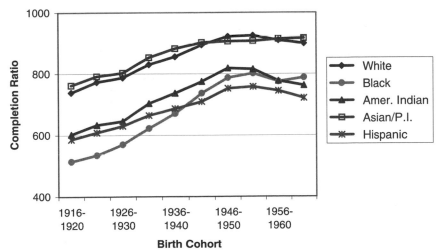

FIGURE 5.2. Educational transition ratio of persons completing 12th grade per 1000 persons who completed 9th grade by birth cohort and race and ethnicity.

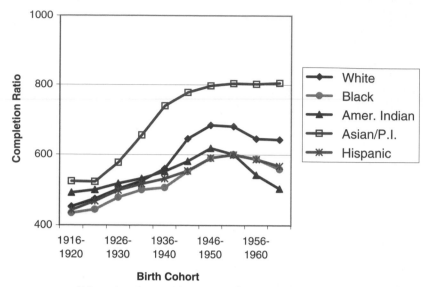

FIGURE 5.3. Educational transition ratio of persons completing some college per 1000 persons who completed high school by birth cohort and race and ethnicity.

Hispanics reached high school. Not all Hispanics and Asian Americans were native born, so their lower educational attainments reflect, in part, the characteristics of immigrants who were schooled in their countries of origin. With the exception of the Hispanic population, the racial gap in

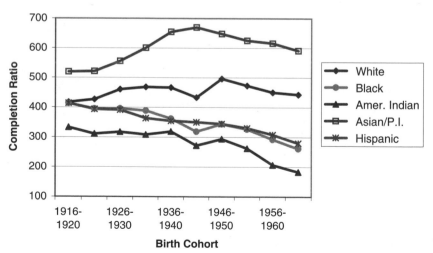

FIGURE 5.4. Educational transition ratio of persons completing bachelor's degree per 1000 persons who completed some college by birth cohort and race and ethnicity.

the proportions reaching high school gradually narrowed over the middle decades of the twentieth century. By the mid-1950s, more than 90 percent of minority groups reached ninth grade or higher, though the figure was only 80 percent for Hispanics as late as the mid-1980s.

The educational transition from ninth grade to high school graduation (Figure 5.2) shows two broad patterns. On one hand, Whites and Asians increased their rate of high school graduation (of those who entered high school) from about 75–80 percent in the 1920s and 1930s to more than 90 percent by the 1960s. These rates have remained at this high plateau for the last three or four cohorts in the time series. Starting at a much lower level (around 50–60 percent), the high school graduation rates of American Indians, Hispanics, and African Americans rose for several decades before reaching a plateau of 70–80 percent for the past few decades. African Americans have made the most progress, rising from approximately 50 percent to 80 percent over these decades. The high school graduation rates for American Indians and Hispanics are only a few points below those of African Americans, but there are troubling signs of decline in the transition to high school graduation during the late 1970s and early 1980s.

Perhaps the most important educational transition is from high school to college. Historically, this figure was about 50 percent, and it may even have declined a bit as the number of students reaching high school increased in the early and mid twentieth century (B. Duncan 1968, p. 623). These data, based on the 1990 Census, show modest gains in the proportions of high school graduates who went on to college from the 1940s to the 1960s (Figure 5.3). The most dramatic rise in this time series is the increasing proportion of Asian American high school graduates who go on to college. Among recent cohorts, about 80 percent of Asian American high school graduates make the transition to college, while the comparable figure is in the mid 60 percent range for Whites and in the 50 percent range for other race and ethnic groups. There has been a slight decline of a few percentage points in the transition from high school to college in the decades after the 1960s (more than 10 percentage points for American Indians). Mare (1995, p. 166) observes that these declines were primarily among men, for whom college attendance was inflated during the 1960s as a means to avoid military conscription during the Vietnam War era.

The final chart, Figure 5.4, shows the transition from entry into college (any postsecondary schooling) to the completion of a bachelors degree. There have been more fluctuations than linear change in this indicator. A little more than 40 percent of Whites who began college completed a bachelors degree in the 1930s; this figure rose to about 50 percent in the late 1960s and then declined to the mid-40s in the 1970s and 1980s. The transition ratio for Asian American students has been 10 to 20 percentage points higher than for White students, while the comparable figures for other minority groups are about 10 percentage points below Whites.

The majority–minority gap for this ratio widened in recent decades, with falling rates of college completion for Black, Hispanic, and American Indian students. For the youngest cohort, those born in the early 1960s, fewer than one in five of American Indian students who begin college receives a bachelors degree.

The Survey of High School Seniors in the Pacific Northwest

To address the potential sources of race and ethnic educational inequality, and the transition from high school to college in particular, we turn to an analysis of plans (abstract and concrete) for college based on two surveys of high school seniors in a metropolitan public school system in the Pacific Northwest in the spring of 2000 and 2002. With the cooperation of the local school administration, we administered an in-school paper and pencil questionnaire to senior students in the five comprehensive high schools in the district. In some schools, seniors completed the survey in regular classrooms, while in others, the students were assembled in an auditorium to take the survey. Overall, student cooperation was very good; fewer than 2 percent of seniors or their parents refused to participate. For seniors who were absent from the school, we conducted four follow-up mailings, using the procedures recommended by Dillman (2000). The follow-up mailings increased our sample by more than 20 percent, for a total of 2,357 respondents (1,156 in 2000 and 1,201 in 2002).

Evaluation of the completeness of coverage of the senior class survey is clouded by the uncertainty in defining the universe of high school seniors, and the logistics of locating students who are nominally registered as high school students, but are not attending school on a regular basis. In theory, high school seniors are students who have completed the eleventh grade, are currently enrolled in twelfth grade, and are likely to graduate from high school at the end of the year. In practice, however, there are considerable variations from this standard definition. Some students consider themselves to be seniors (and are taking senior classes and are listed as seniors in the school yearbook), but are classified in school records as juniors because they have not earned sufficient credits. In addition to fourth-year juniors, there are a number of fifth-year seniors, who were supposed to have graduated the year before. Many of the fifth-year seniors are enrolled for part of the year or are taking only one or two courses in order to obtain the necessary credits to graduate. Because of their infrequent attendance in high school and low level of attachment, both fourth-year juniors and fifth-year seniors are underrepresented in our survey.

About 10 percent of seniors in the school district are not enrolled in regular high schools, but are assigned to a variety of alternative programs for students with academic, behavioral, or disciplinary problems or are being home-schooled. Many of these seniors have only a nominal affiliation with the public schools – the largest number of such students were enrolled in high school equivalency courses at community colleges – and were not motivated to respond to our request to complete a survey of high school seniors. Even among students enrolled in the comprehensive high schools, there were a considerable number of nonmainstream students who completed the survey at lower rates than others. This includes the 6 percent of seniors who were taking community college classes for college credit and another 7 percent of students who were in special education classes for part or all of the school day.

All of these problems affected the response rate to our survey and make it difficult to offer a precise measure of survey coverage. For regular students – graduating seniors at one of the five major high schools – the response rate is around 80 percent. If we consider a broader universe of students, including students with marginal affiliation to high school and other hard-to-contact students, our effective rate of coverage of all potential seniors is probably considerably less – perhaps around 70 percent. Although our rate of survey coverage of all high school seniors is less than desirable, the problems we encountered are endemic in student survey research. Most studies of high school students that are limited to students who are present on the day the survey is conducted will have even lower response rates.

Our primary independent variable in this study is race and ethnicity. Following the new approach to measuring race from the 2000 census, the senior survey allowed respondents to check one or more race categories (Perlmann & Waters, 2002). The responses to the race question were combined with a separate survey question on Hispanic identity to create a set of eight mutually exclusive and exhaustive race and ethnic categories that reflect the considerable diversity in the population of youth in West Coast cities (see the stub of Table 5.1). Although most students have an unambiguous race and ethnic identity, there is a significant minority of students of mixed ancestry and some who refuse to give a response. In future research, we plan to investigate the complexity and nuances of race and ethnic measurement, but here our goal is to assign a single best race/ethnic category to each student. This requires developing a set of procedures for assignment of persons reporting multiple identities and for those who did not respond.

We established a hierarchy of groups to give precedence for assignment to one category if multiple groups were listed. This hierarchy follows the order of groups listed in Table 5.1. For example, if a student responded positively to the question on Hispanic identity, they were assigned to the Hispanic group (first category in Table 5.1) regardless of their response to the race question. About half of Hispanic students checked the other category on the race item and wrote in a Hispanic, Latino, or a specific Latin American national origin. Most of the rest of Hispanics checked White on

TABLE 5.1. *College Plans and Applications Among High School Seniors in 2000 and 2002 in a Metropolitan School District in the Pacific Northwest, by Race and Ethnicity*

Race/Ethnicity	College Plans for Fall			Applied to College	Sample Size
	Four Year	Two Year	No/DK		
	(1)	(2)	(3)	(4)	(5)
Hispanic	28%	41%	32%	49%	209
African American	34%	31%	35%	52%	411
East Asian	52%	28%	20%	70%	137
Cambodian	29%	44%	28%	50%	98
Vietnamese	35%	53%	12%	79%	107
Filipino & Other Asian	32%	38%	30%	48%	92
Am Ind/Hawaii/ Pac Islander	24%	30%	46%	45%	110
White	37%	31%	31%	56%	1,193
TOTAL	36%	34%	31%	55%	2,357

the race item, but there were smaller numbers who identified as Black or some other group. The next category is African American, which includes all non-Hispanic students who checked Black. About one third of students who checked Black also checked one or more additional races (Black/White and Black/American Indian were the most common). Assuming that most students who report partial Black ancestry have experiences similar to those reporting only Black, we have opted for the more inclusive definition, excluding only Hispanics.

The same logic is applied to the other race/ethnic groups, with students of mixed ancestry being included in the group that is higher on the list (in Table 5.1). The net result is that the residual group, White, consists of those who marked only White, while the other categories include students who are partially White. The only group that is affected substantially by this procedure is the category of American Indians/Hawaiian/Pacific Islanders. There are more persons who report mixed American Indian and White ancestry than who report only American Indian ancestry. For the 5 to 6 percent of students who do not report any race, we have substituted the ethnicity reported in school administrative records.

Of this sample of high school seniors, only about half are (only) White. The remainder are incredibly diverse with about 9 percent Hispanic, 17 percent Black, 6 percent East Asian (Chinese, Korean, and Japanese), 4 percent Cambodian, 5 percent Vietnamese, 4 percent Filipino and Other Asian, and 5 percent American Indian, Hawaiian, and Pacific Islander. Although the numbers of students in some of these groups are small, our emphasis is to show as much of the diversity of outcomes as possible within the limits of the data.

Description of Race and Ethnic Disparities in Planning for College

There are two indicators of college ambitions – planning to attend college and applying to college. The first question on college plans was asked as follows:

Do you plan to go on to college or other additional schooling right after high school? That is, do you plan to continue your education THIS FALL?

For students who responded yes to this question, a follow-up question asked:

What is the name and location of the college, professional, or technical school that you will most likely attend in the fall?

For this analysis, we grouped responses into three categories: (1) plan to attend a 4-year college, (2) plan to attend a 2-year community or vocational college, and (3) no or uncertain college plans. This last category includes students who gave inconsistent responses: for example, students who planned to go to college, but did not name a specific college. The second dependent variable on college applications is measured by the responses to a question on whether the student had applied to his/her first or second college of potential interest. Students who had not yet applied to a college (or did not even mention a college of interest) were classified as nonapplicants. The responses to both of these indicators – college plans and college applications – are presented in Table 5.1 by race and ethnicity. More than two thirds of high school seniors in our survey had specific plans for postsecondary schooling for the fall after graduation. Of those planning to go to college, there is about a 50–50 split in those planning to attend a 4-year or a 2-year institution (community colleges and technical schools). Thirty-six percent were planning to attend a 4-year college and 34 percent were planning to attend a 2-year college. Some of those planning to attend a 2-year college may see it as a stepping stone for a future transfer to a 4-year college, whereas for others, community college or technical school is the final objective.

Only a bit more than half of students (55 percent) have actually applied to college. Detailed cross-tabulations (not shown here) reveal that almost all students who plan to attend a 4-year college have submitted a college application, but only about half of those planning to go to a community college have actually applied by the spring of their senior year. It is possible to apply to community college up to a few days before the term begins.

Plans for college among our sample of high school seniors show moderate race and ethnic differentials. The highest level of plans to attend a

4-year college is reported by East Asian students at 52 percent, and the lowest level at 24 percent is evident for American Indians/Hawaiians/Pacific Islanders and for Hispanics at 28 percent. The percentage of Black seniors who have educational plans for attending a 4-year college is comparable to (or just a few points below) that for their White peers – in the mid-30 percent range.

A closer look at the plans for 2-year college and no/uncertain plans reveals the heterogeneity of the Asian American populations. East Asians have higher educational ambitions than Whites. Cambodians and Vietnamese have only average plans for 4-year colleges, but very high levels of planning to go to 2-year colleges. Only one in ten Vietnamese has no or uncertain plans for college. Filipinos and Other Asians are about average in terms of their college plans – only a few points below the levels for Whites.

In general, race and ethnic differentials for the behavioral indicator of applying to college are similar to college plans. About 56 percent of White seniors have applied to college by the spring of their senior year, and at somewhat lower levels are African Americans (52 percent), Hispanics (49 percent), Filipinos (48 percent), and American Indian/Hawaiian/Pacific Islanders (45 percent). Of these, only the gap between American Indian/Hawaiian/Pacific Islanders and Whites is statistically significant. The largest differences for this indicator are between the two groups with very high educational ambitions, East Asians (70 percent) and Vietnamese (79 percent), and all other groups. Although Vietnamese are not distinctive in terms of their plans to attend a 4-year college, their level of college application exceeds even the very high performance of East Asian students.

The objective of the following analysis is to address the question of whether the race and ethnic disparities in educational plans and applications observed in Table 5.1 might be explained by differential social origins. Our first step is to describe the familial and socioeconomic characteristics of the students by race and ethnicity. Then we turn to the multivariate analysis of college plans and applications in order to measure how much of the observed race and ethnic differences is due to their joint association with background characteristics. We also measure how the impact of social background on educational ambitions varies across the major race and ethnic populations of students.

Family and Socioeconomic Backgrounds of Students

Differences in college plans among high school seniors may reflect, in part, the economic and social support available from their families. In Table 5.2, we show race and ethnic variations in five background variables that may be potential sources of economic, social, and cultural support

TABLE 5.2. *Family and Background Characteristics Among High School Seniors in 2000 and 2002 in a Metropolitan School District in the Pacific Northwest by Race and Ethnicity*

Race/Ethnicity	Intact Family	Parent with Some College		Family Owns Home	First or Second Generation	(N)
		Father	Mother			
	(1)	(2)	(3)	(4)	(5)	(7)
Hispanic	46%	38%	44%	61%	49%	209
African American	29%	49%	57%	46%	17%	411
East Asian	64%	50%	42%	69%	83%	137
Cambodian	69%	16%	3%	34%	96%	98
Vietnamese	76%	39%	17%	35%	93%	107
Filipino & Other Asian	53%	41%	53%	67%	74%	92
Am Ind/Hawaii/Pac Islander	46%	48%	44%	55%	21%	110
White	58%	63%	63%	77%	12%	1,193
TOTAL	53%	53%	53%	65%	30%	2,357

Notes: Column 4 is the percent of students who live in owner occupied housing (not renting). Column 5 is the percent of students who are immigrants or the children of immigrants.

for higher education: intact family, father's education, mother's education, home ownership, and immigrant generation. For ease of presentation, all of the background variables are dichotomized in Table 5.2, with unknown and missing responses included in the complement of the category listed at the head of each column. (These variables are coded into more detailed categories in the subsequent multivariate analysis.)

Intact family is indexed by the percentage of students who are living with both their natural (or adopted) mother and father at the time of the survey. Parental education is summarized by the percentage of students whose mother (or father) has some college or more (not applicable and don't know responses are coded as no college education). Home ownership was measured in response to a survey question asking if the student's family owned or rented their home (don't know responses are coded as renters). Generational status is dichotomized into first and second generation (foreign born and the children of the foreign born) relative to third and higher generations.

With the very high rate of marital dissolution in contemporary America, only about half of high school seniors are living with both their mother and father. The question assumed that mother and father were the biological family, but some students may include remarried parents as intact families. Family stability and the presence of both parents in the household may provide social support (and economic support) as students plan for their future (McLanahan & Sandefur, 1994). Asian American seniors, especially Vietnamese, Cambodian, and East Asian, have unusually high levels of intact families (from 64 to 76 percent) while African Americans have the lowest level – fewer than one in three Black seniors lives with both mother and father. In the middle are Whites, Filipinos, Hispanics, and American Indian/Hawaiian/Pacific Islanders. However, Whites are closer to Asian Americans in terms of family stability, and Hispanics and American Indian/Hawaiian/Pacific Islanders are closer to African Americans.

About two-thirds of White seniors have fathers and mothers who have some college education. At the other extreme are Cambodian students, of whom only 16 percent have a father (and 3 percent have a mother) with any college education. In the middle are Blacks, East Asians, and American Indian/Hawaiian/Pacific Islanders, who have parental educational attainments about 10–20 percentage points below those of Whites. Filipinos, Hispanics, and Vietnamese have even lower levels of father's education, and Vietnamese mothers have especially low levels of higher education.

Family socioeconomic resources are also indexed by home ownership. About three quarters of White seniors live with families that own their homes. About 10 percentage points lower are East Asians and Filipinos. Much poorer economic circumstances are evident for Cambodian and Vietnamese students, of whom only one third live in owner-occupied housing. Only slightly higher on the home ownership scale are African Americans at 46 percent.

The rankings by parental education and home ownership – both measures of socioeconomic status – are only moderately associated. White students have more advantaged home environments and the newest immigrant groups, Cambodians and Vietnamese, have the poorest backgrounds. The final column in Table 5.2 shows that more than 90 percent of Cambodians and Vietnamese are immigrants or the children of immigrants. East Asians and Filipinos/Other Asians are not far behind at 83 and 74 percent. In contrast, almost all White, Black, and American Indian/Hawaiian/Pacific Islanders are third or higher generation Americans and most probably have no historical awareness of foreign ancestry. About half of Hispanic students are third generation or higher.

Although newcomer status is associated with somewhat lower socioeconomic status, there is a positive association between recent immigration and family stability. African Americans appear to have the worst of both worlds. Although parental education of Black students is above average, they have poor economic resources (as measured by home ownership) and a very high incidence of single-parent families. As we examine the reasons for race and ethnic differentials in educational ambitions, the diversity of background factors do not yield a simple and consistent portrait of disadvantage between the different racial and ethnic communities

Multivariate Analysis of College Plans

Table 5.3 presents the results of a multinomial logistic regression of college plans and a parallel logistic regression of college applications. For each set of analyses, there are two models. The first model presents a baseline equation with race and ethnicity as the single independent variable. The second model adds the five background variables (introduced in Table 5.2) as covariates to identify potential mediating variables in the relationship between race/ethnicity and the educational outcomes. For the multinomial logistic regression of college plans, there are two categories of the dependent variable: (1) planning to attend a 4-year college relative to no/uncertain college plans, and (2) planning to attend a 2-year college relative to no/uncertain plans. The coefficients are expressed as odds ratios relative to the omitted category, which has a value of 1.0 (for race/ethnicity, the omitted category is White students).

Model 1 shows the observed race and ethnic disparities in college plans in the population, which are similar to the percentage tables in Table 5.1, except the effects of race/ethnicity are expressed as odds ratios. For example, the first coefficient in the first column shows that the odds of Hispanic students planning to go to a 4-year college relative to no (or uncertain) college plans is .74, or 26 percent lower than the same odds for White students (the reference category).

TABLE 5.3. *Multivariate Analysis of Race and Ethnicity and Other Social Background Variables on College Plans and Applications of School Seniors in 2000 and 2002 in a Metropolitan School District in the Pacific Northwest. Effects are Expressed Odds Ratios of Each Category Relative to the Omitted Category*

| | Multinomial Logistic Regression of Planning to Attend Four Year/Two Year College Relative to No/Uncertain Plans | | | | Logistic Regression of Applying to College Relative to Not Applying | |
| | Model 1 | | Model 2 | | Model 1 | Model 2 |
	Four Year	Two Year	Four Year	Two Year	Model 1	Model 2
Race/Ethnicity						
Hispanic	0.74	1.29	1.04	1.49*	0.76+	0.94
African American	0.83	0.91	1.30+	1.00	0.87	1.11
East Asian	2.12***	1.36	2.64***	1.61+	1.87***	2.06***
Cambodian	0.87	1.60+	2.40**	2.34**	0.80	1.39
Vietnamese	2.38**	4.41***	5.52***	5.73***	3.08***	4.77***
Filipino & Other Asian	0.87	1.26	1.08	1.52	0.73	0.83
Am Ind/Hawaii/Pac Islander	0.43***	0.65+	0.59*	0.69	0.64*	0.80
White	omitted	omitted	omitted	omitted	omitted	omitted
Family Structure						
Not Intact			omitted	omitted		omitted
Intact			1.66***	1.24+		1.36***
Mother's Education						
12 years			omitted	omitted		omitted
13–15 years			1.83***	1.41**		1.13
16 or more years			2.58***	1.29		2.04***

Father's Education			
12 years	omitted	omitted	omitted
13–15 years	1.56***	1.23	1.34**
16 or more years	1.74***	0.97	1.45**
Home Ownership			
No	omitted	omitted	omitted
Yes	1.66***	1.03	1.23*
Immigrant Generation			
First generation	0.77	0.89	0.86
Second generation	1.55**	0.94	1.22
Third or higher generation	omitted	omitted	omitted
Pseudo R-Squared	0.02		0.06
(N)	2,357	2,357	2,357

Notes: Observations with unknown (DK) responses on independent variables are included, but the coefficients are not reported.

Model 1 includes only race and ethnicity as an independent variable.

Model 2 includes race and ethnicity and social origins (family structure, parental education, home ownership, and immigrant generation) as independent variables.

+ Significant at the .10 level.

* Significant at the .05 level.

** Significant at the .01 level.

*** Significant at the .001 level.

There are five groups with lower odds of planning to go to a 4-year college than Whites (Hispanic, Black, Cambodian, Filipino/Other Asian, and American Indian/Hawaiian/Pacific Islanders), but all are within the margin of error except for American Indian/Hawaiian/Pacific Islanders. Students in this group are more than 50 percent less likely to have college plans than Whites.

Two Asian American populations, East Asians and Vietnamese students, have odds ratios of planning to attend a 4-year college more than twice those of White students. Both of these coefficients are significant. Recall that Whites and Vietnamese were about equally likely to plan to attend a 4-year college in Table 5.1, but here the odds ratios in Table 5.3 show Vietnamese in a more favorable light. This is because of the much higher odds ratio of Vietnamese students who are planning to attend a 4-year college relative to those having no/uncertain plans (35 percent to 12 percent) than the comparable odds ratio for White students (37 percent to 31 percent).

The patterns for planning to attend a 2-year college (relative to no or uncertain plans) are somewhat more complicated to interpret. Attending a 2-year college indicates higher educational ambitions than not continuing to any tertiary schooling, but the potential for attending a 2-year college is constrained by the proportion planning to attend a 4-year school. For example, the high percentage of East Asian students planning to attend 4-year college leaves a much smaller pool of eligibles for 2-year college enrollment. In the second column of Table 5.3, it appears that Vietnamese and Cambodian students have the highest odds ratios of planning to attend a 2-year college. This indicates high educational ambitions in a setting where economic circumstances may constrain many from attending a 4-year college. American Indian/Hawaiian/Pacific Islanders have the lowest level of planning to attend a 2-year college (relative to no/uncertain plans), though the difference with Whites is just barely statistically significant.

Model 2 shows the results of a statistical experiment with the race/ethnic differentials in college plans purged of the differences in social origins. There are two emergent patterns in Model 2, relative to Model 1. The first is a reduction of the observed differences between Hispanics, Blacks, Filipinos, and American Indian/Hawaiian/Pacific Islanders on one hand and Whites on the other. Only one of these differences was statistically significant in the baseline equation (for American Indian/Hawaiian/Pacific Islanders), and this remains significant in Model 2, but the general pattern appears to suggest that the lower educational plans of these minority groups are in large part explained by impoverished social backgrounds. Indeed, with social background factors held constant, Black students are a little bit more likely to apply to a 4-year college than White students. This finding is consistent with much of the prior research on race and ethnic inequality in educational attainment (Schmid, 2001, pp. 73–75).

The second, and most striking, finding is that the gap between Whites and the two most educationally ambitious Asian American groups, East Asians and Vietnamese, widens when social background factors are held constant. Model 2 also shows that Cambodians emerge as another educationally ambitious Asian American population when social background characteristics are held constant. Recall that the observed levels of educational plans for Cambodians were only about average: a little below Whites for 4-year colleges and a little above Whites for 2-year colleges. These average levels of college plans are observed in a context of very poor socioeconomic origins for Cambodian students. When the social backgrounds of Cambodian students are adjusted to be equal with Whites, the underlying high educational ambitions of Cambodian students are revealed. The same general process is at work for East Asians and especially for Vietnamese students. The observed above-average educational ambitions for these students is strengthened in Model 2 when social background factors are held constant.

The effects of the social origins on educational plans in Model 2 provide additional insights into the ways in which educational ambitions are created and reinforced in American families. Students living in intact families are more likely to plan to attend 4-year colleges, and to a lesser extent 2-year colleges, than students from families with only one parent. This pattern is consistent with a long line of literature on the impact of family stability on the academic success of children (McLahanan & Sandefur, 1994). Highly educated parents, especially a college graduate mother, are significant resources that support student educational plans to attend a 4-year college. Students with a mother who is a college graduate are more than twice as likely as students with only a high school–educated mother to plan to attend a 4-year college. Net of parental education, students who live in owner-occupied housing are 60 percent more likely than students in rental housing to plan to attend a 4-year college than to have no plans beyond high school. Home ownership is an indicator of family economic resources that are independent of parental education. The final social origin variable in Model 2 is immigrant generation. Although one might assume that students who are far removed from their immigrant origins, third generation or higher, would be more familiar with making college plans, it is actually second generation students who have the most positive effect on the education outcome variables.

The preceding analysis of college plans is replicated with a logistic regression analysis of college applications (see the right-hand panel of Table 5.3). In general, the results for applying to college are very similar to those for college plans. Although planning to attend college is an attitudinal variable and applying to college is a behavioral variable, they tap the same general domain. Almost all of those who plan to attend a 4-year college have applied to college, and about half of those who plan to attend a community college have applied to college.

Two of the disadvantaged groups – American Indian/Hawaiian/Pacific Islanders and Hispanics – have lower levels of application to 4-year colleges than Whites in the baseline model (Model 1), but these become statistically insignificant in Model 2, when socioeconomic origins are held constant. Socioeconomic inequality of families is a primary reason for the observed lower level of college applications among disadvantaged minorities. Although Cambodians do not join East Asians and Vietnamese as educationally ambitious Asian Americans for college applications, the overall pattern of coefficients (and change in coefficients) is similar to that for college plans.

The effects of the familial and socioeconomic origins on college applications parallel those on college plans. Growing up in an intact family, having college-educated parents, and living in owner-occupied housing have very strong effects on students who apply to college, relative to those who do not. Although second generation is not a significant predictor of college applications, the overall pattern of coefficients is similar to those for college plans.

There are small differences between the two analyses in Table 5.2 (for college plans and college applications), but similarities are remarkable. There are some disadvantaged minorities, especially American Indian/Hawaiian/Pacific Islanders, whose lower educational outcomes are a function of poorer socioeconomic circumstances. One segment of the Asian American community, East Asians and Vietnamese in particular, has extraordinarily high educational ambitions, which are partially suppressed by their poorer economic backgrounds. Family background is strongly associated with planning for and applying to college. Do these family resources have comparable effects for different race and ethnic groups? This question is addressed in the next section.

Does Social Background Have Comparable Effects Across Ethnic Communities?

In the preceding multivariate analysis, which includes all race and ethnic groups in the same equations, we learned that poorer social background explains some of the lower educational plans of the disadvantaged minorities. However, the high levels of educational ambitions of East Asian and Vietnamese students are not explained by their socioeconomic backgrounds. Indeed, these students would be even more likely to plan and apply for college if their socioeconomic origins were comparable to those of Whites.

In Table 5.4, we ask a related, but different, question, namely, how similar are the relationships between background characteristics and college plans (and application) for each race and ethnic group? Because of the small samples for some groups, we limit this analysis to three populations, Whites, Blacks, and Asian Americans (including all four Asian American populations). Only four independent variables are included in Table 5.4: family structure, mother's education, father's education, and home ownership. There is insufficient variation in generational status within race and ethnic groups for a meaningful analysis. The format of Table 5.4 is comparable to that of Table 5.3; there is a multinomial logistic regression of planning to attend a 4- and 2-year college relative to no or uncertain plans and a parallel logistic regression of applying to college relative to not applying to college.

Family structure, which compares intact relative to nonintact families, is a significant predictor of college plans and college applications for White and Asian students, but not for Black students. This effect is estimated net of the other variables in the model (parental education and homeownership). The majority of Asian and White students live in intact families, but more than two thirds of Black students do not live with both of their biological or adoptive parents. Perhaps the protective advantage of intact families is lessened when the majority of students are growing up in single-parent families. This finding does not mean that family structure is not a major handicap for Black students in other outcomes, but it does not seem to be a major determinant of who plans for and applies to college.

Parental education appears to be much more significant for White than for Black and Asian students. White students with a college-educated father are more than twice as likely to plan to attend a 4-year college than comparable students with a high school–educated father. The effect of a college-educated mother is four times the effect of a high school–educated mother on planning to attend a 4-year college for White students. The same general pattern, if not the same magnitude, is found for college applications among White students.

Mother's education has positive (but inconsistent) effects on college plans and a clear-cut positive effect on college applications for Black students. Father's education, net of mother's education, does not affect the college plans and applications of Black students (it is negative and significant in a couple of cases, but the pattern is too inconsistent to sustain any conclusion). These findings suggest that mothers, much more than fathers, are the primary source of support for the educational ambitions of Black students.

The opposite pattern is found for Asian American students, with father's education appearing to be more important than mother's as the primary influence on educational outcomes. The positive impact of father's education on their children's ambitions must remain a tentative conclusion,

TABLE 5.4. *Multivariate Analysis of Social Background Variables on College Plans (Four Year/Two Year College) and Applications of High School Seniors in 2000 and 2002 in a Metropolitan School District in the Pacific Northwest, Spring 2000, by Race and Ethnicity. Effects are Expressed as Odds Ratios of Each Category Relative to the Omitted Category*

	Multinomial Logistic Regression of Planning to Attend Four/Two Year College Relative to No/Uncertain Plans						Logistic Regression of Applying to College Relative to Not Applying		
	White		Black		Asian		White	Black	Asian
	4-year	2-year	4-year	2-year	4-year	2-year			
Family Structure									
Not Intact	omitted	omitted	omitted	omitted	omitted	omitted	omitted	omitted	omitted
Intact	1.74**	1.10	1.11	1.51	3.13**	2.75**	1.30+	0.94	1.17
Mother's Education									
12 years	omitted	omitted	omitted	omitted	omitted	omitted	omitted	omitted	omitted
13–15 years	2.03**	1.49*	1.68	2.04*	0.44+	0.31*	0.89	1.10	0.51+
16 or more years	3.04***	1.33	1.11	1.38	0.64	0.51	1.67*	1.85	1.39
Father's Education									
12 years	omitted	omitted	omitted	omitted	omitted	omitted	omitted	omitted	omitted
13–15 years	1.81*	1.53*	0.65	0.52+	2.64*	1.55	1.55*	0.70	1.67
16 or more years	1.30	1.00	0.81	0.34*	1.57	1.32	1.33	0.68	0.89
Home Ownership									
No	omitted	omitted	omitted	omitted	omitted	omitted	omitted	omitted	omitted
Yes	2.21**	1.07	1.82+	0.86	1.82	1.11	1.36	2.28**	0.89
Pseudo R^2	0.26		0.23		0.25		0.27	0.21	0.30
N	1,193		411		434		1,193	411	434

Notes: Observations with unknown (DK) responses on independent variables are included, but the coefficients are not reported.
+ Significant at the .10 level.
* Significant at the .05 level.
** Significant at the .01 level.
*** Significant at the .001 level.

however. The patterns are not consistent across the two dependent variables and are of borderline statistical significance.

Homeownership, as an indicator of family economic resources, is found to be important for all groups, but the finding is only consistently significant for White students. Home ownership is a significant predictor of college application, but not of college plans, for Black students, while the reverse is true for Asian American students (just barely significant). We interpret these patterns to suggest weaker socioeconomic differentiation among Black and Asian American students (in terms of college ambitions) than for White students.

Conclusions

American folklore celebrates the United States as a land of opportunity, unlike other societies where social and economic status are inherited from generation to generation. This claim, like most societal myths, has a grain of truth. There is considerable inheritance of poverty and status across generations in American society, but there is also a considerable degree of social mobility (Blau & Duncan, 1967; Jencks, 1979). Education is at the nerve center of the American stratification system, with schooling serving as the primary means of both intergenerational stability and mobility. Advantaged parents are able to pass along their socioeconomic position primarily by ensuring that their children enter and graduate from college. College education is also a passport to prestigious and highly remunerated occupations for many Americans from working-class families.

The fundamental question for research on the American opportunity structure, and the one addressed in this study, is, who is able to enter college? The question is framed here with a particular focus on race and ethnic disparities. Race and ethnic inequality has been a permanent feature of the American stratification system. State-sanctioned segregation and discrimination against African Americans, American Indians, and other racial minorities were ubiquitous until the 1960s, and popular prejudice lingers on. On the other hand, the United States has welcomed millions of immigrants from around the world over the past two centuries, and many of the descendants of these immigrants have moved up the socioeconomic ladder with education from public schools and universities as a primary means of social mobility.

In this empirical study, we are studying educational plans among high school seniors in a metropolitan school system in the Pacific Northwest. Although not generalizable to the United States as a whole, this regional sample provides an opportunity to study the wide range of race and ethnic diversity that is emerging in an age of renewed mass immigration and an increasingly multicultural American society. How are race and ethnic minority students faring, relative to majority White students, in planning and applying for college as they prepare to leave high school and begin their adult lives?

The sample of public metropolitan school system students, by definition, misses students in the suburban and private high schools. If we assume that students in these more advantaged schools are disproportionately White, the observed majority–minority gaps in this analysis may be conservative (underestimates) of the broader societal patterns of racial and ethnic inequality in access to higher education. Another limitation of our study is that only high school seniors were included. Minority students (Hispanics, American Indians, and Blacks) are much more likely to have dropped out of high school and thus to not be represented in our survey. If all members of the original cohort (those eligible to be high school seniors) were included, there would be much greater race and ethnic inequality in college ambitions than those measured here. However, there is no reason to expect that the observed social background influences on college planning and the interactions of social background and race/ethnicity in our data would not also be found in more inclusive population samples.

Given these limitations, the results from this study do not show substantial educational disadvantages for Black students in planning and applying for college (Black students are only 3 to 4 percentage points below Whites). Although this finding may reflect the constricted sample of White students in a metropolitan school district or perhaps the selective migration of African Americans to the Pacific Northwest, there are some troubling signs for Black students. African American students have much higher proportions in nonintact families and in rental housing relative to Whites and other minority groups. Even if Black students have high educational ambitions, the lack of economic resources may make it much more difficult for Black students to actually enroll in college and to graduate. The group with the lowest levels of college plans and applications are American Indian/Hawaiian/Pacific Islanders. Although part of their educational gap relative to White students is due to poorer socioeconomic background, they continued to have lower college plans even when all measured familial and socioeconomic background variables are held constant.

The most complex findings are for Asian Americans. Contrary to popular stereotypes, not all Asian Americans are successful. In the observed data, East Asians have higher levels of college plans and applications than White students, but other Asian national origin populations were average or below average in terms of their levels of college planning and college applications. Vietnamese students are distinctive in terms of their high level of applications to community colleges and extraordinary high level of college applications. Once socioeconomic origins are adjusted to be comparable to the total population of students, however, Vietnamese emerge as the most educationally ambitious population, even above the level of East

Asian students. The same multivariate analysis shows a very high underlying orientation for attending college among Cambodian students, net of their disadvantaged social origins. Among the heterogeneous population of Filipino and Other Asian students, college plans and applications were not significantly different from those for White students.

There is considerable speculation on the reasons for the higher levels of educational ambitions among Asian American students, but relatively little hard evidence. Although the results from this study are not conclusive, they point in several important promising directions. First, it is imperative to break down Asian Americans by national origin groups. In general, East Asians (Chinese, Koreans, and Japanese) have made considerable economic progress in American society, and students in these communities are doing very well in school. Although Cambodians and Vietnamese are sometimes lumped together as Southeast Asian refugee populations, they are quite different communities in terms of their cultural and social characteristics.

Vietnamese share a common Buddhist culture (Mahayana) with East Asia, whereas Buddhism of Cambodia (Theravada) is more closely linked to mainland Southeast Asia (Keyes, 1995; Swearer, 1995). There has also been a strong historical and cultural influence of China on Vietnam, and a significant number of Vietnamese immigrants are of Chinese ancestry. In spite of these cultural differences, there is a very high commitment to pursue a college education in American society for both populations, although economic circumstances mask this finding in the observed proportions planning to attend a 4-year college. The residual group of Asian American students, which includes a substantial number of Filipino students, does not share the very high educational ambitions of the East Asians, Vietnamese, and Cambodians. There is great heterogeneity in this population, and although there are some small groups with very high educational ambitions (e.g., Asian Indians), this is not true for the population as a whole.

The findings here also show that the impact of social origins (as indexed by family structure, parental education, and home ownership) on college plans varies across race and ethnic groups. Paradoxically, social class differences play the strongest role among the White population. There are strong and consistent differences by parental education (especially mother's education), family structure, and homeownership within the White population. There are also social class differences within the Black and Asian American communities, but the patterns are somewhat more muted. Asian American students, in particular, are often able to develop high educational ambitions even though their family backgrounds may be marginal. Two-year colleges, in particular, appear to be a means whereby ambitious but economically disadvantaged students can get started.

One of the most plausible interpretations for the high educational ambitions of Asian Americans, given their relatively poor socioeconomic position and the recency of their immigration to the United States, is "immigrant optimisim" the belief that hard work and perseverance will pay off in America (Kao & Tienda, 1995). The decision to migrate across international border and to accept the role of an outsider requires a powerful ideological motivation. Many immigrants believe that their sacrifices are justified because the lives of their children will be markedly improved in their new homeland. This optimistic orientation – hard work and sacrifice of immigrants will lead to upwardly mobile children – is a pervasive belief of many immigrant cultures in the Untied States. The roots of immigrant optimism must be expressed in intergenerational influences. The very high level of family stability among the Asian populations provides a social base for such influences. The potential interaction between immigrant optimism and family stability is an important question for the future research agenda.

This interpretation finds support in the rapid educational progress among the children of immigrants to the United States in the early twentieth century (Jacobs & Greene, 1994; Lieberson, 1980). This finding is not universal for all groups, however. There is relatively little evidence of a positive second generation effect among Latino students in our sample, and immigrant optimism is rarely mentioned in research on Mexican American educational attainment (Fernandez & Paulsen, 1989; Landale, Oropesa, & Llanes, 1998).

The converse of immigrant optimism is the fatalism expressed by native-born youth that college is beyond their reach. Social class, as measured by parental education and home ownership, is more important for White students than for any minority group. Perhaps there is a culture of pessimism among many poor majority youth who do not develop high aspirations. Lacking the example of parents who have gone to college and sufficient economic resources, many White students may adjust their horizons downward and not put themselves onto the path for college. Perhaps the means by which new immigrants respond to adversity with heightened ambitions might provide valuable insights that would be helpful in providing encouragement for many native-born students.

Acknowledgments

The authors thank John Robert Warren, Paul LePore, Richard Morrill, Susan K. Brown, Jennifer Holsinger, Jason Thomas, Julie Miller, Christine Fountain, and Maya Magarati for their contributions to the larger project from which this paper is derived. The authors are also grateful to Stewart Tolnay and Robert Plotnick, who provided helpful comments on an earlier draft.

APPENDIX TABLE 5.A1. *Educational Transition Ratios per 1,000 Students Who Have Completed the Prior Level of Attainment, By Birth Cohort and Race/Ethnicity: Based on the 1990 United States Census of Population*

Birth Cohorts	From/To: 0–9	From/To: 9–12	From/To: 12–Some Col.	From/To: Some Col.-Bachelor's
1961–1965				
Non-Hispanic White	983	899	643	443
Black	972	788	559	261
American Indian	954	762	504	183
Asian/Pacific Islander	949	916	805	591
Hispanic	807	721	568	280
1956–1960				
Non-Hispanic White	983	909	645	450
Black	967	775	588	292
American Indian	951	777	543	207
Asian/Pacific Islander	931	914	802	616
Hispanic	770	745	587	308
1951–1955				
Non-Hispanic White	981	924	680	473
Black	959	801	601	327
American Indian	950	815	601	262
Asian/Pacific Islander	916	907	804	625
Hispanic	744	758	600	330
1946–1950				
Non-Hispanic White	973	921	684	496
Black	942	787	590	344
American Indian	920	818	619	294
Asian/Pacific Islander	907	906	797	648
Hispanic	716	752	591	345
1941–1945				
Non-Hispanic White	961	894	645	433
Black	912	737	552	318
American Indian	872	775	581	272
Asian/Pacific Islander	892	902	778	670
Hispanic	667	709	554	350
1936–1940				
Non-Hispanic White	938	855	560	466
Black	867	670	507	362
American Indian	811	737	552	318
Asian/Pacific Islander	860	882	739	654
Hispanic	629	686	532	355

(continued)

APPENDIX TABLE 5.A1. *(continued)*

Birth Cohorts	From/To: 0–9	From/To: 9–12	From/To: 12–Some Col.	From/To: Some Col.- Bachelor's
1931–1935				
Non-Hispanic White	909	830	526	468
Black	798	622	500	389
American Indian	739	703	532	308
Asian/Pacific Islander	811	853	655	600
Hispanic	570	664	517	363
1926–1930				
Non-Hispanic White	883	787	503	460
Black	721	570	479	395
American Indian	660	645	518	318
Asian/Pacific Islander	761	803	577	556
Hispanic	522	629	499	391
1921–1925				
Non-Hispanic White	858	773	475	427
Black	637	535	444	395
American Indian	633	633	500	311
Asian/Pacific Islander	691	791	523	521
Hispanic	472	608	468	394
1916–1920				
Non-Hispanic White	811	738	453	417
Black	554	515	434	413
American Indian	591	602	492	333
Asian/Pacific Islander	625	762	524	519
Hispanic	439	586	443	413

References

Ainsworth-Darnell, J. W., & Downey, D.B. (1998). Assessing the oppositional culture explanation for race/ethnic differences in school performance. *American Sociological Review, 63,* 536–553.

Alba, R., & Nee, V. (1999). Rethinking assimilation theory for a new era of immigration. In C. Hirschman, J. DeWind, & P. Kasinitz (Eds.), *The handbook of international migration: The American experience* (pp. 137–160). New York: Russell Sage Foundation.

Blau, P., & Duncan, O. D. (1967). *The American occupational structure.* New York: Wiley.

Caplan, N., Choy, M. H., & Whitmore, J. K. (1991). *Children of the Boat People: A study of educational success.* Ann Arbor, MI: University of Michigan Press.

Correspondents of *The New York Times.* (2001). *How race is lived in America: Pulling together. Pulling apart.* New York: Times Books, Henry Holt.

Day, J. C., & Newburger, E. (2002). The big payoff: Educational attainment and synthetic estimates of work-life earnings. In *Current Population Reports* (pp. 23–210). Washington, DC: U.S. Census Bureau.

Dillman, D. A. (2000). *Mail and Internet surveys: The Tailored Design Method*. New York: Wiley.

Duncan, B. (1968). Trends in output and distribution of schooling. In E. B. Sheldon & W. E. Moore (Eds.), *Indicators of social change: Concepts and measurement* (pp. 601–672). New York: Russell Sage Foundation.

Duncan, O. D. (1969). Inheritance of poverty or inheritance of race? In D. P. Moynihan (Ed.), *On understanding poverty: Perspectives from the social sciences* (pp. 85–110). New York: Basic Books.

Ferguson, R. F. (1998). Teacher's perceptions and expectations and the Black-White test score gap. In C. Jencks & M. Phillips (Eds.), *The Black White test score gap* (pp. 273–317). Washington, DC: Brookings Institution Press.

Fernandez, R., & Paulsen, R. (1989). Dropping out among Hispanic youth. *Social Science Research, 18,* 21–52.

Gibson, M. A. (1988). *Accommodation without assimilation: Sikh immigrants in an American high school*. Ithaca, NY: Cornell University Press.

Gibson, M. A., & Ogbu, J. U. (1991). *Minority status and schooling: A comparative study of immigrant and involuntary minorities*. New York: Garland.

Goyette, K., & Xie, Y. (1999). Educational expectations of Asian American youths: Determinants and ethnic differences. *Sociology of Education, 72,* 22–36.

Hirschman, C. (2001). The Educational enrollment of immigrant youth: A test of the segmented-assimilation hypothesis. *Demography, 38,* 317–336.

Hirschman, C., & Snipp, C. M. (1999). Racial and ethnic socioeconomic attainment in the United States. In P. Moen, H. Walker, & D. Dempster-McClain (Eds.), *A nation divided: Diversity, inequality, and community in American society* (pp. 89–107). Ithaca, NY: Cornell University Press.

Hirschman, C., & Wong, M. G. (1986). The extraordinary educational attainment of Asian-Americans: A search for historical evidence and explanations. *Social Forces, 65,* 1–27.

Jacobs, J. A., & Greene, M. E. (1994). Race and ethnicity, social class and schooling. In S. C. Watkins (Ed.), *After Ellis Island: Newcomers and natives in the 1910 Census* (pp. 209–256). New York: Russell Sage Foundation.

Jaynes, G. D., & Williams, R. M. (Eds.) (1989). *Common destiny: Blacks and American society*. Washington, DC: National Academy Press.

Jencks, C., Bartlett, S., Corcoran, M., Crouse, J., Eaglesfield, D., Jackson, G., McClelland, K., Mueser, P., Olneck, M., Schwartz, J., Ward, S., & Williams, J. (1979). *Who gets ahead?* New York: Basic Books.

Karen, D. (2002). Changes in access to higher education in the United States: 1980–1992. *Sociology of Education, 75,* 191–210.

Kao, G., & Tienda, M. (1995). Optimism and achievement: The educational performance of immigrant youth. *Social Science Quarterly, 76,* 1–19.

Keyes, C. (1995). *The Golden Peninsula: Culture and adaptation in mainland Southeast Asia* (reprint of 1977 edition). Honolulu: University of Hawaii Press.

Landale, N. S., Oropesa, R. S., & Llanes, D. (1998). Schooling, work, and idleness among Mexican and Non-Latino White Adolescents. *Social Science Research, 27,* 457–480.

Lieberson, S. (1980). *A Piece of the pie: Black and White immigrants since 1880*. Berkeley: University of California Press.

Mare, R. D. (1995). Changes in educational attainment and school enrollment. In R. Farley (Ed.), *State of the Union: America in the 1990s: Vol. 1. Economic trends* (pp. 155–213). New York: Russell Sage Foundation.

Massey, D., & Denton, N. (1993). *American Apartheid: Segregation and the making of the underclass*. Cambridge, MA: Harvard University Press.

McLanahan, S., & Sandefur, G. (1994). *Growing up with a single parent: What hurts, what helps*. Cambridge, MA: Harvard University Press.

Ogbu, J. U. (1978). *Minority education and caste*. New York: Academic Press.

Perlmann, J., & Waters, M. (Eds.) (2002). *The new race question: How the Census counts multiracial individuals*. New York: Russell Sage Foundation.

Portes, A., & Rumbaut, R.G. (1996). *Immigrant America: A portrait* (2nd ed.). Berkeley, CA: University of California Press.

Portes, A., & Rumbaut, R. (2001). *Legacies: The story of the immigrant second generation*. Berkeley, CA: University of California Press.

Portes, A., & Zhou, M. (1993). The new second generation: Segmented assimilation and its variants. *Annals of the American Political and Social Sciences, 530,* 74–96.

Schmid, C. (2001). Educational attainment, language minority students, and the new second generation. *Sociology of Education* (Extra issue), 71–87.

Suarez-Orozco, C., & Suarez-Orozco, M. (1995). *Transformations: Immigration, family life, and achievement motivation among Latino adolescents*. Stanford, CA: Stanford University Press.

Swearer, D. K. (1995). *The Buddhist world of Southeast Asia*. Albany, NY: State University of New York Press.

Tienda, M. (1999). Immigration, opportunity and social cohesion. In N. J. Smelser & J. C. Alexander (Eds.), *Diversity and its discontents: Cultural conflict and common ground in contemporary America* (pp. 129–146). Princeton, NJ: Princeton University Press.

Treiman, D. (1970, Spring). Industrialization and social stratification. *Sociological Inquiry, 40,* 207–234.

Walters, P. B. (2001). Educational access and the state: Historical continuities and discontinuities in racial inequality in American education. *Sociology of Education* (extra issue), 35–49.

Waters, M. (1999). *Black identities: West Indian immigrant dreams and American realities*. New York: Russell Sage Foundation and Harvard University Press.

Zhou, M. (1997). Growing up American: The challenge confronting immigrant children and children of immigrants. *Annual Review of Sociology, 23,* 63–95.

Zhou, M., & Bankston, C. L. (1998). *Growing up American: How Vietnamese children adapt to life in the United States*. New York: Russell Sage.

6

Racial and Ethnic Disparities in Crime and Delinquency in the United States

Jeffrey D. Morenoff

Racial and ethnic disparities in the United States criminal justice system are large and persistent. Prison statistics indicate that 28 percent of African American males and 16 percent of Hispanic males will be sent to prison in their lifetime, compared with only 4.4 percent of White males, and that Black and Hispanic minority groups made up 64 percent of the U.S. prison inmate population in 2001 (Bonczar & Beck, 1997). Police statistics showed that in 2000, African Americans were 6 times more likely than Whites to be murdered and 7 times more likely to commit homicides (Fox & Zawitz, 2003). Such stark racial and ethnic disparities polarize researchers and commentators into two opposing camps: those who think that the over-representation of racial and ethnic minorities in the criminal justice system is a reflection of group differences in criminal offending, and those who argue that the disparities in official statistics (e.g., rates of arrest, conviction, incarceration) reflect persistent biases among decision-makers in the criminal justice system (McCord, Widom, & Crowell, 2001; Tonry, 1995; Zimring & Hawkins, 1997). One casualty of this debate is the advancement of criminological research on the fundamental sources of racial and ethnic differences in criminal and delinquent behavior (McCord et al., 2001).

This paper reviews the key empirical findings on race, ethnicity, and criminal/delinquent behavior in the United States. The paper begins by laying out the contours of racial/ethnic disparities in crime and delinquency from three major sources of data – official records on arrest and conviction, self-reports of victimization, and self-reports of offending – and considering reasons for discrepancies between official records and self-reports. This is followed by a discussion of the major explanatory factors for group disparities in offending suggested by prior research: individual differences in so-called "constitutional factors," socioeconomic context, family structure and process, and neighborhood context. The final section considers some initial results from an ongoing multilevel analysis of racial and ethnic disparities in delinquent behavior among adolescents living in Chicago neighborhoods.

Sizing Up Racial/Ethnic Disparities in Crime

Estimates of the size of racial/ethnic disparities in crime vary widely across different sources of crime data. Much of the literature on race/ethnicity and crime relies on official records, such as police reports of known offenses and arrests or court records on conviction. The major criticism of official records is that they confound differences across groups in the prevalence of criminal behavior with differences in the likelihood of arrest and conviction that may result from bias in the criminal justice system. Survey-based self-reports of victimization and offending offer an alternative source of data on criminal behavior that is not affected by bias in criminal justice processing. Estimates of racial/ethnic disparities from all three types of crime data are presented below, after which reasons for discrepancies across data sources are considered in more detail.

Official Crime Statistics

The largest racial/ethnic disparities are typically observed in official crime statistics. The primary source of official crime data in the United States is the Uniform Crime Reports (UCR), a nationwide collection of police reports from nearly 17,000 local law enforcement agencies compiled by the FBI. The UCR includes data on the race (White, Black, American Indian/Alaskan Native, Asian/Pacific Islander) of the offender in all crimes that resulted in an arrest, but it contains no information on the offender's ethnicity. The lack of data on ethnicity in the UCR and many other official sources of crime data is one of the major reasons why there has been so little research on crime among Hispanics and other ethnic groups.[1]

The most recent race-specific arrest data from the UCR, reported in Table 6.1, show that African Americans, who comprised 12.8 percent of the U.S. population in 2001, represented a disproportionate 27.9 percent of total arrests. This overrepresentation of African Americans among arrestees holds for all types of charged offenses except for driving under the influence of alcohol and other liquor law violations. African Americans also comprise a greater share of the arrests for index offenses – crimes that the FBI considers most serious and uses to calculate the Crime Index – than for nonindex offenses. Moreover, among index offenses, race differences are larger for violent crimes, in which the victim is a person (e.g., murder and nonnegligent manslaughter, forcible rape, robbery, and aggravated

---

[1] Official police data on the ethnicity of criminal offenders are available from various state and local law enforcement agencies, but the absence of such identifiers in the UCR means that there is not a unified national source of data on which to base racial/ethnic comparisons.

TABLE 6.1. *Percent Distribution Arrests by Offense Charged and Race: Uniform Crime Reports, 2000*

Offense Charged	Percent			
	White	Black	American Indian or Alaskan Native	Asian or Pacific Islander
Total Population	82.2	12.8	0.9	4.1
Total Arrests	69.7	27.9	1.2	1.2
Total Crime Index	64.5	32.9	1.2	1.5
Violent crime	59.9	37.8	1.0	1.3
Murder and nonnegligent manslaughter	48.7	48.8	1.0	1.5
Forcible rape	63.7	34.1	1.1	1.1
Robbery	44.2	53.9	0.6	1.2
Aggravated assault	63.5	34.0	1.1	1.3
Property crime	66.2	31.0	1.2	1.6
Burglary	69.4	28.4	0.9	1.2
Larceny–theft	66.7	30.4	1.3	1.6
Motor vehicle theft	55.4	41.6	1.1	1.9
Arson	76.4	21.7	0.9	1.0
Total Noncrime Index	73.8	23.4	1.2	1.5
Other assaults	66.0	31.5	1.4	1.1
Forgery and counterfeiting	68.0	30.0	0.6	1.4
Fraud	67.3	31.5	0.6	0.7
Embezzlement	63.6	34.1	0.4	1.9
Stolen property (buying, receiving, possessing)	58.9	39.1	0.7	1.2
Vandalism	75.9	21.6	1.4	1.1
Weapons; carrying, possessing, etc.	61.3	36.8	0.7	1.2
Prostitution and commercialized vice	58.0	39.5	0.8	1.7
Sex offenses (except forcible rape and prostitution)	74.4	23.2	1.1	1.3
Drug abuse violations	64.2	34.5	0.5	0.7
Gambling	30.7	64.4	0.4	4.4
Offenses against family and children	67.6	29.6	1.0	1.7
Driving under the influence	88.2	9.6	1.3	0.9
Liquor laws	85.6	10.6	3.0	0.8
Drunkenness	84.7	13.7	1.1	0.5
Disorderly conduct	65.3	32.6	1.4	0.7
Vagrancy	53.6	43.4	2.6	0.5
All other offenses (except traffic)	65.8	31.6	1.3	1.3
Suspicion	69.0	29.6	0.3	1.2
Curfew and loitering law violations	72.2	24.7	1.1	2.0
Runaways	76.3	17.9	1.4	4.4

Sources: Pastore and Maguire (2002), p. 356; U.S. Census Bureau (2002), p. 13.

TABLE 6.2. *Victimization Race by Type of Crime and Race/Ethnicity of Victim: National Crime Victimization Survey, 2002*

| | Victimization Rate | | | | |
| | Race of Victim | | | Ethnicity of Victim | |
	White	**Black**	**Other**	**Hispanic**	**Non-Hispanic**
All Crime	28.2	35.3	29.1	30.8	28.8
Total Violent Crime[a]	27.1	35.3	20.7	28.4	27.7
Rape/sexual assault	1.1	1.2	1.1	0.5	1.2
Robbery	2.7	7.2	2.8	5.0	3.0
Total assault	23.3	26.9	16.7	23.0	23.5
Aggravated assault	5.4	7.7	5.2	5.6	5.7
Simple assault	17.9	19.2	11.5	17.4	17.8
Personal theft	1.1	1.9	1.8	2.4	1.1
Total Property Crime[b]	173.3	212.2	171.3	227.0	173.4
Burglary	29.4	47.6	32.4	41.7	31.0
Motor vehicle theft	7.9	13.2	10.4	19.7	7.6
Theft	136.0	151.4	128.6	165.6	134.7

[a] Victimization rates for violent crimes are per 1000 persons age 12 years or older.
[b] Victimization rates for property crimes are per 1000 households.
Source: U.S. Census Bureau (2003), pp. 189–190.

assault) than they are for property crimes (e.g., burglary, larceny–theft, motor vehicle theft, and arson). The index crimes with the largest disparities between Whites and African Americans are robbery, murder/nonnegligent manslaughter, and motor vehicle theft.

Victimization Surveys

The largest source of survey-based crime data is the National Crime Victimization Survey (NCVS), an ongoing, nationally representative study of personal and household victimization administered by the United States Census Bureau. The NCVS codes the race and Hispanic origin of the victim, making it possible to estimate both racial and ethnic differences in crime.[2] Table 6.2 summarizes crime rates based on the 2002 NCVS. Racial and ethnic disparities are generally not as pronounced in the NCVS as they are in official statistics. African Americans are more likely than Whites to be victimized by crime, and, as was the case with arrest statistics from the UCR, this difference is greater for violent crimes than it is for property crimes. Racial differences in victimization rates are greatest for robbery

[2] The NCVS also asks victims about the characteristics of the offenders by whom they were victimized and includes a question about the race of the offender (as perceived by the victim), but the response categories do not include ethnicity or Hispanic origin.

(which is consistent with the UCR statistics), followed by motor vehicle theft and burglary. Differences between Hispanics and non-Hispanics are negligible for rates of total victimization and violent victimization, but Hispanics are 1.3 times more likely to be victimized by property crime than non-Hispanics.

Figure 6.1 depicts racial- and ethnic-specific changes over time in violent victimization from 1993 to 1998. The violent victimization rate was consistently highest among American Indians and lowest among Asians. African Americans had the second highest victimization rate, and their rate consistently remained above that of Whites. Hispanics experienced the most change over the time period in their rate of violent victimization, which declined by 45 percent between 1993 and 1998 and converged with the violent victimization rate for Whites. Thus, Whites and Hispanics appear equally likely to be victimized by violent crime.

Self-Reported Offending Surveys

There is no ongoing national survey of self-reported offending comparable in size to the NCVS, but there are a few national studies that collect self-reports of delinquency and risk-related behaviors. One such study is Monitoring the Future (MTF), an annual national survey of secondary school students conducted by the University of Michigan's Institute for Social Research. Table 6.3 summarizes 12-month prevalence rates for self-reported delinquency in the MTF, averaged over three years (1999–2001). Black–White ratios are higher on average for crimes against people than they are for crimes against property – a finding that is consistent with both the UCR and NCVS results – and they are highest for the most severe forms offending (i.e., those that are least prevalent). Unlike the results from both official crime data and victimization statistics, however, these disparities are relatively narrow, with ratios rising above 1.5 only for use of a weapon. Moreover, the MTF data show Whites being *more* involved than African Americans in the most common forms of delinquency, such as petty theft, breaking into a house or building, and damaging property at school or at work.

Another national survey with self-reports of delinquent behavior is the Center for Disease Control's Youth Risk Behavior Surveillance System (YRBSS).[3] Table 6.4 presents summary statistics on delinquency and risk-behavior from the YRBSS. For most of the self-reported behaviors, racial and ethnic disparities are either very small or nonexistent. Whites are more likely than either African Americans or Hispanics to drive drunk or to carry a weapon, and all three groups are almost equally likely to carry a weapon

---

[3] The YRBSS consists of school-based surveys of representative samples of ninth through twelfth-grade students conducted every 2 years by the Centers for Disease Control and Prevention (CDC).

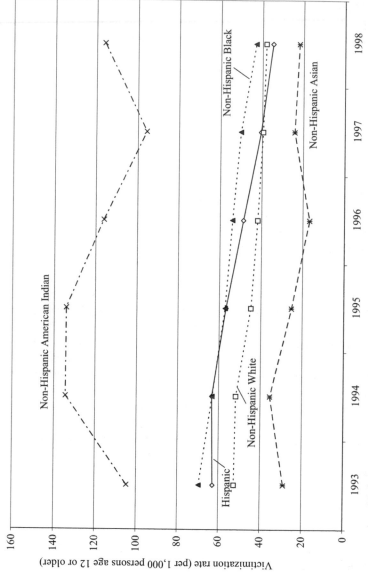

FIGURE 6.1. Violent crime victimization rates by race and ethnicity of victim: National Crime Victimization Sur57.

TABLE 6.3. *Racial Differences in Self-Reported Offending by Offense Type: Monitoring the Future, 1999–2001 (Three-year average rates)*

Delinquency Items (In the last 12 months, have you . . .)	White	African American	AA/White Ratio
Offenses Against Persons			
Used weapon against person to get something?	2.1	4.3	2.1
Hit instructor/supervisor?	2.4	3.4	1.4
Hurt someone requiring medical attention?	11.2	14.5	1.3
Been in Serious fight in school/work?	13.3	14.7	1.1
Been in group fight?	18.6	18.2	1.0
Argued/had fight with parents?	93.8	74.3	0.8
Property Offenses			
Set fire to someone's property on purpose?	2.4	2.7	1.1
Taken part of a car without permission of the owner?	4.0	5.2	1.3
Taken car that didn't belong to your family without owner's permission?	5.5	6.9	1.3
Damaged property at work on purpose?	7.0	6.4	0.9
Taken something not belonging to you worth over $50?	9.8	12.5	1.3
Damaged school property on purpose?	13.7	11.7	0.9
Gone into house or building when you weren't supposed to be there?	24.3	19.8	0.8
Taken something from a store without paying for it?	27.6	29.4	1.1
Taken something not belonging to you worth under $50?	30.6	26.1	0.9
Contact with the Police			
Been arrested or taken to a police station?	8.1	10.0	1.2

Source: Pastore, A. L., & Maguire, K. (Eds.). (2002). *Sourcebook of Criminal Justice Statistics 2001.* (http://www.albany.edu/sourcebook/)

on school property, be threatened or injured with a weapon on school property, or get into a physical fight. Both African Americans and Hispanics are more likely than Whites to experience situations that are related to violent forms of delinquent offending and/or victimization, such as being involved in a fight on school property, being injured in a fight, or feeling too unsafe to go to school.

On balance, the comparison of racial/ethnic disparities across multiple data sources illustrates that differences in criminal involvement between African Americans and Whites appear to be much larger in official statistics than they do in self-reported data, while differences in crime victimization are quite large on some types of crime (e.g., robbery, burglary, personal

TABLE 6.4. *Racial/Ethnic Differences in Delinquent and Risk-Related Behaviors: Youth Risk Behavior Surveillance System, 2001 (Percent reporting engaging in the behavior)*

	White	African American	Latino	AA/White Ratio	Latino/ White Ratio
Injured in a physical fight[a]	3.4	5.3	4.4	1.6	1.3
Felt too unsafe to go to school[b]	5.0	9.8	10.2	2.0	2.0
Carried a gun[b]	5.5	6.5	4.8	1.2	0.9
Carried a weapon on school property[b]	6.1	6.3	6.4	1.0	1.0
Forced to have sexual intercourse	6.9	9.6	8.9	1.4	1.3
Attempted suicide	7.9	8.8	12.1	1.1	1.5
Threatened or injured with a weapon on school property[a]	8.5	9.3	8.9	1.1	1.0
Physically hurt by a boyfriend or girlfriend on purpose[a]	9.1	11.2	9.9	1.2	1.1
In a physical fight on school property	11.2	16.8	14.1	1.5	1.3
Drove after drinking alcohol[b]	14.7	7.7	13.1	0.5	0.9
Carried a weapon[b]	17.9	15.2	16.5	0.8	0.9
Rode with a driver who had been drinking alcohol[b]	30.3	27.6	38.3	0.9	1.3
In a physical fight[a]	32.2	36.5	35.8	1.1	1.1

[a] Refers to one or more times during 12 months preceding the survey.
[b] Refers to one or more times during 30 days preceding the survey.
Source: Pastore, A. L., & Maguire, K. (Eds.). (2002). *Sourcebook of Criminal Justice Statistics 2001.* (http://www.albany.edu/sourcebook/)

theft, and motor vehicle theft) and negligible on others (e.g., assault, rape, and theft). In all three data sources, Black–White disparities are greater for violent forms of offending and also for the most serious types of offenses. There is very little information in published crime statistics (either official records or self-reports) on how Hispanics compare to either African

Americans or Whites. Perhaps the most reliable data on Hispanics come from the NCVS, which suggests that they are no more likely than Whites to be victimized by violent crimes, but are more likely to be victimized by property crimes.

Discrepancies Between Official Records and Self-Reports

Many criminologists interpret the discrepancy between the large racial differences found in official crime statistics and the small to nonexistent differences found in much of the self-reported offending research as evidence that racial and ethnic disparities in crime are largely artifacts of differential processing in the criminal justice system rather than differential involvement in criminal behavior. A recent National Academy of Sciences panel on juvenile crime concluded that this so-called "behavior versus justice system" debate has polarized the literature on race, ethnicity, and crime, leading to a "conceptual and methodological impasse" (McCord et al., 2001, p. 229). One reason for this impasse is no doubt the politically charged nature of the topic, but another, more tractable reason is that criminologists still have not reconciled the discrepancy between official records and self-reports on racial/ethnic differences, and this has deterred researchers from using self-report data to analyze disparities.

Prior to the advent of self-reported delinquency surveys, criminologists relied heavily on studies of individual offending based on official records. Such studies typically consisted of a sample of adolescents (often drawn from school records), on whom researchers would obtain background information (e.g., socioeconomic status, IQ) from administrative records or personal interviews, and official records from police and/or court files. Perhaps the most important of these was Wolfgang, Figlio, and Sellin's (1972) Philadelphia birth cohort study, in which the researchers followed a cohort of 9,945 boys born in 1945 who resided in Philadelphia when they were between the ages of 10 and 18. Using police arrest records, they calculated that 34.9 percent of the cohort was "delinquent" (meaning that they had a recorded police contact between the ages of 7 and 18), and that there were large racial disparities in police contact – 50.2 percent of the non-Whites (most of whom were African American) were delinquent compared to 28.6 percent of the Whites, yielding a Black/White ratio of 1.8. This estimate of the racial gap in police contact is in line with many of other individual-level studies that have used official records (for reviews of this literature, see Hindelang, 1981; Visher & Roth, 1986).

There is also a large literature on self-reported delinquency, dating back to the first systematic study by Short and Nye (1957). The earliest studies of self-reports suggested that there were no racial and ethnic disparities in actual criminal behavior (Chaiken & Chaiken, 1982; Chambliss & Nagasawa, 1969; Gold, 1966; Gould, 1969; Hirschi, 1969). In fact, one review of this literature (Hindelang, Hirschi, & Weis, 1981) found that the mean Black/White delinquency ratio from studies of self-reported delinquency was only 1.1. Hindelang and colleagues (1981) summed up the discrepancy in estimates of racial disparities between official records and self-reports as follows:

The range of ratios in self-report samples restricted to a single sex ... *does not overlap* with the range of ratios found in official data similarly restricted to single-sex groups.... The *very strong* relation between race and delinquency in official data is not present in self-report data. In fact, the self-report relation would have to be characterized as *weak or very weak*. (p. 159; emphasis in the original)

Questioning Validity of Official Records and Self-Reports
How, then, is it possible to reconcile these two seemingly disparate sets of findings? One response has been to question the validity of official records as indicators of criminal involvement and to argue that the biases in the criminal justice system that disproportionately bring minority groups to the attention of police and courts account for much of the discrepancy (Tonry, 1995; Zimring & Hawkins, 1997). In other words, perhaps self-reports are correct, and there are no "true" racial disparities in most types of criminal behavior. Another response has been to question the validity of self-reports and to argue that racial disparities found in official records may be closer to actual disparities in criminal involvement than those found in self-report studies. In an attempt to adjudicate between these two explanations, Hindelang (1978) compared victimization survey reports on the race of violent offenders (for rape, robbery, and assault) from the National Crime Panel (an early version of the NCVS) to UCR data on the racial composition of arrestees for parallel crimes. The results showed that the racial composition of offenders, as reported by victims of violent crime, closely matched the racial composition of offenders from official arrest statistics for parallel offenses, even though victimization statistics include reports of many crimes that never come to the attention of the police and hence do not appear in official records. That estimates of racial disparities from official statistics and victimization surveys were closer to each other than they were to results from self-report studies casts doubt on the validity of self-reports (Hindelang, 1978).

Critics of the self-report method could point to a number of problems with early self-reported delinquency studies. First, most studies did not sample a sufficient number of African Americans to reliably estimate racial differences in criminal behavior, particularly for the most rare forms of crime (Reiss & Roth, 1993). Second, many self-report studies drew samples from in-school populations where African Americans were more likely than Whites to be dropouts, resulting in race-linked sampling bias. A similar problem exists in population-based samples, which still may not cover the most frequent and serious delinquent offenders (Cernkovich,

Giordano, & Pugh, 1985; Reiss & Roth, 1993). Third, most of the questions in early self-report instruments were about relatively minor, nonserious forms of offending, such as under-age drinking, petty theft, and adolescent sexual activity. Given that the Black–White ratio tends to be higher for more serious forms of offending, some scholars believed that the emphasis on less serious forms of offending in self-report studies might account for this inability to detect racial differences.

In response, researchers sought to improve the quality of self-reports by exploring new techniques for constructing self-report instruments and delinquency scales, by moving away from school-based samples in favor of both local and national population-based studies of youth, and by initiating longitudinal designs (Elliott, 1994). Researchers also made important changes to self-report instruments by adding questions on more serious forms of offending, where race disparities may be more visible, and asking survey respondents more detailed questions about the frequency of their involvement in delinquent acts over the past year (early questionnaires included only a small number of response categories such as "never," "once or twice," and "three times or more"), which is important because of evidence suggesting that racial disparities are more pronounced among high-rate offenders, who are also more likely to have police contact (Elliott & Ageton, 1980).

In one of the earliest self-report studies to implement such improvements, Elliott and Ageton (1980) collected longitudinal data on a nationally representative sample of youth and found large racial differences (a Black–White ratio of nearly 2.0) on total delinquency (which included many forms of serious offending), and also significant racial differences in property crime, but no differences for most forms of violent crimes (except aggravated assault and sexual assault). However, Hindelang, Hirschi, and Weis (1981) used a similar questionnaire in a study of youth in Seattle communities and found no racial differences on overall delinquency or on any of their delinquency subscales – they only found racial differences on a few items that involved face-to-face violent offenses. Thus, despite improvements to instrument design, scale construction, and sampling, there remained a discrepancy between official records and self-reports in estimates of racial disparities, prompting concerns about the differential validity of self-reported delinquency across racial and ethnic groups.

Reverse Record Checks
One approach to evaluating the validity of self-reports consists of matching sample members to police and court records and then checking the extent to which sample members self-report offenses for which they have an official record. Although official records are the best criteria available to criminologists for assessing validity, they are by no means a "gold standard." One problem is the likelihood of biases in criminal justice processing that

lead to disproportionately high rates of arrest and conviction for racial and
ethnic minorities (McCord et al., 2001; Tonry, 1995; Zimring & Hawkins,
1997). Also, the process of matching self-reports to official records can be
fraught with error because of differences in the way offenders and official
agencies perceive and classify offenses, the questionable assumption that
the absence of a police record is equated with no involvement in delinquent
behavior, difficulties in obtaining records for offenses that occur outside of
local jurisdictions, and inconsistencies that arise from incorrect identifying
information (e.g., false names, addresses, and social security numbers) in
official records.

Nonetheless, studies that assess the validity of self-reports using reverse record checks have had a profound effect on the course of research
(or lack thereof) on racial and ethnic disparities in crime. In their influential book *Measuring Delinquency*, Hindelang, Hirschi, and Weis (1981)
found substantial racial differences in the propensity of subjects to self-
report crimes for which they had been arrested or convicted. White males
self-reported 90 percent of the offenses on which they had a matching official report, whereas African American males reported only 67 percent
of their official offenses, and these differences were even greater on serious forms of offending – 80 percent of White males self-reported serious offenses on which they had a matching official record compared
with 43 percent of African American males. Similar but smaller differences obtained among females, with 85 percent of Whites self-reporting an
offense when they had a comparable official record compared to 73 percent of African Americans. On serious forms of offending, White females
reported 50 percent of offenses compared with 41 percent for African
Americans. Hindelang and colleagues (1981) concluded that self-reports
were not useful for studying disparities in crime across racial groups, but
that they could still be used for analyzing the etiology of delinquency
within racial groups. Huizinga and Elliott (1986) reported similar results,
finding that only 11 percent of African Americans self-reported all offenses
for which they had a matching arrest record, compared with 57 percent of
Whites. The picture improved when they loosened the criteria for matching self-reports to official records, but substantial race differences remained
(61 percent of the cases matched among African Americans compared with
81 percent among Whites). These studies, and others like them, discour-
aged researchers from using self-reports to conduct cross-race comparisons
(Farrington, Loeber, Stouthamer-Loeber, Van Kammen, & Schmidt, 1996;
Thornberry & Krohn, 2002).

Nonetheless, several recent studies provide more encouraging news on
the validity of self-reports across racial and ethnic groups. Farrington and
colleagues (1996) assessed two forms of criterion validity – concurrent
(when the measure covers the same time period as the criterion) and predictive (when the measure is taken before the criterion) – for White and African

American boys in the Pittsburgh Youth Study (PYS) by comparing self-reported delinquency to records on petitions to the local juvenile court. The validity of self-reports was high for both groups. Concurrent validity was higher for Whites in admitting offenses, but higher for African Americans in admitting arrests, and there were no consistent racial differences in predictive validity. Farrington and colleagues (1996) also found substantial racial disparities in self-reported offending – 33 percent of African Americans in the PYS were serious delinquents compared with 18 percent of Whites. Other recent studies have reported moderate to high levels of validity in self-reported delinquency among both African Americans (Maxfield, Weiler, & Widom, 2000; Paschall, Ornstein, & Flewelling, 2001; Thornberry & Krohn, 2002) and Hispanics (Thornberry & Krohn, 2002).

In sum, the possibility of differential validity by race in self-reports and its potential to bias estimates of racial disparities in crime has stymied research on race and crime for decades (Elliott, 1994). The results of recent studies on the validity of self-report data for African Americans and Hispanics are more encouraging, but there is still very little research on racial and ethnic disparities using survey data, despite the wealth of individual-level data surveys provide on factors that might explain disparities in crime (Thornberry & Krohn, 2002).

Place-Based Disparities in Crime

Because of the dearth of existing individual-level data sets that can be leveraged to study racial and ethnic disparities in criminal behavior, most of the recent research on race, ethnicity, and crime has been conducted at the aggregate level, with official crime data. This literature considers, not disparities between individuals in their propensity to engage in offending, but rather disparities across places with varying racial and ethnic compositions. Many of these studies use homicide rates as the dependent variable because most homicides are eventually detected and reported to the police, thus minimizing potential bias in arrests. The units of analysis in such studies are usually large geographic areas, such as metropolitan areas or central cities. Some studies have considered disparities across smaller geographic units within a particular city, such as census tracts or other approximations of local neighborhoods, but obtaining large enough base rates to reliably estimate crime rates is a problem in such small area analysis.

Although there is a strong tradition of "ecological" research in criminology, dating back to the Chicago School (Bursik & Grasmick, 1993), aggregate-level studies of racial/ethnic disparities in crime gained momentum in recent decades. One fairly consistent finding from ecological studies is that rates of violent crime are higher in cities and metropolitan areas with greater proportions of African Americans (Land, McCall, & Cohen, 1990). Race-linked place disparities in crime persist over time, as documented by studies that together cover a 40-year time period, 1960–1990 (e.g., Land et al., 1990; Messner, 1983; Peterson & Krivo, 1993, 1999; Shihadeh & Flynn, 1996). An analysis of the structural covariates of homicide for 1960 to 1980 by Land, McCall, and Cohen (1990) found the percentage of African Americans in the population was one of only two covariates (the other being the percentage of divorced families) to be statistically and consistently related to homicide rates at the city and SMSA level over time.

Studies of place disparities in offending show that more racially segregated cities and metropolitan areas have higher rates of violent crime (Peterson & Krivo, 1993, 1999; Shihadeh & Flynn, 1996). Thus, place disparities in crime are related to both the racial composition of an area and the geographical separation of African Americans from Whites within an area. Unfortunately, this literature has virtually ignored Hispanics and other ethnic groups.

Several methodological problems cloud the interpretation of place-based disparities in crime. One is the ecological fallacy: It is impossible to draw inferences about individual-level racial disparities from the ecological association between racial composition/segregation and crime rates (Gordon, 1967). Aggregate-level research, by its very nature, cannot disentangle the compositional effects related to being a member of a racial group from contextual effects associated with living in a geographic area that has a high concentration of that group. A true decomposition of racial and ethnic disparities in criminal offending into their within-place (compositional) and between-place (contextual) components requires a multilevel study design that prior research has not attempted.

A second issue concerns the high correlations between racial composition and other predictors of crime (e.g., poverty), which often make it statistically impossible to disentangle the independent effects of racial or ethnic composition on crime from those of other closely related measures. Land and colleagues (1990) showed that it was impossible to identify the independent effects of racial composition on homicide separate from those of other covariates that load onto their "resource deprivation/affluence" index, namely, median family income, the percentage of families living below the poverty line, and the Gini index of family income inequality. Such collinearity makes it difficult to test theoretical explanations for racial disparities in crime on an aggregate level.

A third problem with drawing inferences from race–crime relationships in ecological research involves threats to causal inference posed by the endogeneity of racial composition. The problem is that if crime influences people's decisions on where to move, and if members of some racial groups are differentially able/willing to move in response to fear of crime, then crime rates may be "causing" racial composition, an inversion of the presumed causal path. The classic case of such reciprocal causation involves

White flight from urban areas. If the outmigration of Whites from central cities is spurred in part by the fear of crime, leaving behind a higher minority concentration in those cities, then this could account for part of the correlation between racial composition and crime (South & Messner, 2000). Moreover, such outmigration necessarily undermines residential stability, which in turn could lead to higher crime due to its disruptive effect on social networks and institutions (Sampson & Lauritsen, 1997).

Liska and Bellair (1995) investigated the connection between racial composition and violent crime rates in large U.S. cities over four decades (1950–1990). Using a reciprocal effects model, they found that racial composition predicted changes in violent crime rates in only one of the four decades (1980–1990), but violent crime rates (especially robbery) predicted changes in racial composition across all four decades. In a related study, Morenoff and Sampson (1997) investigated the relationship between homicide rates and population change on a smaller geographic scale, using census tracts in the city of Chicago observed over a 20-year time period (1970–1990). The tract-level homicide rate significantly predicted population decline, as did spatial proximity to high homicide rates in other neighborhoods. Moreover, they found sharp racial differences in the association between homicide and population change: Higher homicide rates were associated with White population loss but Black population gain. The findings from both of these studies are consistent with the idea that high crime rates historically have been an important force in the transformation of urban racial compositions toward higher concentrations of African Americans.

A final caveat about the relationship between racial composition and crime is that the well-known positive association between the population percentage of African Americans and the crime rate weakens or disappears when the crime rate is racially disaggregated. Several studies show either that percent Black has no statistically significant association with Black crime rates (Krivo & Peterson, 1996; Sampson, 1987) or that it is associated with *lower* rates of Black violent crime (Harer & Steffensmeier, 1992; Peterson & Krivo, 1993). Messner (1983) showed that although the percentage of African Americans in metropolitan areas is positively and strongly related to the total homicide rate, the association is nonlinear, such that after a certain threshold of racial composition, the homicide rate stops rising with further increases in percent Black and actually begins to decline at very high levels.

In sum, ecological research on crime highlights the connection between race and place and suggests that racial and ethnic disparities could be connected to the different social contexts in which groups reside. However, it is also important to keep in mind the limitations of making place-based inferences about racial and ethnic disparities – specifically problems related to ecological fallacy, multicollinearity, reciprocal causation, and potentially important interactions and nonlinearities in the aggregate-level race–crime relationship – that continue to thwart efforts to explain what racial and ethnic disparities in crime mean. Nonetheless, previous research – including aggregate-, individual-, and a few multilevel studies – does offer some important potential explanations for racial and ethnic disparities, to which I now turn.

Explaining Racial/Ethnic Disparities in Crime

The following discussion of explanations for racial and ethnic differences in crime is premised on the assumption that the constructs of race and ethnicity hold no distinct scientific credibility as "causes" (Hawkins, 2003), but are more productively viewed as "markers" for a constellation of factors that attach to them (Kraemer et al., 1997). These explanatory factors could be related to individual differences, such as personality traits and other so-called "constitutional" factors that remain relatively stable features of individuals over time (Wilson & Herrnstein, 1985), or they could be characteristics of social contexts that differentiate racial and ethnic groups, such as family and neighborhood environments, the two types of social context that have dominated criminological research on race and crime. For a given factor (or set of factors) to "explain" racial/ethnic disparities in crime, there should be either direct empirical evidence that it accounts for some portion of racial and ethnic gaps in criminal offending, or, given the paucity of previous research that directly addresses racial/ethnic disparities, some evidence that the factor is a durable correlate of criminal behavior and is differentially distributed across racial and ethnic groups.

Constitutional Factors
In their book *Crime and Human Nature*, Wilson and Herrnstein (1985) suggested that constitutional factors established early in life, such as temperament and intelligence (IQ), could explain some share of racial differences in crime. Wilson and Herrnstein acknowledged that constitutional factors alone are unlikely to account for very much of the crime gap between African Americans and Whites because of the large degree of variance *within* groups, but their speculation that racial differences in crime could be partially attributed to differences in impulsivity and IQ was very controversial. There is almost no existing research on the relationship between constitutional factors and crime among Hispanics, so the ensuing discussion of IQ and impulsivity focuses exclusively on Black–White comparisons.

IQ is the most widely studied of all constitutional factors, with a long line of research establishing IQ scores (particularly as measured by verbal tests rather than performance tests) as one of the most robust correlates of delinquency, whether the latter is measured by official records or self-reports (Farrington, 1998; Hirschi & Hindelang, 1977; Lynam, Moffitt, &

Stouthamer-Loeber, 1993; Reiss & Roth, 1993; Wilson & Herrnstein, 1985; Wolfgang et al., 1972). There are, however, several scholars who contend that the IQ–crime relationship, if it exists at all, is very weak (Block, 1995; Cullen, Gendreau, Jarjoura, & Wright, 1997). Many studies have found IQ scores to be differentially distributed across racial groups (Lynam et al., 1993; Wilson & Herrnstein, 1985), but despite the evidence linking IQ to both race and crime, no study has directly assessed how much of the racial gaps in criminal behavior are attributable to differences in IQ.

There are two main perspectives on how IQ may be related to crime. First, low IQ could be an indicator of deficits in "executive functions" of the brain that interfere with a person's ability to inhibit impulses, making it more difficult to monitor and control behavior, sustain attention and concentration, and anticipate and plan accordingly (Farrington, 1998; Lynam et al., 1993). A second possibility is that low IQ is strongly related to school failure, and that children who find it difficult to succeed in school become less committed to education and conformity, making them more likely to engage in delinquent behavior (Farrington, 1998; Hirschi & Hindelang, 1977; Lynam et al., 1993).

Lynam, Moffitt, and Stouthamer-Loeber (1993) assessed both of these mechanisms with PYS data. Their race-specific regressions showed that IQ was significantly related to self-reported delinquency among both Whites and African Americans, but that that there were strong racial differences in the mediators of IQ. Among Whites, the effect of IQ on delinquency was not changed appreciably by the introduction of controls for impulsivity (a test of the executive functioning hypothesis) or school performance (a test of the school failure hypothesis), even though both of these control variables were significantly related to delinquency. However, among African Americans, school performance accounted for virtually all of the IQ–delinquency relationship, whereas impulsivity explained very little. The authors speculated that the reason school achievement appears to be more important for African Americans is that schools provide African American youth with an important source of social control that is often lacking in disadvantaged neighborhoods.

Although there is less research about impulsivity and personality traits than there is on IQ, the results from extant studies suggest that impulsivity, in particular, is a strong correlate of crime, perhaps even stronger than IQ (Block, 1995; Farrington, 1998; Lynam et al., 2000; White et al., 1994; Wilson & Herrnstein, 1985), and that other aspects of personality, such as negative emotionality and constraint, are important sources of individual differences (Caspi et al., 1994). However, few studies have examined whether there are significant racial differences in impulsivity and other aspects of personality, or whether individual differences related to temperament and personality might be important explanations for racial disparities in criminal offending. Moreover, there is no existing literature on the relationship between crime and impulsivity, IQ, or other measures of personality in ethnic groups other than African Americans and Whites.

Socioeconomic Context

In considering the social determinants of racial/ethnic disparities in crime, a seemingly obvious candidate would be the large and persistent group differences in socioeconomic status between Whites and both African Americans and Hispanics (Messner & Rosenfeld, 1997). Although the association between social class and criminal offending is a hotly contested topic in criminology, individual-level research has, by and large, failed to find strong evidence of a relationship, particularly in self-report studies (Dunaway, Cullen, Burton, & Evans, 2000; Tittle & Meier, 1990). Conceivably self-report studies understate the association between social class and crime, just as they understate racial disparities in crime, but there is no evidence of differential validity by social class (Hindelang, 1981; Hindelang, Hirschi, & Weis, 1979; Huizinga & Elliott, 1986; Thornberry & Krohn, 2002). A social class-based explanation for racial/ethnic disparities in crime is also hard pressed to account for why Hispanics, who generally have equal or higher rates of poverty than African Americans, are less touched by crime. Hence, available evidence suggests that racial and ethnic disparities in crime are not attributable to individual or family differences in social class.

Notwithstanding the weak evidence linking individual-level social class and delinquency, aggregate-level research suggests a strong relationship between contextual measures of socioeconomic disadvantage and crime rates of places (Reiss & Roth, 1993; Sampson & Lauritsen, 1994). Two aspects of the relationship between socioeconomic context and crime have received much attention in prior research, namely: (1) whether the most salient dimension of socioeconomic context is relative inequality or absolute deprivation, and (2) whether there are racial differences in the strength of association between crime and socioeconomic context.

In one of the first studies to analyze measures of both relative and absolute deprivation, Blau and Blau (1982) showed that metropolitan areas with greater economic inequality between racial groups exhibited higher rates of murder, rape, robbery, and assault, and that inequality fully mediated the effects of both poverty and racial composition on violent crime. Land and colleagues (1990) took issue with this line of research on the methodological grounds that high correlations between measures of inequality and absolute deprivation often make it impossible to disentangle their effects on crime, and they showed that aggregate-level measures of median family income, the percentage of families living below the poverty line, and the Gini index of family income inequality all load onto the same principal component.

In more recent years, researchers have, by and large, abandoned the effort to disentangle the effects of inequality and absolute deprivation, focusing instead on the related issue of whether the association between socioeconomic context and crime holds for both Whites and African Americans. For example, Harer and Steffensmeier (1992) analyzed race-specific arrest rates for violent crime and found inequality to be a poor predictor of Black violent crime, but a powerful predictor of White violent crime. Other studies using measures of both inequality and deprivation show a similar pattern of weaker associations between socioeconomic context and crime among African Americans compared to Whites (LaFree & Drass, 1996; LaFree, Drass, & O'Day, 1992; Messner & Golden, 1992; Shihadeh & Steffensmeier, 1994).

One explanation for these race differences is that there may be a "ceiling effect" in the relationship between place-based socioeconomic disadvantage and crime such that beyond a certain level of concentrated disadvantage, marginal increases in disadvantage are no longer strongly associated with increasing crime rates. Presumably, the relationship between area disadvantage and crime rates appears weaker for African Americans because they live in more disadvantaged places. In support, Krivo and Peterson (2000) analyzed race-specific homicide rates across 135 central cities and found a weak to trivial association between concentrated disadvantage and homicide at high levels of disadvantage, thus concluding that race-specific differences in the strength of the association are attributable to the different social positions that African Americans and Whites occupy. They also showed that in cities where levels of disadvantage are comparable for African Americans and Whites, there is a strong positive relationship between disadvantage and homicide for both groups. These findings support Sampson and Wilson's (1995) theoretical claim that "the sources of violent crime appear to be remarkably invariant across race and rooted instead in the structural differences among communities, cities, and states in economic and family organization" (p. 41).

Racial and ethnic differences in the spatial context of socioeconomic disadvantage and affluence thus appear to be a promising explanation for racial disparities in crime. The preponderance of evidence supporting this explanation comes from aggregate-level studies, requiring replication using multilevel analyses, as discussed in the following.

Family Structure and Process

Family structure – particularly the prevalence of female-headed families in African American communities (Lichter, McLaughlin, Kephart, & Landry, 1992) – is one of the most frequently invoked explanations for racial/ethnic disparities in crime. In one of the earliest studies of links between "broken homes" – usually defined as families in which at least one biological parent is missing – and delinquency, Monahan (1957) tabulated data on the family structure of youth charged with delinquency in Philadelphia's Municipal Court during the period 1949–1954 ($n = 44,448$). He observed that children in broken homes were overrepresented among delinquents compared to the general population and that there were large racial disparities in family structure. That 62 percent of the African American delinquents were from broken homes, compared to 36 percent for Whites, led him to conclude:

> The relationship [between broken homes and delinquency] is so strong that, if ways could be found to do it, a strengthening and preserving of family life, among the groups which need it most, could probably accomplish more in the amelioration and prevention of delinquency and other problems than any other single program yet devised. (Monahan, 1957, p. 258)

Five years later, in his famous report, *The Negro Family: The Case for National Action*, Daniel Patrick Moynihan (1965) drew on Monahan's findings to argue that racial disparities in crime and delinquency were the product of a "tangle of pathology," rooted in family structure.

Despite the controversy that ensued from the Moynihan Report (Rainwater & Yancey, 1967), researchers have generally failed to find a consistent or strong relationship between broken homes and crime. There are, however, several important limitations to this research. First, many studies identify only one type of broken home (homes in which at least one parent is not living with the family), which ignores potentially important distinctions across different types of broken homes (e.g., single-parent families vs. stepparent families) and differences between the effects of family structure and the marital status of parents (Rebellon, 2002). Second, most research takes a static view of family structure, yet both the timing and cumulative impact of children's exposure to broken homes could be more decisive for delinquency (Hao & Xie, 2001; Wu & Martinson, 1993). For example, some perspectives on family and crime emphasize the influence of early family structure on childhood socialization (e.g., Gottfredson, M. R., & Hirschi, 1990), while others highlight the continuing importance of family structure during late childhood and adolescence, emphasizing the direct control parents can exert in supervising and disciplining adolescents (Hao & Xie, 2001; Rebellon, 2002; Sampson & Laub, 1993). Still other perspectives emphasize the family stress that can ensue from change and instability in family structure (Hao & Xie, 2001; Wu & Martinson, 1993).

A third limitation of the literature on family and crime is the general inattention to family processes that might mediate the effects of family structure, such as parental supervision, monitoring, parental rejection, parent–child closeness, time spent together, and parent–child conflict (Loeber & Farrington, 2000; Rebellon, 2002). Some studies have found that these processes (particularly family conflict) are more important determinants of criminal behavior than family structure *per se* (Loeber & Stouthamer-Loeber, 1986).

A final problem in research on family and crime is that both family structure and family processes are potentially endogenous to delinquency in that similar causes operate on delinquency and family disruption. One possibility is that a third variable, parent quality, is related to both family structure and delinquency. Another threat to causal inferences about family is the possibility of reciprocal causation: the idea that child misbehavior and aggression, which eventually may lead to delinquency, could cause conflicts between parents and potentially threaten the stability of the family unit (Hao & Xie, 2001; Sampson & Laub, 1993).

Surprisingly, despite the long line of research on family structure and crime, only the Pittsburgh study (see later discussion) has directly addressed the role that racial differences in family structure play in explaining racial disparities in crime. Many researchers have explored whether the association between broken homes and delinquency varies by race/ethnicity, and some of this research suggests that broken homes are more influential for African Americans than they are for Whites (e.g., Matsueda & Heimer, 1987; Monahan, 1957). Matsueda and Heimer (1987) contended that this is because broken homes are more likely to foster attitudes among African American youth that are favorable toward delinquency. They also showed that broken homes attenuated parental supervision in both groups, which, in turn, is related to delinquency. However, they used a rather broad, weak measure of antisocial behavior; also, their focus was on broken homes, whereas the large ethnic difference concerns single parenthood. Farrington, Loeber, and Stouthamer-Loeber (2003), using data from the Pittsburgh study to examine violent crime, found that single parenthood had a weaker association with crime in African Americans than in Whites and that family structure could not account for the ethnic difference in level of violent crime (see Maughan, this volume, for a comparable finding in relation to scholastic attainment in the United Kingdom). The sparse findings available to date are, therefore, inconclusive. There is the key need to determine risk effects in each ethnic group, and to test in an appropriate statistical model whether the risk variable accounts for the ethnic difference.

Another dimension of family and crime that is relevant to racial disparities is the ecological context of family organization. In aggregate-level research, the percentage of divorced families is one of the most robust predictors of violent crime rates (Land et al., 1990; Phillips, 1997; Shihadeh & Steffensmeier, 1994). Analyzing city-level violent crime rates, Sampson (1987) found that Black male joblessness – a marker for the scarcity of "marriageable" Black males – strongly predicted the prevalence of Black families headed by single women, which, in turn, was associated with higher offense rates for murder and robbery. Sampson (1987) also found that the percentage of White families headed by females was significantly related to White juvenile and adult robbery offending, suggesting that the same types of ecological conditions may be crime-producing for both groups. Moreover, both Sampson (1987) and Shihadeh and Steffensmeier (1994) found that the association between family structure and crime is particularly strong among juveniles, which supports Sampson's theoretical claim that high concentrations of single-parent families are mainly important for youth because they affect collective child-rearing practices related to social control and guardianship. In sum, the ecological context of family organization and social control is a potentially important piece to the puzzle of racial and ethnic disparities in crime, but these findings await verification using appropriate multilevel methods that simultaneously control for potentially confounding variables at the individual level.

Neighborhood Environment
Despite the long tradition of research on neighborhoods and crime, a dearth of studies that estimate the effects of neighborhood-level characteristics while simultaneously controlling for potentially confounding characteristics of individuals remains a serious limitation. This has begun to change with the publication of several recent multilevel studies that attach contextual data to individual-level self-reports of offending (Elliott et al., 1996; Gottfredson, D. C., McNeill, & Gottfredson, G. D., 1991; Lizotte et al., 1994; Lynam et al., 2000; Peeples & Loeber, 1994; Simcha-Fagan & Schwartz, 1986; Wikstrom & Loeber, 2000).

Two tentative conclusions can be drawn from this research. First, most multilevel studies find the association between neighborhood disadvantage and individual-level delinquency to be weaker than the aggregate-level relationship (Elliott et al., 1996; Gottfredson, D. C., et al., 1991; Lizotte, Thornberry, Krohn, Chard-Wierschem, & McDowall, 1994; Simcha-Fagan & Schwartz, 1986). Peeples and Loeber (1994), however, found that neighborhood disadvantage entirely accounted for disparities between African American and White adolescents in self-reported offending (although a lack of White respondents living in "underclass" neighborhoods precluded racial comparisons in the most disadvantaged neighborhoods). Other multilevel studies demonstrate that the association neighborhood disadvantage and crime varies depending on characteristics of the individual (Lynam et al., 2000; Wikstrom & Loeber, 2000), but there is no consensus on what types of individuals are most susceptible to the risks of living in disadvantaged neighborhoods.

Second, some multilevel studies have documented strong associations between non-Census measures of neighborhood social process and delinquency, net of individual- and neighborhood-level controls. Simcha-Fagan and Schwartz (1986) found that two measures of neighborhood social process – community disorder/criminal subculture and community organizational participation – were related to individual-level delinquency, while Elliott and colleagues (1996) found that social process related to informal networks, informal control, and social integration mediate the association between neighborhood disadvantage and adolescent problem behavior in both Denver and Chicago. Recent aggregate-level research also showed that neighborhood "collective efficacy" – a construct that combines measures of social cohesion and social control – was strongly related to homicide rates in Chicago (Morenoff, Sampson, & Raudenbush, 2001; Sampson et al., 1997) and that this association held in both predominantly African American and predominantly White neighborhoods (Morenoff et al., 2001).

How much racial and ethnic differences in neighborhood context contribute to group differences in crime still remains unclear because of several limitations of prior research. Previous multilevel studies rely on samples that (1) do not contain sufficient cases per neighborhood to conduct within- and between-neighborhood comparisons using appropriate multilevel methods (Raudenbush & Bryk, 2002; Sampson, Morenoff, & Gannon-Rowley, 2002), (2) do not observe African Americans and Whites living under comparable ecological conditions, and (3) contain few Hispanics or members of other ethnic groups. In short, neighborhood context remains one of the most promising explanations for racial and ethnic disparities in crime, but existing research has only begun to explore some of the key questions.

Project on Human Development in Chicago Neighborhoods

In an influential report published nearly a decade ago, the National Academy of Sciences panel on violent crime recognized the dearth of multilevel research and the need for more studies that would attempt to disentangle race/ethnicity from socioeconomic status. The panel called for the creation of a longitudinal cohort study of aggressive, violent, and antisocial behaviors that "would involve studies in multiple communities that vary in their demographic and socioeconomic composition...and their neighborhood and community organization, to investigate how variations and change in these factors alter the probabilities of various developmental sequences" (Reiss & Roth, 1993, p. 159). The Project on Human Development in Chicago Neighborhoods (PHDCN) was designed to study both contextual and longitudinal variation in a range of developmental outcomes, including delinquent behavior.

PHDCN is a longitudinal cohort study of children and adolescents who, along with their primary caregivers, were interviewed in person at three waves of data collection, beginning in 1995 and separated by intervals of approximately 2.5 years, from 1995 to 2002. The study design involved a multistage sampling procedure for selecting neighborhoods, families, and individual children. In the first stage, the project team defined 343 neighborhood clusters (NCs) in Chicago and stratified them by racial/ethnic composition (seven categories) and a scale of socioeconomic status (high, medium, and low). From the resulting 21 cells – three of which contained no observations – 80 NCs were selected, a sample of neighborhoods designed to maximize variation on racial/ethnic composition and socioeconomic status (Sampson, Raudenbush, & Earls, 1997). At the second stage, more than 35,000 dwelling units were enumerated for the 80 clusters, and for selected dwelling units, all households were enumerated, and age-eligible participants were selected with certainty. To be age-eligible, a household member must have had an age within 12 months of one of seven ages: 0, 3, 6, 9, 12,15, and 18 years of age. The resulting sample is representative of families living in a diverse range of Chicago neighborhoods.[4] It is evenly split by gender of the child and is made up of 15% White, 36% African American, and 45% Hispanics. In the same year that the baseline interviews were being conducted for the longitudinal cohort study, PHDCN also conducted a separate community study using a three-stage clustered sample design (see Sampson et al., 1997). The net result is an unusually rich battery of both individual- and neighborhood-level data, drawn from independent sources.

Racial/Ethnic Differences in Self-Reported Offending
The PHDCN cohort study includes an extensive questionnaire on self-reported offending (SRO). Table 6.5 reports summary statistics by race/ethnicity on the percentage of PHDCN respondents in age cohorts 9, 12, 15, and 18 who reported ever having participated in delinquent activities at the first wave of the survey in 1995. The items from the SRO are organized according to scales that were defined in previous research (Raudenbush, Johnson, & Sampson, 2003; Sampson, Morenoff, & Raudenbush, 2005). Within each category, items are ranked in order of prevalence, from lowest to highest. The most consistent result is the low prevalence of offending among Mexican Americans on almost every item. Other group differences vary by item. African Americans exhibit the highest involvement in violence but are less involved in most types of property crime than Whites. Results for other ethnic groups are based on small sample sizes, but it is notable that Puerto Ricans/Other Hispanics have levels of violent offending comparable to those of African Americans and generally higher levels of property offending compared to African Americans. This emphasizes the need to disaggregate Hispanics in studies of crime.

To bring these racial and ethnic differences into sharper relief, Table 6.6 summarizes racial/ethnic differences in three types of delinquency: violent, property, and drug offending. Eight different summary scores are presented for each type of offending to reflect multiple perspectives on how to measure involvement in delinquency. These include two measures

---

[4] The response rate was 78% at wave 1.

TABLE 6.5. *Racial/Ethnic Differences in Percent Who Report Ever Offending, by Type of Offense: PHDCN Cohort Study, Wave 1, Cohorts 9–18*

Delinquency Items (Have you ever . . .)	Total	White	African American	Mexican	Puerto Rican/ other Latino	Other race
Violence Scale						
Used force to rob?	0.55	0.00	0.57	0.31	1.89	0.81
Snatched purse, wallet/picked pocket?	0.89	0.45	0.85	0.72	2.20	0.81
Set fire to house, building, vacant lot?	1.72	2.02	1.98	1.14	1.58	3.28
Attacked someone with weapon?	4.87	3.60	8.11	1.45	5.66	6.50
Been in gang fight?	7.86	7.00	9.90	5.27	9.09	10.57
Carried hidden weapon?	11.80	10.59	16.65	5.79	14.42	14.75
Thrown objects at people?	16.07	10.61	23.19	10.65	17.24	13.82
Hit someone you did not live with?	30.88	28.83	45.28	16.56	30.82	26.83
Property Crime Scale						
Stolen car/motorcycle?	0.76	0.90	0.57	0.62	1.26	1.63
Broke into building to steal?	0.96	1.13	0.75	0.21	1.89	5.74
Stolen from a car?	3.29	4.04	3.48	2.07	4.72	4.88
Bought/sold stolen goods?	6.96	7.24	7.47	5.60	8.52	8.20
Damaged property?	12.83	15.73	12.79	9.32	19.12	13.93
Stolen from household member?	16.98	22.70	19.64	12.11	15.41	15.45
Stole from store?	21.19	25.84	22.86	16.24	24.84	19.51
Drug Crime Scale						
Sold heroin?	0.40	0.00	0.58	0.11	0.97	0.88
Sold cocaine/crack?	2.25	0.93	4.19	0.54	1.92	4.31
Sold marijuana?	4.68	5.05	6.32	2.11	6.03	5.93

(continued)

TABLE 6.5 (continued)

Delinquency Items (Have you ever . . .)	Total	White	African American	Mexican	Puerto Rican/ other Latino	Other race
Other Items						
Taken welfare/unemp. checks that were not yours?	0.11	0.23	0.10	0.00	0.32	0.00
Forced sexual relations with someone?	0.18	0.00	0.48	0.00	0.00	0.00
Used check illegally?	0.41	0.68	0.47	0.21	0.63	0.00
Been paid by someone for having sex with them?	0.50	0.00	0.97	0.21	0.32	0.87
Used false name/alias to obtain something?	1.11	0.69	1.24	0.84	1.58	2.50
Used credit/bank card illegally?	1.31	2.27	0.95	0.83	2.22	2.48
Given false information on form or application?	1.81	2.77	1.62	1.46	2.52	0.83
Been given ticket for driving offense?	5.11	7.88	3.60	4.82	5.99	8.20
Stolen from employer?	6.87	11.59	4.53	6.93	6.30	10.20
Run away from home overnight	7.85	7.64	9.88	5.16	10.03	6.50
Had trouble with police?	11.56	11.65	16.30	5.26	14.24	14.95
Hit someone live you live with?	15.23	17.19	19.32	8.39	19.18	16.39
Caused trouble in public place/acted disorderly?	17.73	22.70	19.11	11.58	23.82	20.33
Driven car without valid license?	18.75	20.95	21.44	14.35	20.06	18.85
Been absent from school without excuse?	20.14	17.86	21.37	17.24	25.95	23.58
N	2,938	446	1,071	978	320	123

TABLE 6.6. *Racial/Ethnic Differences by Category of Offense and Dimension of Offending: PHDCN Cohort Study, Wave 1, Cohorts 9–18*

	White	African American	Mexican	Puerto Rican/ other Latino	Other Race	AA/White Ratio	White/Mex Ratio	AA/Mex Ratio
Violent Offenses								
%Ever	34.38	54.89	24.15	42.01	31.71	1.60	1.42	2.27
%Last year	15.06	22.92	9.12	15.56	11.38	1.52	1.65	2.51
Number of offenses/persons	1.95	4.31	0.50	0.60	1.07	2.21	3.98	8.79
Number of offenses/person-years	0.14	0.32	0.04	0.04	0.08	2.23	3.77	8.39
Number of offenses/persons at risk	12.90	18.74	5.36	3.86	8.86	1.45	2.40	3.49
%1–4 offenses last year	16.82	25.59	12.07	19.06	11.38	1.52	1.39	2.12
%5–9 offenses last year	3.94	6.98	3.56	6.17	3.42	1.77	1.11	1.96
%At least 10 offenses last year	5.98	12.63	3.46	7.74	9.24	2.11	1.73	3.66
Property Offenses								
%Ever	43.37	40.79	29.24	42.95	32.52	0.94	1.48	1.40
%Last year	12.93	14.30	10.17	16.03	14.75	1.11	1.27	1.41
Number of offenses/persons	0.70	0.64	0.45	0.71	2.17	0.92	1.56	1.43
Number of offenses/person-years	0.05	0.05	0.03	0.05	0.16	0.93	1.48	1.38
Number of offenses/persons at risk	5.42	4.48	4.42	4.46	14.56	0.83	1.23	1.01
%1–4 offenses last year	18.83	20.08	14.32	20.00	13.82	1.07	1.32	1.40
%5–9 offenses last year	4.87	4.25	4.35	4.97	4.20	0.87	1.12	0.98
%At least 10 offenses last year	7.78	5.94	4.11	6.49	5.04	0.76	1.90	1.45
Drug Offenses								
%Ever	5.48	7.97	2.41	6.35	7.63	1.45	2.27	3.31
%Last year	0.91	1.05	0.21	0.95	1.70	1.14	4.36	4.99
Number of offenses/persons	0.03	0.02	0.00	0.01	0.04	0.65	15.25	9.98
Number of offenses/person-years	0.00	0.00	0.00	0.00	0.00	0.67	14.41	9.60
Number of offenses/persons at risk	3.50	2.00	1.00	1.00	2.50	0.57	3.50	2.00
%1–4 offenses last year	1.57	2.71	0.92	1.56	1.63	1.73	1.71	2.94
%5–9 offenses last year	0.48	0.69	0.00	0.33	0.89	1.44	–	–
%At least 10 offenses last year	2.84	2.35	0.88	3.24	3.54	0.83	3.22	2.66

of participation in delinquent behavior (cumulative/lifetime participation and current participation within the last 12 months prior to the date of the survey), three measures of frequency (the number of offenses per sample member in the last year, the number of offenses per person-year, and the number of offenses per persons at risk), and three dichotomous measures of high-frequency offenders (those who committed 1–4, 5–9, and 10 or more offenses of a given type within the last year). The table also includes ratios that summarize differences among the three major racial/ethnic groups in the sample: Whites, African Americans, and Mexicans.

The largest disparities between African Americans and Whites are found in violent offending. Black/White ratios for almost all of the violence measures are above 1.5, which is higher than claimed in the self-report studies reviewed by Hindelang and colleagues (1981) and within the range of racial differences found in official data. One exception is the individual frequency rate (number of offenses per persons at risk), which has a Black/White ratio of 1.45 and is still high by self-report standards. This is consistent with the findings of Blumstein, Cohen, Roth, and Visher's (1986) National Academy of Sciences report, which concluded that racial disparities are greater in participation than they are in frequency. Also, racial differences in violence were more pronounced among high-rate offenders, which is consistent with findings from Elliott and Ageton (1980). Mexicans consistently have the lowest levels of violence of any group.

There were no consistent differences between African Americans and Whites in property offending, but Mexicans again had the lowest levels of any group. Whites and Puerto Rican/other Hispanics were most likely to be high-frequency property offenders, while African Americans were more likely to be low-frequency property offenders. Racial differences in drug offending were most sensitive to the type of measurement used. African Americans appeared to be more involved than Whites according to lifetime participation, but Whites were more represented on all of the incidence-based measures. Mexicans continued to have the lowest involvement of any group.

Summary of Major Findings
Given the substantial racial and ethnic disparities in violent offending observed in the PHDCN sample, these data provide a unique opportunity to investigate explanatory factors that account for racial/ethnic differences. Sampson, Morenoff, and Raudenbush (2005) recently conducted a multilevel study of self-reported violent offending in age-cohorts 9, 12, 15, and 18, observed over three waves of the PHDCN study. The authors applied a multilevel modeling strategy that estimated both overall level of violence (the log-odds that a subject was involved in violent behavior over the three waves of the study), adjusting for the "severity" of each item in the violence scale, and subject-specific trajectories of change in violence

across waves of the study. They found that overall levels of violence were significantly higher among African Americans and lower among Mexicans compared to Whites, but there were no significant racial/ethnic disparities in change in violence over the three waves of the study. The individual- and neighborhood-level variables used in the multilevel analysis explained roughly 60 percent of the gap between African Americans and Whites in overall level of violence, and the entire gap between Mexicans and Whites. Neighborhood context accounted for the largest share of the Black–White disparity, accounting for a 33 percent reduction in the gap even after controlling for individual-level explanatory variables. The bulk of the differences between Mexicans and Whites was explained by individual-level immigrant status and neighborhood immigrant composition. Parents' marital status was also a significant predictor of violence, but neither family structure nor family SES were significantly related to violence after controlling for other individual-level factors. Individual-level measures of IQ and impulsivity were significantly associated with violence, but they accounted for very little of the racial and ethnic disparities.

This study by Sampson, Morenoff, and Raudenbush (2005) is perhaps the first to directly investigate the "social anatomy" of racial and ethnic disparities in criminal behavior. It is not surprising that in a city as segregated as Chicago, neighborhood context plays a large role in explaining Black–White differences in crime. However, it may be more surprising to some that differences across neighborhoods remain powerful even after considering variation within neighborhoods related to racial and ethnic group status. This is also one of the first studies to examine delinquency among Mexican Americans, now the nation's largest minority group (Miller, 2003). Despite having lower levels of socioeconomic status than any group in the sample, Mexicans have the lowest rates of involvement in delinquent activity across a wide range of outcomes. Within the Mexican population (and other ethnic groups), crime rates appear to be increasing across generations of immigrants – despite the gains these generations make in socioeconomic status – suggesting either that exposure to American society is in some ways criminogenic or that recent immigrants may differ systematically on some unmeasured attributes related to violence.

Further investigation of why immigrant status is protective against involvement in violence – just as it appears to be protective against other adverse health outcomes such as infant and adult mortality and low birth weight (Palloni & Morenoff, 2001) – is a priority for future research. Equally important, living in a neighborhood with a high concentration of recent immigrants appears to be protective against violence, not just for other immigrants but also for youth in general. These findings undercut some of the prevailing wisdom about socioeconomic deprivation and crime and challenge researchers to move beyond a Black-and-White understanding of race and crime in America.

References

Blau, J. R., & Blau, P. M. (1982). The cost of inequality: Metropolitan structure and violent crime. *American Sociological Review, 47,* 114–129.

Block, J. (1995). On the relation between IQ, impulsivity, and delinquency: Remarks on the Lynam, Moffitt, and Stouthamer-Loeber (1993) interpretation. *Journal of Abnormal Psychology, 104,* 395–398.

Blumstein, A., Cohen, J., Roth, J. A., & Visher, C. A. (Eds.). (1986). *Criminal careers and 'career criminals.'* Washington, DC: National Academy Press.

Bonczar, T., & Beck, A. (1997). *Lifetime likelihood of going to state or federal prison.* Washington, DC: Bureau of Justice Statistics.

Bursik, R., & Grasmick, H. (1993). *Neighborhoods and crime: The dimensions of effective community control.* New York: Lexington Books.

Caspi, A., Moffitt, T. E., Silva, P. A., Stouthamer-Loeber, M., Krueger, R. F., & Schmutte, P. S. (1994). Are some people crime-prone? Replications of the personality-crime relationship across countries, genders, races, and methods. *Criminology, 32,* 163–196.

Cernkovich, S., Giordano, P., & Pugh, M. (1985). Chronic offenders: The missing cases in self-report delinquency research. *Journal of Law & Criminology, 76,* 705–732.

Chaiken, J. M., & Chaiken, M. R. (1982). *Varieties of criminal behavior.* Santa Monica, CA: Rand Corporation.

Chambliss, W. J., & Nagasawa, R. H. (1969). On the validity of official statistics: A comparative study of White, Black, and Japanese high-school boys. *Journal of Research in Crime and Delinquency, 6,* 71–77.

Cullen, F. T., Gendreau, P., Jarjoura, G. R., & Wright, J. P. (1997). Crime and the Bell Curve: Lessons from intelligent criminology. *Crime and Delinquency, 43,* 387–411.

Dunaway, R. G., Cullen, F. T., Burton, V. S., & Evans, T. D. (2000). The myth of social class and crime revisited: An examination of class and adult criminality. *Criminology, 38,* 589–632.

Elliott, D. S. (1994). Serious violent offenders: Onset, developmental course, and termination. *Criminology, 32,* 1–22.

Elliott, D. S., & Ageton, S. S. (1980). Reconciling race and class differences in self-reported and official estimates of delinquency. *American Sociological Review, 45,* 95–110.

Elliott, D. S., Wilson, W. J., Huizinga, D., Sampson, R. J., Elliott, A., & Rankin, B. (1996). The effects of neighborhood disadvantage on adolescent development. *Journal of Research in Crime and Delinquency, 33,* 389–425.

Farrington, D. P. (1998). Individual differences and offending. In M. Tonry (Ed.), *The handbook of crime and punishment* (pp. 241–268). New York: Oxford University Press.

Farrington, D. P., Loeber, R., & Stouthamer-Loeber, M. (2003). How can the relationship between race and violence be explained?" In D. J. Hawkins (Ed.), *Violent crimes: Assessing race and ethnic differences.* New York: Cambridge University Press.

Farrington, D. P., Loeber, R., Stouthamer-Loeber, M., Van Kammen, W. B., & Schmidt, L. (1996). Self-reported delinquency and a combined delinquency seriousness scale based on boys, mothers, and teachers: Concurrent and predictive validity for African-Americans and Caucasians. *Criminology, 34,* 493–518.

Fox, J. A., & Zawitz, M. W. (2003). Homicide trends in the United States: 2000 update. In *Bureau of Justice Statistics Crime Data Brief.* Washington, DC: Bureau of Justice Statistics.

Gold, M. (1966). Undetected delinquent behavior. *Journal of Research in Crime and Delinquency, 3,* 27–46.

Gordon, R. A. (1967). Issues in the ecological study of delinquency. *American Sociological Review, 32,* 927–944.

Gottfredson, D. C., McNeill, R. J., & Gottfredson, G. D. (1991). Social area influences on delinquency: A multilevel analysis. *Journal of Research in Crime and Delinquency, 28,* 197–226.

Gottfredson, M. R., & Hirschi, T. (1990). *A general theory of crime.* Palo Alto, CA: Stanford University Press.

Gould, L. C. (1969). Who defines delinquency: A comparison of self-reported and officially-reported indices of delinquency for three racial groups. *Social Problems, 16,* 325–336.

Hao, L., & Xie, G. (2001). The complexity and endogeneity of family structure in explaining children's misbehavior. *Social Science Research, 31,* 1–28.

Harer, M. D., & Steffensmeier, D. (1992). The differing effects of economic inequality on Black and White rates of violence. *Social Forces, 70,* 1035–1054.

Hawkins, D. F. (2003). Editor's Introduction. In D. F. Hawkins (Ed.), *Violent crime: Assessing race and ethnic differences.* New York: Cambridge University Press.

Hindelang, M. J. (1978). Race and involvement in common-law personal crimes. *American Sociological Review, 43,* 93–109.

Hindelang, M. J. (1981). Variations in sex-race-age-specific incidence rates of offending. *American Sociological Review, 46,* 461–474.

Hindelang, M. J., Hirschi, T., & Weis, J. G. (1979). Correlates of delinquency: The illusion of discrepancy between self-report and official measures. *American Sociological Review, 44,* 995–1014.

Hindelang, M. J., Hirschi, T., & Weis, J. G. (1981). *Measuring delinquency.* Beverly Hills, CA: Sage.

Hirschi, T. (1969). *Causes of delinquency.* Berkeley: University of California Press.

Hirschi, T., & Hindelang, M. J. (1977). Intelligence and delinquency: A revisionist review. *American Sociological Review, 42,* 571–587.

Huizinga, D. A., & Elliott, D. S. (1986). Reassessing the reliability and validity of self-report delinquent measures. *Journal of Quantitative Criminology, 24,* 293–327.

Kraemer, H. C., Kazdin, A. E., Offord, D. R., Kessler, R. C., Jensen, P. S., & Kupfer, D. J. (1997). Coming to terms with the terms of risk. *Archives of General Psychiatry, 54,* 337–343.

Krivo, L. J., & Peterson, R. D. (1996). Extremely disadvantaged neighborhoods and urban crime. *Social Forces, 75,* 619–648.

Krivo, L. J., & Peterson, R. D. (2000). The structural context of homicide: Accounting for racial differences in process. *American Sociological Review, 65,* 547–559.

LaFree, G., & Drass, K. A. (1996). The effect of changes in intraracial income inequality and educational attainment on changes in arrest rates for African Americans and Whites, 1957–1990. *American Sociological Review, 61,* 614–634.

LaFree, G., Drass, K. A., & O'Day, P. (1992). Race and crime in postwar America: Determinants of African-American and White rates, 1957–1988. *Criminology, 30,* 157–188.

Land, K. C., McCall, P. L., & Cohen, L. E. (1990). Structural covariates of homicide rates: Are there any invariances across time and social space? *American Journal of Sociology, 95,* 922–963.

Lichter, D. T., McLaughlin, D. K., Kephart, G., & Landry, D. J. (1992). Race and the retreat from marriage: A shortage of marriageable men? *American Sociological Review, 57,* 781–799.

Liska, A. E., & Bellair, P. E. (1995). Violent-crime rates and racial composition: Convergence over time. *American Journal of Sociology, 101,* 578–610.

Lizotte, A. J., Thornberry, T. P., Krohn, M. D., Chard-Wierschem, D. C., & McDowall, D. (1994). Neighborhood context and delinquency: A longitudinal analysis. In E. M. G. Weitekamp & H-J. Kermer (Eds.), *Cross-national longitudinal research on human development and criminal behavior.* The Netherlands: Kluwer Academic Publishers.

Loeber, R., & Farrington, D. P. (2000). Young children who commit crime: Epidemiology, developmental origins, risk factors, early interventions, and policy implications. *Development and Psychopathology, 12,* 737–762.

Loeber, R., & Stouthamer-Loeber, M. (1986). Family factors as correlates and predictors of juvenile conduct problems. In M. Tonry & N. Morris (Eds.), *Crime and justice: An annual review.* Chicago: University of Chicago Press.

Lynam, D., Moffitt, T., & Stouthamer-Loeber, M. (1993). Explaining the relation between IQ and delinquency: Class, race, test motivation, school failure, or self-control? *Journal of Abnormal Psychology, 102,* 187–196.

Lynam, D. R., Caspi, A., Moffitt, T. E., Wikstrom, P-O. H., Loeber, R., & Novac, S. (2000). The interaction between impulsivity and neighborhood context on offending: The effects of impulsivity are stronger in poorer neighborhood. *Journal of Abnormal Psychology, 109,* 563–574.

Matsueda, R. L., & Heimer, K. (1987). Race, family structure, and delinquency: A test of differential association and social control theories. *American Sociological Review, 52,* 826–840.

Maxfield, M. G., Weiler, B. L., & Widom, C. S. (2000). Comparing self-reports and official records of arrest. *Journal of Quantitative Criminology, 16,* 87–110.

McCord, J., Widom, C. S., & Crowell, N. A. (Eds.). (2001). *Juvenile crime, juvenile justice.* Washington, DC: National Academy Press.

Messner, S. F. (1983). Regional and racial effects on the urban homicide rate: The subculture of violence revisited. *American Journal of Sociology, 85,* 997–1007.

Messner, S. F., & Golden, R. M. (1992). Racial inequality and racially disaggregated homicide rates: An assessment of alternative theoretical explanations. *Criminology, 30,* 421–447.

Messner, S. F., & Rosenfeld, R. (1997). *Crime and the American Dream.* Belmont, CA: Wadsworth Publishing Company.

Miller, S. (2003). Hispanics replace African Americans as largest U.S. minority group. Washington, DC: U.S. Department of State.

Monahan, T. (1957). Family status and the delinquent child. *Social Forces, 35,* 250–258.

Morenoff, J. D., & Sampson, R. J. (1997). Violent crime and the spatial dynamics of neighborhood transition: Chicago, 1970–1990. *Social Forces, 76,* 31–64.

Morenoff, J. D., Sampson, R. J., & Raudenbush, S. W. (2001). Neighborhood inequality, collective efficacy, and the spatial dynamics of urban violence. *Criminology, 39,* 517–559.

Moynihan, D. P. (1965). *The Negro family: The case for national action.* Washington, DC: Office of Policy Planning and Research, U.S. Department of Labor.

Palloni, A., & Morenoff, J. D. (2001). Interpreting the paradoxical in the Hispanic paradox: Demographic and epidemiologic approaches. *Annals of the New York Academy of Sciences,* 140–175.

Paschall, M. J., Ornstein, M. L., & Flewelling, R. L. (2001). African American male adolescents' involvement in the criminal justice system: The criterion validity of self-report measures in a prospective study. *Journal of Research in Crime and Delinquency, 38,* 174–87.

Pastore, A. L., & K. Maguire (Eds.). (2001). *Sourcebook of criminal justice statistics.* Washington, DC: Bureau of Justice Statistics.

Peeples, F., & Loeber, R. (1994). Do individual factors and neighborhood context explain ethnic differences in juvenile delinquency? *Journal of Quantitative Criminology, 10,* 141–157.

Peterson, R. D., & Krivo, L. J. (1993). Racial segregation and Black urban homicide. *Social Forces, 71,* 1001–1026.

Peterson, R. D., & Krivo, L. J. (1999). Racial segregation, the concentration of disadvantage, and Black and White homicide victimization. *Sociological Forum, 14,* 465–493.

Phillips, J. A. (1997). Variation in African-American homicide rates: An assessment of potential explanations. *Criminology, 35,* 527–559.

Rainwater, L., & Yancey, W. L. (1967). *The Moynihan Report and the politics of controversy.* Cambridge, MA: The MIT Press.

Raudenbush, S. W., & Bryk, A. S. (2002). *Hierarchical linear models: Applications and data analysis methods.* Thousand Oaks, CA: Sage Publications.

Raudenbush, S. W., Johnson, C., & Sampson, R. J. (2003). A multivariate, multilevel Rasch model for self-reported criminal behavior. *Sociological Methodology, 33,* 169–211.

Rebellon, C. J. (2002). Reconsidering the broken homes/delinquency relationship and exploring its mediating mechanism(s). *Criminology, 40,* 103–135.

Reiss, A. J., & Roth, J. A. (Eds.). (1993). *Understanding and preventing violence.* Washington, DC: National Academy Press.

Sampson, R. J. (1987). Urban Black violence: The effect of male joblessness and family disruption. *American Journal of Sociology, 93,* 348–382.

Sampson, R. J., & Laub, J. H. (1993). *Crime in the making: Pathways and turning points through life.* Cambridge, MA: Harvard University Press.

Sampson, R. J., & Lauritsen, J. L. (1994). Violent victimization and offending: individual-, situational-, and community-level risk factors. In A. J. Reiss & J. A. Roth (Eds.), *Understanding and preventing violence: Vol. 3. Social influences* (pp. 1–114). Washington, DC: National Academy Press.

Sampson, R. J., & Lauritsen, J. L. (1997). Racial and ethnic disparities in crime and criminal justice in the United States. In M. Tonry (Ed.), *Ethnicity, crime, and immigration: Comparative and cross-national perspectives* (pp. 311–374). Chicago: University of Chicago Press.

Sampson, R. J., Morenoff, J. D., & Gannon-Rowley, N. (2002). Assessing neighborhood effects: Social processes and new directions in research. *Annual Review of Sociology, 28*, 443–478.

Sampson, R. J., Morenoff, J. D., & Raudenbush, S. W. (2005). Social anatomy of racial and ethnic disparities in violence. *American Journal of Public Health, 95*, 224–232.

Sampson, R. J., Raudenbush, S. W., & Earls, F. (1997). Neighborhoods and violent crime: A multilevel study of collective efficacy. *Science, 277*, 918–924.

Sampson, R. J., & Wilson, W. J. (1995). Toward a theory of race, crime, and urban inequality. In J. Hagen & R. Peterson (Eds.), *Crime and inequality* (pp. 37–56). Stanford, CA: Stanford University Press.

Shihadeh, E. S., & Flynn, N. (1996). Segregation and crime: The effect of Black social isolation on the rates of Black urban violence. *Social Forces, 74*, 1325–1352.

Shihadeh, E. S., & Steffensmeier, D. J. (1994). Economic-inequality, family disruption, and urban Black violence – Cities as units of stratification and social-control. *Social Forces, 73*, 729–751.

Short, J. F., & Nye, F. I. (1957). Reported behavior as a criterion of deviant behavior. *Social Problems, 5*, 207–213.

Simcha-Fagan, O., & Schwartz, J. E. (1986). Neighborhood and delinquency: An assessment of contextual effects. *Criminology, 24*, 667–703.

South, S. J., & Messner, S. F. (2000). Crime and demography: Multiple linkages, reciprocal relations. *Annual Review of Sociology, 26*, 83–106.

Thornberry, T. P., & Krohn, M. D. (2002). Comparison of self-report and official data for measuring crime. In J. V. Pepper & C. V. Petrie (Eds.), *Measurement problems in criminal justice research: Workshop summary*. Washington, DC: National Academies Press.

Tittle, C. R., & Meier, R. F. (1990). Specifying the SES delinquency relationship. *Criminology, 28*, 271–299.

Tonry, M. H. (1995). *Malign neglect: Race, crime, and punishment in America*. New York: Oxford University Press.

U.S. Census Bureau (2003). *Statistical Abstract of the United States: 2003* (123rd Edition).Washington, DC: U.S. Government Printing Office.

U.S. Census Bureau (2002). *Statistical Abstract of the United States: 2002* (122nd Edition).Washington, DC: U.S. Government Printing Office.

Visher, C. A., & Roth, J. A. (1986). Participation in criminal careers. In A. Blumstein, J. Cohen, J. A. Roth, & C. A. Visher (Eds.), *Criminal careers and career criminals* (Vol. 1). Washington, DC: National Academy Press.

White, J. L., Moffitt, T. E., Caspi, A., Bartusch, D. J., Needles, D. J., & Stouthamer-Loeber, M. (1994). Measuring impulsivity and examining its relationship to delinquency. *Journal of Abnormal Psychology, 103*, 192–205.

Wikstrom, P-O. H., & Loeber, R. (2000). Do disadvantaged neighborhoods cause well-adjusted children to become adolescent delinquents? A study of male juvenile serious offending, individual risk and protective factors, and neighborhood context. *Criminology, 38*, 1109–1142.

Wilson, J. Q., & Herrnstein, R. J. (1985). *Crime and human nature: The definitive study of the causes of crime*. New York: The Free Press.

Wolfgang, M. E., Figlio, R. M., & Sellin, T. (1972). *Delinquency in a birth cohort.* Chicago: University of Chicago Press.

Wu, L. L., & Martinson, B. C. (1993). Family structure and the risk of a premarital birth. *American Sociological Review, 58,* 210–232.

Zimring, F. E., & Hawkins, G. (1997). *Crime is not the problem: Lethal violence in America.* New York: Oxford University Press.

7

Explaining Ethnic Variations in Crime and Antisocial Behavior in the United Kingdom

David J. Smith

Introduction

This review examines ethnic variations in crime and antisocial behavior in England to consider whether distinct patterns among ethnic groups have tended to persist from one generation to another. Analyzing intergenerational continuities among distinct ethnic groups is challenging because longitudinal data scarcely exist. In their absence, one can only examine ethnic variations in offending rates over time and consider whether these patterns have changed since the initial period of migration and settlement of ethnic minorities. Although the evidence for the early migrant cohorts is fragile, a striking pattern emerges. Crime and antisocial behavior increased among certain groups (African Caribbeans especially), but not at all among certain others (Indians, most clearly). Certain other groups (Bangladeshis, especially) may be intermediate, with signs of a recent increase among the youngest generation. These findings illustrate the great diversity of ethnic minority populations in Britain, and the complexity of their experience of British society. Subsequently I evaluate a range of possible explanations for the striking differences in offending patterns, and for the differences in ethnic continuity and change over the generations.

The reports on a program of research on ethnic minorities in Britain in the mid-1970s highlighted the diversity of the origins, language, religion, and postmigration history of the minority groups in Britain, which was reaffirmed by a subsequent study in the 1990s (Modood et al., 1997; Smith, 1977). Both studies document visible minorities' shared experience of racial discrimination and prejudice, yet highly divergent integration experiences.

The striking point highlighted by existing studies of ethnic minority populations is that the diverse origins and divergent futures of ethnic minorities in Britain do not map onto the differences in rates of offending over the generations, or at least, not in a simple way. There is little evidence that rates of offending are increasing among the second and subsequent generations of Pakistanis and Bangladeshis, who are easily the most deprived group in terms of unemployment, job levels, earnings, and incomes (Tienda, this volume). Nor have rates of offending increased among the successful South Asian groups (Indians and African Asians). Rather, it is among African Caribbeans that the rate of offending is strikingly elevated for second and subsequent generations, but this group occupies a middling position in terms of jobs and earnings. It is often argued that the apparently elevated rate of offending among African Caribbeans reflects discrimination and prejudice within the criminal justice system and the wider society. Given that diverse South Asian groups also suffer discrimination and prejudice, but do not show elevated rates of offending, this seems unlikely.

Instead I argue that the rate of offending among African Caribbeans did actually rise in the second and subsequent generations, which I trace to features of their history, expectations, and life styles that structured interactions with White British people and their predominantly White institutions. African Caribbeans experienced more manifest discrimination and prejudice than South Asians, because they were far more open and outgoing in their approach to living in Britain, resulting, within a couple of generations, in a much higher rate of intermarriage. As part of the legacy of slavery, young African Caribbeans had far more difficulty than young Asians in finding positive sources of identity, and therefore invented a whole new set of styles, symbols, and cultural folkways that took rebellion against White authority as their point of origin. These styles later became popular among White and Asian youths as well, but could not have the same edge of hostility for them. Patterson (1998) argued that the slave plantations (in Jamaica as well as the American South) had long-term consequences for African-American and African-Caribbean families, and for the conception of masculinity and relations between men and women among the descendants of slaves. Although family structures have rapidly evolved among African Caribbeans since the time of their migration to Britain, and also among African Americans over the same period, the course of this evolution is still profoundly influenced by the history of slavery. One view is that common experiences in slavery explain the parallel evolution among the descendants of slaves in the two countries. The resulting patterns of family life may have contributed to elevated rates of crime in subsequent generations, but the underlying mechanisms are highly complex.

There are nevertheless substantial problems and difficulties in establishing these broad conclusions. Evidence about rates of offending among Britain's ethnic minorities before 1980 is fragile, so the evidence for *change* in offending rates between generations is relatively weak, even though the evidence for *elevated* rates of offending among African Caribbeans in later generations is fairly strong. There is a major conflict between different sources of information on rates of offending, and every individual source has a major weakness. Although I argue that identity formation has central importance in offending rates, there is no quantitative evidence to support this claim. Nor is there quantitative evidence on family functioning (as opposed to family structure) among different ethnic groups.

This chapter starts with a critical assessment of the evidence on crime rates among different ethnic groups over the generations. The longest section of the chapter then reviews a number of possible explanations for ethnic variations in crime rates and in doing so summarizes relevant information on explanatory factors such as education and qualifications, unemployment, occupation, and income, racial prejudice and discrimination, neighborhood polarization, cultural resources of different ethnic groups, and identity formation. The final section discusses the main conclusions, identifies the main gaps in the evidence, and reviews the implications for policy.

To elaborate my arguments, I draw extensively on a sequence of four studies of ethnic minorities, racial discrimination, and racial disadvantage in Britain that were carried out in 1966–1967, 1974–1976, 1984, and 1994. The first and second studies (Daniel, 1968; Smith, 1977) were carried out for Political and Economic Planning (PEP); the third and fourth (Brown, 1984; Modood et al., 1997) were carried out for the Policy Studies Institute (PSI), an organization that evolved out of PEP. I also use findings from the British Crime Survey (BCS), a national survey of crime victimization carried out on behalf of the Home Office at roughly 2-year intervals from 1982 (but annually since 2001).

Methodological and Conceptual Issues

Secular Change Versus Intergenerational Change
Since Britain's postcolonial migration began, its social and economic context has changed substantially. Concomitantly, there has been a process of adaptation and development among ethnic minority communities, both within and across the generations. Because of secular change, crime rates among all population groups were substantially higher in 2000 than 50 years before. Relative to other groups, the crime rate among African Caribbeans was elevated in 2000, whereas it probably was not in 1950 (see the following section). However, this change to a *relatively* high crime rate among African Caribbeans may itself result either from secular contextual changes or from a developmental process unfolding among the African-Caribbean population.

Diversity of Ethnic Groups
The diversity of ethnic minority groups in Britain provides a natural experiment, with interesting opportunities for analysis. These groups share certain characteristics and have some common experiences, but are

contrasted in other ways. For example, they all originate from fairly recent migration, have experienced difficult adaptation in deprived urban environments, and have faced substantial discrimination and prejudice. On the other hand, they have contrasting backgrounds in terms of education, language, religion, and family structures (Tienda, this volume; Modood, this volume). Also, they have come to occupy different positions in the occupational hierarchy, and they have different average incomes and different proportions in unemployment and poverty.

The natural experiment arises because cultural similarities among the South Asian groups (for example, in largely maintaining a traditional family structure) cross-cut sharp occupation and income differences. Also, there are wide cultural differences among the South Asian groups on the one hand, and African Caribbeans on the other, yet some South Asian groups are similar to African Caribbeans in socioeconomic status, whereas others are different. This provides an opportunity to "test" whether cultural or economic factors exert stronger influences on changes in crime rates across generations.

Crime and Antisocial Behavior Are Social Constructs

Crime and antisocial behavior cannot be defined in isolation from the response of other people and social institutions. Rather, individuals respond to their *ideas* of the world, which arise out of social interactions, social processes, and institutions (Mead, 1934; Rock, 2003, p. 70). The tradition of labeling theory in criminology placed particular emphasis on the sequence of interactions that leads to the definition of behavior as antisocial or criminal, and to the stigmatization of the individuals concerned (Becker, 1963; Lemert, 1951, 1967).

Symbolic interactionism and labeling theory are potentially of great importance in understanding elevated rates of offending among ethnic minority groups. Hudson (1993) claimed that Black crime is a direct result of the racism inherent in social institutions, particularly the criminal justice system, but Becker (1963) and Lemert (1967) argued that elevated rates of offending develop from a sequence of interactions between people and control institutions in which new symbolic meanings are generated on both sides.

Clearly, the behavior of Black people is often interpreted as criminal or antisocial where similar behavior among Whites would not be. Beyond that, symbolic interactionism and labeling theory raise the possibility that Black identities can be shaped permanently by these ascriptions, thereby affecting the behavior of Black people and their children in the long term.

Measuring Crime and Antisocial Behavior

To a greater or lesser extent, the various methods of measuring or assessing crime and antisocial behavior reflect social reaction as well as the behavior itself. This is most obvious in the case of statistics at various points of the criminal justice process. At the end of the process, for example, the rate of imprisonment is much higher for Black than for White people (Phillips and Bowling, 2002: Table 17.3, p. 605), but this also could reflect selective response and bias at various stages (Morenoff, this volume; White, 2002). Other sources, such as homicide statistics, the reports of victims in crime surveys, and studies of self-reported offending, are much less heavily influenced by social reaction, but are subject to other limitations and biases. For example, surveys exclude or underrepresent marginal groups with high levels of victimization and offending; also, there is evidence (contested by some) of systematic differences among ethnic groups in their willingness to admit to offending in self-report questionnaires (Bowling, 1990; Hindelang, Hirschi, & Weis, 1981; Junger, 1989).

Information About Young People

Like other countries, England and Wales has a separate system of juvenile justice that often diverts young offenders from the courts. The system has been adapted and reformed at various times since the Second World War, and efforts to divert young people from the courts have waxed and waned. Consequently, statistics on the numbers of young people passing through the juvenile justice system are a particularly poor indication of levels of crime or antisocial behavior. Changes over time often reflect changes in the law or the system or the way it was being used (Rutter, Giller, & Hagell, 1998).

Crime Rates Over the Generations

Although there is little hard evidence on which to base an assessment of crime rates among first-generation migrants, ample documentary evidence shows that during the 1950s and 1960s official bodies and ordinary citizens *believed* that African Caribbeans were law-abiding and rather conventional, even old-fashioned, in their morals and behavior. As the flow of migrants from India and Pakistan increased, they also were considered to be quiet and law-abiding, even among natives who disliked other aspects of their way of life. Hall and associates (Hall, Critcher, Clarke, Jefferson, & Roberts, 1978) documented a change in the official view during the mid-1970s. By comparing the reports of the House of Commons Select Committee on Race Relations and Immigration for 1972 and 1976, they noted that the Metropolitan Police claimed the "West Indian community" was law-abiding, but the 1976 report showed a high level of street crime by Black people in London. The press used these reports to raise public anxiety about what was called "mugging" by Black people. Although many of these offences were snatches without violence or threats, Hall et al. (1978) argued that the term "mugging" (which suggests violence) was used to whip up a "moral panic."

More detailed and harder evidence began to accumulate in the 1980s, starting with the PSI study of policing in London (Smith. 1983; Smith &

Gray, 1985). The Police and Criminal Evidence Act of 1984 required that the police keep a record of every person stopped and searched; in time these records were used to compile statistics on police-recorded stops according to the ethnic group of the suspect. From 1985 onward, statistics were compiled on the ethnic composition of the prison population, and since 2000, on persons arrested by the police (Home Office, 2000a, 2000b). Starting in 1982, successive British Crime Surveys (BCS) have provided statistics on the ethnic composition of offenders as described by victims (although in about two thirds of cases, the victim is not able to provide a description).

More recently, two large, national studies of self-reported offending have been conducted, each with substantial subsamples of ethnic minority populations (Flood-Page et al. 2000; Graham & Bowling, 1995). Statistics on homicides are currently available, which reveal ethnicity of both offenders and victims (Home Office, 2000b). Interpretation of this body of evidence remains controversial and difficult, especially in the light of conflicts among different sources. For example, whereas the rate of imprisonment has been seven or eight times higher among Black compared with White people, the rate of self-reported offending among young Blacks and Whites based on national surveys is similar (Graham & Bowling 1995; Flood-Page, Campbell, Harrington, & Miller, 2000). Moreover, several studies of self-reported illegal drug use show lower rates for ethnic minorities compared with White youths (Ramsay, Baker, Goulden, Sharp, & Sondhi, 2001; Ramsay & Percy, 1996; Ramsay & Spiller, 1997).

Taking full account of these conflicts among sources, a careful assessment of the evidence suggests the following consensus among commentators. The crime rate among African Caribbeans and Black Africans is substantially higher than among the White majority. Indian and African Asian youth have low offending rates, probably lower than those of Whites. Among Pakistani and Bangladeshi youth, the crime rate may be slightly higher than among White youth, but the evidence is ambiguous. At the same time, there is evidence that Black people are targeted by the police, and that they are subject to direct and indirect discrimination at several stages of the criminal justice process. Although targeting, bias, and discrimination must influence the crime rate, it is likely that bias accounts for only a small part of the elevated rates of arrest, conviction, and imprisonment among Black people.

Critical Evaluation of the Evidence Base
Data on homicide. As noted by Phillips and Bowling (2002, p. 591), "Homicide data are generally less prone to the well-documented methodological problems of definition and categorization that afflict other offences." Information on the ethnic profile of offenders and victims in homicide cases has recently been published for the first time. Combined results for the 3 years ending 1999–2000 show that 9.7 percent of suspects were Black,

compared with 1.8 percent of the population aged 10 and over, so that Blacks were overrepresented among homicide suspects by a factor of 5.4 (Home Office, 2000b, Table 4.2). Asians and other ethnic groups were also overrepresented among homicide suspects, by factors of 2.2 and 2.5, respectively. Intraethnic crime is a very important factor underlying the elevated Black homicide rate, as 59 percent of the victims of Black homicide suspects were themselves Black; also, 66 percent of the victims of Asian homicide suspects were themselves Asian.

Crime survey evidence: victims' descriptions of offenders. Where victims have been asked to describe offenders in crime surveys, the results have consistently shown a sharply elevated proportion of Black offenders. Victims' reports avoid contaminating rates by possible biases in the criminal justice system, and also include incidents that were not reported to the police. The main disadvantage of victims' reports is that offenders can be described in only about one third of cases, involving mostly personal contact crimes in which Black offenders may be overrepresented.

Several U.S. studies have found that the proportion of Black offenders described by victims was comparable to the number arrested or admitted to prison for the same offenses (Hindelang, 1978; Langan, 1985). A 1981 survey in the United Kingdom found that Black people were represented among offenders about four times the rate of the general population, whereas Asians were substantially underrepresented among offenders described by victims (Smith, 1983, p. 73), in agreement with the British Crime Survey (BCS) results (FitzGerald & Hale, 1996, Table 2.2; Smith, 1997, p. 731). A more focused analysis of the BCS showed that the high rate of offenders described as Black was particularly marked for violence and for muggings, including robbery and snatch theft (Mayhew, Aye Maung, & Mirrlees-Black, 1993).

Victim surveys may exaggerate Black offending because they only adequately represent personal contact crimes, which are the most prevalent types for Black offenders. However, when comparisons are restricted to specific offenses, victim descriptions in Britain (and the United States) account for most of the overrepresentation of Black people in the prison population.

A different criticism of this approach is that victim descriptions are unreliable and systematically biased. The only evidence that directly supports this view is based on a pooled analysis of the 1982, 1984, and 1988 BCS data. Shah and Pease (1992, pp. 198–199, Table 6) showed that recalled incidents involving a White offender were no more recent than those involving a Black offender. This argues against differential recall according to the offender's ethnicity because recall will be better for the more recent incidents, leaving more room for systematic bias in the case of the less recent offenses.

It is conceivable that responses in victim surveys are influenced by implicit social cognitions. Not only do stereotypes influence behavior and recall (Greenwald & Banaji, 1995), but these recall effects themselves are complex. Both incongruency effects (behavior incongruent with character is better recalled) and illusory correlation effects (people interpret experience so as to confirm their stereotypes) can contribute to attribution of crime to Blacks (Garcia-Marques & Hamilton, 1996). Because these processes have contrary effects on recall bias, there is no justification for claims that the net effect would be dominant in the victim survey results. The only directly relevant study, by Shah and Pease (1992), suggests that there is little or no recall bias associated with the offender's ethnicity. Thus, on balance, the evidence from victim surveys indicates that rates of offending are highly elevated among African Caribbeans and Black Africans residing in England.

Targeting and discrimination at various stages of criminal process. The prison population is the last stage in a long series of encounters with the criminal justice system. Differential treatment of ethnic minorities is possible at every stage. For example, police officers might be more likely to stop and search minority youth, and judges might hand out longer sentences to them. Also, deep-rooted properties of the system may tend to work against Black people. For example, a widespread stop and search policy that targets street populations will work to the disadvantage of Black people if they tend to live their lives on the street. Seemingly neutral case processing practices, such as pretrial confinement or reduction of sentences in return for guilty pleas, may systematically work to the disadvantage of ethnic minorities, who are less likely to meet the criteria for release pending trial, and more likely to contest the charges against them.

There is evidence that Black people are significantly more likely than White people to be drawn into the criminal justice process on relatively flimsy evidence. Survey-based measures consistently find that Black people are more likely to be stopped by the police than White people (Smith, 1983, 1997). Official police records for 1999/2000 reveal that the stop and search rate was about five times higher for Black compared with White people (Phillips & Bowling, 2002, p. 594). However, basing the calculations on street populations, rather than the general population, a recent study concluded that White people were actually stopped at a higher rate than Black people (MVA & Miller, 2000). The consequence of these differences for the ethnic profile of persons arrested is limited because only about one fifth of arrests arise from stops (Smith, 1997).

After a suspect has been charged by the police and initial investigations have been completed, the case is passed to the Crown Prosecution Service (CPS) to decide whether prosecution is warranted. The proportion of cases dropped at this stage is higher for ethnic minority than for White defendants (Mhlanga, 1999; Phillips & Brown, 1998), suggesting that Black suspects tend to be charged on weaker evidence than Whites. Moreover, this bias is only partly corrected by later decisions not to prosecute (Phillips & Bowling, 2002, p. 600). Compared with Whites, Black suspects are more

TABLE 7.1. *Representation of Ethnic Groups at Different Stages of the Criminal Justice Process, England and Wales 1999/2000 (Row Percentages)*

	White	Black	Asian	Other	Not Known
Population aged 10+	94.5	1.8	2.7	1.1	0.0
Offenders described by victims[a]	90.0	8.0	2.0	–	n.a.
Stops and searches[b]	85.2	8.2	4.4	0.9	1.3
Arrests[c]	87.0	7.3	4.0	0.8	0.9
Cautions[c]	87.2	5.7	4.1	1.0	2.0
Prison receptions	86.0	8.5	2.5	2.9	0.0
Prison population	81.2	12.3	3.0	3.4	0.1

[a] British Crime Survey 1988 and 1992 (aggregated). Those that are not known (because the victim could not describe them) are excluded from the base for percentages.
[b] Stops and searches recorded by the police under section 60 Criminal Justice and Public Order Act 1994.
[c] Notifiable offenses.
Sources: Home Office (2000b), Table A; FitzGerald & Hale (1996), Table 2.

likely to be remanded in custody, to plead not guilty, and to be committed to the Crown Court (rather than the Magistrates' Court) where severe sentences are more common. Ethnic differences at any particular stage are not large, but the cumulative effect may be large. Hood's (1992) study explained why Black defendants, compared with Whites, were somewhat more likely to be given prison sentences, and why these sentences were longer.

Cumulative effects of bias. Decisions at one stage have to be interpreted in the context of the criminal justice process as a whole: For example, a higher acquittal rate among Black defendants may result from decisions to prosecute on weaker evidence at an earlier stage. Estimating the cumulative effects of bias at all stages is difficult because this depends on the way that different stages interact. Unfortunately, rather than building a model of the whole process, most researchers chart the level of overrepresentation of Black suspects at each stage, and consider whether the observed discrepancies could have been caused by bias (see Blumstein, 1982; Hindelang, 1978).

Table 7.1 shows the representation of ethnic minority groups at different stages of criminal justice according to Home Office statistics. If the cumulative effect of discrimination at each successive stage of criminal process is the main explanation for Black overrepresentation, then the proportion of Black people should consistently increase from one stage to the next. However, as shown in Table 7.1, this is not the case except for the proportion in prison, probably due to longer average sentence lengths for Black defendants than for others. The victim survey results suggest that the proportion of Black people is similar at the beginning and end of the process among arrestees and prison receptions, although the limitations of the victim survey findings (discussed earlier) should also be borne in mind. In any case, the general pattern of findings illustrated in Table 7.1 is not consistent with the view that bias in criminal justice process is the main explanation for elevated rates of conviction and imprisonment of Black people.

The evidence from self-report studies. The findings of self-report studies conflict sharply with the other evidence reviewed here. The Home Office conducted a national survey of 2,500 young people aged 14–25 in 1992–3, with subsamples of about 200 Black people and 500 South Asians. The questioning covered a wide range of property and violent offenses and use of illicit drugs. There were no significant differences in patterns of self-reported offending between Black and White respondents. Self-reported offending was considerably lower among each of the three South Asian groups than among White or Black respondents. Self-reported use of drugs was considerably lower among all four ethnic minority groups compared with Whites (Graham & Bowling, 1995). Another survey carried out in 1999 produced similar findings (Flood-Page et al., 2000).

In the United States, there is also conflicting evidence on race differences in offending rates between victim and other surveys. Self-report studies find little or no ethnic difference in rates of self-reported offending (Huizinga, 1991); yet there are large race differences in victim surveys and official statistics reporting rates of arrest, conviction, and imprisonment. This has raised questions about the validity of self-reported offending rates (see Morenoff, this volume). Although self-reports of offending have some validity, there is ample room for systematic bias among ethnic groups. In the United States, there is evidence that Black males self-reported fewer serious offences than White males (Hindelang, Hirschi, & Weis, 1981, Table 8.7; Huizinga & Elliott, 1986). This systematic bias affects prevalence, incidence, and also seriousness, which is particularly important in explaining the disparity between official and self-report data on ethnic differentials.

A different limitation of self-report studies arises from their sample design, namely that they usually underrepresent serious and persistent offenders, particularly in ethnic minority groups. Many studies have been restricted to very young age groups (e.g., Hindelang et al., 1981), whereas much serious offending occurs among young adults. Furthermore, these studies exclude the institutionalized population (e.g., Graham & Bowling, 1995; Flood-Page et al., 2000). Also, these studies probably achieved fairly low response rates among young African Caribbeans, although no published information is available on this point. A more general limitation is that marginal populations, such as truants from school and the homeless, tend to be excluded from sample surveys. There are strong indications that the exclusion of institutionalized and marginal populations has a substantial effect on estimates of offending rates. Cernkovich, Giordano, and

Pugh (1985) found that the level of self-reported offending among young people defined as "high frequency major offenders" was much lower than among a sample of young people in juvenile institutions. Thus, despite their many strengths, self-report studies do not provide a reliable indication of ethnic differentials in offending.

Summary. These findings suggest that criminal offending, although low among the first generation of African Caribbeans in Britain, rose sharply among the second and subsequent generations. This rise coincided with a secular rise in offending between 1950 and 1980 (Smith & Rutter, 1995), which affected all population groups. However, offending rose more among African Caribbeans compared with other groups, indicating a dramatic change in behavior from the first to the second (and subsequent) generations of African Caribbeans. None of the subcontinental Asian groups witnessed a similar change in offending behavior. There are now signs of a rising rate of offending among Pakistanis, but this increase is smaller, by an order of magnitude, than that characterizing African Caribbeans, and it has taken longer to develop. Although the evidence for elevated rates of offending among African Caribbeans is compelling, there is equally compelling evidence of racism in criminal justice institutions and discrimination at several stages of criminal justice process. This does not negate the evidence for a substantially elevated rate of offending among African Caribbeans.

Explaining Intergenerational Changes

Methodological problems challenge the interpretation of intergenerational offending patterns. The early migrants must presumably have been a highly selected group, with high motivation and determination, and adequate resources to make the journey. Also, not everyone who wanted to come to Britain was admitted, and controls became more stringent over time. Importantly, known criminals would not have been admitted. Presumably, the first generation would be more enterprising, hard working, and conformist than their source population, on average. The same principles of selection would not apply either to children of migrants born in the country of origin who came with their parents or joined them later, or to children born in Britain to migrants. This means that we should expect an increase in crime among second and subsequent generations for reasons that derive only from selection. There is no means of estimating how great the increase due to selection would be, but the striking point about the observed pattern is that intergenerational change was much greater for one ethnic group (African Caribbeans) than for the others. This suggests that the elevated rate of offending among second and subsequent generation African Caribbeans is *not* explained primarily by selective migration effects.

Another problem of method arises because the migrants were concentrated initially in the conurbations, together with the former cotton towns of Lancashire. Although there has been some dispersal since, ethnic minorities remain concentrated in densely populated towns and cities. At the same time, crime rates in Britain, as in other countries, are considerably higher in towns than in suburbs or countryside. Ideally, comparisons should be between ethnic minorities and White people living in the same towns, but most comparisons have been much broader. Nevertheless, when comparisons have been made within London, the same pattern of elevated rates of offending among African Caribbeans only has been found (Smith, 1997). The South Asian groups are more geographically concentrated than African Caribbeans, yet their crime rates increased much less in the second generation. This suggests that the geographical distribution of the ethnic minority populations is not an important part of the explanation for the intergenerational pattern of offending.

Explaining this complex pattern of intergenerational change is a challenging task. What follows is a first, and somewhat speculative, attempt to review possible explanations in the light of the evidence. The comparisons are potentially useful mainly because the four South Asian groups are culturally similar in some ways (traditional family patterns, languages, and religions distinct from the White majority, "culturally enclosed") and different from the African Caribbeans in these respects. At the same time, the four South Asian groups differ appreciably in their socioeconomic position (Tienda, this volume).

The Asian minorities are also internally diverse in terms of socioeconomic status and educational level, whereas the African Caribbeans are less so. In principle this provides the opportunity, especially for Asians, to examine whether socioeconomic factors have an important influence on offending within each ethnic group, and whether the nature of this influence is the same for each ethnic group.

The best available method of analysis is to take a possible explanatory factor, such as level of education, and consider whether the patterns of interethnic differences and crime trends correspond to the equivalent patterns of criminal offending. I argue that the observed patterns permit tentative inferences that, at the very least, rule out a number of factors as likely explanations for the elevated rate of offending among second and subsequent generation African Caribbeans. The limitation of this approach is that detailed analysis of the relationship between an explanatory factor (such as educational level) and criminal offending is not possible for specific ethnic groups because no large data set contains reliable information about both for the same individuals. Having similar information for different periods in history, so as to track change over time, is an even more distant prospect. It is always possible, therefore, that education influences criminal offending in different ways for ethnic groups. It is well known that a relatively small group of persistent and frequent offenders accounts for a high proportion of crime, especially serious crime. It is always possible that there are specific causes of offending among that "hard core" group that are distinctive among African Caribbeans compared with other ethnic groups, and distinctive among "hard core" African-Caribbean offenders compared with the general run of African Caribbeans. That would not be captured by a deductive approach based on coarse patterns of relationships.

Despite this limitation, available information suggests plausible explanations for the remarkable pattern of interethnic differences in criminal offending. For example, if the proportion of Bangladeshis in poverty is much higher than the proportion of African Caribbeans, and if the proportion of African Caribbeans in poverty (and not the proportion of Bangladeshis) has declined, it is perverse to argue that poverty is the cause of the elevated crime rate among African Caribbeans.

Education

Many theorists have proposed that low educational attainment may be a cause of offending because young people who fail to achieve at school are more likely to engage in rude, aggressive, and hostile behavior (Cohen, 1957). It is therefore important to examine the educational background of the migrants, and the educational progress and aspirations of ethnic minority groups in Britain in first and subsequent generations.

The best available source is the Fourth National Survey of Ethnic Minorities, which was carried out by the Policy Studies Institute (PSI) in 1994 (Modood et al., 1997). The authors described the educational qualifications of three groups: (a) migrants – persons who came to Britain at the age of 16 or older; (b) persons aged 25–44 and born in the United Kingdom or 15 years old or less at the time of migration; and (c) young people aged 16–24 (divided into men and women). In the absence of a longitudinal survey, this is the nearest we can get to distinguishing between the first generation (adult migrants), the second generation (those in a middle age group who did not migrate as adults), and the third generation (the young).

Among the migrants (Modood et al., 1997, Table 3.7), Indians were the best-qualified group, followed by African Asians (see Maughan, this volume; Tienda, this volume). The proportion who were highly educated (with degrees) among these groups was much higher than among the native British population at the time. The educational qualifications of migrants from the other two Asian groups, Pakistanis and Bangladeshis, were much lower. Nevertheless, echoing findings from earlier studies (Smith, 1977), the educational background of Pakistani and Bangladeshi migrants was relatively polarized, with a considerable minority having degrees, despite a substantial proportion having no qualifications. The educational background of Caribbean migrants was intermediate with few having university degrees, but more with A-level qualifications, and far more in a skilled manual trade.

Dramatic changes were apparent in the second generation (Modood et al., 1997, Table 3.8). The proportion of second-generation Caribbeans with qualifications at every level was much higher than in the migrant generation.

When we focus on the third generation (Modood et al., 1997, Table 3.9), educational outcomes cannot be fully assessed because many will have not completed their education. Nevertheless, three points can be made. First, the proportion of Asians with degrees was already higher than for Whites. Second, the proportion of Caribbeans with degrees was close to that for Whites, but, overall, the educational profile of young Caribbean women was better than that of men. Third, young Pakistanis and Bangladeshis had much the lowest educational qualifications.

These results however understate the drive to educational attainment among ethnic minorities in Britain because many achieve qualifications later in life. Among all ethnic minorities, the proportion of young people with school leaving qualifications who were still in full-time education was twice as high as among comparable young White people. The proportion of young qualified people staying in full-time education was particularly high among Asians, and, remarkably, was very high among Pakistanis and Bangladeshis, even though this group as a whole had a low level of qualifications. The proportion of qualified young Caribbeans staying on was lower, although still considerably higher than for young qualified White people. These findings indicate a strong commitment to advancement through education among all ethnic minorities, although this was less striking for Caribbeans than for the South Asian groups.

From this pattern it would appear that a low level of educational progress is unlikely to account for the elevated crime rate among African Caribbeans. Caribbeans were less disadvantaged in educational terms than Pakistanis or Bangladeshis at an early stage of the migration, and as a group they made more rapid progress than Bangladeshis especially, but their crime rate increased much more rapidly. Nevertheless, some caution is called for in view of the lack of evidence on the association between educational level and crime within ethnic groups. The findings do not rule out the possibility that crime levels in African Caribbeans are particularly high in a subgroup with educational failure or school dropout; but for educational failure to be a causal factor for the ethnic differences in crime rate, it would have to be the case that either this subgroup of youths failing educationally is larger in African Caribbeans than in other ethnic groups, or that educational failure is a stronger risk factor in African Caribbeans. There is no evidence as yet that either is the case.

Nevertheless, there is evidence that Caribbean males experience very high rates of disciplinary action and exclusion from school, that they have the most confrontational relations with teachers, and that they are the group that teachers feel most threatened by (Modood, 2003). Yet in spite of these problems, there is also evidence that Caribbeans (including Caribbean males) are on balance more likely to want to stay on at school than Whites, and more motivated to achieve educational qualifications (Smith & Tomlinson, 1989), leading to the higher rates of staying on than among Whites.

It has been argued that Black boys draw on a youth street culture that disparages academic achievement as a form of "acting White" and emphasizes living out Black masculinity (Alexander, 1996), leading inevitably to conflict with school authority. This is certainly not true as a general statement about the majority of young Black people. As set out above, overall the story of African Caribbeans in Britain has been one of educational progress, and motivation to educational achievement among most young Black people is exceptionally high. Even so, a significant minority reject and come into conflict with school. It is quite likely that this same minority is responsible in large part for the elevated crime rate among African Caribbeans. The relationship between truancy, rejection of school, and delinquency is very well established (see for example Smith, McVie, Shute, Woodward, & McAra, 2002) but this probably indicates that delinquency and rejection of school are similar behaviors and have common causes, rather than that the educational failure, as such, causes offending.

Unfortunately the debate over the role of educational failure as a factor in ethnic variations in crime has been driven more by ideology than empirical findings so far. There is a need for data on the operation of risk and protective factors as they relate to antisocial behavior within each ethnic group, so that the necessary multivariate analyses can be undertaken in order to determine which factors account for the ethnic group variations.

Unemployment, Poverty, Deprivation

Migrants from all the minority groups tended to suffer a range of disadvantages on arrival and for some considerable time after (Smith, 1977). These disadvantages and deprivations encompassed jobs, earnings, unemployment, large family size (with low resources per family member), area of residence, lack of English (in the case of Asians), and low or unrecognized educational qualifications. There are broadly two ways in which these disadvantages could lead to rising problems for the next generation, including an increase in antisocial behavior. In one version, akin to Merton's (1938) strain theory, young people would see their opportunities to achieve as being blocked, and some would turn to illegal means of attaining their objectives. In a different version, developed in recent years by Sampson and Laub (1993), the difficult living conditions would put a strain on parents, who would consequently become less able to support and control their children effectively. On this second account, deprivation would cause a failure of the normal process of socialization by the family.

In order to assess such explanations, we need to review jobs and living standards among ethnic minorities today, and how these have changed over the past 30 years. The PSI Fourth National Survey of Ethnic Minorities will again be used as the main source.

Study of unemployment trends has shown that ethnic minority unemployment continued to be "hyper-cyclical" from the 1960s up to the present time: that is, unemployment rose and fell faster and further among ethnic minorities than among the general population. Rates of unemployment were higher among ethnic minorities than among Whites at all times, but there were major differences among specific minority groups. In 1994, unemployment rates were about the same among Indians and African Asians as among White people; they were twice as high among African Caribbeans, and about three times as high among Pakistanis and Bangladeshis (Modood et al., 1997, p. 89). The same pattern of contrasts obtains for persons under 35 years of age, but for this age group, unemployment is also strongly related to level of qualifications. Among young people with no qualifications, unemployment was extremely high for African Caribbeans (61 percent) and for Pakistanis/Bangladeshis (43 percent) (Modood et al., 1997, Table 4.3). This indicates that although African Caribbeans have made substantial progress on the whole, there is a group of young African Caribbeans and Pakistanis/Bangladeshis who are socially and economically excluded.

Ethnic minorities have been upwardly mobile relative to White people since their arrival in Britain. For example, between 1982 and 1994, the proportion of men in nonmanual jobs increased much more within each of the ethnic minority groups than within Whites (Modood et al., 1997, Table 4.37). On the other hand, the shift by ethnic minorities from manual to nonmanual jobs has not been accompanied by an improvement in earnings relative to White people. In 1994, Pakistanis and Bangladeshis had much lower earnings than the other groups.

Total household income was also lowest for Pakistanis and Bangladeshis. Incomes of African-Caribbean households were higher, but still substantially below those of White households, whereas incomes of Indian and African Asian households with an earner were almost on a par with those of White households. "Equivalent incomes," which take account of the number of people to be supported, were considerably lower for all ethnic groups compared with Whites, but they were much lower for Pakistanis and Bangladeshis than for the other minority groups. In terms of equivalent incomes, African Caribbeans were the most advantaged of the ethnic minority groups.

As a measure of poverty, the PSI authors also calculated the proportion of households whose equivalent income (taking account of household size and composition) was below half the national average (Modood et al., 1997, Table 5.8). On this measure, the proportion in poverty was far higher for Pakistani and Bangladeshi households than for the other ethnic groups, although the proportion in poverty was also somewhat elevated for Indian, African Asian, and African-Caribbean households.

On a range of measures – unemployment, job levels, earnings, incomes, and poverty – levels of deprivation are thus considerably higher among Pakistanis and Bangladeshis than among African Caribbeans. Moreover, the gap in prosperity between African Caribbeans and Pakistanis and Bangladeshis has remained and, if anything, increased over a period of 30 years and more. Yet the striking change in antisocial behavior has occurred only among African Caribbeans. This makes it clear that deprivation on its own cannot be the explanation. This remains true whether the postulated mechanism is blocked opportunity or inadequate socialization due to the deprived material circumstances of the family. It remains possible that deprivation is part of the story, even a necessary condition of a sharp increase in criminal offending. However, to explain the contrast among ethnic groups, there must be a difference in the way these groups responded to the experience of deprivation.

Family

The family is the most obvious source of intergenerational continuity, as it is the main engine of socialization of the next generation. In the Caribbean, the family was fundamentally altered by slavery, whereas in India family structures evolved continuously among a range of different religious and linguistic groups. In the Indian countryside especially, the family remained the main unit of economic organization. By contrast, in Jamaica and the other plantation territories, as in the American South, the system of slavery utterly destroyed the continuity of African family traditions, along with the original languages, religions, music, and dance of the enslaved people.

The effects of slavery on African Americans after abolition have been the subject of intense controversy among historians and sociologists. The early assumption that slavery had profoundly damaging effects which lasted for many generations was reflected in D. P. Moynihan's 1965 report (Rainwater & Yancy, 1967) on the African American family. As a reaction against this view, revisionist historians wrote new accounts of slavery and its aftermath that argued, for example, that men and women had often maintained stable, quasimarital relationships and been able to look after their children. More recently there has followed a wave of counterrevisionists who have reestablished the damaging effects of slavery on the basis of more detailed factual accounts than before. Orlando Patterson's study *Rituals of Blood: Consequences of Slavery in Two American Centuries* (1998) offers a wide-ranging argument based on the mass of new scholarship, to show that relationships between African American men and women and their children have been profoundly damaged by the long-range effects of slavery and violent racism in the hundred years following abolition. Many or most of the factors discussed by Patterson would also apply to the plantation societies of the West Indies, which were similar in many ways to the American South (it is relevant that Patterson was writing as an African Caribbean settled in the United States).

An apparent difficulty in applying this interpretation to the history of the Caribbean migrants who came to Britain is that according to most commentators, working-class Jamaicans at the time when the migration got under way in the 1940s were monogamous and lived in conventional, old-fashioned, "Victorian" families, although they did tend to be authoritarian in their parenting, which fits with part of Patterson's story. It has been argued that the earliest generation migrating from the Caribbean in the 1940s and 1950s had family structures quite similar to those of working-class families in Britain at the time, with stable lifelong marriages the norm. Possible differences from the British pattern were that the role of the wife was more authoritative and active, and that grandparents played a more active role in the care of grandchildren. The second national survey of ethnic minorities found that lone parents headed 13 percent of West Indian households with children, compared with 9 percent of all families with dependent children (Smith, 1976, p. 38). Thus, although the proportion of single parents was elevated among African Caribbeans, it was not dramatically so. The matter needs more detailed study, but to maintain Patterson's thesis, it would have to be shown that relationships within the migrant families had been shaped by the history of slavery, even though the results were not yet as manifest as they would be later.

Among several of the groups (African Caribbeans and Pakistanis in particular) a substantial proportion of the early migration was of lone males, and it was many years before the balance of the sexes was restored (Brown, 1984; Smith, 1977). This must have had a disruptive effect on family life, particularly where men had left their wives and children in the home country. However, the pattern was less common among African Caribbeans than among several of the Asian groups.

In the years following the migration, radical changes seem to have occurred in the African-Caribbean family. These involved a large rise in the proportion of single mothers, and arguably the growth of a structure in which the woman was the one authoritative and stable figure in the family, whereas her male partners would come and go (echoing relationships at earlier periods of history). To the extent that grandparents (and especially grandmothers) had played an important role in the family in the Caribbean, it may have been important that grandparents rarely migrated to Britain. By contrast, changes in the families of subcontinental Asians seem to have been gradual. The proportion of single parents rose only slightly from a very low figure. Family ties remained close and far-reaching, and the family remained important as an economic unit. With a large and growing number of family businesses, Asians could often raise funds to buy a house or start a business from a wide circle of family members, even when each individual had only small resources (Modood et al., 1997).

Berthoud (2000 and in press) has analyzed these changes by placing family structures and relationships on a continuum running from "modern individualism" to "old-fashioned values." A convenient index of "modern individualism" is the proportion of young women (aged 16–34) who are neither living with their parents nor legally married with children. In Britain there was a dramatic secular increase in the proportion of young women in these "intermediate" structures between 1973 and 2000.

On this model, African-Caribbean family structures in Britain can be regarded as "hyper modern individualist." Thus, for example, among persons aged 25–29, 68 percent of White men and women have lived with a partner, compared with only 38 percent of Caribbeans; among those with a partner, 73 percent of the Whites, but only 51 percent of the Caribbeans, are in a formal marriage. Among those who have married, the proportion who have separated or divorced is twice as high for Caribbeans as it is for Whites across all age groups under 60 (Berthoud, in press, Table 7.1). One in ten White women with children (and under the age of 35) is a single (never-married) mother. No fewer than half of Caribbean mothers are single parents using that definition (Berthoud, in press).

Family structures also vary widely among specific Asian groups. The proportion of those who have ever had a partner is considerably higher among Bangladeshis, Pakistanis, and Indians than among Whites, although it is about the same among African Asians. Again, the proportion of women whose main activity is looking after the house and family is more than twice as high among Bangladeshis and Pakistanis as among Whites, although it is only slightly higher among Indian than among White women, and no higher among African Asian women. Thus Bangladeshis and Pakistanis have very old-fashioned, traditional family structures compared with Whites, whereas African Asians and to a lesser extent Indians have structures quite close to those of Whites.

It is plausible that the rapid change in African-Caribbean families could have played a role in the rise in crime over the generations, whereas the continuing cohesiveness of Asian families may have served a protective function. However, several key questions have still to be answered. First, we need data on the association between family structure and crime within African-Caribbean groups. The findings on education (see Maughan, this volume) indicate that it cannot be assumed that the associations will be the same in ethnic minority groups as in Whites. Second, it is necessary to determine whether family structure (i.e., a single-parent household) is a proximal risk factor for antisocial behavior or, rather, whether it creates risk only when it predisposes to lack of supervision or poor parenting, or whether it simply serves as an index for some other correlated risk factor, such as poverty. In each case, it is necessary to determine the associations with both family structure and crime and to find out whether, in an overall statistical model, the postulated mediating variable accounts for the ethnic variation. Unfortunately, all of that remains a task for the future. There is an association between single parenthood and poverty within African-Caribbean families, as well as within those of Whites (Berthoud, 2000), but it is not known whether poverty predisposes to crime in African Caribbeans, either as a direct or indirect risk factor. A recent natural experiment among Native Americans (Costello, Compton, Keeler, & Angold, 2003) is important in showing that poverty does predispose to disruptive behavior but also that it operates via effects on parental supervision – whether or not something similar is the case among African Caribbeans in the United Kingdom is quite unknown.

A third basic question is why African Caribbeans developed a family pattern that involves a high rate of single parenthood. If Patterson's account of the consequences of slavery is rejected, it becomes even more difficult, since there has to be a particular reason why Black families should be far ahead in the race toward "modern individualism." If Patterson's account is accepted, it is still necessary to explain why these particular consequences of slavery became manifest at this particular time. Since there has been a similar evolution among Black families in the United States, it seems likely that these changes were not brought about primarily by the migration to Britain. In the United States, many Black families also migrated from the South to the North, but in most cases this migration occurred 30 or more years earlier than the accelerated change in family structures. It is all too apparent that basic questions remain unanswered.

Neighborhood

In the early years of immigration to Britain, a few neighborhoods in London and the West Midlands became the nucleus of expanding communities originating from the Caribbean and the Indian subcontinent. Later some further centers of ethnic minority communities became established (for example, in the textile towns of Lancashire and West Yorkshire). There was a fairly strong tendency for ethnic minorities to settle within particular neighborhoods, although spatial segregation between ethnic minorities and White people was never as marked as in the United States. Middle-class and upwardly mobile members of ethnic minority groups were more likely than others to live in predominantly White areas. Those at low job levels, with low earnings, with large families, and (among Asians) with poor English were most likely to live in neighborhoods containing a large proportion from their own ethnic group (Smith, 1977). Essentially these patterns have continued to the present day (Dorsett, 1998).

This poses the question whether the characteristics of neighborhoods where ethnic minorities live can help account for differences in rates of crime between ethnic groups and changes over the generations. In recent years, there has been a return to the idea that community dynamics and the physical and social structure of neighborhoods have an important influence on crime rates (Sampson, Raudenbush, & Earls, 1997).

According to the 1991 UK census, there were no towns or districts in which ethnic minorities comprised a majority: The highest proportion was 44.8 percent in Brent (London). At the level of wards (areas with a total population around 10,000), there were five with a non-White population of 75 percent or above. The highest proportion of Black Caribbeans at ward level was 30 percent. There was one ward in the East End of London where 61 percent of the population was Bangladeshi. At enumeration district level (areas with a total population of around 150) it was rare to find a single ethnic group making up more than half of the population. "It is very clear therefore that nowhere in Britain do we witness the levels of concentration common in North American cities: sustained 100 percent levels for block and tract data being observed in the case of African Americans" (Peach & Rossiter, 1996, pp. 118–119). Focusing on Black people, it can also be shown that at each scale of analysis (cities, wards, enumeration districts) the level of segregation from the White population is much less than in the United States (Peach,1996; Peach & Rossiter, 1996). Also, the level of segregation of Black people in Britain declined steadily between 1961 and 1991 (Peach & Rossiter, 1996, Table 3.13). Bangladeshis were the most geographically concentrated minority group in 1991, followed by Pakistanis. Black Caribbeans were the least segregated minority group, and Indians were midway between Caribbeans and Pakistanis. Hence Black Caribbeans and Bangladeshis were the two most contrasted minority groups in terms of their spatial segregation from White people (Peach & Rossiter, 1996, Tables 3.5–3.8).

There is considerable overlap between the populations of specific ethnic minority groups in Britain, so that many neighborhoods containing substantial numbers of Black residents also contain substantial numbers of residents of Indian or Pakistani origin. However, this overlap is far from complete, so there are many predominantly African-Caribbean or Asian neighborhoods. From the PSI survey of 1994 in conjunction with the 1991 census, Dorsett (1998) found that Bangladeshis lived in the most deprived wards, followed by Pakistanis. In this respect there is a clear difference between Pakistanis and Bangladeshis and the other minority ethnic groups. The level of deprivation at ward level was middling for Caribbeans, and lowest for Indians and African Asians.

On the whole, these findings are not consistent with an interpretation that neighborhoods were an important influence leading to the rise in offending among African Caribbeans. The level of segregation (whether assessed in terms of ethnic concentration or poverty) is considerably higher for Bangladeshis and Pakistanis, who live in more deprived neighborhoods, than for African Caribbeans, but they have not shown the same increase in crime rates over the generations.

The Response to Racial Discrimination and Prejudice

In the first PEP study of *Racial Discrimination in England* carried out in 1966–1967, W. W. Daniel found that the proportion who thought racial discrimination was common and the proportion who claimed they had been victims of it were considerably higher among West Indians than among Asians. Daniel also conducted a series of real-life experiments to test whether someone from an ethnic minority group would be less favorably treated when applying for a job, trying to rent accommodation, or seeking access to various goods and services. These tests monitored the outcomes for four matched applicants: a West Indian, an Asian, a Cypriot, and a White British person. The tests demonstrated massive discrimination against the West Indian and Asian applicants in all situations, and much lower discrimination against the Cypriot. Although perceptions of discrimination had been much higher among West Indians than among Asians, in all situations the tests showed the same level of discrimination against these two visible minorities. Daniel interpreted these findings by arguing that West Indians adopted a far more outgoing style of life than Asians. Consequently, they were far more likely to encounter discrimination and be aware of it. Yet Asians, when they did make themselves vulnerable to discrimination, were just as likely to encounter it (Daniel, 1968).

Subsequent tests have always confirmed that levels of discrimination were the same against different ethnic minority groups, as long as these were groups perceived as racially distinct from the majority (Brown & Gay, 1985; CRE, 1990; Jowell & Prescott-Clarke, 1970; Simpson & Stevenson, 1994; Smith, 1977). Later studies have also confirmed that Caribbeans are more aware of discrimination than other minority groups (Brown, 1984, Table 109; Modood et al., 1997: Table 4.21; Smith, 1977, Table A25). The Fourth National Survey of 1994 showed, further, that the most deprived group, Bangladeshis, were the group least aware of discrimination. This is a highly consistent set of findings over a period of 35 years, suggesting a common level of racial discrimination against different ethnic minority groups, but with different responses to it.

Of course, the level of discrimination against specific minority groups in law enforcement and the criminal justice process has not been rigorously tested in the way that discrimination in employment has been. The results of discrimination testing nevertheless suggest that White people are just as likely to treat Asians unfairly as they are to treat African Caribbeans unfairly. Despite such findings, a theory of "multiple racisms" has gathered supporters in recent years (CMEB, 2000). According to that theory, White people attach specific stereotypes to particular ethnic minority groups (e.g., Pakistanis as quiet, devious, physically fragile; African Caribbeans as loud, easy-going, sexually potent, and so on). A specific case has been made for an anti-Muslim prejudice, which is tied to religion rather than race (Modood et al., 1997; Modood, this volume). It can be argued that a part of the stereotype of African Caribbeans is that they are criminals, and that this causes them to be criminalized. This cannot be directly tested from available evidence, but evidence that has an indirect bearing is available from the British Social Attitudes Survey over the period 1983 to 1998. These surveys asked four questions designed to test prejudices against "Asians" and "Black people." Levels of perceived prejudice and discrimination against these two groups were very similar, with some slight indication that they were greater against Asians than against Black people. Over the whole period, the time trend for prejudice against one group always closely mirrored the trend for the other (see Smith, 2005, for a detailed presentation of these findings). This is a powerful indication of a common factor of perceived hostility, as opposed to "multiple racisms."

From these findings it is not likely that the rising rate of crime among African Caribbeans as distinct from other ethnic minorities can be explained by higher levels of prejudice or discrimination directed against them. Taking up the argument made in Daniel's classic study, however, African Caribbeans may have encountered more prejudice and discrimination than South Asians, they may have become more sharply aware of it, and they may have responded to it differently.

Self-Sufficient Cultural Resources

On Daniel's interpretation of the findings of the first PEP study in 1966–1967, Asians were less likely to encounter discrimination than West Indians because they tended to rely on the resources of their own ethnic group to find jobs, accommodation, and other necessities. Building on this interpretation, it can be argued that Asians and African Caribbeans adopted fundamentally different strategies in adapting to life in Britain (see Modood, this volume). African Caribbean migrants initially thought of themselves as part of a British diaspora. It is the experience of rebuffs that caused strong resentment and hostility. Migrants from the Indian subcontinent, by contrast, saw themselves as going to a deeply alien culture. They tried to maintain most aspects of their way of life in Britain, which meant doing most things through contacts within their own ethnic group. The Asian strategy was to be culturally and economically self-sufficient, even though young Asians soon began to adopt many British styles and habits. In this respect there was an important contrast between the lifestyles of African Caribbeans and subcontinental Asians over the first 30 years after the migration began.

It is plausible that the strategy of cultural self-sufficiency tended to conserve the strength of the family and also to maintain a range of other controls that act as a constraint on antisocial behavior. Also, as demonstrated by Daniel's original research, cultural enclosure tended to protect Asians from direct experience of rejection (although it also closed off potential opportunities). Consequently, young Asians were less likely than young African Caribbeans to be hostile to White authority in response to past rebuffs.

Cultural enclosure is probably related also to the strong motivation to succeed that typifies many immigrant groups. That is because incoming groups that regard themselves as utterly different from the majority feel that they are doing well compared with relatives in their country of origin. Incoming groups that try to integrate feel that they are doing badly compared with the majority in the country of adoption. This makes them less likely to persist in the face of difficulties, and more hostile to the majority who are succeeding better than they are.

Of course, initial cultural enclosure does not help at all to explain the sharp difference in outcomes among different South Asian groups. That seems to be explained by the widely different cultural and financial resources possessed by members of the different South Asian groups at the time of the migration. These differences in resources do not seem to dissipate but rather to increase and multiply over time.

Identity Formation
It seems clear that from the 1970s onward, young African Caribbeans were looking for an identity that would set them apart from their parents, but confirm their sense of self-worth as Black people in Britain (Modood, this volume). They badly wanted to distance themselves from models of hyper-respectability such as the uniformed gospel choir that were valued by the older generation, and they needed to find other badges of a distinctively Black identity. For this they looked to American models in which fashion, music, and, above all, protest were the main ingredients. In many ways, the new sense of Black identity was then constructed in opposition to the dominant institutions, especially those that were thought to be oppressive toward Black people. At its simplest, hostility to the police became one of the building blocks of a new sense of Black self-worth. In more recent developments such as "gangsta rap," involvement in crime and abuse of women as well as protest against the established order are glamorized. Furthermore, styles (such as "gangsta rap") originally adopted as an assertion of Black identity have become extremely popular among White youths as well.

These processes of identity formation among Black youths have been described and analyzed in ethnographic studies such as Claire Alexander's book *The Art of Being Black* (1996). There is a remarkable similarity between the building blocks of Black identity and gender relations in Britain in the 1990s, as described by Alexander, and in the United States over a much longer period, as described by Patterson (1998). In part, this arises from cultural diffusion: Young African Caribbeans in Britain have adopted styles that originated in the United States, or there has been interplay back and forth. If Patterson's argument is correct, the similarity also arises partly from a closely similar history of slavery, although the aftermath of slavery was very different in the Caribbean and America.

Because of the greater self-sufficiency and cultural enclosure of the Asian communities, young Asians have been generally less inclined to adopt protest styles or to make hostility to the police the touchstone of their sense of self-worth. Since the 1990s, young Asians have started to adopt youth styles that originated with Black people, although these are remixed with elements of various Asian cultures. Nevertheless, there is still a clear difference in the salience of hostility to authority within African-Caribbean and Asian youth subcultures. This may help to explain the difference in crime and antisocial behavior among the second and later generations of African Caribbeans and Asians in Britain.

Conclusion

The issues tackled here are very difficult ones, and many of them cannot be resolved from what is known at present. From a careful review of the evidence, it was concluded that crime rates became substantially elevated among second and subsequent generations of African Caribbeans, but not among the South Asian groups. Also, it seems likely that there was a rapid increase in offending among African Caribbeans from the first to the second generation, although hard evidence about rates of offending among the first generation is missing. It is unlikely that these rising and elevated crime rates were the result of general educational failure, because the story of African Caribbeans in Britain has been one of educational progress. Rising crime rates may still have been connected with an oppositional culture among a proportion of African Caribbeans at school, but this suggests that delinquency and rejection of school have common causes. In themselves, unemployment, poverty, and deprivation cannot explain the rising and elevated crime rate among African Caribbeans because their standard of living has improved and is substantially higher than that of Bangladeshis and Pakistanis, who have not shown the same elevated rates of offending. For similar reasons, the explanation cannot lie in the characteristics of neighborhoods where African Caribbeans live. This is because the African-Caribbean population is more dispersed than the Bangladeshi and Pakistani populations, and to the extent that African Caribbeans are concentrated in specific neighborhoods, these are less deprived than the areas where Bangladeshis and Pakistanis live. Nor can the explanation lie in racial prejudice and discrimination, because levels of prejudice and discrimination against Asians and Black people are very similar and have been for at least 30 years.

Although most of the usual explanations lack convincing empirical support, it is much more difficult to justify any positive explanation for elevated crime rates among African Caribbeans in the second and subsequent generations. There are four elements in the explanation put forward here. First, the long-term consequences of slavery have profoundly influenced relations between men, women, and children among the descendants of slaves over many generations. Second, the adoption of an outgoing, integrative style among African-Caribbean migrants led them to encounter more discrimination and prejudice than South Asians, and to compare themselves unfavorably with reference groups in Britain rather than favorably with reference groups in the country of origin. Third, a sequence of interactions between young Black people and the police led to spiraling hostility and the stigmatization of Black people as criminals. Fourth is the growth of oppositional and confrontational styles as sources of identity for young Black men: Although these styles may often be rhetorical rather than literal, and may often be a way of engaging with traditional sources of power rather than rejecting them, they may actually draw young people into dangerous situations and criminal behavior. Although these four elements of an explanation are not firmly established, they may perhaps provide a starting point for deeper research (see also Modood, this volume).

The central paradox of these findings is that young African Caribbeans use protest as a source of identity partly because they have more contact with White people and with White British institutions than do Asians, as evidenced by the high and rising rate of intermarriage. This signals a deep ambivalence in the orientation of young African Caribbeans in Britain. In many ways, they are exceptionally highly motivated to succeed in conventional terms: by doing well at school, college, and university, getting a good job, earning a good living in legitimate ways, and demonstrating status and success through ownership and display of expensive goods. At the same time, aspects of their identity as African Caribbeans in Britain are deeply connected with protest and revolt and are cultivated in response to stigma, and as protection against it. The aim of public policy should be to avoid actions that encourage young African Caribbeans to see deviance as an affirmation of identity.

At various times, the law enforcement system has targeted African Caribbeans, both intentionally and unintentionally. The use of stop and search by the police over the past 40 years is the most obvious example. At other times the system has clearly failed to meet the needs of African Caribbeans, as in the Stephen Lawrence case. As long as this continues, protest against White authority will be an integral part of African-Caribbean culture and will provide a context in which criminality in a substantial minority of young African Caribbeans seems understandable and even justifiable in their circle, even as the majority are aspiring to succeed in conventional terms.

The findings also emphasize the disadvantages of "modern individualism" as a principle for organizing family life, an approach that is pioneered by African Caribbeans. There is little or nothing that the state can do to resist this tide of change. What can perhaps be done is to look for new sources of social engagement and involvement that will help to prevent singletons and single parents from becoming isolated. Equally important are public policies that effectively prevent single parents from falling into poverty. These will help to prevent rising crime among African Caribbeans not because poverty is the major direct cause of crime, but because parenting and family functioning exert a major influence on antisocial behavior and crime in the next generation.

References

Alexander, C. E. (1996). *The art of being Black: The creation of Black British Youth identities*. Oxford: Clarendon Press.

Becker, H. (1963). *Outsiders*. New York: Free Press.

Berthoud, R. (2000). *Family formation in multi-cultural Britain: Three patterns of diversity*. ISER Working Paper 2000–34, University of Essex. Retrieved [20.02.2005] from www.iser.essex.ac.uk/pubs/workpaps/pdf/2000–34.pdf

Berthoud, R. (in press). Family formation in multi-cultural Britain: Diversity and change. In G. Loury, T. Modood, & S. Teles (Eds.), *Ethnicity, social mobility and public policy in the United States and United Kingdom*. Cambridge, UK: Cambridge University Press.

Blumstein, A. (1982). On the racial disproportionality of United States' prison populations. *Journal of Criminal and Criminology, 73*, 1259–1281.

Bowling, B. (1990). Conceptual and methodological problems in measuring "race" differences in delinquency: A reply to Marianne Junger. *British Journal of Criminology, 30*, 483–492.

Brown, C. (1984). *Black and White Britain*. London: Heinemann.

Brown, C., & Gay, P. (1986). *Racial Discrimination: 17 Years after the Act*. London: Policy Studies Institute.

Cernkovich, S. A., Giordano, P. C., & Pugh, M. D. (1985). Chronic offenders: The missing cases in self-report delinquency research. *The Journal of Criminal Law and Criminology, 76*, 705–732.

Cohen, A. (1957). *Delinquent boys*. Glencoe: Free Press.

Commission for Racial Equality (CRE) (1990). *Sorry it's gone: Testing for racial discrimination in the private rented housing sector*. London: CRE.

Commission on Multi-Ethnic Britain (CMEB) (2000). *The future of multi-ethnic Britain*. London: Profile Books.

Costello, E. J., Compton, F. N., Keeler, G., & Angold, A. (2003). Relationships between poverty and psychopathology: A natural experiment. *Journal of the American Medical Association, 290*, 2023–2029.

Daniel, W. W. (1968). *Racial discrimination in England.* Harmondsworth: Penguin.

Dorsett, R. (1998). *Ethnic minorities in the inner city.* Bristol: Policy Press.

FitzGerald, M., & Hale, C. (1996). *Ethnic minorities: Victimization and racial harassment: Findings from the 1988 and 1992 British Crime Surveys.* Home Office Research Study No. 154. London: Home Office.

Flood-Page, C., Campbell, S., Harrington, V., & Miller, J. (2000). *Youth crime: Findings from the 1998/99 Youth Lifestyle Survey.* Home Office Research Study No. 209. London: Home Office.

Garcia-Marques, L., & Hamilton, D. L. (1996). Resolving the apparent discrepancy between the incongruency effect and the expectancy-based illusory correlation effect: The TRAP model. *Journal of Personality and Social Psychology, 71,* 845–860.

Graham, J., & Bowling, B. (1995). *Young people and crime.* Home Office Research Study No. 145. London: Home Office.

Greenwald, A. G., & Banaji, M. R. (1995). Implicit social cognition: Attitudes, self-esteem, and stereotypes. *Psychological Review, 102,* 4–27.

Hall, S., Critcher, C., Clarke, J., Jefferson, T., & Roberts, B. (1978). *Policing the crisis.* London: Macmillan.

Hindelang, M. (1978). Race and involvement in common law personal crimes. *American Sociological Review, 43,* 93–109.

Hindelang, M., Hirschi, T., & Weis, G. (1981). *Measuring delinquency.* Beverly Hills, CA: Sage.

Home Office (2000a). *Prison statistics England and Wales 1999, Cm 4805.* London: The Stationery Office.

Home Office (2000b). *Statistics on race and the criminal justice system 2000: A Home Office publication under section 95 of the Criminal Justice Act 1991.* London: Home Office.

Hood, R. (1992). *Race and sentencing.* Oxford: Oxford University Press.

House of Commons Select Committee on Race Relations and Immigration (1972). *Police/immigrant relations.* HC 71. London: HMSO.

House of Commons Select Committee on Race Relations and Immigration (1976). *The West Indian Community.* HC 180. London: HMSO.

Hudson, B. A. (1993). Penal policy and racial justice. In L. Gelsthorpe & W. McWilliam (Eds.), *Minority ethnic groups and the criminal justice system* (pp. 154–169). Cambridge, UK: University of Cambridge Institute of Criminology.

Huizinga, D. (1991). Assessing violent behaviour with self-reports. In J. S. Milner (Ed.), *Neurophysiology of aggression* (pp. 47–66). Deventer: Kluwer.

Huizinga, D., & Elliott, D. S. (1986). Reassessing the reliability and validity of self-report delinquency measures. *Journal of Quantitative Criminology, 2,* 293–327.

Jowell, R., & Prescott-Clarke, P. (1970). Racial discrimination and white-collar workers in Britain. *Race, 9,* 394–417.

Junger, M. (1989). Discrepancies between police and self-report data for Dutch racial minorities. *British Journal of Criminology, 29,* 273–284.

Langan, P. A. (1985). Racism on trial: New evidence to explain the racial composition of prisons in the United States. *Journal of Criminal Law and Criminology, 76,* 666–683.

Lemert, E. (1951). *Social pathology.* New York: McGraw-Hill.

Lemert, E. (1967). *Human deviance, social problems and social control.* Englewood Cliffs, NJ: Prentice-Hall.

Mayhew, P., Aye Maung, N., & Mirrlees-Black, C. (1993). *The 1992 British Crime Survey*. Home Office Research Study No. 111. London: Home Office.

Mead, G. (1934). *Mind, self and society*. Chicago: University of Chicago Press.

Merton, R. K. (1938). Social structure and anomie. *American Sociological Review, 3*, 672–82.

Mhlanga, B. (1999). *Race and Crown Prosecution Service decisions*. London: The Stationery Office.

Modood, T. (2003). Ethnic differences in educational performance. In D. Mason (Ed.), *Explaining ethnic differences: Changing patterns of disadvantage in Britain* (pp. 53–68). Bristol: Policy Press.

Modood, T., Berthoud, R., Lakey, J., Nazroo, J., Smith, P., Virdee, S., & Beishon, S. (1997). *Ethnic minorities in Britain*. London: Policy Studies Institute.

MVA & Miller, J. (2000). *Profiling populations available for stops and searches*. Police Research Series Paper No. 131. London: Home Office.

Patterson, O. (1998). *Rituals of blood: consequences of slavery in two American centuries*. Washington, DC: Counterpoint/Civitas.

Peach, C. (1996). Black-Caribbeans: Class, gender and geography. In C. Peach (Ed.), *Ethnicity in the 1991 Census: Vol. 2. The ethnic minority populations of great Britain* (pp. 25–43). London: HMSO.

Peach, C., & Rossiter, D. (1996). Level and nature of spatial concentration and segregation of minority ethnic populations in Great Britain, 1991. In P. Ratcliffe (Ed.), *Ethnicity in the 1991 Census: Vol. 3. Social geography and ethnicity in Britain: Geographical spread, spatial concentration and internal migration* (pp. 111–134). London: HMSO.

Phillips, C., & Bowling, B. (2002). Racism, ethnicity, crime, and criminal justice. In M. Maguire, R. Morgan, & R. Reiner (Eds.), The Oxford handbook of criminology (3rd ed., pp. 579–619). Oxford: Oxford University Press.

Phillips, C., & Brown, D. (1998). *Entry into the criminal justice system: A survey of police arrests and their outcomes*. Home Office Research Study No. 185. London: Home Office.

Rainwater, L., & Yancy, W. L. (1967). *The Moynihan Report and the politics of controversy*. Cambridge, MA: MIT Press.

Ramsay, M., Baker, P., Goulden, C., Sharp, C., & Sondhi, A. (2001). *Drug misuse declared in 2000: Results from the British Crime Survey*. Home Office Research Study No. 224. London: Home Office.

Ramsay, M., & Percy, A. (1996). *Drug misuse declared: Results of the 1994 British Crime Survey*. Research Findings No. 33. London: Home Office.

Ramsay, M., & Spiller, A. (1997). *Drug misuse declared in 1996: Latest results from the British Crime Survey*. Home Office Research Study No. 172. London: Home Office.

Rock, P. (2003). Sociological theories of crime. In M. Maguire, R. Morgan, & R. Reiner (Eds.), *The Oxford handbook of criminology* (3rd ed., pp. 51–82). Oxford: Oxford University Press.

Rutter, M., Giller, H., & Hagell, A. (1998). *Antisocial behaviour by young people*. New York: Cambridge University Press.

Sampson, R. J., & Laub, J. H. (1993). *Crime in the making: Pathways and turning points through life*. Cambridge, MA: Harvard University Press.

Sampson, R. J., Raudenbush, S. W., & Earls, F. (1997). Neighborhoods and violent crime: A multilevel study of collective efficacy. *Science, 277,* 918–924.

Shah, R., & Pease, K. (1992). Crime, race and reporting to the police. *The Howard Journal, 31,* 192–199.

Simpson, A., & Stevenson, J. (1994). *Half a chance, still? Jobs, discrimination and young people in Nottingham.* Nottingham, UK: Nottingham & District Racial Equality Council.

Smith, D. J. (1976). *The facts of racial disadvantage.* London: Political and Economic Planning.

Smith, D. J. (1977). *Racial disadvantage in Britain.* Harmondsworth: Penguin.

Smith, D. J. (1983). *Police and people in London: I. A survey of Londoners.* London: Policy Studies Institute.

Smith, D. J. (1997). Ethnic origins, crime, and criminal justice. In M. Maguire, R. Morgan, & R. Reiner (Eds.), *The Oxford handbook of criminology* (2nd ed., pp. 703–759). Oxford: Oxford University Press.

Smith, D. J. (2005). Ethnic differences in intergenerational crime patterns. In M. Tarry (Ed.), *Crime and Justice: An Annual Review of Research.* Chicago: University of Chicago Press.

Smith, D. J., & Gray, J. (1985). *Police and people in London.* Aldershot: Gower.

Smith, D. J., McVie, S., Shute, J., Woodward, R., & McAra, L. (2002). *The Edinburgh Study of Youth Transitions and Crime: Key findings from Sweeps 1 and 2.* Retrieved 4 January 2005 from www.law.ac.uk/cls/esytc/findingsreport.htm

Smith, D. J., & Rutter, M. (1995). Time trends in psychosocial disorders of youth. In M. Rutter & D. J. Smith (Eds.), *Psychosocial disorders in young people: Time trends and their causes* (pp. 763–781). Chichester: Wiley.

Smith, D. J., & Tomlinson, S. (1989). *The school effect: A study of multi-racial comprehensives.* London: Policy Studies Institute.

White, R. (2002). Youth crime, community development, and social justice. In M. Tienda & W. J. Wilson (Eds.), *Youth in cities: A cross-national perspective* (pp. 138–164). Cambridge, UK: Cambridge University Press.

8

Cultural Differences in the Effects of Physical Punishment

Kirby Deater-Deckard, Kenneth A. Dodge,
and Emma Sorbring

Introduction

The predictors of violence and delinquency in childhood and adolescence include attributes of the child (e.g., temperament, intelligence), the home environment (e.g., harsh parenting, maltreatment, domestic violence, family size and structure, parent mental illness, and family antisocial activity), the peer group (e.g., deviant peers, peer rejection), and the community (e.g., school and neighborhood factors; Wasserman et al., 2003). These factors correlate with or predict antisocial behavior in multiple ethnic groups (Rowe, Vazsonyi, & Flannery, 1994; Vazsonyi & Flannery, 1997). However, there is one noteworthy ethnic group difference. The customary use of physical *punishment* is associated with more aggressive behavior problems among European Americans but not among African Americans – although physical *abuse* predicts behavior problems equally well across these and other ethnic groups. Ascertaining the nature and cause of this ethnic group difference is one of the most pressing questions for research on the development of antisocial behavior (Farrington, Loeber, & Stouthamer-Loeber, 2003).

By conducting cross-cultural research, researchers can utilize the discovery of an ethnic group difference to test competing hypotheses about causal mechanisms (Rutter, this volume). In the current chapter, we consider whether the mechanisms linking harsh parenting and children's aggressive behavior problems generalize beyond middle-class Caucasians. Researchers often assume that a mechanism is generalizable across human populations, but the assumption is rarely tested. Discovering whether physical discipline and abuse are universal risk factors for the development of aggressive behavior problems has implications for theory as well as applications in prevention, intervention, and social policy. Moreover, by examining cultural differences, we may elucidate causal mechanisms that account for the link between parenting and children's adaptive and maladaptive development.

We propose that there are cultural differences in child-rearing beliefs and practices that influence children's interpretations of their parents' behaviors. The personalized meaning that the child applies to her or his experiences of discipline is the critical mediating mechanism whereby deleterious effects of harsh parenting practices arise when children interpret these as signs of hostility and rejection (Rohner, 1986). Children's interpretations are influenced by the emotional content of parent–child interactions or relationships (warmth versus animosity), and from beliefs about the appropriateness of parental discipline strategies. Ethnic group differences in parental emotion and children's attitudes may account for the group difference in the effect of physical discipline and for the lack of a group difference in the effect of physical abuse.

Other contributors to this volume highlight interdependent risk factors outside of the home (e.g., deviant peers, deteriorating schools, crime-ridden neighborhoods) that influence the development of antisocial behavior. We focus on harsh parenting because it is proximal to the child and is implicated as a causal mechanism in the intergenerational transmission of aggressive antisocial behavior. However, the effects of physical discipline and abuse must be considered within the context of other correlated risk factors. To this end, we begin by presenting a brief review of the literature on physical punishment, abuse, and the development of aggressive behavior problems, and describe the evidence that points to an ethnic group difference in the link between behavior problems and physical punishment. We then examine the emotional context of the parent–child relationship and children's attitudes about discipline, and whether these account for the ethnic group differences that have been found.

Physical Discipline and Abuse

Parents use discipline to punish misbehavior or reinforce appropriate behavior. Discipline can be preemptive (i.e., strategically changing the environment or redirecting a child's behavior in order to decrease the likelihood of further misbehavior) or reactive (i.e., in response to the current misbehavior). Parents who rely on preemptive strategies are more likely to use positive reinforcement of appropriate behavior and to redirect a child from misbehavior that would warrant punishment. In these families, parenting tends to be more consistent and less punitive, and children are more compliant and well adjusted. In contrast, parents who rely on power-assertive, punitive forms of discipline to punish misbehavior tend to have children who are more aggressive and antisocial (Dishion & McMahon, 1998; Gardner, Sonuga-Barke, & Sayal, 1999).

Physical Punishment

Physical punishment includes spanking, slapping, smacking, or otherwise striking or restraining the child. More than 90 percent of parents in the United States report using spanking as a method of discipline, and it is used by the majority of parents in many other countries as well (Graziano & Namaste, 1990; Straus, 1996). Physical punishment is most common when children are 2 to 3 years old, but as children develop and become more independent, discipline shifts away from power assertion toward verbalized reasoning and loss of privileges (Holden, 1997).

The extent to which a parent is angry and reactive, versus calm and predictable, is an important part of the link between physical discipline, abuse, and child behavior problems. Children who become increasingly aggressive and delinquent are likely to have troubled parent–child relationships that include experiences of harsh, emotionally reactive discipline (Patterson, Reid, & Dishion, 1992). However, the link between physical punishment and aggressive behavior problems is not consistent across studies (for reviews, see Gershoff, 2002a, 2002b; Larzelere, 2000; Straus, Sugarman, & Giles-Sim, 1997).

Parental discipline can cause changes in children's behavior, but children also affect the way their parents behave (Campbell, 1990). Experimental and quasiexperimental studies of children's conduct problems and harsh parenting demonstrate this most clearly. Anderson, Lytton, and Romney (1986) observed boys with and without conduct disorder interacting with their own mothers and the other boys' mothers. It was the boys' conduct disorder status and difficult behaviors that predicted variation in the mothers' harsh behaviors during these observed interactions. In another study, adopted children whose biological mothers were more antisocial elicited harsher discipline from their adoptive mothers (O'Connor, Deater-Deckard, Fulker, Rutter, & Plomin, 1998). Child effects work in conjunction with parent effects, not exclusively or in isolation (Holden, 1997; Patterson et al., 1992).

Physical Abuse

Child maltreatment occurs in many forms, including physical abuse, psychological abuse, sexual abuse, and neglect. Three million children in the United States are referred every year to child protective service agencies for suspected maltreatment, a likely underestimate of actual incidences (U.S. Department of Health and Human Services, 2000). Physical abuse is defined as striking, restraining, or otherwise manipulating the child in a way that leads to lasting physical harm including bruises and wounds, fractures or breaks, disfigurement, or death (Cicchetti, Toth, & Maughan, 2000). Twelve to 20 percent of children in the United States experience physical abuse before adulthood, although its prevalence in the United

States varies over time and across communities (Dodge, Bates, & Pettit, 1990; Straus, 1996).

Parents who use more severe forms of physical punishment are more likely to physically abuse their children, although some nonabusing parents use physical punishment frequently (Chilamkurti & Milner, 1993; Whipple & Richey, 1997). Abuse occurs more often when other risk factors are present, such as poverty, parenting stress, rigid or insensitive information processing (including hostile attributions), marital violence, reactive anger, and child behavioral problems (Montes, de Paul, & Milner, 2001; Thompson et al., 1999; Trickett & Kuczynski, 1986; Woodward & Fergusson, 2002). In addition to its obvious effects on physical health, abuse predicts subsequent violent antisocial behavior (Burke, Loeber, & Birmaher, 2002; Dodge et al., 1990; Lansford, Deater-Deckard, Dodge, Bates, & Pettit, 2004; Loeber, Farrington, & Petechuk, 2003; Wasserman et al., 2003). Physical abuse effects may be stronger for individuals who are at greater genetic risk for aggressive behavioral disorders (Caspi et al., 2002).

Ethnic Group Differences

Mean Differences
Regardless of ethnicity, most parents in the United States report using physical punishment, although there are some group differences in relative frequency. African American parents are more likely to endorse and use physical punishment compared to other ethnic groups (Day, Peterson, & McCracken, 1998; Deater-Deckard & Dodge, 1997; Giles-Sims, Straus, & Sugarman, 1995; Lansford et al., 2004). Some suggest that this difference is indicative of distinct cultural norms, arising in part from adaptation to more stressors faced by African Americans, such as discrimination and poverty (Kelley, Power, & Wimbush, 1992; Pinderhughes, Dodge, Bates, Pettit, & Zelli, 2000). Physical punishment and other methods of power assertion are common in some Asian populations (e.g., Simons, Wu, Lin, Gordon, & Conger, 2000). However, within some African American and Asian communities, strict discipline is seen as evidence of parents' involved caregiving (Chao & Tseng, 2002; Chen & Luster, 2002; Mosby, Rawls, Meehan, Mays, & Pettinari, 1999; Rohner & Pettengill, 1985; Whaley, 2000). These average group differences aside, the variation in the frequency of physical punishment overlaps considerably between ethnic groups. The majority of parents in the United States prefer positive reinforcement of appropriate behavior to more punitive types of discipline, regardless of ethnicity (e.g., Calzada & Eyberg, 2002; Medora, Wilson, & Larson, 2001).

Data on the prevalence of physical abuse shows a similar pattern, with low-socioeconomic status (SES) African Americans being the most overrepresented group (Lansford, Dodge, Pettit, Bates, Crozier, & Kaplow, 2002). Although there are average group differences in the prevalence of abuse, the associations between individual differences in physical abuse or abuse potential, customary use of physical punishment, and a variety of other correlates of child maltreatment are similar cross-culturally (e.g., Buriel, Mercado, Rodriguez, & Chavez, 1991; Tang, 1998). In addition, there are confounds with ethnicity, including SES, marital and family instability and conflict, and neighborhood factors such as levels of crime (Day et al., 1998; Farrington et al., 2003; Pinderhughes, Nix, Foster, Jones, & Conduct Problems Prevention Research Group, 2001). After accounting for these other factors, the ethnic group difference in rates of physical abuse dissipates, but the difference in use of physical punishment remains (Pinderhughes et al., 2000).

Differences in Correlations
The research on cultural differences in mean levels of physical discipline and rates of physical abuse is informative. However, consideration of possible causal mechanisms requires the investigation of ethnic group differences in the correlates or effects of physical punishment and abuse.

Physical Discipline
There is accumulating evidence that the customary use of physical punishment predicts more child aggressive behavior problems for European Americans but not African Americans. Most of the data that we will describe are from Dodge et al.'s (1990) 15-year longitudinal Child Development Project (CDP). The CDP began in 1987, when the children were entering kindergarten, and includes a socioeconomically diverse community sample of 585 children and parents (466 European American, 100 African American). Parents, teachers, peers, and children rated the participants' aggressive behavior problems, and parents completed interviews and questionnaires regarding discipline and physical abuse, all at multiple time points. We assessed customary use of physical punishment, as well as each child's history of physical abuse, as separate variables.

In the CDP, the correlations between several indicators of physical discipline and aggressive behavior problems in middle childhood are positive and significant for European Americans (.13 to .26), but negligible and nonsignificant for African Americans (−.08 to .10; Deater-Deckard, Dodge, Bates, & Pettit, 1996). We found a similar ethnic group difference for adolescents (Lansford et al., 2004). More physical punishment in early childhood and early adolescence predicts more aggressive and delinquent behavior in late adolescence among European Americans, but more physical punishment predicts *less* aggression and delinquency in late adolescence among African Americans.

We reevaluated the ethnicity moderator effect in a second study in the United States. This project also served as the first of several exploratory studies of 5- to 10-year old boys and girls in North America and Europe (unpublished data; see Table 8.1). Rather than recruit matched comparison samples, we invited families from a diverse array of socioeconomic and ethnic groups to participate in order to maximize the descriptive value of each study. Consent was voluntary, so that self-selection biases were present. The U.S. sample is two thirds African American and one third European American, with lower- and middle-SES homes equally represented in both ethnic groups. The families were recruited through several schools that serve families in economically disadvantaged neighborhoods (Conduct Problems Prevention Research Group, 1992). Thus, there are no confounds between ethnicity, SES, school, and neighborhood factors – an advantage over the CDP sample.

Research assistants asked mothers to report on the last time they had threatened, swatted, or spanked their children (1 = within the last year, 3 = within the last month, and 5 = within the last day or two). These items were summed to form a composite physical punishment score ($\alpha = .70$). Mothers also reported on their children's aggressive behavior problems by completing the Aggression subscale of the Child Behavior Checklist (Achenbach, 1991), the Home Behavior Scale (prosocial behavior, adapted from the HOME, Caldwell & Bradley, 1978; reverse scored), and the Behavior Questionnaire (Orrell, 1992). These were summed to derive a composite behavior problems score ($\alpha = .80$). In this study, we replicated the result from the CDP. More physical punishment was associated with more behavior problems among European Americans, $r (27) = .37, p < .05$, but not among African Americans, $r (57) = -.01$.

Other researchers have found the same ethnic group difference, using a variety of sampling and assessment approaches (Gunnoe & Mariner, 1997; McLeod, Kruttschnitt, & Dornfeld, 1994; Slade & Wissow, 2004; Spieker, Larson, Lewis, Keller, & Gilchrist, 1999; Stormshak, Bierman, McMahon, Lengua, & the Conduct Problems Prevention Research Group, 2000). Most recently, Farrington et al. (2003) replicated this finding in the longitudinal Pittsburgh Youth Study. Of the 21 risk factors examined, frequency of physical punishment was the one predictor that differed across ethnic groups in its prediction of violent behavior. Among European Americans, 21 percent of those who were physically punished exhibited violent behavior, compared to 8 percent of those without a history of physical punishment. In contrast, among African Americans, 32 percent of those who were physically punished showed violent behavior, compared to 28 percent of those who were not punished physically. Reviewing the evidence from all of the published studies, Larzelere (2003) concluded that the European American and African American group difference in the correlation between physical punishment and aggressive behavior problems is robust, and this ethnicity moderator effect is strongest in studies with multiple measures and data sources (e.g., parents' and teachers' reports).

Some researchers believe that the ethnic group difference in the correlation between physical discipline and aggressive behavior problems reflects group differences in the relative contribution of child and parent effects (McLeod et al., 1994; Whaley, 2000). According to this view, the data for European American youth represent a bidirectional process, whereby children's behavior problems evoke harsher discipline, which in turn further increments children's aggression. In contrast, the data for African Americans suggest a more unidirectional process in which parents respond to children's misbehaviors with spanking, but this discipline response does not promote escalation in children's aggressive behaviors. In our view, more longitudinal studies are required before inferences about directionality can be drawn.

Physical Abuse. In contrast to the effects of physical discipline, physical abuse consistently and robustly predicts subsequent aggressive behavior problems equally well for ethnic majority and minority youth (Deater-Deckard & Dodge, 1997). In the CDP, there is a moderate positive association between history of physical abuse and level of antisocial behavior for African Americans and European Americans (Lansford et al., 2002). Other studies comparing European Americans, African Americans, Hispanics, and Asians show the same result (Tang, 1998; Wood, 1997). We turn now to consider possible explanations for why the link between physical discipline and child behavior differs for European Americans and African Americans, while the link between physical abuse and child behavior does not.

Children's Interpretations of Parenting

Social learning theory has guided most of the existing research on parental discipline, child abuse, and child maladjustment (for a review, see Maccoby & Martin, 1983). According to this perspective, parents direct aggressive forms of discipline toward their children, who in turn model these aggressive responses to provocation or interpersonal conflict. Evidence from existing correlational studies, quasi-experimental studies (e.g., behavioral genetic designs; Deater-Deckard, 2000), and experiments (e.g., imitating aggressive models; Bandura, Ross, & Ross, 1961) lends some support to this theory. However, social learning theory does not predict, nor does it provide explanations for, ethnic group differences in the link between physical discipline and aggressive behavior – let alone why this group difference would be limited to customary discipline and not abuse. The same is true for a simple genetic determinism explanation, which predicts universal rather than culturally variable effects (Deater-Deckard & Dodge, 1997).

We propose an alternative theory that derives from integration of social learning theory, attachment theory, and social information processing theory (Bowlby, 1969; Crick & Dodge, 1994). According to this perspective, discipline experiences lead the child to learn a "working model" about how interpersonal relationships operate. This model includes all of the "if-then" rules acquired through social learning, but also personalizes the child's experiences by affording a sense of the world as a safe or unsafe place and the child's role in that world as secure or insecure. This perspective emphasizes the meaning that the parent communicates during discipline encounters. The communicated message might range from "You are worthless" to "I love you and want to prepare you for the world, so behave yourself."

Children show problems in development if they come to believe that their parents are rejecting them, because physical and emotional security is essential to healthy psychosocial development (Rohner, 1986). Numerous studies have shown that across cultures, children who think their parents are rejecting them show more problems in mental health (Rohner & Britner, 2002). Thus, the child's perception of parental rejection is an essential and universal mediator that links parenting behavior to children's behavioral problems. However, this mediating psychological mechanism alone cannot account for the European and African American difference in the correlation between physical punishment and aggressive behavior problems. We propose that this universal mechanism is conditioned on or moderated by several aspects of the child-rearing context and children's social cognitions. Furthermore, possible cultural variations in these moderators help explain why there is an ethnic group difference in the effects of physical punishment, and no differences in the effects of physical abuse. In the second half of the chapter, we consider two moderators – the emotional content of the parent–child relationship, and children's attitudes and beliefs about discipline.

Parental Warmth
The emotional tone or quality of the parent–child relationship is one factor that may influence the interpretations children make regarding their physical punishment experiences. This idea stems from theory and research examining the confluence of parental warmth and control in predicting children's development (Baumrind & Black, 1967), and on emotion regulation and security of attachment in parent–child relationships (Cummings & Davies, 1996; Thompson, 1998). The expression of basic emotions (e.g., anger, fear) is universal, and children are able to perceive and interpret, as well as match, their parents' emotion expressions from early in life (Haviland & Lelwicka, 1987; Izard, 1991; Ludemann, 1991). Parents who are hostile toward their children and who spank in anger are more likely to elicit lasting feelings of anger and fear in their children. In turn, the children are more likely to feel rejected (Rohner, 1986). The children also are more likely to show problems in the self-regulation of their emotions and behaviors – an underlying component in the development of hostile aggression (Hubbard et al., 2002).

How does considering cultural differences in emotion expression help explain the ethnic group difference in the link between physical punishment and aggressive behavior? At a general level, display rules regarding when and where particular emotions can or should be expressed differ across cultures – even though the biological and social architecture for expressing and perceiving basic emotions operates in the same way cross-culturally. For example, studies comparing Asians and European Americans show group equivalence in the ability to express and perceive basic emotions including anger, but Asians are less likely than European Americans to express anger in their interactions with others (e.g., Zahn-Waxler, Friedman, Cole, Mizuta, & Hiruma, 1996).

More specific to harsh discipline, there may be ethnic group differences in whether and when emotional expressions of warmth or hostility accompany discipline episodes or other aspects of parental control (Baumrind, 1972; Rohner & Pettengill, 1985). Evidence from narrative accounts and ethnographic studies of African Americans point to the value placed on using physical punishment in a planned and nonreactive way, and showing love and warmth toward the child following discipline. In contrast, the majority of European American parents report feeling angry and remorseful during physical discipline episodes and experience regret afterward (Graziano & Hamblen, 1996; Mosby et al., 1999; Straus, 1996; Ward, 1971; Whaley, 2000; Young, 1970). This group difference in expressed emotions during and following discipline encounters may account for ethnic group differences in the consequences of physical punishment. If true, African American youth are less likely to interpret physical punishment as rejection because it is less often accompanied by parental anger, whereas European American youth are more likely to experience rejection because physical discipline is more often accompanied by parents' reactive anger (Gunnoe & Mariner, 1997).

Data from the CDP are consistent with this proposed mechanism (Deater-Deckard & Dodge, 1997). We computed correlations between an interviewer rating of physical punishment (described above) and teachers' ratings of children's aggressive behavior (kindergarten through sixth grade), separately for two groups of children – those whose mothers were observed to be high in warmth versus low in warmth (median split). The correlations were negligible or modest for the "high warmth" mothers, but were more substantial for the "low warmth" mothers (r from .25 to .34) – regardless of ethnicity. We found the same result using a similar discipline interview in a combined sample of 3-year-old Caucasian British twins and 3- to 12-year-old children adopted from countries in Asia and Europe by Caucasian parents in the United States (Deater-Deckard, Ivy, & Petrill, 2004). Among mothers who were low in warmth, more physical punishment was correlated with more parent-rated child behavior problems, $r(143) = .37$, $p < .001$. In contrast, among mothers who were high in warmth, the correlation was modest, $r(203) = .10$, nonsignificant. Larger studies including European Americans, African Americans,

Hispanics, and Asians yield the same result (McLoyd & Smith, 2002; Simons et al., 2000). Bear in mind that it is difficult to observe physical discipline and abuse episodes as they occur, so researchers must rely on interviews or parents' reports of frequency of physical punishment. We assume that the measures of parental warmth or hostility in these studies also represent the likelihood that the parent shows anger while spanking the child – an assumption that remains to be tested.

Considering parental emotion also helps explain why the effects of physical abuse are universal. Parents who are often angry with their children are more likely to perpetrate abuse, especially when distressed. The endorsement and customary use of physical discipline further increments abuse potential, particularly if the parent is prone to reactive angry outbursts (Crouch & Behl, 2001). Research on children in different cultures and of different ages shows consistent links between parenting stress, physical discipline, reactive anger, and child abuse (e.g., Chan, 1994; Holden & Banez, 1996; Mammen, Kolko, & Pilkonis, 2002; Rodriguez & Green, 1997). Episodes of physical abuse typically include parents' expressions of anger and are likely to be perceived and interpreted by children in different cultures in the same way – as hostility and rejection.

Children's Attitudes About Discipline

Children's attitudes about parenting behaviors are influenced by many factors, including their own experiences with their parents, as well as their understanding of others' beliefs about child-rearing. Individual differences in the strength of conviction of children's attitudes are related to the consistency and emotional content of attitude-relevant information stored in memory, and are as important as the valence (agreement or disagreement) of the beliefs (Judd & Krosnick, 1988 – cited in Sherman, Judd, & Park, 1989).

In cultures in which physical punishment is common, being spanked reinforces the utility of this discipline method in the minds of most children and adolescents, even though physical punishment is often painful and may be interpreted as parental rejection at the time it occurs. In the CDP, more physical punishment in childhood predicts stronger endorsement of spanking in adolescence, regardless of ethnicity (Deater-Deckard, Lansford, Dodge, Bates, & Pettit, 2003). This replicates prior cross-sectional studies that used adults' retrospective recall of their childhoods (Graziano, Lindquist, Kunce, & Munjal, 1992; Kelder, McNamara, Carlson, & Lynn, 1991; Milburn & Conrad, 1996).

Children's attitudes about parental behavior may be crucial determinants of their interpretations of parental discipline and physical abuse. Physical punishment, physical abuse, and biases in social information processing are associated with increases in aggressive behavior problems. Experiences involving physical punishment may constrain children's social knowledge and promote biases in social cognitions that increase the likelihood that they will aggress against others, resist authority, and violate social norms of appropriate behavior (Crick & Dodge, 1994; Dodge et al., 1990). Mothers of aggressive children show similar social cognitive biases – they are more likely to attribute hostile intent in their children's misbehaviors, and they are more likely to respond with harsh discipline (Bugental & Johnston, 2000).

Cultural influences are critical parts of the psychological mechanisms linking actual discipline experiences and beliefs about those experiences. Individuals use norms as the basis for the development of their beliefs about appropriate and inappropriate behavior, and behave in ways that are consistent with those norms because other people reinforce them for doing so. The cultural context includes numerous experiences that provide information about norms and reinforce compliance or punish noncompliance (Lightfoot & Valsiner, 1992). Although the broad socialization goals of parents and communities are universal – all societies want their children to be happy and healthy – cultural differences in child-rearing attitudes are vast (Kelley et al., 1992; Ogbu, 1981).

Through its impact on children's developing attitudes, the cultural context can shape the interpretation that a child makes of her or his physical discipline experiences – as long as the discipline is relatively mild. Some children may experience mild physical discipline as a routine part of growing up and as an indication that they are loved and being cared for properly. Other children may experience the same discipline practice as atypical, signifying something troubling about them or their families. If attitudes do act as a moderator, then those children who believe that physical discipline does not signal "good" and caring parenting are more likely to show higher levels of aggressive conduct problems in the face of higher amounts of harsh parenting, because the experiences are coupled with lasting feelings of rejection. There may be no relation, or even positive behavioral outcomes, for those children who believe that physical discipline indicates involved and caring parenting because these experiences are not coupled with lasting feelings of rejection. In contrast, when children's safety and physical integrity clearly are compromised, any cultural context may have limited power in influencing children's interpretations of their parents' behaviors – most children in most cultures will perceive this as abuse, and will feel rejected and harmed by the perpetrators of the abuse (Deater-Deckard & Dodge, 1997).

Studies of physical aggression norms within peer, neighborhood, and cultural groups provide indirect evidence. Norms influence how it is that aggressive behavior influences group behavior and the relationships within each group. Children are least likely to reject aggressive peers in classrooms where overall rates of aggression are high, and most likely to do so in rooms where rates of aggression are low (Stormshak, Bierman, Bruschi, Dodge, & Coie, 1999). With respect to physical punishment, one study shows that within African American communities, there is no correlation between physical punishment and child behavior problems in neighborhoods where overall rates of spanking are high, but there is a significant positive correlation in neighborhoods where overall rates of spanking are low (Simons, Lin, Gordon, Brody, Murry, & Conger, 2002; cited by Larzelere, 2003). These results may indicate that in groups where aggressive behavior (from peer to peer, or from parent to child) is common, instances of aggression are viewed as typical and normative and are not interpreted as rejection.

Research on discipline practices in schools also is informative about norms, discipline, and children's interpretations of punishment. Rutter, Maughan, Mortimore, Ouston, and Smith (1979) studied schools in central London and examined associations between various forms of punishment and reward and children's disruptive behavior problems. Schools in which punishment – including physical forms – was used sparingly and within the context of a schoolwide set of standards had fewer problem behaviors in classrooms compared to schools in which teachers were left to make their own decisions about discipline. It was in this latter type of school that teachers were more likely to use unofficial forms of physical punishment such as smacks or slaps. This effect held even when incoming students' rates of problem behavior were considered, suggesting a causal effect on pupil behavior. Rutter and his colleagues suggest that these findings point to the importance of schoolwide standards and practices, teacher emotional reactivity to student misbehavior, and the effects of this unofficial reactive physical punishment on children's developing resentment and anger.

More direct evidence of the role of attitudes comes from studies of beliefs about discipline. Children and adults accept physical discipline when they believe that it is deserved (Kelder et al., 1991; Rausch & Knutson, 1991). Children who perceive their parents' use of harsh discipline as unfair are more likely to feel rejected by their parents, which in turn predicts problems in adjustment – a pattern that is consistent across different ethnic groups (Rohner, Bourque, & Elordi, 1996). When compared to European Americans, African Americans are more likely to endorse the use of physical punishment and are less likely to include spanking within their definitions of physical abuse on average, although there also is considerable overlap between groups (Deater-Deckard & Dodge, 1997; Deater-Deckard et al., 2003; Korbin, Coulton, Lindstrom-Ufuti, & Spilsbury, 2000).

None of the existing studies tested whether and how children's beliefs about the appropriateness of physical punishment operate on the correlation between physical punishment and aggressive behavior problems. To this end, we examined children's attitudes about physical punishment and reasoning in the United States, United Kingdom, and Sweden (see Table 8.1). Research assistants conducted 20-minute interviews with the children in their homes (United States) or quiet areas of their classrooms (United Kingdom, Sweden). The structured interview consisted of

TABLE 8.1. *Three Studies of 5- to 10-Year-Old Boys and Girls in Three Countries*

Location	Nashville, USA	London, UK	Lidköping, Sweden
Date	1995	1996	1997
Sample size	102	180	182
Child ages	5–10 years	5–10 years	5–10 years
Ethnic groups	65% African American, 35% European American	75% Caucasian, 25% others	75% Swedish, 25% first/second-generation immigrant

hypothetical vignettes in which a child misbehaves and the mother intervenes. The vignettes varied in terms of the child's behavior (transgression against a peer; transgression against a teacher), the mother's discipline strategy (physical punishment; reasoning and explanation), and the severity of the mothers' physical punishment (spanking or slapping the bottom, paddling the bottom). The vignettes also varied somewhat across the three studies. For example, the vignette depicting a child being spanked with a paddle was excluded in the Swedish study, because it was deemed to be too extreme. Spanking with the hand, let alone an object, has been banned in Sweden since 1979 (described in more detail later), and therefore constitutes physical abuse. Children then stated whether they disagreed or agreed a lot, some, or a little, with four statements – that the mother was trying to harm the child (reverse scored), was showing her love for the child, was trying to prevent future misbehavior, and was being a good parent. We averaged responses to derive composites representing endorsement of physical punishment ($\alpha = .88$) and endorsement of reasoning ($\alpha = .85$).

In the United States and United Kingdom, the vast majority of children endorsed the use of physical punishment, as indicated by high means and restricted variance (on 6-point scale: United States, $M = 4.79$, $SD = .93$; United Kingdom, $M = 5.03$, $SD = 1.11$). In contrast, Swedish children's attitude scores covered the entire range of the scale and were normally distributed; half of the children endorsed physical punishment, and half did not ($M = 3.73$, $SD = 1.21$). By comparison, the distributions of children's attitudes about reasoning were similar across the three samples (on a 6-point scale: United States, $M = 5.26$, $SD = .72$; United Kingdom, $M = 5.58$, $SD = .78$; Sweden, $M = 5.35$, $SD = .79$). This pattern is not surprising, given Sweden's long-standing ban on corporal punishment, and in light of studies in the United States and Australia indicating that children in those countries readily endorse the use of physical punishment (Dadds, Adlington, & Christensen, 1987; Siegal & Barclay, 1985).

In the U.S. study, we examined European American and African American group differences. There was no group difference in average endorsement scores. However, African American children's endorsements of physical punishment and reasoning were moderately correlated, $r = .46$, $p < .001$, while European American children's endorsements of physical punishment and reasoning were independent, $r = .15$ (nonsignificant). Further analyses revealed that only European American children's endorsement of spanking moderated the correlation between frequency of physical punishment and behavior problems, as indicated by a significant three-way statistical interaction after controlling for lower order effects. Among European American children who were least supportive of spanking, more physical punishment was associated with aggressive behavior problems, $r (16) = .71$, $p < .01$, but among European American children who endorsed spanking, more physical punishment was associated with *fewer* aggressive behavior problems, $r (12) = -.65$, $p < .05$. In contrast, the correlation between physical punishment and behavior problems was not significant for African Americans, regardless of whether or not the children endorsed this discipline method.

Thus, although there is some evidence children's attitudes operate as we expected, this is limited to a small sample of European American children. Overall, an ethnic group difference in children's attitudes did not account for the ethnic group difference in the correlation between physical punishment and aggressive behavior problems. In this study as well as the UK and Swedish studies, we used new measures, utilized small convenience samples, and focused on only one aspect of children's social cognitions. We did not investigate the broader set of social cognitive factors operating in the family and cultural group. These include explanations for experiences (i.e., attributions) and comparative evaluation of experiences (e.g., self- and other-efficacy, perceived justice), both of which include systematic biases that are correlated with children's aggressive behavior problems (Bugental & Johnston, 2000). These may be more important than general attitudes to the information processing accompanying children's interpretations of parenting behavior.

Policy Implications

There are wide ranging cultural group differences, and individual differences within each culture, in attitudes regarding the appropriateness and effectiveness of physical punishment and other discipline methods. Individuals differ in whether they regard any, some, most, or all forms of physical punishment as abusive, and whether or not "nonabusive" physical punishment contributes to the development of antisocial behavior. By comparison, there is more agreement about what constitutes physical abuse (e.g., physical contact that results in lasting welts, bruises, or injuries), and about its deleterious effects. Furthermore, there are no apparent cultural differences in the links between parental distress, endorsement and use of physical discipline, and abuse potential. The robust connection between greater likelihood of physical abuse perpetration, greater child abuse potential, and use of harsh discipline practices such as physical punishment is widely replicated in diverse samples of participants (e.g., Dodge et al., 1990; Crouch & Behl, 2001; Haskett, Scott, & Fann, 1995).

There is a consensus that social policies targeting the elimination of physical abuse and other forms of maltreatment can and should be implemented. More controversial is whether and how social policies that target milder forms of physical punishment lead to reductions in child abuse and its ill effects (e.g., Larzelere & Johnson, 1999). Advocates for banning physical punishment propose that doing so will reduce rates of physical abuse, given the connections described previously between physical punishment, abuse potential, and perpetration of abuse (Lansdown, 2000; Straus, 2000). Some countries banned spanking on these grounds. Sweden was the first country to do so, in an effort to eliminate child abuse and to put in place a system of guidelines in which the early signs of physical abuse would be more easily detected (Durrant, 1999). The passage of the legislation was preceded and followed by a continuous decline in Swedes' endorsement of physical punishment – from 53 percent in 1965, to 26 percent in 1978, to only 11 percent in 1994 (Edfeldt, 1996; Ziegert, 1983). Today, Swedish parents are less likely than their Western industrial counterparts to use physical punishment, and those who do use it do so less frequently (Edfeldt, 1996; Palmérus, 1999). Sweden stands in contrast to North America and other parts of Europe, where the majority of adults endorse physical punishment as a discipline strategy. Whether bans on corporal punishment create lasting reductions in rates of physical abuse remains to be seen.

Caution is warranted when deriving implications for policy from data on cultural differences in parenting practices. Knowledge about ethnic or national differences that is well described and widely disseminated, but poorly understood in terms of causes and consequences, can create gaps between majority and minority members of populations. With cultural diversity on the rise in many industrial nations, it may become increasingly difficult for scientists and policy experts to discern whether child-rearing practices in other ethnic groups are indicative of adaptive parenting or child maltreatment (Terao, Borrego, & Urquiza, 2001).

Conclusions

Social learning theory does not explain the difference between European Americans and African Americans in the link between physical punishment and aggressive behavior problems. What is needed is a theory that addresses the role of children's perceptions and understanding of their discipline experiences. Parent–child warmth is likely to be critical to children's interpretations of parenting behaviors. Customary use of physical punishment predicts the development of aggressive behavior problems in parent–child relationships that lack warmth, but does not do so in warm parent–child relationships – regardless of ethnicity. By comparison, there have been few tests of the role of children's attitudes about physical punishment. Our findings suggest that the ethnic group difference in children's attitudes does not account for the difference in the link between physical punishment and behavior problems. Nonetheless, children's attitudes operated as we anticipated within a small sample of European American children. This result, coupled with indirect evidence from other studies of children's and adults' attitudes and group norms, suggests that further exploration of children's beliefs about discipline will yield more insights.

Research that examines a broader array of parenting behaviors and types of parent–child relationships is needed. Scientists also should study fathers and families in a wider variety of cultural groups, given the remarkable variation in child-rearing behaviors between men and women and between cultures. Ideally, some of this research will incorporate immigration research designs in which parenting practices and children's adaptive and maladaptive behaviors are assessed prior to and during the transition to a new country and predominant culture. Such research also can be more thorough in examining the multiple factors and experiences that differ across ethnic and cultural groups, including challenges arising from immigration, risk factors to health and social capital (e.g., disease), discrimination, poverty, neighborhood factors, and peer group influences.

Acknowledgments

The authors are grateful to the study participants and study collaborators and staff in the United States, United Kingdom, and Sweden. We thank our colleagues on the Child Development Project (John E. Bates, Gregory S. Pettit, and Jennifer S. Lanford), the Nashville Parenting Project (Jennifer D. Harnish, Robert Nix, Ellen Pinderhughes), and the studies in London (Yvonne Frasier, Adenike Oyelese) and Sweden (Emma Sorbring, Milena Cvetic, Pia Falk, Josephine Karlsson, Marika Lorén, Frida Sorbring, Miia Sova). The first author was supported by grants from the National Science Foundation (99–07860) and the University of Oregon Foundation. The Child Development Project has been supported by grant MH42498 from the National Institute of Mental Health and HD30572 from the National Institute of Child Health and Human Development, awarded to Kenneth A. Dodge, Gregory S. Pettit, and John E. Bates. The Swedish study was supported by funds provided by the University of Trollhättan-Uddevalla.

Author Note

Kirby Deater-Deckard, Ph.D., is Associate Professor of Psychology at the University of Oregon, Eugene, OR (USA). Kenneth A. Dodge is

William McDougall Professor of Public Policy Studies in the Terry Sanford Institute of Public Policy at Duke University, Durham, NC (USA). Emma Sorbring is a lecturer in the Department for Studies of the Individual and Society, University of Trollhättan-Uddevalla, Vänersborg, Sweden. Address correspondence to Kirby Deater-Deckard, Department of Psychology, 1227 University of Oregon, Eugene, OR, 97403–1227, USA; email: kirbydd@darkwing.uoregon.edu.

References

Achenbach, T. M. (1991). *Integrative guide for the 1991 CBCL/4–18, YSR, and TRF profiles.* Burlington, VT: University of Vermont Department of Psychiatry.

Anderson, K. E., Lytton, H., & Romney, D. M. (1986). Mothers' interactions with normal and conduct-disordered boys: Who affects whom? *Developmental Psychology, 22,* 604–609.

Bandura, A., Ross, R., & Ross, S. (1961). Transmission of aggression through imitation of aggressive models. *Journal of Abnormal and Social Psychology, 63,* 575–582.

Baumrind, D. (1972). An exploratory study of socialization effects on Black children: Some Black-White comparisons. *Child Development, 43,* 261–267.

Baumrind, D., & Black, A. E. (1967). Socialization practices associated with dimensions of competence in preschool boys and girls. *Child Development, 38,* 291–327.

Bowlby, J. (1969). *Attachment and loss* (Vol. 1). London: Hogarth.

Bugental, D. B., & Johnston, C. (2000). Parental and child cognitions in the context of the family. *Annual Review of Psychology, 51,* 315–344.

Buriel, R., Mercado, R., Rodriguez, J., & Chavez, J. M. (1991). Mexican-American disciplinary practices and attitudes toward child maltreatment: A comparison of foreign and native-born mothers. *Hispanic Journal of Behavioral Sciences, 13,* 78–94.

Burke, J. D., Loeber, R., & Birmaher, B. (2002). Oppositional defiant disorder and conduct disorder: A review of the past 10 years, part II. *Journal of the American Academy of Child & Adolescent Psychiatry, 41,* 1275–1293.

Caldwell, B. M., & Bradley, R. H. (1978). *Home observation for measurement of the environment.* Little Rock, AK: University of Arkansas.

Calzada, E. J., & Eyberg, S. M. (2002). Self-reported parenting practices in Dominican and Puerto Rican mothers of young children. *Journal of Clinical Child & Adolescent Psychology, 31,* 354–363.

Campbell, S. B. (1990). *Behavior problems in preschool children.* New York: Guilford.

Caspi, A., McClay, J., Moffitt, T., Mill, J., Martin, J., Craig, I. W., Taylor, A., & Poulton, R. (2002). Role of genotype in the cycle of violence in maltreated children. *Science, 297,* 851–854.

Chan, Y. C. (1994). Parenting stress and social support of mothers who physically abuse their children in Hong Kong. *Child Abuse & Neglect, 18,* 261–269.

Chao, R., & Tseng, V. (2002). Parenting of Asians. In M. H. Bornstein (Ed.), *Handbook of parenting: Vol. 4. Social conditions and applied parenting* (2nd ed., pp. 59–93). Mahwah, NJ: Erlbaum.

Chen, F., & Luster, T. (2002). Factors related to parenting practices in Taiwan. *Early Child Development & Care, 172,* 413–430.

Chilamkurti, C., & Milner, J. S. (1993). Perceptions and evaluations of child transgressions and disciplinary techniques in high- and low-risk mothers and their children. *Child Development, 64,* 1801–1814.

Cicchetti, D., Toth, S. L., & Maughan, A. (2000). An ecological-transactional model of child maltreatment. In A. J. Sameroff, M. Lewis, & S. M. Miller (Eds.), *Handbook of developmental psychopathology* (2nd ed., pp. 689–722). New York: Plenum.

Conduct Problems Prevention Research Group. (1992). A developmental and clinical model for the prevention of conduct disorder: The FAST Track Program. *Development & Psychopathology, 4,* 509–527.

Crick, N., & Dodge, K. A. (1994). A review and reformulation of social information-processing mechanisms in children's social adjustment. *Psychological Bulletin, 115,* 74–101.

Crouch, J. L., & Behl, L. E. (2001). Relationships among parental beliefs in corporal punishment, reported stress, and physical child abuse potential. *Child Abuse and Neglect, 25,* 413–419.

Cummings, E. M., & Davies, P. (1996). Emotional security as a regulatory process in normal development and the development of psychopathology. *Development and Psychopathology, 8,* 123–139.

Dadds, M. R., Adlington, F. M., & Christensen, A. P. (1987). Children's perceptions of time out and other maternal discipline strategies: The effects of clinic status and exposure to behavioural treatment. *Behaviour Change, 4,* 3–13.

Day, R. D., Peterson, G. W., & McCracken, C. (1998). Predicting spanking of younger and older children by mothers and fathers. *Journal of Marriage and the Family, 60,* 79–94.

Deater-Deckard, K. (2000). Parenting and child behavioral adjustment in early childhood: A quantitative genetic approach to studying family processes and child development. *Child Development, 71,* 468–484.

Deater-Deckard, K., & Dodge, K. A. (1997). Externalizing behavior problems and discipline revisited: Nonlinear effects and variation by culture, context, and gender. *Psychological Inquiry, 8,* 161–175.

Deater-Deckard, K., Dodge, K. A., Bates, J. E., & Pettit, G. S. (1996). Physical discipline among African American and European American mothers: Links to children's externalizing behaviors. *Developmental Psychology, 32,* 1065–1072.

Deater-Deckard, K., Ivy, L., & Petrill, S. A. (2004). Maternal warmth moderates the link between physical punishment and child externalizing problems: A shared environmental mechanism. *Submitted for publication.*

Deater-Deckard, K., Lansford, J. E., Dodge, K. A., Pettit, G. S., & Bates, J. E. (2003). The development of attitudes about physical punishment: An 8-year longitudinal study. *Journal of Family Psychology, 17,* 351–360.

Dishion, T. J., & McMahon, R. J. (1998). Parental monitoring and the prevention of child and adolescent problem behavior: A conceptual and empirical formulation. *Clinical Child and Family Psychology Review, 1,* 61–75.

Dodge, K. A., Bates, J. E., & Pettit, G. S. (1990). Mechanisms in the cycle of violence. *Science, 250,* 1678–1683.

Durrant, J. E. (1999). Evaluating the success of Sweden's corporal punishment ban. *Child Abuse and Neglect, 23*, 435–448.

Edfeldt, Å. W. (1996). In Frehsee, D., Horn, W., & Bussman, K-D. (Eds.). *Family violence against children: A challenge for society.* Berlin: de Gruyter.

Farrington, D. P., Loeber, R., & Stouthamer-Loeber, M. (2003). How can the relationship between race and violence be explained? In D. F. Hawkins (Ed.), *Violent crimes: Assessing race and ethnic differences* (pp. 213–237). New York: Cambridge University Press.

Gardner, F., Sonuga-Barke, E., & Sayal, K. (1999). Parents anticipating misbehaviour: An observational study of strategies parents use to prevent conflict with behavior problem children. *Journal of Child Psychology & Psychiatry, 40*, 1185–1196.

Gershoff, E. T. (2002a). Corporal punishment by parents and associated child behaviors and experiences: A meta-analytic and theoretical review. *Psychological Bulletin, 128*, 539–579.

Gershoff, E. T. (2002b). Corporal punishment, physical abuse, and the burden of proof: Reply to Baumrind, Larzelere, and Cowan (2002), Holden, and Parke (2002). *Psychological Bulletin, 128*, 602–611.

Giles-Sims, J., Straus, M. A., & Sugarman, D. B. (1995). Child, maternal and family characteristics associated with spanking. *Family Relations, 44*, 170–176.

Graziano, A. M., & Hamblen, J. L. (1996). Subabusive violence in childrearing in middle-class American families. *Pediatrics, 98*, 845–848.

Graziano, A. M., Lindquist, C. M., Kunce, L. J., & Munjal, K. (1992). Physical punishment in childhood and current attitudes: An exploratory comparison of college students in the United States and India. *Journal of Interpersonal Violence, 7*, 147–155.

Graziano, A. M., & Namaste, K. A. (1990). Parental use of physical force in child discipline: A survey of 679 college students. *Journal of Interpersonal Violence, 5*, 449–463.

Gunnoe, M. L., & Mariner, C. L. (1997). Toward a developmental-contextual model of the effects of parental spanking on children's aggression. *Archives of Pediatrics & Adolescent Medicine, 151*, 768–775.

Haskett, M. E., Scott, S. S., & Fann, K. D. (1995). Child Abuse Potential Inventory and parenting behavior: Relationships with high-risk correlates. *Child Abuse and Neglect, 19*, 1483–1495.

Haviland, J. M., & Lelwicka, M. (1987). The induced affect response: 10-week-old infants' responses to three emotion expressions. *Developmental Psychology, 23*, 97–104.

Holden, G. W. (1997). *Parents and the dynamics of child rearing.* Boulder, CO: Westview Press.

Holden, G. W., & Banez, G. A. (1996). Child abuse potential and parenting stress within maltreating families. *Journal of Family Violence, 11*, 1–12.

Hubbard, J. A., Smithmyer, C. M., Ramsden, S. R., Parker, E. H., Flanagan, K. D., Dearing, K. F., Relyea, N., & Simons, R. F. (2002). Observational, physiological, and self-report measures of children's anger: Relations to reactive versus proactive aggression. *Child Development, 73*, 1101–1118.

Izard, C. E. (1991). *The psychology of emotions.* New York: Plenum.

Judd, C. M., & Krosnick, J. A. (1988). The structural bases of consistency among political attitudes: Effects of political expertise and attitude importance. In A. R.

Pratkanis, S. J. Breckler & A. G. Greenwald (Eds.), *Attitude structure and function.* Hillsdale, NJ: Erlbaum.

Kelder, L. R., McNamara, J. R., Carlson, B., & Lynn, S. J. (1991). Perceptions of physical punishment: The relation to childhood and adolescent experiences. *Journal of Interpersonal Violence, 6,* 432–445.

Kelley, M. L., Power, T. G. & Wimbush, D. D. (1992). Determinants of disciplinary practices in low-income black mothers. *Child Development, 63,* 573–582.

Korbin, J. E., Coulton, C. J., Lindstrom-Ufuti, H., & Spilsbury, J. (2000). Neighborhood views on the definition and etiology of child maltreatment. *Child Abuse & Neglect, 24,* 1509–1527.

Lansdown, G. (2000). Children's rights and domestic violence. *Child Abuse Review, 9,* 416–426.

Lansford, J. E., Deater-Deckard, K., Dodge, K. A., Bates, J. E., & Pettit, G. S. (2004). Ethnic differences in the link between physical discipline and later adolescent externalizing behaviors. *Journal of Child Psychology & Psychiatry, 45,* 801–812.

Lansford, J. E., Dodge, K. A., Pettit, G. S., Bates, J. E., Crozier, J., & Kaplow, J. (2002). A 12-year prospective longitudinal study of the long-term effects of early child physical maltreatment on psychological, behavioral, and academic problems in adolescence. *Archives of Pediatrics and Adolescent Medicine, 156,* 824–830.

Larzelere, R. E. (2000). Child outcomes of nonabusive and customary physical punishment by parents: An updated literature review. *Clinical Child & Family Psychology Review, 3,* 199–221.

Larzelere, R. E. (2003, April). Discussant in symposium (J. Lansford & L. Berlin, Chairs), *Physical discipline and children's development: Cross-cultural perspectives,* at the Biennial Meeting of the Society for Research in Child Development, Tampa, FL.

Larzelere, R. E., & Johnson, B. (1999). Evaluations of the effects of Sweden's spanking ban on physical child abuse rates: A literature review. *Psychological Reports, 85,* 381–392.

Lightfoot, C., & Valsiner, J. (1992). Parental belief systems under the influence: Social guidance of the construction of personal cultures. In I. E. Sigel, A. V. McGillicuddy-DeLisi, & J. J. Goodnow (Eds.), *Parental belief systems: Psychological consequences for children* (2nd ed., pp. 393–414). Hillsdale, NJ: Erlbaum.

Loeber, R., Farrington, D. P., & Petechuk, D. (May 2003). *Child delinquency: Early intervention and prevention.* Child delinquency bulletin series: Child delinquency – Early intervention and prevention. Washington, DC: Office of Juvenile Justice and Delinquency Prevention, U.S. Department of Justice.

Ludemann, P. M. (1991). Generalized discrimination of positive facial expressions by seven-and ten-month-old infants. *Child Development, 62,* 55–67.

Maccoby, E., & Martin, M. (1983). Socialization in the context of the family: Parent-child interaction. In E. M. Hetherington (Ed.), *Handbook of child psychology* (Vol. 4, pp. 1–101). New York: Wiley.

Mammen, O.K., Kolko, D. J., & Pilkonis, P. A. (2002). Negative affect and parental aggression in child physical abuse. *Child Abuse & Neglect, 26,* 407–424.

McLeod, J. D., Kruttschnitt, C., & Dornfeld, M. (1994). Does parenting explain the effects of structural conditions on children's antisocial behavior? A comparison of Blacks and Whites. *Social Forces, 73,* 575–604.

McLoyd, V. C., & Smith, J. (2002). Physical discipline and behavior problems in African American, European American, and Hispanic children: Emotional support as a moderator. *Journal of Marriage & the Family, 64,* 40–53.

Medora, N. P., Wilson, S., & Larson, J. H. (2001). Attitudes toward parenting strategies, potential for child abuse, and parental satisfaction of ethnically diverse low-income U.S. mothers. *Journal of Social Psychology, 141,* 335–348.

Milburn, M. A., & Conrad, S. D. (1996). *The politics of denial.* Cambridge, MA: MIT Press.

Montes, M. P., de Paul, J., & Milner, J. S. (2001). Evaluations, attributions, affect, and disciplinary choices in mothers at high and low risk for child physical abuse. *Child Abuse & Neglect, 25,* 1015–1036.

Mosby, L., Rawls, A. W., Meehan, A. J., Mays, E., & Pettinari, C. J. (1999). Troubles in interracial talk about discipline: An examination of African American child rearing narratives. *Journal of Comparative Family Studies, 30,* 489–521.

O'Connor, T. G., Deater-Deckard, K., Fulker, D. W., Rutter, M., & Plomin, R. (1998). Gene-environment correlations in late childhood and early adolescence. *Developmental Psychology, 34,* 970–981.

Ogbu, J. U. (1981). Origins of human competence: A cultural-ecological perspective. *Child Development, 52,* 413–429.

Orrell, J. (1992). *Assessing parenting competency: A situational approach.* Unpublished master's thesis, Vanderbilt University, Nashville, TN.

Palmérus, K. (1999). Self-reported discipline among Swedish parents of preschool children. *Infant & Child Development, 8,* 155–171.

Patterson, G. R., Reid, J. B., & Dishion, T. J. (1992). *Antisocial boys.* Eugene, OR: Castalia.

Pindherhughes, E. E., Dodge, K. A., Bates, J. E., Pettit, G. S., & Zelli, A. (2000). Discipline responses: Influences of parents' socioeconomic status, ethnicity, beliefs about parenting, stress, and cognitive-emotional processes. *Journal of Family Psychology, 14,* 380–400.

Pinderhughes, E. E., Nix, R., Foster, E. M., Jones, D., & the Conduct Problems Prevention Research Group (2001). Parenting in context: Impact of neighborhood poverty, residential stability, public services, social networks, and danger on parental behaviors. *Journal of Marriage and the Family, 63,* 941–953.

Rausch, K., & Knutson, J. F. (1991). The self-report of personal punitive childhood experiences and those of siblings. *Child Abuse & Neglect, 15,* 29–36.

Rodriguez, C. M., & Green, A. J. (1997). Parenting stress and anger expression as predictors of child abuse potential. *Child Abuse and Neglect, 21,* 367–377.

Rohner, R. P. (1986). *The warmth dimension: Foundations of parental acceptance-rejection theory.* Thousand Oaks, CA: Sage.

Rohner, R. P., Bourque, S. L., & Elordi, C. A. (1996). Children's perceptions of corporal punishment, caretaker acceptance, and psychological adjustment in a poor, biracial Southern community. *Journal of Marriage and the Family, 58,* 842–852.

Rohner, R. P., & Britner, P. A. (2002). Worldwide mental health correlates of parental acceptance-rejection: Review of cross-cultural and intracultural evidence. *Cross-Cultural Research: The Journal of Comparative Social Science, 36,* 15–47.

Rohner, R. P., & Pettengill, S. M. (1985). Perceived parental acceptance-rejection and parental control among Korean adolescents. *Child Development, 56,* 524–528.

Rowe, D. C., Vazsonyi, A. T., & Flannery, D. J. (1994). No more than skin deep: Ethnic and racial similarity in developmental process. *Psychological Review, 101,* 396–413.

Rutter, M., Maughan, B., Mortimore, P., Ouston, J., & Smith, A. (1979). *Fifteen thousand hours: Secondary schools and their effects on children.* Cambridge, MA: Harvard University Press.

Sherman, S. J., Judd, C. M., & Park, B. (1989). Social cognition. *Annual Review of Psychology, 40,* 281–326.

Siegal, M., & Barclay, M. S. (1985). Children's evaluations of fathers' socialization behavior. *Developmental Psychology, 21,* 1090–1096.

Simons, R. L., Lin, K-H., Gordon, L. C., Brody, G. H., Murry, V., & Conger, R. D. (2002). Community differences in the association between parenting practices and child conduct problems. *Journal of Marriage & the Family, 64,* 331–345.

Simons, R. L., Wu, C., Lin, K., Gordon, L., & Conger, R. D. (2000). A cross-cultural examination of the link between corporal punishment and adolescent antisocial behavior. *Criminology, 38,* 47–79.

Slade, E. P., & Wissow, L. S. (2004). Spanking in early childhood and later behavior problems: A prospective study of infants and young toddlers. *Pediatrics, 113,* 1321–1330.

Spieker, S. J., Larson, N. C., Lewis, S. M., Keller, T. E., & Gilchrist, L. (1999). Developmental trajectories of disruptive behavior problems in preschool children of adolescent mothers. *Child Development, 70,* 443–458.

Stormshak, E. A., Bierman, K. L., Bruschi, C., Dodge, K. A., & Coie, J. D. (1999). The relation between behavior problems and peer preference in different classroom contexts. *Child Development, 70,* 169–182.

Stormshak, E. A., Bierman, K. L., McMahon, R. J., Lengua, L. J., & the Conduct Problems Prevention Research Group (2000). Parenting practices and child disruptive behavior problems in early elementary school. *Journal of Clinical Child Psychology, 29,* 17–29.

Straus, M. A. (1996). Spanking and the making of a violent society. *Pediatrics, 98,* 837–842.

Straus, M. A. (2000). Corporal punishment and primary prevention of physical abuse. *Child Abuse and Neglect, 24,* 1109–1114.

Straus, M. A., Sugarman, D. B., & Giles-Sims, J. (1997). Spanking by parents and subsequent antisocial behavior of children. *Archives of Pediatrics and Adolescent Medicine, 151,* 761–767.

Tang, C. S. (1998). The rate of physical child abuse in Chinese families: A community survey in Hong Kong. *Child Abuse and Neglect, 22,* 381 391.

Terao, S. Y., Borrego, J., & Urquiza, A. J. (2001). A reporting and response model for culture and child maltreatment. *Child Maltreatment, 6,* 158–168.

Thompson, R. A. (1998). Early sociopersonality development. In W. Damon (Ed.), *Handbook of child psychology* (Vol. 3, pp. 24–104). New York: Wiley.

Thompson, R. A., Christiansen, E. H., Jackson, S., Wyatt, J. M., Colman, R. A., Peterson, R. L., Wilcox, B. L., & Buckendahl, C. W. (1999). Parent attitudes and discipline practices: Profiles and correlates in a nationally representative sample. *Child Maltreatment, 4,* 316–330.

Trickett, P. K., & Kuczynski, L. (1986). Children's misbehaviors and parental discipline strategies in abusive and nonabusive families. *Developmental Psychology, 22*, 115–123.

U.S. Department of Health and Human Services (2000). *Child maltreatment 1998: Reports from the States to the National Child Abuse and Neglect Data System.* Washington, DC.

Vazsonyi, A. T., & Flannery, D. J. (1997). Early adolescent delinquent behaviors: Associations with family and school domains. *Journal of Early Adolescence, 17,* 271–293.

Ward, M. (1971). *Them children: A study in language learning.* New York: Holt, Rinehart & Winston.

Wasserman, G. A., Keenan, K., Tremblay, R. E., Coie, J. D., Herrenkohl, T. I., Loeber, R., & Petechuk, D. (April 2003). *Child delinquency bulletin series: Risk and protective factors of child delinquency.* Washington, DC: Office of Juvenile Justice and Delinquency Prevention, U.S. Department of Justice.

Whaley, A. L. (2000). Sociocultural differences in the developmental consequences of the use of physical punishment during childhood for African Americans. *Cultural Diversity and Ethnic Minority Psychology, 6*, 5–12.

Whipple, E. E., & Richey, C. A. (1997). Crossing the line from physical discipline to child abuse: How much is too much? *Child Abuse & Neglect, 21*, 431–444.

Wood, J. M. (1997). Risk predictors for re-abuse or re-neglect in a predominantly Hispanic population. *Child Abuse & Neglect, 21*, 379–389.

Woodward, L. J., & Fergusson, D. M. (2002). Parent, child and contextual predictors of childhood physical punishment. *Infant & Child Development, 11*, 213–236.

Young, V. H. (1970). Family and childhood in a southern Negro community. *American Anthropologist, 72*, 269–288.

Zahn-Waxler, C., Friedman, R. J., Cole, P. M., Mizuta, I., & Hiruma, N. (1996). Japanese and United States preschool children's responses to conflict and distress. *Child Development, 67*, 2462–2477.

Ziegert, K. A. (1983). The Swedish Prohibition of corporal punishment: A preliminary report. *Journal of Marriage and the Family, 45*, 917–926.

9

Ethnicity and Mental Health

The Example of Schizophrenia in the African Caribbean Population in Europe

Peter B. Jones and Wai Lun Alan Fung

Introduction

The relatively common occurrence of schizophrenia in African-Caribbean populations living in Europe is used in this chapter as a model to discuss relationships among ethnicity, migration, and mental health. The phenomenon will be described, and possible causes will be discussed in the context of the theoretical framework that underpins the migration paradigm, set out by Rutter in Chapter 1.

Ødegaard (1932) was the first to moot the idea that certain migrant groups may be susceptible to schizophrenia in the years following their journey. He noted the phenomenon in Norwegian migrants to the Midwest of the United States in the early years of the 20th century. Studies in the United Kingdom began to report a much higher than expected incidence of schizophrenia in this group soon after their arrival in the 1950s and first half of the 1960s. Initial reports were confirmed and explored in a series of progressively more rigorous and sophisticated studies that will be reviewed in what follows (Hemsi, 1967; Kiev, 1965).

The schizophrenia incidence rate[1] appears to be elevated 5- to 10-fold compared with the general population. Such an effect is almost as large as the association between smoking and lung cancer, something that, 30 years earlier, revolutionized understanding of the causes of that disease and paved the way for major and extant public health initiatives the world over. However, the schizophrenia and ethnicity association remains contentious and unexplained. It is a tantalizing window to shed light on the origins of schizophrenia and other mental illness, as well as on the meaning of ethnicity. The phenomenon is subject to vicissitudes from the stigma, prejudice, and misunderstanding that pervade mental illness in

---

[1] Incidence rate defined in this chapter as number of new (incident) cases per 100,000 population per year.

general and schizophrenia in particular. Some, though increasingly few, even feel that the relationship between ethnicity and schizophrenia may be spurious (Sashidharan, 1993).

The concept of ethnicity is debated elsewhere in this volume, so it is not considered at length here. Definitions in standard, English dictionaries show extensive cross-referral among ethnicity, race, and culture. In the psychiatric literature, the term generally includes notions of minority groups within majorities, and interactions and reactions between and within these groups. Furthermore, the idea of *recent* coexistence and migration is implied when the term *ethnic minority* is used. The recent migration, rather than minority status, per se, may be important; certainly they are two dimensions to be investigated. It is worth noting that the comparison "White" populations in many of the studies cited here are given very little consideration as to the meaning of the reference category as an ethnic group in itself. Such populations are almost all heterogeneous in terms of migration histories over the past two millennia, with continuing migration of newly displaced people, particularly from Eastern Europe and the Balkan region. The processes of integration and assimilation have, in some cases, had many generations over which to operate, albeit not always resulting in harmony.

The African-Caribbean population residing in the United Kingdom and Europe (predominately, the Netherlands), occurred during the 1950s and early 1960s, although there has been substantial bidirectional movement since. The first-generation migrants came for employment and, although suffering unexpected levels of negative attitudes and racially motivated abuse, were relatively successful economically, particularly compared with subsequent generations. The first, second, and third generations of this movement now form a coherent and culturally vibrant component of UK culture, identified within the self-ascription categories of the recent UK and Dutch censuses and population registration systems. Glover et al. (2001) provided an excellent review and analysis of recent migrations to the United Kingdom.

What Is Schizophrenia?

Schizophrenia is a severe mental illness that affects a variety of the systems within the brain or mind. It is best understood as a clinical syndrome or collection of features, rather than a precise diagnosis that infers specific causes or outcome. Perception, inferential judgment, thought structure, concepts of self, cognitive processes, volition, emotional capacity, and motor systems can all be involved, with highly damaging effects on personal functioning that generally last months or years. Table 9.1, which is adapted from a review by Andreasen (1995), summarizes the component parts of this syndrome and the underlying brain systems that can go awry.

TABLE 9.1. *The Syndrome of Schizophrenia*

Symptom	System
Hallucinations	Perception
Delusions	Inferential thinking
Disorganized speech	Language
Bizarre/catatonic behavior	Behavioral monitoring
Alogia	Conceptual fluency
Affective disturbance/blunting	Emotional expression
Anhedonia	Experiencing pleasure
Avolition	Will or volition
Movement disorder	Extrapyramidal control

Modified from Nancy Andreasen (1995). Symptoms, signs and diagnosis. *Lancet, 346,* 477–481, with the addition of movement disorder and extrapyramidal control.

Psychiatrists have been debating the more precise definitions for over a century, but most would recognize contemporary operational definitions such as ICD-10 (World Health Organization, 1992) that is reproduced in Appendix 9.1. The edges of the syndrome are interestingly unclear in terms of normal versus abnormal experiences, and between it and other psychotic illnesses. Indeed, current clinical and research interest has returned to the notion of a less clearly drawn diagnosis within the psychotic syndrome. Clinicians concentrate on interventions targeting individual symptoms; researchers acknowledge that the diagnostic boundaries between psychotic disorders that are suggested by operational criteria have not cleaved these syndromes in terms of causes or mechanisms. However, a syndrome with phenomena in several domains outlined in the ICD criteria is dramatic and would be recognized the world over. Current views posit differences in brain function under considerable genetic control as the basis of the syndrome, which interact extensively with social and personal environment. The latter view is crucial for understanding how ethnicity and schizophrenia may be linked.

There is evidence that brain systems are different in the early development of children who will, as adults, develop the syndrome (Jones, Rodgers, & Murray, 1994). At the time of onset of that syndrome, there is evidence of abnormalities in both cognitive function and, subtly, brain structure. Thus, current views about the syndrome are far from the antipsychiatry views of the 1960s and '70s that posited schizophrenia as a myth or concoction of maladaptive societies and families (Laing, 1960; Szasz, 1961). The components of schizophrenia have a mechanistic basis in neurobiology, although the multilevel impact of the disorder may be better understood in the language and constructs of other disciplines, as may parts of their origins.

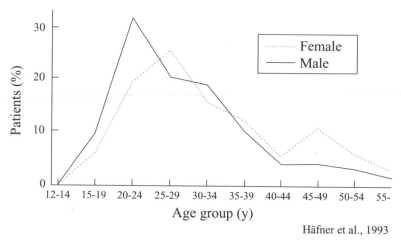

Häfner et al., 1993

FIGURE 9.1. Age at onset of schizophrenia (Häfner, Maurer, Loffler, & Riecher-Rossler, 1993).

Who Gets Schizophrenia?

The general epidemiology and natural history of the schizophrenia syndrome has been described extensively (e.g., Jones & Cannon, 1998). It affects something less than 1 percent of people during their lifetime, roughly 500 people in every 100,000 at any one time (or about 10 people on the list of a primary care physician). It arises de novo in about 10 people per 100,000 per year, accounting for about half of all psychotic mental illness. About 10 to 15 percent of people who develop the disorder kill themselves.

Much of the personal, societal, and economic impact of the schizophrenia syndrome stems from its characteristic age at onset, which is most commonly in the late teens, twenties, or thirties (Figure 9.1). This is in marked contrast to the majority of morbidity and mortality that occurs at the extremes of life. The early adult phase is the time in the life course when people are establishing their "social capital" for the rest of their lives (Putnam, 1995) and beginning to repay the investments of parents and communities during earlier development.

Where in the World Does Schizophrenia Occur?

Questions about whether schizophrenia occurs all over the world, or is confined to Western civilization or to cultures influenced by the practice of psychiatry, are directly relevant for establishing an association with particular ethnic groups. A major attempt to answer them was mounted by the World Health Organization with a series of important clinical and epidemiological studies in the 1960s, 1970s, and 1980s.

One of the major enquiries, the "Ten Country Study" (Jablensky et al., 1992), investigated the incidence of schizophrenia in different centers around the world, including settings in industrial, developed, and developing countries, as well as urban versus rural and Western versus Asian comparisons. Schizophrenia was found in all these societies, though with interesting differences in clinical outcome. In the context of the antipsychiatry movement prevalent at the time, this finding of worldwide occurrence emphasized schizophrenia as a real medical condition, rather than a by-product of certain cultures and attitudes toward interpersonal differences and personal styles. There were a few differences in incidence, but for narrowly defined schizophrenia the incidence did not differ substantially across centers. The findings are summarized in Figure 9.2.

The study was never designed (and so was not large enough) to investigate and define detailed differences in incidence. Nevertheless, the interpretation of *uniform* incidence of narrowly defined schizophrenia in different cultures around the world was almost universally accepted. This has had an adverse effect on the acceptance and interpretation of emerging findings showing increased incidence among certain ethnic groups who had migrated, such as had been suggested by Ødegaard (1932). Such findings were at odds with the view that schizophrenia has uniform incidence in all cultures.

However, these views were, themselves, inconsistent with earlier findings showing, for instance, clear evidence of a gradient in incidence according to socioeconomic status of neighborhood of residence. The classic studies of Faris and Dunham in 1920s Chicago had demonstrated this clearly (Faris & Dunham, 1960). They exploited the concentric rings of social advantage and disadvantage in that city where the inner area is the poorest, and socioeconomic status improves toward the suburbs (Figure 9.3a). Figure 9.3b shows that the incidence of schizophrenia estimated over 10 years is tightly related to social advantage. Causation is another matter, although the notion of drift into cities by vulnerable or ill people has been shown not to account for this (Dauncey, Giggs, Baker, & Harrison, 1993).

The main conclusion from existing studies is that the level of country is probably far too crude to understand underlying population heterogeneity in terms of many characteristics, ranging from social to genetic, that might help explain the group-specific variation in the incidence of schizophrenia. The study of ethnicity and schizophrenia almost certainly needs to take account of personal social and microenvironmental characteristics more than it does features defined at the level of country or even culture. This thesis is explored further in what follows.

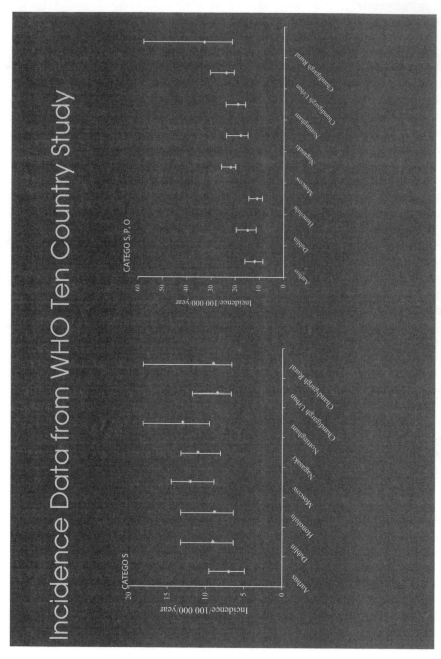

FIGURE 9.2. Taken from Jones & Cannon (1998), *who used the data published in Jablensky et al. (1992) in order to calculate the 95 percent confidence limits indicated by the error bars surrounding the incidence points for a narrow definition of schizophrenia (CATEGO S) on the left, and a broad definition of the disorder (CATEGO, P & O) on the right-hand panel, for eight sites with useable data from the WHO 10-country study of the incidence of schizophrenia.*

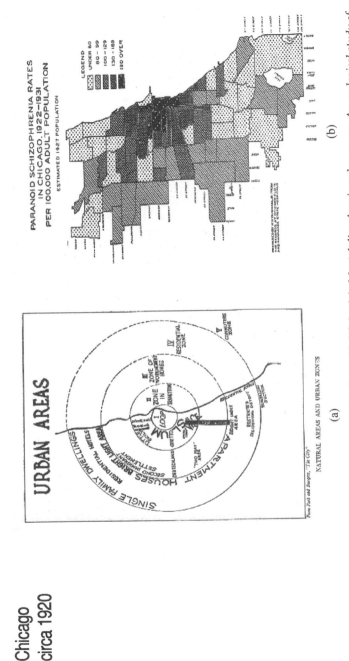

FIGURE 9.3. (a) and (b) from: Faris, R. E. L., & Dunham, H. W. (1960). *Mental disorders in urban areas. An ecological study of schizophrenia and other psychoses* (2nd ed.). New York: Hafner. Part (a) occurs as Chart 1 on p. 3, and Part (b) as Map XIX on p. 86.

233

Is Schizophrenia Really More Common
in the UK African-Caribbean Population?

Following the initial reports of higher than expected occurrence of schizophrenia among African-Caribbean people living in England (Hemsi, 1967; Kiev, 1965), the relevant, formal, epidemiological studies of incidence can be divided into two phases, according to the adequacy of the population denominator available. This is a key methodological issue in this epidemiological niche. For unraveling the association between ethnicity and schizophrenia, the UK 1991 census is a watershed, as it was the first to record ethnicity in a systematic way according to self-ascription.

Studies Using Census Data Prior to the 1991 Census
Eleven studies (see Table 9.2) reported an incidence rate ratio (compared with the White population) for schizophrenia in the African-Caribbean community ranging from 1.7 to 13.2. However, no single study was methodologically satisfactory (discussed by Castle, Wessely, Der, & Murray, 1998) because of the uncertainty about the ethnic makeup of the population. Reliable statistics were available only for place of birth, not ethnicity, and several scholars considered it likely that many young Black people of both British and Caribbean birth did not register for either the 1971 or 1981 census (Cruickshank & Beevers, 1989). A number of assumptions relating to the place of birth and the head of the household probably considerably underestimated the true population, inflating the relative risks. Part of the apparent excess could have been due solely to a large, "hidden" population in the period of risk for schizophrenia.

Cochrane and Bal (1989) used the now defunct Mental Health Enquiry that was equivalent to a national discharge register, but with many methodological problems involving both case ascertainment and the definition of ethnicity. The study by McGovern and Cope (1987) recorded ethnicity and place of birth, but did not operationally define schizophrenia. Confined to inpatients, the study was prone to referral bias; young Black men with schizophrenia may have been preferentially referred or admitted (often compulsorily) compared with their White counterparts.

Detailed, local case registers have the advantage of covering a circumscribed geographical area with a well-defined population at risk, albeit where ethnicity remains opaque. They, too, have a raft of biases associated with them. The study by Harrison, Owens, Holton, Neilson, and Boot (1988) in Nottingham overcame many, but not all, of the methodological difficulties that affected earlier studies. It was the first study of its kind among migrants in the United Kingdom that was based on sound epidemiological principles, including prospective case finding within a defined catchment area, standardized assessments of mental state, operational diagnostic criteria, and extensive use of collateral history (Harrison, 1990).

TABLE 9.2. *Incidence Studies on Schizophrenia in African Caribbeans Compared to Whites, Using Denominator Data Prior to the 1991 Census*[a]

Authors	Year	Location	Case Ascertainment	Number of African Caribbean Cases	Incidence Rate Ratio
Hemsi	1967	London (Camberwell Lambeth)	Case notes; first admissions	12	3.8
Giggs	1973	Nottingham	Case register	43	6.0
Rwegellera	1977	London	Case register	25	7.6
Carpenter & Brockington	1980	Manchester	Case notes (inpatients)	47	1.7
Bebbington et al.	1981	London (Camberwell)	Case register	180	3.7
Dean et al.	1981	Southeast England	Hospital admissions (national)	55	5.5
McGovern & Cope	1987	Birmingham	Hospital (inpatients)	51	6.5
Harrison et al.	1988	Nottingham	Prospective first-contact study	28	13.2
Cochrane & Bal	1989	England & Wales	Mental health enquiry; hospital admissions (national)	56	3.9
Castle et al.	1991	London (Camberwell)	Case register	36	5.9
Thomas et al.	1993	Manchester	Hospital admission	193	10.0

[a] Rates given in per 100,000 person-years at risk.

TABLE 9.3. *Incidence Studies of Schizophrenia in African Caribbean Compared with White Population, Using 1991 Census Data*[a]

Author	Year	Location	Case Ascertainment	Study Period	Age Group (years)	Number of A-C Cases	Broad Schizophrenia[b]			Narrow Schizophrenia		
							Whites	A-C[c]	Rate Ratio	Whites	A-C	Rate Ratio
King et al.	1994	London	Prospective first contact	July 1991–June 1992	16–54	9	20	89	4.5	12	53	4.4
Van Os, Castle, et al.	1996	London (Camberwell)	First admission	1988–92	16 or above	32	–	–	–	–	–	3.1[d] (95% CI 2.0–4.7)
Harrison et al.	1997	Nottingham	Prospective first contact	1992–94	16–64	32	16.9	149.6	8.8 (95% CI 5.9–12.9)	5.7	46.7	8.5 (95% CI 4.4–16.5)
Bhugra et al.	1997	London	Prospective first contact	April 91–Mar 93	18–64	38	29	51	1.7 (95% CI 1.1–2.8)	–	–	–

[a] Rates given in per 100,000 person-years at risk.
[b] Diagnoses made according to ICD-9 for King et al.; Research Diagnostic Criteria (RDC) for van Os et al.; ICD-10 for Harrison et al.; CATEGO for Bhugra et al.
[c] A-C stands for African Caribbeans.
[d] The value given is the standardized mortality ratio (SMR).

Diagnoses of schizophrenia were made according to the ICD-9 and DSM-III criteria.

Harrison and colleagues (1988) found that the incidence rates of schizophrenia were more than 12 times higher in the African-Caribbean community compared with the general population. The finding caused a furor. However, the study suffered from the problems of the 1981 census, and the bias arising from the fact that referrals of African-Caribbean cases were solicited by the investigators. Nevertheless, this study represented a step change in quality of methods, building as it did upon the experience of Nottingham as a center in the WHO study (1992).

Studies Using the 1991 Census

This trend for improvement in methods continued because the 1991 census included comprehensive data on the ethnic composition of the general population. Unfortunately, there was systematic underenumeration of young adults in particular ethnic groups because of the apparent link between registering for the census and liability for a recently introduced poll tax.

Four published studies using these data are shown in Table 9.3. Three of them employed a prospective design and ascertained cases by first contact of services. The London (Bhugra et al., 1997) and second Nottingham (Harrison et al., 1997) studies published in 1997 both employed a methodology for case ascertainment and assessment similar to that of the WHO Ten Country study. The incidence rates of schizophrenia in these studies were elevated in the African-Caribbean group; even major uncertainties in the denominator could not account for the higher incidence rates.

Is This Phenomenon Confined to Migrants to the United Kingdom?

This is an important question. Migration from the Caribbean to the United States, for instance, has been considerable, but there is no literature suggesting a raised incidence of schizophrenia for this population. Furthermore, the socioeconomic circumstances of U.S. Caribbean migrants are thought to be considerably better than those of their European counterparts (see Chapter 3). Studies in Europe suggest that the rate of schizophrenia for African-Caribbean migrants to European countries is higher than the indigenous populations in these countries (Table 9.4).

Two studies of migrants to the Netherlands from the Surinam, Dutch Antilles, and Morocco (Selten, Slaets, & Kahn, 1997; Selten et al., 2001), and one study of immigrants to Sweden from East Africa (Zolkowska et al., 2001) indicate higher incidence of schizophrenia and other psychotic illnesses for these groups. The Surinamese population residing in the Netherlands is ethnically diverse, as is the one for population in Surinam – with around 40 percent each from Asian and African background.

TABLE 9.4. *Incidence Studies of Schizophrenia in African-Caribbean Immigrants in Other European Countries*

Authors	Year	Location	Case Ascertainment	Diagnostic Criteria	Incidence Rate Ratios (95% Confidence Interval)
Selten et al.	1997	The Netherlands	Case registry (first hospital admission)	ICD-9 (broad schizophrenia)	Surinamese: 3.8 (3.5–4.1) Antillean: 3.9 (3.5–4.5)
Selten et al.	2001	The Netherlands	First contact of services	DSM-IV (all nonaffective psychoses)	Morocco: 4.5 (1.4–8.5) Surinam: 3.2 (1.8–5.7) Dutch Antilles: 2.9 (0.9–9.5)
Zolkowska et al.	2001	Sweden (Malmo)	Hospital admission	DSM-IV (all nonaffective psychoses)	All immigrants: 1.4 (1.1–1.8) East Africans: 11.3 (6.4–19.9)

Is the Rate of Schizophrenia Raised in the Country of Origin?

The findings from the WHO Ten Country Study suggest that demonstrably elevated schizophrenia rates would not be found in the country of origin, although the study did not include any Caribbean centers. It is important to exclude this possibility, though, in order to consider selective migration as a possible explanation (see later discussion).

Three major incidence studies have been conducted in the Caribbean in the 1990s (Table 9.5). They cover Jamaica (Hickling & Rodgers-Johnson, 1995), Trinidad (Bhugra et al., 1996), and Barbados (Mahy, Mallett, Leff, & Bhugra, 1999), three islands from which the majority of UK migrants hail. These three studies employed a prospective design to ascertain all cases making first contact with services. The studies in Trinidad and Barbados both employed the screening and measurement instruments of the WHO study. The incidence rates of schizophrenia in Jamaica, Trinidad, and Barbados were similar to the rate for the White population in the United Kingdom reported in previous studies, and were significantly lower than the comparable rate for UK African-Caribbean people. These findings suggest that environmental factors – rather than genetic (or genetic factors alone) – raised the incidence of schizophrenia and other psychotic illnesses among African Caribbeans in the United Kingdom.

Is the Increased Incidence Confined to Schizophrenia Among the Psychoses, and to African-Caribbean Migrants as Opposed to Groups with Other Origins?

Although not strictly within the model being used in this article, these are highly relevant questions. The answer to both appears to be no. There is little specificity in either dimension. Briefly, Leff, Fisher, and Bertelsen (1976), Bebbington et al. (1981), and Hunt et al. (1993) have all demonstrated more mania in African-Caribbean populations in the United Kingdom compared with the indigenous population. A middle syndrome between this and schizophrenia – so-called schizo-mania – has also been reported as more common among African Caribbeans (van Os, Takei, et al., 1996). Higher mania levels may reflect a type of stress reaction (Tyrer, 1982), as discussed in the following. Furthermore, Selten and colleagues (2001) demonstrated the increase in all psychotic disorders among Caribbean migrants to the Netherlands.

Regarding other migrant ethnic groups, the situation is less clear. King and colleagues (King, Coker, Leavey, Hoare, & Johnson-Sabine, 1994) demonstrated an increase in psychoses among all groups residing in an ethnically diverse area of North London. In the Netherlands (Selten et al., 2001), in Denmark (Mortensen, Cantor-Graae, & McNeil, 1997), and in Sweden (Zolkowska et al., 2001), similar findings have been shown, with an interesting replication of *no* significant differences in psychoses incidence

TABLE 9.5. *Incidence Studies of Schizophrenia in the Caribbean Islands*

Authors	Year	Location	Age group (years)	Incidence Rate[a] for Narrow Schizophrenia[b]	Incidence Rate for Broad Schizophrenia	Remarks
Hickling & Rodgers-Johnson	1995	Jamaica	15–54	20.9	—	—
Bhugra et al.	1996	Trinidad	15–54	16	22	Rates are similar to those from the WHO study in Honolulu and Aarhus, and much lower than the rates for African Caribbeans in London.
Mahy et al.	1999	Barbados	18–54	28	32	Identical methodology to two previous studies in Trinidad (Bhugra et al., 1996) and London (Bhugra et al., 1997).

[a] Incidence rates given in per 100,000 person-years at risk.
[b] For all three studies, diagnoses were made according to the CATEGO system, as used in the WHO DOS study.

rates between Turks and the indigenous populations. These findings implicate migration, rather than ethnicity per se, and encourage focus on detailed experiences rather than generalized effects. Presumably, different groups will have quite varied experiences, just as will the individuals within any one group.

New Evidence from Nottingham

Following the series of relevant studies from this city, a new investigation was begun in 1997 in conjunction with two other UK centers that have contributed to the area, Bristol and London. The Medical Research Council "ÆSOP (Aetiology and Ethnicity in Schizophrenia and Other Psychoses) Study" (Fearon et al., 2005; Kirkbride et al., 2005) was designed as a population-based case control study with two sets of aims. The first set involved the confirmation and further exploration of the extent and specificity of the schizophrenia and ethnicity association. The goal was to confirm the existence of an association between African-Caribbean ethnicity and schizophrenia using the best possible methods, and to document the extent of the association. In particular, the researchers sought to ascertain whether schizophrenia was the only psychotic syndrome that was more common among African-Caribbean persons, and whether other ethnic minority populations presented similar psychiatric disorders. Second, and more important, the research team sought to design models and test hypotheses concerning causation. Some results of the descriptive goals are presented briefly here as preliminary data from one center, Nottingham. The prevalent models and hypotheses are then reviewed.

The collection of incident cases of all psychotic disorders (that is, schizophrenia, similar syndromes that do not meet criteria because the length of time is too short for schizophrenia, psychotic syndromes associated with drug use, depression with psychosis, and mania with psychosis) followed closely the methods that had been used in the WHO study (Jablensky et al., 1992) and thence by subsequent investigators (e.g., Harrison et al., 1997, in Nottingham, and Bhugra et al., 1997, in London).

Any person who contacted mental health services with evidence of delusion, hallucination, thought disorder, or negative symptoms of schizophrenia (see Table 9.1) during the 2 years mid-1997 to mid-1999 was included in the study. A comprehensive "leakage" study was undertaken so as to include people who were, for any reason, excluded from this system. Detailed psychopathological assessment was undertaken using a standard interview (SCAN) and extracted from clinical records. These data were presented to a panel of diagnosticians, who classified the clinical picture according to the ICD 10 (World Health Organization, 1992), blind to information about ethnicity that was obtained by self-ascription wherever possible, according to the classification used in the UK 1991 census (see http://census.ac.uk/casweb/ for full details and data).

TABLE 9.6. *Incidence Rate Ratios (IRRs) with Corresponding 95% Confidence Intervals for Different Diagnostic Groups in African Caribbeans (Using Whites as Baseline) in Nottingham, UK, 1997–99*

Diagnostic Category	Crude (Uncorrected for Underenumeration)	Crude (Corrected for Underenumeration)	Adjusted for Gender	Adjusted for Age	Adjusted for Age and Gender
All psychoses	8.2 (5.4–12.4)	8.1 (5.4–12.3)	8.2 (5.4–12.4)	8.1 (5.4–12.4)	8.3 (5.5–12.6)
ICD 10 Schizophrenias and related syndromes (F 20–29)	9.7 (5.8–16.2)	9.5 (5.7–16.0)	9.7 (5.8–16.2)	9.4 (5.6–15.9)	9.6 (5.7–16.3)
ICD 10 Narrowly defined schizophrenia (F20)	8.8 (4.3–17.8)	8.6 (4.3–17.5)	8.8 (4.3–17.9)	8.2 (4.0–16.7)	8.5 (4.2–17.3)
ICD 10 Bipolar disorders (F30–31)	14.9 (5.5–40.3)	14.7 (5.4–39.8)	14.8 (5.4–40.0)	14.3 (5.2–38.9)	14.4 (5.3–39.3)
ICD 10 Depressive psychoses (F32–33)	5.1 (1.5–16.6)	5.0 (1.5–16.4)	5.0 (1.5–16.3)	5.7 (1.7–18.9)	5.7 (1.7–18.8)
ICD10 Drug-related disorders (F10–19)	2.1 (0.3–15.6)	2.1 (0.3–15.4)	2.1 (0.3–15.8)	2.0 (0.3–14.5)	2.1 (0.3–15.3)

The denominator, or population at risk, was defined as the Nottingham population at that census age 16–64 years, multiplied by 2 so as to estimate the number of person-years at risk for psychotic disorders during the study period.[2] Systematic underenumeration of certain ethnic and age groups was dealt with by using published correction factors (OPCS, 1994). Details of the method and results are presented elsewhere (Fung, 2002), as is confirmatory analysis using information from the subsequent, 2001 census (ÆSOP Study Group, 2005).

Table 9.6 shows the incidence of a variety of psychotic syndromes during the study period for the African-Caribbean population compared with the White, indigenous population. The preliminary calculation of rates of *all* psychotic syndromes indicates that they are increased in the African-Caribbean population (incident rate ratios (IRRs) greater than 1), even after taking into account the group age and gender structure as well as the underenumeration at the census. The only diagnostic category where the effect may be due to chance (the 95 percent confidence interval includes one) is for the drug-related psychoses. This is of considerable interest because one of the reasons put forward for the raised rate is increased drug use among African-Caribbean men (see later discussion). However, there is no evidence of excess drug-induced psychoses for this group that could be mimicking schizophrenia and, moreover, there is no corroborating evidence of increased use of drugs in this population group (see later discussion).

Lack of specificity for the psychotic diagnostic effect among African Caribbeans (Table 9.6) is also apparent from a comparison of different migrant groups (Table 9.7). For ease of presentation, the substantial non-White ethnic groups in Nottingham (South Asian Indian, Pakistani, Black African, and Chinese) are classified together and compared with the White European group. This is not meant to indicate similarities among these groups other than a migrant origin. The effects reported in Table 9.7 indicate that all psychoses, and both broadly and narrowly defined schizophrenia, are more common in these groups compared with the White Europeans.

Thus, an increased incidence of schizophrenia and other psychotic disorders has consistently been reported in the African-Caribbean population in the United Kingdom and is present in the largest and most recent investigation. The increase in incidence has also been reported among migrants from certain ethnic groups to other European countries, and this lack of specificity is also confirmed by the ÆSOP study. There does not appear to be a major effect of generation, with increased rates of schizophrenia-like psychosis being found in the elderly first generation in London (Reeves, Saurer, Stewart, Granger, & Howard, 2001). However, the rates in the Caribbean host countries do not seem to be increased.

---

[2] The population at risk used here does not include four of the electoral wards in Nottingham.

TABLE 9.7. *Incidence Rate Ratios (IRRs) with Corresponding 95% Confidence Intervals for All Psychoses, Broad Schizophrenia (ICD-10 F20–29), and Narrowly Defined Schizophrenia (F20) in Other Ethnic Groups[a] (Using Whites as Baseline), Nottingham, UK, 1997–99*

Diagnostic Category[b]	Crude (Uncorrected for Underenumeration)	Crude (Corrected for Underenumeration)	Adjusted for Gender	Adjusted for Age	Adjusted for Age and Gender
All psychoses	4.2 (2.7–6.6)	4.2 (2.6–6.5)	4.1 (2.6–6.5)	3.72 (2.4–5.9)	3.7 (2.4–5.9)
F20–29	3.9 (2.1–7.4)	3.9 (2.1–7.3)	3.9 (2.1–7.2)	3.6 (1.9–6.7)	3.5 (1.9–6.6)
F20	4.3 (2.0–9.4)	4.2 (1.9–9.3)	4.2 (1.9–9.3)	3.7 (1.7–8.2)	3.7 (1.7–8.2)

[a] Including Indians, Pakistanis, Black Africans, Chinese.
[b] See Table 9.6 for ICD coding.

What might be the causes of these differentials? If we could understand them, we might understand much about the possible causes of psychotic illnesses in general and be better prepared to help migrant groups who experience these disorders. Sharpley and colleagues (Sharpley, Hutchinson, McKenzie, & Murray, 2001) have carefully reviewed a number of possibilities that are discussed in what follows and that are the focus of the second phase of the ÆSOP study.

Possible Causes of the Raised Rates of Schizophrenia in the European African-Caribbean Population

Misdiagnosis

Interpreting mental states as abnormal requires shared beliefs and understanding of mental norms between observer and patient; emic and etic considerations are paramount (Cochrane & Bal, 1987). Strategies to judge whether conditions are the same or different generally include examination of overlap or points of rarity in clinical features, differences in outcome, and different causation. All have been used to investigate this problem.

Some observers have suggested that the features of the schizophrenia syndrome cannot be called schizophrenia when they occur in some ethnic groups. Others suggest that the increased rates are due to misinterpretations of normal phenomena by culturally myopic researchers or psychiatrists (Littlewood & Lipsedge, 1981; Sashidharan, 1993). For example, Lewis, Croft-Jeffreys, and David (1990) showed that, in fact, British psychiatrists were rather loath to diagnose schizophrenia on the basis of clinical vignettes about African-Caribbean people, and that there were no differences in diagnostic practices on the basis of their own country of origin. The best study to date on this issue comes from Hickling, McKenzie, Mullen, and Murray (1999). They undertook two sets of assessments on the same patients, one by a Jamaican psychiatrist, the other by British doctors. Both sets diagnosed a similar proportion as having schizophrenia, though these were the same patients in only half the cases. Thus, the clinical diagnosis was not very reliable, but not obviously ethnically biased in terms of patients' or assessors' culture.

Arguments about whether the syndrome represents pathology or whether its constituent phenomena are to be regarded as culturally normal are unresolved (al-Issa, 1995). This may result in reporting biases for some groups who feel that what western cultures view as abnormal is, in fact, normative. What would take them to the psychiatrist in the first place is not clear. The possibility that such migrants would be referred to services disproportionately was excluded in two case-control studies, one by Wessely, Castle, Der, and Murray (1991), the other by Mortensen et al. (1997). Furthermore, McGovern and Hemmings (1994) found that the majority of African-Caribbean and White patients and relatives conceptualized the person diagnosed with schizophrenia as "mentally ill" and supported compulsory admission where it was used (Mercer, 1986).

More frequent and severe positive psychotic symptoms have been reported in African Americans compared with Whites (Adebimpe, Chu, Klein, & Lange, 1982; Adebimpe, Klein, & Fried, 1981; Lawson, Yesavage, & Werner, 1984; Mukherjee et al., 1983); a comparable phenomenon has been reported in Britain (Ndetei & Vadher, 1985). Other British data include excess reporting of hallucinations in a large population-based study (Johns, Nazroo, Bebbington, & Kuipers, 1998), and delusional ideas in a detailed psychological assessment (Sharpley & Peters, 1999). These findings also pose general questions as to the boundaries of the schizophrenia syndrome.

Misdiagnosis of Depression and Affective Psychoses
The idea that affective (depressive or manic) syndromes may be selectively misdiagnosed as schizophrenia is a less attractive explanation of the schizophrenia excess, given that these disorders seem also to be more common (see previous discussion). However, it is still possible that the syndrome presents somewhat differently among ethnic groups (Zigler & Glick, 1988). Hutchinson and colleagues (1999) used factor analysis to investigate the underlying symptom structure of the psychosis in different ethnic groups. They demonstrated more affective symptoms (mania–catatonia) in schizophrenia in African-Caribbean people compared with their White counterparts, though there are no differences in terms of the core symptoms of schizophrenia. This may be something important clinically. Conversely, Kirov & Murray (1999) showed more schizophrenia-like symptoms in affective disorders for this group. Overall, systematic misdiagnosis does not seem an adequate explanation for an excess of either schizophrenia or affective disorders, particularly given the ÆSOP study findings of a lack of specificity regarding increased incidence of several diagnoses rather that a systematic overrepresentation of one or other. However, the presentation of any syndrome may be affected by ethnicity to some degree.

Outcomes Are Similar: This Suggests Similar Illnesses
There have been several studies comparing the outcome of schizophrenia in African-Caribbean and the remaining populations in the United Kingdom (Bhugra et al., 1997; Birchwood et al., 1992; Harrison, Amin, Singh, Croudace, & Jones, 1999; Harvey, Williams, McGuffin, & Toone, 1990; McGovern & Cope, 1991; McGovern & Hemmings, 1994; McKenzie et al., 1995; Sugarman, 1992; Takei et al., 1998; Thakker & Ward, 1998; also see the review by McKenzie & Murray, 1999). Follow-up periods ranging from 1 to 18 years provide ample evidence of differences in pathways to and experiences with care, with the African-Caribbean group having uniformly worse experiences. There is also some evidence to support the lack of

identification and treatment of affective symptoms in this group. However, convincing evidence of differences in fundamental domains of symptomatic or functional outcome is lacking. Variability among studies is slight and, in our view, is consistent with sampling errors. The field would be helped by a meta-analysis.

Causal Hypotheses

This is the third plank of a nosological approach. In general, there are a number of competing models one might suggest for the excess schizophrenia. First, different groups might have different disorders and, logically, different causes. Second, there may be common factors causing the same disease across groups, who differ in the prevalence of the causal factors. Third, there may be causes that theoretically would modify risk in any group, but that occur only in one. For example, stress from racial discrimination may occur only or predominantly among racially distinct groups. Fourth, there may be effect modification due to differential vulnerability (perhaps genetic) where causes have an effect only in one group despite being prevalent in all. These last two mechanisms would represent extra, novel causes leading to excess disease.

Genetic Predisposition

This is known to be important in the cause of schizophrenia (Jones & Cannon, 1998), so it is important to know whether there exist differences among ethnic groups. Two studies have shown that there is a much higher risk of schizophrenia in siblings than in the parents of African-Caribbean people with schizophrenia (Hutchinson et al., 1996; Sugarman & Craufurd, 1994). This suggests environmental factors acting on second-generation African Caribbeans, although it was clear from the latter study that different families have radically different baseline risks. Thus, gene–environment interactions are likely to be involved.

Predisposition to Migration

Ødegaard (1932) suggested a shared predisposition to migration and to schizophrenia as an explanation of the excess schizophrenia among Norwegian migrants to Minnesota. Furthermore, the new, concentrated gene pool might amplify the effect in subsequent generations (Thomas, Stone, Osborn, Thomas, & Fisher, 1993). Literature reviews (Canadian Taskforce on Mental Health Issues, 1988) and empirical studies suggest this is not the answer. For instance, about half the inhabitants of Surinam migrated to the Netherlands, making selective migration unlikely (Selten et al., 2002). However, it is important to consider the disparate reasons for migrating within any one apparently homogeneous group coupled with potentially differing incorporation experiences thereafter (Cheng & Chang, 1999).

Early Life Influences

Part of the vulnerability to schizophrenia may be established in very early life, when the most profound events are occurring in terms of brain development. Although genes may very likely trigger onset at this time, many putative modifiers of early development are thought of as environmental, despite the probability of interactions. Prenatal viral infections have been suggested as an early causal factor for schizophrenia, with influenza (Mednick, Machon, Huttenen, & Bonett, 1988; O'Callaghan et al., 1991) and rubella (Brown, A. S., & Susser, 1999) finding support. Young African-Caribbean immigrants to the United Kingdom during the 1950s had little or no immunity to rubella (Nicoll & Logan, 1989). Their children had high rates of the congenital rubella syndrome when mothers were exposed to the virus that was common in the United Kingdom before the present vaccination programs (Parsons, 1963). Thus, some have proposed that high rates of schizophrenia may be a late sequel (Glover, 1989; Harrison, 1990), though there is no direct empirical support. Prenatal and perinatal complications may be associated with later risk of schizophrenia, possibly through a mechanism involving hypoxia (reviewed by Cannon, Jones, & Murray, 2002). Hutchinson and associates (1997) suggested that an excess of such complications in African-Caribbean mothers may be important but, again, there is no evidence supporting this; indeed, the contrary seemed more plausible (McKenzie, 1999; McKenzie et al., 2002).

Thus, one set of hypotheses to explain the excess incidence of schizophrenia – that early life factors attenuating brain development are more common in African-Caribbean people, rendering them more vulnerable to later illness – can be rejected on current evidence. Eliminating this explanation, along with the lack of evidence to support a genetic diathesis, is a step forward in this area. It puts the spotlight on more proximal factors stressing later vulnerability and triggering or precipitating events; many of the hypothesized agents are in the realm of psychosocial stresses, as discussed in what follows, rather than biological toxins.

Developmental Risk Factors Later in Childhood

That children who develop schizophrenia as adults differ from their peers in a number of domains suggests antecedent causes (Cannon et al., 1999; Davies, Russel, Jones, & Murray, 1998; Jones et al., 1994). Sharpley et al. (2001) emphasize that African-Caribbean children in England achieve less academically and have higher than expected rates of learning disability (Wing, 1979). They are also more frequently exposed to a variety of privations that increase risk for nonpsychotic mental illness (Maughan, 1989). Some, such as disrupted schooling, may be important triggers for schizophrenia in the general population (Mortensen et al., 2002, though cause and effect is unclear). Despite all the clues about early life, the data indicate, if anything, lower risks of early or developmental insults among European African-Caribbean people who develop schizophrenia. Thus, excess vulnerability established in this way seems an unlikely explanation for the excess schizophrenia in this population.

Drug Use

Prospective, epidemiological data (Andreasson, Allebeck, & Engstrom, 1987) show that cannabis use is more common in young Swedish men who later develop schizophrenia over subsequent decades, a phenomenon confirmed by a number of recent, longitudinal studies (Arseneault et al., 2002; van Os et al., 2002) including an extension of the original Swedish material (Zammit, Allebeck, Andreasson, Lundberg, & Lewis, 2002). High levels of cannabis use have been suggested as relevant in the excess psychosis in the African-Caribbean population, though this is yet another area surrounded by uncertainty and contrary evidence (Callan & Littlewood, 1998; Ghodse, 1986; Littlewood, 1998; McGuire et al., 1994, 1995; Thornicroft, 1990). Indeed, cannabis use was *less* prevalent in immigrants to The Netherlands compared with Dutch people (Selten & Sijben, 1994; Selten et al., 1997). In summary, there is some evidence to suggest that cannabis use, particularly high levels early in life, contributes to the causes of schizophrenia, in general, but there is no support for the excess of the disorder in African-Caribbean people being due to its use.

Results of an Urban Environment

We have already noted the association between social disadvantage and schizophrenia seen in 1920s Chicago, and commented that this heterogeneity at the level of neighborhood may be masked when high-level units, such as countries, are studied. The findings have been replicated in the United Kingdom (Giggs & Cooper, 1987; Ineichen, Harrison, & Morgan, 1984) and Europe, with studies suggesting that being brought up in a city is the relevant exposure (Lewis, David, Andreasson, & Allebeck, 1992; Marcellis, MacIver, & Soomans, 1998), rather than drift after diagnosis (Freeman, 1994). The variety of suggested explanations is extensive (Sharpley et al., 2001). It includes social factors such as adverse life events (Brown, G. W., & Prudo, 1981), social isolation (Burnett et al., 1999), overcrowding (Magaziner, 1988), psychosocial overstimulation (Wing, 1989), higher crime levels (Dekker et al., 1997) and lower socioeconomic class (Castle, Scott, & Wessely, 1993); physical insults such as air, lead, or other pollution (Dekker et al., 1997); and other physical factors that may interfere with development (Jablensky, 1988; Takei, O'Callaghan, & Sham, 1992; Torrey & Bowler, 1991).

Other community-level factors, such as social capital (Putnam, 1995), may also be compromised more commonly in the African-Caribbean population, and this may contribute to excess schizophrenia. Boydell et al. (2001)

demonstrated an apparent interaction between person and place by showing that African-Caribbean people who lived in areas with a low proportion
of people from the same ethnic group appeared to be at particularly high
risk of schizophrenia. Apart from that interaction, most African-Caribbean
people in the United Kingdom may be exposed to these putative, routine,
individual-level risk factors, given that most live in cities, though not in
higher shares than their White counterparts. Thus, part of the excess rate
of schizophrenia may be attributable to causes that tend to concentrate in
cities; if persons at risk moved to the countryside, this mechanism would
lower the risk. However, it doesn't really explain the excess if comparable populations are contrasted. We still need to find some factors that are
unique.

Racially Based Life Events and "Racism"

Adverse life events are known to cluster before the onset or relapse of
psychosis (Bebbington et al., 1993). Although having face validity as a
cause of mental distress, there is no good evidence to support either an
excess in general (Gilvarry et al., 1999) or racially related life events as
unique causes of any mental illness in this group (Sharpley et al., 2001).
This is not to say that discrimination, bullying, or racial persecution are
not extremely stressful and damaging.

If these factors were important one would expect an increase in so-
called minor psychiatric morbidity. Evidence of an excess of nonpsychotic
disorders in African-Caribbean people is scanty and contradictory (Jenkins
et al., 1997; Nazroo, 1997, 1998; Shaw et al., 1999). This excess has been
studied largely through a veil of factors related to help seeking and health
services (Burke, 1984; Gillam, 1990; Kleinman, 1980; Leff, 1988; Nazroo,
1998; Rack, 1982; Rathwell, 1984). If stresses interact with genetic or other
diathesis for schizophrenia, then increased exposure to such triggers in one
population compared with another will result in excess disorder. Further
research is required to investigate these complex models; the case control
design of the MRC ÆSOP study (see previous discussion) is intended to
investigate this in detail.

One area that is attracting attention is not merely the differential occurrence of risk factors, but differences in their psychological meaning to
individuals who may differ by ethnicity, culture and identity, age, gender,
and other factors. Some formulate these ideas in terms of personality and
the genetically mediated concept of "schizotypy"; others do so in a clinical psychological sense of style of attribution of events. Thus, Gaupp and,
later, Kretschmer suggested that someone's long-term sensitive style of
attribution may predispose that person to schizophrenia, ideas that have
remained popular (Bentall, Jackson, & Ilgrim, 1988; Bentall, Kinderman,
& Kaney, 1994; Colby, Fraught, & Parkinson, 1979; Garfield, Rogoff, &
Steinberg, 1987; Kinderman & Bentall, 1996; Robey, Cohen, & Gara, 1989;

Schneider, 1959). Original ideas of sensitive personalities have now developed into more complex psychological theories of the initiation and maintenance of some psychotic phenomena, particularly delusion, in the face of certain external events (Kinderman & Bentall, 1996; Sharpley et al., 2001). Only provisional evidence for different attribution styles in ethnic groups exists at present (Sharpley & Peters, 1999).

Brain Structure, Function, and Cognition

Whereas there is a reasonably large literature about epidemiological, social, and psychological explanations of the excess of schizophrenia in European African-Caribbean populations, there is virtually nothing in the areas of brain structure, function, or cognition. This is remarkable given common contemporary ideas on schizophrenia as a brain disease (Andreasen, 1995). This dearth of understanding reveals more about social factors as they impinge (rightly) upon science than it does about the causes of any excess burden of schizophrenia in an already disadvantaged group. Psychiatry has saddled itself with a rather curious convention of excluding from the definition of schizophrenia any cases where the brain pathology is obvious. Current evidence suggests that this paradox seems to be less pertinent for the ethnic excess than in the general population.

Conclusions

There is no doubt that the schizophrenia syndrome occurs far more commonly in African-Caribbean migrants to Europe than might be expected. This increased risk of 5- to 10-fold is huge in relative terms. Although the original reports attracted some opprobrium, linking the most stigmatizing mental illness with a considerably disadvantaged group in historical terms, recent work suggests that a range of psychotic mental illnesses are more commonly found in several recently migrant, ethnic minority populations in the United Kingdom and elsewhere. There is no evidence to support hypotheses suggesting either selective migration of vulnerable people, or vulnerability caused by early developmental insults. Thus, we must look to predisposing and triggering factors that are likely to be found in the realms of the psychosocial effects of being a young adult from a minority group living in contemporary UK society.

Somehow, the interactions among individuals, ethnic groups, and societies are played out in the brains and minds of some people as the mental phenomena of psychotic syndromes with a neurobiological basis and with multidimensional implications. Interestingly, these interactions appear most toxic not immediately after migration, but in later years and across generations. This is partly due to the fact that people are at risk of schizophrenia only during the adolescent and young adult years, and many migrants are older than this at the time of entry. However, this also suggests that the experience of the second and subsequent generations of migrants, who have not themselves migrated, may be of particular importance.

If we could explain these effects, we would learn much about schizophrenia and other psychoses, as well as providing practical guidance for particular population groups. We might also define risk factors for morbidity even more widespread than the particular psychotic syndromes that have been the focus of this chapter. The increasing movements of populations in the modern world and the dreadful burden of mental illness make this endeavor ever more urgent. In this area, the migration paradigm is more than a research tool, but a social and political fact that has implications in terms of the association with psychotic illness. An imperative is to establish health services that are accessible and acceptable to migrant groups, alongside efforts to tackle the stigma that will influence those who are affected and the communities from which they come.

Acknowledgments

The authors gratefully acknowledge funding from the UK MRC and Stanley Medical Research Institute (PJ) and from the Commonwealth Scholarship Commission (WLAF), and the major contribution of the ÆSOP Study Group and its investigators.

APPENDIX 9.1

ICD-10: Schizophrenia (WHO, 1992)

General Criteria for Paranoid, Hebephrenic, Catatonic and Undifferentiated Schizophrenia

G1. Either at least one of the syndromes, symptoms and signed listed under (1) below or at least two of the symptoms and signs listed under (2) should be present for most of the time during an episode of psychotic illness lasting for at least 1 month (or at some time during most of the days).
  1. At least one of the following must be present:
     (a) thought echo, thought insertion or withdrawal, or thought broadcasting;
     (b) delusions of control, influence or passivity, clearly referred to body or limb movements or specific thoughts, actions or sensations; delusional perception;
     (c) hallucinatory voices giving a running commentary on the patient's behaviour, or discussing the patient between themselves, or other types of hallucinatory voices coming from some part of the body;

(d) persistent delusions of other kinds that are culturally inappropriate and completely impossible (e.g. being able to control the weather, or being in communication with aliens from another world).

2. Or at least two of the following:

(e) persistent hallucinations in any modality, when occurring every day for at least 1 month, when accompanied by delusions (which may be fleeting or half-formed) without clear affective content, or when accompanied by persistent overvalued ideas;

(f) neologisms, breaks or interpolations in the train of thought, resulting in incoherence or irrelevant speech;

(g) catatonic behaviour, such as excitement, posturing or waxy flexibility, negativism, mutism and stupor;

(h) "negative" symptoms, such as marked apathy, paucity of speech and blunting or incongruity of emotional responses (it must be clear that these are not due to depression or to neuroleptic medication).

G2. Most commonly used exclusion clauses

(1) If the patient also meets the criteria for manic episode (F30.) or depressive episode (F32.), the criteria listed under G1(1) and G1(2) above must have been met before the disturbance of mood developed.

The disorder is not attributable to organic brain disease (in the sense of (F00-F09) or to alcohol- or drug-related intoxication (F1x.0), dependence (F1x.2) or withdrawal (F1x.3 and F1x.4).

References

Adebimpe, V. R., Chu, C. C., Klein, H. E., & Lange, M. H. (1982). Racial and geographic differences in the psychopathology of schizophrenia. *American Journal of Psychiatry, 139*, 888–891.

Adebimpe, V. R., Klein, H. E., & Fried, J. (1981). Hallucination and delusions in black psychiatric patients. *Journal of the National Medical Association, 73*, 517–520.

al-Issa, I. (1995). The illusion of reality or the reality of illusion. Hallucinations and culture. *British Journal of Psychiatry, 166*, 368–373.

Andreasen, N. C. (1995). Symptoms, signs and diagnosis of schizophrenia. *Lancet, 346*, 477–481.

Andreasson, S., Allebeck, P., & Engstrom, A. (1987). Cannabis and schizophrenia: A longitudinal study of Swedish conscripts. *Lancet, ii*, 1483–1485.

Arseneault, L., Cannon, M., Poulton, R., Murray, R., Caspi, A., & Moffitt, T. E. (2002). Cannabis use in adolescence and risk for adult psychosis: Longitudinal prospective study. *British Medical Journal, 325*(7374), 1212–1213.

Bebbington, P. E., Hurry, J., & Tennant, C. (1981). Psychotic disorders in selected immigrant groups in Camberwell. *Social Psychiatry, 16*, 43–51.

Bebbington, P. E., Wilkins, S., Jones, P., Foerster, A., Murray, R., Toone, B., & Lewis, S. (1993). Life events and psychosis. Initial results from the Camberwell Psychosis Study. *British Journal of Psychiatry, 162,* 72–79.

Bentall, R. P., Jackson, H. F., & Ilgrim, D. (1988). Abandoning the concept of schizophrenia: Some implications of validity arguments for psychological research into psychotic phenomena. *British Journal of Clinical Psychology, 27,* 303–324.

Bentall, R. P., Kinderman, P., & Kaney, S. (1994). The self, attributional processes and abnormal beliefs: Towards a model of persecutory delusions. *Behaviour Research and Therapy, 32,* 331–341.

Bhugra, D., Hilwig, M., Hossein, B., Marceau, H., Neehall, J., Leff, J., Mallett, R., & Der, G. (1996). First-contact incidence rates of schizophrenia in Trinidad and one-year follow-up. *British Journal of Psychiatry, 169,* 587–592.

Bhugra, D., Leff, J., Mallet, R., Der, G., Corridan, B., & Rudge, S. (1997). Incidence and outcome of schizophrenia in Whites, African–Caribbeans and Asians in London. *Psychological Medicine, 27,* 791–798.

Birchwood, M., Cochrane, R., MacMillan, F., Copestake, S., Kucharska, J., & Carriss, M. (1992). The influence of ethnicity and family structure on relapse in first-episode schizophrenia. A comparison of Asian, African-Caribbean and White patients. *British Journal of Psychiatry, 161,* 783–790.

Boydell, J., van Os, J. J., McKenzie, K., Allardyce, J., Goel, R., McCreadie, R. G., & Murray, R. M. (2001) Incidence of schizophrenia in ethnic minorities in London: Ecological study into interactions with environment. *British Medical Journal, 323,* 1336–1338.

Brown, A. S., & Susser, E. S. (1999) Plausibility of prenatal rubella, influenza and other viral infections as risk factors for schizophrenia. In A. S. Brown & E. S. Susser (Eds.), *Prenatal exposures in schizophrenia. Progress in psychiatry.* Washington, DC: American Psychiatric Association.

Brown, G. W., & Prudo, R. (1981). Psychiatric disorder in a rural and an urban population. I. Aetiology of depression. *Psychological Medicine, 11,* 581–599.

Burke, A. (1984). Racism and psychiatric disturbance among West Indians in Britain. *International Journal of Social Psychiatry, 30,* 50–68.

Burnett, R., Mallett, R., Bhugra, D., Hutchinson, G., Der, G., & Leff, J. (1999). The first contact of patients with schizophrenia with psychiatric services: Social factors and pathways to care in a multi-ethnic population. *Psychological Medicine, 11,* 581–599.

Byrne, M., Agerbo, E., & Mortensen, P. B. (2002) Family history of psychiatric disorders and age at first contact in schizophrenia: An epidemiological study. *British Journal of Psychiatry, 181*(Suppl. 43), s19–s25.

Callan, A., & Littlewood, R. (1998). Patient satisfaction: Ethnic origin or explanatory model? *International Journal of Social Psychiatry, 44,* 1–11.

Canadian Taskforce on Mental Health Issues (1988). *After the door has opened.* Ottawa: Ministry of Supply and Services.

Cannon, M., Jones, P. B., Huttunen, M. O., Tanskanen, A., Huttunen, T., Rabe-Hesketh, S., & Murray, R. M. (1999) School performance in Finnish children and later development of schizophrenia. A population-based longitudinal study. *Archives of General Psychiatry, 56,* 457–463.

Cannon, M., Jones, P. B., & Murray, R. M. (2002) Obstetric complications and schizophrenia: Historical and meta-analytic review. *American Journal of Psychiatry*, 159, 1080–1092.

Carpenter, L., & Brockington, I. F. (1980). A study of mental illness in Asians, West Indians and Africans living in Manchester. *British Journal of Psychiatry*, 137, 201–205.

Castle, D., Wessely, S., Der, G., & Murray, R. M. (1991). The incidence of operationally defined schizophrenia in Camberwell, 1965–1984. *British Journal of Psychiatry*, 159, 790–794.

Castle, D., Scott, K., & Wessely, S. (1993). Does social deprivation during gestation and early life predispose to later schizophrenia? *Social Psychiatry and Psychiatric Epidemiology*, 28, 1–4.

Castle, D., Wessely, S., Van Os, J., & Murray, R.M.(1998) *Psychosis in the inner city: The Camberwell First Episode Study* [Maudsley Monograph]. Hove: Psychology Press.

Cheng, A. T. A., & Chang, J. C. (1999). Mental health aspects of culture and migration [Editorial review]. *Current Opinions in Psychiatry*, 12, 217–222.

Cochrane, R., & Bal, S. S. (1987). Migration and schizophrenia: An examination of five hypotheses. *Social Psychiatry*, 22, 181–191.

Cochrane, R., & Bal, S. S. (1989). Mental hospital admission rates of immigrants to England. *Social Psychiatry and Psychiatric Epidemiology*, 24, 2–11.

Colby, K. M., Fraught, W. S., & Parkinson, R. C. (1979). Cognitive therapy of paranoid conditions: heuristic suggestions based on a computer simulation model. *Cognitive Therapy and Research*, 3, 55–60.

Cruickshank, J., & Beevers, D. (1989). *Ethnic factors in health and disease*. Sevenoaks: Wright.

Dauncey, K., Giggs, J., Baker, K., & Harrison, G. (1993) Schizophrenia in Nottingham: Lifelong residential mobility of a cohort. *British Journal of Psychiatry*, 163, 613–619.

Davies, N., Russel, A., Jones, P., & Murray, R. M. (1998). Which characteristics of schizophrenia predate psychosis? *Journal of Psychiatric Research*, 32, 121–131.

Dean, G., Walsh, D., Downing, H., & Shelley, E. (1981). First admission of native born and immigrants to psychiatric hospitals in South-East England 1976. *British Journal of Psychiatry*, 139, 506–512.

Dekker, J., Peen, J., Gardien, R., de Jonghe, F., & Wijdenes, W. (1997). Urbanisation and psychiatric admission rates in the Netherlands. *International Journal of Social Psychiatry*, 43, 235–246.

Faris, R. E. L., & Dunham, H. W. (1960). *Mental disorders in urban Areas. An ecological study of schizophrenia and other psychoses* (2nd ed.). New York: Hafner.

Fearon, P., Kirkbride, J., Morgan, P., Mallett, R., Leff, J., Harrison, G. L., Murray R. M., Jones, P. B., and the ÆSOP Study Group. (2005). Schizophrenia and other psychotic syndromes are more common in migrant groups in the UK – evidence from the Medical Research Council ÆSOP study. Manuscript submitted for publication.

Freeman, H. (1994). Schizophrenia and city residence. *British Journal of Psychiatry*, 164(Suppl. 23), 39–50.

Fung, W. L. A. (2002) *Incidence of psychotic illness in UK migrant populations*. Unpublished master's thesis, University of Cambridge, Cambridge, UK.

Garfield, D. A., Rogoff, M. L., & Steinberg, S. (1987). Affect recognition and self-esteem in schizophrenia. *Psychopathology, 20,* 225–233.

Ghodse, H. (1986). Cannabis psychosis. *British Journal of Addiction, 81,* 473–478.

Giggs, J. (1973) High rates of schizophrenia among immigrants in Nottingham. *Nursing Times, 69,* 1210–1212.

Giggs, J. A., & Cooper, J. E. (1987). Ecological structure and the distribution of schizophrenia and affective psychoses in Nottingham. *British Journal of Psychiatry, 151,* 627–633.

Gillam, S. (1990). Ethnicity and the use of health services. *Postgraduate Medical Journal, 66,* 989–993.

Gilvarry, C., Walsh, E., Samele, C., Hutchinson, G., Mallett, R., Rabe-Hesketh, S., Fahy, T., van Os, J., & Murray, R. M. (1999). Life events and perceptions of racism in a sample of community care patients with psychotic illnesses. *Social Psychiatry and Psychiatric Epidemiology, 24,* 49–56.

Glover, G. R. (1989). The pattern of psychiatric admission of Caribbean-born immigrants in London. *Social Psychiatry and Psychiatric Epidemiology, 24,* 49–56.

Glover S., Gott C., Loizillon A., Portes J., Price R., Spencer S., Srinivasan V., & Willis C. (2001). *Migration: an economic and social analysis. RDS Occasional Paper 67.* London: HMSO. 1st July 2003 http://www.homeoffice.gov.uk/rds/pdfs/occ67-migration.pdf

Häfner, H., Maurer, K., Loffler, W., & Riecher-Rossler, A. (1993). The influence of age and sex on the onset and early course of schizophrenia. *British Journal of Psychiatry, 162,* 80–86.

Harrison, G. (1990). Searching for the causes of schizophrenia: The role of migrant studies. *Schizophrenia Bulletin, 16,* 663–671.

Harrison, G., Amin, S., Singh, S. P., Croudace, T., & Jones, P. (1999). Outcome of psychosis in people of African–Caribbean family origin. Population-based first-episode study. *British Journal of Psychiatry, 175,* 43–49.

Harrison, G. L., Glazebrook, C., Brewin J., Cantwell, R., Dalkin, T., Fox, R., Jones, P., & Medley, I. (1997). Increased incidence of psychotic disorders in migrants from the Caribbean to the United Kingdom. *Psychological Medicine, 27,* 799–806.

Harrison, G., Owens, D., Holton, A., Neilson, D., & Boot, D. (1988). A prospective study of severe mental disorder in African-Caribbean patients. *Psychological Medicine, 18,* 643–657.

Harvey, I., Williams, M., McGuffin, P., & Toone, B. K. (1990). The functional psychoses in African-Caribbeans. *British Journal of Psychiatry, 157,* 515–522.

Hemsi, L. K. (1967). Psychotic morbidity of West Indian immigrants. *Social Psychiatry, 2,* 95–100.

Hickling, F. W., McKenzie, K., Mullen, R., & Murray, R. (1999). A Jamaican psychiatrist evaluates diagnosis at a London psychiatric hospital. *British Journal of Psychiatry, 175,* 283–285.

Hickling, F. W., & Rodgers-Johnson, P. (1995). The incidence of first-contact schizophrenia in Jamaica. *British Journal of Psychiatry, 167,* 193–196.

Hunt, N., Adams, S., Coxhead, N., Sayer, H., Murray, C., & Silverstone, T. (1993). The incidence of mania in two areas in the United Kingdom. *Social Psychiatry and Psychiatric Epidemiology, 28,* 281–284.

Hutchinson, J., Takei, N., Bhugra, D., Fahy, T. A., Gilvarry, C., Mallett, R., Moran, P., Leff, J., & Murray, R.M. (1997). Increased rate of psychosis among African–Caribbeans in Britain is not due to an excess of pregnancy and birth complications. *British Journal of Psychiatry, 171,* 145–147.

Hutchinson, J., Takei, N., Fahy, T. A., Bhugra, D., Gilvarry, C., Moran, P., Mallett, R., Sham, P., Leff, J., & Murray, R.M. (1996). Morbid risk of schizophrenia in first-degree relatives of White and African–Caribbean patients with psychosis. *British Journal of Psychiatry, 169,* 776–780.

Hutchinson, J., Takei, N., Sham, P., Harvey, I., & Murray, R. M. (1999). Factors analysis of symptoms in schizophrenia: Differences between White and Caribbean patients. *Psychological Medicine, 29,* 607–612.

Ineichen, B., Harrison, G., & Morgan, H. G. (1984). Psychiatric admissions in Bristol. I. Geographical and ethnic factors. *British Journal of Psychiatry, 145,* 600–604.

Jablensky, A. (1988). Schizophrenia and environment. In A. S. Henderson & G. D. Burrows (Eds.), *Handbook of social psychiatry.* Amsterdam: Elsevier.

Jablensky, A., Sartorius, N., Ernberg, G., Anker, M., Korten, A., Cooper, J. E., Day, R., & Bertelsen, A. (1992) Schizophrenia: Manifestations, incidence and course in different cultures. A World Health Organization ten-country study [Monograph supplement]. *Psychological Medicine, 20,* 1–97.

Jenkins, R., Lewis, G., Bebbinton, P., Brugha, T., Farrell, M., Gill, B., & Melzer, H. (1997). The National Psychiatric Morbidity Surveys of Great Britain – Initial findings from the household survey. *Psychological Medicine, 27,* 775–789.

Johns, L. C., Nazroo, J. Y., Bebbington, P., & Kuipers, E. (1998). Occurrence of hallucinations in a community sample. *Schizophrenia Research, 29,* 23.

Jones, P., Rodgers, B., & Murray, R. M. (1994). Child developmental risk factors for schizophrenia in the British 1946 cohort. *Lancet, 344,* 1398–1402.

Jones, P. B., & Cannon, M. (1998). The new epidemiology of schizophrenia: Common methods for genetics and the environment. *The Psychiatric Clinics of North America,* 21, 1: 1–25.

Kiev, A. (1965) Psychiatric morbidity of West Indian immigrants in an urban group practice. *British Journal of Psychiatry, 111,* 51–56.

Kinderman, P., & Bentall, R. P. (1996). Self-discrepancies and persecutory delusions: Evidence for a model of paranoid ideation. *Journal of Abnormal Psychology, 105,* 106–113.

Kirkbride, J., Fearon, P., Morgan, C., Dazzan, P., Morgan, K., Tarrant, J., Lloyd, T., Holloway, J., Hutchinson, G., Leff, J., Mallett, R., Harrison, G. L., Murray, R. M., & Jones, P. B., on behalf of the ÆSOP study team. (2005). *Incidence of schizophrenia and other psychotic syndromes from a multi-centre investigation: findings from the ÆSOP study.* Manuscript submitted for publication.

King, M., Coker, E., Leavey, G., Hoare, A., & Johnson-Sabine, E. (1994). Incidence of psychotic illness in London: Comparison of ethnic minority groups. *British Medical Journal, 309,* 1115–1119.

Kirov, G., & Murray, R. M. (1999). Ethnic differences in the presentation of bipolar affective disorder. *European Psychiatry, 14,* 199–204.

Kleinman, A. (1980). *Patients and healers in the context of culture* (pp. 138–145). Berkeley, CA: University of California Press.

Laing, R. D. (1960) *The divided self: An existential study in sanity and madness.* London: Routledge.

Lawson, W. B., Yesavage, J. A., & Werner, P. D. (1984). Race, violence and psychopathology. *Journal of Clinical Psychiatry, 45,* 294–297.

Leff, J. (1988). *Psychiatry around the globe. A transcultural view* (2nd ed.). London: Gaskell.

Leff, J., Fisher, M., & Bertelsen, A. (1976). A cross-national epidemiological study of mania. *British Journal of Psychiatry, 129,* 428–442.

Lewis, G., Croft-Jeffreys, C., & David, A. (1990). Are British psychiatrists racist? *British Journal of Psychiatry, 157,* 410–415.

Lewis, G., David, A., Andreasson, S., & Allebeck, P. (1992). Schizophrenia and city life. *Lancet, 340,* 137–140.

Littlewood, R. (1998). *The butterfly and the serpent: Essays in psychiatry and religion.* New York: Free Association Books.

Littlewood, R., & Lipsedge, M. (1981). Some social and phenomenological characteristics of psychotic immigrants. *Psychological Medicine, 11,* 289–302.

Magaziner, J. (1988). Living density and psychopathology: A re-examination of the negative model. *Psychological Medicine, 18,* 419–431.

Mahy, G. E., Mallett, R., Leff, J., & Bhugra, D. (1999). First-contact incidence-rate of schizophrenia on Barbados. *British Journal of Psychiatry, 175,* 28–33.

Marcellis, M., MacIver, S., & Soomans, A. (1998). Area, class and health: Should we be focusing on places or people? *Journal of Social Policy, 22,* 213–234.

Maughan, B. (1989). Growing up in the inner city. *Paediatric and Perinatal Epidemiology, 3,* 195–215.

McGovern, D., & Cope, R. (1987). First psychotic admission rates of first- and second-generation African–Caribbeans. *Social Psychiatry, 22,* 139–149.

McGovern, D., & Cope, R. (1991). Second-generation African–Caribbeans and young whites with a first-admission diagnosis of schizophrenia. *Social Psychiatry and Psychiatric Epidemiology, 26,* 95–99.

McGovern, D., & Hemmings, P. (1994). A follow-up of second generation African-Caribbeans and White British with a first admission diagnosis of schizophrenia: Attitudes to mental illness and psychiatric services of patients and relatives. *Social Science and Medicine, 38,* 117–128.

McGuire, P. K., Jones, P., Harvey, L., Bebbington, P., Toone, B., Lewis, S., & Murray, R.M. (1994). Cannabis and acute psychosis. *Schizophrenia Research, 13,* 161–168.

McGuire, P. K., Jones, P., Harvey, I., Williams, M., McGuffin, P., & Murray, R. (1995). Morbid risk of schizophrenia for relatives of patients with cannabis-associated psychosis. *Schizophrenia Research, 15,* 277–281.

McKenzie, K. (1999). Moving the misdiagnosis debate forward. *International Review of Psychiatry, 11,* 153–161.

McKenzie, K., Jones P. B., Lewis S. W., Williams, M., Toone, B., Sham, P., & Murray, R. M. (2002). Lower prevalence of pre-morbid neurological illness in African-Caribbean than White psychotic patients in England. *Psychological Medicine 32,* 1285–1291.

McKenzie, K., & Murray, R. M. (1999). Risk factors for psychosis in the UK African–Caribbean population. In D. Bhugra & V. Bahl (Eds.), *Ethnicity: An agenda for mental health* (pp. 48–59). London: Gaskell.

McKenzie, K., van Os, J., Fahy, T. A., Jones, P., Harvey, I., Toone, B., & Murray, R. (1995). Psychosis with good prognosis in African-Caribbean people now living in the United Kingdom. *British Medical Journal, 311,* 1325–1328.

Mednick, S. A., Machon, R. A., Huttenen, M. O., & Bonett, D. (1988). Adult schizophrenia following prenatal exposure to an influenza epidemic. *Archives of General Psychiatry, 47,* 875–876.

Mercer, K. (1986). Racism and transcultural psychiatry. In P. Miller & N. Rose (Eds.), *The Power of Psychiatry.* Cambridge, UK: Polity.

Mortensen, P. B., Cantor-Graae, E., & McNeil, T. F. (1997). Increased rates of schizophrenia among immigrants: some methodological concerns raised by Danish findings. *Psychological Medicine, 27,* 813–820.

Mukherjee, S., Shukla, S., Woodle, J., Rosen, A.M., & Olarte, S. (1983). Misdiagnosis of schizophrenia in bipolar patients: A multiethnic comparison. *American Journal of Psychiatry, 140,* 1571–1572.

Nazroo, J. (1997). *Ethnicity and mental health.* London: Policy Studies Institute.

Nazroo, J. (1998). Rethinking the relationship between ethnicity and mental health: The British Fourth National Survey of Ethnic Minorities. *Social Psychiatry and Psychiatric Epidemiology, 33,* 145–148.

Ndetei, D. M., & Vadher, A. (1985). A comparative cross-cultural study of the frequencies of hallucination in schizophrenia. *Acta Psychiatrica Scandinavica, 70,* 545–549.

Nicoll, A., & Logan, S. (1989). Viral infections of pregnancy in childhood. In J. Cruikshank & D. Beevers (Eds.), *Ethnic factors in health and disease* (pp. 95–102). London: Wright.

O'Callaghan, E., Sham, P., Takei, N., Glover, G., & Murray, R.M. (1991). Schizophrenia after exposure to 1957 A2 influenza epidemic. *Lancet, 337,* 1248–250.

Ødegaard, O. (1932). Emigration and insanity: A study of mental disease among Norwegian-born population in Minnesota. *Acta Psychiatrica et Neurologica Scandinavica, 7*(suppl. 4), 1–206.

Office of Population Censuses & Surveys (OPCS) (1994). *1991 census user guide: Vol. 58. Under-coverage in Great Britain.* United Kingdom: Office of Population Censuses and Surveys.

Parsons, C. (1963). West Indian children with multiple congenital defects. *Archives of Diseases in Childhood, 38,* 454–458.

Putnam, R. D. (1995). Bowling alone. America's declining social capital. *Journal of Democracy, 6,* 65–78.

Rack, P. (1982). *Race, culture and mental disorder* (pp. 101–112). London: Tavistock.

Rathwell, T. (1984). General practice, ethnicity and health service delivery. *Social Science and Medicine, 19,* 123–130.

Reeves, S. J., Saurer, J., Stewart, R., Granger, A., & Howard, R. J. (2001). Increased first-contact rates for very late-onset schizophrenia-like psychosis in African- and Caribbean-born elders. *British Journal of Psychiatry, 179,* 172–174.

Robey, K. L., Cohen, B. D., & Gara, M. A. (1989). Self-structure in schizophrenia. *Journal of Abnormal Psychology, 98,* 436–442.

Rwegellera, G.G. (1977) Psychiatric morbidity among West Africans and West Indians living in London. *Psychological Medicine, 7,* 317–29.

Sashidharan, S. P. (1993). African-Caribbeans and schizophrenia: The ethnic vulnerability hypothesis re-examined. *International Review of Psychiatry, 5*, 129–144.

Schneider, K. (1959). *Clinical psychopathology*. New York: Grune & Stratton.

Selten, J. P., Cantor-Graae E., Slaets, J. P. J., & Kahn, R. S. (2002). Ødegaard's selection hypothesis revisited: Schizophrenia in Surinamese immigrants to The Netherlands. *American Journal of Psychiatry, 159*, 669–671.

Selten, J. P., & Sijben, N. (1994). First admission rates for schizophrenia in immigrants to the Netherlands. The Dutch National Register. *Social Psychiatry and Psychiatric Epidemiology, 29*, 71–77.

Selten, J. P., Slaets, J. P. J., & Kahn, R. S. (1997). Schizophrenia in Surinamese and Dutch Antillean immigrants to The Netherlands: Evidence of an increased incidence. *Psychological Medicine, 27*, 807–811.

Selten, J. P., Veen, N. N., Feller, W., Blom, J. D., Schols, D., Camoenie, W., Oolders, J., van der Velden, M., Hoek, H. W., Rivero, V. M., van der Graaf, Y., & Kahn, R. (2001). Incidence of psychotic disorders in immigrant groups to The Netherlands. *British Journal of Psychiatry, 178*, 367–372.

Sharpley, M. S., & Peters, E. (1999). Ethnicity, class and schizotypy. *Social Psychiatry and Psychiatric Epidemiology, 34*, 507–512.

Sharpley, M., Hutchinson, G., McKenzie, K., & Murray, R. M. (2001). Understanding the excess of psychosis among the African-Caribbean population in England. Review of current hypotheses. *British Journal of Psychiatry* (Suppl. 40), 60–68.

Shaw, C. M., Creed, F., Tomenson, B., Riste, L., & Cruickshank, J. K. (1999). Prevalence of anxiety and depressive illness and help seeking behaviour in African-Caribbeans and white Europeans: two phase general population survey. *British Medical Journal, 318*, 302–306.

Sugarman, P. A. (1992). Outcome of schizophrenia in the African-Caribbean community. *Social Psychiatry and Psychiatric Epidemiology, 27*, 102–105.

Sugarman, P. A., & Craufurd, D. (1994). Schizophrenia in the African-Caribbean community. *British Journal of Psychiatry, 164*, 474–480.

Szasz, T. S. (1961) *The myth of mental illness: Foundations of a theory of personal conduct*. St Albans: Paladin.

Takei, N., O'Callaghan, E., & Sham, P. (1992). Winter-birth excess in schizophrenia: Its relationship to place of birth. *Schizophrenia Research, 6*(Special issue), 102.

Takei, N., Persaud, R., Woodruff, P., Brockington, I., Murray, R. M. (1998). First episodes of psychosis in African-Caribbean and White people. An 18-year follow-up population-based study. *British Journal of Psychiatry, 172*, 147–153.

Thakker, J., & Ward, T. (1998). Culture and classification: The cross-cultural application of DSM-IV. *Clinical Psychology Review, 18*, 501–529.

Thomas, C. S., Stone, K., Osborn, M., Thomas, P. F., & Fisher, M. (1993). Psychiatric morbidity and compulsory admission among UK-born Europeans, African-Caribbeans and Asians in central Manchester. *British Journal of Psychiatry, 163*, 91–99.

Thornicroft, G. (1990). Cannabis and psychosis. Is there epidemiological evidence for association? *British Journal of Psychiatry, 157*, 25–33.

Torrey, E. F., & Bowler, A. (1991). Geographical distribution of insanity in America: Evidence for an urban factor. *Schizophrenia Bulletin, 16*, 591–604.

Tyrer, S. P. (1982). Mania: Diagnosis and treatment. *British Journal of Hospital Medicine, 28,* 67–73.

van Os, J., Bak, M., Hanssen, M., Bijl, R.V., de Graaf, R., & Verdoux, H. (2002). Cannabis use and psychosis: A longitudinal population-based study. *American Journal of Epidemiology, 156,* 319–327.

van Os, J., Castle, D. J., Takei, N., Der, G., & Murray, R. M. (1996). Psychotic illness in ethnic minorities: clarification from the 1991 Census. *Psychological Medicine, 26,* 203–208.

van Os, J., Takei, N., Castle, D. J., Wesseley, S., Der, G., MacDonald, A. M., & Murray, R. M. (1996). The incidence of mania: Time trends in relation to gender and ethnicity. *Social Psychiatry and Psychiatric Epidemiology, 31,* 129–136.

Wessely, S., Castle, D., Der, G., & Murray, R. M. (1991). Schizophrenia and African-Caribbeans. A case-control study. *British Journal of Psychiatry, 159,* 795–801.

Wing, J. K. (1979). Mentally retarded children in Camberwell, London. In H. Hafner (Ed.), *Estimating needs for mental health care* (pp. 77–91). New York: Springer.

Wing, J. K. (1989). The concept of negative symptoms. *British Journal of Psychiatry, 155*(Suppl. 7), 10–14.

World Health Organization. (1992). *The ICD-10 classification of mental and behavioural disorders: Clinical descriptions and diagnostic guidelines.* Geneva: WHO.

Zammit, S., Allebeck, P., Andreasson, S., Lundberg, I., & Lewis, G. (2002). Self reported cannabis use as a risk factor for schizophrenia in Swedish conscripts of 1969: Historical cohort study. *British Medical Journal, 23; 325* (7374), 1199.

Zigler, E., & Glick, M. (1988). Is paranoid schizophrenia really camouflaged depression? *American Psychologist, 43,* 284–290.

Zolkowska, K., Cantor-Graae, E., & McNeil, T. F. (2001). Increased rates of psychosis amongst immigrants to Sweden: Is migration a risk factor for psychosis? *Psychological Medicine, 31,* 669–678.

Ethnic Variations in Youth Suicide

Jewelle Taylor Gibbs

Suicide is the third leading cause of death among American youth in the 15 to 24 age group. While the overall youth suicide rate has nearly doubled since 1960, the rate for African American youth has tripled, yet is still lower than the rate for non-Hispanic Whites (Centers for Disease Control, 2001). However, with the exception of Native American youth, the rates for other ethnic minority youth have remained fairly stable over the past 4 decades, and Black youth are still less likely than White youth to commit suicide or engage in suicidal behavior.

An examination of youth suicide rates in the United States reveals a curious paradox: Since 1960 African American youth, both males and females, have consistently recorded lower rates than White youth despite their relatively greater exposure to multiple risk factors and behaviors that are associated with youth suicide (Dryfoos, 1990; Garland & Zigler, 1993). Although the gap in suicide rates between White and non-White males has narrowed since the mid-1980s, the differences persist in the face of continuing racial discrimination, family poverty, and exposure to stressful environments that disproportionately affect the health and mental health of youth of color (see Gibbs & Huang, 2003; U.S. Department of Health and Human Services, 2001).

The purpose of this chapter is to examine this seeming paradox of lower suicide rates among Black youth in a society in which they are economically and socially disadvantaged and lack access to affordable health care. The goals are (1) to summarize the current epidemiological data and clinical studies of youth suicide in the United States; (2) to summarize what is known about the risk and protective factors associated with adolescent suicidal behavior; and (3) to consider ethnic variations in these factors in order to examine possible mediating mechanisms for the ethnic differences in youth suicide. This paper focuses primarily on a comparison of suicidal behaviors among Whites, African Americans, and Hispanics, because there is an adequate research literature about them. Data about Asian American

TABLE 10.1a. *Suicide Rates per 100,000 According to Ethnicity and Age,*
1960–1999: Males (Centers for Disease Control, 2001)

	1960	1970	1980	1990	1995	1999
White Male (Non-Hispanic)						
15–24 yrs.	8.6	13.9	21.4	24.4	23.8	18.8
25–44 yrs.	18.5	21.5	24.6	26.4	27.3	25.4
45–64 yrs.	36.5	31.9	25.0	6.8	24.8	23.8
65 and over yrs.	46.7	41.1	37.2	45.4	39.2	35.3
Black Male						
15–24 yrs.	4.1	10.5	12.3	15.1	18.0	14.4
25–44 yrs.	12.6	16.1	19.2	19.6	18.6	15.4
45–64 yrs.	13.0	12.4	11.8	13.1	11.8	10.1
65 and over yrs.	9.9	8.7	11.4	14.9	14.3	13.1
Hispanic Male[a]						
15–24 yrs.	–	–	–	14.7	18.3	11.9
25–44 yrs.	–	–	–	16.2	15.5	13.1
45–64 yrs.	–	–	–	16.1	14.2	11.9
65 and over yrs.	–	–	–	23.4	19.9	17.4

[a] Suicide statistics were not recorded separately for persons of Hispanic descent before the Census of 1990. Prior to that, Hispanics were included with Whites.

and Native American youth are noted briefly when appropriate data could be located.

Adolescent Suicide Behaviors, Rates, and Trends

In 1999, the overall suicide rate among youth ages 15–24 was 10.3 per 100,000 (Centers for Disease Control, 2001). However, the rates varied widely by age, sex, and ethnicity (see Tables 10.1a and 10.1b). First, in all groups, suicide is a much more common occurrence in males than females. However, other data have been consistent in showing that attempted suicide is more common in females (Diekstra, Kienhorst, & deWilde, 1995; Shaffer & Gutstein, 2000).

Second, in the 15 to 24 age group of males, the youth suicide rate was highest in non-Hispanic Whites (18.8 per 100,000), next highest in Blacks (14.4), and lowest in Hispanics (11.9). In females, again the highest rate was in non-Hispanic Whites (3.2), with the rate in Blacks and Hispanics both lower at 2.0. Suicide rates of American Indians are extremely high, but questions have been raised about the validity and reliability of these statistics, which vary widely among tribal groups and are skewed by a small population base-rate (LaFromboise & Dizon, 2003). Similarly, overall suicide rates (7.3 per 100,000) among Asian American youth, 15–24, are generally lower than rates for the other three ethnic groups, but these

TABLE 10.1b. *Suicide Rates per 100,000 According to Ethnicity and Age,*
1960–1999: Female (Centers for Disease Control, 2001)

	1960	1970	1980	1990	1995	1999
White Female (Non-Hispanic)						
15–24 yrs.	2.3	4.2	4.6	4.2	3.9	3.2
25–44 yrs.	7.0	11.0	8.1	6.6	6.3	6.3
45–64 yrs.	10.9	13.0	9.6	7.7	6.7	6.8
65 and over yrs.	8.8	8.5	6.4	6.8	5.7	4.6
Black Female						
15–24 yrs.	*	3.8	2.3	2.3	2.2	2.0
25–44 yrs.	3.0	4.8	4.3	3.8	3.4	2.5
45–64 yrs.	3.1	2.9	2.5	2.9	2.0	1.8
65 and over yrs.	*	2.6	*	1.9	2.2	1.5
Hispanic Female[b]						
15–24 yrs.	–	–	–	3.1	2.6	2.0
25–44 yrs.	–	–	–	3.1	2.7	2.5
45–64 yrs.	–	–	–	2.5	2.7	2.5
65 and over yrs.	–	–	–	*	*	2.2

* Fewer than 20 deaths in that year in this group.
[b] Suicide statistics were not recorded separately for persons of Hispanic descent before the Census of 1990. Prior to that, Hispanics were included with Whites.

rates mask the underlying variations within the Asian and Pacific Islander subgroups. However, young Asian American females had higher suicide rates than all other minority females.

Third, the peak age for suicide varies by ethnicity, with the rate highest in young people among Blacks and Hispanics, whereas in non-Hispanic Whites the highest rates occur in old age in males and late middle age in females, suggesting that the most stressful periods in the life cycle may be different for Whites and for ethnic minorities (Gibbs, 1988). However, it should be noted that, whereas the rates of suicide in older people have been falling over time in non-Hispanic Whites, they have risen in Blacks. The data on Hispanics are available for too short a time period for reliable conclusions about temporal changes.

Risk Factors for Suicide

Risk and protective factors for suicide need to be conceptualized under several different headings. First, numerous studies have shown that individuals who experience suicidal ideas or who make suicidal attempts have a much greater likelihood of dying later from suicide (Shaffer & Gutstein, 2002). About 40 percent of suicides have made a previous known suicide attempt. Nevertheless, some caution is needed when making links between suicidal attempts and completed suicide, not only because the former are much more frequent (that is, that many people who attempt suicide do not die from suicide), but because the epidemiological associations are so different. Thus, attempted suicide is much more common in females, whereas suicide is much more frequent in males. Moreover, in most White populations, suicide continues to rise in incidence with increasing age, whereas that is not the case for attempted suicide, which is predominantly a feature of late adolescence and early adult life.

Second, major depressive disorder is associated with a greatly increased risk of suicide compared with the general population – as shown both by follow-up studies of youths with depression and by psychological autopsy studies of young people who commit suicide (Shaffer & Gutstein, 2002). However, conduct disorders are also associated with a much increased suicidal risk. In part, this probably arises because conduct disorders are accompanied by an increased predisposition to depression and in part by a likelihood of behaving in an impulsive fashion and of using drugs that reduce inhibitions.

Third, suicide is associated with both chronic psychosocial adversities, as indexed by features such as poor parent–child communication, family conflict, or physical/sexual abuse, and acute stressors, such as disciplinary crisis, examination failure, or rejection by friends or a family quarrel (Garland & Zigler, 1993; Shaffer, Garland, Gould, Fisher, & Trautman, 1988; Shaffer & Gutstein, 2002).

These first three sets of features are all concerned in one way or another with a liability to experience mental states that include feelings of despair or a wish to die, or styles of risk-taking behavior that could lead to life-threatening acts when suffering from suicidal thoughts. In addition, it is necessary to consider nonpsychological factors that increase the probability either that there will be suicidal acts or that they will result in death. Thus, alcoholic intoxication reduces inhibitions, and the availability of potentially lethal drugs or of firearms provides the means to bring about death.

Finally, there are protective factors that serve to counter risk mechanisms (Garland & Zigler, 1993; Shaffer et al., 1988). Those that have been most prominent in discussions of suicide are family support (presumably because it fosters successful coping) and religiosity (because it provides inhibitions against using suicide as a means of response to despair and hopelessness). High self-esteem and a strong sense of self-competence also appear to be protective. In all three cases, however, the evidence that they do serve this role is not strong.

In considering possible mediating mechanisms for the ethnic differences in suicide rates, it is necessary to determine whether the differences stem from ethnic variations in the exposure to risk factors, or in the availability of protective factors, or the pattern of responses to either.

Suicidal Ideation

Several large-scale surveys, including the Youth Risk Behavior Survey of 13,601 high school students (Centers for Disease Control, 2002), the National Longitudinal Study of Adolescent Health as studied in 10,803 youth (Blum et al., 2000) and the Commonwealth Fund (1997) survey of 3,586 adolescent females have all found that Black youths were less likely than either Whites or Hispanics to report either suicidal ideation or suicidal attempts. Accordingly, the relatively low rate of suicide in Blacks is in line with the findings on suicidal ideation; the need is to account for both, rather than the translation of suicidal thoughts into lethal acts. The findings for Hispanics, by contrast, were different. Their rates of suicidal ideation were generally comparable to those of Whites and were above those for Blacks, despite the evidence that their suicide rates were low (see Tables 10.1a and 10.1b). For Hispanics, therefore, it is necessary to consider why suicidal ideation is less likely to result in lethal suicidal acts.

Depression

The findings for depressive symptomology tend to follow the same general pattern (Kleykamp & Tienda, in press; Roberts, Roberts, & Chen, 1997; Roberts & Sobhan, 1992; Siegel, Aneshensel, Taub, Cantwell, & Driscoll, 1998; Stiffman, Cheuh, & Earls, 1992). That is to say, depression is less frequently reported by Black youth than by Whites or Hispanics, whereas the rate in Hispanics is generally the highest of the three main ethnic groups. Most of the evidence derives from questionnaire responses, raising the possibility that the ethnic variations reflect reporting tendencies rather than clinically significant disorders. It is necessary to turn to the findings from large-scale surveys in which the number and pattern of depressive features are used to diagnose disorders (Kessler, Borges, & Walters, 1999; Weissman, Bruce, Leaf, Florio, & Holzer, 1991). They concern adults rather than young people, but they are informative in showing a broadly similar picture to that provided by questionnaires. The rates of depressive disorders tend to be unusually low in Blacks but on the high side in Hispanics. Thus, in the Epidemiologic Catchment Area (ECA) (Weissman et al., 1991) study, the lifetime prevalence of affective disorders in males was 3.4 percent in Blacks, 5.2 percent in Whites, and 6.1 percent in Hispanics. The comparable figures for females were 8.7 percent, 10.5 percent, and 9.5 percent, respectively. Combining the ECA data with the Hispanic Health and Nutrition Epidemiologic Survey data, Oquendo et al. (2001) showed that, compared with non-Hispanic Whites, Puerto Ricans and Mexican Americans of both sexes and Cuban American females (but not males) had a particularly low suicide rate relative to their rate of major depression. The finding suggests that the main issue with

Black youths is why their rate of depression is low, as much as why their rate of suicide is low. On the other hand, the issue with Hispanic youths is why their relatively high rate of depression does not result in a correspondingly high rate of suicide.

Before drawing that conclusion, however, it is necessary to ask whether the association between depression and suicide found in numerous studies of Whites applies in the same way in Blacks and Hispanics. The evidence on this point is rather limited but several small-scale studies of selected groups have suggested that the associations may be weaker in Blacks than Whites (Kempton & Forehand, 1992; King, Raskin, Gdowski, Butkus, & Opipari, 1990; Rotheram-Borus & Trautman, 1988; Summerville, Abbate, Siegel, Serravezza, & Kaslow, 1992), although probably generally similar between Hispanics and Whites (Dembo, 1988; Hovey & King, 1996; Walter et al., 1995). Possibly, too, White youth are more likely than Blacks to report suicidal ideation as a precursor to suicidal behavior (Lester & Anderson, 1992; Molock et al., 1994). If the tentative evidence that suicidal ideation and depression are weaker predictors of suicide in Blacks than Whites and Hispanics is accepted, that opens up the question of what does predict suicide in Blacks (Gibbs, 1997).

Conduct Disturbance and Antisocial Behavior

One possibility concerns antisocial behavior. There is extensive evidence from national statistics that the rate of crime in African Americans is much higher than in Whites. Questions need to be raised about the validity of these statistics in view of the evidence that there is racial bias in both policing practice and the operation of the youth justice system (see Morenoff, this volume; also Smith, this volume). Nevertheless, although the majority of young Blacks are law-abiding, it is evident that a disproportionate number become embroiled in some form of crime. As already noted, conduct disorder constitutes an important risk factor for suicide. It is necessary to recognize, however, that the suicidal risk is associated with conduct disturbance (i.e., a broader pattern of socially maladaptive behavior) rather than with crime per se. In adults, the Epidemiologic Catchment Area (ECA) study showed that, although crime was more frequent in Blacks, antisocial personality disorder was not particularly increased in Blacks relative to Whites (Robins, Tipp, & Przybeck, 1991). The evidence with respect to young people is decidedly limited, but a similar difference may apply. It is also possibly relevant that Black and Hispanic youth tend to express fewer reservations than Whites about antisocial behavior (Dembo, 1988; Organista, 2003). Insofar as that is a solid observation, it suggests that antisocial activities in Blacks and Hispanics may be less likely to be associated with general social malfunction than is the case with Whites, as Dembo (1988) found in his study of a multiracial sample of juvenile detainees in

Florida. If that were to be the case, the association with suicidal risk might be expected to be lower in Blacks and Hispanics. Unfortunately, there seems to be a lack of good evidence on whether or not that is so.

The starting point with respect to antisocial behavior is that the relatively high rate in Blacks and Hispanics would seem to lead to the paradoxical expectation that the rate of suicide should be similarly raised, whereas clearly it is not. The dilemma is that the crucial piece of missing information concerns the extent to which there are ethnic variations in the social malfunction associated with crime. The findings on antisocial behavior are of no help in suggesting a mediating mechanism for the low rate of suicide in Blacks and Hispanics but they may not be quite as paradoxical as they seem to be at first sight. Clearly, the topic warrants further study.

Substance Use

National surveys have consistently shown ethnic differences in drug and alcohol use, with the highest rates of overall substance use reported by Native American, White, and Hispanic youth, and the lowest rates in Black and Asian youth – apart from marijuana use in Blacks (Blum et al., 2000; Centers for Disease Control, 2002; Commonwealth Fund, 1997; Wallace & Bachman, 1991). White and Hispanic youth also tend to initiate substance use at an earlier age than Blacks (Dembo, 1988; Wallace & Muroff, 2002). They are also more likely than Blacks to express favorable attitudes to substance use, to enjoy "getting high" at parties, and less likely to perceive negative consequences of substance use (Hawkins, Catalano & Miller, 1992; Wallace & Muroff, 2002). The lower rate of alcohol and drug use in Blacks, and the accompanying likely lower rate of disinhibition, may provide a possible partial explanation for the low rate of suicide. However, that could not account for the lower rate of suicide in Hispanics.

School Failure

Young people committing suicide may tend to have lower than average levels of scholastic attainment, and exam failure or school disapproval or poor performance are apparent fairly common precipitants of suicidal acts (Brent, Baugher, Bridge, Chen, & Chiapetta, 1999; Garland & Zigler, 1993; Gould, Fisher, Parides, Flory, & Shaffer, 1996; Kessler et al., 1999; Shaffer & Gutstein, 2002; Walter et al., 1995). Accordingly, the educational performance of Blacks and Hispanics relative to Whites could be a relevant feature with respect to ethnic variations in suicide. The available evidence shows that, on average, both African Americans and Hispanics tend to be less successful academically than Whites, and especially than Asians (see Hirschman & Lee, this volume; Tienda, this volume). The reasons for these variations remain ill understood (see also Maughan, this volume), but their existence does not help in accounting for the suicide rate findings. The somewhat lower rate (on average) of educational performance in Black and Hispanic youth would argue for a higher rate of suicide in these ethnic groups, but that is the opposite of what is found.

However, in that connection, it would be crucial to know whether poor academic performance is as strong a risk factor for suicide in Blacks and Hispanics as it is in Whites. Good data on that point are limited, but it has been suggested that poor school performance constitutes less of a risk for suicide in Black youth than in White or Hispanic youth (Dembo, 1988; Dornbusch, Mont-Reynard, Ritter, Chen, & Steinberg, 1991; Vega, Zimmerman, Warheit, Aposproi, & Gil, 1993). Also, Gould et al. (1996) found that failing a grade at school was a risk factor only in non-Hispanic Whites, and not in either Blacks or Hispanics. Possibly, Black and Hispanic youth are more likely than Whites to develop negative attitudes to educational achievement (Organista, 2003) and therefore less likely to become despairing over poor academic performance.

Sexual Intercourse

Although several studies report that an early initiation into sexual intercourse is associated with suicidal behavior (Blum et al., 2000; King et al., 2001; Walter et al., 1995), the mediating mechanisms remain uncertain. In part, this association probably reflects the timing of pubertal maturation, with the suicidal risk greater for physically mature youth. In part, however, the association may index the stresses associated with sexual activity (in terms of decision-making, unwanted pregnancies, teenage parenthood, or broken love relationships). Be that as it may, the finding that Blacks have an earlier initiation into sexual activities than Whites and Hispanics (Blum et al., 2000) would seem to suggest a higher suicide risk – the opposite of what is found.

Again, it would be important to know if attitudes toward sexuality differed among ethnic groups, but few data on this point are available. One study (Cooper, Pierce, & Huselid, 1994) found that the risks for problem behavior associated with drug taking and sexual intercourse were greater in Whites than Blacks, but the specific effects on suicide risk were not explicitly examined.

Family Adversities

A large literature attests to the statistical associations between family adversities and stresses and suicide risk (Shaffer & Gutstein, 2002). It is not at all clear whether such adversities are more common in some ethnic groups than in others. Research has focused on more easily measured features such as being reared in a single-parent family. That is a more common experience for African Americans than for European Americans or Hispanics (see Morenoff, this volume). However, being reared in a single-parent home is unlikely to serve as a direct risk factor for suicide (or for other outcomes). The question concerns the extent to which family structure indexes other family adversities and, especially, whether this varies by ethnic group. Good data on this point are lacking. However, there is some (albeit inconsistent) evidence that single parenthood is less of a risk factor for problem behavior in Black youth than in Whites (Blum et al., 2000; Wallace & Bachman, 1991). Whether or not that is the case with respect to suicide risk is not known.

Poverty, Social Disadvantage, and Neighborhood Adversity

Psychosocial disadvantage has been found to be a distal risk factor for a wide range of problem behaviors in young people; however, the association with suicide is weak and inconsistent. Because it is clearly evident that both Blacks and Hispanics are more likely than Whites to experience such disadvantage at both a family and neighborhood level, it might be supposed that this would be associated with a high level of suicide, but what has to be explained is the opposite – an unusually low rate. However, Gould et al. (1996) found that African American suicide victims had a significantly *higher* socioeconomic status than their matched controls, so social disadvantage may not be a relevant mediator of suicidal risk. Quite apart from the stress and adversity aspects of psychosocial disadvantage, suicide risks might be expected to be increased as a result of the greater exposure to substance abuse, to drugs, and to violence in socially disorganized inner city ghettos (Centers for Disease Control, 1998; Hammond & Yung, 1993). So why is the suicide rate unexpectedly low?

Some investigators have suggested that the effects of adverse neighborhoods may be less for Black youth because strong local institutions, adequate social resources, and family support mitigate negative effects (Furstenburg, 1993; Williams et al., 2002) or because they perceive neighborhood quality more positively (Seidman, 1991; Stiffman, Hadley-Ives, Elze, Johnson, & Dore, 1999). However, Wallace and Muroff (2002) found that Black youth were more likely than Whites to express dissatisfaction with the areas in which they lived. Moreover, the Chicago study (see Morenoff, this volume) suggested that neighborhood disadvantage constitutes the main mediating variable for the higher rate of antisocial behavior in African Americans. In any case, there is a lack of evidence that Blacks living in adverse neighborhoods have more social resources and family support than Whites living in the same area. Others have suggested that the ability to purchase inexpensive guns, together with the severe deterioration of inner-city ghettos, has contributed to the rising rates of gun-related crime, homicide, and suicide among ethnic minority youth (Centers for Disease Control, 1998; Gibbs, 1988; Hammond & Yung, 1993). However, that runs counter to the finding of the *lower* rate of suicide in both Blacks and Hispanics; it also does not explain the apparent rise in suicide among middle-class Black youth for whom economic disadvantage is not an issue (Centers for Disease Control, 1998; Gould, et al., 1996).

Family Support and Parental Supervision

Parental supervision may be protective against antisocial behavior in African American youth (Spencer & Dornbusch, 1990; Taylor, Seaton, & Rodriguez, 2002), and it might similarly protect against suicide. Authoritarian child-rearing practices are associated with fewer problem behaviors in Black youth, suggesting that firm discipline and structured rules in urban low-income environments may serve a protective function (McCabe, Clark, & Barnett, 1999; Taylor et al., 2002). It is noteworthy that physical punishment in African American families does not have the risk effect generally found in White families (see Deater-Deckard et al., this volume). Nevertheless, firm discipline and good supervision are not obvious mediators for the ethnic differences in suicide – both because there is a lack of evidence on any association with suicide, and because they are being suggested as protective in relation to both antisocial behavior (for which the rate is high in African Americans) and suicide (for which the rate is low).

Possibly, kinship support could serve to mitigate the effects of poverty and racial discrimination (McCabe et al., 1999; Nettles & Pleck, 1994). It has been argued that the active support of an extended kin network is more characteristic of the cultural pattern in Blacks and Hispanics than in Whites for whom the modal pattern is that of the nuclear family (Billingsley, 1992; Garcia-Preto, 1996). In line with that suggestion is the evidence of the important role of grandparents in African American families (Burton, Dilworth-Anderson, & Merriwether-deVries, 1995). However, we lack good quantitative evidence on ethnic variations in the extent and nature of support from an extended kinship, and on the associations between support and rate of suicide.

Religiosity

Much the same applies to the alleged protective role of religiosity. There is evidence that a high level of church involvement or a high level of expression of religious commitment is associated with a reduced likelihood of using cigarettes or marijuana (Wallace & Muroff, 2002), of antisocial behavior (Wallace & Bachman, 1991; Zimmerman, Ramirez-Valles, Zapert, & Maton, 2000), and poor school performance (Williams, Davis, Cribbs, Saunders, & Williams, 2002). Various aspects of religiosity have been initially linked to lower suicide rates in minority youth, but empirical evidence of a direct link is lacking. Cultural values and traditional attitudes against suicide in the African American community are often cited as deterrents to suicide in Black youth (Early, 1992; Stack, 1998; Weddle & McKenry, 1995), as they have been, too, in Hispanic youth (Garcia-Preto, 1996; Hovey & King, 1996; Organista, 2003). The suggestion is plausible; there is some evidence that religiosity is somewhat protective against suicide in all ethnic groups, but adequate testing of its protective role and its postulated mediation of ethnic variations in suicide remains to be undertaken (Nettles & Pleck, 1994; Wallace & Bachman, 1991).

Self-Esteem and Effective Coping

Since the 1970s, many studies have found that self-esteem tends to be at a higher level in African American youths than in Whites and Hispanics, after controlling for socioeconomic status (Commonwealth Fund, 1997; Rosenberg & Simmons, 1972; Rotherham-Borus, 1989). However, findings vary by the domain of self-esteem. Black and Hispanic youth score lower on esteem in relation to academic prowess, but equal or higher on social skills and athletic ability (Martinez & Duke, 1987; Turner & Turner, 1983) – to some extent mirroring their actual performance. On the whole, African American girls report higher self-esteem than Whites and Hispanics, who do not differ greatly (Gibbs, 1985; Kleykamp & Tienda, in press; Martinez & Duke, 1987). Global self-esteem tends to diminish in preadolescence, but this may not be the case in Black girls (Brown & Gilligan, 1992; Robinson & Ward, 1991).

It seems reasonable to suppose that self-esteem should be linked with antisocial behavior, substance abuse, and suicide (Harter, 1990), but the direction of association remains uncertain, and the protective effect of high self-esteem has still to be established. Moreover, there is some indication that the effects found in Whites may not apply to Blacks and Hispanics (Leung & Drasgow, 1986). Some researchers have connected strong ethnic identity with high self-esteem (Chavira & Phinney, 1991; Parham & Helms, 1985; Phinney, 1990), and Whaley (1993) has suggested that cultural identity may be more important than self-esteem for good psychological functioning. However, for the most part, causal hypotheses have yet to be put to the test in rigorous fashion. Also, it remains to be explained why supposedly similar features in Blacks and Hispanics should lead to similar outcomes with respect to suicide but different outcomes with respect to depression and suicidal ideation.

Acculturative stress (meaning the stresses accompanying the processes by which immigrants adopt the values of the dominant host culture – Alvarez & Ruiz, 2001) has been proposed as a risk factor in Hispanic youths (Berlitz & Valdez, 1997; Chavez, Randall, & Swain, 1992; Hovey &

King, 1996; Swanson, Linskey, Quintero-Salinas, Pumariega, & Holzer, 1992). That may well be the case, but this does not seem to explain why Hispanics have a high rate of depression and suicidal ideation but a low rate of suicide.

Similar issues apply to suggestions that Black youths exercise superior coping strategies (Dembo, 1988; Dornbusch et al., 1991; Vega et al., 1993). There appear to be differences between Black boys and Black girls in the efficacy of particular coping strategies (Grant et al., 2000). Also, it remains unclear why coping should be effective in relation to suicide but not to low scholastic achievement or antisocial behavior, although Dornbusch and his colleagues (1991) suggested that Blacks may have adapted to high levels of stress by externalizing rather than internalizing it, thus explaining the apparent inconsistency.

Conclusions

This review of risk and protective factors as they might be relevant to ethnic variations in suicide has raised more questions than answers. The starting point seems solid enough – namely, the low rate of suicide in African Americans and Hispanics as compared with Whites. However, in addition to the low rate of suicide, it is necessary to account for the narrowing of the ethnic difference over time (at least with respect to Blacks and non-Hispanic Whites) and the quite different age profile (with the rising incidence of suicide in Whites but not in Blacks and Hispanics). The background to the low rate of suicide in Blacks and Hispanics also differs strikingly. The rate of suicidal ideation and of depression is low in Blacks but high in Hispanics. Accordingly, the main challenge with Blacks is to account for an overall low rate of depression and suicidal ideation, whereas the challenge with Hispanics is to explain why depression and suicidal ideation are less likely to lead on to suicide than is the case with Whites.

The next issue is whether the risk factors for suicide are indeed high in Blacks and Hispanics; in other words, is there any reason to expect a high rate of suicide? With respect to psychosocial risk factors, the available evidence suggests that poverty and social disadvantage per se are *not* important risk factors for suicide, although they are for other adverse psychological outcomes. The pervasiveness of racial discrimination is real enough, but it has not been a major factor in studies of the precipitants of suicide. The better-documented precipitants include acute stresses such as disciplinary episodes, personal humiliation or failure, or social rejection. It might well be that these are more common in Blacks and Hispanics, but evidence is lacking on whether or not that is actually the case. Early-onset sexual intercourse is statistically associated with suicide risk, but the mechanisms remain ill understood, and it may well be that there is not the same risk effect in African Americans.

Although most people who experience suicidal thoughts or who attempt suicide do not die from suicide – probably at least 90 percent do not do so – some two fifths of completed suicides have been preceded by suicide attempts, and suicide attempts constitute a major risk factor. Similarly, the vast majority of suicidal victims have suffered from some overt mental disorder, of which depression and conduct disorder are the most common. In these respects, Hispanics would be expected to have a high rate of suicide, but they do not. Personal psychological factors (such as religious conviction and strong ethnic identity), together with cultural features (such as kinship support, suicide taboos, and community cohesion), constitute plausible protective factors, but there is only weak empirical evidence that they actually serve this role. Although these features could play a role in the low suicide rate of African Americans, it is less plausible that they do so because the evidence that they protect against depression is weaker.

A low rate of alcohol and substance use (apart from marijuana) could be protective against both depression and suicide in African Americans (but not Hispanics). Although depression has been proposed as a mechanism mediating substance use (because of self-medication effects), the empirical evidence suggests that the main causal arrow runs in the opposite direction; high rates of alcohol and substance use predispose to depression (see Rutter, 2002).

The conclusions appear to be that, although the risk factors for suicide may not be as high in Blacks and Hispanics as usually presumed, the levels would not seem to predict an unusually low rate of suicide. Accordingly, there is a paradox to be explained (Gibbs, 1997). The answer could lie in ethnic variations in the meaning of risk factors or the presence of important protective factors, but which it is remains uncertain. In this chapter, the main focus has been on psychological and sociocultural risk and protective factors, but the possibility remains that the answer lies in protective genetic/biological factors (see Rutter & Tienda, this volume). The existence of such factors has been well demonstrated (Shaffer & Gutstein, 2002), but whether their prevalence differs among ethnic groups is not known.

The findings point to the clear recommendation that the issue of ethnic variations in suicide rates warrants much more study than it has received up to now. Quite apart from the value of such research in elucidating the reasons for ethnic differences in suicide, the findings are likely to be more broadly informative on the risk and protective factors for suicide in young people more generally. Both quantitative and qualitative research is needed, adequate-sized representative samples will be essential, proper attention will need to be paid to the varied meanings of ethnicity, both within-group and between-group differences will have to be studied, and research strategies will have to be devised to test competing hypotheses on mediating mechanisms. This will often require prospective longitudinal samples, combined with the choice of "natural experiments" that pull apart variables that ordinarily go together (see Rutter, this volume).

As ethnic minorities continue to increase in the United States, comprising more than one third of the youth population, there is a demographic imperative for researchers to design studies that incorporate culturally appropriate measures, ethnically diverse samples, and data analytic strategies that recognize the complexity of the multiple meanings of ethnicity, of the interplay between risk and protective mechanisms, and of the importance of social context in predisposing to particular outcomes.

Advances in research on adolescent suicide are critically needed to provide a greater understanding of this tragic phenomenon, to design effective prevention and early intervention programs, and to influence public policy initiatives promoting healthy child and adolescent development.

References

Alvarez, L. R., & Ruiz, P. (2001). Substance abuse in the Mexican-American population. In S. L. Straussner (Ed.), *Ethnocultural factors in substance abuse treatment* (pp. 111–136). New York: The Guilford Press.

Berlitz, J., & Valdez, D. (1997). A sociocultural context for understanding gang involvement among Mexican-American male youth. In J. G. Garcia and M. C. Zea (Eds.), *Psychological interventions and research with Latino populations* (pp. 56–72). Boston: Allyn and Bacon.

Billingsley, A. (1992). *Climbing Jacob's ladder: The enduring legacy of African American families.* New York: Simon & Schuster.

Blum, R. W., Beahring, T., Shaw, M. L., Bearinger, L. H., Sieving, R. E., & Resnick, M. D. (2000). The effects of race/ethnicity, income, and family structure on adolescent risk behaviors. *American Journal of Public Health, 90,* 1879–1884.

Brent, D. A., Baugher, M., Bridge, J., Chen, T., & Chiapetta, L. (1999). Age- and sex-related risk factors for adolescent suicide. *Journal of the American Academy of Child and Adolescent Psychiatry, 38,* 1497–1505.

Brown, L. M., & Gilligan, C. (1992). *Meeting at the crossroads: Women's psychology and girls' development.* Cambridge, MA: Harvard University Press.

Burton, L. M., Dilworth-Anderson, P., & Merriwether-deVries, C. (1995). Context and surrogate parenting among contemporary grandparents. *Marriage & Family Review, 20,* 349–366.

Centers for Disease Control. (1998). Suicide among Black youth: United States, 1980–1995. *Morbidity and Mortality Weekly Report, 47,* 193–206. Rockville, MD: National Center for Health Statistics.

Centers for Disease Control. (2001). Deaths: Leading causes for 1999. *National Vital Statistics Report, 49*(11), Oct. 12. Rockville, MD: National Center for Health Statistics.

Centers for Disease Control. (2002). Youth risk behavior surveillance – United States, 2001. *Morbidity and Mortality Weekly Report, 51*/SS4, June 28. Rockville, MD: National Center for Health Statistics.

Chavez, E. L., Randall, C., & Swaim, R. C. (1992). An epidemiological comparison of Mexican-American and White non-Hispanic 8th and 12th grade students' substance use. *American Journal of Public Health, 82*, 445–447.

Chavira, V., & Phinney, J. (1991). Adolescents' ethnic identity, self-esteem, and strategies for dealing with ethnicity and minority status. *Hispanic Journal of Behavioral Sciences, 13*, 226–227.

Commonwealth Fund. (1997). *Survey of the health of adolescent girls*. New York: Commonwealth Fund.

Cooper, M. L., Pierce, R. S., & Huselid, R. F. (1994). Substance use and sexual risk-taking among Black adolescents and White adolescents. *Health Psychology, 13*, 251–262.

Dembo, R. (1988). Delinquency among Black male youth. In J. T. Gibbs (Ed.), *Young, Black and male in America: An endangered species* (pp. 129–165). New York: Auburn House.

Diekstra, R. F. W., Kienhorst, I. W. M., & deWilde, E. J. (1995). Suicide and suicidal behaviour among adolescents. In M. Rutter & D. J. Smith (Eds.), *Psychosocial disorders in young people: Time trends and their causes* (pp. 686–761). Chichester, UK: Wiley.

Dornbusch, S. M., Mont-Reynard, R., Ritter, P. L., Chen, Z., & Steinberg, L. (1991). Stressful events and their correlates among adolescents of diverse backgrounds. In M. E. Cotton and S. Gore (Eds.), *Adolescent stress: Causes and consequences* (pp. 111–130). New York: Aldine de Gruyter.

Dryfoos, J. (1990). *Adolescents at risk: Prevalence and prevention*. New York: Oxford University Press.

Early, K. E. (1992). *Religion and suicide in the African American community*. Westport, CT: Greenwood Press.

Furstenberg, F. F. (1993). How families manage risk and opportunity in dangerous neighborhoods. In W. J. Wilson (Ed.), *Sociology and the public agenda* (pp. 231–258). Newbury Park, CA: Sage.

Garcia-Preto, N. (1996). Latino families: An overview. In M. McGoldrick, J. Giordano, & J. K. Pearce (Eds.), *Ethnicity and family therapy* (pp. 141–154). New York: The Guilford Press.

Garland, A. F., & Zigler, E. (1993). Adolescent suicide prevention: Current research and social policy implications. *American Psychologist, 48*, 169–182.

Gibbs, J. T. (1985). City girls: Psychosocial adjustment of urban Black adolescent females. *Sage, 2*, 28–36.

Gibbs, J. T. (1988). Conceptual, methodological, and sociocultural issues in Black youth suicide: Implications for assessment and early intervention. *Suicide and Life-Threatening Behavior, 18*, 73–89.

Gibbs, J. T. (1997). African American suicide: A cultural paradox. *Suicide and Life-Threatening Behavior, 27*, 68–79.

Gibbs, J. T., & Huang, L. N. (2003). *Children of color: Psychological interventions with culturally diverse youth*. San Francisco, CA: Jossey-Bass.

Gould, M. S., Fisher, P., Parides, M., Flory, M., & Shaffer, D. (1996). Psychosocial risk factors of child and adolescent completed suicide. *Archives of General Psychiatry, 53*, 1155–1162.

Grant, K. E., O'Koon, J. H., Davis, T. H., Roache, N. A., Poindexter, L. M., Armstrong, M. L., Minden, J. A., & McIntosh, J. M. (2000). Protective factors affecting low-income urban African American youth exposed to stress. *Journal of Early Adolescence, 20,* 388–417.

Hammond, W. R., & Yung, B. (1993). Psychology's role in the public health response to assaultive violence among young African American men. *American Psychologist, 48,* 142–154.

Harter, S. (1990). Self and identity development. In S. Feldman and G. R. Elliott (Eds.), *At the threshold: The developing adolescent* (pp. 352–387). Cambridge, MA: Harvard University Press.

Hawkins, J. O., Catalano, R. F., & Miller, J. Y. (1992). Risk and protective factors for alcohol and other drug problems in adolescence and early adulthood: Implications for substance abuse prevention. *Psychological Bulletin, 112,* 94–105.

Hovey, J. D., & King, C. A. (1996). Acculturation, stress, depression, and suicidal ideation among immigrant and second generation Latino adolescents. *Journal of the American Academy of Child and Adolescent Psychiatry, 35,* 1183–1192.

Kempton, T., & Forehand, R. L. (1992). Suicide attempts among juvenile delinquents: The contribution of mental health factors. *Behavior Research and Therapy, 30,* 537–541.

Kessler, R. C., Borges, G., & Walters, E. E. (1999). Prevalence of and risk factors for lifetime suicide attempts in the National Comorbidity Survey. *Archives of General Psychiatry, 56,* 617–626.

King, C. A., Raskin, A., Gdowski, C. L., Butkus, M., & Opipari, L. (1990). Psychosocial factors associated with urban adolescent female suicide attempts. *Journal of the American Academy of Child and Adolescent Psychiatry, 29,* 289–294.

King, R. A., Schwab-Stone, M., Flisher, A. J., Greenwald, S., Dramer, R. A., Goodman, S. H., Lahey, B. B., Shaffer, D., & Gould, M. S. (2001). Psychosocial and risk behavior correlates of youth suicide attempts and suicidal ideation. *Journal of the American Academy of Child and Adolescent Psychiatry, 40,* 837–846.

Kleycamp, M., & Tienda. M. (in press). Physical and mental health status of adolescent girls: A comparative ethnic perspective. In D. B. Bills (Ed.), *The shape of inequality: Social stratification and ethnicity in comparative perspective – Essays in honor of Archibald O. Haller.* San Francisco: Elsevier Scientific Publishing Series.

LaFromboise, T., & Dizon, M. (2003). American Indian children and adolescents. In J. T. Gibbs and L. N. Huang, *Children of color: Psychological interventions with culturally diverse youth* (pp. 45–94). San Francisco: Jossey–Bass.

Lester, D., & Anderson, D. (1992). Depression and suicidal ideation in African-American and Hispanic American high school students. *Psychological Reports, 71,* 618.

Leung, K., & Drasgow, F. (1986). Relation between self-esteem and delinquent behavior in three ethnic groups: An application of item response theory. *Journal of Cross-Cultural Psychology, 17,* 151–167.

Martinez, R., & Duke, R. L. (1987). Race, gender and self-esteem among youth. *Hispanic Journal of Behavioral Sciences, 9,* 427–443.

McCabe, K. M., Clark, R., & Barnett, D. (1999). Family protective factors among urban African American youth. *Journal of Clinical Child Psychology, 28,* 137–150.

Molock, S. D., Kimbrough, R., Lacy, M. B., McClure, K. P., et al. (1994). Suicidal behavior among African-American college students: A preliminary study. *Journal of Black Psychology, 20,* 234–251.

Nettles, S. M., & Pleck, J. H. (1994). Risk, resilience, and development: The multiple ecologies of Black adolescents in the United States. In R. J. Haggerty, L. R. Sherrod, M. Garmezy, & M. Rutter, *Stress, risk and resilience in children and adolescents* (pp. 147–181). New York: Cambridge University Press.

Oquendo, M. A., Ellis, S. P., Greenwald, S., Malone, K. M., Weissman, M. M., & Mann, J. J. (2001). Ethnic and sex differences in suicide rates relative to major depression in the United States. *American Journal of Psychiatry, 158*, 1652–1658.

Organista, K. C. (2003). Mexican American children and adolescents. In J. T. Gibbs & L. N. Huang, *Children of color: Psychological interventions with culturally diverse youth* (pp. 344–381). San Francisco, CA: Jossey-Bass.

Parham, T. A., & Helms, J. E. (1985). Attitudes of racial identity and self-esteem: An exploratory investigation. *Journal of College Student Personnel, 26*, 143–151.

Phinney, J. S. (1990). Ethnic identity in adolescents and adults: Review of research. *Psychological Bulletin, 108*, 499–514.

Roberts, R. E., Roberts, C. R., & Chen, Y. R. (1997). Ethnocultural differences in prevalence of adolescent depression. *American Journal of Community Psychology, 25*, 95–110.

Roberts, R. E., & Sobhan, M. (1992). Symptoms of depression in adolescence: A comparison of Anglos, African and Hispanic Americans. *Journal of Youth and Adolescence, 21*, 639–651.

Robins, L. N., Tipp, J., & Przybeck, T. (1991). Antisocial Personality. In L. N. Robins & D. A. Regier (Eds.), *Psychiatric disorders in America: The Epidemiologic Catchment Area Study* (pp. 258–290). New York and Toronto: Macmillan.

Robinson, T., & Ward, J. V. (1991). "A belief in self far greater than anyone's disbelief": Cultivating healthy resistance among African American female adolescents. In C. Gilligan, A. J. Rogers, & D. Tolman (Eds.), *Women, girls, and psychotherapy: Reframing resistance* (pp. 87–103). Binghamton, NY: Harrington Park.

Rosenberg, M., & Simmons, R. G. (1972). *Black and White self-esteem: The urban school child*. Rose Monograph Series. Washington, DC: American Sociological Association.

Rotheram-Borus, M. J. (1989). Ethnic differences in adolescents' identity status and associated behavior problems. *Journal of Adolescence, 12*, 361–374.

Rotheram-Borus, M. J., & Trautman, P. D. (1988). Hopelessness, depression, and suicidal intent among adolescent suicide attempters. *Journal of the American Academy of Child and Adolescent Psychiatry, 27*, 700–704.

Rutter, M. (2002). Substance use and abuse: Causal pathways considerations. In M. Rutter & E. Taylor (Eds.), *Child and adolescent psychiatry* (4th ed., pp. 455–462). Oxford: Blackwell Scientific.

Seidman, E. (1991). Growing up the hard way: Pathways of urban adolescents. *American Journal of Community Psychology, 19*, 173–205.

Shaffer, D., Garland, A., Gould, M., Fisher, P., & Trautman, P. (1988). Preventing teenage suicide: A critical review. *Journal of the American Academy of Child and Adolescent Psychiatry, 27*, 675–687.

Shaffer, D., & Gutstein, J. (2002). Suicide and attempted suicide. In M. Rutter & E. Taylor (Eds.), *Child and adolescent psychiatry* (4th ed., pp. 529–554). Malden, MA: Blackwell.

Siegel, J. M., Aneshensel, C. S., Taub, B., Cantwell, D. P., & Driscoll, A. K. (1998). Adolescent depressed mood in a multi-ethnic sample. *Journal of Youth and Adolescence, 27*, 413–427.

Spencer, M. B., & Dornbusch, S. M. (1990). Challenges in studying minority youth. In S. Feldman & G. R. Elliott (Eds.), *At the threshold: The developing adolescent* (pp. 123–146). Cambridge, MA: Harvard University Press.

Stack, S. (1998). The relationship between culture and suicide: An analysis of African Americans. *Transcultural Psychiatry, 35*, 253–269.

Stiffman, A. R., Cheuh, H. & Earls, F. (1992). Predictive modeling of change in depressive disorders and counts of depressive symptoms in urban youths. *Journal of Research on Adolescence, 2*, 295–316.

Stiffman, A. R., Hadley-Ives, E., Elze, D., Johnson, S., & Dore, P. (1999). Impact of environment on adolescent mental health and behavior: Structural equation modeling. *American Journal of Orthopsychiatry, 69*, 73–86.

Summerville, M. B., Abbate, M. F., Siegel, A. M., Serravezza, J., & Kaslow, N. J. (1992). Psychopathology in urban female minority adolescents with suicide attempts. *Journal of the American Academy of Child and Adolescent Psychiatry, 31*, 663–668.

Swanson, J. W., Linskey, A. O., Quintero-Salinas, R., Pumariega, A. J., & Holzer, C. E. (1992). A binational school survey of depressive symptoms, drug use, and suicidal ideation. *Journal of the American Academy of Child and Adolescent Psychiatry, 31*, 669–678.

Taylor, R. D., Seaton, E., & Rodriguez, A. U. (2002). Psychological adjustment of urban, inner-city ethnic minority adolescents. *Journal of Adolescent Health, 31*, 280–287.

Turner, C. B., & Turner, B. F. (1983). Gender, race, social class, and self-evaluations among college students. *The Sociological Quarterly, 23*, 491–507.

U.S. Department of Health and Human Services. (2001). Mental health: Culture, race, and ethnicity. In *Supplement to mental health: A report of the Surgeon General.* Rockville, MD: Office of the Surgeon General.

Vega, W. A., Zimmerman, R. S., Warheit, G. J., Aposproi, E., & Gil, A. G. (1993). Risk factors for early adolescent drug use in four ethnic and racial groups. *American Journal of Public Health, 83*, 185–189.

Wallace, J. M., & Bachman, J. G. (1991). Explaining racial/ethnic differences in adolescent drug use: The impact of background and lifestyle. *Social Problems, 38*, 333–357.

Wallace, J. M., & Muroff, J. R. (2002). Preventing substance abuse among African American children and youth: Race differences in risk factor exposure and vulnerability. *The Journal of Primary Prevention, 22*, 235–261.

Walter, H. J., Vaughan, R. D., Armstrong, B., Krakoff, R. Y., Maldonado, L. M., Tiezzi, L., & McCarthy, J. F. (1995). Sexual, assaultive, and suicidal behaviours among urban minority junior high school students. *Journal of the American Academy of Child and Adolescent Psychiatry, 34*, 73–80.

Weddle, K. D. & McKenry, P. C. (1995). Self-destructive behaviors among Black youth: Suicide and homicide. In R. L. Taylor (Ed.) *African American youth: Their social and economic status in the United States* (pp. 247–279). Westport, CT: Praeger.

Weissman, M. M., Bruce, M. L., Leaf, P. J., Florio, L. P., & Holzer, C. E. (1991). Affective disorders. In L. N. Robins & D. A. Regier (Eds.), *Psychiatric disorders in America: The Epidemiologic Catchment Area Study* (pp. 53–80). New York and Toronto: Macmillan.

Whaley, A. L. (1993). Self-esteem, cultural identity, and psychosocial adjustment in African American children. *Journal of Black Psychology, 19*, 406–422.

Williams, T. R., Davis, L. E., Cribbs, J. M., Saunders, J., & Williams, J. H. (2002). Friends, family, and neighborhood: Understanding academic outcomes of African American youth. *Urban Education, 37*, 408–431.

Zimmerman, M. A., Ramirez-Valles, J., Zapert, K. M., & Maton, K. I. (2000). A longitudinal study of stress-buffering effects for urban African American male adolescent problem behaviors and mental health. *Journal of Community Psychology, 28*, 17–33.

11

Ethnicity and Intergenerational Identities and Adaptations in Britain

The Socio-Political Context

Tariq Modood

Exclusion and Inclusion

Ethnic identities as publicly projected self-concepts have proved to be un-expectedly popular in Britain among members of ethnic minorities, es-pecially compared to earlier migrant groups and their descendants, say, Jews from eastern Europe. Minority groups have played a major role in determining the public character of these identities, as well as in relation to the prevalence and decline of specific labels. A key feature of these self-concepts has been their politically oppositional character. This was less salient initially – when one might have expected migrants to have had a greater sense of "otherness" – and became more prominent as migrants be-came more settled and a new generation reached adulthood. Oppositional stances increased as interaction with mainstream British society and policy participation rose, when one would have expected, if not assimilation, a softening of ethnic identities.

The explanation of this paradox begins with racism: Non-Whites were perceived and treated as racially defined groups of inferiors, outsiders, and competitors whose right to be in Britain and to be treated as equal citi-zens was not fully accepted. That they were marked out as "racial" groups and understood as racialized ethnicities has three implications (Modood, Berthoud, & Nazroo, 2002). First, migrants were perceived as a collectivity or more precisely as collectivities rather than merely as individuals, neigh-bors, fellow-workers, citizens, and so on. Second, they were perceived by the White British and publicly labeled in terms of specific collectivities, such as Black or Asian, whether they approved or not, and, consequently, minority groups were forced to accept, resist, or negotiate these labels and

I am most grateful for very useful comments offered on an earlier version of this paper by the editors of this volume, and the other contributors and participants of the conference at which the paper was presented, especially David Smith; and also to Michael Banton, Gregor McLennan, and James Nazroo.

their implied identities. Third, they had to draw attention to and resist various forms of discrimination and unfavorable treatment, whether in personal interactions or through mobilizing and organizing public protest and campaigns.

Identity, then, both as self-concept and as social fact, had considerable salience for the migrants and their offspring, with complex, negative and positive personal meanings, and became a socio-political obstacle or re-source. It was a site for contestation and collective assertiveness concerned with overthrowing demeaning stereotypes and stigma. Adopting and pro-jecting an identity simultaneously conveyed pride in family origins while seeking acceptance by the White British. Explanation for this paradox does not lie merely in racism. It lies also in the public challenge to externally imposed identities by campaigns promoting collective self-concepts, in re-sistance to racism through appeals to ethnicity. Critical to explaining the paradox of accentuated ethnic identity while seeking to belong is the wider political context that not only permitted assertions of identity as opposition to racism, but seemingly required them as a path to citizenship.

This oppositional character of ethnic minority self-concepts has demon-strated that political mobilization and participation, especially protest and contestation, can be an effective means of integration in Britain. As ac-tivists, spokespersons, and a plethora of community organizations come to interact with and modify existing institutions, there is a two-way pro-cess of mutual education and incorporation: Public discourse and political arrangements are challenged, but adjust to accommodate and integrate the challengers. Political contestation seems to be a necessary for integration when identities and the solidarities and divisions they create or constrain are shaped by public sphere discourses. However, in Britain "ethnicity" or "Blackness" has come to be experienced less as an oppositional identity than as a way of being British. A similar process appears to characterize being "Muslim" at the moment. Perhaps because of the success of the op-position period, minority identities, especially among young people, are now less oppositional.

These are rather large, general propositions about a complex phe-nomenon over a period of time. How can they be made persuasive? Much of the subject matter is not amenable to quantitative analysis, and in any case only limited relevant quantitative data are available. Moreover, as yet there are no techniques for measuring the social functions of self-concepts. Some aspects of ethnic identity can be understood as relationships among variables, but most aspects are too large and imprecise for that kind of inquiry. My interest is in ethnic identity as a particular phenomenon, as a feature of contemporary Britain. In this chapter, I explore (1) how a unique set of social relationships and social understandings hang together as a historical event, and (2) the evolution of ethnicity and its social contours, recognizing that there is a great degree of contingency that cannot possibly be the basis of scientific predictions. Accordingly, I do not follow a singular or well-defined methodology, but pursue a syncretic approach to illustrate that different perspectives yield mutually consistent conclusions. I also utilize systematic quantitative data produced for analyses of ethnicity, but my interpretations rely on knowledge or experience that go beyond the data because I connect survey findings with events, trends, and discourses in ways that transcend relationships among variables. My claim is that second-generation identities and cultural adaptations must be interpreted in terms of the larger picture I sketch. My overview is both descriptive and explanatory because it organizes and conceptualizes empirical phenomena in ways that render ethnic expressions intelligible, even when the attributed causation is not susceptible to quantitative analysis or testable by repeatable experiments. I focus on the socio-political here rather than the socioeconomic, not because it is less relevant, but because some of the relevant points about the socioeconomic character of ethnic minorities and intergenerational trends in Britain are made elsewhere in this volume.[1]

Briefly, I argue that the British imperial legacy has been a source of racism and therefore an obstacle to the integration of ethnic minorities. It has, however, also constituted a set of opportunity structures for an easy acquisition and exercise of citizenship, for political opposition to racism, and for ethnic minority assertiveness, partly influenced by developments elsewhere, especially the United States. Hence, as data show, there is very little erosion of group identification across the generations, though the *kind* of identity that is espoused varies: "Color" is salient for Caribbeans and religion for South Asians. Some of these identities are sustained by communal practices, for example, the high levels of endogamy among South Asians, but also by socio-political conflict, which is especially evident for Muslims at present. Hence these identities persist even when participation in distinctive cultural practices declines.

It would be mistaken to think that racial and religious identities are weak or "symbolic" when they can serve as a basis for political mobilization. Yet, the trend is for less oppositional and for "hyphenated" identities, such as "British Indian," indeed, for fluid, multiple identities. The Caribbeans, who originally led the way with oppositional identities, are ahead on this trend toward multiple identities. This is related to the high level of social mixing and success in popular culture that they have achieved. Although both political assertiveness and socio-cultural prominence have contributed to integration, it so far has brought the Caribbeans few economic dividends. This suggests perhaps that a good integration strategy sometimes may require delaying assimilation until entry into a middle-class environment has been achieved. This may be the trajectory of groups such as the African

---

[1] See in particular chapters by Tienda, Maughan, and Smith in this volume; for a systematic presentation on various aspects of the socioeconomic, see Modood et al. (1997); for a quantitative analysis of the relationship between ethnic identities and health, see Karlsen and Nazroo (2002); and for the bases of that analysis, see Nazroo and Karlsen (2003).

Asians, Chinese, and Indians, for whom ethnic difference has served as a protective factor. Hence some might conclude that the Caribbean strategy has not been successful. However, Britain exhibits different kinds of multiculture, including a mixing and style-setting hybridity and an ethnoreligious communitarian development. Minority groups have their own distinct character and so are likely to develop distinctive forms of integration. Meanwhile it is important to see that by replacing assimilation with assertiveness, not only is racism challenged, but space is opened up for a model of integration that allows minorities to retain some self-pride. No one form of integration, then, should be elevated to a paradigmatic status, either theoretically or in the area of policy.

Opportunity Structures and the "Host" Country

The postwar "New Commonwealth" immigration was led by West Indians, some of whom or their relatives had voluntarily fought for Britain during the Second World War, hoping to "better themselves" while assisting in the economic reconstruction of the "Mother Country." They were soon joined by large numbers of Indian and Pakistani young men, who also had a British Imperial connection, though a much less developed sense of British identity; instead, their identities revolved around tightly organized lines of kinship, custom, religion, language, and postimperial nationhood, which gave them a clear and confident sense of not being British even while admiring their former ruling power (this sentiment being at least as common as any residual anticolonialism). Few of these (mainly male) migrants came with the idea of settling in Britain; rather, the idea was to send remittances to family back home and/or save up to return with some capital. Only the Indian-origin refugees from East Africa, who arrived during the late 1960s to mid-1970s, came as intact families looking new homes. Partly through the Indians' example, the Pakistanis and later the Bangladeshis set in motion a process of family reunification precisely when British-born and/or British-schooled West Indians were reaching adulthood. But successively tightening immigration procedures left the family reunification process incomplete, particularly for the late-arriving Bangladeshis. These immigrant colonial groups, then, did not all arrive or commit themselves to raising a family in Britain at the same time: roughly speaking, as family units the Caribbeans are a generation ahead of the Pakistanis, with Indians and African Asians in between.

Except for African Asians, who had become a commercial and professional elite in countries such as Uganda and Kenya (but arrived mainly penniless in Britain), most UK-bound migrants arrived with poor qualifications and skills. Partly for this reason, and partly because of the racial discrimination in the labor market, which included devaluing overseas qualifications, the migrants entered the British economy at the bottom and were residentially concentrated in rundown neighborhoods. All groups have experienced some upward educational and economic mobility, especially the African Asians, who through self-employment and higher education have to a large extent restored their lost prosperity. Most groups remain socioeconomically disadvantaged by most measures compared with Whites. The most severely disadvantaged are the Bangladeshis, Pakistanis, and Caribbeans, roughly in that order. Given their longer settlement in the United Kingdom, the low social position of Caribbean males is especially problematic because they do not display to the same extent the educational and economic optimism of most migrants. Indeed, intergenerational progress seems to have halted or reversed for Caribbean males (Modood et al., 1997, Chapters 3 and 4; Tienda, this volume; Maughan, this volume; for the relationship to deviant behavior, see Smith, this volume).

In the main, these ethnic immigrant groups have not only been able to make socioeconomic progress, but they also have managed to oppose and reduce racism in British society, though sometimes reduction in one kind of racism is accompanied by an increase in another. A commonplace observation is that Britain, like its European neighbors, is an "old" country and not as hospitable to immigrants as, say, Canada, the United States, and Australia – countries that have been historically constituted by immigration. Yet, in relation to some groups of immigrants and in particular cities such as London, Britain has been remarkably receptive and self-transformative. This is related to the course of ethnic minority political mobilization in Britain, which began with circumstances conducive to ideological assertiveness, prominence, and civic impact to a scale and in a limited period of time without parallel in western Europe. A set of opportunity structures constituted by the following are responsible for the successful assertiveness of Britain's minority population, including:

The British imperial connection, felt by many migrants and politically acknowledged by at least some White British;
The perceived right to live in Britain and acquire a British identity;
Automatic British citizenship and franchise from day of arrival (later qualified);
Absence of large-scale antiracist struggles elsewhere in the English-speaking world, especially in the US, in which notions of "migrants and hosts" were absent, and that were borrowed from or emulated in Britain, creating a confidence and assertiveness that among migrants-as-guests would be regarded as intolerable by the "hosts."

In each of these respects, the West Indians, who thought of themselves as culturally British in the way that New Zealanders arriving in England in the 1950s did, took the lead in forging a minority political discourse and assertiveness into which South Asians gradually assimilated and either adapted for their own use, or used as a point of departure to press for a less racial dualist, Black–White orientation in favor of an ethnic pluralism (Modood, 2005). I speculate that if the West Indian migration had not preceded or accompanied that from South Asia, the latter group would have been less politically assertive. Once minority assertiveness becomes part of a political culture and is regarded as legitimate, perhaps even necessary to establish a degree of group dignity, then it can take forms that owe nothing to the original source. They can take, for example, the form of the Muslim campaign against *The Satanic Verses*, which to many observers initially bore no relation to antiracism, but has increasingly come to be seen in that light (Modood, 1990).

Ethnic, Racial, and Religious Identities

Ethnic identity – like gender and sexuality – not only has become politicized, but for some people has become a primary focus of their politics. While less prominent than in the United States, yet more so than on the European mainland (Baldwin-Edwards & Schain, 1994), ethnic assertiveness in Britain arises from perceptions of not being respected and lacking access to public space, and it consists of counterposing "positive" images against traditional or dominant stereotypes. By projecting identities in order to challenge racism and existing power relations, the politics of ethnic identity seeks not just toleration for ethnic difference, but also public acknowledgment, resources, and representation. The key political identity has been a Black identity, derived from and paralleling the Black pride and Black power discourses in the United States. However, in Britain, the political project encompassed within this identity not just those of African descent, but also South Asians (the latter being more numerous than the former from the early 1970s). This unified identity achieved a temporary and fragile hegemony during the 1980s, but is simply one feature of a plurality of non-White public identities (Modood, 1994). The latter now prominently includes a Muslim identity that among many, especially younger Pakistanis and Bangladeshis, tends to eclipse more specific ethnic identities. In part this is because domestic and transnational political crises and conflicts have pushed Muslims and Islam into the public spotlight (Modood, 2002a).

Having set out the socio-political backdrop in which ethnic identity formations and cultural adaptations are being forged, I examine data from Fourth National Survey of Ethnic Minorities in Britain to portray the magnitude and pace of the key trends on ethnic differentiation.[2] Despite the

[2] Fieldwork was undertaken in 1994 and covered many topics besides those of culture and identity, including employment, earnings and income, families, housing, health, and racial harassment. The survey was based on interviews, of roughly about an hour in length, conducted by ethnically matched interviewers, and offered in five South Asian languages and Chinese as well as English. More than 5,000 persons aged 16 or over were interviewed from the following six groups: Caribbeans, Indians, African Asians (people of South

limitations of survey data for portraying complex topics such as identity, this unique survey has the potential to offer what small-scale ethnographic studies, armchair theorizing, and political wishful thinking cannot. Crucially, it offers a sense of scale.

The survey explored only certain dimensions of culture and ethnicity. For example, it did not cover youth culture and recreational activities such as music, dance, and sport. These cultural dimensions are likely to be as important to self- and group identities of some respondents, especially the Caribbeans, as the features included in the survey. Moreover, almost all the questions asked in the survey provided indications of how closely people affiliated to their group of origin. We did not explicitly explore ways in which members of the minorities had adopted, modified, or contributed to ways of life of other groups, including the White British.

The survey revealed that members of minority groups, including those born and raised in Britain, strongly associated with their ethnic and family origins and thus there was little erosion of group identification across the generations. Although individuals described themselves in multiple and varied ways, groups had quite different conceptions of the kind of group identity that was important to them. Skin color ("Black") was prominent in the self-descriptions of Caribbeans, whereas religion was so in the self-descriptions of South Asians. This is not surprising because the legacy of slavery imposed color as a persistent identity in the relations between European and African-origin peoples in the Atlantic area, especially in the English-speaking area. Indeed, as African-origin people became part of European and colonial cultures, color signified an even larger burden of differentiation. Post–World War II West Indian migrants thought of themselves as culturally British, but the experience of racial exclusion developed in them, and especially in the generation that arrived as children, a fierce sense of Black oppositional identity, allied with a similar Black pride movement in the United States. The "child migrant" generation persuaded their elders and generations to follow of the value of "Black" as a positive identity (cf. Banton, 1983, pp. 328–329).

Thus color as an identity became the basis of a pan-ethnic antiracist Black identity that included all non-Whites, especially the South Asians. In the absence of supporting data, race egalitarians asserted that Asians accepted this identity. However, the Fourth Survey shows that, despite several decades of antiracist politics focused around a Black identity, only one fifth of South Asians considered themselves Black. Moreover, contrary to those who suggest that "Black" is a popular but "situational identity"

Asian descent whose families had spent a generation or more in East Africa), Pakistanis, Bangladeshis, and Chinese, though the Culture and Identity questions were asked of only about half the sample. Additionally, nearly 3,000 White people were interviewed, in order to compare the circumstances of the minorities with that of the ethnic majority. Further details on all aspects of the survey are available in Modood et al. (1997).

among Asians (Drury, 1990), the survey revealed that Blackness is not a context-specific identity for them, even for those who consider themselves non-White. Rather, it is perceived to be a fundamental aspect of themselves (at least in Britain) (Modood et al., 1997, pp. 295–297). This tallies with our earlier study showing that only a minority of Asians regarded themselves "Black," and that among those who did so, color was such an important aspect of their identity that it often subsumed all others (Modood, Beishon, & Virdee, 1994). Specifically, for Asians, "Black" identity was slightly less common among the young and the British-born, and more frequently mentioned among migrants with 25 years of British residence.

Just as Black identity has important historical roots for African origin people, religious identities are prominent community and nationalist identities in South Asia. The South Asian identification and prioritization of religion, however, is more than nominal. Nearly all South Asians reported having a religion, and 90 percent said that religion was important to them. In some ways Caribbeans also cleave to religion. About one third of Caribbean and White people, and even more Chinese, report not having any religion. For every ethnic group, younger people are less connected to a religion than their elders (though perhaps to become more like their elders as they age). Nevertheless, while only 5 percent of White 16- to 34-year-olds said that religion was *very important* to how they led their lives, nearly one fifth of Caribbeans, more than one third of Indians and African Asians, and two thirds of Pakistanis and Bangladeshis in that age group so reported (see Table 11.1). Non-White Anglicans are three times more likely than White Anglicans to attend church weekly, and well over half of the members of Black-led churches do so. Black-led churches are a rare growth point in contemporary British Christianity. Indeed, the presence of the new ethnic minorities is changing the character of religion in Britain not simply by diversifying it, but also by giving it an importance that is out of step with native trends.

The centrality of religion to the constitution of South Asian communities and ethnic identities can be further illustrated in a number of ways. Very

TABLE 11.1. *Age and Ethnic Variation in Salience of Religion: Percent Reporting "Very Important"; Cell Percentages (Weighted)*

	White	Caribbean	Indian	African Asian	Pakistani	Bangladeshi	Chinese
All	13	34	47	43	73	76	11
16–34	5	18	35	37	67	67	7
35–49	13	43	56	40	81	92	8
50+	20	57	59	64	83	81	31
Unweighted count	2,857	587	627	373	595	298	109

Source: Modood et al. (1997), p. 308.

few Asians marry across religious and caste boundaries, and most expect that their children practice their religion. Despite the fact that at least five major South Asian languages are spoken in Britain, and most Asians have some facility in more than one of these languages, each linguistic community is strongly connected to a religious community (Modood et al., 1997, pp. 308–312). Moreover, the salience of religion is nourished by conflict. Religious dress codes that require adherents to wear turbans or headscarves or to cover their legs continue to be resisted by acts of discrimination and exclusion at schools and workplaces and are the objects of legal rulings. The demand, especially by Muslims, that children be allowed to conduct acts of worship in their parents' religion in state schools, and that the state should fund Muslim schools (on the same basis as the Christian and Jewish schools are funded) has been an object of political activism and conflict. Half of the Muslims supported the idea of religious schools within the state sector, compared to only 20 percent of Sikhs, 13 percent of Hindus, and two fifths of White Catholics. However, relatively few parents would send their children to such schools, even if they were available: fewer than 10 percent of Hindus and Sikhs, 28 percent of Muslims, and 38 percent of White Catholics did so or would do so (Table 11.2). The affirmative answers for 16- to 34-year-olds was lower than these aggregate figures, as was also the case with persons with higher education (except in the case of Catholics).

Religion, moreover, is particularly worth exploring in relation to British socialization because it marks a significant cultural difference between the migrants and British society. Not only did most of the migrants have a different religion than the natives, but all the indications are that they, including the Christians among them, were more religious than the society they were joining. This was the case at the time of migration and during the early years of settlement, and it remains so today. The secular decline of indigenous religious observance and faith among native Britons makes religious diversity an important test case for the effect of British socialization. In general, most migrant cultural practices decline with the length of their stay in the host society across generations. This occurs with language, dress, arranged marriages, and so on. It is also the case with religion, though perhaps descendants of migrants are more likely to keep alive a distinctive religion rather than a distinctive language. This has certainly been the case with the Jewish and Indian diasporas, for example, though not with the Chinese. Rather, what makes religion exceptional is that, if not generally, at least in British society, religion is now strongly correlated with age: The older a Briton is, the more religious he or she is likely to be. Yet, the longer a migrant has been in Britain, the more likely it is that his or her original culture becomes muted. So, in the particular case of religion, age and length of residence in Britain work against each other in the maintenance of ethnic difference.

In fact, although the actual pattern is not uniform or perfectly linear, longer tenure in Britain is associated with a reduced importance of religion.

TABLE 11.2. *Preference for Schools of One's Own Religion; Cell Percentages (Weighted)*

				Church of England		Roman Catholic		Old Protestant		New Protestant
	Hindu	Sikh	Muslim	White	Others	White	Others	White	Others	Others
All	6	9	28	17	11	38	37	12	13	30
16- to 34-year-olds	9	1	23	13	10	34	24	15	15	30
Persons without qualifications	11	21	35	20	10	36	37	9	5	26
Persons with A-levels or higher education	3	2	18	14	13	41	45	11	23	37
Unweighted count	*419*	*363*	*1,033*	*1,395*	*131*	*317*	*75*	*201*	*102*	*101*

Source: Modood et al. (1997), p. 324.

Testing for the independent effects of age and length of residence or the extent of religiosity using logistic regression reveals that for Indians and Pakistanis, these effects more or less cancel each other out. However, among Bangladeshis and African Asians, length of residence exerts about twice the effect on religiosity as age does. This means that, in the case of the latter, the decline in religion through British socialization is only partially offset by age (Modood et al., 1997, pp. 305 – 308).[3]

The Fourth Survey data is from 1994, and since then dramatic political events have surrounded British Muslims. For at least a decade, a Muslim assertiveness – sometimes expressed as a political identity; sometimes as a religious revival; sometimes both – has been evident in Britain and elsewhere, especially among the young (Jacobson, 1997; Modood, 1990; Saeed, Blain, & Forbes, 1999). In 2001, Muslim identity manifested itself in the violent disturbances in some Northern cities, which some of the protagonists referred to as an *intifada*. It is mainly nourished, however, by events outside Britain, especially by despair at the victimization and humiliation of Muslims in places such as Bosnia, Kashmir, Afghanistan, Iraq and above all, Palestine. For many British Muslims, such military disasters and humanitarian horrors evoke a strong desire to express solidarity with oppressed Muslims through the political idea of the *Ummah*, the global community of Muslims, which must defend and restore itself as a global player. In the aftermath of September 11, media vilification and increases in physical attacks on the Muslim community have increased the salience of "Muslim" as an identity (Modood, 2002b).

New Forms of Ethnicity

The Fourth Survey also offers for the first time reliable evidence that ethnicity is coming to mean new things. Distinctive cultural practices having to do with religion, language, marriage, and so on still command considerable allegiance. For example, nearly all South Asians can understand a community language, and more than two thirds use it with family members younger than themselves. More than half of the married 16- to 34-year-old Pakistanis and Bangladeshis had their spouse chosen by their parents. There was, however, a visible decline in the extent to which subsequent generations participate in distinctive cultural practices such as these. This is particularly evident among younger South Asians, who, compared with their elders, are less likely to speak to family members in a South Asian language, regularly attend a place of worship, or report an arranged marriage.

Yet, these indicators of acculturation do not mean that immigrant minority groups cease to identify with their ethnic or racial or religious group. In

---

[3] I am grateful to my former colleague, Professor Richard Berthoud, for assistance with this analysis and that reported in Table 11.3.

this respect, the survey clarifies and makes explicit what recent "identity politics" left implicit. Ethnic identification is no longer necessarily connected to personal participation in distinctive cultural practices, such as those of language, religion, or dress. Some people expressed an ethnic identification even though they did not participate in distinctive cultural practices. Hence it is fair to say that a new conception of ethnic identity has emerged; or, if it is not entirely new as such, it is more widespread and more theoretically recognized as a phenomenon.

Ethnic identity has been implicit in distinctive *cultural practices*, and this continues as the basis of a strong expression of group membership. Additionally, however, an *associational* identity has emerged, which takes the form of pride in one's origins, identification with certain group labels, and sometimes a political assertiveness. The ethnic identities of the second generation may have a weaker component of behavioral difference, but it would be misleading to portray them as weak identities as such. During the past couple of decades the bases of identity formation have undergone important changes, but minority assertiveness has not disappeared. Rather, identity has moved from the implicit and presumed obvious in distinctive cultural practices, to conscious and public projections of group membership and the explicit creation and assertion of politicized ethnicities. Of course, identities so formed are necessarily fluid and susceptible to change with the political climate, but to consider them weak is to overlook the pride with which they may be asserted, the intensity with which they may be debated, and their capacity to generate community activism and political campaigns. This is clearly evident in the United States, too, as Rubén Rumbaut argues in the following chapter. In any case, what is described here as cultural-practices-based group and associational identities are not mutually exclusive. They depict ideal types that find concrete expression in highly variable ways. Moreover, a reactive pride identity can generate new cultural practices or revive old ones.

Some of the reported differences in culture and identity can be partly explained by place of birth, period of residence in Britain, or occupational class, or by a combination of these and related factors. Easily the strongest influence on South Asians' identity is their age at time of arrival to Britain. Nearly half of those who migrated after age 35 exhibited a "strong" behavioral identity; one eighth of them were in the "weak" group (Table 11.3; full details in Modood et al., 1997, pp. 334–336). By contrast, half of the British-born South Asians were members of the "weak" behavioral category. Underlying these differences, however, is an important contrast between African Asians and Indians (about 90 percent of whom are Sikhs and Hindus) and Pakistanis and Bangladeshis (more than 95 percent of whom are Muslims), which is perhaps rooted in religion. On a range of issues to do with religion, arranged marriages, choice of schools, and use of

TABLE 11.3. *South Asian Behavioral Identity, by Age at Migration*

	Born in United Kingdom	Up to 4	5–10	11–15	16–24	25–34	35 plus
Weak behavioral identity							
Indians and African Asians	60	49	41	26	21	17	17
Pakistanis and Bangladeshis	28	31	16	3	5	15	2
Strong behavioral identity							
Indians and African Asians	4	6	16	24	25	24	35
Pakistanis and Bangladeshis	11	11	33	47	47	52	56
"Strong" minus "weak"							
Indians and African Asians	−56	−43	−25	−2	+4	+7	+18
Pakistanis and Bangladeshis	−17	−20	+17	+44	+42	+37	+54

Source: Modood et al. (1997), p. 336.

Asian clothes, the latter take a consistently more "conservative" view than the former, even when age on arrival, British birth, and economic position are taken into account. The explanation for these differences derives from several sources. First, Pakistanis and Bangladeshis are more likely to come from rural backgrounds, and, in particular, from poorer rural backgrounds, than Indians. Second, their attitudes and practices in relation to gender roles, marriage, and ties of kinship also are more conservative (Ballard, 1990). The sense of "siege" and "threat" that some Muslim peoples have historically felt in the context of Western colonialism and cultural domination, and to which rural peoples in particular responded through a "defensive traditionalism," is a third explanatory factor (Modood, 1990).

Britishness and Popular Culture

Besides color and religion, respondents of the Fourth Survey mentioned other ethnic identities, too, and for some ethnic/racial/religious identification was not salient. For example, one in six British-born Caribbean-origin people did not think of themselves as being part of an African Caribbean ethnic group; this was not just related to the growing issue of mixed descent (discussed in the following). East African Asians mentioned their jobs as being as important an aspect of self-identity as any other. While more than one third of Caribbeans and about one quarter of South Asians wished to send their children to schools where half the pupils were from their ethnic group, only one tenth of Chinese wished to do so.

Clearly, the identities just discussed, varied as they are, do not necessarily compete with a sense of being British. More than two thirds of Asians claimed that they felt British, and these proportions were, as one might expect, higher among young people and those who had been born in Britain. The majority of respondents had no difficulty with the idea of hyphenated or multiple identities (Hutnik, 1991; Modood et al., 1994; see also Runnymede Trust, 1998). While the highest assimilation level (self-identification as British only) was registered by 18 percent of British-born Caribbeans, the highest disassociation with British identity was expressed by 35- to 49-year-old Caribbeans (47 percent). This indicates not only a high degree of intragroup variation but, more specifically, that some of the younger Caribbeans (some of whom are "mixed race" or of "mixed origins") appear to be reviving the assimilative hopes of the earliest West Indian migrants who saw themselves as coming to the "Mother Country." Nevertheless, there also is evidence of alienation from or a rejection of Britishness among the young. For example, more than a quarter of British-born Caribbeans did not regard themselves as British. In-depth interviews revealed that most of the second generation considered themselves as mostly, but not entirely, culturally and socially British. However, some of them considered being British only a legal title. In particular, some found it difficult to call themselves "British" because they felt that the majority of White people did not accept them as British because of their race or cultural background; through hurtful "jokes," harassment, discrimination, and violence, some experience denial of their claim to be British (Modood et al., 1994, Chapter 6). Of course, "British" is a problematic and declining feature of identification among some White people, too, especially, the young. Always resisted by many Irish in Britain, British identity is being eclipsed by "Scottish" in Scotland. Indeed, there seems to be less subjective incompatibility between being British and Pakistani than being British and Scottish, particularly among the young.

It seems that Asians in Scotland, like other Scots, consider themselves in terms of their Scottishness rather than Britishness (Saeed et al., 1999).[4] However, in England, where the issue of English identity is full of complexity and ambivalence, of implicit superiority and suspicion of nationalism, "English" has been treated by the new Britons as a closed ethnicity rather than an open nationality. Hence, while many ethnic minorities have

---

[4] Interestingly, non-Whites in Scotland and Wales do often have a sense of identification with these nations (Saeed et al., 1999), but non-Whites in Britain rarely think of themselves as Europeans (Runnymede Trust, 1998).

come to think of themselves as hyphenated Brits, they have only recently started to think of themselves as English. Indeed, for Whites, too, English as a prominent public identity has only recently emerged as a feature of British cultural life, and largely as a consequence of a Scottish disavowal of British. Even now, however, it is most popularly associated with a football team. Consequently, the Caribbeans, who are strongly overrepresented as players on the England team, are placed at the center of English national identity. Indeed, this is one of many examples in which Caribbean people have become an integral feature of popular British culture and the public imagination of self – a remarkable phenomenon, given their disadvantaged socioeconomic profile, not to mention population size.

The unusual position of the Caribbeans is manifested in other ways, too. Although the trend for all groups is away from cultural distinctness and toward cultural mixture and intermarriage, it is not equally strong among the various groups, and disproportionately characterizes the Caribbeans. For example, among the British-born with a partner, half of Caribbean men and one third of Caribbean women, compared to one fifth of Indian and African Asian men, one tenth of Pakistani and Bangladeshi men, and very few South Asian women, had a White partner. This does need to be interpreted carefully because the rate of marriage or partnerships is not uniform across groups. Forty percent of Caribbean men and women did not have a partner compared to the national average of 20 percent. However, that is not in itself evidence that Caribbean–White unions are less likely than the data first suggest. Rather, given that Caribbeans are more likely to be multiple partnering and in a series of relationships, it may be that the level of interracial partnerships is greater than the averages reveal. In the Fourth Survey, 40 percent of Caribbean children who were living with two parents reported one White parent. This too may exaggerate the number of mixed Caribbean–White origin children as a proportion of all children of Caribbean ancestry, because the figure is based on two-parent households, which are not the modal pattern among Caribbeans. About half of Caribbean-origin children are living with only one parent (compared to a sixth of children nationally).

This important qualification has to be balanced against the fact that many Caribbean-origin children are likely to be brought up by a White mother without the presence of the father in the household. Unfortunately, I am unable to quantify this because this type of household was not included in this survey. The Caribbean–White social, cultural, sexual, and generational mix is, I believe, very deep in Britain. Low ethnic segregation has made this possible and stands in contrast to the high segregation of African Americans in the United States (Johnston, Forrest, & Poulsen, 2002). Moreover, the segregation of the Caribbeans in the United Kingdom is much less than that of the South Asians. That the Caribbean migrants in the United Kingdom started off much closer to the White British, not least in the possession of the English language, but also in norms of sexual contact and behavior and marriage partner selection, facilitated their mixing with Whites. This stands in radical contrast to the experience of South Asians.

This deep mix, which requires going beyond survey data to appreciate, is bound to have a profound impact on the idea of a Black identity and of a Black community. As yet these matters are not discussed publicly. What leading Black analysts and public intellectuals openly discussed by the mid-1990s is the vibrant strength of a Black British cultural identity. Darcus Howe makes reference to Black people having "a social ease and confidence now that we have not had before" (Younge, 1995). Henry Louis Gates, Jr., believes that "a culture that is distinctively Black and British can be said to be in full flower" (Gates, 1997, p. 196), and Stuart Hall has argued not only that "Black British culture could be described as confident beyond measure in its own identity"(Hall, 1998, p. 39), but also that young Black people have made themselves *the* defining force in street-oriented British youth culture" (Hall, 1998, p. 40). A group comprising less than 2 percent of the population has, in terms of both quantity and quality, established itself as a leading-edge presence in urban youth culture in the face of racism, social deprivation, and relative exclusion from positions of power and wealth. Thus, far from being pariahs, many Black people have become objects of desire, with many young Whites envying and imitating their "style" (cf. Hall in Gates, 1997, p. 196).

Black British cultural success, like some other aspects of Caribbean settlement in Britain, has been highly inclusive. Although born of an assertiveness and a search for dignity, and at times oppositional in expression, Caribbean ethnic identity has also been a movement of integration, of wanting to be included into the British mainstream, of sharing and mutual respect (Phillips & Phillips, 1998, and Part 4 of the BBC television series *Windrush*, to which this book is an accompaniment). It has, inevitably, been largely a Black–White relationship, but some young Asians and others have been drawn into it as well. This sociability does not occur in a color-blind assimilationist, "passing for White" context in which racism is ignored. For some young people it can take place in ways in which Black ethnicity and antiracism are emphasized or, indeed, are the point. Black persons can be admired not in spite of, but because of, their Blackness, for their aesthetics, style, and creativity as well as for their antiracist resistance and sometimes even for their outcast or deviant status. For example, at a typical performance of controversial Black nationalist rap bands, more than half of the audience will be White (cf. Smith, this volume).

It is interesting to consider this situation in the light of Min Zhou's observation that in the United States assimilation is not always the path to social mobility (Zhou, 1997). So too in Britain, Caribbean ethnicity has brought remarkable social dividends, but few economic ones, and with Indians the reverse obtains. Asian Muslim ethnicity is currently under massive political attack for producing segregation and religio-political militancy. Often overlooked is Pakistanis' refusal to assimilate into local White working-class cultures that has sustained their hopes of social advancement and permitted a cohort of higher education entrants on a scale that exceeds what the government has achieved for the White working classes (Modood, 2003; Maughan, this volume). As Zhou notes, for some groups an effective integration strategy often requires delayed assimilation until entry into a middle class environment has been achieved (Zhou, 1997). British-born African Asian and Indian men are gradually increasing rates of intermarriage, and their female counterparts appear to be moving in this direction. I expect this trend to increase for both sexes, but unlike the Caribbeans, intermarriage is mainly a middle-class phenomenon. There is, however, no conclusive evidence for this emergent trend yet. In any case, different minorities will relate to the mainstream in their own way. Although some ways may prove more successful in furthering integration than others, an approach characteristic of one group should not be elevated to a paradigmatic status, either theoretically or in the area of policy.

Group differences of the sort discussed in this chapter used to be regarded by antiracists as of negligible significance for public policy on grounds that the important policy goal was eradicating racism and that all non-White groups in Britain experience the same racism. As the research evidence of differential stereotyping has accumulated, some theorists discovered what they alleged was a "new racism," though the differential stereotyping and treatment of Asians and Blacks seems to be as old as the presence of these groups in Britain (Modood, 1997). The Fourth Survey strongly supports the contention of differential prejudice targeted at Britain's minority groups. There is now a consensus across all groups that prejudice against Asians is much the highest of any ethnic, racial, or religious group. Moreover, Asians themselves believe that the prejudice against them is primarily a prejudice against Muslims (Modood et al., 1997, pp. 133–134). No doubt perceptions of Asian cultural practices, and the extent to which they are adhered to, determines the strength of prejudice against Asians. Thus the important prejudice in Britain now may be a cultural racism rather than a straightforward color racism. But it would be wrong to assume that the most culturally distinct or culturally conservative groups are least likely to feel British and vice versa. That the Caribbeans are the culturally and socially closest to the White British, but also were most likely to dismiss identification with Britishness – more than the Pakistanis and the Bangladeshis, who are the most culturally conservative and separate of these groups – testifies to this point.

Conclusion

Although there is, then, much empirical support for those theorists such as Stuart Hall who have emphasized the fluid and hybridic nature of contemporary postimmigration ethnicities in Britain, his suggestion that groups are so internally complex that they have become "necessary fictions" is much exaggerated (Hall, 1987, p. 45, and 1992, p. 254). Moreover, the theoretical neglect of the role of religion reflects a bias of theorists of "difference" rather than developments on the ground (Modood, 1998). British theorists of "race" had assumed that there was a deep racial/color divide. Contemporary developments suggest that ethno-religious divisions may prove equally, if not more, persistent.

The kind of intergenerational identities and adaptations witnessed in Britain partly reflect the positive and negative features of British society. The pursuit of political demands and interventions by ethnic and religious minorities, although not frictionless of course, represents a process of political participation, negotiation, and integration. Discourses of identities and the formation of new collective self-concepts have been critical to these politics because they mediate between members of the majority and the minorities. They challenge and change the terms on which members of the minorities and the rest of Britain interact. Compared to interest-based politics, identity politics may seem inefficient and even intractable, but it has been in this case a critical symbolic dimension of the integration process. By replacing assimilation with assertiveness, not only is racism challenged, but a model of integration that allows minorities to retain some self-pride by positing a two-way or multiway dynamic of cultural adaptation is articulated. Yet, one of the most notable developments is that increasingly "ethnicity" or "Blackness" is experienced less as an oppositional identity than as a way of being British. Significantly, though, "Muslim" has not fully begun this transition.

However, many theorists and social critics have only slowly recognized the important differences among the minorities and that they seem destined for different socio-cultural locations within a plural, but stratified, Britain. Vague talk about "multiculturalism" obscures to most people at least two simultaneous developments underway. One is a mixing and style-setting hybridity, typified by the Caribbeans, with "color" remaining a stigmatic attribute while also becoming desirable because it is stigmatic. Second is the development of ethno-religious communities, typified by Asian Muslims, whose presence generated a moral panic after 9/11 but who in their own way are also becoming institutionally integrated. The latter are no less hybridic in that their emergence and evolution in the social structure is a product of British opportunity political imperatives. The point is that integration/hybridity is not just a matter of degree; there are different modes of integration and hybridity. Moreover, all minority groups have their own distinct character. Even where it is accurate to say that they have a similar set of circumstances, their responses will be culturally mediated. An important policy implication is to not use one group as a "model" for integration in relation to others.

References

Baldwin-Edwards, M., & Schain, M. A. (Eds.). (1994). The politics of immigration in Western Europe [Special issue]. *West European Politics, 17*, 2–16.

Ballard, R. (1990). Migration and kinship: The differential effect of marriage rules on the process of Punjabi migration to Britain. In C. Clarke, C. Peach, & S. Vertovec (Eds.), *South Asians overseas*. Cambridge, UK: Cambridge University Press.

Banton, M. (1983). *Racial and ethnic competition*. Cambridge, UK: Cambridge University Press.

Drury, B. (1990, May). *Blackness: A situational identity*. Paper presented at the New Issues in Black Politics conference, University of Warwick.

Gates, H. L. (1997, April 28–May 5). Black London. *The New Yorker*.

Hall, S. (1987). Minimal selves. In L. Appignanesi (Ed.) *The real me: The question of identity and postmodernism*. London: Institute of Contemporary Arts.

Hall, S. (1992). New ethnicities. In J. Donald & A. Rattansi, *'Race', Culture and Difference*, London: Sage.

Hall, S. (1998). Aspiration and attitude...Reflections on Black Britain in the Nineties. *New Formations*, Frontlines/Backyards Special Issue, 33.

Hutnik, N. (1991). *Ethnic minority identity, a social psychological perspective*. Oxford: Clarendon Press.

Jacobson, J. (1997). Religion and ethnicity: Dual and alternative sources of identity among young British Pakistanis. *Ethnic and Racial Studies, 20*, 238–256.

Johnston, R., Forrest, J., & Poulsen, M. (2002). The ethnic geography of EthniCities: The "American Model" and residential concentration in London. *Ethnicities, 2*, 209–235.

Karlsen, S., & Nazroo, J. Y. (2002). Agency and structure: The impact of ethnic identity and racism on the health of ethnic minority people. *Sociology of Health and Illness, 24*, 1–20.

Modood, T. (1990). British Asian Muslims and the Rushdie affair. *Political Quarterly, 61*, 143–160; reproduced in J. Donald and A. Rattansi, *'Race', Culture and Difference*, London: Sage.

Modood, T. (1994). Political blackness and British Asians. *Sociology, 28*, 859–876.

Modood, T. (1997). "Difference", cultural racism and anti-racism. In P. Werbner & T. Modood (Eds.), *Debating cultural hybridity: Multi-cultural identities and the politics of anti-racism*. London: Zed Books.

Modood, T. (1998). Anti-essentialism, multiculturalism and the "recognition" of religious minorities. *Journal of Political Philosophy, 6*, 378–399; reproduced in W. Kymlicka & W. Norman (Eds.), *Citizenship in diverse societies*. Oxford: Oxford University Press.

Modood, T. (2002a). The place of Muslims in British secular multiculturalism. In N. Alsayyad & M. Castells (Eds.), *Muslim Europe or Euro-Islam: Politics, culture and citizenship in the age of globalisation*, New York: Lexington Books.

Modood, T. (2002b). Muslims and the politics of multiculturalism in Britain. In E. Hershberg & K. Moore (Eds.), *Critical views of September 11: Analyses from around the world*. New York: New Press.

Modood, T. (2003). Ethnic differences in educational performance. In D. Mason (Ed.), *Explaining ethnic differences: Changing patterns of disadvantage in Britain*. Bristol: Policy Press.

Modood, T. (2005). Ethnicity and political mobilisation in Britain. In S. Teles, T. Modood, & G. Loury (Eds.), *Race, ethnicity and social mobility: A comparative study of the US and Britain*. Cambridge, UK: Cambridge University Press.

Modood, T., Beishon, S., & Virdee, S. (1994). *Changing ethnic identities*. London: Policy Studies Institute.

Modood, T. Berthoud, R., Lakey, J., Nazroo, J., Smith, P., Virdee, S., & Beishon, S., (1997). *Britain's Ethnic Minorities: Diversity and Disadvantage* London: Policy Studies Institute.

Modood, T., Berthoud, R., & Nazroo, J. (2002). "Race," Racism and Ethnicity: A Response to Ken Smith. *Sociology, 36*, 419–427.

Nazroo, J. Y., & Karlsen, S. (2003). Patterns of identity among ethnic minority people: Diversity and commonality. *Ethnic and Racial Studies, 26*, 902–930.

Phillips, M., & Phillips, T. (1998). *Windrush: The irresistible rise of multicultural Britain*. London: HarperCollins.

Runnymede Trust, in partnership with the Commission for Racial Equality (1998). *Young people in the UK: Attitudes and opinions on Europe, Europeans and the European Union*. London.

Saeed, A., Blain, N., & Forbes, D. (1999). New ethnic and national questions in Scotland: Post-British identities among Glasgow Pakistani teenagers. *Ethnic and Racial Studies, 22*, 821–844.

Younge, G. (1995, March 20). Black in Britain: Where are we now? *The Guardian*.

Zhou, M. (1997). Growing up American: The challenge confronting immigrant children and children of immigrants. *Annual Review of Sociology, 23*, 63–95.

12

Assimilation, Dissimilation, and Ethnic Identities

The Experience of Children of Immigrants in the United States

Rubén G. Rumbaut

Introduction

The immigrant-stock population of the United States – the foreign born and their U.S.-born children – surpassed 60 million people in the year 2000, a total larger than the entire population of the United Kingdom. The Current Population Survey estimated that there were 32.5 million foreign-born persons in the United States in 2002, and nearly another 30 million U.S.-born persons with at least one foreign-born parent, comprising 22 percent of the total U.S. population (Rumbaut, 2002; Schmidley, 2003). The foreign born are fairly recent arrivals: almost half arrived in the United States since 1990, and another quarter entered during the 1980s. This "new" immigration – largely from Asia, Latin America, and the Caribbean, with smaller but growing components from Europe, Africa, and the Middle East – has been changing fundamentally the racial and ethnic composition and stratification of the American population, as well as the social meanings of race and ethnicity and of American identity. The immigrants and their children are forming the emerging ethnic groups of the United States in the 21st century, even as they are themselves being transformed into the newest Americans. Their intergenerational evolution may produce new ethnic formations and identities, even as the process of "becoming American" has come to include the adoption or rejection of a set of officially constructed pan-ethnic labels such as "Hispanic" and "Asian/Pacific Islander," which lump together scores of nationalities into one-size-fits-all minority group categories – and which may, unwittingly, institutionalize not their assimilation but their dissimilation.

What do we actually know of the psychosocial adaptations and self-identities of the millions of young people of foreign parentage growing up and coming of age in the complex multiethnicity of the contemporary United States? The way that these youths define themselves is significant, revealing much about their social attachments as well as their sites of belonging, and how and where they perceive themselves to "fit" in the society of which they are the newest members. Self-identities and ethnic loyalties can often influence long-term patterns of behavior and outlook as well as intergroup relations, with potential long-term political implications. Whether (or how) they will be able to maintain an attachment to the nation of their birth or of their parents' birth, or identify instead with the ethnoracial categories into which they are pervasively classified by their adoptive society, or forge new identities in a process of ethnogenesis – all these are open empirical questions.

We know, for instance, of new and robust evidence of rapid English language assimilation among children of immigrants in the United States (Portes & Rumbaut, 1996, 2001). The data confirm that, regardless of national origins, these young people learn to speak English proficiently and come to prefer it to their mother tongue. Indeed, in view of the historic fate of immigrant languages in America, the findings underscore anew why the United States has been aptly called a "language graveyard." But is there a similar assimilative shift over time in their ethnic self-identities and sense of belonging? If so, what explains it? If not, how *do* they identify? Is ethnic self-identity mainly a function of natal and filial–familial attachments, degree of acculturation, or experiences of discrimination (and attendant "memories of wounds" experienced in the present and not solely remembered or reenacted from the group's collective past)? Or is it also shaped by a host of other factors? This chapter is an effort to address those questions systematically by examining the results of the Children of Immigrants Longitudinal Study (CILS), to be described in what follows.

Theoretical Considerations: The Twilight of Ethnicity?

Conventional accounts of ethnic identity shifts among the descendants of European immigrants, conceived as part of a larger, linear process of assimilation, have pointed to the "thinning" of their ethnic self-identities in the United States. For their descendants, at least, one outcome of widespread acculturation, social mobility, and intermarriage with the native population is that ethnic identity became an optional, leisure-time form of "symbolic" ethnicity (Gans, 1979). As the boundaries of those identities become fuzzier and less salient, less relevant to everyday social life, the sense of belonging and connection to an ancestral past faded "into the twilight of ethnicity" (Alba, 1985; Waters, 1990). Indeed, Florian Znaniecki once memorably depicted the melting pot of the United States, where ancestral identities were dissolved, as the "euthanasia of memories."

This mode of ethnic identity formation, however, was never solely a simple linear function of socioeconomic status and the degree of acculturation – that is, of the development of linguistic and other cultural similarities with the dominant group – but hinged also on the context of reception and the degree of discrimination experienced by the subordinate group. Milton Gordon (1964), in his seven-stage portrayal of assimilation in American life, saw "identificational assimilation" – a self-definition as an unhyphenated American – as the culmination of a complex sequence made possible only if and when it was accompanied by an absence of prejudice and discrimination in the core society. Whether ethnicity will become similarly optional – a matter of individual choice – for the descendants of immigrants who are today variously classified as non-White, or whether they will be collectively channeled into enduring, engulfing, racially marked subordinate statuses and forge oppositional identities, remain open questions.

Drawing on the European experience and on the eve of the new immigration from Asia and Latin America, the prevailing view of the matter was framed succinctly by Nahirny and Fishman (1996 [1965]: 266): "The erosion of ethnicity and ethnic identity experienced by most (but not all) American ethnic groups takes place in the course of three generations . . . ethnic heritage, including the ethnic mother tongue, usually ceases to play any viable role in the life of the third generation." However, compared to language loyalty and language shift, generational shifts in ethnic self-identification are far more conflictual and complex. To those authors the "murky concept of ethnic identification" did not lend itself to intergenerational analysis along a unidimensional attitudinal continuum because the parents, children, and grandchildren differed among themselves not only in the *degree* but also in the *nature* of their identification with ethnicity. Thus, paradoxically, despite rapid acculturation, as reflected in the abandonment of the parental language and other ethnic patterns of behavior, the second generation remained *more* conscious of their ethnic identity than were their immigrant parents.

The parents' ethnic identity was so much taken for granted and accepted implicitly that they were scarcely explicitly aware of it. For the children, however, their marginality made them acutely self-conscious and sensitive to their ethnicity, especially when passing through adolescence. Moreover, at least under reigning conditions of dissonant acculturation,

the generational discontinuity between the formative experiences and dominant environments of most immigrant [parents] and [children] rendered the family ineffective as an agency for the transmission of traditional ethnicity. So pronounced was this generational gap that by the time the [children] reached adolescence the immigrant family had become transformed into two linguistic sub-groups segregated along generational lines (Nahirny & Fishman, 1996 [1965], pp. 267, 277–78).

Finally, by the third generation the grandchildren became "literally outsiders to their ancestral heritage," and their ethnic past an object of symbolic curiosity more than anything else. There was no doubt about the national identity of the grandchildren – they were simply Americans of one particular (if not mixed) ethnic ancestry. And neither was there any trace left of the "wounded identity" of the children, for in contrast with them, the grandchildren had never experienced "the full brunt of marginality."

Indeed, as is the case with respect to language maintenance and language shift, the decisive turning point for change in ethnic and national self-identities can be expected to take place in the second rather than the first generation. Relative to the first generation, the process of ethnic self-identification of foreign-born immigrant children and the U.S.-born children of immigrants is more complex and ambiguous, and it often entails the juggling of competing allegiances and attachments. Situated within two cultural worlds, they must define themselves in relation to multiple reference groups (sometimes in two countries and in two languages) and to the classifications into which they are placed by their native peers, schools, the ethnic community, and the larger society. Pressure from peers and from parents can tauten the tug-of-war of ethnic and national loyalties, contributing unwittingly to a sense of marginality. This state of affairs can be further complicated when identities are racialized, group boundaries are sharpened by a visible color line, and the metaphorical definition of who one is on the "inside" conflicts with the definition of who one is on the "outside," raising questions about the "authenticity" of either identity and doubts about fully belonging to any group.

To their parents, who came of age before they came to America, such concerns are almost entirely irrelevant. Immigrants who arrive as adults seldom lose their original linguistic allegiances or accents, even while learning English; neither, for that matter, do they readily shed their homeland memories and self-images, even after becoming naturalized American citizens. On the contrary, they come with preexisting and fully formed identities, along with their hopes for the future. Their experience of migration, nostalgia for the homeland, desire to instill in their children a sense of pride in their cultural heritage, and anxiety over their children's rapid Americanization may all actually deepen the parents' own sense of identification with "home," perhaps most poignantly among exiles and sojourners who migrate reluctantly and sustain ritually affirmed hopes of an eventual return. The central theoretical and empirical question is rather what happens to their children and how it is that they come to define their ethnic identities and sites of belonging, particularly during their passages to adulthood – the youthful years of "identity crisis" and heightened self-consciousness when the self-concept is most malleable (Erikson, 1968; Phinney, 1990; Rosenberg, 1965, 1979). That developmental process can be complicated for U.S.-reared children of immigrants by experiences of intense acculturative and generational conflicts as they strive to adapt in American contexts that may be racially and culturally dissonant, and in family contexts where the differential acculturation of parents and children may take a variety of forms.

Youths see and compare themselves in relation to those around them, based on their social similarity or dissimilarity with the reference groups that most directly affect their experiences – especially with regard to such socially visible and categorized markers as gender, phenotype, accent, language, name, and nationality. Their social identities, forged in terms of those contrasts with others, represent the way they self-consciously define the situation in which they find themselves and construct an ongoing account of who "we" – and "they" – are. Ethnic identification begins with the application of a label to oneself in a cognitive process of self-categorization, involving not only a claim to membership in a group or category, but also a contrast of one's group or category with other groups or categories. Such self-definitions also carry affective meaning, implying a psychological bond with others that tends to serve psychologically protective functions – indeed, they may be adopted in part because they protect the individual's self-esteem, whereas negative self-esteem can precipitate an alteration of identification (Deaux, 1996; Tajfel, 1981). Ethnic self-awareness is heightened or blurred, respectively, depending on the degree of dissonance or consonance of the social contexts that are basic to identity formation. For majority-group youths in an ethnically consonant context, ethnic self-identity tends to be taken for granted and is not salient, but contextual dissonance heightens the salience of ethnicity and of ethnic group boundaries. People whose ethnic, racial, or other social markers place them in a minority status in their group or community are more likely to be self-conscious of those characteristics. Youths may cope with the psychological pressure produced by such dissonance by seeking to reduce conflict and to assimilate within the relevant social context – the modal response of the children of European immigrants in the American experience. An alternative reaction may lead in an opposite direction to the rise and reaffirmation of ethnic solidarity and self-consciousness.

That latter reaction can be provoked when the dominant social context is perceived to be one of hostile exclusion and not of inclusion and acceptance. Thus, for example, Proposition 187, an initiative put to the voters of California in the fall of 1994, exacerbated ethnic tensions throughout a state that accounts for more immigrants than any other by far (about a third of the U.S. total reside in California). The measure aimed to "Save Our State," as Proposition 187 was called, by denying social and nonemergency health care services – and access to public schools – to undocumented immigrants and their children. It also required school districts to verify the legal status of students' parents or guardians and to report to state officials any persons suspected of being in the United States unlawfully so that they might be detained and deported. Many highly acculturated teenaged children of immigrants (especially those from Mexico) reacted by joining with friends who were organizing their schools' anti-187 movement and by affirming, even reveling in, the identity of their parents' ancestry. Proposition 187 won

in a landslide, getting 59 percent of the statewide vote; in populous San
Diego and Orange Counties, south of Los Angeles, the measure passed with
67 percent of the votes cast. But for many 1.5- and second-generation youth,
a Mexican ethnic self-identity was "thickened" in the process, a sense of belonging made more salient than ever as they came to define who they were
and where they came from *in opposition to* who and what they were not.
The divisive campaign had the unintended consequences of accentuating
group differences, heightening group consciousness of those differences,
hardening ethnic identity boundaries between "us" and "them," and promoting ethnic group solidarity and political mobilization.

This process of forging a *reactive ethnicity* in the face of perceived threats,
persecution, discrimination, and exclusion is not uncommon (Aleinikoff &
Rumbaut, 1998; Portes & Rumbaut, 2001). On the contrary, it is one mode
of ethnic identity formation, highlighting the role of a hostile context of reception in accounting for the rise rather than the erosion of ethnicity –
including oppositional identities and their attendant "memories of
wounds." (Indeed, identity-defining reaction formation processes in situations of ethnic conflict and social exclusion have their parallel in the
way national self-definitions have been forged in international conflicts,
rivalries, and particularly wars.) Just 2 years before Proposition 187, for example, second-generation Korean-Americans saw more than 2,300 Korean-
owned stores in Los Angeles' Koreatown targeted by African Americans
and burned during the rioting that followed a "not guilty" verdict in the
1992 trial of four White police officers charged with the brutal beating of a
Black motorist. The event caused many young Koreans born or raised in
the United States to become self-conscious about their common fate and
distinctiveness as Koreans. They too reacted by participating in multigen-
erational solidarity rallies and by moving to organize politically to protect
the interests of the parent generation and the image of the group in the
larger society.

In the remainder of this chapter, relying primarily on survey data
from the CILS panel study, I examine various factors shaping ethnic self-
identification in our sample of immigrant-origin youths. I hypothesize
that the process of language learning and acculturation, as well as experiences of racial–ethnic discrimination, among other factors, will – in
given sociohistorical contexts – be accompanied by changes in the character and salience of ethnicity – ranging from "linear" to "reactive" forms,
from "thick" to "thin" identities – and hence by divergent modes of ethnic
self-identification. In particular, I address these questions: What are their
ethnic (or pan-ethnic) self-identities? How salient or important are they to
these youths, and how have they shifted over time? What characteristics
distinguish the different types of ethnic (or pan-ethnic) identities from each
other? And among those characteristics, which are the main predictors of
different types of ethnic (and pan-ethnic) identities?

The Children of Immigrants Longitudinal Study: Forms of Ethnic Self-Identification

The Children of Immigrants Longitudinal Study (CILS), carried out in Southern California (San Diego) and South Florida (the greater Miami area), has followed a large sample of more than 5,000 youths from immigrant families representing 77 different nationalities from the junior high school grades in 1991–92 (when most were 14 or 15 years old), to the end of senior high school in 1995–96 (when most were 17 to 18 years old). The sample attrition rate was less than 20 percent between surveys. [CILS respondents were again located and reinterviewed in 2001–02 (when they were in their mid-20s)], wherever they were then residing, but these latest results are not yet available at this writing.) Respondents were eligible to enter the sample if they were U.S.-born but had at least one immigrant (foreign-born) parent, or if they themselves were foreign-born and had come to the United States at an early age (most before age 10). The baseline sample was evenly divided by gender and nativity (half were foreign-born, half were born in the United States of foreign-born parents). The main nationalities represented in the San Diego sample are Mexican, Filipino, Vietnamese, Laotian, Cambodian, Chinese, and smaller groups of other children of immigrants from Asia and Latin America. In the South Florida sample, the main national-origin groups consist of Cubans, Nicaraguans, Haitians, Jamaicans, Colombians, Dominicans, and others from Latin America and the Caribbean (for details of the study see Portes & Rumbaut, 2001; Rumbaut & Portes, 2001).

In both the 1992 and 1995–96 CILS surveys, an open-ended question was asked to ascertain the respondent's ethnic self-identity. No closed categories or checklists were provided, requiring the respondents to write their answers in their own words and in their own hand. Those written self-designations were then coded and quantified, and they comprise the main outcomes that I seek here to describe and explain. From the variety of responses given, four mutually exclusive types of ethnic self-identities became apparent, which accounted for more than 95 percent of the answers given in both surveys. These four types were classified as follows: (1) a foreign national identity (e.g., Mexican, Vietnamese); (2) a hyphenated-American identity, explicitly recognizing a single foreign national origin (e.g., Cuban-American, Filipino-American); (3) a plain American national identity, without a hyphen; and (4) a pan-ethnic minority group identity (e.g., Asian, Black, Hispanic, Latino). The first two of these identify with the immigrant experience and original homeland, if at different degrees of closeness, whereas the last two types are exclusively identities "made in the USA." The first three also involve chiefly national identifications (past or present, or a bridging of both); the fourth reflects a denationalized identification with racial–ethnic minorities in the United

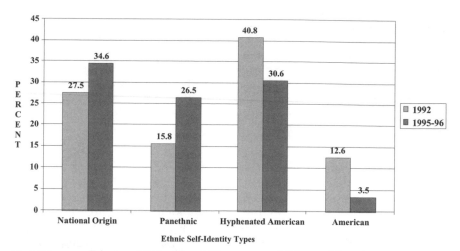

FIGURE 12.1. Ethnic self-identity shifts among children of immigrants, 1992 to 1995–96. See text for description of ethnic self-identity types. Not shown are mixed identities chosen by about 4 percent of the respondents in both surveys. *Source:* CILS (longitudinal sample).

States and self-conscious differences in relation to the White Anglo majority population.

Ethnic Identity Shifts

Figure 12.1 presents the frequency distribution of the results from both surveys for the longitudinal sample as a whole. In the 1992 survey, when these youths were in the eighth and ninth grades, just more than a quarter (27 percent) identified by the foreign national origin; a plurality (41 percent) chose a hyphenated-American identification; 13 percent identified as American; and 16 percent selected pan-ethnic self-identifications. By the 1995–96 survey, as they were finishing high school, more than a third (35 percent) of the same respondents now identified by national or ethnic origin; fewer than a third (31 percent) chose a hyphenated-American identification; only 3.5 percent identified as American; and more than a quarter (27 percent) selected pan-ethnic self-identifications. Among the last, "Hispanic" was reported by 12 percent of the sample in the first survey and by 18 percent in the follow-up; a "Latino" self-designation was selected by a much smaller number of youths of Latin American origin, but it increased more rapidly from 0.5 to 1.4 percent. Whereas hardly any youth had identified as "Asian" or "Asian American" in the first survey (0.3 percent), that category grew noticeably to 4.5 percent in the second survey. "Black" self-identities doubled from 0.9 to 1.9 percent.

These results show substantial change over time, underscoring the malleable character of ethnicity. The magnitude of the change, however, is moderate: nearly half (44 percent) of the youths reported exactly the same ethnic self-identity in their written responses to the open-ended question in the follow-up survey. (Preliminary results from the 2001–02 survey similarly show that half of the respondents reported the same ethnic self-identity as they had in 1995–96.) This degree of stability takes on added significance when it is considered that several years had passed between surveys, spanning a relatively volatile developmental period from middle to late adolescence in changing cultural contexts. If ethnic identity does not emerge here as a "fixed" characteristic, then, neither is it so "fluid" as to be reducible to a set of changing situations. Still, the fact that more than half of the respondents reported a change in their ethnic self-definitions in the span between surveys underscores the need not to take such identities as givens, but to track their evolution across the life course.

Moreover, the direction of the shift was unexpected. If their rapid language shift to English documented previously were to have been accompanied by a similar acculturative shift in ethnic identity, then we should have seen an increase over time in the proportion of youths identifying as American, with or without a hyphen, and a decrease in the proportion retaining an attachment to a foreign national identity. But as shown in Figure 12.1, the results of the 1995 survey (conducted in the months after the passage of Proposition 187 in California) pointed in exactly the opposite direction. In 1992, more than 53 percent identified as American or hyphenated-American, but only 34 percent did so 3 years later – a net *loss* of nearly 20 percentage points. Meanwhile, both the foreign national origin and pan-ethnic identifications combined for a net *gain* of almost 20 percentage points. The shift, therefore, had been not toward mainstream identities but toward a reaffirmation of the immigrant identity for some groups (notably Mexicans and Filipinos in California, and Haitians and Nicaraguans in Florida), and toward pan-ethnic minority group identities for most others, who become increasingly aware of and adopt the ethnoracial markers in which they are persistently classified by the schools and other American institutions. How and why this occurred is a complex story. One part of it has to do with the stability and salience of the different types of ethnic self-identities, and I turn first to that issue.

Stability and Salience

Table 12.1 presents a detailed cross tabulation of these results. For each of the identity types chosen in 1992, the table shows the proportion of respondents who reported exactly the same identity in 1995–96 (a measure of the *stability* of that identity), as well as the proportions who shifted to a different type of ethnic self-identification. As Table 12.1 shows, 58 percent of the youths who identified by their own or their parents' foreign national origin in 1992 did so again 3 years later (the most stable and "fixed" type of self-identification), compared to 47 percent of those choosing

TABLE 12.1. *Continuity and Change in the Ethnic Self-Identities of Children of Immigrants, 1992 and 1995–96*[a]

| Ethnic Self-Identity Reported in 1992 | Ethnic Self-Identity in 1995–96 | | | | | Total |
	National Origin	Pan-ethnic	Hyphenated American	American	Mixed, Other	N in 1992 (%)
National origin	57.7	20.2	17.4	1.2	3.6	1181 (27.5)
Pan-ethnic	32.5	46.5	16.8	0.6	3.5	677 (15.8)
Hyphenated American	28.1	20.6	44.6	2.7	4.0	1748 (40.8)
American	10.7	33.8	32.8	14.8	7.9	542 (12.6)
Mixed, other	22.9	27.9	26.4	3.6	19.3	140 (3.3)
TOTAL	1482	1135	1314	150	207	4288
N in 1995–96 (%)	(34.6)	(26.5)	(30.6)	(3.5)	(4.8)	(100.0)

[a] Figures are row percentages, indicating the proportion of respondents who reported in the 1995–96 survey the same or a different type of ethnic identity as that given in 1992. Overall, 44% of the respondents reported the same identity in the follow-up survey, while 56% reported a different type. See text for a description of ethnic identity types.

Source: CILS (longitudinal sample).

pan-ethnic identities, 45 percent of those reporting a hyphenated-American identity, and a mere 15 percent of those who had identified as plain Americans (by far the most unstable and "fluid" type of self-identification). Of those shifting to other identities, Table 12.1 suggests the patterning of the shifts: They either added a hyphen or dropped the hyphen in favor of a pan-ethnic or a foreign nationality identity. Very few shifted to a plain American identity by the second survey (overall it plummeted from 13 percent to 3.5 percent); among those who had initially identified as American only, a third shifted to a hyphenated-American identity, while another third adopted a pan-ethnic type.

In the 1995–96 survey, the youths were asked how important their reported ethnic self-identity was to them. The responses, on a 3-point scale from "very important" to "not important," provide a measure of the *salience* of the different identity types. We can thus compare the different identity types by their degree of stability (the percent reporting the same identity years later) and salience (the percent reporting their identity as "very important"). Once again foreign national-origin identities command the strongest level of allegiance and attachment: more than 71 percent of the youths so identifying considered that identity to be "very important" to them, followed by 57 percent of the hyphenates, 53 percent of the pan-ethnics, and only 42 percent of those identifying as plain American. The last emerges as the "thinnest" identity, with the lowest stability and salience scores – fitting theoretical expectations for a highly acculturated, majority-group self-image in socially consonant contexts. The foreign national identity, in contrast, emerges as the "thickest" identity, with the highest stability and salience scores – fitting theoretical expectations for a less-acculturated, more acutely self-conscious image in socially dissonant contexts. In the salience–stability hierarchy of ethnic identities, the pan-ethnic and hyphenated-American types fall in between those two poles.

Multivariate logistic regressions (not shown) were carried out to identify the factors most likely to predict ethnic identity and salience. A large array of possible predictors was examined – but only a handful emerged as significant determinants of stability and salience. Identities tended to be most stable among less-acculturated respondents (i.e., those who reported lesser preferences for English and American ways of doing things) and those high in perceptions of discrimination (i.e., those who reported experiences and expectations of unfair treatment because of their ethnicity or race). Identities were also more stable among those youths whose parents were both born in the same country and who spoke the parental language at home. Females were also more likely than males to have retained the same ethnic identity over time. Those same predictors also determined salience, except that gender had no significant effect on salience, whereas our measure of family cohesion did – that is, net of other factors, the more cohesive the family was, the more likely were the youths to consider their ethnicity as being very important to them. Put another way, "thicker" (stable and salient) ethnic self-identities were least likely to be found among second-generation youth who experienced little discrimination, had become more acculturated, and spoke English in homes with low family cohesion – a recipe for dissonant acculturation and ancestral disidentification.

Ethnic Self-Identities by National Origin

How did these patterns of ethnic self-identification vary among the major nationalities in the study? Table 12.2 provides a breakdown by national origin, showing both the percent selecting the four main ethnic identity types in the most recent survey, as well as the percent change ($\pm$) in each identity since the initial survey. In addition, "internal ethnicity" (the presence of different ethnic groups within an immigrant nationality – see Bozorgmehr, 1997) is considered in this table by separating the Vietnamese and the ethnic Chinese from Vietnam, and the Lao and the Hmong from Laos – the ethnic Chinese and the Hmong were segregated and disparaged minority groups in their country of origin, and as such their identity choices and homeland attachments bear closer comparative scrutiny. A number of points merit highlighting.

First, a glance at Table 12.2 reveals that the patterns discussed so far do not apply equally to every nationality, and that in fact there are very large discrepancies in some cases. For example, 35 percent of the total sample identified by a foreign national origin in the second survey, a gain of 7 percent from the first survey. But that figure is an average that ranges from a high of 67 percent among the Lao (compared to 48 percent of the Hmong), 58 percent of the Vietnamese (compared to 26 percent of the ethnic Chinese-Vietnamese), and more than 50 percent of the Filipinos and Nicaraguans, to a low of only 5 percent of the Dominicans and 6 percent of the Cubans in private schools. The Mexicans and Filipinos – in California – registered the strongest gains in foreign national-origin identities from the baseline survey (each increasing by 24 percent), vividly documenting (especially in the Mexican case) the Prop-187-induced process of reaction formation noted earlier. Most of the Mexican shift came from youths who had identified as Chicano, Hispanic, or Latino in the 1992 survey.

Other groups registered significant losses in national-origin identification, especially Dominicans, West Indians, and the Hmong, Chinese, and smaller Asian-origin groups. All of these smaller groups instead posted very large increases in pan-ethnic identities, with 72 percent of the Dominicans choosing "Hispanic" or "Latino" self-identities, as did 62 percent of the Colombians. The Hmong and the Chinese, virtually none of whom had identified pan-ethnically as "Asian" in 1992, made large inroads into this type of racialized self-identification by 1995. This result is clearly not explained by socioeconomic factors, since the Hmong had the lowest family socioeconomic status of all the groups in this study (and the highest

TABLE 12.2. *Ethnic Self-Identities of Children of Immigrants, by National Origin Groups, 1995–96*

| | Type of Ethnic Self-Identity[a] | | | | | | | |
| National Origin Groups | National Origin | | Pan-Ethnic Identities | | Hyphenated American | | American Identity | |
	% in 1995–96	(% Change since 1992)	% in 1995–96	(% Change since 1992)	% in 1995–96	(% Change since 1992)	% in 1995–96	(% Change since 1992)
Latin America:								
Cuba (private school)	6.2	(+2.7)	19.2	(+15.1)	70.5	(+13.0)	2.1	(−32.9)
Cuba (public school)	16.5	(−0.4)	31.5	(+23.2)	42.0	(−11.1)	6.1	(−14.6)
Dominican Republic	5.1	(−20.5)	71.8	(+44.9)	10.3	(−15.4)	2.6	(−16.7)
Mexico	41.2	(+23.5)	25.0	(−21.0)	28.9	(−2.0)	1.2	(−1.8)
Nicaragua	54.1	(+19.6)	25.6	(−13.2)	17.4	(+2.1)	0.4	(−8.2)
Colombia	15.7	(−7.6)	62.7	(+36.8)	13.0	(−17.3)	3.2	(−15.7)
Other Latin America	16.7	(−10.0)	43.3	(+33.2)	23.3	(−7.1)	13.3	(−16.7)
Haiti and West Indies:								
Haiti	37.8	(+6.7)	4.4	(−7.4)	43.7	(+5.2)	0	(−14.1)
Jamaica	39.0	(−13.6)	15.3	(+10.2)	29.7	(+2.5)	2.5	(−10.2)
Other West Indies	14.5	(−13.3)	55.4	(+47.0)	16.9	(−10.8)	2.4	(−24.1)
Asia:								
Vietnam (Vietnamese)	57.9	(+13.1)	11.9	(+11.5)	29.4	(−18.3)	0	(−4.0)
Vietnam (ethnic Chinese)	25.9	(−1.7)	29.3	(+29.3)	39.7	(−10.3)	1.7	(−1.7)
Laos (Lao)	66.7	(+4.9)	11.8	(+9.0)	19.4	(−9.7)	0.7	(+0.0)
Laos (Hmong)	48.0	(−14.0)	38.0	(+36.0)	12.0	(−14.0)	0	(−4.0)
Cambodia	48.3	(+7.9)	21.3	(+19.1)	30.3	(−15.7)	0	(−3.4)
Philippines	55.1	(+24.0)	1.9	(+1.2)	37.0	(−22.8)	1.7	(−3.6)
Chinese, Other Asia	19.4	(−12.9)	43.9	(+42.6)	23.2	(−24.5)	5.8	(−8.4)
Europe, Canada:	8.8	(−14.0)	7.0	(−3.5)	10.5	(−10.5)	57.9	(+15.8)
TOTALS	34.6	(+7.0)	26.5	(+10.7)	30.6	(−10.1)	3.5	(−9.2)

[a] See text for description of ethnic self-identity types. Not shown is a residual category of mixed identities chosen by 4.8% of the respondents in the 1995–96 survey. Figures are row percentages.

Source: CILS (longitudinal sample).

poverty rate in the United States, for that matter), whereas the Chinese in this sample mostly came from professional families. By contrast, virtually none of the Filipinos identified in pan-ethnic terms (fewer than 2 percent), as did only 4 percent of the Haitians. The Filipinos and Haitians stand out from all other groups in that they almost entirely identified either by national origin or as hyphenated-Americans, maintaining an explicit symbolic attachment to their parents' homeland.

Every group, with one exception, posted losses in the plain American identity by the latest survey. Even upper-middle-class private-school Cubans, more than a third of whom had identified as American in 1992, abandoned that identity almost entirely by 1995–96 (a loss of 33 percent). The sole – and telling – exception involve the Europeans and Canadians: Not only were they the only groups who increased (by 16 percent) their proportion identifying as plain American, but by the last survey more than half (58 percent) had adopted that majoritarian, mainstream identity as their own. All other groups were in the low single digits by comparison, marking a sharp segmentation of identities. Socioeconomic status alone would not explain this divergence; as noted, the high-status private-school Cubans dropped that identity, and another relatively high-status group – the Filipinos – consistently posted minuscule numbers identifying as un-hyphenated Americans. Neither would acculturation to American ways by itself explain it; again the Filipinos, easily the most highly acculturated Asian-origin group, serve as a counterexample. In the following I attempt to disentangle this puzzle.

Origins and Identity

Ethnic identity is, in part, a way of answering the question "Where do I come from?" The answers given are often expressed in a metaphorical language of kinship (e.g., "homeland," "fatherland," "mother tongue," "blood ties") with reference to a "birth connection" to nation and family – to an imagined common origin or ancestry (Cornell & Hartmann, 1998; Horowitz, 1985). Even the "thinnest" ethnicities tend to be rooted in such kinship metaphors. Thus, although ethnic identities may be socially and politically constructed, they are experienced and expressed as "natural." In this regard, nativity variables (where one was born, to whom one was born, where one's parents were born) are clearly important to ethnic and national self-definitions. For children of immigrants, they are also variables that can significantly complicate a clear-cut answer to basic questions of ethnic self-definition, particularly when the country of birth of the parents differs from that of the child and (in cases of interethnic marriage) from each other. The extent of such differences in the nativity patterns of our respondents and their parents is depicted in Table 12.3, broken down by national origin groups.

TABLE 12.3. *Nativity Patterns of Children of Immigrants and of Their Parents*

National Origin Groups	Nativity of Children[a]		Nativity of Father and Mother		
	Foreign-Born (1.5 Generation) %	U.S.-Born (2nd Generation) %	Both Born in Same Country %	In Different Countries %	One Parent Born in United States (2.5 Generation) %
Latin America:					
Cuba (private school)	8.9	91.1	85.6	9.6	4.8
Cuba (public school)	32.2	67.8	74.8	14.1	11.1
Dominican Republic	32.1	67.9	79.5	1.3	19.2
Mexico	38.2	61.8	73.0	9.5	17.5
Nicaragua	92.9	7.1	85.8	13.2	1.1
Colombia	48.1	51.9	64.9	25.9	9.2
Other Latin America	53.9	46.1	74.3	7.1	18.6
Haiti and West Indies:					
Haiti	54.8	45.2	85.9	9.6	4.4
Jamaica	63.6	36.4	78.0	11.9	10.2
Other West Indies	32.5	67.5	50.6	24.1	25.3
Asia:					
Vietnamese	84.2	15.8	89.0	8.1	2.9
Laos (Lao)	98.6	1.4	95.1	4.9	0
Laos (Hmong)	94.0	6.0	90.0	10.0	0
Cambodia	96.6	3.4	80.9	19.1	0
Philippines	42.5	57.5	79.1	3.9	17.0
Other Asia	43.9	56.1	64.5	7.1	28.4
Europe, Canada:	14.0	86.0	22.8	3.5	73.7
TOTALS	49.9	50.1	76.8	10.4	12.9

[a] Figures are row percentages.

Source: CILS (longitudinal sample).

Half of the children of immigrants in the CILS sample were born in the United States (the second generation), whereas the other half was foreign-born (the 1.5 generation). However, as Table 12.3 shows, there are wide differences by national origin. Well more than 90 percent of the Laotians, Cambodians, and Nicaraguans were foreign-born, as were 84 percent of the Vietnamese. By contrast, more than 90 percent of the Cubans in private school were U.S.-born, as were 86 percent of the Europeans and Canadians, and well more than half of the Mexicans, Filipinos, and other Asians and West Indians. Note that only three-fourths of the children in the sample had parents who were both born in the same country – and hence who could transmit to their children a common national origin. These rates of homogamy vary widely by nationality, with the highest proportions of endogamous conational parents (between 85 and 95 percent) found among the Laotians, Vietnamese, Haitians, Nicaraguans, and Cubans in private school, while fewer than one fourth (23 percent) of the Europeans and Canadians had conational parents – indicative of high levels of interethnic marriage.

How do these nativity patterns affect ethnic self-identification? That question is graphically answered in Figure 12.2, which depicts each of the main types of ethnic self-identity by the place of birth of the child and his/her parents. Among those who reported a foreign national-origin identity, 75 percent were foreign-born, compared to 31 percent of those who reported a hyphenated-American identity and a minuscule 8 percent of those identifying as plain American. Fewer than half (47 percent) of those

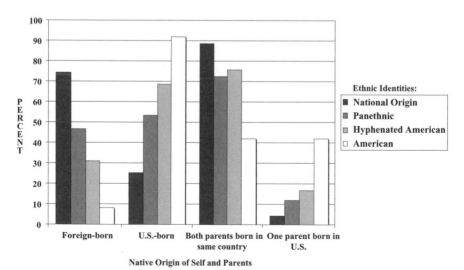

FIGURE 12.2. Ethnic self-identities, 1995–96, by native origin of self and parents. The probability of differences being due to chance is less than 1 in 1,000 for all associations shown.

identifying by pan-ethnic categories were foreign-born. In families where both parents came from the same country of birth, their offspring were much more likely to incorporate that national origin as part of their own identity (either wholly or as a hyphenated-American identity). In families where both parents were foreign-born but came from different countries of birth, their offspring were more likely to simplify the complexity of mixed origins by adopting either a pan-ethnic (minority) or plain American (majority) identity, thus resolving the conflict of identifying with one parent rather than the other.

Acculturation and Identity

Of course, even when the nativity patterns of the youths and of their parents are held constant, many other factors are likely to impinge independently on the process of ethnic self-identification. Table 12.4 lists a variety of factors related to patterns of acculturation of both parents and children (measured in the 1992 survey) that are strongly predictive of the children's identity outcomes (measured 3 to 4 years later in the 1995–96 survey). These data make clear that each identity type has a distinct social profile that differs significantly from each of the others. For example, the parents' length of residence in the United States provides an indicator of their own level of acculturation. The longer the parents had resided in the United States, the more likely their children were to assimilate their identities along the continuum from foreign national to pan-ethnic to hyphenated-American to plain American. That same linear gradient is evident for each of the different indicators of parental socioeconomic status shown (home ownership, occupation, and education), of foreign and English language proficiency and use, and of preference for "American ways" reported separately by both the youths and their parents. Language, in particular, is closely connected to the formation and maintenance of ethnic identity. The shift to English is associated with a shift in self-definition and seems to entail abandoning not only a mother tongue but also a personal identity. Those youths most loyal to the mother tongue were also most loyal to a national-origin identity; conversely, those youths who preferred English and spoke only English with their parents and close friends were much more likely to identify as an unhyphenated American.

Finally, Table 12.4 presents selected indicators pertaining to the youths' attitudes toward and attachment to their parents and family, and the effect of those on ethnic self-identifications. One item asked at both surveys – measuring the youths' response to a question about feeling embarrassed about their parents' ignorance of American ways – provides an empirical indicator of dissonant acculturation within the family. Again, the same linear relationship obtains as with the other measures of acculturation: Least embarrassed were youths who identified by national origin, and

TABLE 12.4. *Nativity, Social Status, Language, Acculturation, and Attitudes Toward Parents: Selected 1992 Predictors of Ethnic Self-Identities Reported by Children of Immigrants in 1995–96*

Predictor Variables, 1992[b]	Ethnic Self-Identity in 1995–96[a]				
	National Origin %	Pan-Ethnic %	Hyphenated American %	American %	Total Sample %
Child's nativity:					
Foreign-born	74.5	46.6	31.1	8.0	49.9
U.S.-born	25.5	53.4	68.9	92.0	50.1
Parents' nativity:					
Both born in same country	88.9	72.3	75.7	42.0	76.7
Born in different countries	6.5	15.8	7.5	16.0	10.4
One parent born in United States	4.6	11.9	16.8	42.0	12.9
If both parents foreign-born, year of immigration to U.S.:					
Before 1970	4.5	14.2	20.9	40.2	13.0
In 1970s	15.8	26.8	35.4	37.9	25.8
In 1980s	79.7	59.0	43.7	21.8	61.2
Socioeconomic status:					
Family owns home	48.7	52.8	66.4	73.3	56.6
Parent is a professional	20.6	24.3	26.2	40.0	24.3
Education 12 yrs+ (mother)	53.3	58.9	64.6	76.7	59.7
Language and acculturation:					
Speaks foreign lang. "very well"	37.9	38.5	26.9	14.0	33.0
Speaks English "very well"	66.6	79.1	84.6	95.3	77.4
Parent speaks English "very well"	22.3	26.9	38.5	59.4	30.3

Speaks English with parents	32.7	48.7	70.0	40.2
Speaks English with friends	30.3	34.4	62.0	32.8
Prefers English	64.4	79.8	91.3	72.9
Prefers "American ways"	34.8	46.4	74.7	41.9
Parents prefer "American ways"	19.8	28.1	60.1	25.6
Attitudes toward parents/family:				
Embarrassed of parents, 1992	22.9	27.1	30.0	24.6
Embarrassed of parents, 1995–96	26.5	31.2	42.0	29.3
Believe that only relatives can help with serious problems, 1992	19.6	12.2	7.3	15.5
Believe that living close to family is "very important," 1995–96	46.8	39.7	24.8	42.0

[a] Figures are column percentages. The probability that the differences by type of identity are due to chance is less than 1 in 1,000 for all variables in the table. The ethnic self-identities are those reported in the follow-up survey of 1995–96. For simplicity of presentation, a small residual category of mixed identities is not included.

[b] Predictor variables were measured in the baseline survey of 1992, unless otherwise noted; parent's English ability was measured at the time of the separate parental interviews in 1995–96.

Source: CILS (longitudinal sample).

most embarrassed were those who identified as plain American (with the proportion widening over time). A different set of items tapped attitudes expressing felt collective obligations toward the family; two of them are shown in Table 12.4 (believes that only relatives can help with serious problems, and that living close to family is very important). The higher the level of agreement on these items, the more likely that the youth identified by national origin; the lower the level of agreement, the more likely that the youth identified as plain American, with the other two identity types falling in between.

Clearly the family plays a central role in the process of ethnic socialization. It is the crucible of the child's first notions of belonging and of "home," and it is within the family that the child first learns about and forms ethnic attachments and self-concepts. Even in the sometimes bumpy passage through adolescence and under varying degrees of differential acculturation, how these youths think and feel about themselves continue to be affected by the parents' modes of ethnic socialization and by the strength of the attachment that the child feels to the parents.

Discrimination and Identity

The story of the forging of an ethnic self-identity in the second generation, however, plays out on a much larger stage than that of the family. Earlier I focused attention on social forces outside the family that shape both the creation of racial–ethnic categories and of ethnic self-definitions, particularly those involving discrimination and the politics of reactive ethnicity and not only those involving acculturation and the psychology of linear ethnicity. I now return to those concerns.

Regional location (in Southern California or South Florida) and the type of school these youths attended (inner-city or suburban, public or private schools) are two such extrafamilial contextual factors. They delimit the youths' exposure to different social worlds, shape differential associations with peers in those contexts, and influence attendant modes of ethnic socialization and self-definition. As Table 12.5 shows, slightly more than half of the sample (52 percent) was located in South Florida, and slightly less than half (48 percent) in the San Diego area. But two thirds (67 percent) of those identifying by a foreign national origin were in San Diego, while about four fifths (79 percent) of those identifying as plain American were in South Florida. The distribution of the main types of pan-ethnic identities – as specified in Table 12.5 – is even more skewed by location, reflecting the varieties of groups that have settled in those areas. The location of the school attended in junior high school – which is in part a function of family socioeconomic status – remains associated with the self-identities reported by the youths several years later. Those identifying as plain Americans were most likely to have attended suburban schools (73 percent), followed

321

TABLE 12.5. *Location, Experiences of Discrimination, Perceptions of the United States, and Self-Reported Race, by Main Types of Ethnic Self-Identities Reported by Children of Immigrants in 1995–96*[a]

Predictor Variables	Ethno-National Self-Identity in 1995–96			Pan-Ethnic Self-Identity in 1995–96			Total Sample %
	National Origin %	Hyphenated American %	American %	Hispanic, Latino[b] %	Asian %	Black %	
Location:							
Southern California	67.3	47.6	21.3	19.8	75.1	16.3	48.1
South Florida	32.7	52.4	78.7	80.2	24.9	83.7	51.9
School attended in 1992:							
Inner-city school	37.4	30.4	26.7	38.4	43.0	48.8	35.4
Suburban school	62.6	69.6	73.3	61.6	57.0	51.2	64.6
Experienced discrimination:							
Reported in 1992	60.3	53.5	44.0	44.7	57.0	68.8	54.5
Reported in 1995–95	66.4	62.0	52.7	51.4	66.8	80.0	62.2
Expects discrimination:							
Reported in 1992	36.6	33.0	22.7	21.7	33.2	61.3	32.0
Reported in 1995–96	39.7	35.3	27.3	25.4	34.2	62.5	35.1
Agrees that "The U.S. is the best country to live in":							
Reported in 1992	57.7	65.9	73.3	58.3	66.8	47.5	60.8
Reported in 1995–96	67.9	76.0	78.0	72.2	72.0	54.4	71.3

(continued)

TABLE 12.5 (continued)

Predictor Variables	Ethno-national Self-Identity in 1995–96			Pan-Ethnic Self-Identity in 1995–96			Total Sample %
	National Origin %	Hyphenated American %	American %	Hispanic, Latino[b] %	Asian %	Black %	
Child's self-reported "race":							
White	6.0	17.4	58.7	20.8	–	–	14.3
Black	5.7	6.7	2.7	0.8	–	85.0	6.6
Asian	40.4	23.1	3.3	–	92.2	–	25.8
Multiracial	5.1	15.0	16.0	11.5	6.2	13.8	11.4
Hispanic, Latino	16.4	17.2	10.0	57.8	–	–	23.5
Nationality	23.3	18.0	2.7	4.8	0.5	–	14.9
Other response	3.2	2.7	6.7	4.4	1.0	1.3	3.6
Parent's self-reported "race":							
White	16.8	32.9	63.8	60.8	0.9	4.7	30.2
Black	6.2	7.4	1.4	1.4	0.9	81.4	7.4
Asian	39.7	29.9	13.0	0.7	76.9	2.3	29.2
Multiracial	8.9	8.6	10.1	15.6	0.9	2.3	9.6
Hispanic, Latino	2.6	2.4	1.4	6.7	–	–	3.2
Nationality	20.1	13.0	2.9	6.3	18.8	–	14.2
Other response	5.7	5.9	7.2	8.4	1.7	9.3	6.3

[a] Figures are column percentages. The probability that the differences by type of identity are due to chance is less than 1 in 1,000 for all variables in the table. The types of self-identities are those reported in the 1995–96 survey. For simplicity of presentation, a small residual category of mixed identities is not included.

[b] Reported self-identity as "Hispanic," "Latino," or "Chicano."

Source: CILS (longitudinal sample, N = 4,288).

by those identifying as hyphenated Americans (70 percent); by comparison, the youths identifying by each of the different varieties of pan-ethnic labels were more likely to have attended inner-city schools with peers who tend to be primarily native racial and ethnic minorities. Although only a third (35 percent) of the sample attended schools in the inner city, half of those identifying as Black did so (49 percent), as did 43 percent of the Asians, and 38 percent of the Hispanics or Latinos.

The process of growing ethnic awareness among the children of immigrants in the CILS sample is especially evident in their perceptions, experiences, and expectations of racial and ethnic discrimination. As Table 12.5 shows, reports of actual discriminatory experiences increased from 54 percent to 62 percent of the sample in the last survey. Virtually every group reported more such experiences of rejection or unfair treatment against themselves as they grew older, with the highest proportions found among the children of African-Caribbean and Asian-origin immigrants, followed by Mexicans and other Latin Americans, and the lowest proportions among Cuban youth in Miami.

As seen in Table 12.5, there are significant associations between experiences and expectations of discrimination reported at both surveys, and the types of ethnic and pan-ethnic self-identities expressed in the latest survey. Indeed, discrimination sharpens ethnic–racial identity boundaries and increases the salience of the category on the basis of which persons experience unfair treatment. Among the three main types of ethno-national identities, the highest proportions of experienced and of expected discrimination were reported by those who identified by national origin, and the lowest by those who identified as American, with hyphenates in between. Among the three main types of pan-ethnic identities, by far the highest proportions were seen among "Black"-identified respondents, with "Asian"-identified pan-ethnics in the middle, and the lowest among "Hispanic"-identified youth. This last result was most clearly seen among Latin American-origin youth in South Florida, where they constitute a numerical majority in dense ethnic enclaves that buffer them from external discrimination.

Still, it is important as well to underscore the fact that despite their growing awareness of racial and ethnic inequalities, most of the youth in the sample (almost two thirds) continued to affirm a confident belief in the promise of equal opportunity through educational achievement. Even more tellingly, as Table 12.6 shows, 61 percent of these youths agreed in the 1992 survey that "there is no better country to live in than the United States," and that endorsement grew to 71 percent 3 years later – despite a growing anti-immigrant mood in the country and especially in California during that period. Again there were significant differences by ethnic identity types, and even wider differences by national origin groups. Tellingly, the groups *most* likely to endorse that view were the children of political exiles who found a favorable context of reception in the United States: the

TABLE 12.6. *Self-Reported "Race" of Children of Immigrants and their Parents, by National Origin Groups, 1995–96*

National Origin Groups	Respondent (Child/Parent)	White (%)	Black (%)	Asian (%)	Multiracial (%)	Hispanic, Latino (%)	Nationality (%)	Other (%)
					Self-Reported "Race"[a]			
Latin America:								
Cuba	*Child*	41.2	0.8	–	11.5	36.0	5.5	4.9
	Parent	93.1	1.1	0.3	2.5	1.1	0.5	1.4
Mexico	*Child*	1.5	0.3	–	12.0	25.5	56.2	4.5
	Parent	5.7	–	2.1	21.6	15.9	26.1	28.5
Nicaragua	*Child*	19.4	–	–	9.7	61.8	2.7	6.5
	Parent	67.7	0.5	1.6	22.0	5.4	0.5	2.2
Other Latin America	*Child*	22.8	1.9	–	14.7	52.9	4.6	3.1
	Parent	69.5	4.6	0.8	17.8	2.3	1.9	3.1
Haiti and West Indies:								
Haiti	*Child*	–	75.9	–	8.4	–	9.6	6.0
	Parent	–	85.5	1.2	–	–	6.0	7.2
Jamaica, West Indies	*Child*	3.4	66.4	7.6	15.1	–	–	–
	Parent	8.4	65.5	5.0	8.4	–	6.7	5.9
Asia:								
Philippines	*Child*	1.1	–	61.6	13.2	–	23.0	1.1
	Parent	0.3	0.5	44.1	11.1	–	41.4	2.7
Vietnam	*Child*	–	–	89.8	1.6	–	7.0	1.6
	Parent	–	–	99.6	–	–	–	0.4
Laos, Cambodia	*Child*	0.4	–	87.8	3.4	–	7.2	1.1
	Parent	–	–	74.9	–	–	23.6	1.5
Other Asia	*Child*	1.5	–	82.4	13.2	–	2.9	–
	Parent	2.9	1.5	76.5	1.5	–	8.8	8.8
Europe, Canada:	*Child*	76.0	–	–	8.0	12.0	–	4.0
	Parent	84.0	–	–	8.0	4.0	–	4.0
TOTALS	*Child*	12.1	6.5	32.1	10.3	20.3	15.5	3.2
	Parent	30.2	7.4	29.2	9.6	3.2	14.2	6.3

[a] Figures are row percentages.

Source: CILS.

Cubans and the Vietnamese. The groups *least* likely to agree with that statement were those who had most felt the weight of racial discrimination: the children of immigrants from Haiti, Jamaica, and the West Indies. As they learn how they are viewed and treated within their contexts of reception and rejection, of social inclusion and exclusion, the youths form and inform their own attitudes toward the society that receives them – and their own identities as well.

Race and Identity

Near the end of the 1995–96 follow-up survey, the respondents were asked to answer a semistructured question about their "race." They were given the option to check one of five categories: "White," "Black," "Asian," "multiracial," or "other"; if the last was checked, they had to write in their own words what that "other race" was. The results (also presented in Table 12.5) are revealing.

Less than half of the total sample checked the conventional categories of White, Black, or Asian; 11 percent reported being multiracial; and more than 40 percent checked "other." Nearly a quarter of those who responded "other" wrote down "Hispanic" or "Latino" as their "race," and another 14 percent reported their nationality as their "race." Among those youths adopting pan-ethnic identities, as Table 12.5 indicates, there is an obvious conflation of race and ethnicity in the way they define their identities: 92 percent of those who identify as "Asian" give that as their race, as do 85 percent of those who identify as "Black" – while 58 percent of those who identify as "Hispanic" or "Latino" extend racial meaning to that label as well. Among those youths identifying by the other ethno-national types, racial self-definition as "White" makes a decisive difference: 58 percent of the plain American youths said they were White, compared to 17 percent of the hyphenated Americans and 6 percent of those identifying by a foreign national origin.

The explicit racialization of the "Hispanic" or "Latino" categories, as well as the substantial proportion of youths who conceived of their nationality of origin as a fixed racial category, are noteworthy both for their potential long-term implications in hardening group boundaries, and for their illustration of the arbitrariness of racial constructions. The latter point is made particularly salient by directly comparing the youths' notions of their "race" with that reported by their own parents (the same "race" item was used in the parental interviews of 1995–96). Those results are cross-tabulated in Table 12.6.

The closest match in racial self-perceptions between parents and children is evident among the Haitians, Jamaicans, and other West Indians (most of whom self-report as Black), among the Europeans and Canadians (most of whom label themselves White), and among most of the Asian-origin groups except for the Filipinos. The widest mismatches by far occur among the Latin-American-origin groups. For example, 93 percent of Cuban parents identify as White, compared to only 41 percent of their children; 68 percent of Nicaraguan parents see themselves as White, but only 19 percent of their children agree, as is the case among all other Latin-origin groups except Mexicans. The children of the former, instead, largely adopt "Hispanic" or "Latino" as a racial label, whereas scarcely any of their parents do so, as Table 12.6 vividly shows. Among the Mexicans, whose pattern differs from all of the others, the children preponderantly racialize the national label, whereas Mexican parents are more likely to use "other" (mestizo) and "multiracial" as descriptors.

These remarkable results point to the force of the acculturation process and its impact on children's self-identities. Fully exposed to American culture and its racial definitions, children learn to see themselves more and more in these terms and even to racialize their national origins. We turn now to a multivariate analysis of these self-perceptions and their determinants.

Determinants of Ethnic Self-Identities

Thus far I have examined several correlates that are theoretically and empirically linked to specific patterns of ethnic self-identification. Among these factors are parental socioeconomic resources, nativity and national origin, parent–child relations within the family, acculturation and language, discrimination, and race. To consider which factors predict ethnic and pan-ethnic identity labels, I estimated a series of multivariate logistic regressions (not shown) with each separate identity type as the dependent variable. To establish unambiguously the temporal ordering of effects, the predictors in the equations were measured in 1992, whereas the dependent variables were measured in 1995–96. The patterns that emerge from the multivariate analyses confirm a continuum of determination from national-origin to hyphenated to plain American self-definitions, as well as distinct profiles for the main pan-ethnic identities.

First, controlling for other predictors, nativity variables remain powerfully linked to self-identity. Being born in the United States was by far the strongest *negative* predictor of identifying by the parental national origin. It was also the strongest *positive* predictor of identifying as a hyphenated American, and it was a significant *positive* predictor of selecting a plain-American identity as well. Among pan-ethnic identities, being born in the United States was also *positively* predictive of the made-in-the-USA identities of Hispanic and Black. Becoming a naturalized U.S. citizen adds to the pattern above for all three of the ethno-national identities – negatively predicting a foreign nationality identity, positively predicting American self-definitions, with or without a hyphen – but it washes out of the equations for all three of the pan-ethnic identities. Citizenship influences national self-definitions, over and above nativity, but it seems to be irrelevant for the adoption of denationalized, racialized identities. The acquisition of citizenship may be interpreted as signaling a stake in the society as a full-fledged member, legally as well as subjectively, with an accompanying shift in one's frame of reference. Nativity and citizenship exerted far stronger influences on ethnic self-identification than our measure of years in the United States. Thus, it is not so much the length of residence in the receiving country but rather the nature of one's sociopolitical membership status in it that appears to be more determinative of the psychology of ethnic belonging.

The parents' own nativity in turn exerts a strong independent influence on the ethnic socialization of the child. Having both parents born in the same nation strongly boosts the odds that the child will identify with the parents' nationality, or at least keep part of it by identifying binationally as a hyphenated American. When the parents were not conationals, having one parent born in the United States also strongly increased the probability of adopting a hyphenated-American identity. Conversely, children whose parents were born in different (typically Latin American) foreign countries were more likely to identify pan-ethnically as Hispanic or Latino, showing again the impact of parental intermarriage on the lack of continuity of ancestral identities. Parental intermarriage blurs the boundaries of ethnicity for the children and clearly complicates and may derail the transmission of an ancestral identity.

Second, among the set of predictors involving the children's perceptions of their parents and family, two variables retained significant effects on ethnic identification: the embarrassment and familism indices. Respondents who reported feeling embarrassed by their parents were less likely to identify by national origin, and more likely to identify as a hyphenated American. This index was also the strongest determinant of choosing an "Asian" self-identity: the more embarrassed children felt about their parents, the more likely they were to adopt that pan-ethnic identity. By contrast, those high on the attitudinal familism index were more likely to identify by national origin. These results point to the varying effects on ethnic self-identity of the loosening of family ties – and of the maintenance of family attachments. In general, the preceding set of variables involving various aspects of the parent–child relationship underscores the fundamental influence of the family as a crucible of ethnic socialization in this diverse population of children of immigrants.

Third, parental socioeconomic status washed out in most of these regressions, suggesting that its effect on modes of self-identification is indirect and more likely to be mediated through other variables. However, the two cases where direct effects are observable are noteworthy. Immigrant parents who are higher-status professionals were *more* likely to influence their children's selection of a foreign national identity. Conversely, a Hispanic minority identity was associated with *lower*-status parents, suggesting that, with other predictors held constant, more vulnerable low-SES youths were also more susceptible to that pan-ethnic mode of self-definition. In more resourceful, upper-middle-class immigrant families the child may have more reason to associate social honor with and to feel pride in the national identity of the parents – and to affirm it for themselves. This finding is in accord with theoretical expectations that identity shifts tend to be from lower to higher status groups and not vice versa, all other things being equal.

Fourth, acculturation and language use, preference and proficiency remain significantly but only moderately linked to most of the forms of ethnic self-identification. Youths who did not prefer English or American ways (low acculturation scores) and who were not proficient in English (as measured in the 1992 survey) were somewhat more likely to identify by a foreign national origin in the latest survey. Youth who identified as Hispanic, by contrast, also did not prefer English or American ways (low acculturation scores) yet were proficient in English while also regularly speaking Spanish at home. Highly acculturated respondents who preferred and were proficient in English *but who also used the foreign language frequently at home* were most likely to identify binationally as hyphenated Americans. If they were equally acculturated but spoke only English at home, they were more likely to drop the hyphen and identify as plain American. In sum, these identity choices reflect not only varying levels of linguistic fluency but also the nuances of how and which languages are used with significant others in varying social contexts. As noted earlier, the switch to English is part of a larger acculturation process bound to entail the abandonment not only of an ancestral language but also of an ancestral identity. What the switch to English per se does not predict is the form that these alternative self-identities will take.

Finally, discrimination and racialization exert among the strongest net effects on modes of ethnic self-identification. Youths who reported more experiences of discrimination were strongly disposed to identify with a foreign national origin, without any "American" qualifier attached. Such experiences and perceptions of exclusion and rejection on ascribed racial–ethnic grounds clearly undercut the prospect of identificational assimilation into the mainstream. It is worth noting that in analyses of national-origin identities, the strength of the discrimination effect was cut in half *after* two "race" dummy variables were entered into the regression (for those reporting their "race" either as White or as their nationality). This suggests that a substantial part of the discrimination measure was absorbed by those racial categories. Holding other factors constant, a non-White racial self-designation was strongly predictive of a foreign national identity. And those who understood their nationality of origin in fixed, racial terms – as a "race" – were even more likely to define themselves by national origin. Only a foreign birth had a stronger net effect on the probability of adopting a foreign national origin self-identity.

On the other end of the identity continuum, respondents who reported more experiences of discrimination were significantly *less* likely to identify as plain American. The effect of the discrimination measure was negative and significant *before* the same two racial self-definitions were entered into the equation. The strength of the discrimination effect was attenuated to insignificance once the two "race" variables were entered. Indeed, when a "White" racial self-conception was entered into the equation, that variable had by far the strongest effect on the determination of plain American identities. *An "American" ethnic identity and a "White" racial identity emerge as nearly synonymous in these results.* What is more, when national-origin groups were entered in the models, the *only* ones who retained strong and positive net effects on the odds of selecting a plain American identity were Europeans and Canadians. Without exception, none of the Latin American, Caribbean, or Asian groups in the sample had a significant positive association with that particular identity outcome.

Among the various pan-ethnic identity types, high scores on experiences of discrimination were significantly associated only with the selection of a Black self-identity. But discrimination had a strong *negative* effect on the selection of a Hispanic identity, underscoring the observation made earlier about the comparatively protective aspects of the Miami enclave as a buffer against experiences and expectations of discrimination among Latin-origin youths. In this regard, a contextual variable – the type and location of the school (and by inference, of the neighborhood and the proximal peer groups) in which these youths were placed – made an additional difference in the process of self-definition. With all other predictor variables held constant, having attended inner-city schools in junior high school where most students were racial–ethnic minorities significantly increased the likelihood of developing a racial or pan-ethnic identity (particularly for youths reporting a Black or Hispanic/Latino self-identity), while decreasing the probability of identifying ancestrally by national origin. These results provide empirical support for a segmented assimilation perspective, here applied to the process of ethnic (and racial) self-definition.

Did specific national origins continue to affect the types of ethnic self-identification once the other predictors were taken into account? In many cases they did not; that is, despite the wide range of differences between them, many nationalities (entered as dummy variables into the regression equations) retained no significant effects in the models tested. In some cases, however, they did – suggesting that there is more about those national-origin groups and their contexts of reception that is not explained by the set of predictors included in the model. For example, a strong independent effect of European and Canadian national origins was observed for the selection of a plain American identity. More than any other nationality, Cubans stood out for their strong attachment to a hyphenated-American identity, and they were followed closely in this propensity by the Vietnamese, net of all other factors. Two other important cases involve the Mexicans and Filipinos, both of whom retained strong positive effects on the likelihood of adopting a foreign national identity.

As shown earlier (in Table 12.2), those two California-based nationalities shifted to the foreign national identity by a greater percentage than any other group on either coast. And in the case of the Mexicans in particular, our qualitative evidence suggested how the California sociopolitical context in which the divisive Proposition 187 campaign was conducted had heightened the salience of ethnic and racial boundaries and accompanying processes of reaction formation. As a test of this effect, I entered into the regression a dummy variable for regional location. When this contextual factor was accounted for, the Mexican nationality effect completely washed out of the equation – but the Filipino effect, although reduced in magnitude, remained strong. The results suggest that the propensity of the Mexican-origin youths to identify by national origin at the time of the 1995 survey was accounted for by the effect of the California context. However, the similar propensity of Filipino youths was not explained by any of the predictor variables in the model, raising intriguing theoretical and empirical questions as to why this may be so. Perhaps the history of U.S. colonialism in the Philippines and the valence of that colonial past in Filipino collective consciousness may have more to do with the identity choices of Filipino youth, as forms of ethnicity that react as much against that past as to their present circumstances. Indeed, the larger theoretical significance of national-origin groups as proxies for their contexts of reception in the United States – and as proxies for the histories of the relations of those countries with the United States – further underscores the complexity of the factors that may impinge on the determination of ethnic self-identities in the second generation.

Limitations and Implications

The foregoing analysis of ethnic self-identity and the factors that shape it stem from a single open-ended question asked at two points in time, 3 years apart, in a mostly structured survey of representative samples of adolescent children of immigrants in the United States. Those surveys were supplemented by separate interviews with their parents, in which we were able to ask some equally worded questions for comparative analysis, including items on racial self-identification. Nonetheless, there are significant limitations involved in this analysis – both substantively and methodologically. Some of these are briefly considered here, focusing on their implications for comparative research on ethnicity.

Ethnic identities are contextually malleable and may be hypothesized to vary across different social situations, across different developmental stages throughout the life course, and across different historical contexts. Our survey instruments did not examine the situational contexts in which ethnic self-identities may be differentially, and multiply, deployed; yet, in theory, the way an ethnic identity may be expressed in one's presentation of self can differ depending on one's audience. Multiple identities, moreover, may reflect mixed ethnic origins as well as multiple markers of ethnic difference from others – including race and religion and region or nation of origin – that are not reducible to a single identity (as official data are wont to do by reducing ethnicity to fixed-choice categories). And in the data here presented, we surveyed our respondents from their mid- to their late teens. But adolescence is, among other things, a developmental period of "identity crisis" and identity formation; the CILS results reported here are thus limited to that period of the life course and may not apply, for example, to samples of middle-aged adults with children of their own in whom they may be trying to inculcate a sense of ethnic attachment. And as seen especially among Mexican-origin respondents with respect to reactive self-identifications expressed in the aftermath of the Proposition 187 campaign in California, the larger sociopolitical and historical context matters. But our surveys were limited to the same locales in the mid-1990s.

Although the quantified coded responses given by thousands of individuals from dozens of diverse national origins revealed a handful of distinct patterns that advance our explanation of complex processes of self-identification, they do not tell us much about the (likely varying) subjective meanings that particular ethnic or racial labels may have had for individual respondents, the degree to which ethnicity is racialized in the respondents' own notions of these modes of group identity, or for that matter the possibility that the same label (e.g., "Latino") may take on different meanings for the same individual at a later time (e.g., in young adulthood) or in different circumstances (e.g., in college). Such considerations underscore the need to both broaden and deepen our research by incorporating mixed methods as appropriate to get at those dimensions of varying subjectivity and situationality, and to facilitate a more thoroughly contextualized study of ethnic identity and social belonging, and their cumulative causation. In particular, they suggest the need to extend our study longitudinally into adulthood, and to complement the survey methods we have employed in CILS – and the representative sample on which the study is based – with in-depth qualitative interviews, oral histories, and targeted ethnographies.

Conclusion

Ethnic identities are not inevitable outcomes, but complex products of people's ongoing efforts to interpret, understand, and respond to the social structural, cultural, and historical situations in which they find themselves, within their sets of resources and vulnerabilities. To be sure, now as in the past, immigration begets ethnicity, but the modes and contexts of immigrant incorporation are not the same today as they were in the past. For today's immigrants to the United States and their offspring, the processes of adaptation and ethnogenesis unfold in an era of civil rights, affirmative action, and ethnic revivals that differ in kind from those which obtained during the heyday of hegemonic Americanization in the early 20th century. Nonetheless, today's newcomers are recategorized in broad racialized pan-ethnic clusters that the host society deems appropriate for those sharing (or imagined to share) a particular language or phenotype – and that convey the symbolic message, with its attendant stereotypes, that the newcomers belong to a subordinate status in the national hierarchy. Although the state, the school system, the media, and the society at large may insist on redefining these immigrants and their children into one-size-fits-all pan-ethnic labels such as "Hispanics" and "Asians," the children themselves are quite plural in their ethnic self-definitions. Challenged to incorporate what is "out there" into what is "in here" and to crystallize a sense of who they are, they "translate themselves" and construct a variety of self-identities in constant interaction with both internal and external circumstances. Some cling tenaciously to their parents' national loyalties and retain their parents' national identities, with or without a hyphen. Others shift to an unhyphenated American self-image and identify symbolically with the mainstream, banking on their unaccented English and consonant phenotypic traits. Still others internalize the racial and pan-ethnic categories into which they are constantly classified and identify symbolically with national minorities.

As we have seen, the paths to those different forms of ethnic self-definition are shaped by a variety of social and psychological forces. The results of our surveys show major differences in patterns of self-identification among teenage children of immigrants from scores of sending countries growing up in two distinct corners of the United States. They suggest some of the complex, conflictive, often incongruous and unexpected ways in which race and class, discrimination and acculturation, family relationships and personal dreams can complicate their sense of who they are. And they suggest that identities are neither fixed nor irreversible, but always a function of relational processes whose meaning is embedded in concrete social and historical contexts. If for some the search for identity may with time and acceptance blur and fade into the twilight of ethnicity, for others it may with sharpened salience lead into the high noon of ethnicity – and for still others something in the wide range between those poles. But the underlying process is one in which all children of immigrants are inescapably engaged and of which they are acutely aware: making sense of who they are and finding a meaningful place in their adoptive society.

Acknowledgment

An earlier version of this paper was presented to the Jacobs Foundation Conference on "Ethnic Variations in Intergenerational Continuities and Discontinuities in Psychosocial Features and Disorders," Schloss Marbach, Ohningen, Germany, October 2002. I gratefully acknowledge the support provided to the Children of Immigrants Longitudinal Study (CILS) by research grants from the Russell Sage Foundation, and by the Andrew W. Mellon, Spencer, and National Science Foundations, to Alejandro Portes and Rubén G. Rumbaut, Principal Investigators.

References

Alba, R. D. (1985). *Italian Americans: Into the twilight of ethnicity.* Englewood Cliffs, NJ: Prentice-Hall.

Aleinikoff, T. A., & Rumbaut, R. G. (1998). Terms of belonging: Are models of membership self-fulfilling prophecies? *Georgetown Immigration Law Journal, 13,* 1–24.

Bozorgmehr, M. (1997). Internal ethnicity: Iranians in Los Angeles. *Sociological Perspectives, 40,* 387–408.

Cornell, S., & Hartmann, D. (1998). *Ethnicity and race: Making identities in a changing world.* Thousand Oaks, CA: Pine Forge.

Deaux, K. (1996). Social Identification. In E. T. Higgins & A. W. Kruglanski (Eds.), *Social psychology: Handbook of basic principles.* New York: Guilford.

Erikson, E. H. (1968). *Identity: Youth and crisis.* New York: W. W. Norton.

Gans, Herbert J. (1979). Symbolic ethnicity: The future of ethnic groups and cultures in America. *Ethnic and Racial Studies, 2,* 1–20.

Gordon, M. (1964). *Assimilation in American life: The role of race, religion, and national origins.* New York: Oxford University Press.

Horowitz, D. L. (1985). *Ethnic groups in conflict.* Berkeley: University of California Press.

Nahirny, V. C., & Fishman, J. A. (1996) [1965]. American immigrant groups. Ethnic identification and the problem of generations. In W. Sollors (Ed.), *Theories of ethnicity: A classical reader* (pp. 266–281). New York: New York University Press.

Phinney, J. S. (1990). Ethnic identity in adolescents and adults: Review of research. *Psychological Bulletin, 108,* 499–514.

Portes, A., & Rumbaut, R. G. (1996). *Immigrant America: A portrait* (2nd ed.). Berkeley, CA: University of California Press.

Portes, A., & Rumbaut, R. G. (2001). *Legacies: The story of the immigrant second generation.* Berkeley and New York: University of California Press and Russell Sage Foundation.

Rosenberg, M. (1965). *Society and the adolescent self-image*. Princeton, NJ: Princeton University Press.

Rosenberg, M. (1979). *Conceiving the self*. New York: Basic Books.

Rumbaut, R. G. (2002). Severed or sustained attachments? Language, identity, and imagined communities in the post-immigrant generation. In M. C. Waters & P. Levitt (Eds.), *The changing face of home: The transnational lives of the second generation* (pp. 43–95). New York: Russell Sage Foundation.

Rumbaut, R. G., & Portes, A. (Eds.) (2001). *Ethnicities: Children of immigrants in America*. Berkeley and New York: University of California Press and Russell Sage Foundation.

Schmidley, D. (2003). The foreign-born population in the United States: March 2002. *Current Population Reports* P20–539. Washington, DC: U.S. Census Bureau.

Tajfel, H. (1981). *Human groups and social categories*. London: Cambridge University Press.

Waters, M. C. (1990). *Ethnic options: Choosing identities in America*. Berkeley, CA: University of California Press.

13

Deciphering Ethnicity

Reflections on Research Opportunities

Marta Tienda and Michael Rutter

Conceptualizing and empirically demonstrating how ethnic differences emerge, why they persist over time, and their consequences for youth development has proven to be a formidable research challenge. The highly fluid character of ethnicity coupled with temporal and spatial variation in its definition and measurement are two difficulties analysts must surmount, but inadequate conceptualization is perhaps the greatest hindrance to understanding how ethnic differences matter. Many analysts implicitly assume that ethnicity constitutes an explanation for variation in myriad psychosocial outcomes, rather than a phenomenon to be explained. This assumption hinders research into causal mechanisms. Whether by design or default, ethnic variation is often derived as a statistical residual rather than as a starting point for sharp theoretical questions about which of its multiple facets operates to produce the outcome of interest, what circumstances trigger ethnically differentiated responses, and which ethnic differences persist over time.

The chapters assembled in this volume illustrate the inherent difficulties not only of drawing causal inferences about *how* and *why* ethnic differences emerge, but also of generalizing about the circumstances through which ethnicity becomes a risk or protective factor for adolescents. In Chapter 3 we characterized ethnicity as a multifaceted phenomenon that is socially constructed and hence highly pliable. Subsequently, we identified possible mediators of ethnic effects, including individual and group identity, religion, language use, and myriad cultural practices that differentiate populations, irrespective of whether they send migrants elsewhere. Using different methodological approaches and focusing on diverse outcomes, including educational attainment, socialization practices, antisocial behavior, mental health, and identity development, the foregoing chapters attempt to disentangle proximal from more distal correlates of psychosocial outcomes in order to identify the circumstances that generate and/or accentuate ethnic group differences. Temporal variation is essential to establish whether and what forms of ethnic variation are likely to become enduring features of a population. Generational comparisons are especially instructive to this end, yet by themselves cannot reveal why ethnic differences diminish for some groups but not others.

In the Preface to this volume we highlighted key substantive insights from each of the chapters, which need not be repeated. However, as a testimonial to their success in questioning what factors give rise to ethnic differences and how these change over time and across social settings, the authors raise as many questions as they answer. Therefore, in this concluding chapter, we highlight several key insights about the mechanisms that produce ethnic differences in order to suggest promising research lines and to draw selective policy lessons.

Ethnic Continuities and the Migration Paradigm

Two features of this volume provide analytical leverage for understanding the emergence and evolution of ethnic differences in psychosocial outcomes. First, paired comparisons of ethnic group experiences in the United Kingdom and the United States permit selected inferences about how context – notably reception factors and modes of incorporation (Portes & Rumbaut, 1996) – contributes to the emergence and consolidation of ethnic differences. Despite the shared history and cultural affinities of the two settings, the United States and United Kingdom differ appreciably in their migration histories and apparently also in the trajectories of second-generation youth. Situational factors define the contours of ethnicity at the time of migration and through the process of settlement, cultural adjustment, and structural integration. Nonetheless, the cross-site comparisons of specific groups provide a foundation for generalizations beyond single case studies, while also aiding in the identification of puzzles based on divergent experiences of specific national origin groups.

For example, better understanding of how situational factors operate to produce ethnic differences is needed to decode the paradox of apparently lower educational achievement of Caribbean Blacks in the United Kingdom compared with the relatively better performance of their U.S. ethnic counterparts. This paradox may reflect dissimilar selection regimes, or different reception factors that raise the risks associated with being a foreign-born Black youth more for those destined to the United Kingdom than for those who settle in the United States (Waters, 1999). However, more investigation is needed to ascertain whether Caribbean Blacks bound for the United States are more positively selected, and what place-specific circumstances elevate the risks associated with Caribbean origin in the United Kingdom, if, in fact, that hypothesis is borne out empirically.

A second set of insights derives from efforts to identify the mechanisms that trigger differential responses among ethnic groups. Situations where the migrant group differs appreciably from the host society offer the richest opportunities to understand the emergence and evolution of ethnic variation. Socio-demographic approaches to migration distinguish among three mechanisms, namely, selection, disruption, and assimilation – all of which can influence the production of ethnic differences, albeit to differing degrees. That assimilation became the key concept in the study of immigration and ethnicity in the United States conveys the expectation that newcomers will, with the passage of time, become integrated into the host society (Portes & Rumbaut, 2001, 1996; Alba & Nee, 1999). The amount of time required to render ethnic differences inconsequential was of less concern to most early analysts of immigrant integration than the theorized inevitable direction of change, which Milton Gordon (1964) characterized in three variants of assimilation: anglo conformity, melting pot, and cultural pluralism. These variants reflect different ways cultural diversity manifests itself, not degrees of integration or ethnic variation in psychosocial outcomes.

Among U.S. social scientists, assimilation tends to be viewed as a largely positive goal. By contrast, among UK social scientists, it involves many negative connotations because it implies a required loss of a separate identity. Thus, many Jews wish to retain their own religious schools, festivals, diet, and customs and, to that extent, do not wish to be placed in a "melting pot." On the other hand, other than Hassidic Jews, who remain rather separate from the main Jewish community, they do not wish to dress differently and they do not wish to be treated first as a Jew rather than as a fellow Britisher. Of course, they wish to be successful in the broader British society (and many of them are) and they do not want to be discriminated against (and in most circumstances they no longer are to any marked extent, although anti-Semitism remains in some groups). The Chinese community in both the United States and the United Kingdom has also chosen to remain relatively separate in many ways. They are largely "integrated" in the sense that they are accepted and not subject to substantial discrimination. The Amish in the United States are even more separate and wish to remain so. The Welsh in the United Kingdom are fiercely proud of their separate culture and language and have no wish to be assimilated in a global sense, but they are not discriminated against.

In short, it is not an acceptable goal to seek an elimination of ethnic differences with respect to culture and identity. It is, however, a desirable goal both to get rid of discrimination against ethnic (or any other sort of) groups, and to avoid the processes by which ethnic variations lead to, or become associated with, social (or other forms of) disadvantage.

In that connection, too, the notion of "the host society" is similarly misleading and offensive to many. British politicians on the extreme right have long argued that immigrants must accept all the mores and customs of this hypothetical society, totally ignoring the varied nature of such mores and customs. There are many British "host societies" and not just one. The situation in the United States is the same. Although integration continues to reflect the socioeconomic acceptance of immigrants into a multicultural nation, recent scholarship has questioned Gans's (1979) notion of "straight-line" integration, which implies a predictable, temporal, positive progression. The straight-line perspective is overly simplistic because it overlooks numerous deviations from the predicted upward trajectory of immigrant integration (Alba & Nee, 1999). Portes and Zhou's (1993) segmented concept conveys the idea that the process of immigrant integration need not follow an upward trajectory from lower to higher status locations in the social structure. Studying the diverse integration trajectories of immigrant groups across national contexts will help identify necessary and sufficient conditions for ethnic prejudice and exclusion to disappear or to become accentuated (Portes & Rumbaut, 2001, p. 148).

Selection and disruption mechanisms are the less well-studied facets of the migration paradigm. Demographers have studied disruption effects on fertility to determine whether completed family size of migrants differs from that of natives, or whether disruption effects of migration on fertility manifest themselves mainly as changes in spacing of births. However, few demographic surveys contain the requisite data to distinguish selection from disruption effects empirically. Unless migrant women are compared with their nonmigrant counterparts in the sending communities, selection effects cannot be easily disentangled from disruption effects. As Jones and Fung (this volume) aptly demonstrate, both mechanisms are crucial for understanding ethnic variation in the incidence of schizophrenia among Caribbean Blacks residing in the United Kingdom because the migration experience itself can trigger physical and psychological responses that can be misconstrued as genetic predispositions to poor mental health. Few studies have theorized how disruption effects play out and what forms of disruption produce deleterious effects and which do not.

Unfortunately, few analysts have access to data that characterize the circumstances surrounding the migratory experience; hence disruption effects are seldom assessed indirectly, as inferences based on outcomes. Yet, the stresses experienced by voluntary migrants whose departure is planned and orderly may be quite different from those, such as political refugees and asylum seekers, whose departure from their country of origin may be chaotic and sudden. Rumbaut (1985) has documented how the circumstances of departure affect the mental health status of Southeast Asian refugees subsequent to arrival, and it is no surprise that groups whose migration experience was precipitated by fear of persecution and family breakup experienced higher levels of stress in their host community. The displacement and resettlement involved in the process of international migration is itself stressful, but all the more so when the cultural and social differences between the host and migrant populations are large, and/or when the move occurs under traumatic circumstances, as often occurs for refugees. Ethnic differences so produced may have more to do with the circumstances of migration rather than with psychosocial and cultural differences among the groups compared. This is so in both the United States and the United Kingdom.

Although several authors exploit comparisons of first and second generations of immigrants to characterize trajectories of integration, only Jones and Fung were able to compare migrants with their source populations. Such comparisons proved essential for isolating the migration process and its sequelae as stress-inducing experiences that can trigger mental illness. Thus, until both selection and disruption effects are suitably represented, inferences about ethnicity and segmented or straight-line integration will remain tentative.

Research Opportunities

Given the practical and theoretical purposes that motivated the conference, two indicators signaling a successful research undertaking are the richness of new questions raised for further inquiry, and the guides for practical interventions to lessen the association of ethnicity with various indicators of disadvantage and maladjustment. Collectively, the chapters underscore that ethnicity is of limited theoretical or practical relevance without a solid understanding of the mechanisms that produce and perpetuate ethnic variations over time. Whatever the outcome of interest, the challenge of deciphering causal mechanisms that produce ethnic differences requires longitudinal data that capture both developmental processes and intergenerational continuities and discontinuities. Without this requirement, the pitfalls of correlational designs will continue to blur understanding of the mechanisms through which ethnic differences are generated and maintained.

Generational Transitions

Although it is commonplace to draw inferences about assimilation from intergenerational comparisons, with few exceptions, these differences usually conflate third-generation immigrants with ethnic minority groups whose migration history may be in the very distant past. This measurement problem is particularly applicable for studies based on census-type data, which are unable to distinguish the third- from higher-order generations (Suro & Passel, 2003). Beyond measurement, however, the more formidable challenge is to conceptualize how and why ethnic differences persist among nonimmigrant groups whose parents and grandparents did migrate. Simply put, Native Americans and African Americans are not immigrant minorities whose integration experiences can be represented or directly compared with those of first- and second-generation immigrants. In fact, early critics of Gordon's assimilation paradigm were explicit in noting that many U.S. minority groups were "unmeltable," and hence required an alternative framework to explain their social and economic marginality.

Additional puzzles from the educational experiences of immigrant and minority youth can derive productive analytical leverage from the migration paradigm (see Oropesa & Landale, 1997, for an example based on Puerto Ricans). For example, the seeming nonlinear association between generational status and educational attainment warrants more careful disaggregation of the so-called third generation, which in census-type surveys is an aggregation of third- and higher-order generations (Smith, 2003). The growing volume of U.S. research about the second generation has begun to fill that necessary gap (Portes & Rumbaut, 2001), but these school-based studies are unable to monitor the selection regimes underlying the flows or how disruption effects play out over the short and long term. Oropesa and Landale's (1997) study is a noteworthy exception because their design includes respondents at origin and destination.

Massive U.S. immigration from Asia and Latin America provides promising future opportunities to consider whether ethnic differences persist into the third generation, for which groups, and under what circumstances. During the next 20 years, the second generation – children of immigrants from Latin America – will constitute almost half of Hispanic population growth in the United States, whereas their offspring, "the true third generation," will make up just over one-quarter of projected growth (Suro & Passel, 2003). Looking forward, this demographic phenomenon represents a unique opportunity to understand not only the emergence and transformation of Hispanic ethnicity across generations and among diverse national origin groups, assuming appropriate longitudinal data are collected, but also how Hispanics are transforming the ethno-racial landscape of the United States. Comparisons of first- and second-generation ethnic minority immigrants with nonimmigrant minority groups, such as Native Americans, African Americans, and "Hispanos" who do not identify with recent immigrants but, instead, trace their roots to the original settlers of the American Southwest, should further deepen understanding of the mechanisms that produce and consolidate ethnicity and its attendant consequences.

The United Kingdom provides similar opportunities with respect to the migration from the Caribbean in the 1950s, and the more recent migration from both Africa and the Indian subcontinent. However, in order to make best use of the migration paradigm, it will be necessary to include comparisons with the country of origin (as the Jones and Fung chapter well illustrates), and to examine intergenerational continuities and discontinuities within, as well as between, families, including all offspring, in order to examine variations among siblings (see Rutter, 2004). In order to appreciate better the meaning of the processes and the causal mechanisms involved, it will often be desirable to combine quantitative and qualitative research strategies (see Laub & Sampson, 2002).

Despite its richness for distilling causal mechanisms for some psychosocial outcomes, there are limits to the utility of the migration paradigm. As noted earlier, it is not particularly helpful for understanding the disadvantaged status of nonimmigrant minority groups, such as the U.S. Native American and African American populations. The distinction between immigrant and minority youth is important for future analyses of ethnic variation (Vincent, 1974). For third- and higher-order immigrant groups, as for nonimmigrant minority youth, the temptation for ethnicity to stand for explanation may regain force unless the mechanisms undergirding ethnic differentiation are better clarified.

Educational Outcomes
Both the United Kingdom and the United States exhibit wide variation in youth educational attainment, with minority groups usually at both the lowest and highest scholastic achievement levels. While the race gap in educational attainment has been narrowing in the United States, particularly in high school graduation rates, educational gaps have widened for other groups, notably Hispanic immigrants (Mare, 1995). That Asian Americans – another immigrant minority group – have the highest attainment levels challenges simplistic explanations about the educational risks associated with either immigrant or minority group status and forces a search for deeper causes. The United Kingdom also features large differences in educational achievements of young people from South Asia, with Indians faring significantly better than Pakistani and Bangladeshi youth.

That pervasive ethnic variation in psychosocial outcomes is generally attributed to systematic group differences in socioeconomic standing inadvertently reduces ethnicity to social class, whether or not researchers admit to reductionism. However, group differences in educational attainment cannot be reduced to social class because temporal changes in schooling levels reveal both convergent and divergent educational assimilation vis-à-vis the dominant majority in both the United Kingdom and United States. Furthermore, the divergent educational trajectories of immigrant minorities in both countries implicate reception factors and context-specific circumstances as contributors to persisting ethnic differences in educational attainment of immigrant and minority youth.

The puzzling experience of West Indian youth residing in the United Kingdom and United States illustrates this point and calls into question the relative importance of selection factors versus context-reception factors in producing the divergent educational pathways for youth. In the absence of clear evidence establishing whether Black Caribbean migrants to the United States and United Kingdom differ in their achievement motivation and/or parental resources to promote their offspring's educational goals, selection remains a viable competing explanation for the segmented assimilation trajectory in the United Kingdom compared with the seemingly more positive experience of Black Caribbean youth residing in the United States. Prejudice-based social exclusion may also operate to compound educational disadvantages of UK Caribbean Blacks (Gillborn & Mirza, 2000; Gillborn, 1996), but given the legacy of racial discrimination in the United States, their seemingly different fate is odd. A comparison of Haitian and Jamaican youth residing in different contexts would provide some insight into this puzzle, particularly if social class differences can be minimized. It is also conceivable that the apparent puzzle merely reflects the fact that, in the United States, Caribbean Blacks are compared with African Americans – a nonimmigrant minority – whereas in the United Kingdom, the core comparison is with their first-generation counterparts (usually their parents). Such comparisons that confound temporal and cross-section ethnic variation cannot possibly clarify whether and how context-reception factors operate to produce the apparent differences.

Socialization and Social Context

One of the longest standing debates in social science revolves around the relative influence of environment and socialization versus heredity on developmental psychosocial outcomes. Although arguments are frequently posed in polemical terms, there is general agreement (as well as strong evidence) that both are important to varying degrees in all facets of human development, and that these two broad sets of forces interact, often synergistically, in their influence on individual outcomes (see Rutter, 2004). The scientific evidence discussed in Chapter 3 does not find compelling proof that biology is the major determinant of ethnic differences in psychosocial outcomes, yet beliefs that heredity is directly responsible for race and ethnic variation in scholastic and economic attainment remain pervasive, even among scientists and educators (Morning, 2004). Several chapters invoke the importance of social environment in shaping distinct futures for immigrant and minority youth, but beyond the family context, there remains much ambiguity about how institutional settings, such as schools, neighborhoods, and other organizational settings, produce and/or reinforce ethnic differentiation. This state of affairs largely reflects the limited availability of data suitable for estimating context effects rather than researchers' failure to acknowledge their influence.

For example, it is unclear under what circumstances ethnic residential segregation operates as a protective factor for ethnicity and youth. The urban underclass debate emphasized the social exclusion aspects of segregation by which the effects of concentrated poverty are magnified through spatial arrangements (Massey & Denton, 1993). Yet, for new immigrants whose culture and language differ from that of the host society, residential propinquity with compatriots can also serve a protective function during the initial period of cultural adaptation. How long such protections operate is an empirical question deserving research attention. These same protections, which would tend to maintain ethnic differentiation, can become risk factors for youth if ethnic density also implies concentration of social disadvantages and opportunities for behavioral transgressions (Heitmeyer, 2001). The often fine lines between the risks and protections afforded by ethnically homogeneous neighborhoods make it difficult to tease apart ethnic variation from social class influences that are frequently conflated. This represents a priority research for future investigation.

Perception also is a powerful force in the social construction of ethnicity and ethnic identities because much social behavior, including discrimination, is predicated on belief systems, whether justified or not. The attempt by Deater-Deckard and his colleagues to clarify the mechanisms producing differences in the link between punishment and aggression is promising for understanding the sources of ethnic variation in youth conduct problems and aggressive behavior. However, their focus on developed countries, and their exclusion of Hispanics and Asians from the U.S. comparisons, warrant further replication involving a broader range of ethnic groups in the United States and elsewhere, a more representative sample of communities, and a longer longitudinal perspective.

Both Smith and Morenoff document wide ethnic variation in rates of adolescent antisocial behavior in the United Kingdom and United States, respectively. Although the national origin composition of ethnic groups differs in each nation, the pattern of variation is similar in that immigrant youth exhibit lower offending rates than their second- and higher-order generation ethnic counterparts. This apparent paradox raises questions about whether segmented integration is involved, why the downward trajectories appear to be steeper for some groups, and what circumstances are responsible for ethnic differences. In light of the difficulties of accurately measuring generational status, it is also conceivable that the misrepresentation of generations using the conventional "native born of native-born parents" to define the third generation distorts the generational comparisons by conflating the experiences of immigrants with those of ethnic minority groups (Vincent, 1974).

Because they are less fraught with measurement difficulties, comparisons between first- and second-generation youth still beg the question of which factors protect recent immigrants from engaging in antisocial behavior. Situational factors that foster offending, together with racism in the criminal justice system, probably contribute to the observed ethnic differences in crime (White, 2001), but social context factors by themselves seem insufficient to account for increases in the incidence of antisocial behavior among native-born youth from ethnic minorities, whether they have immigrant parents or not. That many recent immigrants live in economically disadvantaged ethnic neighborhoods complicates the puzzle of ethnic differences in offending rates from the opposite direction because this circumstance should elevate, not depress, deviant activity. Unfortunately, data limitations preclude further adjudication of the mechanisms that underpin ethnic variation in offending, but resolving the generational puzzle promises valuable insights not only about causal mechanisms, but also about how segmented assimilation and deviance might be related.

Perhaps the most difficult task confronted by researchers of ethnic variation is identifying ethnic-linked genetic influences on psychosocial outcomes. Jones and Fung exploit the migration paradigm to understand the elevated rates of schizophrenia among Caribbean Blacks residing in the United Kingdom and elsewhere. By comparing population rates across diverse settings, and with sensitivity to ethnic biases in (mis)diagnosis, these authors disentangle predisposing from precipitating and perpetuating factors that contribute to their high schizophrenia prevalence rates. Systematically comparing migrants with their nonmigrant counterparts at origin and destination also gives some purchase on migrant selectivity, a frequent confounding factor for understanding nativity differentials, while longitudinal comparisons help them pinpoint the timing of onset. Their hypothesis that the migration experience itself operates as a triggering mechanism is compelling enough, but also warrants further scrutiny to document the necessary and sufficient conditions for onset. At a minimum, future research should seek to identify other ways that stressful migration episodes might trigger psychosocial disorders. Study of the integration experiences of refugee populations should prove instructive in this regard.

Ascription and Ethnic Variation

Two additional research domains that promise original insights about the causes and consequences of ethnic variation in psychosocial outcomes concern sex differences and biracialism. First, although sex differences are not the main focus of this volume, several chapters highlight the value of comparing boys and girls for decoding ethnic differences. For example, cultural differences in the acceptability of physical discipline differ not only by ethnicity, as Deater-Deckard and colleagues demonstrate, but also by sex. Comparing the migration experiences of boys and girls from highly gender-stratified countries, such as Japan or Middle-Eastern nations, with those of boys and girls from societies featuring low levels of gender differentiation could prove to be highly instructive about the construction of ethnic differences. For instance, women have very low social standing in Muslim societies, and they are subject to some of the most egregious physical violence and abuse. How these normatively sanctioned behaviors carry over to societies that do not tolerate extreme physical abuse of women should prove instructive for understanding not only sex differences in aggressive behavior in the host society, but also the circumstances that structure divergent trajectories for migrants from a common culture.

Second, biracialism offers another opportunity to better understand the mechanisms that produce ethnic variation in psychosocial outcomes because it triggers ambiguity about ethnic identity, unless official classification policy imposes group membership based on phenotype or national origins, as in Apartheid South Africa or the U.S. antebellum South. The increased prevalence of multiracial admixtures, recognized in the United States by the 2000 census guidelines that permit individuals to self-classify using multiple racial categories, offers promising opportunities to investigate how racial categories are socially constructed (Morning, 2004). Moreover, in the United States, designation as "Hispanic" has greatly complicated the racial classification system because well over 40 percent of Hispanics do not self-identify as one of the six major racial groups, but rather opt for the residual "other" (Pew Hispanic Center, 2002). This response pattern is highly consistent across census and surveys that involve adults and youth, but these self-ascribed racial classifications are not well understood.

Identifying what circumstances encourage individuals to classify themselves as multiracial can further illuminate factors that are particularly salient in the social construction of racial categories, while comparisons of individuals who self-classify as single or multiple races can illustrate some of the socioeconomic consequences. For example, Udry, Li, and Hendrickson-Smith (2003) maintain that mixed-race origins are a source of great stress for adolescents, leading to higher levels of depression and deviant behavior (for example, truancy and use of alcohol and nicotine). The authors speculate that the apparent high-risk status of biracial youth derives from the struggle with identity formation and its associated lack of self-esteem and social isolation.

Nevertheless, further research is needed to confirm that mixed-race status triggers higher levels of stress – under which circumstances and why. Whether similar results would obtain if, instead of respondents' self-report of racial identity, parents' racial designations were used is another promising future direction both to corroborate their findings and to investigate whether respondents whose self-classification was at odds with that based on their parents' report experienced comparable levels of stress to those whose racial classifications were consistent. Given the fluidity of ethnic identity and inconsistency in its measurement over time, such comparisons would give some purchase on whether Udry's inference that ambivalence about identity is in fact a causal mechanism.

Policy Considerations

Ethnic variation in psychosocial outcomes is practically important when it involves unequal life chances for members of ethnic groups, which is why policymakers might be interested in the origins and evolution of ethnic differences. For example, personal decisions to don traditional dress should be inconsequential for life chances. However, if ethnic garments serve as markers that trigger prejudice and discrimination, they can produce all forms of social exclusion. To illustrate this point further, if teachers use ethnic group membership – whatever criteria are used to classify individuals as belonging to an ethnic group – as signals for expected performance or beliefs about ability, then ethnic differences in scholastic outcomes are likely. Yet, in this instance, teacher expectations rather than ethnic traits are the causal mechanism producing diversity in scholastic achievement, not ethnicity per se. Losing sight of this crucial point often results in blaming the victim – quite a serious error in the policy arena.

Explorations into the factors responsible for ethnic variation in education, ethnic identity, offending behavior, and mental health yield a set of practical lessons that can be translated into concrete policy recommendations. The social costs of economic deprivation of immigrant and minority youth, which play out in elevated rates of youth crime rates, poor mental health, and educational underachievement, are potentially profound because they accumulate over the entire life course and may promote intergenerational continuities. Such continuities do not by themselves imply causal mechanisms, yet policy designed to break cycles of disadvantage must be based on solid understanding of the transmission processes and causal mechanisms.

Accepting the dictum that problem prevention is usually cheaper and more efficient than amelioration and remediation, uncoupling the associations between ethnicity and psychosocial and economic disadvantage requires a shift from immigration policy to immigrant integration policy. The former is concerned largely with selection regimes, notably who is admitted under specific auspices; the labor needs of the domestic economy; and historically unique geopolitical ties. Policy for youth development takes these conditions as given and focuses on the socioeconomic integration of immigrants and their offspring. Whether and how much acculturation is necessary for structural integration remains a highly emotional and contested research topic. However, its practical significance looms large, particularly as the second generation comes of age (Suro & Passel, 2003), and as nation-states take official stances on the acceptability of ethnic markers (such as attire) in public places. The recent debate in France over whether Muslim women can wear head covers is a case in point. Whether such pressure cooker integration policies designed to homogenize culturally distinct groups will further the integration project, or precipitate reactive ethnicity and intergroup hostility, remains to be seen. The jury is still out, but forced assimilation should not be viewed as necessarily positive. Perhaps the concept used by many Canadians of a "cultural mosaic" might be more appropriate than that of a "melting pot."

Youth-centered integration policy is guided by a focus on investment in young people and the institutions that serve them. A few general principles follow from the evidence presented in the foregoing chapters. First, given the strong link between educational achievement and family attitudes toward education, both youth and parents should be involved in strategies to promote educational success of minority and immigrant youth. This would include providing language training for new arrivals. Moreover, the design of intervention programs should use established principles of social learning.

Second, youth-centered interventions should strive to reduce ethnic segregation that accentuates class differences. The deleterious consequences of residing in poor, socially isolated neighborhoods are well documented and require deliberate strategies to revitalize ethnically dense communities by investing in social infrastructure while respecting the right to cultural diversity. The distinction between heterogeneity and inequality must not be confused lest cause and consequence become confounded. Tawney (1952) expressed the issue particularly clearly:

While ... natural endowments differ profoundly, it is the mark of a civilised society to aim at eliminating such inequalities as have their own source, not in individual differences, but in its own organisation. ... Individual differences that are the source of social energy are more likely to ripen and find expression if social inequalities are, as far as practical, diminished. (p. 49)

Third, the elevated stress levels associated with the process of migration and the prolonged process of cultural and socioeconomic adaptation require attention to the mental health of both parents and youth. That is, a better understanding of the disruptive aspects of the migration experience can serve public policy by focusing on the causes rather than on the correlates of mental distress. Furthermore, the educational underachievement of some immigrant and minority youth warrants strengthened school-to-work transition programs to facilitate their economic integration and break the cycle of disadvantage between them and future generations.

References

Alba, R., & Nee, V. (1999). Rethinking assimilation theory for a new era of immigration. In C. Hirschman, P. Kasinitz, & J. DeWind (Eds.), *The handbook of international migration* (pp. 137–160). New York: Russell Sage.

Gans, H. J. (1979). Symbolic ethnicity: The future of ethnic groups and cultures in America. *Ethnic and Racial Studies, 2,* 1–20.

Gillborn, D. (1996). Exclusions from school. *University of London Institute for Education Viewpoint*, No. 5.

Gillborn, D., & Mirza, H. S. (2000). *Educational inequality: Mapping race, class and gender.* London: Office for Standards in Education Institute of Education. Retrieved April 6, 2003, from http://www.OFSTED.gov.uk/publications/docs/447.pdf

Gordon, M. (1964). *Assimilation in American life: The role of race, religion, and national origins.* New York: Oxford University Press.

Heitmeyer, W. (2001). Have cities ceased to function as "integration machines" for young people? In M. Tienda & W. J. Wilson (Eds.), *Youth in cities* (pp. 87–112). New York: Cambridge University Press.

Laub, J. H., & Sampson, R. J. (2002). *Shared beginnings, divergent lives: Delinquent boys to age 70.* Cambridge, MA: Harvard University Press.

Mare, R. D. (1995). Changes in educational attainment and school enrollment. In R. Farley (Ed.), *State of the Union: America in the 1990s.* New York: Russell Sage Foundation.

Massey, D. S., & Denton, N. (1993). *American apartheid.* Chicago: University of Chicago Press.

Morning, A. (2004). *The nature of race: Teaching and learning about human difference.* Unpublished doctoral dissertation, Princeton University.

Oropesa, R. S., & Landale, N. S. (1997). Immigrant legacies: Ethnicity, generation and children's familial and economic lives. *Social Science Quarterly, 78,* 399–416.

Pew Hispanic Center (2002). *2002 national survey of Latinos.* Washington, DC: Pew Hispanic Center and Kaiser Family Foundation.

Portes, A., & Rumbaut, R. G. (1996). *Immigrant America.* Berkeley: University of California Press.

Portes, A., & Rumbaut, R. G. (2001). *Legacies: The story of the immigrant second generation.* Berkeley and New York: University of California Press and Russell Sage Foundation.

Portes, A., & Zhou, M. (1993). The new second generation: Segmented assimilation and its variants. *Annals of the American Academy of Political and Social Sciences, 530,* 74–96.

Rumbaut, R. G. (1985). Mental health and the refugee experience: A comparative study of Southeast Asian refugees. In Tom C. Owan (Ed.), *Southeast Asian mental health: Treatment, prevention, services, training and research* (pp. 443–486). Rockville, MD: National Institute of Mental Health.

Rutter, M. (2004). Pathways of genetic influences on psychopathology. *European Review, 12,* 19–33.

Rutter, M. (2004). International continuities and discontinuities in psychological problems. In P. L. Chase-Lansdale, K. Kiernan, & R. Friedman (Eds.), *Human development across lives and generations: The potential for change* (pp. 239–277). Cambridge, UK: Cambridge University Press.

Smith, J. P. (2003). Assimilation across the Latino generations. *American Economic Review, 93,* 315–319.

Suro, R., & Passel, J. S. (2003). *The rise of the second generation: Changing patterns in Hispanic population growth.* Washington, DC: Pew Hispanic Center. Retrieved December 27, 2003, from http://www.pewhispanic.org/site/docs/pdf/PHC%20Projections%20final.pdf

Tawney, R. H. (1952). *Equity*. London: Allen and Unwin.

Udry, J. R., Li, R. M., & Hendrickson-Smith, J. (2003). Health and behavior risks of adolescents with mixed-race identity. *American Journal of Public Health, 93,* 1865–1870.

Vincent, J. (1974). The structuring of ethnicity. *Human Organization, 33,* 375–379.

Waters, M. (1999). *Black identities: West Indian immigrant dreams and American realities.* New York: Russell Sage Foundation.

White, R. (2001). Youth crime, community development and social justice. In M. Tienda & W. J. Wilson (Eds.), *Youth in cities* (pp. 138–164). New York: Cambridge University Press.

Author Index

Abbate, M. F., 267
Abbott, R. D., 3
Achenbach, T. M., 209
Acosta, D., 61
Adams, S., 239
Adebimpe, V. R., 246
Adlington, F. M., 216
Ageton, S. S., 149, 166
Ahituv, A., 42
Ahmad, N., 13
Ainsworth-Darnell, J. W., 111
Alba, R. D., 43, 50, 55, 109, 302, 338
Alberti, K. G., 13
Albrecht, R., 69
Alderman, M. H., 13
Aleinikoff, T. A., 306
Alexander, C. E., 188, 197
al-Issa, I., 245
Allardyce, J., 249
Allebeck, P., 249
Alvarez, L. R., 272
Amin, I., 67
Anand, I. S., 14
Anderson, D., 267
Anderson, K. E., 206
Andreasen, N. C., 228, 251
Andreasson, S., 249
Aneshensel, C. S., 266
Angold, A., 66, 193
Anker, M., 231
Aposproi, E., 269
Arel, D., 51, 54, 65
Armstrong, B., 267
Arseneault, L., 249
ÆSOP Study Group, 241, 243
Ataman, S., 13

Aye Muang, N., 180
Ayers, C. D., 3

Bachman, J. G., 268, 270, 271, 272
Baiyewu, O., 7
Baker, J., 231
Baker, P., 179
Bal, S. S., 234, 245
Baldwin-Edwards, M., 286
Ball, D., 7
Ballard, R., 293
Baluja, K. F, 71
Banaji, M. R., 181
Bandura, A., 210
Banez, G. A., 213
Bankston, C. L., 109, 110
Banton, M., 287
Barclay, M. S., 216
Barham, C., 42
Barnett, D., 271
Baron, R. M., 14, 63
Bartusch, D. J., 172
Bates, J. E., 207, 208, 213
Battle, J., 44
Baugher, M., 268
Baumrind, D., 211, 212
Beahring, T., 266
Bean, F. D., 52
Bearinger, L. H., 266
Bebbington, P. E., 239, 246, 250
Beck, A., 139
Becker, H., 177
Beckett, C., 12
Beevers, D., 234
Behl, L. E., 213, 218
Beishon, S., 81, 174, 285

Bell, J. F., 90, 95
Bell, R. Q., 4
Bellair, P. E., 153
Belsky, J., 2
Bennet, P., 14
Bennett, F., 13
Bentall, R. P., 250
Berger, M., 8
Berglund, P., 62
Berk, R. A., 2
Berlitz, J., 272
Berridge, D., 91
Bertelsen, A., 231
Berthoud, R., 24, 81, 174, 192, 193, 281, 285
Bertin, T. K., 61
Bhatnagar, D., 14
Bhopal, R., 13
Bhugra, D., 237, 239, 241, 246
Bierman, K. L., 209, 214
Bifulco, G. W., 6
Billingsley, A., 271
Birchwood, M., 246
Birmaher, B., 207
Bjerregard, B., 2
Black, A. E., 211
Blain, N., 291, 294
Blatchford, P., 90
Blau, J. R., 156
Blau, P. M., 131, 156
Block, J., 155
Blom, J. D., 237
Blum, R. W., 266, 268, 269
Blumstein, A., 166, 182
Bonczar, T., 139
Boot, D., 234
Borge, A. I. H., 11
Borges, G., 266
Borrego, J., 218
Bourque, S. L., 215
Bowcock, A. M., 61
Bowlby, J., 210
Bowler, A., 249
Bowling, B., 178, 179, 181, 183
Boxer, A. M., 69
Boydell, J., 249
Bozorgmehr, M., 312
Bradley, R. H., 209
Braithwaite, A., 14, 62
Brent, D. A., 268
Brewer, M., 43
Bridge, J., 268
Britner, P. A., 2, 211

Brodie, M., 52
Brody, G. H., 215
Brooks, J. S., 3
Brooks-Gunn, J., 29, 34, 68
Brown, A. S., 248
Brown, C., 176, 181, 191, 195
Brown, G. W., 249
Brown, L. M., 272
Brozovic, M., 7
Bruce, M. L., 266
Brugha, T., 246
Bruschi, C., 214
Bryk, A. S., 161
Bugental, D. B., 214, 217
Burchard, E. G., 8, 60, 61
Buriel, R., 208
Burke, A., 250
Burke, J. D., 90, 207
Burnett, R., 249
Bursik, R., 151
Burton, L. M., 271
Burton, V. S., 156
Butkus, M., 267

Caldwell, B. M., 209
Callan, A., 249
Calzada, E. J., 207
Camoenie, W., 237
Campbell, S., 179
Canadian Taskforce on Mental Health
    Issues, 247
Cann, H. M., 61
Cannon, M., 247, 248
Cantor-Graae, E., 237
Cantwell, D. P., 266
Caplan, N., 109
Carlson, B., 213, 215
Carriss, M., 246
Caspi, A., 2, 9, 14, 62, 69, 154, 155, 207
Castle, D., 234, 249
Catalano, R. F., 3, 268
Cavalli-Sforza, L. L., 61
Centers for Disease Control, 262, 263, 266,
    268, 270, 271
Cernkovich, S. A., 148, 183
Chadwick, O. F. D., 57
Chaiken, J. M., 147
Chaiken, M. R., 147
Chambliss, W. J., 147
Champion, L., 3
Chan, Y. C., 213
Chandrasekhar, Y., 14

Chang, J. C., 247
Chao, R., 207
Chapman, M., 4
Chard-Wierschem, D. C., 160
Chaturvedi, N., 13
Chavez, E. L., 272
Chavez, J. M., 208
Chavira, V., 272
Chen, C., 69
Chen, F., 207
Chen, T., 268
Chen, Y. R., 266
Cheng, A. T. A., 247
Chenz, Z., 269
Cheuh, H., 266
Chilamkurti, C., 207
Chiu, H., 61
Christensen, A. P., 216
Christensen, H. T., 69
Christiansen, E. H., 207
Cicchetti, D., 206
Clark, R., 271
Clark, T., 43
Clarke, J., 178
Clegg, J. B., 7
Cline, T., 90, 103
CMEB (Commission on Multi-Ethnic Britian), 195
Coccaro, E. F., 62
Cochran, R., 246
Cochrane, R., 234, 245
Cohen, A., 186
Cohen, J., 3, 166
Cohen, L. E., 151
Cohen, P., 3
Coie, J. D., 204, 214
Colby, K. M., 250
Cole, P. M., 212
Coleman, D., 23
Collier, D., 7
Colman, R. A., 207
Commonwealth Fund, 266, 268, 272
Compton, F. N., 66, 193
Conduct Problems Prevention Research Group, 208, 209
Conger, R. D., 207, 213, 215
Conrad, S. D., 213
Cooper, J. E., 231, 249, 269
Cooper, R. S., 13, 60, 62
Cope, R., 234, 246
Copestake, S., 246
Cornell, S., 314

Correspondents of the New York Times, 109
Corridan, B., 237
Costello, E. J., 66, 193
Côte, S., 11
Coulton, C. J., 215
Coxhead, N., 239
Coyle, N., 60
Craig, I. W., 14, 62, 207
Craufurd, D., 247
CRE (Commission for Racial Equality), 195
Creed, F., 14, 250
Crick, N., 210, 214
Critcher, C., 178
Croft-Jeffreys, C., 245
Crouch, J. L., 213, 218
Crowell, N. A., 139
Crozier, J., 207
Cruickshank, J. K., 13, 234
Cullen, F. T., 155, 156
Cummings, E. M., 211

Dadds, M. R., 216
Daniel, W. W., 67, 82, 176, 195
Dauncey, K., 231
David, A., 245
Davies, N., 248
Davies, P., 211
Davies, R., 91
Davies, S. C., 7
Davis, F. J., 51, 56
Day, J. C., 107
Day, R., 231
Day, R. D., 207, 208
de Abreu, G., 90
de Paul, J., 207
Deater-Deckard, K., 69, 70, 206, 207, 208, 210, 212, 213, 214, 215
Deaux, K., 305
Dekker, J., 249
Dembo, R., 267, 268, 269, 273
Demie, F., 97
Demler, O., 62
Denton, N. A., 28, 109, 342
Der, G., 237
Devlin, B., 8
deWilde, E. J., 263
Dickens, R., 43
Diekstra, R. F., 263
Dillman, D. A., 116
Dilworth-Anderson, P., 271
Dishion, T. J., 205, 206

Dizon, M., 263
Dodge, K. A., 14, 70, 207, 208, 210, 212, 213,
    214, 215, 218
Dohrenwend, B. P., 66
Dornbusch, S. M., 269, 271, 273
Dornfeld, M., 209
Dorsett, R., 193
Downey, D. B., 111
Drasgow, F., 272
Drinkwater, S., 91, 98
Driscoll, A. K., 266
Drury, B., 288
Dryfoos, J., 262
Duke, R. L., 272
Dumaret, A.-C., 12
Dunaway, R. G., 156
Duncan, B., 112, 115
Duncan, G. J., 29, 34, 66
Duncan, O. D., 108, 131
Dunham, H. W., 231
Dunn, G., 94
Durrant, J. E., 218
Durrington, P. N., 14
Duyme, M., 12

Earls, F., 68, 194, 266
Early, K. E., 272
Eaves, L., 2, 5, 8, 14, 15, 66
Ecob, R., 102
Edfeldt, Å. W., 218
Edmonston, B., 24
Elliott, D. S., 149, 150, 156, 160, 166, 183
Ellis, S. P., 71
Ellwood, D., 43
Elordi, C. A., 215
English and Romanian Adoptees (ERA)
    Study Team, 2, 12
Engstrom, A., 249
ERA Research Team, 5, 6
Erikson, E. H., 304
E-Risk Study Team, 4
Erkanli, A., 14
Ernberg, G., 231
Erting, C., 58
Esparza, J., 14
Eugene, E., 58
Evans, T. D., 156
Eyberg, S. M., 207

Fahy, T., 250
Fang, J., 13
Fann, K. D., 218

Faris, R. E. L., 231
Farquhar, C., 90
Farrell, M., 246
Farrington, D. P., 69, 70, 150, 151, 154, 155,
    204, 207, 208, 209
Feinberg, S., 8
Feldman, M. W., 61
Feller, W., 237
Ferguson, R. F., 111
Fergusson, D. M., 6, 207
Fernandez, R., 134
Ferrell, R., 62
Figlio, R. M., 147
Fihosy, C., 90
Fisher, M., 247
Fisher, P., 268
Fishman, J. A., 303
FitzGerald, M., 180
Fix, M., 67
Flanagan, K. D., 211
Flannery, D. J., 204
Flewelling, R. L., 151
Flood-Page, C., 179, 183
Florio, L. P., 266
Flory, M., 268
Flynn, N., 152
Fogel, R. W., 59
Foner, N., 44
Forbes, D., 291, 294
Ford, T., 88
Forehand, R. L., 267
Forrest, J., 295
Forrester, T., 13
Foster, E. M., 208
Fox, J. A., 139
Fraser, H., 13
Fraught, W. S., 250
Fried, J., 246
Friedman, R. J., 212
Fulker, D. W., 206
Fung, W. L. A., 243, 338
Furstenburg, F. F., 270

Gans, H. J., 55, 302, 338
Garcia-Marques, L., 181
Garcia-Preto, N., 271, 272
Gardien, R., 249
Gardner, F., 205
Garfield, D. A., 250
Garland, A. F., 262, 265, 268
Gates, H. L., 296
Gatwood, R., 88

Gay, 195
Gayle, V., 91
Gdowski, C. L., 267
Gelernter, J., 62
Gendreau, P., 155
Gershoff, E. T., 206
Ghodse, H., 249
Gibbs, J. T., 262, 264, 267, 271, 272, 274
Gibson, M. A., 110
Giggs, J. A., 231, 249
Gil, A. G., 269
Gilchrist, L., 209
Giles-Sim, J., 206, 207
Gill, B., 246
Gillborn, D., 33, 34, 88, 90, 94, 99, 100, 101, 342
Giller, H., 14
Giller, M., 178
Gilliam, S., 250
Gilligan, C., 272
Gilvarry, C., 250
Giordano, P., 148
Gipps, C., 88, 99, 101
Girodano, P. C., 183
Glick, M., 246
Glover, S., 228, 248
Goel, R., 249
Gold, M., 147
Goldblatt, P., 82
Golding, J., 10, 14
Goldscheider, C., 54
Goldstein, J., 28
Gomez, S. L., 60
Goodman, A., 43
Goodman, R., 57, 88
Goodnow, J., 1
Gordon, L. C., 207, 213, 215
Gordon, M., 55, 303, 337
Gordon, R. A., 152
Gott, C., 228
Gottfredson, D. C., 160
Gottfredson, G. D., 160
Gould, L. C., 147
Gould, M. S., 268, 269, 270, 271
Goulden, C., 179
Goyette, K., 111
Graham, J., 179, 183
Graham, P., 57
Grasmick, H., 151
Granger, A., 243
Gray, H., 90
Gray, J., 179

Graziano, A. M., 206, 212, 213
Green, A. J., 92, 213
Greene, M. E., 134
Greenwald, A. G., 181
Greenwald, S., 71
Greenwood, R., 10, 14, 63
Gulley, B. L., 4
Gunnoe, M. L., 209, 212
Gureje, O., 7
Gutstein, J., 263, 264, 265, 268, 269, 274

Hagell, A., 14, 178
Hague, Z., 90, 95
Hale, C., 180
Hall, K. S., 7
Hall, S., 178, 296, 298
Halpern, D., 65
Hamblen, J. L., 212
Hamilton, D. L., 181
Hammond, W. R., 270, 271
Hanis, C. L., 61
Harer, M. D., 153, 157
Harland, J., 13
Harrington, H. L., 14, 62
Harrington, V., 179
Harris, T., 6
Harrison, G., 231, 234, 237, 241, 246, 248
Harter, S., 272
Hartmann, D., 314
Harvey, I., 246
Haskell, M. E., 218
Hatano, G., 1
Haviland, J. M., 211
Hawkins, G., 139, 148, 150, 154
Hawkins, J. D., 3
Hawkins, J. O., 268
Heath, A., 92, 93, 101
Heimer, K., 70
Heitmeyer, W., 54, 343
Helms, J. E., 272
Hemmings, P., 245
Hemsi, L. K., 227, 234
Hendrickson-Smith, J., 345
Hendrie, H. C., 7
Herrenkohl, T. I., 204
Herrnstein, R. J., 59, 67, 154, 155
Hewett-Emmett, D., 61
Hickling, F. W., 3, 239, 245
Hindelang, M. J., 147, 148, 149, 150, 154, 155, 156, 166, 178, 180, 182, 183
Hindley, P., 58
Hirschi, T., 147, 149, 150, 154, 155, 178, 183

Hirschman, C., 109, 110, 112
Hiruma, N., 212
Hoek, H. W., 237
Holden, G. W., 206, 213
Holton, A., 234
Holzer, C. E., 266, 273
Home Office, 179, 180
Hood, R., 182
Horowitz, D. L., 314
Horwood, L. J., 6
Hotz, V. J., 42
Hovey, J. D., 267, 272
Howard, R. J., 243
Howe, D., 296
Hsu, C.-C., 69
Huang, L. N., 262
Hubbard, J. A., 211
Hudson, B. A., 177
Hui, S. L., 7
Huizinga, D. A., 150, 156, 183
Hunt, N., 239
Hurry, J., 239
Hutchinson, J., 246, 247, 248
Hutnik, N., 294

Ineichen, B., 249
Izard, C. E., 211

Jablensky, A., 231, 241, 249
Jackson, S., 207
Jacobs, J. A., 134
Jacobsen, K. C., 59
Jacobson, J., 291
Jaffe, S. R., 14
Jarjoura, G. R., 155
Jaynes, G. D., 109, 112
Jefferson, T., 178
Jencks, C., 131
Jenkins, R., 250
Jensen, A. R., 58
Jensen, P. S., 154
Jin, R., 62
Johns, L. C., 246
Johnson, B., 218
Johnston, C., 214, 217, 218
Johnston, R., 295
Jones, D., 208
Jones, P. B., 229, 247, 248, 338, 344
Jowell, R., 195
Joynson, R. B., 60
Judd, C. M., 213
Junger, M., 178

Kadiri, S., 13
Kahn, R. S., 237
Kalaria, R. N., 62
Kandel, D. B., 4
Kao, G., 134
Kaplow, J., 207
Karen, D., 108
Karter, A., 60
Kasinitz, P., 44
Kaslow, N. J., 267
Kaufman, J. S., 13, 60
Kaur, D., 13
Kazdin, A. E., 154
Keaveney, L., 12
Keeler, G., 66, 193
Keenan, K., 204
Kelder, L. R., 213, 215
Keller, T. E., 209
Kelley, M. L., 207, 214
Kempton, T., 267
Kenney, D. A., 14, 63
Kephart, G., 70
Kertzer, D. I., 51, 54
Kessler, R. C., 62, 154, 266, 268
Keyes, C., 133
Kidd, J. R., 61
Kidd, K. K., 61
Kienhorst, I. W., 263
Kiernan, K., 57
Kiev, A., 227, 234
Kimbrough, R., 267
Kinderman, P., 250
King, C. A., 267, 269, 272, 273
King, M., 239
Kingue, S., 13
Kirov, G., 246
Kitamura, S., 69
Klein, H. E., 246
Kleinman, A., 250
Kleykamp, M., 266, 272
Knutson, J. F., 215
Kobrin, S., 69
Kolko, D. J., 213
Korbin, J. E., 215
Koretz, D., 62
Korten, A., 231
Kraemer, H. C., 154
Krakoff, R. Y., 267
Kranzler, H., 62
Kreppner, J. M., 12
Krivo, L. J., 152, 153
Krohn, M. D., 150, 151, 156

Krosnick, J. A., 213
Kruttschnitt, C., 209
Kucharska, J., 246
Kuczynski, L., 207
Kulkarni, A., 13
Kunce, L. J., 213
Kupfer, D. J., 154

Lacey, M. B., 267
LaFromboise, T., 263
Lahiri, D. K., 7
Laing, R. D., 229
Laker, M., 13
Lakey, J., 81, 174, 285
Lanbert, H., 90
Land, K. C., 151, 152, 156, 159
Landale, N. S., 134, 340
Landry, D. J., 70
Langan, P. A., 180
Lansdown, G., 218
Lansford, J. E., 207, 208, 210, 213
Larson, J. H., 207
Larson, N. C., 209
Larzelere, R. E., 206, 209, 215, 218
Laub, J. H., 14, 188, 341
Lauritsen, J. L., 153, 156
Lawrence, S., 199
Lawson, W. B., 246
Leaf, P. J., 266
Lee, S-Y., 69
Leff, J., 237, 239, 249, 250
Lelwicka, M., 211
Lemert, E., 177
Lengua, L. J., 209
Leslie, D., 91, 98
Lester, D., 267
Leung, K., 272
Leventhal, T., 68
Levin, M., 59
Levin, R., 52
Levine, R. A., 1
Lewis, D., 102
Lewis, G., 245
Lewis, S. M., 209
Lewis, S. W., 248, 249
Li, R. M., 345
Lichter, D., 70
Lieberson, S., 54, 108, 109, 112, 134
Lightfoot, C., 214
Lin, K.-H., 207, 213, 215
Lindquist, C. M., 213
Lindstrom-Ufiti, H., 215

Linskey, A. O., 273
Lipsedge, M., 245
Liska, A. E., 153
Littlewood, R., 245, 249
Lizotte, A. J., 160
Llanes, D., 134
LLoyd, K., 28, 37, 41
Loeber, R., 66, 69, 150, 160, 204, 207,
  209
Logan, J., 43
Logan, S., 248
Loizillon, A., 228
Lotrich, F., 62
Ludemann, P. M., 211
Luster, T., 207
Lutz, A., 43
Lynam, D., 67, 154, 155, 160
Lynn, R., 59
Lynn, S. J., 213, 215
Lynskey, M. T., 6
Lytton, H., 206

Maccoby, E., 210
Mackness, M. I., 14
MacLeod, D., 93, 104
MacMillan, F., 246
Macpherson of Cluny, Sir W., 101
Madhavan, S., 13
Magaziner, J., 249
Magnuson, K., 66
Maguire, M., 92
Mahy, G. E., 239
Maldonado, L. M., 267
Mallett, R., 237, 239, 249
Malone, K. M., 71
Mammen, O. K., 213
Mann, J. J., 71
Marcellis, M., 249
Mare, R. D., 35, 109, 112, 115, 341
Mariner, C. L., 209, 212
Markus, H., 1
Marmot, M. G., 13
Martin, J., 14, 62, 207, 208, 209
Martin, M., 210
Martinez, R., 272
Marvin, S., 2
Massey, D. S., 28, 109, 342
Matseuda, R. L., 70
Maughan, A., 206, 215
Maughan, B., 3, 94, 102, 248
Maxfield, M. G., 151
Mayhew, P., 180

Mays, E., 207
McCabe, K. M., 271
McCall, P. L., 151
McCarthy, J. F., 267
McClay, J., 14, 62, 207
McClure, K. P., 267
McCord, J., 139, 147, 150
McCracken, C., 207
McCreadie, R. G., 249
McDowall, D., 160
McGee, D., 13
McGovern, D., 234, 245, 246
McGuffin, P., 246
McGuire, P. K., 249
McHenry, P. C., 272
McKeigue, P. M., 13
McKenzie, K., 3, 246, 248
McLanahan, S., 122, 127
McLaughlin, D. K., 70
McLeod, J. D., 209, 210
McLoyd, V. C., 213
McMahon, D., 93, 101
McMahon, R. J., 205, 209
McNamara, J. R., 213, 215
McNeil, T. F., 237
McNeill, R. J., 160
Mead, G., 177
Meadow-Orlans, K. P., 58
Mednick, S. A., 248
Medora, N. P., 207
Meehan, A. J., 207
Meier, R. F., 156
Meltzer, H., 88, 94, 246
Mercado, R., 208
Mercer, K., 246
Merikangas, K. R., 62
Merriwether-deVries, C., 271
Merton, R. K., 188
Messner, S. F., 152, 153, 156
Mhlanga, B., 181
Miele, F., 58
Milburn, M. A., 213
Miles, W., 2
Mill, J., 207
Miller, J. Y., 179, 181, 268
Miller, P., 1
Miller, S., 167
Milner, J. S., 207
Minch, E., 61
Mirrlees-Black, C., 180
Mirza, H. S., 33, 34, 90, 94, 342
Miyares, I., 44

Mizuta, I., 212
Modood, T., 24, 63, 68, 70, 81, 82, 84, 85, 92, 93, 95, 98, 101, 174, 176, 186, 187, 188, 189, 190, 192, 195, 281, 285, 286, 288, 289, 291, 292, 293, 294, 297
Moffitt, T. E., 2, 4, 9, 14, 62, 63, 67, 70, 73, 154, 155, 207
Moloch, S. D., 267
Montes, M. P., 207
Mont-Reynard, R., 269
Morenoff, J. D., 153, 161, 166, 167, 343
Morning, A., 28, 342, 345
Mortensen, P. B., 239, 245, 248
Mortimore, P., 102, 215
Mosby, L., 207, 212
Mosisa, A. T., 42
Mountain, J., 60
Moynihan, D. P., 70, 190
Mukherjee, S., 246
Mullen, R., 3
Muna, W., 13
Munjal, K., 213
Muroff, J. R., 268, 270, 271
Murray, C., 59, 239
Murray, R. M., 2, 3, 5, 8, 14, 66, 229, 234, 246, 248
Murry, V., 215
MVA, 181
Myers, D., 71

Nagasawa, R. H., 147
Nahirny, V. C., 303
Namaste, K. A., 206
Nazroo, J. Y., 81, 174, 246, 250, 281, 285
Ndetei, D. M., 246
Neale, J., 90
Nee, V., 55, 109, 338
Needles, D. J., 155
Neilson, D., 234
Nelson, C., 56
Nettles, S. M., 271
New, M., 62
Newburger, E., 107
NICHD Early Child Care Research Network, 2
Nicoll, A., 248
Nikapota, A., 2, 69
Nix, R., 208
Noel, D. J., 54
Northstone, K., 10, 14
Novac, S., 154
Nye, F. I., 147

O'Callaghan, E., 248
O'Connor, T. G., 2, 5, 6, 12, 206
Ødegaard, O., 4, 227, 231, 247
Office for Standards in Education
    (OFSTED), 102
Office of Population Censuses and Surveys,
    243
Offord, D. R., 154
Ogbu, J. U., 110, 111, 214
Ogunniyi, A. O., 7
Olrick, J. T., 2
Oolders, J., 237
Opipari, L., 267
Oquendo, M. A., 71
Organista, K. C., 267, 269, 272
Ornstein, M. L., 151
Oropesa, R. S., 134, 340
Osborn, M., 68, 247
Osotimehin, B., 13
Osuntokun, B. O., 7
Ouston, J., 215
Owen, D., 92
Owens, D., 234
Owoaje, E. E., 13
Oxford English Dictionary, 50

Palloni, A., 167
Palmérus, K., 218
Parham, T. A., 272
Parides, M., 268
Park, B., 213
Park, J., 71
Parker, E. H., 211
Parkinson, R. C., 250
Parsons, C., 248
Paschall, M. J., 151
Passel, J. S., 339, 340, 346
Patel, D. J., 14
Patel, S., 13
Pathak, S., 33, 34, 43
Patterson, G. R., 206
Patterson, O., 175, 190
Paulsen, R., 134
Peach, C., 68, 194
Pearce, D., 82
Pease, K., 180, 181
Peen, J., 249
Peeples, F., 69, 160
Percy, A., 179
Perez-Stable, E. J., 60
Perlmann, J., 51, 64, 117
Persaud, R., 246

Petechuk, D., 204, 207
Peters, E., 246
Petersen, A. C., 69
Petersen, W., 51, 52
Peterson, G. W., 207
Peterson, R. D., 152, 153
Pettinari, C. J., 207
Pettingill, S. M., 207, 212
Pettit, G. S., 207, 208, 213
Pew Hispanic Centre, 345
Phillips, C., 178, 179, 181
Phillips, J. A., 159
Phillips, M., 296
Phillips, T., 296
Phinney, J., 272
Phinney, J. S., 304
Pickles, A., 2, 3, 5, 8, 12, 14, 15, 66
Pilkington, A., 100
Pilkonis, P. A., 213
Pinderhughes, E. E., 207, 208
Pitcher, J., 92
Pleck, J. H., 271, 272
Plewis, I., 90
Plomin, R., 4, 206
Pollock, B., 62
Portes, A., 25, 55, 68, 93, 104, 110, 302, 306,
    307, 336, 338, 340
Portes, J., 228
Poulsen, M., 295
Poulton, R., 14, 62
Power, T. G., 214, 207
Prescott-Clarke, P., 195
Prewitt, K., 42, 54, 64
Price, R., 228
Prince, M., 61
Pritchard, J. K., 61
Prudo, R., 249
Pryor, J., 70
Przybeck, T., 267
Pugh, M., 148
Pugh, M. D., 183
Pumariega, A. J., 273
Putnam, R. D., 230, 249

Quintero-Salinas, R., 273
Quinton, D., 3, 68

Rabe-Hesketh, S., 250
Rack, P., 250
Rainwater, L., 190
Ramsay, M., 179
Ramsden, S. R., 211

Randall, C., 272
Raskin, A., 267
Rathwell, T., 250
Raudenbush, S. W., 68, 161, 166, 167, 194
Rausch, K., 215
Ravussin, E., 14
Rawls, A. W., 207
Reardon, S. F., 40
Reeves, S. J., 243
Reid, J. B., 206
Reiss, A. J., 68, 148, 155, 156, 161
Resnick, D., 8
Resnick, M. D., 266, 268
Richards, M. H., 69
Richey, C. A., 207
Ridley, M., 62
Risch, N., 8, 60
Riste, L. K., 13, 250
Ritter, P. L., 269
Rivero, V. M., 237
Roberts, B., 178
Roberts, C. R., 266
Roberts, R. E., 266
Robey, K. L., 250
Robins, L. N., 267
Robinson, T., 272
Rock, P., 177
Rodgers, B., 70, 229
Rodgers-Johnson, P., 239
Rodriguez, A. U.,
Rodriguez, C. M., 213
Rodriguez, J., 208
Roeder, K., 8
Rogoff, M. L., 250
Rohner, R. P., 205, 207, 211, 212, 215
Romney, D. M., 206
Rosenberg, M., 272, 304
Rosenberg, N. A., 61
Rosenfeld, R., 156
Ross, R., 210
Ross, S., 210
Rossiter, D., 194
Roth, J. A., 147, 148, 155, 156, 161, 166
Rotheram-Borus, M. J., 267, 272
Rothon, C., 92, 94
Rotimi, C. N., 13
Rowe, D. C., 4, 59, 68, 204
Roy, P., 12
Rubinzstein, D. C., 7
Rudge, S., 237
Ruiz, P., 272
Ruiz-Linares, A., 61

Rumbaut, R. G., 25, 55, 63, 65, 68, 110, 301, 302, 306, 307, 336, 338, 340
Runnymede Trust, 294
Rush, A. J., 62
Russel, A., 248
Russell, G., 69
Rutter, M., 2, 3, 5, 6, 8, 9, 10, 11, 12, 14, 15, 57, 62, 63, 66, 68, 69, 71, 73, 102, 178, 184, 206, 215, 340, 342

Saeed, A., 291, 294
Sagi, A., 2
Salt, J., 23
Samele, C., 250
Sammons, P., 90, 97, 102
Sampson, R. J., 14, 68, 153, 156, 159, 161, 162, 166, 167, 188, 194, 341
Sandefur, G., 122, 127
Sartorius, N., 231
Sashidharan, K., 228, 245
Saurer, J., 243
Sayal, K., 205
Sayer, H., 239
Scarr, S., 59, 60
Scazufca, M., 61
Schain, M. A., 286
Schellenberg, G. D., 7
Schmid, C., 127
Schmidley, D., 301
Schneider, B., 42
Schneider, K., 251
Schoenhals, M., 42
Schols, D., 237
Schuerman, L., 69
Schull, W. J., 61
Schulz, L., 14
Schwartz, J. E., 160
Schweder, R. A., 1
Scott, A., 82
Scott, S. S., 218
Seaton, E.,
Seidel, U. P., 57
Seidman, E., 270
Sellin, T., 147
Selten, J. P., 237, 239, 247, 249
Serravezza, J., 267
Sewell, T., 97, 100
Shaffer, D., 263, 264, 265, 268, 269, 274
Shah, B., 13
Shah, R., 180, 181
Sham, P., 248
Sharp, C., 179

Sharpley, M. S., 245, 246, 248, 249, 250
Shaw, C. M., 250
Shaw, M. L., 266
Sheppard, D., 60
Sher, K., 2
Sherman, S. J., 213
Shihadeh, E. S., 152, 159
Shiner, M., 92, 101
Short, J. F., 147
Shukla, S., 246
Siegal, M., 216
Siegel, A. M., 267
Siegel, J. M., 266
Siever, L. J., 62
Sieving, R. E., 266, 268
Sijben, N., 249
Silberg, J., 14, 62, 71
Silva, P. A., 2, 9, 14
Silverstone, T., 239
Simcha-Fagan, O., 160
Simmons, R. G., 272
Simons, R. L., 207, 213, 215
Simpson, A., 195
Skogan, W. G., 69
Slaets, J. P., 237
Small, S., 63
Smith, A., 215
Smith, D. J., 67, 82, 90, 102, 174, 176, 178, 180, 181, 184, 185, 186, 188, 191, 193, 195, 343
Smith, J., 213
Smith, J. P., 24, 340
Smith, P., 81, 174, 285
Smithmyer, C. M., 211
Snipp, C. M., 109
Sobhan, M., 266
Social Exclusion Unit, 83
Sondhi, A., 179
Sonuga-Bourke, E., 205
South, S. J., 153
Spencer, M. B., 271
Spencer, S., 228
Spieker, S. J., 209
Spiller, A., 179
Spilsbury, J., 215
Srinivasan, V., 228
Stack, S., 272
Steffensmeier, D., 153, 157, 159
Steffenson, A., 52
Steinberg, L., 269
Steinberg, S., 250

Stepick, A., 45, 58
Stepick, C. D., 58
Stevenson, H. W., 69
Stevenson, J., 195
Stewart, R., 243
Stiffman, A. R., 266, 270
Stigler, J. W., 69
Stoll, L., 102
Stone, K., 247
Stormshak, E. A., 209, 214
Stoutham-Loeber, M., 66, 67, 69, 150, 155, 204, 209
Straus, M. A., 206, 207, 212, 218
Struyk, R. J., 67
Stults, B., 43
Suarez-Orozco, C., 110
Suarez-Orozco, M., 110
Sugarman, D. B., 206, 207, 246, 247
Sugden, K., 62
Summerville, M. B., 267
Suro, R., 52, 339, 340, 346
Susser, E. S., 248
Swain, R. C., 272
Swanson, J. W., 273
Swearer, D. K., 133
Syme, S. L., 13
Szasz, T. S., 229

Tajfel, H., 305
Takei, N., 246, 248, 249
Tang, C. S., 208, 210
Tang, H., 8, 60
Taub, B., 266
Tavridou, A., 13
Tawney, R. H., 347
Taylor, A., 14, 62
Taylor, M., 88, 97
Taylor, R. D., 271
Teed, D., 58
10/66 Dementia Research Group, 61
Tennant, C., 239
Terao, S. Y., 218
Thomas, C. S., 247
Thomas, P. F., 247
Thompson, R. A., 207, 211
Thornberry, T. P., 2, 150, 151, 156
Thornicroft, G., 249
Thorpe, K., 10, 14, 63, 73
Tienda, M., 28, 37, 41, 42, 52, 56, 109, 134, 266, 272
Tiezzi, L., 267
Tipp, J., 267

Tittle, C. R., 156
Tizard, B., 90
Tizard, J., 8, 59
Tomenson, B., 250
Tomenson, D., 14
Tomfohrde, J., 61
Tomkiewicz, S., 12
Tomlinson, S., 90, 102
Tonry, M. H., 139, 148, 150
Toone, B. K., 246, 248
Torrey, E. F., 249
Toth, S. L., 206
Trautman, P. D., 267
Tremblay, R. E., 11, 204
Trickett, P. K., 207
Trieman, D., 109
Trull, T., 2
Tseng, V., 207
Tully, L. A., 14
Turner, B. F., 272
Turner, C., 13
Turner, C. B., 272
Tyrer, S. P., 239

Udry, J. R., 345
UK DWP, 43
UK Office of National Statistics, 28, 31
Unverzagt, F. W., 7
Unwin, N., 13
Urquiza, A. J., 218
US Census Bureau, 23, 26
US Department of Health and Human
    Services, 206, 262
US DHHS, 35
US DOE, 37

Vadher, A., 246
Valdez, D., 272
Valdez, J., 52
Valencia, M. E., 14
Valsiner, J., 214
van den Oord, E. J., 59
van der Graaf, Y., 237
van der Velden, M., 237
van Gent, T., 58
van IJzendoorn, M. H., 2
Van Os, J., 234, 239, 249
Varghese, M., 61
Vaughn, R. D., 267
Vazsonyi, A. T., 204
Veen, N. N., 237
Vega, W. A., 269, 273

Vincent, J., 56, 341, 343
Virdee, S., 81, 174, 285
Visher, C. A., 147, 166

Waldmann, I. D., 59, 60
Walker, L., 13
Wallace, J. M., 268, 270, 271, 272
Walsh, E., 250
Walter, H. J., 267, 268
Walters, E. E., 62, 266
Walters, P. B., 108
Wandsworth Education Department, 97
Wang, Q., 62
Ward, J. V., 272
Ward, M., 212
Ward, R., 60
Ward, T., 246
Warder, G. S., 14
Warheit, G. J., 269
Wasserman, G. A., 204, 207
Waters, M. C., 44, 51, 58, 64, 109, 110, 117,
    302
Watson, B., 13
Weatherall, D. J., 7
Weber, J. L., 61
Weddle, K. D., 272
Weiler, B. L., 151
Weinberg, R. A., 59
Weis, J. G., 148, 149, 150, 178, 183
Weissman, M. M., 71, 266
Werner, P. D., 246
Wessely, S., 234, 245
Whaley, A. L., 207, 210, 212, 272
Whipple, E. E., 207
White, A., 30, 43
White, J. L., 155
White, M., 13
White, R., 178, 343
Widom, C. S., 139, 151
Wild, S., 13
Wilks, R., 13
Wilkstrom, P-O. H., 154, 160
Williams, J. H., 3
Williams, M., 246, 248, 270, 271
Williams, R. M., 109, 112
Willis, C., 228
Wilson, J. Q., 154, 155
Wilson, S., 207
Wilson, W. J., 5, 28, 66, 67, 69
Wimbush, D. D., 207, 214
Wing, J. K., 248, 249
Winterbotham, M., 14

Wolfgang, M. E., 147, 155
Wong, M. G., 109
Wood, J. M., 210
Woodle, J., 246
Woodruff, P., 246
Woodward, L. J., 207
World Health Organization, 229, 241
Woulbroun, E. J., 4
Wright, J. P., 155
Wu, C., 207, 213
Wyatt, J. M., 207

Xie, Y., 111

Yallop, J., 13
Yancy, W. L., 190
Yesavage, J. A., 246
Youdell, D., 101
Young, V. H., 212
Younge, G., 296

Youth Cohort Study, 83
Yu, C. E., 7
Yule, B. A., 8
Yule, W., 8, 57
Yung, B., 270, 271

Zahn-Waxler, C., 212
Zajacova, A., 28, 37, 41
Zammit, S., 249
Zawitz, M. W., 139
Zelli, A., 207
Zhivotovsky, L. A., 61
Zhou, M., 109, 110, 296, 297, 338
Ziegert, K. A., 218
Zigler, E., 246, 262, 265, 268
Zimmerman, R. S., 269, 271
Zimring, F. E., 139, 148, 150
Ziv, E., 8, 60
Znaniecki, F., 302
Zolkowska, K., 237, 239

Subject Index

abuse. *See* physical abuse
acculturative stress, 272
adoption
   IQ levels and, 59
affective syndromes
   schizophrenia v., 246
African Americans
   antisocial behaviors in, 267
   Caribbeans (Black) v., 44
   college enrollment rates for, 112
   college graduation rates for, 116
   college plans and, 132
   crime rates for, 267
   cultural acceptance of, 108
   depressive disorders and, 266
   early sexual behavior of, 269
   educational attainment for, 108
   family support within, 271
   high school graduation rates for, 115
   index offenses by, 140
   IQ-delinquency relationship for, 155
   murder rates for, 139
   parental education levels for, 35
   in PHDCN, 162
   physical discipline by, 207, 212
   population demographics for (U.S.), 26
   poverty rates for, 35, 109
   prison attendance rates for, 139
   residential segregation of, 56, 109
   reverse record checks for (males), 150
   self-esteem levels for, 272
   state-sponsored segregation against, 109,
      194
   suicide rates for, 71
   teachers' expectations for, 111
   in UCR, 140
   unemployment for, 159
   white IQ levels v., 59
   youth suicide rates for, 263
   in YRBSS survey, 145
Africans
   UK migration patterns for, 81
aggression. *See* physical aggression
Alzheimer's disease, 7, 61
   APO-E-4 allele and, 7, 62
anglo conformity, 337
antisocial behavior. *See also* UK crime
      statistics
   in African Americans, 267
   in Chicago Neighborhood Study, 270
   conduct disorders and, 267–268
   drug/alcohol usage and, 71
   Dunedin longitudinal study for, 9
   educational levels and, 67–68
   IQ and, 67
   measurement factors for, 177–178
   physical abuse's influence on, 207
   predictive validity tests for, 9
   punitive disciplinary methods and, 205
   risk factors for, 9, 205
   sex difference in, 9–10
   as social construct, 177
   symbolic interactionism theory and, 177
   UK crime statistics and, 174
apartheid, 56, 345
APO-E-4 allele, 7, 62
The Art of Being Black (Alexander), 197
Asian Americans
   Cambodians as part of, 133
   college graduation rates for, 115
   college plans for (U.S.), xiii
   discrimination against, 109

East Asians as part of, 133
educational attainment for, 341
educational transitions for, 115
high school graduation rates for, 115
national origin groups for, 133
physical discipline by, 207
Vietnamese, 133
youth suicide rates for, 263
"Asian trajectory," 104
Asians (continental)
cultural self-sufficiency of, 196, 197, 198
educational levels for, xii, 33
family structure and, effects of, 192
"host society" residence periods and,
influence of, 292–293
household income levels for, 189
linguistic diversity for, 39
physical discipline by, 207
population demographics for (UK), 26, 52
poverty rates for, 82
religious identity for, 288
"situational identity" of, 287, 293
ÆSOP study (for schizophrenia), 241, 246,
250
parameters for, 241
assimilation. *See also* integration
anglo conformity as, 337
cultural pluralism and, 337
identificational, 303
language, 302
limited, as theory, 110
melting pot theory of, 337
in migration paradigm, 337
paradigm for, 339
segmented hypothesis of, 110
in UK, levels of, 294
in U.S., 337
assimilation model (racial/ethnic
inequality), 109
assimilation paradigm, 339
minority status in, 340
assimilation typology
in ethnic classification schemes, 55
in migration paradigm, 337
"associational" identity (ethnic), 292
political impact of, 292
attachment theory, 210
attitudinal familism index, 327

Bangladeshis (UK), 34
achievement levels of, 96
English language fluency for, 97

female education levels for (UK), 33
household income levels for, 31
male education levels for, xii
migration patterns for, 81
poverty rates for, 82
unemployment rates for, 189
B-CAMHS99 Survey, 88, 94, 95, 96, 97, 98
cumulative disadvantage indicators, 99
BCS (British Crime Surveys), 176, 179, 180
See also UK Crime statistics
criticisms of, 180
illusory correlation effects in, 181
incongruency effects in, 181
offender descriptions in, 180
social cognitions in, 180
Behavior Questionnaire, 209
biracialism, 345. *See also* mixed race persons
as stress factor, 345
birth cohorts study
delinquency in, 147
educational attainments and, 112
educational transitions in, 115, 135
parameters for, 112–115
Philadelphia, 147
Black–White poverty ratio, 35
British Crime Surveys. *See* BCS
British Social Attitudes Survey, 196

Cambodian American, 133
Canada
family care data for, 11
capital (human)
cultural, 95
educational attainment and, 93–94
parenting as, 94
Caribbeans (Black)
African Americans v., 44
"child migrant" generations of, 287
disciplinary actions against (UK), 187
discrimination against, 175
education levels for, xii
educational attainment (UK), 104
female education levels for (UK), 33
household income levels for (UK), 31, 189
"hyper-modern individualism" in, 192,
193
identity formation for (in UK), 196, 197,
199
institutional exclusion of, 187
interracial marriage for, 295
police interactions with, 199
religiosity of, 288

Caribbeans (black) (*continued*)
  schizo-mania and, 239
  schizophrenia and, 227, 237, 238, 239,
    246–247, 251–252
  self-identity for, 287
  single-parent households and, xii–xiii,
    191, 193
  slavery and, 175, 190, 199
  social position of (UK), 285, 296, 336, 342
  UK crime statistics and, 175, 198, 199
  UK migration of, 44, 80, 81, 196, 197–198,
    284, 340–341
  unemployment rates for, in UK, 189
  in U.S., 44, 45
Caucasians. *See* Whites
causal mechanisms
  alternative, 3–8, 9
  for antisocial behavior, 9–10
  association validity for, 2–3
  evidence factors for, 2
  for family care/group care, 11
  hazards for, 3
  individual differences and, 9
  for institutional deprivation, 12
  key assumptions for, 9
  for language impairment, 10–11
  measurements for, 2–3
  for migration designs, 12–13
  research strategies for, 8–13
  residential care and, 11–12
  risk exposure processes for, 9
  sampling for, 2, 8
  statistical analyses for, 3
CDP (Child Development Project), 208, 210,
    212, 213
  Behavior Questionnaire as part of, 209
  Child Behavior Checklist as part of, 209
  ethnicity moderator effects in, 208
  Home Behavior Scale as part of, 209
  parameters of, 208
Center for Disease Control, 143
  YRBSS survey by, 143
Chicago Neighborhood Study, xiv
  antisocial behavior in, 270
Child Behavior Checklist, 209
child development
  emotional warmth during, 211–213, 218
  parental rejection during, 211
Child Development Project. *See* CDP
child poverty
  minority/immigrant differentials for
    (UK), 30–34

  in UK, 43
  in U.S., 34, 35
child rearing beliefs, 205
  emotional content within, 205
Children of Immigrants Study, xvi
Chinese youth
  educational levels for, 34
CILS (Children of Immigrants Longitudinal
    Study), 302, 307–314
  acculturation in, 317–320, 328
  adolescence as factor in, 331
  attitudinal familism index in, 327
  demographics for, 307
  English language fluency as factor in, 309,
    317
  ethnic self-identity in, 307, 324, 325–326,
    332
  family structure variable in, 320
  generational gaps in, 303–304, 310
  Hispanic Americans in, 325
  identity shifts in, 308–309
  identity stability in, 309–312
  limitations of, 330–331
  multivariate logistic regressions in, 311
  national origins as variable in, 312–317
  parental socioeconomic status in, 327–328
  parental U.S. residence length in, 317
  racial discrimination as variable in,
    320–323, 325, 328–329
  regional location variable in, 320
  situational contexts in, 331
  socioeconomic status in, 317
Civil Rights Revolution (U.S.), 112
"collective efficacy," 161
college attendance, 41
  Hispanic Americans and, 41, 112
  minority/immigrant youth and, 41
college enrollment rates, 40–41
  for African Americans, 112
  ethnic differentials for, 41
college graduation rates
  for African Americans, 116
  for Asian Americans, 115
  as educational transition, 115
  for Hispanic Americans, 116
  for Native Americans, 116
  for Whites, 115
college plans
  for African Americans, 132
  application as part of, 119, 127, 132
  for Asian Americans, xiii, 132–133
  demographic rates for (U.S.), xiii

ethnic differentials in, 120
for Hispanics Americans, xiii
multivariate analyses of, 123–128
for Native Americans, 132
in Pacific Northwest Study (High
    School seniors), 118, 119, 120, 123–127,
    129
racial differentials in, 120
for Whites (U.S.), xiii
Commonwealth Fund, 266
Commonwealth Immigration Act of 1962,
    23
Commonwealth Immigration Act of 1968,
    23
conduct disorders
    antisocial behavior and, 267–268
    physical discipline and, 206
    suicide as result of, 265
congenital rubella syndrome, 248
"constitutional factors"
    for crime, 139, 154–156
    IQ as, 154–155
    temperament, 155
CPS (Crown Prosecution Service) (UK), 181
crime. *See* generational crime patterns (UK);
    murder rates; NCVS; place-based
    disparities (crime); UK crime statistics;
    U.S. crime statistics
Crime and Human Nature
    (Herrnstein/Wilson), 154
Crime Index, 140
criminal justice system, 139. *See also* U.S.
    crime statistics
    statistics for, by ethnicity, 139
criminology studies, 147
    ecological research in, 151, 153–154
Crown Prosecution Service. *See* CPS
cultural capital, 95
    as educational attainment, 97–98
    parental education as, 95–96
"cultural enclosure," 197
"cultural mosaic"
    "melting pot" v., 347
cultural pluralism, 337
cultural racism, 297
cultural self-sufficiency
    of Asians (continental), 198
    of Indians (Asian), 196, 197
Current Population Survey, 301

day care (group)
    family care v., 11

delinquency
    in birth cohorts study, 147
    Black/White ratios for, 146, 148, 149
    educational rejection and, 188
    IQ and, 154, 155
    predictors of, 204
    reverse record checks and, 150
    self-reported, 147
depressive disorders
    African Americans' expressions of, 266
    ethnicity as factor for, 266–267
    Hispanic Americans' expressions of, 266
    serotonin transporter genes and, 62
    suicide as result of, 265
disciplinary methods. *See also* physical
        discipline
    beliefs about, 215
    cultural differences in, 205
    parental strategies for, 205
    physical punishment as, 205–206, 207
    positive reinforcement as, 205
    preemptive, 205
    punitive, 205
    reactive, 205
discrimination, xiv. *See also* racial
        discrimination
    "statistical," 56
distal starting points, 7
"dose-response" relationships, 6
drug/alcohol abuse
    antisocial behavior and, 71
    cannabis, 249
    by ethnicity, 268
    religiosity as factor for, 271
    schizophrenia as result of, 249
Dunedin longitudinal study, 9

ECA (Epidemiologic Catchment Area), 266,
    267
Education Authority (UK), 84
education levels, xii, xiii. *See also* parental
        education; schooling
    anti-social behavior and, 67–68
    for Asians (continental), xii
    for Bangladeshis, xii
    for Caribbeans (Black), xii
    for Chinese youth (UK), 34
    as ethnic effect, 67–68
    ethnic variances in (UK), 32, 33
    family structure's influence on, xiii
    for Hispanic Americans, 37
    income and, 31, 107

education levels (*continued*)
    parental, influence of, xiii, 35, 37, 38, 95–96
    for Whites (UK), 31
    for women (UK), 31–33
educational attainment, 107–108, 341–342
    for Asian Americans, 341
    birth cohorts study and, 112
    for Caribbeans (Black) (UK), 104
    cultural capital and, 97–98
    data sources for, 83–84
    Education Authority (UK) and, 84
    educational continuation ratios and, 112
    English language fluency and, 97
    ethnic diversity and, 92–103
    ethnic inequality in (U.S.), 108–111,
        112–116
    family influences on, 98–99
    gender norms as factor for, 94
    for Hispanic Americans, 109, 341
    human capital and, 93–94
    for Indians (Asian), 186–187
    institutional segregation and, 112
    institutional systems and, 99–101
    Islamic values on, 97
    longitudinal data for (UK), 90–91
    migrant generation and, 84–85
    migration as influence on, 81
    for Native Americans, 109
    opportunities for, 101–102
    post-compulsory schooling (UK) and,
        91–92, 101
    primary school testing (UK) and, 89–90
    during primary school years (UK), 88–89
    pupil-teacher conflicts and, 100
    "school persistence" rates and, 98
    social gradients and, 94
    social/economic status as factor for,
        81–83, 94–95
    suicide and, 268–269
    teachers' expectations as part of, 100, 346
    in UK (minority groups), 81, 83–92
    in U.S., 107
educational continuation ratios, 112
educational enrollment, 112
    Civil Rights Revolution's (U.S.) influence
        on, 112
educational institutions
    in CILS, as variable, 320
    educational attainment and, 99–101
    effectiveness of, 102–103
    exclusion data for, 100
    marketization of, 101

    racial harassment in, 100
    school experiences in, 99–101
educational transitions
    for Asian Americans, 115
    in birth cohorts study, 115, 135
    college graduation, 115
    high school to college, 115
    for Whites, 115
emotional warmth
    during child development, 211–213, 218
    cultural differences and, 211–212
    physical discipline and, 212, 213
emotional/behavioral disturbance rates
    residential care and, 11
employment
    ethnic identity as result of, 293
    nonmanual (by ethnicity), 189
English language fluency, 43
    for Bangladeshis (UK), 97
    in CILS, role of, 309, 317
    educational attainment and, 97
    ethnic variances in, 40
    for immigrant youth, 34
    immigration and, 71
    immigration as factor for, 71
    for migrant generations, 85
    migrant generations and, 85
    for Pakistanis (UK), 97
"Englishness," 294
environment (social)
    personal effects on, 4
    in social selection, 3
Epidemiologic Catchment Area. See ECA
"equivalent incomes," 189
    poverty measures and, 189–190
ethnic bias
    in self-report studies, xiii
ethnic classification schemes, 54–58
    assimilation typology within, 55
    construction of, 54
    government agencies and, 54
    group membership as facet of, 55
ethnic effects, 63–72
    education as, 67–68
    family structure as, 70–71
    genetics as, 72
    immigration as, 71
    mediators of, 335
    minority status as, 71–72
    native language and, 65
    neighborhood influence as, 68–69
    personal group identity as, 63–64

racial discrimination as, 72
religion as, 64–65
social community as, 65
social context of, 69–70
ethnic identity, xvi, 305
"associational," 292
biracialism and, 345
in CILS, 307
cross-national variance for, 52
definitions of, 50
employment as factor for, 293
fixed categorical features and, 6
formation of (in UK), 196, 197–198, 199,
281, 286–291
gender and, 344
genetic construction of, 61–63, 344
group boundaries and, 56
"host society" residence period and, 292
"hyphenated," 283
immigration's effect on, 54–55
institutional definitions for, 58
inter-group contact and, 54, 55
inter-racial marriage as factor for, 327
labeling theory and, 56
language as basis for, 52–53
legal classifications of, 51
"new," 291–293
"one-drop" rule and, 51
in Pacific Northwest Study (high school
seniors), 117, 124
physiognomy as part of, 56
politicization of, 286–288
predetermined categories for, 51
racism and, 58
reactive ethnicity and, 55, 306, 331
reciprocal adaptation processes and, 55
religiosity and, 288, 289–291, 298
research, 339–345
as risk factor, 6
as self-description, xvi, 51–54, 64
self-esteem as result of, 272
social construction of, 54–58, 343
social context for, 342–344
social locations of, 54
social policy creation and, 346–347
in U.S., 108, 131
variations in, 344–345
youth responses to, 305
ethnic identity research, 339–345
generational transitions as part of,
339–341
measurement problems in, 339

ethnic minorities
in assimilation paradigm, 340
definition of, 50
immigrant youth and, 21, 341
in UK (population), 25
in U.S. (population), 26
ethnic minority/immigrant youth, 21
college attendance for, 41
educational access for, 42
linguistic diversity for, 39
poverty differentials for (UK), 30–34
social class differences for, 42
socioeconomic differentiation for, 29–31,
42
ethnic neighborhoods
"collective efficacy" in, 161
community order/disorder effects in,
160
community/individual interaction in, 69
crime in, 69, 160–161
genetic designs for, 69
in PHDCN, 167
place-based disparities (crime) and, 153
social support within, 68
socioeconomic context of, xiv
suicide in, 270
in UK, 68, 193–194, 195
in U.S., 68
U.S. census measures for, 160
ethnicity. *See* ethnic identity
EU (European Union), 23
"euthanasia of memories," 302
"executive function" deficits
IQ and, 155

family care
day care (group) v., 11
epidemiological data (Canada) on, 11
maladaptive, 11
physical aggression and, 11
social selection and, 11
family structure
for Asians (continental), 192
in CILS, as variable in, 320
educational attainment and, influence on,
98–99
as ethnic effect, 70–71
for Indians (Asian), 190
Pacific Northwest Study (high school
seniors) and, 121, 122, 129
poverty as result of, 70
single parenthood, effects of, 70

family structure (*continued*)
   suicide and, 265, 269–270
   varieties of, 192
fatalism, 134
fixed categorical features, 6
   direct proximal mechanisms and, 6
   ethnic identity and, 6
Fourth National Survey of Ethnic
    Minorities, 186, 189, 195, 286
   "new" ethnic identities in, 291–293

GCSE (General Certificate of Secondary
    Education), 89
   White v. Black attainment of, 89
gene environment correlations, 14
General Certificate of Secondary Education.
   See GCSE
General Household Survey, 92
generational crime patterns (UK). *See also*
   UK crime statistics
   changes in, 178–179, 184–198
   education as factor in, 186–188
   selection principles in, 184
genetic mediations, 4–5
   ethnic features as part of, 5, 7
   migration designs and, 14
genetics
   Alzheimer's disease and, 61
   as ethnic effect, 72
   ethnicity and, as factor in, 61–63, 344
   schizophrenia and, 247
Germany, 51
   Jews in (WWII), 51

high school dropout rates
   ethnic differences and, 39
high school graduation rates, 107–108
   for African Americans, 115
   for Asian Americans, 115
   for Hispanics, 115
   for Native Americans, 115
   for Whites, 115
Higher Education Statistics Agency, 91
Hispanic Americans
   in CILS, 325
   college attendance and, 41, 112
   college graduation rates for, 116
   college plans for (U.S.), xiii
   crime and, 156
   depressive disorders and, 266
   educational attainments for, 109, 341
   high school graduation rates for, 115

   in NCVS, 147
   parental education levels for, 37
   in PHDCN, 162
   population demographics for (U.S.), 26, 52
   poverty rates for, 35, 36
   prison attendance rates for, 139
   self-esteem levels for, 272
   youth suicide rates for, 263
   in YRBSS survey, 145
Hispanic Health and Nutrition
    Epidemiologic Survey, 266
Hispanic–White poverty ratio, 35
HND (Higher National Diploma), 91
Home Behavior Scale, 209
home ownership
   Pacific Northwest Study (high school
    seniors) and, 122–123, 127, 131
"host society"
   Asians (continental) in, residence periods
    for, 292–293
   ethnic identity in, 292–293
House of Commons Select Committee on
    Race Relations and Immigration, 178
household income levels
   for Bangladeshis (UK), 31, 189
   for Caribbeans (UK), 31, 189
   "equivalent incomes" and, 189
   for Indians/Asians (continental), 189
   for Pakistanis (UK), 31, 189
hyperactivity/inattention rates, 12
"hyper-modern individualism," 192, 193,
   200
"hyphenated" identities (ethnic), 283, 294
hypoxia, 248

illusory correlation effects, 181
"immigrant optimism," 134
   fatalism v., 134
immigration
   cultural concentration as result of, 28
   "cultural enclosure" as response to, 197
   English language fluency and, 71
   as ethnic effect, 71
   ethnic identity as result of, 54–55
   intergenerational educational mobility
    and, 33
   mobility as result of, 56
   parental socioeconomic resources and, 28
   race as factor in, 44
   residential settlement patterns' influence
    on, 28
   as risk factor, 6

segregation as result of, 28
social dislocation as result of, 45
social impact of, 24
socioeconomic status and, 188–190
to UK, rates of, 24, 81
unemployment trends and, 189
unskilled, 41
to U.S., rates of, 24
Immigration and Nationality Act, 24
U.S. migration and, 24
imperialism
racism as result of, 283
income levels
education levels and, 31, 107
in UK, 30
incongruency effects, 181
index offenses, 140
Indians (Asian), 34
cultural self-sufficiency of, 196, 197
family structures for, 190
female educational levels for, 33
general educational attainment for,
186–187
household income levels for, 189
UK migration patterns from, 81
information processing theory, 210
institutional deprivation, 12
IQ and, influence on, 12
integration, 298
assimilation strategies for, 283–284, 297
political contestation and, 282
"straight-line," 338
in UK, 282
youth centered policies for, 347
Intelligence Quotient. *See* IQ
intergenerational differences
as ethnic effect, 65–66
women and, 66
inter-racial marriage, xvi
Caribbeans (Black) and, 295
ethnic identity and, 327
in U.S., 26
intifada, 291
IQ (Intelligence Quotient), xiv
adoption's influence on, 59
African American delinquency and, 155
antisocial behavior and, 67
as "constitutional factor," 154–155
controversial studies for, 59, 60
criminal behavior and, xiv
delinquency and, 154, 155
"executive function" deficits and, 155

heritability of, 60
institutional deprivation's influence on,
12
Minnesota Transracial Adoption Study
and, 59
in PHDCN, influence of, 167
racial differences in, 58–60
Islam
educational attainment and, 97

Jews
in Germany (WWII), 51
hereditary laws among, 51

labeling
individual identification and, 57
physical handicaps and, 57
social category reification in, 57
as social construction, 57–58
stigmatization as result of, 57
labeling theory, 56
crime/delinquency applications within,
56, 177
Labour Force Surveys, 91
"language graveyard," 302
language impairment
inference criteria for, 10
obstetric risk analysis for, 10
in twins, 10–11
languages
ethnic identities and, role in, 52–53, 65
limited assimilation theory, 110
linguistic diversity, 40
for minority/immigrant youth, 39
London Study (for schizophrenia), 237

Measuring Delinquency
(Hindelang/Hirschi/Weis), 150
"melting pot" theory, 337
"cultural mosaic" v., 347
Mental Health Inquiry, 234
Mexican Americans
in PHDCN, 167
migrant generations
downward occupational mobility of,
94
educational attainment and, 84–85, 186
educational qualifications for, 85, 86, 87
employment skills for, 284
English language fluency and, 85
gender differences between, 85, 87
"new," 87, 187

migrant generations (*continued*)
  second, 85–87, 187
  "third," 340
migration designs, 12–13
  environmental influences on, 14
  genetic mediations and, 14
  mortality rates and, 13
  "New Commonwealth," 284
  paradigms for, 45
  place-based disparities (crime) and,
    153
  psychological outcomes and, 13–15
  schizophrenia rates and, 247
migration paradigm, 336–339
  assimilation's influence on, 337
  displacement/resettlement in, 338–339
  disruption effects in, 338
  incorporation modes in, 336
  reception factors in, 336
  selection mechanisms in, 338
  situational factors within, 336
  socio-demographic approaches to, 337
  stress levels from, 347
migration rates
  educational attainment and, 81
  for UK, 23
  for U.S., 23
Millennium Cohort Study, 104
Minnesota Transracial Adoption Study, 59,
    60
mixed race persons, 51
  U.S. census reporting on, 51
Monitoring the Future. *See* MTF
mortality rates
  migration as factor for, 13
The Moynihan Report, 70
MTF (Monitoring the Future), 143
  delinquency rates (by ethnicity) in, 143
multiple racisms theory, 195–196, 197
murder rates. *See also* U.S. crime statistics
  for African Americans, 139
  for Whites, 139
Muslims, 286
  intifada and, 291
  in UK, 291
  Ummah for, 291

National Crime Panel, 148
National Crime Victimization Survey. *See*
  NCVS
National Longitudinal Study of Adolescent
  Health, 266

Native Americans, 54
  college graduation rates for, 116
  college planning for, 132
  cultural acceptance of, 108
  educational attainment for, 109
  high school graduation rates for, 115
  youth suicide rates for, 263
NCs (neighborhood clusters), 161
NCVS (National Crime Victimization
  Survey), 142
  Hispanics in, 147
  racial differences in, 142
  U.S. Census and, 142
NCWP (New Commonwealth and
  Pakistan), 23
neighborhood clusters. *See* NCs
noncausal mechanisms, 3–8
  genetic mediations in, 4–5
  risk mis-specification in, 5–6
  social selection in, 3–4
  third variable effects in, 5
Nottingham Study (for schizophrenia), 237,
    241–245
  ÆSOP study and, 241
  Caribbeans (Black) v. Whites in, 235, 236
  incidence rate ratios in, 242, 244
  risk population in, 243

"one-drop" rule, 51
  mixed race persons and, 51
opportunity structures (in UK), 284–285,
    286
  British identity as, 285
  citizenship accessibility as, 285
  imperial history and, 285
  racism and, 285
oppositional-defiant symptoms, 66

Pacific Northwest Study (high school
  seniors), 116–118
  college applications in, 118, 119, 120, 127
  college planning disparities in, 119, 120,
    123–127, 128, 129
  demographics for, 116, 118–119
  ethnic identity as factor in, 117, 124
  family structure as factor in, 121, 122, 129
  generational status in, 122, 123, 127
  home ownership as factor in, 122–123,
    127, 131
  parental education variable in, 122, 127,
    129
  race as factor in, 117

socioeconomic contexts in, 120–123,
128–131
variables in, 117–118
Pakistanis (UK), 34
achievement levels of, 96
English language fluency and, 34, 97
female education levels for (UK), 33
household income levels for (UK), 31
migration patterns for, 81
poverty rates for, 82
unemployment rates for, 189
parental earning capacity, 35
parental education
as cultural capital, 95–96
influence of, xiii, 35, 37, 38
maternal, 95, 129
Pacific Northwest Study (high school
seniors) and, 122, 127, 129
reading scores and, 95
parenting
child rejection and, 211
children's interpretations of, 210–217
as human capital, 94
PEP (Political and Economic Planning), 176,
195, 196
personal group identity, 63–64
intermarriage rates and, 63
PHDCN (Project on Human Development
in Chicago Neighborhoods), 161–167
African Americans in, 162
Black/White violence ratios in, 166
ethnic neighborhood context as part of,
167
Hispanic Americans in, 162
individual frequency rates in, 166
IQ and, influence of, 167
Mexican Americans as part of, 167
NCs in, 161
offense categories in (by ethnicity), 165
parameters of, 161–162
self-reported offenders in, 162–166
summary scores in, 162
physical abuse
aggressive behaviors as result of, 210
antisocial behavior as result of, 207
against children, in U.S., 206
discipline and, 205–207, 210
risk factors for, 207
social policies about, 218
socioeconomic status and, 207
physical aggression
family care and, 11

norms for, 214
physical abuse and, 210
physical discipline, 205–206, 208–210
abuse and, 205–207
African American parents and, 207,
212
age-based, 206
Asians and, 207
CDP and, 208
children's attitudes about, 213–217
cohort studies of, 216
conduct disorder and, 206
cultural context for, 214
ethnic differences in, 207–210
legal responses to, by nation, 218
parental warmth and, 212, 213
in schools, 215
in social learning theory, 210
social policies about, 217, 218
in U.S., by parents, 206
physical punishment. *See* physical
discipline
Pittsburgh Youth Study. *See* PYS
place-based disparities (crime), 151–154
See also US crime statistics
ecological fallacy in, 152
ethnic neighborhoods as factor in, 153
methodological problems for, 152–153
outmigration as factor in, 153
race as factor in, 151
racial composition and, 152
reciprocal effects model for, 153
residential segregation and, 152
"resource deprivation/affluence" index's
influence in, 152
urban areas and, 151
The Police and Criminal Evidence Act of
1984, 179
Policy Studies Institute. *See* PSI
Policy Studies Institute survey. *See* PSI
Policy Study Institute Studies, 67
Political and Economic Planning. *See* PEP
popular culture
in UK, 293–297
post-compulsory schooling (UK)
educational attainment and, 91–92, 101
general participation in, 91
for South Asian immigrants, 103
poverty differentials
for minority/immigrant youth (UK),
30–34
in U.S., 34–42

poverty rates. *See also* child poverty
  for African Americans, 35, 109
  for Asians (continental), 82
  for Bangladeshis (UK), 82
  Black–White ratio, 35
  child (US), 34, 35
  differentials, 30–42
  "equivalent incomes" and, 189–190
  family structure's influence on, 70
  for Hispanic Americans, 35, 36
  Hispanic–White ratio, 35
  oppositional-defiant symptoms and, 66
  for Pakistanis (UK), 82
  psychological functioning as result of, 66
  social costs of, 346
  suicide and, 270–271
poverty ratios
  Black–White, 35
  Hispanic–White, 35
predictive validity tests
  for antisocial behavior, 9
prenatal viral infections
  congenital rubella syndrome, 248
  schizophrenia and, 248
primary school testing
  educational attainment and, 89–90
  gender differences within, 90
  social class effects on, 90
Project on Human Development in Chicago
    Neighborhoods. *See* PHDCN
Proposition 23, 305
  election demographics for, 305
  reactive ethnicity as result of, 312, 331
  sociopolitical context for, 330
PSI (Policy Studies Institute) survey, 82, 83,
    84, 85, 92, 176, 178, 186
pupil–teacher conflicts, 100
PYS (Pittsburgh Youth Study), 151, 209
  African Americans in, 151

racial discrimination, xiv. *See also*
    segregation
  in CILS, as variable, 320–323, 325, 328–329
  as ethnic effect, 72
  opportunity access and, 72
  from racial grouping, 281
  stigmatization as result of, 72
Racial Discrimination in England (Daniel),
    195
racial grouping, 50, 281–282. *See also* ethnic
    identity
  collective perceptions as result of, 281

  discrimination from, 281
  "hyphenated" identities and, 283
  labeling as result of, 281
racism
  cultural, 297
  in educational institutions, 100
  ethnic identity and, 58
  imperialism and, 283
  "new," 297
  schizophrenia as result of, 250–251
  social factors and, influence on (U.S.), 108,
    131
  sociopolitical conflicts and, 283
  in UK, 281
Rampton/Swann Inquiry, 88
reactive ethnicity
  ethnic identity and, 55, 306, 331
  from Proposition 23, 312, 331
reciprocal effects model, 153
"refugee" system, 23
religiosity
  by age, 288
  of Caribbeans (Black), 288
  dress codes as result of, 289
  drug/alcohol abuse and, 271
  as ethnic effect, 64–65
  ethnicity and, 288, 289–291, 298
  school choice and, 290
  suicide and, 265, 271–272, 274
  of Whites, 288
replacement fertility rates
  for U.S./UK, 22
residential care, 11–12
  emotional/behavioral disturbance rates
    and, 11
  hyperactivity/inattention rates and, 12
residential segregation, 342
  for African Americans, 56, 109
  immigration's influence on, 28
  place-based crimes and, 152
  social exclusion from, 342
  in UK, 28, 83
"resource deprivation/affluence" index,
    152, 156
reverse record checks
  for African American males, 150
  concurrent validity in, 151
  crime and, 149–151
  delinquency analysis through, 150
  differential validity (by race) in, 151
  predictive validity in, 151
  for White males, 150

risk factors
  for antisocial behavior, 9
  "dose-response" relationships and, 6
  ethnicity as, 6, 7
  fixed categorical features and, 6
  immigrant status as, 6
  levels of, 6–7
  mis-specifications of, 5–6
  for schizophrenia, 248–249
  for suicide, 264–265
risk mechanisms. *See also* risk factors
  direct proximal, 6
  levels of, 6–7
Rituals of Blood: Consequences of Slavery in Two American Centuries (Patterson), 190

The Satanic Verses, 286
"Save Our State," 305. *See also* Proposition 23
schizo-mania
  schizophrenia v., 239
schizophrenia, xv, 227, 344
  affective syndromes v., 246
  brains systems and, 229, 251
  in Caribbean Islands (Jamaica/Trinidad/Barbados), 240
  in Caribbeans (Black), 227, 237, 239, 246–247, 251–252
  causal hypotheses for, 247
  census data for, 234–237
  drug/alcohol abuse and, 249
  early life influences and, 248
  environmental factors for, 249, 250
  genetic predispositions for, 247
  geographic demography for, 230–231
  hypoxia as cause for, 248
  incidence rates for, 227, 230, 234, 238
  late childhood risk factors for, 248–249
  London Study for, 237
  Mental Health Inquiry for, 234
  migration as variable for, 247
  misdiagnoses for, 245–246
  in Norwegian migrants, 227
  nosological approach to, 247
  Nottingham Study for, 237
  prenatal viral infections and, 248
  in psychiatric literature, 228
  racism as factor for, 250–251
  schizo-mania v., 239
  social capital as factor for, 249
  social factors for, 249

  sociological impact of, 230
  symptoms for, 228–229, 252
  "Ten Country Study" for, 231
"school persistence" rates, 98
schooling, 88–89. *See also* educational attainment
  National Curriculum assessments and, 88
  physical discipline and, 215
segmented assimilation hypothesis, 110
  cultural acceptance as part of, 110
segregation
  educational, 112
  residential, 28, 56, 83, 109
  state-sponsored (U.S.), 109, 131
self-competence
  suicide and, 265
self-esteem
  acculturative stress and, 272
  African American youth and, levels of, 272
  ethnic identity as factor in, 272
  Hispanic American youth and, levels of, 272
  suicide and, 265, 272–273
  White youth and, levels of, 272
self-identity
  for Caribbeans (Black), 287
  categorical approach to, 53–54
  in CILS, 307, 324, 325–326, 332
  determinants of, 326–330
  ethnicity and, xvi, 51–54
  pan-ethnic, 325
  religious, 288–289
  "situational," 287
  skin-color as part of, 287
  U.S. citizenship and, 326–327
self-report studies, xiii
  ethnic bias in, xiii
  limitations of, 183–184
  in UK crime statistics, 183–184
self-reported offending surveys
  Black/White ratios in, 143, 145, 183
  crime and, 143–147
  criticism of, 148–149
  "high frequency" participants in, 184
  MTF, 143
  in PHDCN, 162–166
  race-linked sampling bias in, 148
  validity of, 148
serotonin transporter genes
  depressive disorders and, 62

"settlement system," 23–24
 source country composition and, 23
sexual behavior
 African Americans and, 269
 early-onset, 269, 273
 suicide and, 269
single-parent households
 among Caribbeans (Black), xii–xiii, 97,
  191, 193
 Caucasian women and, xiii
skin color
 self-identity and, 287
slavery, 199
 Caribbeans (Black) and, 175, 190, 199
social affluence, 66–67. *See also* poverty
  rates
social capital
 schizophrenia and, 249
social community
 as ethnic effect, 65
social dislocation
 immigration and, 45
social learning theory, 210, 218
 physical discipline and, 210
social policy creation
 ethnic identity and, 346–347
 for integration, 347
 youth development and, 346
social selection
 environments' role in, 3
 family care and, 11
 in noncausal mechanisms, 3–4
social stigmatization, 57, 342
socioeconomic contexts
 in CILS, 31, 327–328
 for ethnic neighborhoods, xiv
 in Pacific Northwest Study (high school
  seniors), 120–123, 128–131
 in U.S. crime statistics, 156–160
Somalis
 UK migrations patterns for, 81
South Africa, 51, 56, 345
 apartheid in, 51, 56, 345
"statistical" discrimination, 56
stigmatization
 from labeling, 57
 from racial discrimination, 72
 social, 57
"straight-line" integration, 338
strain theory, 188
suicidal ideation, 264, 266, 273
 ethnicity as factor for, 266, 267

suicide, xv
 adolescent behaviors for, 263–264
 African Americans and, rates for, 71
 age variables for, 264
 attempts, by gender, 263, 264
 cause of death rates and, 262
 conduct disorders as factor for, 265
 cultural attitudes towards, 272, 274
 depressive disorders as factor in, 265
 educational attainment and, 268–269
 ethnic neighborhoods as factor for, 270
 ethnicity/gender variables for, 263, 264
 family structure as factor for, 265, 269–270
 ideation for, 264, 266
 nonpsychological factors for, 265
 parental supervision as factor for, 271
 poverty as factor for, 270–271
 protective factors against, 265, 274
 psychosocial adversity as factor in, 265
 religiosity as factor for, 265, 271–272, 274
 risk factors for, 264–265, 273, 274
 self-competence and, 265
 self-esteem and, 265, 272–273
 sexual behavior and, 269, 273
symbolic interactionism theory, 177

teachers' expectations, 100, 346
 for African Americans, 111
"Ten Country Study," 231, 237
 country of origin variable in, 239
third variable effects
 in noncausal mechanisms, 5

UCR (Uniform Crime Reports), 140
 African Americans in, 140
 Crime Index and, 140
 index offenses in, 140, 141, 142
 race data (offender) in, 140
UK (United Kingdom). *See also* UK crime
  statistics
 African migration patterns to, 81
 age structures in, 26
 Asian (African) populations in, 26, 52
 "Asian trajectory" in, 104
 Asian youth educational levels in, 33
 assimilation levels in, 294
 Bangladeshi migration patterns to, 81
 Caribbeans (Black) in, 44, 80, 81, 196,
  197–198, 284, 285, 296, 336, 340–341
 child poverty levels in, 43
 Commonwealth Immigration Act of 1962
  in, 23

Commonwealth Immigration Act of 1968
in, 23
crime rates in, 176
demographic context for, 22–29
Education Authority in, 84
educational attainment in (minority
groups), 81, 83–92, 341
"Englishness" in, 294
ethnic identity formation in, 196, 197–198,
199, 281, 286–291
ethnic neighborhoods in, 68, 82–83,
193–194, 195
ethnic pluralism in, 285
ethnic religiosity in, 289–291, 298
ethno-racial composition in, 25, 176–177
immigration increases in, 24
income distribution quintiles for, 30
income level definitions in, 30
Indian migration patterns to, 81
institutional ethnic identification in, 58
integration in, 282
migration patterns for, 23, 81
minority population in, 25, 27, 43, 81
multiple racisms theory in, 195–196
NCWP and, 23
"New Commonwealth" migration to,
284
opportunity structures in, 284–285, 286
Pakistani migration patterns to, 81, 284
popular culture effects in, 293–297
poverty differentials in, 30–34
projected population demographics for,
42
racial discrimination responses in,
195–196
racism in, 281, 286
"refugee" system in, 23
replacement fertility rates for, 22
residential segregation in, 28, 83
secular changes in, 176
self-sufficient cultural resources in, 196,
197
"settlement system" in, 23
social policies in, 43
Somali migration patterns to, 81
total population for, 22, 42
Vietnamese migration patterns to, 81
UK crime statistics, 178
antisocial behavior and, 174
Caribbeans (Black) and, 175, 199
ethnic variations in, 174
evidence evaluation for, 179–184

generational changes for, 178–179,
184–198
homicide data, 179–180
intra-ethnic crime as factor in, 180
prison population and, 181
self-report studies in, 183–184
youth reports as part of, 178
UK justice system processes
bias effects in, 182–183
case processing within, 181
CPS in, 181
discrimination within, 181–182
ethnic group representation in, 182
prosecution rates in, 181
Ummah, 291
unemployment rates
for Caribbeans (Black), in UK, 189
Uniform Crime Reports. *See* UCR
United Kingdom. *See* UK
U.S. (United States). *See also* U.S. crime
statistics
African American population
demographics in, 26
age demographics for, 26
Asian Americans in, 109
Caribbeans (Blacks) in, 44, 45
child poverty in, 34, 35
criminal justice system in, 139
crude migration rates for, 23
cultural assimilation in, 337
demographic context for, 22–29
"economic well-being" in, 34
educational inequalities in, 37, 107, 131
ethnic identity in, as social factor, 108, 131
ethnic neighborhoods in, 68
ethno-racial composition of, 25
high school graduation rates in, 107–108
Hispanic American population
demographics in, 26, 52
housing/employment audit studies in, 67
identificational assimilation in, 303
"immigrant optimism" in, 134
Immigration and Nationality Act's effect
on, 24
immigration increases in, 24, 340
immigration populations for, 301
institutional ethnic identification in, 58
inter-racial marriage rates in, 26
language assimilation in, 302
as "language graveyard," 302
minority population in, 26, 27, 43
Native American population in, 54

U.S. (United States) (*continued*)
  physical discipline and, by parents, 206
  police statistics in, 139
  population demographics for, 301
  poverty differentials in, 34–42
  projected population demographics for,
    42
  race in, as social factor, 108, 131
  replacement fertility rates for, 22
  social mobility in, 131
  state-sponsored segregation in, 109, 131
  working-age population in, 42
  youth suicide rates in, 262, 263
U.S. Census
  Current Population Survey, 301
  ethnic neighborhoods and, measures for,
    160
  NCVS and, 142
  sub-national categories in, acceptance of,
    52
U.S. crime statistics, 140–142
  "behavior v. justice system" debate for,
    147
  cause v. markers for, 154
  "constitutional factors" for, 139, 154
  ethnic neighborhoods and, 69, 160–161
  Hispanic Americans and, 156
  I.Q. levels and, xiv
  place-based disparities in, 151–154
  reverse record checks and, 149–151
  self-reported offending surveys and,
    143–147
  socioeconomic context for, 156–160
  UCR and, 140
  victimization surveys and, 142–143

victimization surveys
  for crime, 142–143
  NCVS, 142
Vietnamese
  UK migration patterns for, 81
Vietnamese Americans, 133
"voluntary" minorities, 111

Whites
  African American IQ levels v., 59

college graduation rates for, 115
college plans for (U.S.), xiii
educational levels for, 31
educational transition rates for, 115
high school graduation rates for, 115
household incomes for (UK), 31
murder rates for, 139
prison attendance rates for, 139
religiosity of, 288
reverse record checks for (males),
  150
self-esteem levels for, 272
social class differences among, 133
in YRBSS survey, 143
Windrush, 296
women
  attempted suicides and, 263
  educational attainment (UK) and, 94
  educational levels for (UK), 31–33
  ethnic identity for, 344
  intergenerational differences and, 66
  within migrant generations, 85, 87
  post-primary schooling for, 90
World Health Organization, 231

YCS (Youth Cohort Study), 89, 90
  analyses of, 91
Youth Cohort Study. *See* YCS
Youth Risk Behavior Study, 266
Youth Risk Behavior Surveillance System
  survey. *See* YRBSS
youth suicide rates
  for African Americans (in US), 263
  for Asian Americans, 263
  for Hispanic Americans, 263
  for Native Americans, 263
  in U.S., 262, 263
  for Whites (in U.S.), 263
YRBSS (Youth Risk Behavior Surveillance
  System) survey, 143
  African American criminal behavior in,
    145
  Hispanic American criminal behavior in,
    145
  racial disparities in, 146
  White criminal behavior in, 143